Making Sense of Social Research Methodology

For our students, who are also our teachers and dialogue partners.

Sara Miller McCune founded SAGE Publishing in 1965 to support the dissemination of usable knowledge and educate a global community. SAGE publishes more than 1000 journals and over 800 new books each year, spanning a wide range of subject areas. Our growing selection of library products includes archives, data, case studies and video. SAGE remains majority owned by our founder and after her lifetime will become owned by a charitable trust that secures the company's continued independence.

Los Angeles | London | New Delhi | Singapore | Washington DC | Melbourne

Making Sense of Social Research Methodology

A Student and Practitioner Centered Approach

Pengfei Zhao
University of Florida

Karen Ross
University of Massachusetts Boston

Peiwei Li
Lesley University

Barbara Dennis
Indiana University Bloomington

**$SAGE

ⓈSAGE

FOR INFORMATION:

SAGE Publications, Inc.
2455 Teller Road
Thousand Oaks, California 91320
E-mail: order@sagepub.com

SAGE Publications Ltd.
1 Oliver's Yard
55 City Road
London, EC1Y 1SP
United Kingdom

SAGE Publications India Pvt. Ltd.
B 1/I 1 Mohan Cooperative Industrial Area
Mathura Road, New Delhi 110 044
India

SAGE Publications Asia-Pacific Pte. Ltd.
18 Cross Street #10-10/11/12
China Square Central
Singapore 048423

Acquisitions Editor: Leah Fargotstein
Editorial Assistant: Kenzie Offley
Content Development Editor: Chelsea Neve
Production Editor: Rebecca Lee
Copy Editor: Talia Greenberg
Typesetter: Hurix Digital
Proofreader: Theresa Kay
Indexer: Integra
Cover Designer: Karine Hovsepian
Marketing Manager: Victoria Velasquez

Copyright © 2022 by SAGE Publications, Inc.

All rights reserved. Except as permitted by U.S. copyright law, no part of this work may be reproduced or distributed in any form or by any means, or stored in a database or retrieval system, without permission in writing from the publisher.

All third party trademarks referenced or depicted herein are included solely for the purpose of illustration and are the property of their respective owners. Reference to these trademarks in no way indicates any relationship with, or endorsement by, the trademark owner.

Printed in Canada

Library of Congress Cataloging-in-Publication Data

Names: Zhao, Pengfei, 1984- author.

Title: Making sense of social research methodology : a student and practitioner centered approach / Pengfei Zhao, Karen Ross, Peiwei Li, Barbara Dennis.

Description: First edition. | Thousand Oaks, California : SAGE Publications, Inc., [2022] | Includes bibliographical references and index.

Identifiers: LCCN 2020042717 | ISBN 978-1-5063-7868-8 (paperback) | ISBN 978-1-5063-7866-4 (epub) | ISBN 978-1-5063-7867-1 (epub) | ISBN 978-1-5063-7869-5 (ebook)

Subjects: LCSH: Social sciences—Research. | Social sciences—Methodology.

Classification: LCC H62 .Z49 2022 | DDC 300.72/1—dc23

LC record available at https://lccn.loc.gov/2020042717

This book is printed on acid-free paper.

MIX
Paper from responsible sources
FSC® C103567

21 22 23 24 25 10 9 8 7 6 5 4 3 2 1

BRIEF CONTENTS

Preface	xvii
About the Authors	xxii
Chapter 1: Our Research Story: A Prelude	1

CLUSTER 1 • UNDERSTANDING RESEARCH: MAKING SENSE OF UNDERLYING ASSUMPTIONS — 19
Roots and Branches

Chapter 2 •	How Do We Know? That Is the Question	23
Chapter 3 •	Research, Identity, and Relational Processes	41
Chapter 4 •	Ethical Considerations Across the Spectrum of Research	59
Chapter 5 •	Knowledge and Meaning in Research	83
Chapter 6 •	Sociopolitical Conditions of Research	113
Chapter 7 •	Validity in the Context of Research	137

CLUSTER 2 • WHAT IS THE MEANING OF "DATA"? — 167
Roadmap

Chapter 8 •	What Am I Looking For?	171
Chapter 9 •	Defining Data	197
Chapter 10 •	Generating and Acquiring Data	217
Chapter 11 •	How Do I Know I Have "Enough" Data? How Do I Know I Have "Good" Data?	243

CLUSTER 3 •	**HOW DO WE CONCEPTUALIZE "INFERENCE"?**	**267**
	Connecting the Dots	
Chapter 12 •	Understanding Inference as a Process	273
Chapter 13 •	Description and Inference in the Research Sphere	301
Chapter 14 •	Making Inferences About Trends and Experiences	327
Chapter 15 •	Writing Up Research	351
Chapter 16 •	Coming Back Full Circle: Implications of the Inferential Process	377
Chapter 17 •	Postlude	405

Appendix A: Statistical Tests Used to Establish Causal Inferences	**419**
Appendix B: Statistical Tests Used to Establish Correlational Inferences	**425**
Appendix C: Getting Clarity About the Vision of Your Class Project	**429**
Appendix D: A Generic Rubric for Evaluating Empirical Research Articles	**433**
Glossary of Terms	**437**
About the Contributors	**449**
References	**455**
Index	**465**

DETAILED CONTENTS

Preface	xvii
About the Authors	xxii

Chapter 1 • Our Research Story: A Prelude — 1
- Paths Toward Research — 1
  - **Barbara's Story** — 1
  - **Peiwei's Story** — 3
  - **Karen's Story** — 4
  - **Pengfei's Story** — 4
  - **Coming Together** — 5
  - **Emerging Research** — 7
- Making Implicit Explicit: Our Intentions and Assumptions — 8
  - **Holding Complexity** — 8
  - **Bridging Binaries** — 9
  - **Accessible but Not Simplified** — 11
  - **Acknowledging Our Position** — 12
- About Reading This Book — 13
  - **Cluster Structure** — 14
  - **Book Features** — 15
- Further Readings — 17

CLUSTER 1 • UNDERSTANDING RESEARCH: MAKING SENSE OF UNDERLYING ASSUMPTIONS — 19
- Roots and Branches — 19

Chapter 2 • How Do We Know? That Is the Question — 23
- Musing Upon the Everyday: Enquiring Minds Want to Know — 23
- Narrative and Conceptual Interludes: The Meaning of "Research" — 25
  - **Epistemology: How Do We Know What We Know?** — 26
  - **Criticalism: Not Taking Knowledge for Granted** — 28
  - **Partisanship** — 29
  - **Intersubjectivity** — 31
  - **Reflection** — 31
- Research Scenario: Researching Through Collective Values: The Feminist Research Collective — 32

- Synthesis: An Open Dialogue — 36
  - **Conceptual Synthesis** — 36
    - *Is Research a Way to Solve Problems?* — 37
    - *Are Researchers Experts?* — 37
    - *Is Research Science?* — 37
    - *Is Research a Situated Form of Practice?* — 38
  - **Methodological Synthesis** — 38
  - **Personal Synthesis** — 39
- Moving Forward — 39
- Further Readings — 39

Chapter 3: Research, Identity, and Relational Processes — 41

- Musing Upon the Everyday: The Presentation of Self — 41
  - **Narrative and Conceptual Interludes: Exploring Identity in Research** — 43
  - **Identity/Claims** — 44
  - **Legitimate Knowledge** — 47
- Research Scenario: A Collaborative Action Research Project — 50
- Synthesis: Points for Reflection — 55
  - **Conceptual Synthesis** — 55
  - **Methodological Synthesis** — 56
  - **Personal Synthesis** — 56
- Moving Forward — 57
- Further Readings — 57

Chapter 4: Ethical Considerations Across the Spectrum of Research — 59

- Musing Upon the Everyday: What Would You Do? — 60
  - **Ethics in Research** — 62
  - **Procedural and Situational Ethics in Research** — 63
- Narratives and Conceptual Interludes: On Being Ethical in Research Practices — 65
  - **Positionality** — 67
  - **Intersubjectivity** — 69
  - **Care and Openness** — 70
  - **Power** — 72
- Research Scenario: Marginalia: Sara McClelland — 74
- Synthesis: Points for Reflection — 78
  - **Conceptual Synthesis** — 78
  - **Methodological Synthesis** — 79
  - **Personal Synthesis** — 80
- Moving Forward — 80
- Further Readings — 81

Chapter 5: Knowledge and Meaning in Research — 83

   Musing Upon the Everyday: Understanding Meaning — 83
   Narrative and Conceptual Interludes: Different Ways of Knowing — 85
      Epistemology and Ontology — 86
      Epistemology, Methodology, and Method — 87
      The Contour of Typical Epistemology and Ontology Stances — 89
         Positivism — 90
         Post-Positivism and Critical Realism — 90
         Diverging Epistemologies — 91
      Three Types of Knowledge Claims — 93
         Objective Claims — 94
         Subjective Claims — 94
         Normative Claims — 95
      Understanding Meaning — 96
   Research Scenario: My "Fat Girl Complex" — 99
      Questions for the Guest Contributors (and to You) — 101
      A Critical Realist Response to the Research Scenario: Joseph Maxwell — 101
      A Constructivist Response to the Research Scenario:
         Sabine Siekmann and Joan Parker Webster — 103
   Synthesis: Points for Reflection — 108
      Conceptual Synthesis — 108
      Methodological Synthesis — 109
      Personal Synthesis — 109
   Moving Forward — 109
   Further Readings — 110

Chapter 6: Sociopolitical Conditions of Research — 113

   Musing Upon the Everyday — 114
      How Should I Dress for My First Job Interview? — 114
   Narrative and Conceptual Interludes — 115
      Conceptualizing Social Action Through Looking at an
      Environmentalist's Dilemma — 115
      Social Norms and Everyday Life — 115
      Social Structure and Agency — 119
      Structural and Interactive Power — 123
   Research Scenario: Making
     a Difference as a Researcher — 127
      Representation of Women Scholars in the Hybrid Space of
         Knowledge: Wei Luo — 127
      An Essay on My Positionality: Payal P. Shah — 130
   Synthesis: Points for Reflection — 133

Conceptual Synthesis	133
Methodological Synthesis	134
Personal Synthesis	134
Moving Forward	134
Further Readings	135

Chapter 7: Validity in the Context of Research — 137

Musing Upon the Everyday: Validity in (Mis)understanding	137
Narrative and Conceptual Interludes: Do We *Really* Know the Truth?	138
Validity, Truth, and Objectivity	**140**
Defining Validity	*140*
Truth, Validity, and Epistemological Assumptions	*140*
Validity in the Context of Quantitative Research	**144**
Validity in the Context of Qualitative Research	**145**
A Meta-Discussion: Validity in the Context of Understanding Meaning	**147**
Meaning and Validity: Intersubjectivity	*147*
Meaning and Validity: Meaning Field, Meaning Horizon	*148*
Meaning and Validity: An "as if" Quality	*150*
Meaning and Validity: Uncertainty	*151*
A Unifying Approach to Validity: Validity Criteria for Different Types of Knowledge Claims	**153**
Validity Criteria for Objective Knowledge Claim	*153*
Validity Criteria for Subjective Knowledge Claims	*154*
Objectivity–Subjectivity Dualism	*154*
Validity Criteria for Normative Knowledge Claims	*155*
Validity in Research: A Recap	**156**
Research Scenario: Validity and Assessment: David Rutkowski	157
Synthesis: Points for Reflection	162
Conceptual Synthesis	**162**
Methodological Synthesis	**163**
Personal Synthesis	**163**
Moving Forward	163
Further Readings	164

CLUSTER 2 • WHAT IS THE MEANING OF "DATA"? — 167

Roadmap	167

Chapter 8: What Am I Looking For? — 171

Revisiting Research and Identity in the Context of Data	171
Musing Upon the Everyday: Solving Problems That Matter to Us	171
Research-ability	**173**
Openness	**174**

Systematicity	**174**
Standardization	**174**
Narrative and Conceptual Interludes: A Researcher and Their Organizing	175
Reviewing Existing Knowledge and Establishing the Conversation	**177**
Context: Establishing Interpretive Guideposts	*178*
Background Knowledge and More: Literature Review	*179*
Existing Knowledge and More: Meta-analysis	*181*
Informed Decision-Making: Justifying One's Decisions	*182*
Formulating Research Interests, Questions, and Hypotheses	**182**
Research Interests	*183*
Research Questions	*183*
Hypotheses	*184*
Generating Data	**185**
Designing Research or Creating Research Designs	**186**
Fixed Designs	*187*
Flexible Designs	*189*
Research Scenario: Studying a Rare Condition: Jenny Downs	191
Synthesis: Points for Reflection	193
Conceptual Synthesis	**193**
Methodological Synthesis	**193**
Personal Synthesis	**194**
Moving Forward	194
Further Readings	194

Chapter 9: Defining Data — 197

Musing Upon the Everyday: How Much Should I Pay for My First Home?	197
Narrative and Conceptual Interludes	198
Generating and Acquiring Data as Social Action	**198**
The Intention of Generating Data	**200**
Intentionally Foregrounding the Rationale of Data Generation and Acquisition	*202*
Different Levels of Goal-Orientedness	*203*
Operationalization	*204*
Generating Data as Communicative Action	**206**
Putting the Two Dimensions Together	**209**
Research Scenario: The Effects of Power on Ethnographic Research: Ke Li	211
Synthesis: Points for Reflection	214
Conceptual Synthesis	**214**
Methodological Synthesis	**215**
Personal Synthesis	**215**

Moving Forward	215
Further Readings	216

Chapter 10: Generating and Acquiring Data — 217

Musing Upon the Everyday: How Should I Make That Lasagna?	217
Narrative and Conceptual Interludes: A Day in the Life of a Researcher	218
Data as Process: Generating and Acquiring Data	**219**
The Process of Generating and Acquiring Data: What Researchers Do	**225**
Data, Not Phenomenon	**229**
Data as Product	**231**
Research Scenario: Making Choices About Data Generation	233
A Day in the Life, I: Student Example	**233**
A Day in the Life, II: Student Example	**236**
Synthesis: Points for Reflection	241
Conceptual Synthesis	**241**
Methodological Synthesis	**241**
Personal Synthesis	**241**
Moving Forward	241
Further Readings	242

Chapter 11: How Do I Know I Have "Enough" Data? How Do I Know I Have "Good" Data? — 243

Musing Upon the Everyday: How Did the Lasagna Turn Out?	243
Narrative and Conceptual Interludes: Creating the Perfect Recipe	244
Sampling	**245**
Data Saturation	**252**
Missing Data	**253**
Generalizability and Transferability	**255**
Research Scenario: Evaluating the Data Generation and Acquisition Process	257
How Do You Know You Have Enough Data? The Example of the Changing Fate Project: Pengfei Zhao	**257**
Global Survey of LGBT NGOs Working in Education: Oren Pizmony-Levy	**260**
Synthesis: Points for Reflection	265
Conceptual Synthesis	**265**
Methodological Synthesis	**265**
Personal Synthesis	**265**
Moving Forward	266
Further Readings	266

CLUSTER 3 • HOW DO WE CONCEPTUALIZE "INFERENCE"? 267

    Connecting the Dots 267

Chapter 12: Understanding Inference as a Process 273

    Musing Upon the Everyday: The World of Iris 273

    Narrative and Conceptual Interludes I: Making Sensible Interpretations 275

        Correspondence Thinking and Its Problems **277**

            Problems With the Correspondence Theory and Its Representational Theory of Meaning *280*

        What Are Inductive and Deductive Reasoning? What's Their Relationship to Inference? **281**

            Induction *282*

            Deduction *283*

            Induction and Deduction in Social Science *283*

        Developing a Critical Pragmatist Perspective on Meaning Fields and Reconstruction **285**

            Reconstructing Meaning Fields *286*

            Contrast Between Correspondence and Reconstructive Approaches to Interpretation *288*

    Narrative and Conceptual Interlude II: Applying the Insights of Critical Pragmatism to Social Research 289

        Reconstructing Meaning Fields as Social Science Inferencing **290**

            Starting With Low-Level Inferences *291*

        The Role of Substantive Theory **292**

        Reconsidering Bias **293**

    Research Scenario: Understanding and Serving Today's College Students. The Problem of Basic Needs Insecurity: Katharine Broton 294

    Synthesis: Points for Reflection 297

        Conceptual Synthesis **297**

        Methodological Synthesis **298**

        Personal Synthesis **298**

    Moving Forward 299

    Further Readings 299

Chapter 13: Description and Inference in the Research Sphere 301

    Musing Upon the Everyday: The Process of Making Choices 301

    Narrative and Conceptual Interludes: What to Make of the GRE? 302

        Description and Inference in Our Decisions About Data **303**

- Description and Inference With Numerical Data: An Introduction to Statistics — 305
  - *Descriptive Statistics* — 305
  - *Inferential Statistics* — 309
- Description and Inference With Textual and Visual Data — 311
- Missing Data and Outliers in the Inferential Process — 316
- Coming Back to Validity — 317
- Research Scenario: Making Decisions — 319
  - Network Analysis: Jeffrey Pugh — 319
  - Photovoice in Our Community: Danielle Lansing — 321
- Synthesis: Points for Reflection — 323
  - Conceptual Synthesis — 323
  - Methodological Synthesis — 324
  - Personal Synthesis — 324
- Moving Forward — 325
- Further Readings — 325

Chapter 14: Making Inferences About Trends and Experiences — 327

- Musing Upon the Everyday: Obesity Is Contagious — 328
- Narrative and Conceptual Interludes: Making Inferences That Matter — 330
  - Moving Beyond Description: Categories of Inferences — 330
    - *Causation* — 331
    - *Making Relational Inferences* — 334
    - *Reconstructing Logical Relationships* — 336
    - *Metaphors* — 337
    - *Making Structural Inferences* — 337
    - *Modeling* — 338
    - *Social Network Analysis* — 339
    - *Frame Analysis* — 340
  - Bringing Inferences Into Dialogue With One Another — 340
    - *Insights and Consciousness-Raising* — 341
    - *Theory Building* — 342
  - For Whom: Predictability, Generalizability, Transferability, and Commitments — 342
    - *Predictability* — 343
    - *Generalizability* — 343
    - *Transferability* — 343
    - *Commitments to and for Whom* — 344
- Research Scenario: Youth Encounter Programs in Israel: Karen Ross — 345
- Synthesis: Points for Reflection — 348
  - Conceptual Synthesis — 348
  - Methodological Synthesis — 348
  - Personal Synthesis — 349
- Moving Forward — 349
- Further Readings — 350

Chapter 15: Writing Up Research — 351

Musing Upon the Everyday — 351
   Professional Writing Revisited — 351
Narrative and Conceptual Interludes — 352
   A Morning With Metaphors — 352
   Writing as a Process — 353
   Writing As a "Relationally Responsible Practice" — 356
      Accessibility — 357
      Informativeness — 358
      Transparency — 359
   Expanding the Author–Reader Relational Responsibility — 359
      The Relationship Is Multifold — 359
      Authors' Responsibility to Themselves — 361
   Genres and Voices, Conventions, and Innovations — 362
      Genre and Convention — 362
      The Change of Genre — 365
      A Continuum of Academic Authorial Voice — 366
      Write to Your Own Voice — 368
Research Scenario: Double Writing in Participatory Action Research: Meagan Call-Cummings — 368
Synthesis: Points for Reflection — 373
   Conceptual Synthesis — 373
   Methodological Synthesis — 373
   Personal Synthesis — 374
Moving Forward — 374
Further Readings — 374

Chapter 16: Coming Back Full Circle: Implications of the Inferential Process — 377

Musing Upon the Everyday: What Is in My Food? — 377
Narrative and Conceptual Interludes: Research Impact—for What, for Whom, and by Whom? — 379
   What Does It Mean for Research to Have an Impact? — 381
      Explanation Versus Understanding — 382
      Nature of Research and Forms of Research Impact — 384
   How Do We Evaluate Research Impact? — 389
      Impact and Value — 389
      Is Generalizability Always Desirable? — 390
      Research Impact and Social (In)justice — 390
      Research as Power and Empowerment — 393
      Othering, Epistemological Violence, and Ethics — 394
Research Scenario: Extrapolating Social Change From Research: Positionality, Iterativity, and Envisioning: Hakim Mohandas Amani Williams — 397

Synthesis: Points for Reflection	401
Conceptual Synthesis	**401**
Methodological Synthesis	**402**
Personal Synthesis	**402**
Moving Forward	402
Further Readings	403

Chapter 17: Postlude   405

Appendix A: Statistical Tests Used to Establish Causal Inferences   419

Appendix B: Statistical Tests Used to Establish Correlational Inferences   425

Appendix C: Getting Clarity About the Vision of Your Class Project   429

Appendix D: A Generic Rubric for Evaluating Empirical Research Articles   433

Glossary of Terms   437

About the Contributors   449

References   455

Index   465

Teaching Resources

This text includes an array of instructor teaching materials designed to save you time and to help you keep students engaged. To learn more, visit **sagepub.com** or contact your SAGE representative at **sagepub.com/findmyrep**.

PREFACE

If you're reading this textbook, who are you? Well, if you're like our students, you are enrolled in graduate school (in the social sciences). We would guess that you might be enrolled in an MA program, likely one that is oriented toward professional training rather than direct preparation for a PhD. Or perhaps you are an instructor like us, who teaches research methodology courses to students like ours.

This book is written with all of you in mind. In our combined decades of experience teaching introductory, graduate-level social science methodology courses, we found that the available texts didn't resonate as much with our students as we had hoped. To be sure, there are plenty of research methodology texts and other resources out there! Yet we have found that these tend to be written with one of two audiences in mind: doctoral students or those students who are preparing to engage in academic research—or students who are expected to *consume* research, as readers of the research studies others conduct. But almost all of our students do research—as professionals, in their academic studies, and in their personal lives. This is true even as most of them are in terminal MA programs and not planning on continuing study toward a PhD or other research degree. Such a narrow focus on PhD students has limited the benefits for both teachers and learners.

Thus, this text is guided by multiple goals. For students: First, we aim to provide a resource that can help you think about research as it *applies* to your everyday lives and to your professional practice—as well as to academic research settings, should you be conducting formal research studies. This goal is rooted in our deep-seated belief that research is something we *all* do in our everyday personal and professional settings. That is, all of us engage in a search for information that can help us answer questions and provide solutions to problems. Related to this, we hope to help you develop a sense of efficacy as a researcher, based on a critical understanding of research and what it can be. This means not only doing research but also interpreting it: Through this text we hope you develop the ability to critically understand research studies, so as to more effectively integrate research into professional and personal practice. Indeed, throughout the text, we strive to make explicit the connections between research and practice, to illustrate how these are connected as forms of praxis. Finally, this textbook aims to bring processes of doing and interpreting research, and their many taken-for-granted concepts, into the conversation. In particular, we aim to create opportunities for reflection and dialogue about underlying assumptions that drive our understandings of "truth," "impact," "expertise," and other concepts that shape the decisions we make about doing and disseminating research—concepts that are rarely discussed during the process of doing research studies, let alone in introductory research methodology texts.

For instructors: Our goals, as stated above, reflect the core of what we believe needs to be part of the conversation in research methodology courses, especially courses in the social sciences for MA or professional degree students. While particularly oriented toward students in applied or professional fields such as education and counseling, this text will be beneficial for students in any area of the social sciences.

This textbook follows a different format than many introductory methodology texts. Rather than taking a procedural or linear approach to research (e.g., focusing primarily on the "how to" and the technical components of undertaking a research study), we explore the process of social inquiry in a *dialogical, integrative* manner. Our commitment to dialogue in this text is reflected in a number of ways. First, this is a multivocal text: In addition to our four voices, we include the voices of other scholars, as well as our students, through **Research Scenarios** in each chapter that apply concepts from that chapter to a specific research context. We explicitly present these scenarios in dialogue with our own discussion of research concepts, which we approach from a critical, praxis-oriented perspective. We also frame this text as a conversation, where student perspectives are welcomed, in order to emphasize the openness of research to new voices and points of view. The **Pause and Reflect** sections integrated into each chapter are explicitly oriented toward such a conversation. These sections also offer instructors possible discussion questions or guided activities for making concepts discussed in the chapter more concrete.

Students and instructors will both notice our integrative approach to research, which is reflected in the structure of the textbook. We have organized the text into three clusters of chapters. The first cluster introduces concepts that are fundamental to all aspects and steps of the research process but are often discussed in limited ways, if they are discussed at all, in introductory research texts. These concepts include relationality, identity, ethics, epistemology, validity, and the sociopolitical context within which research occurs.

Our second and third clusters focus on the concepts of data and inference. These clusters engage concretely with steps we take in the research process, including decisions about designing research, generating data, making inferences, and so on. Within each of these chapters, we build on interconnections from other chapters within the cluster, as well as add nuance in our discussion of concepts introduced in the first cluster to illustrate how they permeate the research process.

By presenting social inquiry in this way, we draw attention to the inherently complex and tightly integrated nature of research in a way that is unique, not only in introductory research textbooks but in research methodology texts as a whole.

For instructors: We have organized each chapter of the textbook in a way that is oriented toward providing readers with opportunities to consider how research concepts apply to their personal, professional, and academic lives. We begin each chapter with a feature we call **Musing Upon the Everyday,** which utilizes an ordinary situation to introduce concepts that are then discussed in the context of formal research. The range of situations presented in these introductory sections is meant to ensure that readers with different backgrounds, experiences, and/or interests will be able to find resonance with the content discussed; it provides entry points that instructors can draw on (or draw inspiration from) to introduce and then dive more deeply into the concepts as they manifest in the research sphere. Within each chapter, we also include multiple opportunities for readers to **Pause and Reflect** on the material discussed. As discussed above, in this section, we use structured questions to guide readers in applying material to their own experiences and thus scaffold their understanding of the concepts.

Finally, while much of the text focuses on conceptual elements of research, we provide readers with concrete strategies for connecting these concepts to their own academic and professional work in the **You and Research** section at the end of each chapter. For students: In this section, we suggest how material referenced in the chapter might be applied in the context of developing a research proposal or empirical research study, as well as how existing empirical studies can be read with the substance of the chapter in mind.

As with all texts, creating this book has been a collective effort, and there are numerous individuals we wish to thank. First and foremost, we thank students in multiple sections of EDUC-Y520 at Indiana University, whose dialogues with us as instructors created the impetus for this textbook and whose reflections and assignments we have incorporated into the text. In addition, we wish to thank our students in ConRes 635 and GGHS 780 at UMASS Boston, PSYC610-Fall 2017 and Psyc715-Spring 2018 at Springfield College, GCOUN 6101-Spring 2019 at Lesley University, as well as later cohorts of students in EDUC-Y520 at Indiana University, for their feedback on draft chapters and their substantive insights, which have helped us write in a clearer, more accessible manner and get our ideas across more directly. Thank you also to Ian Arthur. And we especially wish to thank Allyson Bachta, whose detailed feedback on every one of our draft chapters helped us see when we were including too much jargon, too much (or not enough) detail, and undoubtedly made this textbook more student-friendly.

Our guest contributors provided research scenarios that lent additional perspectives to this textbook and have undoubtedly strengthened it as a result. Thank you to Katharine Broton, Meagan Call-Cummings, Jenny Downs, the Feminist Research Collective, Danielle Lansing, Ke Li, Wei Luo, Joseph Maxwell, Sara McClelland, Oren Pizmony-Levy, Jeffrey Pugh, David Rutkowski, Payal Shah, Sabine Siekmann, Joan Webster, and Hakim Williams.

Indiana University's Scholarship of Teaching and Learning (SoTL) program provided us with two grants that funded retreats for us to write the textbook proposal and lay out the structure of this book. An Indiana University Institute of Advanced Studies grant (awarded to Barbara) helped fund additional meetings.

At SAGE, Leah Fargotstein and Chelsea Nave have helped guide this textbook from its initial proposal to the textbook you hold in your hands. Their advice and suggestions have been immeasurably helpful, and it is hard to see them as anything but a part of this collaborative project! Thanks also to Natalie Elliot for her assistance with obtaining copyright permissions, and to the Production team at SAGE, especially Rebecca Lee and Talia Greenberg for their work in helping us move this textbook from words on a page to completed text. Talia dialogued with us through the copyediting phase and contributed to refining the text. The authors and SAGE would also like to thank the following reviewers for their comments and assistance in developing the book:

Amy B. Thistlethwaite, Thomas More University

Cheryl Heykoop, Royal Roads University

Denise Mitten, Prescott College

Diane Bagwell, The University of West Florida

Erica D. McCray, University of Florida

Gerardo Blanco-Ramirez, University of Massachusetts Boston

Jean Beaman, Purdue University

Jessie L. Krienert, Illinois State University

Mary Christopher, Hardin-Simmons University

Marco Gemignani, Duquesne University (Pittsburgh, PA) and Universidad Loyola de Andalucía (Seville, Spain)

Natalie Boero, San Jose State University

Petra A. Robinson, Louisiana State University

Rhonda Matthews, Edinboro University

Rod Carveth, Morgan State University

Shannon J. Storch, Mount St. Mary's University

Tracy Walker, Virginia State University

Wenfan Yan, UMSS Boston

Xyanthe N. Neider, Washington State University

Finally, our colleagues, students, and families have played a large role in bringing this textbook into the light of day. Barbara acknowledges her colleagues at Indiana University in the Inquiry Methodology Program and especially Drs. Ginette Delandshere and Lucinda and Phil Carspecken, who provided critical food for thought. She would also like to thank her family, Cicada, Kabara, Jordan, Michael, Chelsea, Burris, Ignatius, and Ovilee, who continually encourage her laughter, playfulness, imagination, and inquisitiveness while supporting her heart toward social justice inquiry and activism.

Karen wishes to thank her colleagues in the Department of Conflict Resolution, Human Security and Global Governance for encouraging this project since she joined the faculty there in 2015, and the faculty in the Inquiry Methodology Program at Indiana University—especially Phil Carspecken, Ginette Delandshere, and Barbara Dennis—for the mentorship that nurtured her development as both a methodologist and as a teacher. Love and thanks also to her family—Neil, Alon, and Sonya—for providing the space to write, the support to keep going, and the reminder to stay grounded and stop thinking about research methodology once in a while.

Similar to others, Peiwei would like to express her deep gratitude to the Inquiry Methodology community at Indiana University, especially Drs. Phil Carspecken and Barbara Dennis. Those critical readings, dialogues, and mentorships fundamentally shape how she engages with social inquiry. She also acknowledges Springfield College and Lesley University for their support on this project. Gratitude also to her partner, Arjan, and her daughter, Maeve, who has flourished alongside this project. Their love, support, laugher, and hugs keep Peiwei rooted and hopeful.

Pengfei is very grateful for the unfailing support she received from the Inquiry Methodology Program at Indiana University. The insights, wisdom, and kindness of the faculty members in the Program have greatly nurtured her inquiry into critical theory and research methodology. She would also like to thank her colleagues in the Research and Evaluation Methodology Program at the University of Florida, whose support has been critical to her more recent intellectual development. Her partner, Guojun Wang, has been inspiring, encouraging, and supportful of her intellectual pursuit since 2003. Her daughter, Yunzhi, is a source of happiness and creativity in her life. Her deepest love and gratitude go to both Guojun and Yunzhi.

ABOUT THE AUTHORS

Pengfei Zhao is an Assistant Professor of Qualitative Research at the University of Florida in the Research and Evaluation Methodology Program. She has an interdisciplinary background in inquiry methodology, sociology, and cultural studies. In her research and teaching, Pengfei draws from a wide spectrum of theories—from critical theories to contemporary pragmatism and feminism—to formulate a praxis- and social justice–oriented research methodology. Primarily using ethnographic, narrative, and participatory methodologies, she is interested in the challenges of and innovative approaches to conducting research in culturally diverse and politically troubled contexts. Such efforts are manifested in her writing on doing research in authoritarian states, the institutionalization of research regulation in East Asian contexts, and translation in qualitative research. Currently, Pengfei is completing a book manuscript based on her critical ethnographic study of rural youth's coming-of-age experience during China's drastic transition from socialism to late-socialism.

Karen Ross is an Assistant Professor of Conflict Resolution in the Department of Conflict Resolution, Human Security, and Global Governance at the University of Massachusetts–Boston. Previously, she was an adjunct instructor at the Global and International Education Program at Drexel University and the Inquiry Methodology Program at Indiana University. Karen's teaching and research focus on issues at the intersection of dialogue, peace-building, social activism, and education. She conducts basic and applied research to help understand the impact of grassroots peace-building interventions and the way these interventions fit into societal-level peace-building efforts. Karen's research also focuses on methodological issues related to *how* we conduct research about peace-building and social justice work, how we can do so in more inclusive ways, and how to broaden conceptions of expertise and legitimate knowledge in social inquiry.

Peiwei Li is an Associate Professor of Counseling and Psychology and the Research Coordinator for the PhD program of Counseling and Psychology in Transformative Leadership, Education, and Applied Research at Lesley University. Peiwei's cross-cultural experiences as an immigrant and a Chinese woman growing up in the late socialist/emerging capitalist era in China have fueled her interest in understanding the intersection of culture, class, race, gender, and complex power relations that fuel and reproduce social and systemic pathologies and psychological sufferings. Her scholarship is located in the borderland of critical psychology and critical qualitative methodologies, pertaining to identity development, emancipatory interest, consciousness-raising, recognition, solidarity, and potentials for liberatory actions. Substantively, she has engaged in research on diversity and social justice education, immigration and detention, violence against women, and spiritual development.

Barbara Dennis is a daughter, sister, mother, grandmother, and partner who is located professionally as a Professor of Qualitative Inquiry at Indiana University in the Inquiry Methodology Program. She most consistently engages in critical participatory ethnographies to study core theoretical and practical methodological concepts such as participation, validity, and ethics. As an activist and a scholar, Barbara has been engaged with communities that fight against social injustice and work toward the futures of liberation now. For example, she has been involved with a LGBTQ+ youth community committed to providing educational programming for educators around the country. Their goal is to explore how schools can become sites through which marginalized queer kids can thrive. Barbara values the contributions research makes toward those efforts and welcomes the critique of research that sustains inequity.

Teaching Resources

This text includes an array of instructor teaching materials designed to save you time and to help you keep students engaged. To learn more, visit **sagepub.com** or contact your SAGE representative at **sagepub.com/findmyrep.**

1

OUR RESEARCH STORY

A Prelude

PATHS TOWARD RESEARCH

We begin this book with a multivoiced story of the four people whose paths converged to produce this text. Instead of speaking to you in a distant, third-person voice, we would like to make connections on a more personal level. This may not be an approach that you are familiar with when it comes to research textbooks. But since we are taking a *dialogic* approach to strive for our student-centered intention, we find it necessary to bring ourselves and our stories to the foreground as we open the text. As in any dialogue, it is important to know who are the people talking. Also, when we say "dialogue," the concept goes beyond an actual dialogic situation where people go back and forth with one another. For us, dialogue is a larger concept, where people are engaged in communication explicitly or tacitly. For instance, reading is, also, such a communicative context, where dialogue takes place between the author and the reader, and within the readers themselves. Dialogue is an important feature that we cherish in our approach. In fact, there are various places where we will continue to bring our stories into this text. We hope to make connections and honor the relational nature of social inquiry, which we will unpack later. We also hope that our stories might inspire you to think about what brought you to your current area of study and career orientation. What does "research" mean to you? What do you find intriguing and meaningful to inquire about? From here we can start to discuss the nature of social inquiry and research practices through dialogues.

Barbara's Story

I have always been a shy people-watcher, wanting to understand from the outside. Impossible in some ways, inevitable in others. Watching from the outside versus understanding from my own experience was a difference between somehow identifying things *about* the person versus identifying *with* the person I was observing. Early on, I had come to associate research with the former, not the latter.

In high school, I had personal reactions to my biology class when I was asked to dissect animals. As a longtime vegetarian, I actually felt sick to my stomach when asked to take apart the dead animals in a lab. I did not know where the animals had come from, nor why their lives had been sacrificed so I could do science. This experience again reinforced the idea that to do science was to distance one's feelings and self from the object of inquiry. Were my moral inclinations antithetical to science? Was the idea of knowledge in the service of good to override my individual moral sensibilities?

Also, during my youth, the constitutionality of the death penalty was being debated. I was deeply interested in this debate. I remember tussling with a distinction between the facts and the norms. Could science help us with issues like this?

In my early 20s, I was a special education teacher. As part of my training I was taught to use single-subject designs, or applied behavioral analysis, in my teaching. Single-subject design works by describing observable behaviors in response to particular educational interventions, usually one child at a time, avoiding any efforts to understand what was going on for the child. One was just to make notes about exactly what was observable. Understanding what the child was experiencing was considered irrelevant to explaining the behavioral outcomes of the child. One's intentions to best serve the child's educational needs through this approach demanded a suspension of those personal motivations in order to abstract oneself as the observer from the child's behavior as the observed.

This way of thinking about research, where the procedures themselves force an unquestioned distinction between the researcher and what is being researched, permeated my early ways of thinking about scientific inquiry. In this way of thinking, the researcher is completely *different* than the subject of her research. What connected the researcher to the research subject was the use of precise and legitimate procedures and instruments. But when I was actually engaged with a student, trying to figure out what was going on, I did not really experience this strict separation. The main image-metaphor I had for thinking of research in this way was the scientist in a lab coat looking through a microscope and accurately depicting what she saw. But, alas, that way of thinking about research contrasts with how I think about research now. As an activist researcher, I think of all research as engaged—not disengaged, as informed by particular perspectives rather than neutral, and as recursive and creative rather than strictly linear and procedural. I see that research is never just about the facts but will always necessarily and positively include the values through which the facts become both relevant and interesting. The main metaphor I have for thinking about research now is a conversation. Imagine people bringing questions to a table to talk. This is my image of good research. This looks really different than that lab-coated scientist looking through a microscope!

Peiwei's Story

I could not imagine I would be doing what I'm doing today 15 years ago, when I was a freshman studying chemistry in China. Despite excelling in language, history, and literature, I was expected to pursue a career as a scientist by my parents and teachers. In my home country, a narrow view of "success" prevailed that favored "hard" sciences over "soft" ones. I tacitly inherited this cultural value, studied chemistry in college, and then moved along the pipeline to become a doctoral student in biochemistry at Indiana University in 2003. I'm tremendously grateful for my cross-cultural experience, which created a critical space for self-reflection. I realized that blindly following a path defined by others would not make a meaningful life. I had to attend to the part of me that yearned to be expressed. I consider that this ongoing journey of self-discovery is itself a fundamental inquiry process, which perhaps always accompanies any formal inquiries and research endeavors that I'm drawn to engage with. To me, the process of pursuing knowledge is always shaped by our unique and similar life experiences and thus from a certain vantage point. It carries a deep interest of knowing who we are, why we are doing what we are doing, and what is a good and just life for ourselves and others.

As a little girl, I remember how much I loved to watch my parents, two literature majors, reciting lines from *Hamlet*—vibrant and full of passion. It resonated in me the desire to experience people and the world with sensitivity and intuition, which eventually led me to counseling psychology and inquiry methodology. Thanks to the open and nourishing learning environment at Indiana, I never experienced "research" as something that is external to other aspects of my life. It is a constant unfolding journey to inquire about human nature and the universe with openness and curiosity.

Research is also a process of critical thinking and reflection that does not take things for granted. It always involves asking questions, including of ourselves and our ideas. This helps us closely examine our assumptions and biases as individuals and as a society, to explicate and challenge oppressing cultural norms and social structures, and to create conditions through actions toward positive social change. In this sense, research is not just an academic activity but also a way of thinking and being integrated, guided by specific values and commitments to be in the world and relate to others. This requires open and democratic communication among multiple voices, and a willingness to reach understanding with *the other*, especially those who have very different views from our own. This understanding of research certainly has shaped my identity as a scholar, a teacher, and a person, and how I approach this book.

Karen's Story

Research is a word I have heard all my life. Both of my parents are scientists; from a young age I heard terminology associated with "scientific research," and was encouraged to take math and natural science courses all through high school. Even though I was fairly certain my passions didn't lie in these areas, it was a point of pride for me to be one of only two females in an advanced math class as a high school senior. The support and encouragement I received from family and teachers allowed me to avoid feeling that I couldn't do well because I was a girl.

So it was with some sense of "letting others down" that I turned my attention as a college student to areas about which I was much more passionate. As I thought about who I might be letting down by doing so, their (possible) perspectives became less important to me than focusing on the things I felt would help me engage in work that might contribute to positive social change. This was the thought that initially motivated my graduate studies as well, which I began in an applied professional field.

In fact, it was only partway through my master's degree that I began to think again about the concept of "research" and what it meant. Questions about the impact of the professional field I was involved in led me to my PhD studies and to asking questions about what "impact" meant and how it could be understood. Even at that point, my only real framework for thinking about research was research in the natural sciences. However, as I dug deeper into my graduate work and thought about how to use research to contribute to positive social change, I found my perspective on what research could look like expanding in ways that really resonated with how I see myself in the world. Research and approaches to research have become not secondary to the substantive issues on which I focus professionally, but an integral part of my thought process whenever I think about a problem and how I might solve it. I am reflective about the approaches I take to applied work and about ways of integrating research and application in ways that are consistent with the social justice orientation I bring to my professional, academic, and personal life. My vision of "research" is that it is not only iterative and nonneutral (rather than "linear" and "objective"), but also that it is always contributing to a conversation that, ultimately, is about shaping the world in which we live.

Pengfei's Story

I remember that when I was a kid, I began to explore the world with great curiosity. Living in a small, isolated town in North China, I did not have many opportunities to get exposed to various forms of cultural life or scenic natural views. One thing that really compensated for this disadvantage was reading, which opened a window for the little me to "travel" imaginatively to other countries or to "talk" with great people who had passed away centuries ago. I was so into reading that I spent most of the spare time in my childhood diving into novels and poems. I found myself fascinated by the myriad of experiences that the characters in the books had gone through. I resonated with these experiences so much that sometimes I almost felt like I was living in dual worlds—the world of reality and the world of my books. Now, after many years, I have grown up and become a researcher, yet the interest in people's life experiences has continued, which constantly drives me to read more, think more, and talk more with people.

Like many of my colleagues in academia, I can always feel deep-seated anxiety to produce more. The reasons are rather realistic: One needs to graduate, to find a job, to support her family, to get tenure, and so on. However, I find that doing research merely for these reasons is not the path worth pursuing. For me, doing research is connected to much deeper needs in my life, such as communicating with people, learning insights from them, and working with them to make the world better. Yes, making the world better—this is where my intercultural experience comes into play. Because of the opportunity to live in very distinctive cultures such as China and the United States, I have noticed how different people understand what a "better world" is and how we can make it happen. As I am learning and challenging American culture, some values that I used to hold firmly have started to shake. For instance, I am reluctant to say "democracy is a universal value good for every country in the world," and I have become aware of how my understanding of modern Chinese history is distorted by political power. Doing research, teaching research, and writing about research in this sense are also ways for me to wrestle with my being in-between two cultural worlds and to forge a better future.

Coming Together

Now, we hope that you have learned a little bit about each of us—what drew us to do research and what research means to us. We open the book with these stories to acknowledge that research does not happen in a vacuum. Research is never an endeavor separated from who we are and our life experiences. What is your story of understanding "research"? What are your thoughts on what research is and should be? You may also ponder how we came together to write this book. What is our approach? In fact, the very idea of this book grew out of a research collaboration where we wanted to understand how our own students conceptualize "research."

Back in 2011, three of us (Peiwei, Karen, and Pengfei) were doctoral students in the Inquiry Methodology Program at Indiana University (IU) Bloomington, where Barbara is a faculty member. As indicated in our stories, we all encountered moments when we experienced disconnects from our learning processes. Some of those disconnections involved a common image of "research" sharply separated from our everyday lives and professional experiences. As graduate students, we were expected to learn *about* highly specialized and expert knowledge such as intermediate and advanced statistics. These are important and helpful topics to learn about. However, such knowledge is often positioned as if it exists independently of who we are, and the learning process demands very little self-reflection or conscious effort to integrate our learning into our lives as a whole. But intuitively, we all felt research is more than what we knew and were told earlier in our studies. Fortunately, in the Inquiry Methodology Program at IU, we experienced an alternative way of understanding and practicing research. It was cultivated by an *inquiry-oriented* culture that creates space for both *knowing* and *being*, research and practice, as well as the connections between theoretical/philosophical insights and concrete social issues. Being exposed to two different cultures of inquiry at times created tensions in our experiences. But this also deepened our understanding and primed open critical spaces for new visions.

Later in our doctoral training, Peiwei, Karen, and Pengfei all had opportunities to teach a graduate-level research methodology course and to participate in a teaching affinity group facilitated by Barbara, who also taught this same introductory course on a regular basis. Together, we became more aware of various kinds of disconnects our students experienced in relation to the notion of "research." Most of our graduate students identified themselves as practitioners in applied fields such as teaching, instructional technology, counseling, language education, educational leadership, higher education administration, student affairs, and so on. Even for those students who anticipated becoming researchers themselves, we discovered that their learning experiences could flounder without some way of anchoring this knowledge *about* research to the *lived* experiences they brought with them.

As we paid closer attention to our students' understandings of "research," we began to notice how their conceptions influenced the ways they identified (or not) with the class and their level of engagement (and lack thereof). For example, many students came to the class with preconceived images of "research" as "experiments," "numbers," "statistics," or "dry and boring research articles." They had a hard time connecting those ideas with their experiences as teachers, counselors, educational specialists, or administrators—the very passions that brought them to graduate school in the first place. Many of them considered research to be something academic experts do, and not something they themselves might participate in through their daily (professional and personal) practices. Consequently, they were not too motivated to learn and considered the course somewhat superfluous to their own goals, needs, and interests. Do you resonate with any of those experiences? Have you ever experienced similar disconnects?

Through teaching and conversations about our teaching, we could not help but wonder: Are we (students and instructors alike) embedded in a certain educational climate that favors a narrow way of thinking about research (e.g., primarily as controlled experiments or statistical analyses, carried out by someone in a lab coat)? If so, how was this culture formed? What has shaped the dynamic where students are positioned as passive recipients of specialized knowledge by the experts? Is this all that research is about? If not, what can or should research be? Is there a need to transform this rather hierarchical understanding of research toward a more inclusive and relational one?

These questions inspired us to further explore our students' conceptions of research. We were particularly interested in students' perspectives, since *your* voices were often missing from both the existing literature and pedagogical discussions. For example, we were able to find only scant literature on graduate students' perceptions of "research." In fact, this body of literature seems to further reinforce the idea that "research" is a canon of knowledge one must acquire as a graduate student irrespective of their own conceptualizations. We found this very troublesome. Ultimately, our desire to learn more from our students, and the desire to move beyond the image portraying research as a set canon of information to be learned, paved the way for our long-term research collaboration, pursuing a *student-centered* approach to teaching research methodology.

Emerging Research

This text is a direct "outcome" of this collaboration, initiated in 2011 during a dinner conversation between Karen and Peiwei. As they shared their respective teaching experiences, they were struck by the similar challenges they had both encountered. They were both interested in student engagement in the introductory research methodology course and the tension that surfaced between students' identities and the course design. Their concerns and curiosities quickly found echoes in Barbara and Pengfei's experiences. The four of us decided to form a research team and carved out a research study, which we called "Researching 'Research.'" The key question we asked was: How do graduate students in an introductory research methods course conceptualize the notion of "research"? In fact, as a sidenote, we will unpack and draw from this particular project to situate our discussions throughout this textbook. You will hear directly from some of the students in our class, although the excerpts and quotes that we took from student assignments sometimes have been modified, shortened, or condensed for clarity. Also, we have published our work in a couple of research articles (Li, Ross, Zhao, & Dennis, 2017; Ross, Dennis, Zhao, & Li, 2017). Interested readers can find full references in the Further Readings section at the end of the chapter.

This research collaboration provided a catalyst and useful insights for us to imagine, conceptualize, and develop this textbook. Immersing ourselves in student participants' own narratives made us further question basic assumptions about research. For example, we often say that the purpose of research is to "produce knowledge," but what is the nature of what we consider "knowledge"? Why do we even want to produce knowledge? What types of knowledge can or should be generated? How can we generate knowledge that is genuine and valid? Who benefits from knowledge production? For what and for whom is it produced? Who should be producing knowledge? Who is producing knowledge?

These underlying questions have been intimately embedded in the process of designing and writing this textbook. These questions touch on various aspects of research, including understanding the nature, purpose, and process of research, and the relationship between the researcher, the participants, and the larger social, cultural, and political contexts. They also bring up key concepts such as epistemology, identity, intersubjectivity, validity, ethics, and more, which we will unpack across various chapters. You can count on these key questions and concepts to resurface in the text in various iterations. There is no need to worry if those terms do not sound familiar at this point.

MAKING IMPLICIT EXPLICIT: OUR INTENTIONS AND ASSUMPTIONS

Before we introduce the specifics of the book, we find it important first to walk you behind the scenes. We would like to share some of the major decisions and dilemmas with which we wrestled as we developed this book. By making our assumptions and values explicit, we hope that you gain a better understanding of the inner workings of the book.

Holding Complexity

First, we anticipate that many readers are new to the topic of research methodology. Therefore, there is a need to introduce the conventional foundations of social inquiry so that novice research readers can build a platform to enter the dialogue. Meanwhile, our challenge here is to avoid, on the one hand, perpetuating a fundamentalist orientation that promotes the belief that one particular approach to research is the *best* or the *only* way to generate legitimate knowledge. Conventional or classic knowledge is vulnerable to this fundamentalist orientation because it is often taken for granted as a given. On the other hand, we also want to avoid throwing readers into the deep complexity of social research without sufficient scaffolding built from the "classics." As a whole, our intention is to hold both sides and to strive for a dynamic balance. That is, we work to facilitate dialogue between canonical knowledge and other perspectives, honoring the open nature of knowing and facilitating critical thinking about the very notion of knowing.

As an example of this intention of holding complexity, we introduce traditional methodological terms such as "validity," "data collection," and "research designs," but we also reflect on them through a set of principles, like inclusivity, dialogue, and power analysis. In this way, conventions are not taken up as a given without being reflected on and questioned. Similarly, this text crosses disciplinary boundaries of social sciences. We draw out shared concerns and core concepts of social inquiry across disciplines and fields of practice. In contrast, many existing texts are situated primarily within a particular field or discipline (e.g., education, psychology, health sciences, etc.). We acknowledge that substantive disciplinary differences are important to attend to, and yet we hope to focus on methodological concepts and practices that may transcend disciplines.

Bridging Binaries

To hold complexity also means to be vigilant about the potential traps of entrenched binaries. In this text, we aspire to bridge what we view as a somewhat superficial divide between qualitative and quantitative research. The demarcation between the qualitative and quantitative research "camps" has important historical roots (more discussion in Chapters 5 and 7), and the quantitative and qualitative research traditions have different methodological underpinnings. And yet we disagree with common perceptions that essentialize those differences and make their boundary unnecessarily rigid. We believe that holding the differences while examining the potential for unification can help us more critically and creatively engage with research endeavors.

Thus, we envision a nonbinary approach to inquiry, reconceptualizing research not as primarily anchored to specific methods or a set of procedures. Foremost, we view research as a fluid inquiry process that has both universal and context-specific features (more discussion in Chapters 8 and 9). We strive to hold both aspects. A prefigured separation between quantitative and qualitative research risks closing up the potential for a "meta"-level understanding that enables us to examine underlying assumptions associated with research. With this exploration, we can more critically recognize differences and make fluid or porous seemingly fixed borders.

At the same time, we would like to shift away from understanding knowledge through picture-like metaphors—for instance, thinking of research studies as "building blocks" that accumulate in time to form a larger knowledge base. This kind of metaphor implies that knowledge is like solid and independent "pieces" that are "out there" once produced. Together, they can lead to a more "complete" picture. In contrast, one possible alternative

FIGURE 1.1 ◆ Metaphor of Knowledge: Building Blocks vs. Dialogue

Source: iStock.com/mangpor_2004; iStock.com/jacoblund.

is to think of knowledge as claims that people make. From this perspective, a knowledge claim is not an entity-like object but a form of communication made by a speaker, which always has an implicit relational intent. Thus, to develop knowledge requires that we bring competing perspectives into dialogue with one another. Something new might emerge from the endless process of disagreement, persuasion, and agreement. We also would like to acknowledge that any knowledge claim, including what we say in this text, needs to stay open to being questioned, challenged, and being brought into further discussion. Any claim is potentially fallible. Thus, for us, knowledge necessitates a process of continued reflection and dialogues. The metaphor of research articulated by Barbara in her story, as people talking together, serves as the overarching metaphor for this text as well.

In practice, to bridge binaries means that we do not "stick" to any end of the "pole"; we dynamically move in-between the poles, wandering in the "gray area." Here are a few concrete applications in the text guided by this intention:

- We strive to honor the inherent connection between theory and practice. In our view, theory serves an important function of explaining, illuminating, raising awareness, and so on. But theory should never be separated from concrete contexts of practice. Thus, we anchor all of our theoretical and conceptual discussions in either ordinary circumstances or concrete professional and research contexts, where we hope readers find resonance.

- We want this text to be conceptually strong, but we also see the need to include the "nuts and bolts" and "how-to" types of content material (e.g., guidelines, resources, checklists, technical/procedural information, examples, and so on). But space is limited. We address this inevitable tension through deliberately foregrounding and backgrounding certain materials. For example, we use the

Appendix feature to accommodate supplemental materials that are important to include but may clutter the conceptual integrity of the main text.

- We debated whether to develop a glossary for the text. We certainly find it important to help readers more easily track research concepts and key terms. But we also worry that they may see how *we* define research concepts as the only or best way. As a result, we may mislead readers and counter our own understanding that concepts can be interpreted, defined, and applied very differently in the research community. Divergent views are vital for the livelihood of our thinking. We would like to convey the importance of embracing multiple perspectives. Therefore, we decided to include a glossary but stress that the glossary is more a *conceptual* than a *technical* attempt to articulate key research terms. Also, our definitions are always open to alternative articulations, and they may even evolve across chapters as those concepts grow more complex. We encourage readers to use the glossary in this open and dynamic way, and perhaps even add your own understanding as you gain confidence.

Accessible but Not Simplified

In this text, we are committed to a *student-centered* approach. We intend to write this text as a conversation *with* you rather than talking *to* you or *at* you. We also feel strongly that this student-centered approach does not mean *student-simplified*. For us, being student-centered is primarily a pedagogical issue, related to developing ways to inspire motivation and create resonance. Student-centered does *not* mean "watering down" or oversimplifying the content or writing level, but it does involve eliminating jargon and non-engaging style of writing to make the text accessible. In fact, we would argue that learning to hold complexity of ideas without quickly flattening and simplifying is an essential learning outcome for graduate students, because this metaskill is a key component of critical thinking. Being able to think and act with complexity can go a long way in your professional and life experiences.

Meanwhile, it is likely that you may run into some dense and challenging content in this text. We hope that those moments may not stem primarily from writing accessibility in terms of the overuse of jargon and abstract expressions. Instead, we anticipate that this dense and challenging feeling will likely relate to the need to wrestle with and grasp complex ideas, and to a demand for critical reflection. We firmly believe that graduate students are capable of thinking with complexity, and as a matter of fact, yearn for deeper and critical understanding. To be clear, we surely fall short in places, even with the best intention of striving for a balance between accessibility and complexity. We are open to hearing from you and learning about how we have succeeded or failed to realize this goal.

Acknowledging Our Position

Last but not least, we would like to acknowledge that we do not aim for a "bird's eye view" that encompasses all different schools of thought and ideas, or to offer you a *complete* picture of research. We disagree with the common understanding (or myth) that knowledge should be or can be "value-free" or neutral. Our stance is that the act of producing knowledge is always already embedded within a constellation of interests and value orientations, and from a given position. Carrying values and interests is inevitable and does not automatically equal to "bias," although research certainly can be biased (more discussions on this in Chapters 2, 3, 5, 6, and 16).

All four of us share a critical orientation toward research, significantly influenced by critical theories and feminist theories such as the work of German social theorist Jürgen Habermas. This stance guides how we approach this text in a fundamental way (more discussions on our theoretical and philosophical assumptions in Chapters 2 and 5). At the same time, we consciously work to avoid centering our perspective *at the expense of* exposing readers to other orientations/possibilities. We would like to keep our values and assumptions explicit so that readers can disagree with our views and we can enter a dialogue. As a matter of fact, a genuine critical approach welcomes multiple views, disagreements, and critiques so that self-reflection and further dialogues are possible. Figure 1.2 sums up our four guiding intentions in the process of generating this text.

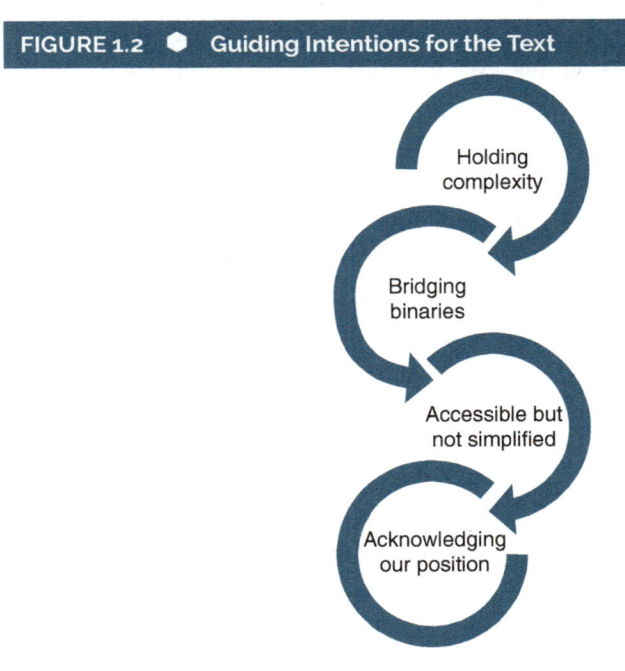

FIGURE 1.2 • Guiding Intentions for the Text

- Holding complexity
- Bridging binaries
- Accessible but not simplified
- Acknowledging our position

ABOUT READING THIS BOOK

Readers may have already noticed that we are taking a unique approach to this textbook. A typical research methods textbook usually starts with a definition of research, and then a rather linear process of choosing a research question, deciding on a research design, collecting and analyzing data, and writing up research. Research is often portrayed as a type of specialized knowledge that stands on its own. Students are positioned to absorb such knowledge passively. In contrast, this text grounds the discussion of research in ordinary experiences and foregrounds your own understanding and feelings about research as informed by your experiences. We move *away from* a didactic view of knowledge that suggests knowledge exists external to your experience and who you are. Instead, we move *toward* the premise that learning and knowledge are interactional and relational, always forming, and formed through intimate connections to your life experiences.

To create a more organic learning process, we use a *dialogical* approach in the text that draws on the concept of "dialectic" as originally discussed by the German philosopher Georg Wilhelm Friedrich Hegel (see Hegel, 1971).[1] Dialectical ideas are also prominent in the works of other scholars such as sociologist W. E. B. Du Bois (see Du Bois, 1920) and Brazilian educator Paulo Freire (see Freire, 1972). In line with this approach, we first introduce and explain concepts as they arise within the context of a given chapter. As we return to these concepts further along in the book, we add complexity and nuance to how they are discussed. Our goal, as we noted above, is not to bring you as readers to a point of "complete" understanding, but rather, through reading this text, to begin an ongoing, holistic, and nuanced conversation about the meaning of research. This is also the reason why we intentionally *stay away* from putting the emphasis on clear-cut, singular, and fixed definitions of terms and concepts—something you might be expected to memorize in some other learning contexts. We hope to create a space for dialogue and the development of a deeper understanding about research concepts over time.

---

[1] The essence of Hegel's dialectical approach, which builds upon the work of earlier philosophers and is discussed most extensively in Part I of his *Encyclopaedia of Philosophical Sciences*, is the idea that ideas or concepts are defined in relation to other ideas or concepts. According to Hegel, we initially understand concepts in a "fixed," stable way. However, this understanding is soon followed by a realization that our initial understanding of a concept is one-sided; in this moment, our understanding is destabilized. Hegel suggests that our initial, fixed understanding then "self-subulates," or passes into its opposite. In other words, the one-sidedness of an initial moment of understanding leads to a destabilization of that understanding that then leads to a new, opposite moment of understanding that negates previous understanding, while at the same time preserving the essence of that initial understanding within a new, broader understanding of the concept. The dialectical approach is reflected in this textbook in the way that we expand upon, complicate, and draw new, broader understandings of concepts into our discussion throughout the text.

Cluster Structure

We organize the textbook into three "clusters," each consisting of several chapters (see Figure 1.3 for a visual overview). Our choice to use the term *cluster* instead of *section* or *part* is intentional. For us, "cluster" signifies a nonhierarchical and nonlinear relationship among the content domains, while emphasizing the internal connections between those domains. Each cluster has its own emphasis, while a set of underlying key concepts is progressively "thematized" across clusters. This idea of *thematizing* is also illustrated in Figure 1.4: Each cluster, like a single layer of the spirals, has a distinct form. And yet, various clusters, like layers of spirals, are deeply embedded in one another. Together, they spiral as a boundless whole, where a previous movement becomes increasingly unpacked and *made explicit* in the *next* movement. Concepts become *thematized* through such progressive movements across chapters and clusters.

Specifically, Cluster 1 introduces a number of "big picture" issues that are relevant across the full spectrum of the research process. Each chapter in Cluster 1 simultaneously introduces new ideas and builds on concepts addressed in earlier chapters. Key concepts discussed and synthesized in Cluster 1 include knowledge, epistemology, meaning, criticalism, partisanship, intersubjectivity, reflection, issues of identity, research ethics, social norms, structure and power, and validity (see Chapters 2–7). Building upon Cluster 1, Clusters 2 and 3 explore the research process. Chapters in Cluster 2 address questions related to the concept of "*data*"—what data are and how data can be generated or acquired. Concepts such as identity, ethics, meaning, intersubjectivity, validity, and so on become further thematized in Cluster 2 in the context of understanding data (see Chapters 8–11).

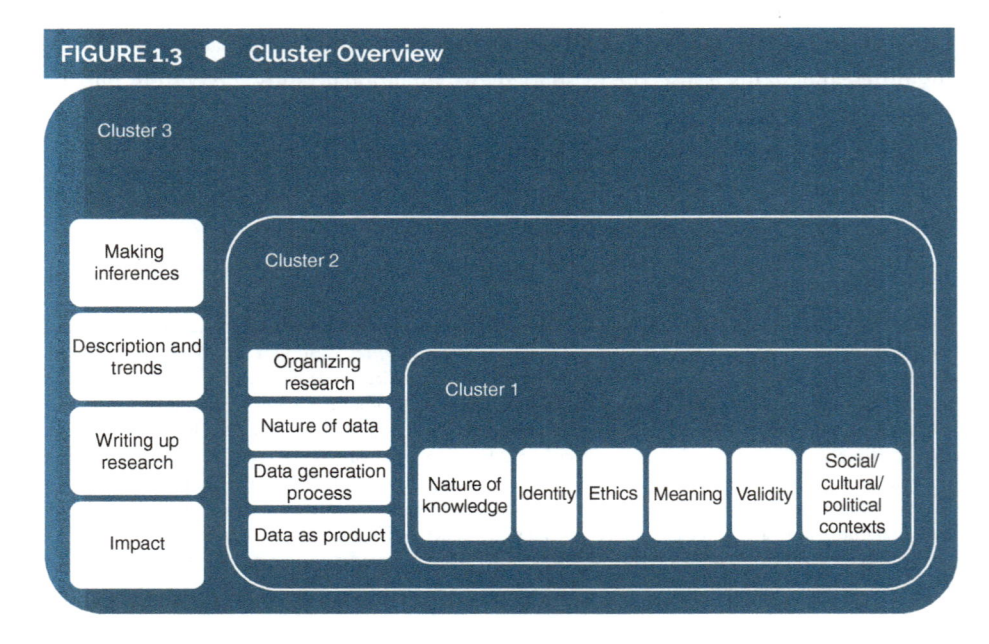

FIGURE 1.3 Cluster Overview

Cluster 3
- Making inferences
- Description and trends
- Writing up research
- Impact

Cluster 2
- Organizing research
- Nature of data
- Data generation process
- Data as product

Cluster 1
- Nature of knowledge
- Identity
- Ethics
- Meaning
- Validity
- Social/cultural/political contexts

FIGURE 1.4 ● **The Idea of Thematization**

Source: iStock.com/JianGang Wang.

In Cluster 3 we focus on the concept of *making inferences* through research, and discuss various ways to make inferences, including lower-level or higher-level inferences across quantitative and qualitative research contexts. A demarcation between description and large trends and patterns of experiences is also relevant in understanding inferences. Throughout Clusters 2 and 3, key concepts introduced in Cluster 1 become increasingly thematized through more concrete contexts of research practice. Cluster 3 also expands the discussions on inference-making to the process of disseminating research findings and academic writing, and to the understanding of research impact.

Book Features

Structurewise, we contextualize our discussions in concrete research examples and bring in the voices and perspectives of other researchers/practitioners/students. We raise questions and provide space for critical thinking and deeper reflection in various features, while working to undermine our voices as unquestionable experts. Each chapter (except Chapter 1) is written following the same structure for consistency. After a short introduction, each chapter begins with a feature we call Musing Upon the Everyday. The feature usually presents an ordinary situation that you might experience as a student, a professional, or in everyday life, which we hope provides a bridge between your everyday experiences and research concepts. Following this section, we introduce a Narrative that highlights the main conceptual ideas in the chapter. Within this narrative we include Conceptual Interludes that highlight and explain conceptual ideas that the narrative sparks. This is followed by a Research Scenario that applies concepts discussed to one or more concrete research studies, written by different researchers from a variety of disciplines.

Toward the end of each chapter, we add two features that provide opportunities for further reflection and applications. The You and Research section includes two subcategories—namely, When Interpreting Research, and When Doing Research. The When Interpreting Research subsection speaks to students who may continue to engage with research through reviewing and dissecting research findings for the purposes of, for example, guiding or evaluating professional practice. In contrast, the When Doing Research subsection is oriented to those students who are currently engaged in or may in the future engage in conducting an empirical research study. In both cases, we aim to provide practical knowledge and concrete applications for readers regarding the specific chapter content.

The Synthesis: Points for Reflection section, as the name suggests, serves to summarize the chapter, but it is more than just a summary of what has been discussed. Instead, in line with our dialogical approach, this section is an invitation for readers to continue the conversation in a few different ways. In the Conceptual Synthesis, we reflect back on key concepts discussed in the chapter, addressing how these discussions have built upon concepts introduced in previous chapters and engaged with them in integrated ways. We also recap key methodological ideas in the Methodological Synthesis, reflecting on how these link back to the conceptual discussion. We then create a space for Personal Synthesis, facilitating readers to draw your own connections to the chapter content as it relates to your personal and/or professional experiences. Finally, we end each chapter with a Moving Forward section that begins to make connections between concepts discussed and what will be introduced in the following chapter. We also provide a list of Further Readings, pertinent to key ideas discussed, and/or additional publications by the guest contributor(s).

Overall, chapters are written in a conversational style that aligns with the dialogic principle, which is at the core of this textbook. Our *language* (and content) *choices* also reflect a second key principle of our writing: inclusivity. To this end, we use the *pronouns* "they/them/theirs/themself" to move beyond gender-binary language. However, we do use "he/his" and "she/her/hers" in places where we are referencing individuals who we know identify as male or female, and in sections written by our guest contributors. We also include both first and last names of authors when we cite these authors for the first time in the text. This is to counter a historical erasure where women's contributions to the academy and to the human intellectual history at large were significantly obscured.

In sum, we hope this prelude serves not only as a map to help you grasp the big picture of where we came from and where we are going, but also a Pandora's box that gives a sneak peak of surprises and hopefully treasures for you to discover from new horizons. We are excited to have you on board!

Further Readings

Li, P., Ross, K., Zhao, P., & Dennis, B. (2017). Critical action research: How do graduate students in an introductory research class conceptualize "research"? In *SAGE Research Methods Cases, 2017*. Thousand Oaks, CA: SAGE.

Ross, K., Dennis, B., Zhao, P., & Li, P. (2017). Exploring graduate students' understanding of research: Links between identity, validity, and research conceptions. *International Journal of Teaching and Learning in Higher Education*.

UNDERSTANDING RESEARCH

Making Sense of Underlying Assumptions

ROOTS AND BRANCHES

Our journey of this text starts with seven interconnected chapters organized in Cluster 1. This cluster introduces fundamental research concepts that serve as the foundation for social research. Imagine that the research process is like a growing tree. Cluster 1 chapters explore the root system of the tree, which is mostly underground. Without a robust root system, a tree cannot sustainably grow into its full potential with lush branches. And when some branches of the tree show problems, they might be traceable to what is happening in the roots or the soil. This is why we are starting our discussion with a set of fundamental concepts and ideas that are always relevant to any research (the "roots" of social inquiry). This includes underlying sociological and cultural dynamics and conditions that either enable or limit the very possibilities, conception, and processes of research.

This orientation might seem unusual, but it is intentional. As mentioned in Chapter 1, we have taken a unique approach to building the infrastructure and organization of this book. Many introductory research methodology textbooks start by defining research, providing a brief history of social research, and then delineating common types of research and the process of conducting a research study. This strategy certainly has its merits. It provides a well-defined framework and a relatively linear and procedural understanding of the research process. This may appear helpful and appealing for students who are new to research.

However, it is also the very approach from which we hope to depart. In our view, a genuine, *student-centered* pedagogy demands a reconceptualization of how research is typically presented—for instance, as a kind of expert knowledge, or as a formal, top-down monologue. This form of knowledge is also often perceived as independent from students' lived experiences, and from the social and cultural contexts of our time. On the contrary, a student-centered approach needs to center on a *dialogue* that engages students as whole people and sees them as collaborating members at the table, who have valuable perspectives and expertise to offer for understanding research.

FIGURE CL1.1

What does this mean, concretely? It means we turn the table around, shifting away from presenting research from a third-person perspective and challenging the idea of "pure" research that only experts do. It means, instead, that we build the very conception of "research" as deeply rooted in *personal*, *relational*, and *sociocultural* contexts from the bottom up—not seeing those contexts as peripheral dimensions that can be *added* onto what would typically be considered the fundamentals of research. This is precisely what Cluster 1 chapters aim to accomplish.

To grow the tree of this lived and contextualized understanding of research requires a different root system. This root system consists of rudimental knowledge and principles that are constitutive of this new tree. Such root knowledge is rarely clear-cut; nor is it easily presented in linear or procedure-based forms. It necessarily taps into philosophical, sociological, and ethical perspectives of knowing, which are not separated from practical applications of research. In fact, *philosophical* understanding is often pitted against *practical* applications as a mutually exclusive binary. We hope to challenge this problematic divide.

Meanwhile, we also would like to acknowledge that our approach may likely provoke unfamiliarity and perhaps even create an initial sense of confusion. It could be due to the fact that this approach runs counter to some readers' existing perceptions and images of research, or that it does not adhere to the typical shape of narratives associated with a research text. If you feel this way, that is to be expected. The leap to new understanding usually involves surprises and confusion. As articulated in Chapter 1, the book is designed with an iterative structure that the key ideas and concepts introduced in Cluster 1 will be repeatedly revisited, further developed, and applied in later clusters and chapters.

To offer a more detailed overview, there are six chapters in Cluster 1: a chapter that establishes a basic understanding of research as a relational and reflective endeavor (Chapter 2), and then chapters that focus on researchers' identity and positionality (Chapter 3), research ethics (Chapter 4), the theoretical and philosophical foundations of research (Chapter 5), the social-cultural-political embeddedness of research (Chapter 6), and lastly, research validity (Chapter 7). More specifically,

- Chapter 2 introduces the concept of "research" and lays the groundwork for further discussions on the foundations of research. Readers likely already have some existing images and perceptions of what research is. Chapter 2 engages you to examine those taken-for-granted notions of research and introduces a way of conceptualizing research, most fundamentally, as a relational, critical, and reflective endeavor and process. This nature of research also requires certain commitments and responsibilities for the researcher.

- Chapter 3 focuses on issues of identity in research. Building on the relational conception of research introduced in Chapter 1, this chapter raises the question, "Who am I?" in relation to the research process. One goal of the text is to help readers integrate theoretical learning with professional and everyday practice. This inevitably requires an awareness of identity and positionality, as the researcher and practitioner themselves cannot be bracketed out of the research process. In fact, our claims to identity shape how we engage with research—and every aspect of the research process. How we position ourselves to research also brings out the question of what counts as legitimate knowledge, which we will critically examine. Actually, this theme will be present throughout the entire text.

- Chapter 4 addresses ethics as a topic permeating all research processes. It challenges the common conception of ethics that understands ethics primarily as a set of procedures, or in close relation to institutional review boards (IRBs). Chapter 4 builds on the discussions of the fundamentally intersubjective nature of research in Chapter 2 and on why positionality matters in social inquiry, as discussed in Chapter 3. It grounds the premise of ethics foremost as an ethical understanding of ourselves in relation to others, and as situational. Concepts such as care, openness, and fallibility are unpacked in this context.

- Chapter 5 lays out the philosophical foundation for the pursuit of social inquiry. It focuses on the basic nature of knowledge, knowing, and meaning. This foundation is not considered external to or independent from research practice. Rather, philosophical assumptions operate with or without our awareness, and are always an integral part of the inquiry process. In this chapter, we introduce some basic vocabulary to enter this discussion. For instance, we discuss concepts such as "ontology" and "epistemology," and an array of assumptions about what is real and what is genuine knowledge. We demonstrate how those assumptions influence how we conceptualize and carry out research. In addition, this chapter explores the nature of meaning and how we understand meaning, which is relevant to all types of research.

- Chapter 6 connects the concepts discussed in previous chapters to the broader socio-cultural-political context within which research takes place. Specifically, this chapter focuses on how social and cultural contexts shape our positionality, how we engage in research practice, and how we may interpret our findings. We explore often-taken-for-granted questions such as, What is "culture"? What is the nature of social structure and how it operates? How should we understand the notion of "power"? Meaningfully engaging with these concepts can deepen our understanding of sociological, contextual, and systemic accounts of research.

- Chapter 7, the last chapter of Cluster 1, focuses on issues related to "validity." It builds upon the discussions in Chapter 5 and further explores principles and criteria that we apply to warrant or verify research claims. Although validity is relevant to all research, this concept has been taken up in a rather siloed manner between the quantitative, mixed methods, and qualitative research communities. This chapter addresses validity in an integrated manner that transcends this traditional divides. Readers will examine how you already intuitively apply the concept of validity in everyday life, and learn related validity strategies and requirements during the research practice.

As you read through these chapters, we encourage readers to pay attention to the internal connections across them, since roots always intersect and intertwine to form a root system. Also keep in mind the spiral image presented in Chapter 1, which may remind you that the concepts introduced in this cluster will continue to unfold across the book. We are excited to move forward with you on this journey.

2

HOW DO WE KNOW? THAT IS THE QUESTION

We are curious about how you understand "research"—not in the sense of a (right or wrong) formal definition, but in terms of your own starting place in understanding what research means to you and how that understanding makes you feel. How about if you take just a few minutes to jot down some of your ideas?

In this chapter, we explore some basic underlying assumptions of research and knowledge. To do this, we first present two ordinary scenarios where one is seeking information to figure something out. Then, we discuss five core concepts that help us articulate underlying assumptions associated with knowing. This is followed by a research scenario. There is a chapter synthesis to tie these three pieces together, followed by a list of further resources. Throughout the chapter, we intend to involve readers in thinking about their own assumptions of research and knowledge. It is not our goal to provide a set of definitions, but rather to engage in a process of articulating ways we might think about research and knowledge. For example, can you identify something about which you would like to learn more? Why is this topic interesting to you? Do you have an idea about what to do to learn what you want to learn? What would you say is the same and different between learning and research?

MUSING UPON THE EVERYDAY: ENQUIRING MINDS WANT TO KNOW

Remember the first time you felt butterflies in your stomach around someone you liked? You might remember it like this: Your heart would beat so fast when you walked close to that person, although you tried hard to pretend you were indifferent. Before you knew it you had become focused on learning as much as you could about this person—googling,

Facebooking, checking with mutual friends, spotting your love interest from a distance (involuntarily), and soliciting every "coincidence" to be nearby despite a rush of anxiety. Eventually, you collected sufficient courage to drop a hint indicating your interest—words just poured onto the screen (or paper) across hours and several drafts with an eye to integrating the perfect amount of self-disclosure with a desired level of protection.

Time forward. It's 10 o'clock at night. You are situated at your favorite corner of the library. In front of you sits a huge coffee, your laptop, and a stack of articles with yellow highlights covering the pages. Your smartphone vibrates regularly with pop-ups that always successfully lure you away from those books. "Focus!" you remind yourself. A 10-page research paper is due tomorrow morning! Your professor insisted that it should include at least 20 sources. Although you are genuinely attempting to avoid another late-night work session, you just can't keep your fingers on the keyboard. Instead of squeezing out "scientifically" crafted sentences, your mind seems to wander in a stream of consciousness, something like this: What does the professor want from me? Am I just repeating what "she says, he says," or can I write about my own ideas, too? Why am I doing this? What does this have to do with me? Why does grad school have to be like this? Boring.

> **Pause and Reflect.** Perhaps you can take a moment to do a quick body scan—how do you feel in your body in each of these scenarios? Are they different? If so, why do you experience them differently, despite the fact that both situations involve collecting and making sense of some kinds of "data"? How do you think of yourself in relation to the two experiences? What sort of narratives do you generate about yourself from each story? What aspects of the experiences are important to how you think of yourself as a person?

One of the obvious distinctions between both scenes is that one's motivations and engagements with them are different. Differences in motivation are among the many ways in which we notice that the learner is involved in the process of learning regardless of the topic to be learned. We are invested for varying reasons in the knowledge we seek. Thus, efforts to get to know something are not merely efforts to know something outside of ourselves, but efforts that ultimately have something more or less at stake for us as learners.

In this text, you are going to be asked to learn about research itself. Well, that doesn't happen in a vacuum. You come to the book with motivations, assumptions, experiences, ideas, and a history of learning about "research"—you are not just beginning with a blank page. Those existing experiences likely will explicitly or implicitly impact your new learning. For example, what kinds of images and feelings come up for you when you think about the word *research*? Would you think of either of these two scenes as research? Why or why not?

NARRATIVE AND CONCEPTUAL INTERLUDES: THE MEANING OF "RESEARCH"

We will begin by developing a specialized vocabulary and set of concepts. Some of the words might seem vaguely familiar and some will be unfamiliar to you. As we begin using these concepts, we will anchor them in ordinary understandings. All five of the concepts introduced here speak specifically to ways one might think about knowledge and its relationship to research. Before jumping into these new concepts, let's articulate where we are starting.

> **Pause and Reflect.** Draw a picture depicting the relationship between knowledge and research. For example, does one lead to the other? Once you have completed your drawing, take a closer look and ask these questions:
>
> - What elements did you include in the drawing?
> - Was there a person in the picture?
> - How difficult was it to create the drawing?

It was a lovely spring break day. Karen, Pengfei, and Barbara were at the park with other friends. The three of them were working together in a class using photography for research. They decided to take pictures of each other taking pictures.

In this photo you can see Karen taking a photo of Barbara taking a picture of Karen. You can even see the shadows of them both. What you can't see is Pengfei, the photographer of the actual photo you see in Figure 2.1.

FIGURE 2.1 ● Karen Taking a Picture of Barbara Taking a Picture of Karen

FIGURE 2.2 ● Barbara Took a Picture of Pengfei

FIGURE 2.3 ● Pengfei Took a Picture of Barbara While Barbara Was Taking Pictures

Interestingly, what appears to be happening in Figure 2.1 is different than what actually occurred. If you look closely you can guess that Barbara was not really taking a picture of Karen. Barbara took a picture of Pengfei, while Karen took a picture of Barbara (see Figure 2.2); all the while, Pengfei took a picture of Barbara (Figure 2.3).

These images introduce some of the core ideas we hope to draw out through this conceptual interlude. The five concepts we present in this chapter include epistemology, criticalism, partisanship, reflection, and intersubjectivity. What do you guess these concepts mean?

Epistemology is a large term we use to talk about theories of knowledge. **Criticalism** is one epistemological orientation—that is, one theory of knowledge. The concepts of **partisanship, intersubjectivity**, and **reflection** are characteristics of a critical epistemology. We can imagine knowledge development as a conversation. The structure of the conversation represents epistemology. The values and norms entailed in how the conversation is carried represent criticalism. The conversation requires that we take one another's position in the conversation in order to understand each other. Taking each other's perspective in the conversation is best described through the concepts of partisanship, reflection, and intersubjectivity.

Epistemology: How Do We Know What We Know?

Our assumptions about "research" are linked with our basic views on what constitutes knowledge. Philosophers use the word *epistemology* to refer to the study of knowledge and knowing. We can use this philosophical term to say that research will always be linked to epistemological claims—that is, research will always be linked to assumptions we implicitly make about knowledge and knowing. Engaging in research will be an epistemological endeavor, but we are also epistemologically engaged every time we are using, claiming, developing, and acquiring knowledge—including knowledge about a love interest or a topic for a research paper.

For a long time in Western philosophy, "seeing" was a primary metaphor for knowing—"seeing is knowing," "let me *see* the evidence," "I *saw* it with my own eyes," and so on (see Carspecken, 2003). However, seeing is already interdependent with language, culture, self-identity, and power, for example. To say that we know what is going on in that photograph of Karen and Barbara taking pictures on that sunny day in the park involves more than just our visual acuity. What kinds of things can you say you know from that photograph just by looking at it? Does the image give you information about the two women—who they might be culturally and racially, whether or not they seem to know each other? Would different people "see" the photo differently? What about the assumption that we are "seeing" the same thing? What are the differences between the image itself and your interpretation and understanding of that image?

This chapter started with a scenario of interest toward some potential romantic partner. In addition to how we might learn about such a person through observations and interactions, we can also search potential information sources. Internet surfing is a typical way to learn about persons of interest. Perhaps we find a Facebook page or an article the person wrote, or we see that the person is involved in a club. Some of this information is written about the person, some is written by the person, and some is written to the person (like when a friend posts on the person's Facebook page). In order to expect that we might actually learn something about our beloved through this process we have to make a few assumptions, such as that people can be identified on the internet and that we can understand the language being used. Some of our assumptions will be more subtle. For example, we will think differently about what we read depending on the source and the content. A friend who posts something sarcastic on Facebook might indirectly indicate that a love interest has a sense of humor. Discovering that our beloved has a police record might point to a different kind of information and alternative types of interpretations. Our interpretation of the information is what constitutes our developing knowledge about this beloved. Our interpretations will also depend on our own values.

In the second example at the beginning of the chapter, we asked readers to imagine being in the middle of writing a paper. Typically, when people are writing a research report, they might find articles that support one perspective and articles that contradict that information. By seeking a balance of information, writers are able to develop and articulate previously held ideas about the topic and potentially shift earlier ways of thinking. They also are able to identify different perspectives on understanding the information. Let's say we are writing a paper on capital punishment. We will find some legal and historical information, some information about what people believe, and some information about the actual practices. We might even find statements from victims or family members of those executed through the use of the death penalty. We will find different information about organizations that oppose the death penalty and some that favor it. Our own ideas are likely to change in some way by examining the various claims to knowledge that are out there. When you think about knowledge of a person you might love and knowledge of a topic you might research, how are these kinds of knowledges and knowledge-seeking activities the same or different?

In both of these endeavors, epistemological claims are embedded in our information-seeking. We can also use the word *epistemology* to talk about the body scan you performed earlier in the chapter when thinking about how you felt in each of the scenarios posed at the beginning of this chapter. Knowledge of yourself, your own feelings, desires, and motivations is also part of the field we think of as epistemology. However, this kind of knowledge is not something we can look up on the internet as you access it in a different way.

Another epistemological aspect of these two scenarios has to do with our ideas of what is good and bad, right and wrong. For example, it might be perfectly okay to look up a love interest on the internet, but most of us agree that taking this to an extreme would not be. Also, in order to understand the legal history of the death penalty, we would have to understand what the community agrees is the right thing to do. Following Habermas (1984), community agreements are communicatively established and referenced when members of a group hold each other accountable to a norm or value. For example, we might have community agreements that killing is not okay. Knowledge of this sort is different than knowledge about our own feelings (fear of criminals or sorrow over the loss of a loved one, for example) and knowledge about the facts about the use of capital punishment (for example, who has been put to death in the last 3 years). Chapter 5 focuses specifically on questions of epistemology, knowledge, and meaning. In Chapter 5 you will learn more about these three differing epistemological categories.

Criticalism: Not Taking Knowledge for Granted

Criticalism is an umbrella term that houses a range of social theories, all bearing a *critical epistemological* orientation: Knowledge is a communicative, social achievement and knowing is the process that engages one in the social communicative efforts to know, *including the questioning of claims to knowledge*. There are important characteristics of *criticalism* that are embedded in the way all four of us think about research. The most important one is not to take knowledge itself for granted. In other words, all knowledge and assumptions associated with that knowledge should be open to question, in principle. In practice, it would be impossible to call everything into question, because even our questions have assumptions embedded in them. The point here is that criticalists assume the questionability of knowledge as one of the most basic assumptions (Habermas, 1972, 1981). Another important characteristic of a critical orientation toward knowledge is an understanding that social actors can use knowledge to make the world better or worse. Researchers who assume a criticalist orientation share an explicit value orientation toward positive social change and justice, and as a result attend to subtle and covert forms of privilege, inequality, and oppression, and aim for developing ways to raise awareness and balance unequal situations (Freire, 1970/2000).

Anything we find out about our love interest or about the death penalty should be subject to relevant questions because as knowledge-seekers we explore relevant questions in order to better understand that which grabs our interest. This is what is meant by the word *critical*. The phrase *critical epistemology* will be used at the start to imply that knowledge is questionable. Even factual knowledge about the external world—scientists are constantly posing questions of existing knowledge. For example, between the world's 1970s knowledge about both Pluto and planets and 2015 knowledge about both Pluto and planets, Pluto's status as a planet came under question. At one point Pluto was declassified as a planet and then reclassified. Science depends on the ability to question and re-question established knowledge, even knowledge that has the status of being a fact.

Partisanship

Our common ways of thinking about *partisanship* equate it with bias. Under this way of thinking, it would be bad to think of one's research as partisan. However, criticalists acknowledge that all knowledge is partisan. Let's look closely at what that means. Are you familiar with the example of blind people touching different aspects of an elephant and drawing conclusions about what they touch? Each one comes to a different idea about what they are touching. Aspects of this story will help us understand what we mean by partisanship. The idea that we cannot be all-knowing when we are knowledge-seeking is depicted through the metaphor of blindness, which is dependent upon that visual association we mentioned earlier. There is no way to know that you "see" the whole picture. In other words, the metaphor indicates the challenge of being able to identify the *whole*, or take a perspective from that whole. Everyone's "sight" is limited. When we try to find out information about a potential love interest, we are aware that there is no way we can know everything there is to know about the person. The information gleaned from each of the people seeking knowledge about the elephant is valid when understood from the perspectives through which that knowledge was generated. A description of the tail makes sense when you know where the describer is standing and what they are touching. This assumption that all knowledge is generated from a perspective is what we mean when we use the word *partisanship*. We must do our best to articulate and understand the positions and perspectives through which we are seeking and generating knowledge.

Whether trying to learn as much as we can about our love interest or about the death penalty, it becomes quite clear that the source of the information is vital to knowing how to interpret the information. There is no knowledge that does not come from a source or from a particular perspective. Think about it. Start with something you know to be true and trace that knowledge in your mind to its source. This doesn't mean the knowledge is biased; it just means that it is embedded within a perspective and an interest (Habermas, 1972). Some philosophers use the world *relative* to express this idea that all knowledge is relative to/related to its community, its context, and its source. Other philosophers use the word *partisanship* to indicate that knowledge is not neutral, and that it seems always both to assume particular perspectives and have outcomes in the world. By assuming that knowledge is not neutral, researchers challenge the conception of knowledge as something outside the knower. This challenge shows the existence of conflicting *epistemological assumptions*, in this case between the assumption that knowledge is not neutral and always involves the perspective of a knower, and the assumption that knowledge exists as something outside the knower. *Critical epistemology* has the assumption that knowledge is not neutral, including knowledge of knowing. Methodology is a kind of knowledge of knowing; thus, by drawing on a critical epistemology, researchers do not assume their own methodological decisions and practices are neutral.

Across our two primary examples, we can see that in the first place the knowledge-seeking itself is motivated and positioned by the seeker. Thus, anything produced as an outcome of these efforts will bear the mark of that motivation and seeking. The motivations and positions taken up by the seeker should be accounted for when discussing what one has learned. Likewise, each of the sources of information we might turn to bring to bear a particular perspective. For example, information from the love interest's Facebook friends will bring a different perspective than information from the police record search. Both are valid, but they are different and must be interpreted in light of these differences. This is what is meant by *partisanship*. We must be mindful of the perspectives that are engaged through the knowledge we obtain. Each perspective is always partial, and that partialness is best understood when the engaged perspective is well articulated. The old saying that there are two sides to every argument comes up here. Think about the last argument in which you were engaged and see if you can identify at least two sides. How do the "sides" and the "arguments" go together?

When you saw the photograph of Karen and Barbara seemingly taking each other's pictures, you implicitly knew that there was another photographer involved—the one who was not in the frame of the picture itself. Given what you saw in the photograph, you could almost guess where this other photographer, Pengfei, was standing when she took her picture. Then, when you looked more closely at the photo, you could recognize that Barbara was not actually taking a photo of Karen. We want to think of these visual effects as metaphors for understanding the interpretive positions that are involved in research. Interpretive positions are a topic we discuss more in the remaining chapters of this cluster.

Our epistemological orientation is critical. We wrote about this in Chapter 1 and we will continue to develop it throughout the text. This means that you should query that perspective and interpret the knowledge we offer through this perspective.

Intersubjectivity

Another important aspect of *critical epistemology* is something philosophers refer to as *intersubjectivity*. Habermas (1981) uses this concept to imply the possibility that two subjects can expect to understand one another. One's basic experience with knowledge suggests that it relies on this expectation. For example, when someone posts something about my beloved on Facebook, the one posting expects that people will be able to read and understand the posting. Now, perhaps not everyone will understand it and not everyone will be able to read it, but in order to post, one relies on this expectation. If someone replies to the post writing: "What do you mean?" the replier is also relying on the expectation that the original poster will understand the question. When questions surface, efforts are made to explain, again relying on the idea that this communicative effort can, in principle, be understood. Knowledge is fundamentally a subject-to-subject phenomenon, rather than a subject-to-object phenomenon (this particular claim is an example of an epistemological claim). Even if a researcher is studying the pros and cons of the death penalty, the point is that this knowledge is of value because of the subject-to-subject relationship—what those pros and cons mean for the social use and understanding of the death penalty. Therefore, knowing and knowledge are fundamentally relational and are constituted in dialogues between subjects rather than in a monologue by a single person. In this way of thinking, a metaphor for research is *a conversation*. Most of those conversations are indirect. For example, when you are looking up information about your love interest, you are indirectly conversing with those whose perspectives you find on the internet about your beloved. You are also using a language that you share.

Pengfei's photograph of Barbara and Karen provides a visual example of this expectation. That is, Pengfei expects that those who see the photograph will share the cultural knowledge necessary to notice that cameras are being used, that the picture takers are aware they are photographing one another, and that a conversation about this activity could ensue.

> **Pause and Reflect.** Think of the most deeply personal knowledge you have. Some people say that our most deeply held knowledge cannot be communicated—perhaps a spiritual knowledge or a deep feeling you have associated with a person or place. Perhaps it is some knowledge that illustrates an awareness of yourself. Notice any communicative or imaginative aspects of that specific knowledge. What would it take to share this knowledge with others?

Reflection

We engage in *Reflection*, as a process, when we are looking at how the subject–subject relationship is tied up in the knowledge. If we take seriously the idea that knowledge is a subject–subject endeavor rather than a subject–object endeavor, then we have to see how the subject-to-subject relationship is embedded within all forms of knowledge. This means that knowledge will inevitably reflect that subject–subject relationship. Remember from the section on criticalism that a most basic similarity across researchers who describe their work as critical involves a willingness to call assumptions into question, including assumptions about the research process itself. Being aware of the subject-to-subject nature of knowledge is one of the first aspects of reflection. Additionally, reflections on assumptions of knowing that one brings into the research process or self as knowers/subjects are implied through the knowledge itself. For example, when one is seeking information about a beloved, the ideas of what kind of lover one deserves, how loveable one is, and so forth are nestled within the act of seeking to know the beloved other. One can engage in reflective practices by articulating these notions of subjectivity and the feelings one has about oneself alongside the feelings one has toward this particular love interest.

In quite obvious ways, Pengfei's photograph of Karen and Barbara taking pictures is a reflection of her own activity in the scene. In order to get at this, we have to talk about how the photograph is being taken and what that means for the photographer. The photographer-as-subject is part of the overall conversation, and part of what it means to think about the photograph itself.

RESEARCH SCENARIO: RESEARCHING THROUGH COLLECTIVE VALUES: THE FEMINIST RESEARCH COLLECTIVE

Through this research scenario we hear from the Feminist Research Collective (FRC) regarding its commitments and values as a collective and how those commitments and values drew it to create its WomenWeLove research project. As you read its narrative, you will see how tightly its values and interests are linked with the project.

The historically significant Combahee River Collective (CRC) was an outgrowth of the U.S. National Black Feminist Organization of the 1970s. The CRC promoted equality, intersectionality for Black men and women, the inclusion of lesbians in the Black feminist movement, peace, and togetherness. The CRC was clear in its purposes and steadfast with its commitments. Feminist collective examples are important history for the formation of our Feminist Research Collective, which began at Indiana University in the fall of 2017.

The vision for our group focused on three areas: activism, shared collective feminist scholarship, and support of individual and collective academic endeavors. Democratization, equity, inclusion, and justice were important principles as we gathered and began to coalesce into a dedicated, engaged, diverse group of women. During the spring semester (2019), we spent time focusing on a research project to guide us all in our pursuit of doing feminist research. We wanted to find a project idea that everyone would enjoy working on. In a moment of pure collaboration and cohesion we found ourselves enthralled with a project that allowed us to map out the stories of women in our lives, later to be known as the WomenWeLove Project (ofwomenwelove.org). In the conception of the project, ideas and agreeance occurred organically and surprisingly. We found connections, inspiration, and synergy that brought us all together. For example, Pengfei had an idea of telling stories of the women in our lives, which could be located on a world map so that we could visualize the global experiences of being a woman. Sam chimed in that she had a family member who worked for ARCgis, a storymapping digital tool. Sam's sister-in-law was able to guide us in the use of the software, which was available free to us through Indiana University. It is difficult to describe how this special moment unfolded, but our experience speaks to the way in which the FRC has continued its becoming a collective.

Through our WomenWeLove project we establish connections amongst women from disparate places and times, and connect scholarship with those outside the academy. To begin the project, FRC members conducted interviews with ordinary, everyday women they love in order to learn about that person's life. Oftentimes pictures, newspaper articles, yearbooks, and photo albums from the person's life were included as well. The researcher then created an online digital story space using the ARCgis storymapping software to build a personally focused set of narratives with our participants. The FRC created a website through which the stories are brought together on a single landing page. Once fully developed, people from around the world will be invited to interview a woman they love and add to the page. This project embodies our values and commitments. Namely, we believe in drawing on our love for women (mothers, grandmothers, daughters, friends, lovers) to establish a knowledge base of often-erased women's lives. The project also puts expertise into the hands of ordinary folks. The project requires active collaboration based on equity, justice, and respect. Perhaps it is easy to see how our values as a collective translated into the values of this project.

We entered the interviews with our loved ones, open and ready to hear whatever they wanted to share with us. We listened to them with care and interest—their lives were already considered important to us. Each participant was active in the development of their storymap and in reviewing their interviews. However, our participants did more than this. For example, during the first workshop we led on the project (in 2019), two of our participants were present (one in person and one over the phone) to help us facilitate the workshop and to share their experiences with the project.

The values we hold in relation with one another are values we carry forward into our research, which is aligned through love with those values. For example, our value of difference and inclusion is seen in the following conversation:

> **Dajanae:** *What is our definition of women? What's our definition of women's centered voices? We need to acknowledge the history of the definition of women, and say how we challenge that. We need to deconstruct the traditional notion of "women's voice at the center."*
>
> **Barbara:** *Keeping "women's voice at the center" is saying that it is a unified place. We are actually trying to dislodge that.*
>
> **Pengfei:** *Women's voices are not one voice.*
>
> **Barbara:** *The image people will get is that we have a solid, unified center. This is problematic because such spaces are inevitably marked as a white woman's space.*

We also value a capacity to speak freely, both in terms of disagreeing with others, but also in terms of protecting the collective.

> **Barbara:** *Effective collectives can work through confrontations, but we need to rethink the idea that, in order for the group to be legitimate and authentic, there have to be confrontations. The queer youth group I work with wouldn't talk about their activities using the concepts "confrontation" or "disagreement." Members of the group do disagree with one another, yet their way of being inclusive refers to honoring both the positiveness of the group and what individual people care about and do. Forcing members of a (minoritized) group to publicly air their differences would increase their vulnerability as a group and as individual members. If you allow multiple perspectives, then differences do not have to be erased.*
>
> **Sam:** *Thinking about confrontation in this way is also a very paternalistic way of thinking about disagreement, and it has a violent connotation to it. It also stereotypes women's groups.*
>
> **Pooja:** *It's creating binaries about how groups should work. There's a confrontational theory operating in elitist scientific institutions in India. Open confrontation and aggression is a symbol of maleness in Indian academia. There's also a lot of disagreement and conflict showcased in entertainment.*
>
> **Lucy:** *Our discussions are a part of a safe space. People may disagree in a safe space. If you don't allow multiple perspectives, then reaching consensus is very*

superficial. I used to be part of a community-building group in Houston, where it was considered important that people were able to express divergent views. The key was not to do this in an accusatory way—"You did this"—but in an honest way—"I felt this."

Lucy: *What matters most is not whether we are a collective or individuals but how power is distributed within the group.*

Our commitment to equity and justice demands that we stay aware of structural and interactive power differences without, but also within. For example, as a collective and in our research, we are diligent to undermine traditional hierarchies, to destabilize roles that rely on hierarchical power relationships, and to give everyone a chance to participate and to set the priorities. Our agendas are mutually established and we take turns facilitating and taking notes. We seek to express our work as a mutual collaboration while also allowing for varying availabilities, energies, and interests. Through our collaborative research, and as seekers of justice, we build community and scholarship as manifestations of our love for and commitment to women in the world both near and far. Pengfei said, "This space allows for multiple interpretations to coexist. For example, the interviews all mean very different things to us and our relationship with our participants/women we love, but also collectively, we are creating some synergy, forging some conversations, and so on."

As part of this unique collaborative community, it is our responsibility to destabilize existing hegemonic social structures and simultaneously be open and frank about our (and our participants') burdens, limitations, and discomfort. So, while we are not personally accountable for the statements made by our participants, the onus is on us, in the future, to work as allies and subtly restate our positionality and inclusivity to defuse any potential instances of disquiet and/or distress.

Having read the research scenario, we can locate some of the concepts at work within this research study. In what ways do you think the study is critical in its epistemological orientation? In other words, how is knowledge being called into question? The study is unapologetically partisan—that is, oriented toward telling the often-left-out stories of ordinary women, through loving perspectives and within a context of love. Intersubjectivity is established between the researchers and their participants through dialogue, but also in the generation of the storymap pages that make it possible to think about the lives of women across time and space as it puts those lives in dialogue with one another. How would you describe the subject-to-subject reflection in the knowledge of women being produced through the study?

> ### ✓ YOU AND RESEARCH
>
> How are these conceptions of research similar or different to the two ordinary examples with which we started the chapter? What is the difference between thinking of yourself as a knowledge-seeker in the sense of these first two examples and thinking of yourself as a researcher? How does thinking of yourself as a researcher connect or not with other ideas you have about yourself as a professional? It is important to be aware that knowledge is not produced in a vacuum and that it is never a matter of neutrality or a reflection of disinterest on the part of the knowledge-seeker. Let's draw on the metaphor of the conversation as we imagine what the insights of this chapter contribute to both our interpreting and our doing of research.
>
> #### When Interpreting Research
>
> When interpreting research, we take a critical orientation toward the knowledge produced through research, recognizing that this knowledge is being produced with purposes, perspectives, and assumptions already in place. We want to encourage all of us as researchers and practitioners to take this questioning and open orientation into how we interpret research with which we are presented. This contrasts with the idea that one could just read the results section of a study and apply those results to their own work without taking into account purposes, perspectives, and assumptions.
>
> #### When Doing Research
>
> The questions and concepts of this chapter are brought into our efforts to do research through reflection. We want to encourage researchers to think about the assumptions and everyday practices of knowledge-seeking and how these might be carried forward in the research process. Take care to make your perspectives, motivations, and epistemological assumptions clear for those with whom you will be doing the research and sharing the outcomes of the study.

SYNTHESIS: AN OPEN DIALOGUE

At the beginning of this chapter, we introduced two ordinary scenarios for us to start to ponder the idea of "research" and how you may (or may not) relate to it. You did a body scan to check on how you *feel* about research, and you contemplated what research means to you. In Chapter 1, you also read our story of becoming researchers, and a description of how we approach research projects, including the specific project that was a catalyst for writing this textbook.

Conceptual Synthesis

Looking back at your response to describing what "research is," did you talk about solving a problem, answering a question, or gathering information? Did you list examples of things you might research? We noticed that there was, at times, a disconnect between how our students defined and described research and how they related to it themselves. Almost all of our students defined research in very formal terms, using formal language and describing it as a very formal activity. Yet, when they described their relationship as a person to research, they expressed uncertainty and used informal language. Such a contrast implied that the students experienced a disconnect between who they imagined themselves to be and what they envisioned as the work of research. Below, we provide some examples from our students and the study we conducted. Perhaps you can compare how you defined research with these examples.

Is Research a Way to Solve Problems?

Perhaps you, like many of our students, think of research as a way to "solve a problem," "answer a question," or "gather information." As one student put it, "I now can research anything I want at my fingertips. Broadly, I believe research to be a quest for further knowledge about a desired topic. We research everything: products to buy, vacations to go on, job descriptions." Another student wrote, "Research is not that unapproachable. Everyone can design and conduct a research project. And even, research shares the similar logic with the process of problem solving in our daily life." These students drew a parallel between the act of research and everyday activities. They described themselves as people who are regularly engaging in research to solve ordinary problems in life. Can you relate to this type of conceptualization? Why or why not? Do you think this type of conceptualization captures the essence of research? If not, what could be missing, in your opinion?

Are Researchers Experts?

Some of our students thought of research as a form of expertise that required specialized knowledge and skills. For instance, one student noted that research was a "serious" endeavor with "more opportunities to mess things up." Students who conceptualized research in this way tended to assume that they lacked the expertise to be involved in doing research. Our students expressed feelings of "intimidation," cynicism, or alienation toward being that kind of expert. In other words, when students thought of research as a form of expertise, they also imagined themselves outside of that expertise. One student commented that research constitutes "an academic process that requires enormous amounts of talent, time, and effort in hopes of boosting one's reputation in the overly competitive world of academia." Can you relate to those emotional qualities in your own experiences? Have you ever felt intimidated by research or statistics? If so, where do you think those feelings come from?

Is Research Science?

Another conceptualization is one in which students equated research with science and presented research as a process of testing hypotheses, or acquiring evidence to prove or disprove certain beliefs. Students who conceptualize research in this way often focus on the position of a scientist in relation to research. Their conceptualizations emphasize notions of "objectivity," "scientific methods," "numbers," "experimentations," quantitative methods, and statistics. One student described research specifically as "the pursuit of information through the scientific method." With respect to this conceptualization of research, our data indicate both complementary and mutually exclusive student identity claims. For instance, the identity claims that emerged from the assignment of one student who was raised by two parents working in professions related to natural sciences, and who also was an undergraduate researcher in a university-based laboratory, suggests that he perceives himself as someone who is both comfortable with and who can be a part of the research process. On the other hand, another student with a similar conceptualization of research described herself as being "overwhelmed" by the research process when encountering it in an undergraduate class; her narrative presented her position as being "intimidated" by the research process. What is your view on the similarities and differences between "research" and "science"? Do you think they are the same thing? *Science* and *scientific* are buzzwords that are used quite often in our professional life nowadays, but have you thought of what they mean when you use them?

Is Research a Situated Form of Practice?

Finally, a very small number of our students discussed research in terms of it being a set of practices of very particular communities of people, like academics. For these students, research entailed members of particular communities reaching some kind of communicative agreement on norms and standards for their research, and for how they will relate with one another. For instance, one student noted, "Sharing the results with the scientific community is an essential part of research. The objectivity and the validity of research can be confirmed by others within the community by the discussions and further explorations of the topic by others in the field." Students who conceptualized research in this way could imagine themselves as part of a research community, even if they presently considered themselves on the sidelines for the moment. Looking back to your definition of research, how did you position yourself in relation to the broader research community? Did you see yourself inside or outside of such a community? Do you know the norms and standards of a research community, perhaps in counseling or the field of peace and social justice?

Methodological Synthesis

"Research" is certainly not one thing, although we often have a stereotypical image or perception associated with it. Looking back at what you wrote, do you think it reflects or, on the contrary, is in conflict with how research is generally portrayed or understood?

This question is closely related to some of the findings from the "researching research" project we first described in the Prelude (Ross et al., 2017). Remember that one of our findings involved a relationship between how our former students defined "research" and how they positioned themselves as either insiders or outsiders to the research process they defined. Our analysis helped us see that our former students tended to define or conceptualize research in one of four ways on the content level—that is, research as a means of problem solving, research as a form of expertise, research as science, and research as a situated practice.

Personal Synthesis

As you read through those examples of conceptualizations, is there anything that resonates with you and your own experiences? Do you experience any tension between your thinking and feeling about research? If you consider that "research" is something external to you and feel intimidated and alienated from it, you certainly are not alone. As revealed in our analysis, many students perceive research to be truncated to a set of steps and techniques that are presumed to follow in a linear manner and in a "scientific" fashion, and are conducted and practiced by experts. This may create a sense of alienation for you if your own internalized conceptualizations of research don't resonate with how you identify with knowledge in your ordinary life.

MOVING FORWARD

The next chapter focuses on research, identity, and relational processes. The chapter will build upon the five core concepts introduced here. We want to think even more subtly about how research is relational and will always involve the identity of the researcher and assumptions about what it means to know *with* others.

Further Readings

Ali-Khan, C. (2011). Seeing what we mean: Visual knowledge and critical epistemology. *International Journal of Qualitative Studies in Education, 24*(3), 303–322.

Ambroise, J. R., & Broeck, S. (Eds.). (2015). *Black knowledges/Black struggles: Essays in critical epistemology.* Oxford, UK: Oxford University Press.

Crawford, M., & Marecek, J. (1989). Feminist theory, feminist psychology: A bibliography of epistemology, critical analysis, and applications. *Psychology of Women Quarterly, 13*(4), 477–491.

Forsyth, T. (2008). Political ecology and the epistemology of social justice. *Geoforum, 39*(2), 756–764.

Habermas, J. (2006). Political communication in media society: Does democracy still enjoy an epistemic dimension? The impact of normative theory on empirical research. *Communication Theory, 16*(4), 411–426.

Morrow, R. A., & Torres, C. A. (2002). *Reading Freire and Habermas: Critical pedagogy and transformative social change.* Columbia, NY: Teachers College Press.

Scotland, J. (2012). Exploring the philosophical underpinnings of research: Relating ontology and epistemology to methodology and methods of scientific, interpretive, and critical research paradigms. *English Language Teaching, 5*(9), 9–16.

Shearmur, J. (1988). Habermas: A critical approach. *Critical Review: A Journal of Politics and Society, 2*(1), 39–50.

Supa, D. W. (2009). The origins of empirical versus critical epistemology in American communication. *American Communication Journal, 11*(3), 1–11.

Williams, M. (2001). *Problems of knowledge: A critical introduction to epistemology.* Oxford, UK: Oxford University Press.

Further Readings by the Feminist Research Collective and Feminist Research

The Combahee River Collective. https://combaheerivercollective.weebly.com/the-combahee-river-collective-statement.html. Accessed March 7, 2020.

Dennis, B., Carspecken, L., Zhao, P., Silberstein, S., Bose, S., Saxena, P., Palmer, D., Washington, S., & Elfreich, A. (2020, July, online first). Digital migrating and storyworlding with women we love: A feminist ethnography. *Journal of Contemporary Ethnography.* https://doi.org/10.1177/0891241620937758

Martin, E. (1991). The egg and the sperm. How science has constructed a romance based on stereotypical male–female roles. *Signs, 16*(3), 485–501.

3

RESEARCH, IDENTITY, AND RELATIONAL PROCESSES

In this chapter, we build on the discussion in the previous chapter to explore two key concepts: the role of identity in research and the idea of research as relational. As in Chapter 2, we first present several examples from the contexts of our everyday experiences. We use these examples to introduce the core concepts about the nature of research as relational and closely linked to our identities, which we alluded to in our Chapter 1 narratives and which are the focus of the narrative and conceptual interludes. We then apply these concepts to our own action research project in the Research Scenario section of the chapter.

MUSING UPON THE EVERYDAY: THE PRESENTATION OF SELF

> **Pause and Reflect.** We begin with a question for you: Who are you? Or, more specifically, what is your **identity**—that is, what are the qualities that make you your own, unique person? Before we get into the chapter, take a few minutes to jot down three to five characteristics that you feel are salient in how you define or express who you are.

Now, let's think about a few scenarios where identity plays a role.

It is late at night, and you are sitting at your computer, browsing Facebook and revising your profile. What do you include? You ask yourself, "How should I describe my personality? What should I say about my hobbies? My unique characteristics? What unique quote should I include?" You ponder these questions for a while, hesitating over the keyboard.

Now, you are in a classroom, starting your first week of graduate school courses for the semester. Most of the students are unfamiliar to you, and you to them. You look around and see some talking and laughing together. Another student is sitting on their own with a scowl on their face as they pull books out of their bag. "That person looks angry," you think to yourself. "Maybe not somebody I want as a study partner this semester." You keep scanning the room, looking for someone to sit next to who seems friendly. As you scan, you wonder, "What are these other students thinking about me?"

A few days later, you are seated in the lounge of a university research center, waiting to meet with the director to interview for a job as a research assistant on a new project. Earlier that day, you reviewed the job description, and now, as you wait, your thoughts turn to how you can best show the director how you embody what they are looking for. "What do I emphasize in response to their questions?" you ponder. "How can I demonstrate my passion and commitment in just a few words and minutes?"

You might have noticed that all of these scenarios ask you to engage with how one expresses themselves and/or is perceived by others. As you imagine yourself in each of these situations, different aspects of your identity might be emphasized: your hobbies, your studiousness, your diligence. In other situations, different characteristics might be at the forefront of how you choose to present yourself. Why might this be the case? No matter what the context, there are aspects of our identities that we choose to bring to the fore, and alternately things that we try to keep hidden from others, at least initially. Even as we sit alone in a room, creating a social media profile on a computer, we are thinking about how others will perceive that profile—we make choices about how to identify ourselves based on our own knowledge and assumptions about the audience. In other words, even when we are alone, we are in relationship with others, and these relationships with others shape what we foreground in terms of identity claims.

In this chapter, we will focus on these issues as a way of emphasizing different facets of identity and their implications for conducting research. We want to emphasize in the chapter that identity is an intrinsic aspect of all social actions, not just those that require us to explicitly think about how we are presenting ourselves. Indeed, our focus in this chapter is on relational or interpersonal aspects of identity and not identity as a mode of self-expression. As we will discuss in the following pages, our implicit assumptions—about our audience, about social norms in relation to that audience, and so on—shape which of our identity claims are foregrounded and which are not. Our goal is to help you think through the ways your own identity and relationships with others are both shaped by and shape your learning, ideas, and how you engage with research.

NARRATIVE AND CONCEPTUAL INTERLUDES: EXPLORING IDENTITY IN RESEARCH

In this section, we introduce concepts related to identity, identity claims, and legitimate knowledge, concepts that we hope help begin to clarify some of the ways in which identity and research are inextricably linked. We do so by starting with an "everyday" research situation—preparations for and experiences during a trip Karen took to visit her brother when he was living overseas—and using it as the basis for discussing how these concepts emerge within more formal research contexts.

In the summer of 2002 Karen was on a bus from Johannesburg, South Africa, to Maputo, Mozambique, to visit her brother, who was living in Mozambique at the time. As the bus neared the South Africa–Mozambique border, she found herself getting more and more excited that she was going to see where her brother lived, meet his friends, and learn a bit more about his life after not seeing him for over a year. And then, all at once—she panicked. She had never checked whether she needed a visa to enter Mozambique from South Africa! What if she were turned away at the border? Thankfully, a visa was not needed, and she was able to get to her brother's village. Even as she crossed the border, however, she realized that she needed to rethink her approach to trip planning and beginning new adventures.

In the context of planning and carrying out her trip to Mozambique, Karen found herself faced with a number of dilemmas that required investigation. For instance, what kind of budget should she set? How should she plan on getting to her brother's village in central Mozambique from Maputo, the capital? What were the necessities she should pack—things that she absolutely would need and might be unable to acquire while there?

In planning for the trip, Karen relied almost entirely on her brother for information. He had a cell phone, but this was before the age of smartphones and applications like WhatsApp that we can use these days to communicate with friends and family around the world. Their communication was limited to one or two phone calls a month and postal letters that could take up to a month to arrive. And since he was her brother and they missed each other and wanted to keep one another informed about their lives, their communication, when it happened, focused on a wide range of topics that didn't necessarily include budgeting or other pertinent logistical issues related to Karen's trip. Needless to say, as a result, her trip planning was less than comprehensive, and she arrived in Johannesburg, South Africa (to where she had booked her flight) less than prepared. Hence the panic attack she experienced on the way to the Mozambique border.

What, you might ask, does this story have to do with research and, more specifically, with the concepts above? Let's tease some of this out.

Identity/Claims

When we talk about identity, many things come to mind: who I am, who you are, how the way we present ourselves or experience our relationships shifts in different contexts, and so forth. When planning for her Mozambique trip, Karen's relationship with her brother significantly shaped the way she presented herself in relation to acquiring new information. She made the choice to rely primarily on him as her source of knowledge. When she communicated with him about the trip, however, what was foregrounded was not "Karen as traveler to Mozambique" but, rather, "Karen as loving sister who can't wait to see her brother." And as noted above, this had important implications for the kind of information Karen obtained prior to arriving in South Africa and Mozambique.

Conceptually, what is important to understand from this is that the part of our identity that is most foregrounded at any moment is based on relationships. This is true both in explicit contexts (for example, in a job interview where someone is choosing to emphasize aspects of their identity that will present them in the best light possible) and in the context of social actions that are not explicitly about self-expression (as written about by Erving Goffman), as in the case of Karen's focus when planning her travel to Mozambique (for more on this, see Goffman, 1956). Of central importance here is the idea that whenever we act, we are making a claim about who we are through that action—hence, our use of the term **identity claim**.

For example, when Barbara brushes her teeth, in addition to ideas about being healthy and liking the feel of clean teeth, she is enacting an identity claim about being a person who cares for herself. The identity claim is not at the foreground of this action when Barbara brushes her teeth routinely (before bed, for instance)—in other words, being someone who cares for herself is not what she is most explicitly thinking about when she engages in tooth brushing. However, if Barbara were getting ready for a job interview, she might brush her teeth even though it would not be typical for her to brush them at that time. The act of tooth brushing in this instance would foreground not only the claim that Barbara is a person who takes care of herself, but also that she is trying to make a good impression, that she is professional, and maybe even meticulous and pleasant. She is also claiming not to be a slob. These are the kinds of things Barbara would be explicitly hoping the interviewer would notice about her, and these would be in part signaled by the tooth brushing. In other words, while preparing for and during the interview, Barbara would foreground identity claims in the way she presents herself in order to create a certain kind of relationship with her interviewer.

In the previous chapter, we wrote about intersubjectivity as a key concept related to critical epistemology and knowledge (and we will expand on this concept in Chapter 5). The main idea is that our basic experiences with knowledge are relational, constituted through explicit or implicit dialogues between multiple subjects. Likewise, our relationships with other people shape how we present ourselves, regardless of whether we are consciously focused on self-presentation or engaged in activities where identity is in the background. This means that identity is *intrinsic* to all social action, no matter the context—trip planning, job interviewing, or going on an outing with friends, as well as collecting data utilized to answer research questions.

Although identity is always a part of social action, another concept to keep in mind is that there is always more to any one of us than our identity claims, or than what is experienced as part of our relationship with others. In other words, identity claims are partial—in two ways. First, they are always enacted as part of an existing or potential relationship with one another and must be understood in that relational context. As the examples in the "Musing Upon the Everyday" section above underscore, our identity claims vary based on what kind of relationship we establish and with whom that relationship exists. Second, at any given moment, whatever is explicit about our identity contrasts with an aspect of the self that is beyond the identity claims we make about ourselves. We are always aware of ourselves and being more than any claim we might make about ourselves. It is not possible to be known in total, but only in part. For example, when you present yourself in a job interview, on social media, or during the first day of class, as in the scenarios at the start of this chapter, the claims you are making about yourself are partial—they don't tell the whole story of you. There is always a part of you that is beyond that presentation. The two ways in which identity claims are partial are illustrated in Figure 3.1. In this figure one sees that identity claims are always *part,* but not the whole, of our identity. They are also always constituted in relation with another person.

In fact, there is always a part of us that is even beyond our ability to reflect about with respect to our own selves. The philosopher Immanuel Kant (1996) described this concept in what he referred to as the "**transcendental I**." By that he meant that when we articulate our identity, even in the form of self-reflection, there is always a part of our self that is beyond that reflection. The process of reflection is itself a way of making claims about oneself, meaning that when we reflect we already transcend or go beyond that reflection or

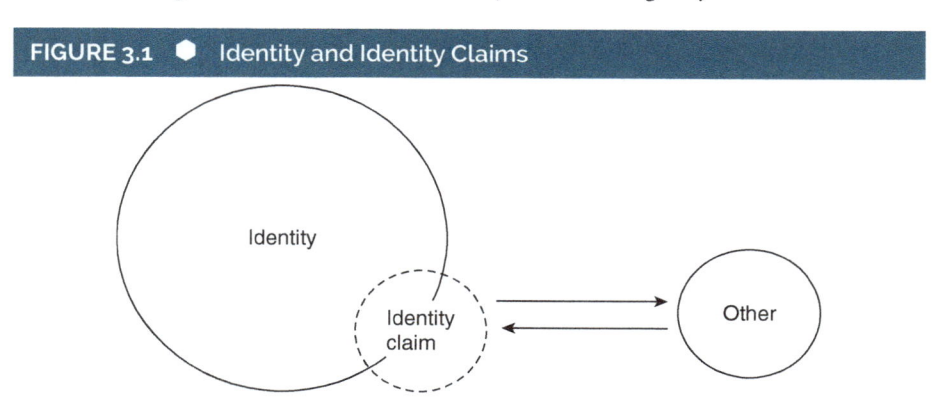

FIGURE 3.1 ● Identity and Identity Claims

what is being reflected upon. What *is* conveyed as an identity claim always already assumes a shared communicative context (either explicitly in what we express or present to others, or implicitly in terms of how we think of ourselves). In other words, building on the idea of intersubjectivity that we discussed in Chapter 2, when we express our identity in any way (even to ourselves), we do so with the expectation of a shared cultural and linguistic context—and with the expectation that others will be able to understand us in that context.

Let's try to make these concepts a little bit more concrete. In any one of the scenarios at the start of the chapter, you might think to yourself, "Who am I" or "How should I present myself?" Even though your thoughts may be focused on how you express *your* identity, this thought process already assumes, implicitly, that you are expressing that identity for someone else and in a way that would be recognized by that someone else: what we refer to as **position-taking**. In all three of the scenarios articulated, this is the case—even as you sit in your room by yourself, you make choices about what to put on your social media profile because you assume that the profile will be viewed by (and will elicit reactions from) other people. But *what* you write on that profile might be quite different from the part of yourself you emphasize in a job interview or on the first day of class.

In a different kind of context, such as trip planning, the kinds of questions asked also are shaped by the kind of relationship you have with the person you are asking for information: In Karen's case, the questions she asked her brother about how to prepare were shaped by her relationship with him and how she generally expresses her identity to him. Indeed, the way she positioned herself in relation to her brother when seeking knowledge about her trip likely would have differed quite a bit from how Karen might have presented herself if seeking the same information from a travel agent. This points to the fact that even though there might be some persistent similarities in identity claims across various contexts, what you emphasize or not—what you foreground or background in your identity claim—is not static. In other words, our identity claims change based on the context, and in particular, what is foregrounded may change based on how we think others will react and how others have reacted, or what we know to be appropriate in a given context.

Ultimately, the ways in which we express our identity or know what to foreground about our identity in any given context are relational, including in the context of formal research. Choices about what we foreground in terms of our identity shape not only the topics we research and the kinds of research questions we ask, but also the kind of information (data) we might hope to generate as part of the research process. Here is an example of what that means: Karen does much of her research in Israel with organizations that bring together Jewish and Palestinian citizens for the purposes of promoting positive social change. She herself was born in Israel to two Jewish parents (one Israeli and one American), and grew up both in Israel and the United States. As Karen has written about elsewhere with her colleague Na'amah Razon (Razon & Ross, 2012), when Karen meets with Jews and Palestinians in Israel for interviews, the way she presents herself matters in terms of the kinds of relationships she builds with her research participants. For instance, there is a difference between presenting herself as a "researcher from the United States" and an "Israeli American researcher." Neither one is more or less correct, but each of these represents a way of highlighting certain parts of her identity and leaving other aspects of her identity further in the background. And the choices that she makes about what aspects of her identity to highlight can really make a difference in terms of the kinds of relationships she is able to establish with individuals she interviews, and therefore how much they might trust her and be willing to open up during interviews in terms of participating in an interview that is meant to help answer research questions. In other words, these relationships shape the depth of data collected and Karen's ability to address the research questions guiding her studies.

In a formal research context, explicit discussion about a researcher's identity claims and how they shape the inquiry process is often referred to as a discussion about **positionality** or **reflexivity** (in other words, following on what we wrote in Chapter 2: reflection on oneself; we return to the concept of positionality in Chapter 4). However, the degree to which these issues are discussed at all depends on the epistemological assumptions of the researchers (which we started to discuss in Chapter 2 and to which we will return in Chapter 5) and, following from that, on what are considered legitimate knowledge and legitimate knowledge production processes. Furthermore, while we discuss self-reflection here in relation to how one's background shapes engagement with research, reflection plays an important role throughout the research process—for instance, when addressing ethical dilemmas (as we discuss in Chapter 4) and making decisions about how and with whom to collect and analyze data.

Legitimate Knowledge

In Chapter 2 we talked about epistemology as constituting the assumptions we make about knowledge and how it can be acquired (we will return to this in Chapters 5 and 7). When we talk about legitimate knowledge, the concept is directly tied to epistemology in the sense that what is considered legitimate or valid knowledge—that is, what knowledge to take up as "true" or "valid" in a given context—depends upon our underlying worldviews regarding what knowledge is and how we acquire it. Thus, when we judge knowledge to be valid, what we are doing implicitly is deciding how we determine something is true.

We will talk more about the nature of "legitimate" or "valid" knowledge in Chapters 5, 6, and 7, but let's consider it briefly here in relation to Karen's trip to Mozambique. At the end of her trip, Karen returned from the village where her brother was living to Maputo prior to catching a flight back to the United States. She had spent the previous

2 weeks with her brother and had not needed to manage independent travel. Since Karen didn't know her way around, her brother explained where she should get off of the bus in Maputo and how to get from the bus station to the airport. Karen made her way south from his village, and at the end of the ride received different advice from a fellow bus passenger than she had received from her brother about where to go next. She was stumped for a while, trying to decide whose advice to heed, before she saw a Peace Corps volunteer she had met earlier in the week (and who happened to be in Maputo at the same time). He was going to the same place Karen was and planned to get there the way her brother had suggested, so she decided to follow him.

The issue of legitimate knowledge manifests here in Karen's hesitation over which way to go when given differing advice by her brother and by her fellow bus passenger, a Mozambican from Maputo. More concretely, the issue relates to whose perspective she considered trustworthy, and on what basis. With her brother, Karen had a long-standing relationship, and she was confident that his directions were provided in order to help her arrive at her destination quickly and comfortably. Karen trusted his advice—she trusted *him*—and therefore she was confident in his knowledge. She had no such relationship with the bus passenger, and thus no basis for trusting the advice given—even though it was given by someone likely more familiar with the location than Karen's brother. The information Karen saw as most legitimate in this case was based upon the nature of her relationship with the person presenting that information, including his knowledge of her and what might make sense for her personally.

In an explicitly research-focused context, the issue of legitimate knowledge is likewise present, but it manifests in slightly different ways. Here is one example: In one of Barbara's research methods courses, a student who was the mother of an infant raised questions in class about childrearing practices and how she might engage in research that would help her be (in her view) a better mother. Essentially, she was interested in **action research** about childrearing—that is, she asked research questions about a concrete set of problems with an explicit goal of resolving or addressing those problems (we will discuss action research further in Chapter 8). Another student in the class thought the conversation about childrearing did not belong in a graduate course on research methodology. This second student wrote to Barbara asking her to take steps to intervene and end the discussion about what this one student considered an inappropriate topic for class. The complaining student did not consider the childrearing questions (or the knowledge they reflected) to be legitimate, because they did not think a mother in the midst of childrearing could possibly construct a legitimate research project on that topic if her own experiences were too entangled in what she wanted to study. In this case, the topic was perceived as *not* legitimate, in part because the identity claim of the student as a mother was foregrounded not only in relation to her own childrearing experiences but also in the context of conducting research.

If we think of the mother's childrearing questions as a form of action research, then her status as a mother and the various ways she identifies with that status strengthen the legitimacy of the research project rather than weaken it. As we will discuss later in the text, this is a form of research that places the researcher and their identity claims at the foreground of the research process. Action research has come under criticism because dominant approaches to research are based on the epistemological stance that there should be a separation between the researcher and the focus of inquiry. However, as Phil Carspecken (1996) notes, the researcher's own identity claims are always involved in the research process. This is true, for instance, in terms of what topics we focus on, what questions we ask, what choices we make about how to collect data, and so on. It is not possible to engage in the act of doing research and not make identity claims through the act. The question we wish to raise, therefore, is not *whether* identity claims are a legitimate part of the research process, or whether knowledge linked to our identity claims are legitimate, but rather which identity claims are foregrounded explicitly, in the research process itself as well as in how we write about it.

The question about whether it is appropriate or legitimate to explicitly foreground identity claims in the process of doing research illustrates once again the fact that there are multiple perspectives on what constitutes legitimate knowledge. In some traditional forms of research, foregrounding the position of the researcher is not considered legitimate because, as we discuss in Chapter 5, researchers are perceived to be separate from what (or who) they research, and this separation is assumed to make the research more "objective" (a concept we will discuss at length in Chapter 5). In fact, this perspective is perpetuated not only within research spheres but also in the way that research is presented in popular media: specifically, in a way that promotes expertise and expert culture as linked to this separation of inquiry and identity claims, impeding the opportunities for practitioners to engage in research. (We will also discuss this point further in Chapter 6 as part of our discussion of power and context in research.) Moreover, traditional academic writing, in which the third person is used and authors are discouraged from inserting themselves into what is written, also reflects long-standing cultural norms in research about what is considered legitimate knowledge and how that knowledge should be presented. Writing characterized by use of the third person is perceived in many contexts to be related to legitimacy and expertise. As we will discuss in Chapter 6, this perception is partially due to power structures and how they shape dominant approaches to engaging in different aspects of the research process.

It is important to note that not all approaches to research encourage this separation. Indeed, the norms discussed above are just that—norms (indeed, norms that largely developed in the context of research conducted by male, Caucasian scholars in the Global North), which are open to criticism. They are not universally shared but instead reflect understandings within this particular research culture. Another way of putting this is that knowledge (legitimate knowledge) is contextual. In other words, what is considered legitimate knowledge is community based, and the norms of any given community will inevitably be a part of how knowledge in that community is developed. Thus, we believe it is important to consider research cultures other than the dominant one, and to introduce approaches that allow for a more inclusive approach to thinking about intellectual contributions and communities of inquiry. As alluded to above, action research blurs the researcher/practitioner boundary. Moreover, in research based in critical, feminist, participatory, and certain other epistemological stances (discussed further in Chapter 5), it is expected that a researcher will make explicit their own identity both in terms of its motivation for, and in terms of its role in, the research process.

As we end this section, we encourage you to reflect for a minute on your own identity as a student and scholar, and how this is related to what you or others perceive as legitimate knowledge.

> **Pause and Reflect.** Issues of legitimacy and expertise are culturally connected to the separation of researcher and identity both in terms of substance and in terms of form. Here is an example to consider: Why do you think researchers often use the third person (he, she, it, they) when they write their studies for journals, instead of the first person (I, me, we)? What message does the *form* of this writing send, and when might it be a better choice to write in the first person? Also, when does this choice seem like a *stylistic* choice, and when does it seem like an *ethical* choice? More broadly: How do you think that the way in which arguments are expressed connects with norms or expectations we have about the perceived authority of our ideas?

RESEARCH SCENARIO: A COLLABORATIVE ACTION RESEARCH PROJECT

In Chapter 1 we introduced to you the project—"Researching Research"—that set our work on this textbook into motion. Our decision to write this textbook came out of the sense we encountered from our students that it was difficult for them to "see themselves" within the realm of research. It also grew out of confirmation of our intuition, through data we collected in our collaborative project, that many students had fixed ideas about research and about themselves that were, in some cases, almost diametrically opposed. As we discussed in Chapter 1, this had implications for how students approached research methodology courses as well as their levels of engagement with course material.

We mentioned in Chapter 1 that the project that became the basis for this textbook is a collaborative action research project. We characterized it this way because the basis for asking our research question is a desire to understand our own teaching *with an explicit desire to modify it*. Much research exists in order to provide better theoretical or empirical knowledge about natural or social phenomena in this world, sometimes with the hope that it might become the basis for changes in, say, policy or medical treatment. But as we discussed earlier in this chapter, action research is conducted so that the data that answer research questions can be used immediately, in very concrete ways. For us, the research question, "How do graduate students in an introductory research methods course conceptualize the notion of 'research'?" was a question that arose directly out of our desire to better meet the needs of students in our research methodology classes.

Another aspect of our research project that characterizes it as an action research project is the way that it foregrounds our own identities as teacher-scholars. In our "Researching Research" project, it was precisely our desire to learn about our own teaching endeavors that set the stage for the project. Our identity claims *as teachers* as well as researchers were central to the process as a whole. For instance, we framed the project this way in how we approached our students (the participants in the study), making explicit that we were starting from the perspective of researchers who wanted to know more about the experiences of our students, in order to become better teachers.

Identity also became a core concept in the way we framed our analysis. During the process of analyzing data generated through the project, we came up with a concept we (Karen, Barbara, Pengfei, and Peiwei) refer to as *pragmatic fissures* (Ross et al., 2017). This concept relates to the interrelationship between the way our students defined the concept of research, what they see as valid or appropriate ways of discussing research, and their own identity claims as related to research—that is, the way they position themselves in relation to research, as illustrated in Figure 3.2.

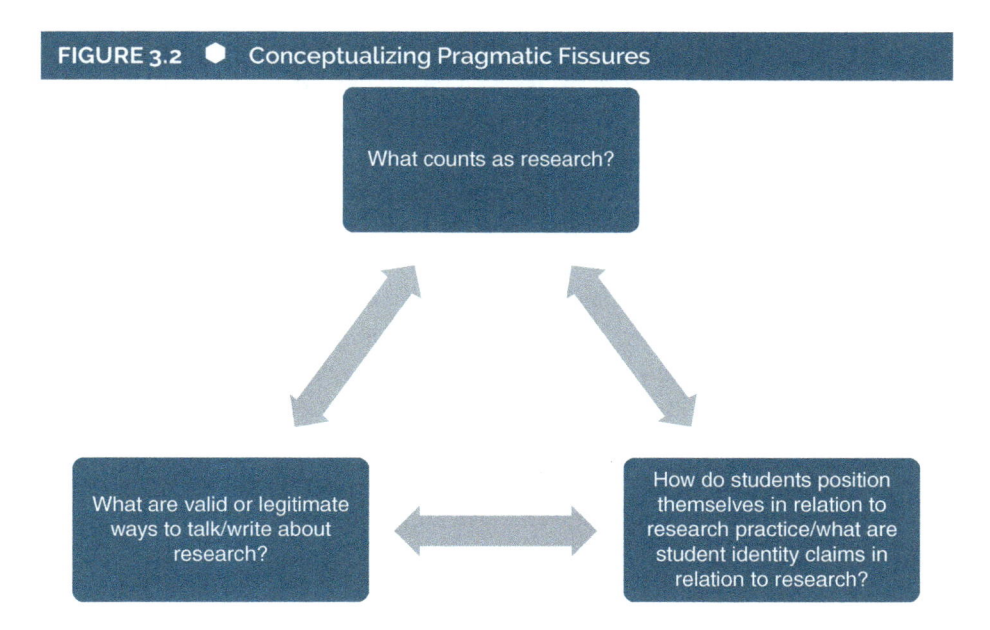

FIGURE 3.2 ● Conceptualizing Pragmatic Fissures

- What counts as research?
- What are valid or legitimate ways to talk/write about research?
- How do students position themselves in relation to research practice/what are student identity claims in relation to research?

When we analyzed students' definitions of the concept of research and their discussions of aspects of their own background and experiences shaping those definitions, we found that there were often significant contrasts, or tensions, in how students wrote about these two things—this is what we refer to as "pragmatic fissures." In essence, this term illustrates tensions that occur when students wrote about research in one way (e.g., as an endeavor that "experts" participate in, or as something requiring a lot of mathematical knowledge), but wrote about themselves in a very different way—for example, as non-experts, or as being "not good with numbers." We called these tensions "*pragmatic fissures*" to highlight the fact that the tensions we saw came across not only in the specific words students used to write about how they conceptualized research contrasted with their own identity claims, but also in the *pragmatics* of their writing: the kind of language they used (formal or informal writing), the overall tone, and so forth.

Let's look at a few examples of these pragmatic fissures to make this point more clear. During the first couple of weeks of class, we each asked our students to write a response to an essay prompt asking them to define research and inquiry and discuss anything in their background related to how they came up with these definitions. The following examples are drawn from responses to that essay assignment. (These essay responses were among the many data sources we drew upon in the "Researching Research" project.)

The first example is one where there is a clear tension expressed between the student's understanding of research and their identity in relation to research. The student understands research as one thing and expresses this as something that contrasts with their view of themselves. On the other hand, the student's actual identity claim in relation to research is not expressed clearly, and we understand it mostly implicitly from what is written:

> *To be completely honest, the words* research *and* inquiry *are and have been very difficult words for me to digest. I have always been intimidated by these words despite my desire to understand them better. When I took my required research class during my undergraduate studies it was not a pleasant experience for me. I felt overwhelmed by the terminology and the entire process of research. When it came time for the final project and designing my own research study I felt completely unprepared and at a loss for how to even begin such an endeavor. I like to think that I have learned a little more about research and inquiry since that time and have become a little more aware and understanding of these terms, but the beginning of this class has brought back a lot of feelings of insecurity in my ability to understand and approach this topic. I am trying to maintain an open mind and approach this class with an attitude to learn and absorb all that I can in the hopes of gaining confidence and better understanding.*
>
> *When I have considered research in the past, one of the reasons I believe it has intimidated me so much is because I have thought of research as this elaborate*

> *process with intricate details and a mind to imagine it that is very specific about the design. I have also mostly considered research as an extension of math and science. With this in mind I have always thought that you needed to have a good grasp of both subjects in order to do well as a researcher. While it is clear that you do need to understand aspects of math and science, it is not the driving force behind research. I have also always thought of research as "something well-qualified people do."*

When we look carefully at what this student wrote, we can see a few ways in which identity claims are articulated in ways that stand in tension with the way the research experience is defined. For example, research is described as an extension of math and science and a process with "intricate details." At the same time, this student described their experience as an undergraduate taking a research methods class as "an unpleasant experience" and spoke about feeling "overwhelmed" by terminology and "unprepared" to undertake an independent research project. While this student acknowledged that their perspective on research has shifted somewhat since that time, they also mentioned the "insecurity" that returned upon beginning the graduate-level research methodology class for which they wrote this essay.

So in this essay we see very explicitly that this student does not see "research" or "doing research" as something that aligns with how they see themself. On the other hand, their own identity claims are more implicit. For example, the essay suggests that this student does not see themself as someone who is especially good at math or science. Their essay also suggests implicitly that they are not someone who finds "elaborate processes" that require very precise, specific designs to be something appealing. But none of this is stated outright. It requires us to consider the essay as a whole, and some of the things that are not said or only vaguely alluded to, in order to reach an understanding with the student.

Here is another student essay response, which presents what we might call congruence rather than tension between the student's identity and how they conceptualize research. In other words, through the student's writing, we can see that they do not see research as something that contrasts with how they see themself, but rather that they are claiming an identity as part of the world of research:

> *I recall being a young child in grade school and learning the definition of the term, "hypothesis." To me, research is investigation. It starts with a question, idea, or hypothesis, and involves investigation to obtain information on the initial thoughts. I think of research in terms of formal, clinical research, and informal research that is part of our daily lives. Anytime we Google information on the internet, read a magazine article, or compare prices at stores for a desired purchase, we are conducting research. When we research, we are obtaining information to help support a knowledge base. In my opinion, the premise of research is to learn more about a particular thought or concept.*

This essay also did not explicitly address the student's identity. But in this example, the way that the essay is written—that is, the *form* of this essay—suggests that the student identifies themselves within the definition and description of research. For instance, they talk about research as constituting multiple things: "formal, clinical research, and informal research that is part of our daily lives," which indicates—though it is not explicit—that they view what they do as part of their daily life as constituting research. This student also uses the word *we* multiple times in the essay when talking about research, which suggests that they see themself as part of that "we." Again, as with the previous example, none of this is explicit in the words that the student wrote, but we can understand the possible meaning they are trying to convey through the pragmatics of their communication.

As we wrap up the core of the chapter, we want to address some of the implications of what we have discussed for your own engagement with research—either in the context of reading others' research or in the context of conducting your own research study. We will then end with a synthesis of what we have discussed in the preceding pages of the chapter. Before doing so, however, we want to offer one more opportunity for reflection based on what you have just read.

> **Pause and Reflect.** Go back to the definition of research you came up with in the previous chapter. Now, think about your own sense of self. When you revisit your definition, do you see yourself within it, or outside of it? In other words, does your definition include you as an engaged researcher, or does it suggest that you are someone who is observing a researcher?

✓ YOU AND RESEARCH

Let's take what we have been talking about through this chapter and think about how it might apply in the context of your own engagement with empirical research.

When Interpreting Research

When you read a research article, there may or may not be an explicit discussion of identity on the part of the author(s). Generally, this discussion is more likely to appear when the research conducted is primarily qualitative, although this is not always the case. It is often indicated by sections entitled "Reflexivity," "Positionality," or something similar. These sections include a narrative by the author or authors of the research publication that reflect on how the researchers position themselves in relation to the focus of their research, in terms of the topic, methodological approach, and/or relationship to the research participants. As you read research, you should pay close attention to whether this kind of reflection is included in the manuscript.

If it is not, look for other narratives or clues in the manuscript that can help you better understand the motivation of the researchers for undertaking this project. For instance, this information might be found in parts of the manuscript that talk about steps the researcher took to ensure the validity of their research (something we will discuss more in Chapter 7).

When Doing Research

As you begin to engage in the research process, it is important to reflect on your own identity and how different aspects of your identity shape not only relationships with research participants, but also what kinds of research questions you ask, what techniques for generating data most "speak" to you, and so forth. In research proposals and academic manuscripts, if they are articulated, these aspects of identity are discussed in sections often titled "Reflexivity," "Positionality," or that otherwise indicate a focus on how the researcher views themself in relation to the research project. Good preparation for doing research and writing these sections includes taking some time to explicitly reflect upon the ways that your identity intersects with the project you plan to undertake. This reflection should primarily address how your background, experiences, or personal/professional commitments have led you to conduct this research, and it should also help you gain a better sense of how directly you think your research project might be intertwined with aspects of your identity (for instance, you may find through your reflection that an action research project where your identity is intricately intertwined with the process makes sense; you may also realize that while aspects of your background have shaped what it is that you want to research, you want to take a bit more of a "distant" approach to engaging with the topic in the research process). It is also important to reflect upon ways that your identity may shape with whom you engage during the research process—in particular, to whom you may most naturally gravitate during the process of data generation—as well as how you might emphasize different aspects of your identity as you engage with your participants in different ways. Some of this reflection and how you discuss those emphases in the context of planning for and writing about your research also have implications for the validity of your research—something we will discuss more in the coming chapters, especially Chapter 7.

In most research that is based on positivist approaches (something we will discuss more in Chapter 5), there is almost no discussion or reflection about identity included in research proposals or write-ups. Even so, we encourage you to take some time to jot down a few thoughts about what is motivating you to engage in this research process.

SYNTHESIS: POINTS FOR REFLECTION

In this section, we synthesize some of the key elements of the discussion in this chapter.

Conceptual Synthesis

In the previous pages, we built on the concepts introduced in Chapter 2 to show how identity and relationships are integral to the research process. Throughout the chapter, we have tried to address the relationship between identity and research in a few different ways: in terms of the intersubjective nature of identity, and in relation to the way that our identity claims are foregrounded and backgrounded in different contexts and relationships, and especially in different types and aspects of research. We also highlighted the way that this relationship between identity and research emerged as an important concept from our own collaborative action research project, highlighting the way that identity is linked to the way that individuals see themselves within or as part of the research endeavor as a whole. In this way, we hope we have helped you develop a more complex way of thinking about the central role of identity within the research process. As we move forward through the textbook, we will engage with issues related to identity with these ideas in mind.

Methodological Synthesis

In the textbox questions throughout this chapter, we have asked you to reflect on your own experiences in relation to the concepts addressed. And in each of the scenarios beginning the chapter, you were asked about how you present yourself. When we look at these queries and scenarios together, we can see that they ask you to think about how you might present yourself differently in different contexts—how you might foreground or background different aspects of your identity, depending on the situation. As we have seen through the chapter, this isn't so different from research contexts, in which we need to think about *what* identity claims we will communicate, to *whom*, *how* we will communicate them, and which claims we choose to highlight or leave in the background. In other words, from a methodological standpoint, the key takeaways from this chapter relate to the way that our identity claims shape our engagement with the research process. As we have noted throughout the previous pages, identity plays a role in all aspects of the research process. For instance, identity is always present as a motivating factor for our research questions and how we engage with the research process. Identity claims also play a role in how we engage with our research participants. Moreover, although identity is always present, it is not always discussed. The degree to which identity claims are made explicit or left in the background of research relates to our assumptions about what constitutes knowledge and what is considered legitimate or valid knowledge.

Personal Synthesis

Finally, from a personal perspective, a concept discussed in this chapter that we feel is important to reemphasize relates to the *pragmatic fissures* finding from our own research project, in particular the tension that we see articulated by students who see themselves as "outside" of research because they are not experts. The idea that research requires "expertise" is a norm in the scholarly community that reinforces an "expert culture" and tends to exclude individuals who are not (or not yet) socialized into the norms and rules of academia. Throughout this textbook, our aim is to critique this idea of "expertise" as a necessary aspect of the identity of researchers or prerequisite for claiming a researcher identity. Instead, we wish to advocate for a more open and inclusive community of researchers, and we invite you to reflect upon how you see yourself as a part of that community.

MOVING FORWARD

In the next chapter we will explore issues related to ethics in research. Our discussion will build on the concepts in this chapter, with a particular focus on the relational elements of research and ethical implications that arise from those relationships.

Further Readings

Bensimon, E. M., Polkinghorne, D., Bauman, G., & Vallejo, E. (2004). Doing research that makes a difference. *The Journal of Higher Education, 75*(1), 104–126.

Fine, M., Torre, M. E., Boudin, K., Bowen, I., Clark, J., Hylton, D., Martinez, M., Roberts, R. A., Smart, P., & Upegui, D. (2003). Participatory action research: Within and beyond bars. In P. Camic, J. E. Rhodes, & L. Yardley (Eds.), *Qualitative research in psychology: Expanding perspectives in methodology and design* (pp. 173–198). Washington, DC: American Psychological Association.

4

ETHICAL CONSIDERATIONS ACROSS THE SPECTRUM OF RESEARCH

If we want to talk about research ethics, which question seems most pressing: *What does it mean for a researcher to behave ethically in the conduct of a study?* or *What constitutes ethical research?* Do you think that methods themselves are ethically neutral but that researchers can engage with methods in more or less ethical ways? For example, let's say a researcher is going to use a questionnaire to conduct a study of attitudes toward people who are homeless. Would you consider decisions about who will be included or how the items will be analyzed to not really involve ethics? Do we think about ethics as something the researcher brings in through their behavior in the research process, or do we think about ethics as something that also involves the structure and design of the study itself?

Most of the academic writing about ethics centers on the researcher as the locus of ethical activity in a study. Institutional review boards (IRBs) examine proposed studies to be sure that the researcher has plans to protect human subjects/participants through the research process. In designing one's studies and in thinking about how one should behave as a researcher we tap into how we think we should behave as people more generally. Perhaps, though, being a researcher adds a layer of ethical accountability. These are some of the issues we want to grapple with in this chapter as we introduce ideas about what it means to think and act ethically through our research.

Many of us learned moral adages as children. For example, we might have learned "Do unto others as you would have them do unto you," or "Walk a mile in another person's shoes before judging them," or "Swallow your pride."

Philosophers of old distinguished between morals and ethics by locating morality as an individual's accounting of themselves to their own specific standards of behavior in ways with which they would not have expected everyone else to agree. For example, some vegetarians do not eat meat for religious reasons. Not eating meat for vegetarians with religious motivations might constitute moral behavior for them, but they would not expect everyone else to engage in this same form of morality. In this example, the reasons for being vegetarian are personal and not expected to be largely applicable to diverse communities. On the other hand, not stealing from someone can have a myriad of motivations behind it but would be something we would reasonably expect from and commit to our social circles. We would hold each other accountable to the same expectations. We would probably even carry forward this ethical principle in unfamiliar situations or social circles of which we are not a part. The ethical principle is "Do not take things that do not belong to you," which is backed up by additional ethical principles such as "Do unto others as you would have them do unto you." There is a whole branch of philosophy devoted to ethics. The word itself is derived from an ancient Greek word (ἦθος) for custom or habit and involves the study of right and wrong *doing*. When we think about this ethics, we will not be thinking of principles alone, but rather actions through which we can talk about ethical ideas, principles, and judgments.

Aaron Kuntz (2015) recently published a book titled *The Responsible Methodologist*. In the book he argued that researchers must take responsibility for our actions in the social contexts we have entered. We invite readers to think carefully and critically about what it means to conduct research ethically.

MUSING UPON THE EVERYDAY: WHAT WOULD YOU DO?

Have you heard the following ethical dilemma? A person needs medicine for a loved one who is facing a life or death situation, but the medicine costs more than the person can afford. Is it right or wrong for the person to steal the medicine in order to keep their loved one alive? This dilemma is known as the Heinz Dilemma, and it is often used to illustrate that the reasons people give to support their response is what helps us understand how they are thinking of the dilemma in terms of morality and ethics. Our responses to ethical and moral dilemmas help define us as people. In fact, just thinking that a particular situation is a moral or ethical dilemma is itself an indicator of how we locate ourselves ethically. Sometimes a situation one person experiences as an ethical dilemma is not a dilemma at all for another person. When was the last time you faced a dilemma that was about ethics?

> It's been a long day. You stopped at a local multipurpose department store on your way home to pick up a lot of supplies for a party the next day. The line to

check out was long. You are ready to get home. The bill totals $163.44 and you pay with four 50 dollar bills ($200.00). You are not really paying attention, and in the hustle you take the change and the receipt and dash out of the store shoving both the receipt and the change into your pocket. You head to your vehicle and load the bags of stuff into the back of your car. At this point, you take the receipt and money out of your pocket and you realize the cashier gave you too much change—four dollars too much. You shop at that department store often and you could just bring the change back in another time. Of course, you could choose to walk back in then. You are tired, but you know the right thing to do. *What do you do? Is this an ethical dilemma? Why or why not?*

You are walking along a city sidewalk in the evening. There are people sitting next to the sidewalk bundled up with blankets. One of the people you pass, a young woman, looks up at you and asks if you have some money you can share with her. You are not sure what to do. You happen to have a small bit of change, but you have always been advised that it was not a good idea to give money to needy people on the street. In fact, you recall seeing a sign nearby asking people not to give money to panhandlers. You could make sure the struggling woman knows where the nearest homeless shelter is or how to get food from a community pantry. You could stop and buy a meal for the person. But money? Do you make eye contact with her? Should you give her money? Do you say no? Do you say you don't have any? Do you offer her helpful information? Do you offer to buy her supper? Do you say anything? *Is this a dilemma for you? Why or why not? What is the intersection of moral and ethical behavior in this example?*

You are in a bookstore and you see an adult grab a youngster by the arm—probably the child is about 7 years old and probably the adult is the child's parent. The adult is reprimanding the child for not coming when having been called. The child wants to keep reading a book, but the parent is ready to go. You feel uncomfortable in your stomach about the way the child is being treated and in some ways it reminds you of times you felt impatient and talked harshly to your own children. *Is this an ethical or moral dilemma for you? Why or why not? What do you do?*

Pause and Reflect. Take a moment to think about your answers to the above scenarios. What, at last, compels you to act in a particular way? What are the factors you consider when pondering those situations? Think about the person you are as you act in response to the situations presented. We connect our ideas of ourselves with our beliefs about ethics. Because ethics involves our ideas of acting right, ethical actions or inactions carry a judgment with them about being a good person. What would a "good" person do in the scenarios above?

Ethics in Research

Following World War II, U.S. social psychologists began exploring concepts of obedience, social manipulation, authority, and evil with an interest in understanding how ordinary people could have consented to, participated in, and perpetuated the horrible atrocities of this Holocaust. In contrast with the idea that such evil behavior was primarily the result of a psychopathology, American social psychologists of the mid-20th century wanted to better understand how it was that ordinary, otherwise moral people could engage in the horrific crimes committed by Nazi Germany and Imperialist Japan. Researchers realized that it would be difficult to study how human beings might act in particular situations if they were informed up-front about what the researcher was studying. Knowing the objective of the research (for example, understanding obedience and social manipulation) would necessarily impact how people would act in the research study itself and thereby limit the researcher's ability to understand how obedience, for example, might work in the everyday context. Thus, social psychologists developed a research tradition that involved useful deception. Stanley Milgram conducted a series of studies looking at obedience to/compliance with authority. In these studies, a research participant was assigned the role of "shocker." The participant was told that the study was about the effectiveness of shock punishment in promoting learning. The participant was ostensibly enlisted to administer the negative shock as punishment whenever the "learner" got an answer wrong. The researcher was the authority figure and, when they expressed reluctance, would encourage the all-male participants to administer the shock. Also, the voltage of shock escalated incrementally as the learner continued to make mistakes. However, instead of studying the effects of punishment on the learning process, Milgram was actually studying obedience and authority. Both the "researcher" and the "learner" were actors hired by the actual researcher. The "learner" pretended to get hurt by the increased levels of shock voltage. The "researcher" acted in an authoritarian way, expecting the subject to continue administering shocks at increasing voltages even when this became visibly uncomfortable for the "learner." The subject administering the shock could see and hear the "learner" through one-way glass. Milgram was interested in how far the participant would go in obedience to the researcher–authority figure. You can see why Milgram had to deceive the participant. The study had to be set up in such a way as to produce the conditions of authority. Some subjects got visibly upset with being asked to continue increasing the voltage in light of painful pleas by the learner to stop. Still, the subjects were admonished to continue and most did, while only a few refused.

Milgram's study is used as an example of research that does not live up to contemporary standards of ethical practices. Deceit is still considered an acceptable part of a research protocol if it is deemed necessary for the kinds of results one is interested in obtaining. However, at the conclusion of duping the subjects, researchers are expected to inform participants of the real purposes of the study, and it is at that point that they are given an opportunity to consent to the actual study. Do you think it is ethical to use deceit like this in research?

> **Pause and Reflect.** Use the internet to check out other studies through which ethical debates have emerged. Consider looking up these: the Tuskegee Syphilis Study; Genie—a 20th century wild child language study; Alice Goffman's *On the Run*. What ethical lessons can researchers learn from these studies?

Procedural and Situational Ethics in Research

Institutional review boards (IRBs) were established in part to help researchers design studies that avoided ethical problems. The boards are responsible for assessing whether or not a proposed study lives up to ethical requirements. IRBs particularly focus on the protection of human subjects in the social sciences. For example, when deciding whether or not to approve a study that involves deceit or harm, IRBs balance the merits of the knowledge to be gained with the potential harm for participants so long as participants are informed (even if after the fact) of the requirements of participation and potential harms/benefits and are able to consent. IRBs also give special attention to caring for human subjects from three types of vulnerable populations (children, prisoners, and people with disabilities).

Institutional review boards provide fundamental and necessary, yet minimal, oversight for each given research project. Review boards, by their very nature, have to take a **procedural approach to ethics**. What this means is that review boards will examine the procedures of the study to ensure that those procedures are fair and transparent, provide ample opportunity for non/participation and non/consent, and ensure that risks are identified and minimized in relation to anticipated benefits. As you might imagine, IRBs cannot help researchers with all ethical decisions that might arise when conducting a study. Researchers must draw on a more contextual approach for this. **Situational ethics** requires researchers to take the complexity of the situation into account when engaging as an ethical researcher. For example, perhaps a young person agrees to have their photo included as part of a study, but you realize that the photo might produce challenges for the person's future job-seeking. In this case, perhaps you decide not to use the photo, even though you have permission from the youth and IRB approval.

A procedural approach to ethics would ask the following questions of studies like Milgram's:

- Are subjects able to say no to participating in the study at any point throughout the research process?
- Is the deceit necessary to obtain the findings?
- Are the risks of participating appropriate, including the emotional labor of administering shocks to someone in pain?

- Does the deceit produce negative consequences for the participants that are not easily mediated and/or are not justified by the value of the findings for the world?
- Is the participant properly informed of the study's purpose and given a free and clear opportunity to withhold consent?

This approach focuses its ethical concerns one-directionally: What is the researcher doing to the subject in terms of costs (time requirement, emotional demands, for example)? What is the researcher offering the subject in terms of benefits? And how is the researcher obtaining informed consent, providing confidentiality/anonymity, and accounting for risks? Journal editors will not publish studies that have not secured IRB approval.

A situational approach to ethics, such as the one described above, could complement a procedural approach, but the premise is always that research ethics are at first internal to the research situation at hand. In the above example, there could be procedures used to minimize the risks of using photos (a procedural approach), but those procedures would need to make sense within the particular situation (by taking a situated approach). Such procedures could be helpful for the researcher, but they would not be sufficient for ensuring the ethical behavior of the researcher. Research situations will have a more or less micro-level context. For example, in a large-scale international testing study, math scores obtained internationally do not involve interpersonal contact with the subjects of the study, possibly not even with anyone in the country from which the scores were obtained. A situated approach to ethics in this scenario would have to take into account whether or not the subject was becoming too distressed in the process. For example, the very research topic of asking a subject to obey the researcher's authority and administer a shock even when the "learner" was clearly being harmed was duplicated inadvertently between the "researcher" and the subject. Some subjects became distraught with having to administer the shock, and still the pretending researcher would continue to admonish the subject to administer the shock regardless of how distraught that subject had become. There was no consideration for the contextualized situation, or the person. What should an ethical researcher do in this situation?

The American Psychological Association offers five guidelines for avoiding ethical quandaries, as outlined by Deborah Smith (2003). These guidelines are intended to keep ethical problems at bay. They include:

1. Discuss intellectual property frankly. For example, establish who has contributed to the development of ideas, identify whose ideas are being drawn on, and provide participants with appropriate credit for their ideas.
2. Be conscious of multiple roles. That is, acknowledge that people will engage in the research through multiple roles, such as facilitator and friend. These roles might be fluid and contradictory.

3. Follow informed consent rules. As researchers we establish, usually through IRBs, what rules of consent we are agreeing to follow with our participants, and we must follow these. For example, we might agree to destroy audio files after a particular length of time.

4. Respect confidentiality and privacy. Refrain from using names, stories, or information outside of the research context. For example, confidentiality and privacy can be compromised if we initiate, engage in, and otherwise discuss our work with friends or colleagues. It is important to keep these concerns in mind.

5. Tap into ethics resources. There are a variety of online and institutional resources that help us think about and respond ethically to research situations. This would include scholarly publications on ethics, but also professional codes of ethics and other such resources.

Much of the rest of this chapter focuses on the situational aspects of engaging ethically in research. At the end of the chapter, we will return to a discussion on the procedural aspects of ethical studies.

NARRATIVES AND CONCEPTUAL INTERLUDES: ON BEING ETHICAL IN RESEARCH PRACTICES

In this section of the chapter, we will build on concepts to which you have already been introduced, namely positionality and intersubjectivity. We will move these concepts forward to bring in the concepts of care and openness. We will also begin to talk about power dynamics and how they can be linked to ethical action and social justice endeavors. Philosophers and methodologists have long considered ethics to be practical—that is, linked to action. As we explore important concepts for ethics, we will use an example of research on bullying.

Bullying has received a lot of policy and research attention. There are both quantitative and qualitative studies on bullying and policies that link to those research studies. The study topic in itself has a social justice orientation with a concern for not only being able to describe and understand bullying, but ultimately with the hope that research can inform practice in such a way as to decrease or eliminate bullying. Jing Wang, Ronald Iannottie, and Tonja Nansel (2009) examined the prevalence of bullying across four modes (physical, verbal, relation, and cyber) among U.S. adolescents. They used self-report questionnaires and already existing survey data to report the distribution of bullying activities and victimization according to demographic characteristics. Kathryn Modecki, Jeannie Minchin, Allen Harbaugh, Nancy Guerra, and Kevin Runions (2014) looked at bullying across two contexts—cyber and traditional face-to-face. They analyzed published research studies reporting on prevalence of both cyber and traditional bullying/aggression in order to locate the trends related to bullying across a variety of contexts and characteristics. This way of conducting research about bullying in schools is helpful because it contributes to our ability to take social action to reduce bullying. Understanding the distribution and prevalence of bullying and victimization is important for society. We are able to ask important questions about bullying, and we know that the answers to those questions have ethical implications. The methodological decisions also have ethical ramifications.

As someone who conducts long-term school ethnographies, Barbara has had the unfortunate opportunity to witness and hear talk of bullying in schools. At one time, she was in a school that had a growing population of non-native English-speakers. Anecdotally, her research team was hearing a lot of stories about bullying, and members of the team were witnessing bullying. In the high school, the newcomer students (as they were called) were being bullied by other students as well as by educators. Barbara first wrote about this as an ethical question: What happens when an ethnographer intervenes? She was trying to locate what it meant to intervene in the ongoing activities of a research site and when not intervening resulted in perpetuating harmful, ongoing activities that were being regularized among people at the site. Barbara wasn't just in this site as a researcher; she was there as a person—a person who would hold herself accountable to being ethical. Jette Kofoed and Dorthe Staunæs (2015) ask researchers to refrain from intervening in bullying scenarios when conducting school studies. They argue that researchers should focus instead on the research contribution. They also suggest that by resisting the urge to intervene, researchers can take a more critical stance toward the community's sense of goodness/badness or rightness/wrongness. They argue that hesitancy is an ethical stance in the research context, and they use the example of witnessing bullying, imploring researchers not to intervene. In what ways might intervention be talked about using ethical principles?

According to Barbara, there was a teacher in the school who was not treating one of the newcomer students very respectfully. The particular student, Yu-Ting,[1] told Barbara's research team (and the English-as-a-second-language teacher at the high school) that she felt uncomfortable in the offending teacher's class, and that she did not know how to succeed in that class. Yu-Ting was nervous even talking with the teacher. At that time, Barbara's research team read over transcripts of the class and became more and more convinced that Yu-Ting was being academically intimidated and emotionally disrespected. What was Barbara to do? She had promised her participants (which included both the teacher and the student) that the research would not be used to harm them. Protecting the student seemingly required Barbara to put the teacher at risk. What ethical principles are involved, and which ones should be prioritized?

---

[1] A pseudonym.

The dilemma for Barbara involved how to act ethically in relation to both concerns: concern for Yu-Ting's well-being and concern that none of her research participants (in this case, the teacher) be harmed as a direct result of participating in the study (which seemingly ruled out reporting the offense to a principal using research data).

> **Pause and Reflect.** When we are faced with certain dilemmas we *feel* that there is something we must do, some way to act. And we can sense that by doing one thing or another we are being a particular kind of person. A philosopher named Martin Heidegger (1889–1976) helped us think about ethical action as noticing an *impending me*—that is, who I would be if I acted in particular ways. For example, what if I see a friend cheat on an exam? I might think that if I report the cheating, I am being a *snitch*. What if I don't report the cheating, but instead talk with the friend about how to help them prepare better so they do not feel the need the cheat? Then, perhaps, I will think of myself as a "mentor" or "guide" to my friend. Can you think of research scenarios where a researcher might respond one way or another, and in so doing be recognized as a particular kind of person?

Positionality

In Chapter 2 we were introduced to the concept *partisanship*. Remember that partisanship is our acknowledgment that all knowledge is claimed from specific perspectives and through specific assumptions. In Chapter 3 we were introduced to the concept *identity* as claims we make both explicitly and implicitly through our words and deeds. These two concepts can help us understand the idea of positionality. Researchers write about positionality in a variety of ways. Alan Peshkin (1988) writes about the subjectivity of the researcher (for example, that the researcher's feelings and experiences are involved in how the researcher is positioned in the project). Feminist Nancy Hartsock (1983) writes about positionality as a standpoint perspective from which to engage research through an existing set of value commitments (such as valuing equity across gender), through a sociopolitical orientation (as we might find if someone were disadvantaged by a sexist political system), and through a set of epistemological assumptions (like knowledge is socially constructed). Each of the various ways of thinking about researcher positionality contributes important details to our thinking. For our purposes in this chapter, we want to bring together the concept of positionality as a way to explore how one might ethically engage in research. Acknowledging that we bring into a research project a particular perspective and set of values helps us begin to locate ethical positions. We carry the task forward if we think about either how we identify through those values and perspectives *and/or* how they play out in the resolution of what we experience as an ethical dilemma. When Barbara was experiencing the situation with Yu-Ting and one of her teachers, she was aware of her own partisanship—a passion for disrupting inequity and injustice in schools and a concern for students who have been marginalized in schools.

Barbara has long considered herself an advocate for social justice, both inside and outside her academic work with schools. If you review Barbara's work you will see a history of identifying with disadvantaged children, including her early years as a special education teacher in a small rural school. These values and identity claims are connected to how Barbara imagines herself behaving ethically. In some ways, positionality will always, in part, have an ethical dimension. As we are positioned through our actions, we are partly to be known as (positioned as) ethical (or not) through those same activities. In other words, our activities can always be interpreted with respect to ethics and, consequently, the ethics of our own positions as relative to those actions can be questioned.

Because our positionality is established in relation to/with others, the ethical dimensions of our positionality are contextual. Barbara was not content just to witness what seemed to her and others an example of a teacher being harsh with a culturally and linguistically different student—she had to act. She had to contribute to making things better for Yu-Ting, but she also had a commitment to protect the teacher as a research participant. The dilemma about what to do showed its face through Barbara's positionality as a social justice researcher.

Researcher positionality is a common part of the language of doing qualitative research, but what does this mean for people who conduct quantitative studies? How can we locate researcher positionality if it is not directly written about? Just above, we referred to a meta-analysis study by Modecki et al. (2014). Let's take this one as an example. A meta-analysis is a research project that looks closely at existing research studies. Researchers systematically find and examine literature adhering to a particular scope or type and then they analyze the results of the studies to find patterns across them. Modecki et al. located 80 quantitative studies that reported prevalence rates for both traditional and cyberbullying/aggression among adolescents. They did not involve any human subjects directly to conduct their research. In their findings they concluded that the variation across measurement approaches of the different studies accounted for the variability of the results that were reported across the different studies. Modecki et al. do not have a "positionality" statement in their paper. Even so, we can locate their values and surmise an ethical position from statements they do make. In the introduction, they wrote, "Before translating findings [of studies on bullying] for advocacy and intervention, it is crucial to first present accurate estimates regarding the extent of the problem and to demonstrate how varying concepts and measures influence results" (Modecki et al., 2014, p. 604). The authors also take care to acknowledge psychologists' concerns that there are more negative consequences of cyberbullying (in contrast with traditional bullying). Although this concern was not addressed through their study, they wanted to be sure that the lower prevalence rates associated with cyberbullying were interpreted within this context of existing concern, without having to claim that the concern emerged through their study.

At the start of the article, the authors position themselves as part of a community of people who care about reducing bullying and other forms of aggressive behavior among adolescents. They do this in a number of ways. For example, in the first paragraph of the paper they write, "The realization that bullying in any context can have lasting physical and emotional consequences has led parents, educators, and policymakers to embrace intervention efforts, and there is now substantial educational and clinical interest in programs that help to mitigate bullying's harmful outcomes" (p. 602). We are led to interpret the researchers as positioning themselves in this cause. Further along, they continue, "For policies and programs to safeguard youth against detrimental consequences of bullying, it is first . . ." (p. 603). This is further confirmation of our interpretation. The authors are beginning to locate themselves in a project that has a social justice motivation—that is, to better understand the prevalence of aggressive activities (including bullying) in order to contribute to effective policies and practices aimed at decreasing these activities and alleviating their effects. Their genuine research questions emerge from this perspective.

Just a few more things to notice. Modecki et al. specifically selected studies involving adolescent self-reports of an adjacent experience. This means that they prioritized getting the voices of the youth. While there are likely a myriad of reasons for focusing on self-report studies, one must minimally take such reports to be valid and important. One would not be of the mindset that reports of bullying and aggression are overrated or predominantly false if one were using them to document prevalence rates. These positions carry forward an ethical orientation toward what is right and what is wrong complicit with a particular way of enacting research that has the potential of helping us create a better world.

Intersubjectivity

We first encountered the concept *intersubjectivity* in relation to the concept *epistemology* (Chapter 2). We explored the intersubjective basis for all communication and knowledge—that is, communication and knowledge as a subject-to-subject endeavor. Now we can locate intersubjectivity specifically in the context of ethical action because behaving ethically requires some understanding of others and our relationships with them. Intersubjectivity helps us think about how we can position-take with others so we understand our actions from their perspectives, even if in a relative and imperfect way. This **position-taking** also constitutes our ethical understanding of ourselves in relation to others. It might take a rudimentary form—like "do unto others as you would have them do unto you," which basically suggests that we treat others as though they were like us. However, it can also mean that we learn to position-take with our research participants because we are listening to them and coming to understand them. We can be with our participants in this way, working toward understanding. Ethics seems to need this *being-with* character and *being-with one another* depends on diversity and difference (Dennis, 2018).

It was not easy for Barbara to relate to Yu-Ting through her own experiences, but she was able to listen to Yu-Ting talk about how she felt. Barbara cared about Yu-Ting. Barbara wanted Yu-Ting to be understood and appreciated as a learner by her teachers. Through dialogue Barbara and Yu-Ting and other educators at the site could work ethically together to care for Yu-Ting's well-being. In the end, even the offending teacher was included in the *being with*. The teacher felt inadequate in their ability to teach Yu-Ting. The teacher did not want to treat Yu-Ting specially by accommodating her needs. The teacher did not want to change what they were doing. The teacher, however, was happy for us to find a different teacher for Yu-Ting. In the end, that was what happened. *With* one another, the group found an ethical resolution. This term *one another* is a good way to heighten our sense of ethics in the research process. The questions of right and wrong are practical and contextual questions. The intimacy of imaging ethical activity seems also to involve the context of specific imaginable others.

How would this idea of intersubjectivity, as grounds for understanding ethical activity, pertain to studies like Modecki et al. (2014), where there are no direct interactions with human subjects—no sense of *one another*? In these cases perhaps the ethical accountability is both greater and smaller. Intersubjectivity is still involved in the interpretive process in a layered way. As Modecki et al. analyzed the studies they included in their research, they specifically looked up the instruments used to see how bullying and aggression were both defined and measured. They also asked the primary researchers of the studies if they had any questions related to interpreting the study. This way they gave the researchers a chance to answer those questions. When researchers clarify their analytic interpretations with others, the check-in bolsters the ethics of the study because it is more inclusive and fosters a *with one another* attitude within the research process. The alternative might be to impose one's own interpretation. As another example, Modecki et al. (2014) found some contradictory information regarding prevalence and suggested that "further research is needed to reconcile these different interpretations" (p. 607). What these examples illustrate is that even in research where human subjects are not directly being studied, intersubjectivity (that is, the relationship between the researcher and other interpreters) still grounds the interpretive process. Moreover, it is possible to locate ethical action as involving researchers in an interpretive process that is inclusive, multipositional, and has a *with* orientation—in this case, *with* researchers who study bullying and *with* adolescents who are reporting on their experiences.

Care and Openness

As a subject-to-subject endeavor, research involves engaging *with* others, even when one is the lone researcher and one is not engaging directly with human subjects. The intersubjective milieu creates a space for caring in the context of being open to the other. *With*, as a contextualized way of thinking about research ethics, calls us to care about and with our participants, our research communities, the communities that stand to benefit from the research, and so forth. These networks of care ask us to be open emotionally, intellectually, and culturally. What we mean by openness is researchers being open to their own fallibilities, to the experiences and claims of others, and to learning *with* others about the communities within which we live. Care is a way to act and feel, but one does not have to feel a certain way in order to behave in a caring way. Through care, one commits to acting with an attitude of least harm and most beneficence for those affected. This care does not work like a rule book, but instead works through position-taking. Caring involves asking oneself questions like "How will this research decision affect the participants?" and "How will this research decision affect the community?" and "How will people feel about engaging in this way?" and so forth.

Among qualitative researchers, the link between care and ethics is made of common dialogue points. However, for quantitative researchers, the concept of care has not been acknowledged as relevant, in part because quantitative researchers do not tend either to talk about their work in subject-to-subject terms or emphasize the relationship aspects of their work. Nevertheless, care with procedures is a form of care for and care with research subjects and communities. For example, institutional review boards require researchers to identify how they intend to protect participants' confidentiality. All researchers, including those who engage in quantitative approaches, will have to think carefully about how to do this, given the specifics of their studies. For quantitative researchers it might mean being sure to separate the data from identifiers, like contact information and consent forms. For qualitative researchers it may mean using pseudonyms and being sure the data are kept in a secure place.

Being open to one's own **fallibility**—to the idea that perhaps one's interpretation might be faulty or one's expectations might not hold up—contributes to ethical action by enabling researchers to hear and understand perspectives, experiences, and interpretations that are different than their own so that they might take these differences seriously when it comes to understanding and care. Our abilities to act ethically in relation with others benefits from being open to those others. Doing what is right, doing the next right thing, in terms of our research practices is dependent upon what it means for others. How can we imagine the relevance of openness for quantitative studies where part of the craft of doing the research involves tightening (rather than opening) the range of potential interpretations? For example, quantitative researchers often define terms in quite precise ways. Well, if a quantitative researcher is concerned about how to define things being studied, that researcher could examine a broad range of definitions and think carefully about whom the definitions serve/benefit and whom they harm. Simultaneously, a researcher might articulate what is made invisible through specific definitions and what is made visible. For example, if one defines caring as "providing verbal support," then one might make invisible (or fail to see through one's research) the way a person cares for another nonverbally. These same questions might be examined when thinking about who to include or how to get a sample of subjects from the general population of interest. Choosing specific ways and places to recruit has ethical consequences. One way to remain open is to be as broadly inclusive and reflective as possible when making methodological decisions. For researchers engaging in qualitative studies, being open involves listening to what participants have to say about the design, data collection approaches, and findings. It also means hearing when one's expectations are not being met and when there are surprising things to hear. Doing these things would be considered ethical in the context of a research project because they afford the researcher an opportunity to authentically secure perspectives and engage in position-taking with participants. When that happens, the research is less likely to harm its participants.

Power

We suspect that the concept of *power* has been lurking in the back of your mind. Perhaps you were thinking that care counteracts power or uses power to carry out its good deeds. Maybe you wondered if the degree of one's openness was relative to the effects of power in particular situations. Power is conceptualized differently across varying philosophical clusters. For example, some philosophies define power as the motor that produces all knowledge. In this way of thinking, knowledge always serves those in power, maintaining the status quo in how people act and what people think. Another way of thinking about power is that it distorts truth and forces people to abandon the goal of understanding as the primary focus in our interactions and quests for knowledge. In this way of thinking, power is used strategically to achieve outcomes that keep people from reaching understanding with one another. Instead of thinking of researching *with* one another, power would be invoked *on* or *over* others. When power is invoked, responses by others are forced and truncated. Let's look at an example. What if a researcher wants to **prove** that their antibullying program gets the best results? If that researcher is invested only in the outcomes and not toward understanding how the antibullying program is actually doing and why it is working or not working, that researcher might create a questionnaire in which respondents are forced into choosing only positive responses about the program. In such situations, we would say that power has intruded on the research process. Can you spot this problem in the following question?

How positive was your experience in the Supercalifragilisticexpialidocious Antibullying Program?

FIGURE 4.1 ● How Positive Was Your Experience in the Supercalifragilisticexpialidocious Antibullying Program?

★	★★	★★★	★★★★
Positive	Quite Positive	Very Positive	Extremely Positive

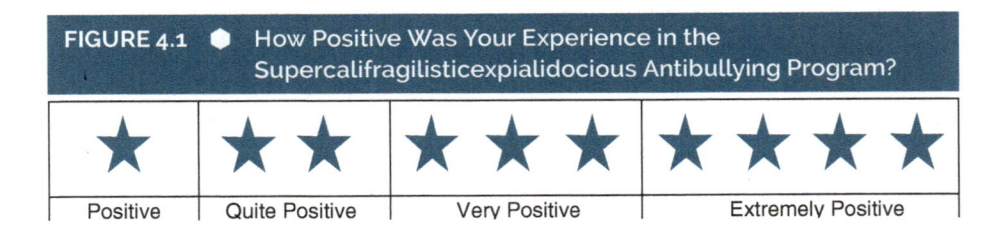

Power can influence the outcomes of research even in unintended ways. Imagine that the researcher asks respondents to answer questions in order to receive a $15 pass to a local movie theater. If the respondent wants the movie pass, they might decide to participate on the researcher's terms even if the questionnaire forces them to describe their experiences only in positive terms. In this case, the respondent might participate in order to get the movie pass, even when unable to respond authentically to the questions.

Recall the Milgram study? The researcher used his authority to test obedience. This was done in a way that withheld care for the research participants who begged the fake researcher to let them stop administering the shock. The researcher used his authority as power over the subjects and even though this was part of the research question itself, the power caused harm to some of the participants.

Sometimes power enters the research process through cultural and social structures. For example, researchers often have cultural power, and subjects might make extra efforts to please the researcher. According to Jim McCambridge, John Wilton, and Diana Elbourne (2014), the Hawthorne Effect in research is conceived as what happens when subjects try to provide the answers they think the researcher wants. We could use the term *power* to explain this as an effect of the hierarchical status relationship that is cultural in nature, which rests on who holds authority in the culture. Likewise, other sociocultural structures could be involved, such as the gender and ethnicity of the researcher.

The potential negative effects of the uses of power must be held in check. IRBs will monitor studies for the use of power in recruiting, for example, asking researchers what their relationships are with potential subjects (Are you their teacher? Are you their client? Do you have any authority over them?), but the more subtle forms of negative power must be attended to through conscious awareness/reflection, dialogue with participants, and openness.

Empowerment is also a form of power. This form of power energizes people to act on their own behalf to the benefit of the communities important to them. We also use empowerment as a way of thinking about research potential for members of disadvantaged communities. We have to do this with some caution. If researchers go into communities intending to empower them, then the researcher is not taking a *with* attitude, because the researcher would be assuming both that the participants need empowering and that the researcher themself knows how to go about doing this. Drawing on a *with* attitude, researchers would, instead, enter communities open to participants locating their own possibilities for empowerment; then empowerment is more likely.

Power can disturb a researcher's ethical orientation as it limits intersubjectivity, truncates positionality, and works against care and openness. Empowerment, on the other hand, can be an outcome of ethically enacted research and should, in practice, foster intersubjectivity, care, and openness.

In the research scenario below we see how one researcher has committed themself to studying the way people speak *into* and *with* survey researchers. As you read through the scenario, we encourage you to think about how this methodological interest deepens our understanding of research ethics with respect to positionality, intersubjectivity, openness, care, and empowerment.

RESEARCH SCENARIO: MARGINALIA: SARA MCCLELLAND

Dr. Sara McClelland, from the University of Michigan, explores what it means when what survey responders write in the margins raises technical questions about the status or meaning of the commentary for data analysis. We might also think about what these marginalized comments bring up for our ethical consideration.

Have you ever left a note in the margin of a survey? Perhaps you wanted to explain your answer or reword the question to better fit your experience. Maybe you wrote "sometimes" as your answer since the only response options were "all the time" or "never." These kinds of comments are called "marginalia." Comments and markings in the margins of a survey offer researchers an opportunity to listen when participants "speak back" about their lives and the research process. Unfortunately, marginalia are nearly always disregarded and often seen as unimportant by researchers. I argue, instead, that marginalia are an invaluable tool for any researcher who wants to understand more about the phenomenon, person, or group they are studying (McClelland, 2016).

Leaving comments in the margins of a survey, crossing out words, and changing the text of the survey are all ways that participants can make their voices heard, even if a researcher did not ask for their input (or asked for input only in a specific format, as in "check all that apply"). Marginalia is often a way of a participant saying, "You won't know the answer by asking like this," or "I can't make my experience fit here" or "This is what you need to know" (Smith, 2008). Marginalia, therefore, offer an important way for researcher and participant to communicate with one another during a study, even if they are not physically in the same place. When participants are faced with survey questions that do not match their experience, the person may reject the survey, accommodate their experience to fit the questions, or reformulate the questions to accommodate their experience (in other words, provide inaccurate data). Without greater attention to the feedback that participants leave (when researchers provide the opportunity), those asking the questions risk not knowing what we have missed in the process of trying to learn something.

In one study of marginalia, I examined comments left by participants in a study of women diagnosed with metastatic breast cancer. I analyzed comments participants left next to and around survey items about female sexual function. The participants in this study left lots of notes and other kinds of marks on the paper surveys, and rather than ignore these notes, I used them to develop new information about the women in the study. For example, participants often explained their responses to certain questions and offered more detail than the survey question allowed them to share. Most dramatically, when I used the marginalia to guide my analysis of the survey data, there were several key findings that changed as a result of the marginalia analysis. This highlights the role that marginalia can and should play in survey research. I developed several guidelines for researchers to use when pursuing studies of survey marginalia and offered three categories for analysis: 1) marginalia that aim to clarify or explain survey responses, 2) marginalia that aim to correct the survey, and 3) marginalia that communicate a survey item is not applicable (see McClelland & Holland, 2016, for more detail).

Marginalia challenge researchers' assumptions (about the world, about those they are studying, about the research process) and bring heightened attention to the ethical dimensions of research. Studies of marginalia extend calls from feminist scholars of color who have argued that margins of all kinds should be recognized as locations of political knowledge and power. Writers such as bell hooks (1984), Gayatri Spivak (1990), and Linda Tuhiwai Smith (2006) have called for attention to the power of "speaking back from the margins" of a group, society, or nation as an essential way to bring greater attention to those who are routinely ignored in political decision-making, and indeed, marginalized. This perspective is also part of a long tradition in psychology, including feminist psychology (Unger, 1998), participatory action research (Stoudt, Fox, & Fine, 2012), and critical psychology (Fox, Prilleltensky, & Austin, 2009). These writers and their colleagues encourage researchers to listen more carefully to participants' demands to be heard. These demands should, in fact, change the way that research is done and incorporate more voice and experiences in any study. Analysis of marginalia provides one of the many available methodological tools to see this promise through.

Marginalia are a gift, a form of labor, and a challenge from the participant— they should be viewed as an invitation to understand more and understand better. It is key, therefore, that researchers respect the time, energy, and insight that participants offer over the course of any study. Researchers too commonly come to think of participants as "cheap" labor, especially with the increased use of online data collection such as Amazon's Mechanical Turk (MTurk) and other data collection systems that pay participants a few cents to answer a survey question. Data collection, however, should never be "cheap." It is unethical to think about study participants merely as disembodied labor providing data for lower and lower prices. Regardless of the study design, asking someone to participate in research is—and should be—respected as important work and rewarded as such. Rather than looking for ways that we can cheapen data collection, marginalia research encourages researchers to communicate with participants, listen to their feedback, and change our methods in response to this priceless interaction.

Dr. McClelland's insights indicate a subtle way of thinking about survey research where there is a tendency to ignore what's in the margins and thereby erase participant responses. We can learn from her ethical interest in the respondents' full participation, even when it exceeds the boundaries originally set by the researcher. Notice, also, that ignoring what is in the margins is to assume power over the respondents rather than to assume equity and accept that respondents have something important to offer the researcher that should not be erased.

✓ YOU AND RESEARCH

When Interpreting Research

It is difficult to judge the ethical aspects of a research study only through published accounts, but it can help if we establish some questions oriented toward ethics that we might bring into our interpretations of studies. Can you think of ethical questions that might help guide your reading of research? For example, will you be able to determine the extent to which respondents or participants were afforded opportunities to disagree with the researcher?

As scholars involved in reading, making sense of, and applying published research, it is important to be sure that we attend to the ethics of the research, in the first place, and then that we use research findings in ethical ways, in the second place.

It is not always easy to assess the ethics of published studies. On the procedural level, we can use institutional and organizational certifications. For example, it is nearly impossible to publish research without certifying to the journal that the study was approved by an IRB. Therefore, it is pretty safe to assume that studies published in research journals have been approved by an IRB. Also, studies conducted by members of a professional organization like the American Psychological Association or the American Educational Research Association will adhere to those organizations' stated ethical standards. However, in this chapter we have encouraged you to think more broadly and deeply about research ethics. This will require you to pose questions of studies regarding positionality and power—for example, looking for answers to those questions as you read. If I were reading a study that reported on findings of international testing, I would want to know:

- who paid for the study (power),
- what opportunities for refusing participation were reasonably available (power),
- how members of the community were described (e.g., as members of a poor, "developing" nation) (positionality),
- how the measures were culturally attuned (intersubjectivity),
- who from the community/nation was involved in the development of the measures (intersubjectivity), and
- how the community was able to first use the test data (openness and care).

In the second place, we want to think about the ethics of using the findings in our own context and for our own purposes. This question has a double-sided ethical issue. Is there any potential risk for participants in my applying the data to other communities like our own, *and* what will be the effects/risks for our own community? The ethical issue involves whether or not the use of the findings contributes to making the world a better place—more egalitarian, more socially just and equitable, more caring and open. Do the same ethical principles we want to see upheld in research practice also hold up to how the research findings affect the social life of communities? Research does things in the world. When we use research, we must hold ourselves accountable to what's being done.

When Doing Research

As someone actively engaged in doing research, you will be expected to meet the procedural requirements of institutional review boards. For example, even in situations that are not under institutional review, as researchers we hold ourselves accountable to the same procedural standards because we recognize their important ethical value. However, this cannot be the end of our ethical thinking when we are conducting studies. One of the best ways to be sure your research is not harmful is to persistently ask yourself ethical questions about the relationship and effects of the research on and for participants. Taking a *with* attitude helps us orient our research with respect to positionality, intersubjective awareness, openness, caring, and power/empowerment in ways that decrease the likelihood our research will cause harm, particularly in unforeseen ways. We must never assume that we have settled all ethical issues just by having obtained IRB approval. Finding ways to better understand our participants' experiences with the research can help us stay ethically tuned to them. We can build these opportunities into our research design, for example, by making space for participants to give us feedback specifically about the research process itself.

Sometimes people assume that minimal face-to-face contact with participants produces minimal ethical considerations, but we must be careful with any assumptions

(Continued)

(Continued)

that seem to suggest we can minimize our ethical concerns in research. Instead of beginning with a minimalist approach, we can raise ethical questions as potential concerns and see where they lead us. For example, if drawing on already existing data, we can ask more questions of the data-gathering process rather than just assuming we do not need to be concerned about the ethics of data collection. IRBs will typically exempt studies using already existing large-scale data sets, but this does not mean there are no ethical concerns. If you want to tap into such data sets for your own research, you should be well informed about the ethics of the data collection. What did researchers do with missing data, for example? You should be sure that your own use of the data is consistent with what participants might have expected. For example, perhaps participants were told the study was about economic achievement, but your study is about gender differences. Would those participants have agreed to participate in a study on gender differences in economic achievement? You should consider ways in which participants were treated by the research—asking, for example, how power might have influenced participant responses. Because research is never neutral, we are never free to give ourselves a pass on ethical concerns as researchers. It is possible to broadly apply the principles presented in this chapter to help you raise ethical questions from *within* any particular research study. In much the same way that Dr. McClelland opens up her research to what participants have to say in the margins, we want to create opportunities for participants to speak back to us, to resist our power, to take matters into their own hands.

SYNTHESIS: POINTS FOR REFLECTION

In this chapter, we have started thinking about research ethics. Our ethical actions are not just a matter of being an ethical researcher; when we behave ethically, even in the research context, we identify ourselves with what is right. One thing we did not talk about is how to assess our own ethics in reflection on the ethics of others. Can we reflect on the ethicality of our behavior? Can we reflect with others on the ethicality of their behavior? What would this look like? Though being an ethical researcher requires adhering to institutional review board expectations and concerns, one's ethical activity as a researcher is an ongoing aspect of one's work in the project. It is a doing that can be spoken of through research decisions, interaction points, writing, and returning. We begin thinking of our ethical actions as intersubjective, positioned, caring, and open. We see ourselves as oriented toward understanding rather than oriented toward strategically achieving some *a priori* goal.

Conceptual Synthesis

In addition to thinking of ethics through both procedural and situational categories, we have tried to lay out some basic principles through which to raise ethical questions.

These principles are themselves interrelated. For example, intersubjectivity infuses our capacities to care and is affected by how open we are to others. Power distorts our capacities to engage in caring and open ways. Positionality is given through intersubjectivity. Positionality is always a matter of power/empowerment. That is, positions themselves are not neutral. This orientation toward ethics is communicative and relational in nature. Imagine there is a problem that needs to be solved. We have a diverse group of people sitting at the table, including those who are most likely to be affected by the problem. At this table, everyone is open and oriented toward understanding one another as part of the effort to solve the problem. We genuinely care for each other, and we are able to act on this care. We recognize our positions at the table as equal. We do not have to hide from others at the table. In this situation we are able to proceed with all taking on ethical commitments for both the way in which the conversation happens (for example, making sure everyone gets to talk) and for the outcomes of the conversation (the solutions to the problem that are the result of the conversation). This image guides how we think about research. It enables us always to locate ourselves with ethical questions as a legitimate and important part of the conversation, and the image reminds us that we are accountable for how we structure the way the conversation is going to happen (our methodology, so to say) as well as how the outcomes of the conversation get put into place to solve the problem (what it means to disseminate and use findings).

Methodological Synthesis

These questions force us to think about the behavior and whether or not it could be considered ethical. But we can also question the ethics themselves. What makes such and such ethical? Here's an example:

> We might suggest to you that "*It is unethical to publish research without making it available to your participants, even when you do not directly have participants* (as in the Modecki et al. study)."

> You might respond, "*What makes that ethical? Being committed to that might mean that you are limited in what you present, that you do not present the raw truth. Wouldn't it be unethical to hold back on the truth?*"

Your response would have pushed our conversation on ethics forward.

> We respond by saying, "*We have to be able to do both to a certain extent, but maybe the raw whole truth does more harm than good. We wouldn't want to do harm, and certainly the best way to be sure we are not doing harm is to the let the participants speak back to us.*"

And so the conversation goes on. What we can notice is that conversations about ethics will continue as each person makes reference to alternative ethics that seem to support the claim. Similarly, alternative ethical claims might support a counterclaim. This kind of conversation on ethics is the way to assess and dialogue about ethical action. Such dialogue is always implicitly possible. This holds regardless of whether we are trying to establish the ethics through a procedural approach or through a situational approach. For example, if the IRB asks us as researchers to provide information about psychological services to adolescents we interview about bullying experiences, we might ask, "What are the consequences of this, and for whom? How is this ethical?"

These kinds of questions can be turned toward research practices themselves, producing a methodological orientation on ethics. The textboxes in this chapter asked you to think through research ethics from a relational perspective. Each of those opportunities for reflection have assumed that methodology is not a neutral set of actions and that research always has consequences that are embedded in what we do methodologically. This applies even to the use of the scientific method.

Personal Synthesis

Think about a time when you did something you knew was wrong. How did you know what you were doing was wrong? What was the motivation for doing it? How did you feel afterward?

Sometimes we do not behave as ethically as we know how to. When this happens, we can assess our motivations. We can recognize the conditions under which doing the right thing would have been more likely.

Sometimes we realize later, after acting, that something was not ethical in terms of the activity or its consequences. For example, like us, you might like chocolate. Not all chocolate companies derive their chocolate from ethical sources. Some companies employ child slaves. Perhaps you unwittingly purchased chocolate from such a place. Was your purchase unethical if you were unaware of the slavery? Is there any way to be an ethical consumer in contemporary Western societies? One unintended consequence of the chocolate purchase is a prolonging of child slavery.

MOVING FORWARD

In the next chapter, we will look at knowledge and meaning. This chapter makes our ideas about intersubjectivity and criticism even more explicit. We get ideas about how our beliefs about knowledge affect what it is we know. This will give us an opportunity also to see how our sense of ethics might intersect with our beliefs about knowledge and meaning.

Further Readings

Dennis, B. (2018). Working without/against a compass: Ethical dilemmas in educational ethnography. In D. Beach, C. Bagley, & S. Marques da Silva (Eds.), *Handbook on ethnography of education* (pp. 51–70). Hoboken, NJ: Wiley Press.

Hugman, R., Pittaway, E., & Bartolomei, L. (2011). When "do no harm" is not enough: The ethics of research with refugees and other vulnerable groups. *The British Journal of Social Work, 41*(7), 1271–1287.

Lahman, M. K., Geist, M. R., Rodriguez, K. L., Graglia, P., & DeRoche, K. K. (2011). Culturally responsive relational reflexive ethics in research: The three Rs. *Quality & Quantity, 45*(6), 1397–1414.

Oliver, P. (2010). *The student's guide to research ethics* (2nd ed.). Berkshire, UK: McGraw Hill. Open University Press.

Panter, A. T., & Sterba, S. K. (Eds.). (2011). *Handbook of ethics in quantitative methodology.* London, UK: Taylor & Francis.

Resnik, D. (2011). What is ethics in research and why is it important? *National Institute of Environmental Health Sciences, 1*(10), 49–70.

Further Readings by Sara McClelland

McClelland, S. I. (2011). Who is the "self" in self-reports of sexual satisfaction? Research and policy implications. *Sexuality Research and Social Policy, 8*(4), 304–320.

McClelland, S. I. (2016). Speaking back from the margins: Participant marginalia in survey and interview research. *Qualitative Psychology, 3*(2), 159–165.

McClelland, S. I. (2017). Vulnerable listening: Possibilities and challenges of doing qualitative research. *Qualitative Psychology.* Online first at: http://psycnet.apa.org/psycinfo/2016-62665-001/

McClelland, S. I., & Fine, M. (2008). Writing *on* cellophane: Studying teen women's sexual desires; Inventing methodological release points. K. Gallagher (Ed.), *The methodological dilemma: Creative, critical and collaborative approaches to qualitative research.* London, UK: Routledge, pp. 232–260.

McClelland, S. I., & Holland, K. J. (2016). Toward better measurement: The role of survey marginalia in critical sexuality research. *Qualitative Psychology, 3*(2), 166–185.

McClelland, S. I., Rubin, J. D., & Bauermeister, J. A. (2016). "I liked girls and I thought they were pretty": Initial memories of same-sex attraction in young lesbian and bisexual women. *Archives of Sexual Behavior, 45*(6), 1375–1389.

McClelland, S. I., Rubin, J. D., & Bauermeister, J. A. (2016). Adapting to injustice: Young bisexual women's interpretations of microaggressions. *Psychology of Women Quarterly, 40*(4), 532–550.

5

KNOWLEDGE AND MEANING IN RESEARCH

In this chapter, we dig deeper into the philosophical assumptions and understandings that are always backgrounded in any research endeavor. We often call this "foundations of research," which we began discussing in Chapter 2. We revisit and build more complexity and connections with those concepts introduced in Chapter 2, starting with an everyday example followed with a narrative that draws on ordinary experiences. We then introduce a conceptual interlude that focuses on a set of basic philosophical ideas related to research. This is followed with a research scenario and responses to that scenario by different researchers. We would like to emphasize that research does not take place in a vacuum but always has certain assumptions embedded. Some of the concepts introduced here may be quite new to you, and they can be a bit abstract to grasp. Meanwhile, try to trust that you also already have some intuitive understanding of these ideas.

MUSING UPON THE EVERYDAY: UNDERSTANDING MEANING

Have you ever attended a funeral of someone you didn't know well? Imagine you get the news that a distant family member just passed. The funeral is in the midst of the semester, and you have multiple deadlines coming up. But it is only an hour away and will take place during the weekend. You feel ambivalent and obligated at the same time.

Eventually you decide to go, since most of your nuclear family members will not be able to make it. You start to make some plans: Should I send some flowers? Should I send a card? Should I attend all the events or just some? Which ones might be appropriate to skip? What should I say to the family?

The day comes quickly. You put on a black formal outfit and arrive early at the church where the service is taking place. You run into a lot of people you know but haven't seen for a while. You are busy carrying on small conversations to catch up with people while trying to blend in the atmosphere of commiserating about the death. You find this is somewhat awkward—you are not really very sad since you did not have a relationship with the passed person, who seemed to have lived a very good life until the end. Still, you feel out of place because you do not feel as sad as everyone else, you assume. You try to conceal your true feelings inside but you worry that it will show on your face; other people may notice. This makes you feel anxious.

Putting yourself in this scenario, how would you know what is appropriate and what is expected of you? How would you approach the discrepancy between how you feel and how you are supposed to feel and appear? What kind of prior knowledge would you need to draw from to understand how to act in that situation? What if you grew up in a very different culture? Would you understand the situation in the same way?

As you "live" through the scenario, you have tacitly engaged in various ways of knowing and, for that matter, acquiring knowledge. For example, the knowledge you gain from reading someone's obituary is different from knowing what is appropriate to wear and say at a funeral. Similarly, knowing how you feel inside is different from observing and interpreting other people's reactions to the funeral. There are different types of knowledge, and we recognize their difference through the ways we have access to the knowledge. In this chapter we will demonstrate that knowing and knowledge in such ordinary experience do not differ fundamentally from how we generate research claims about a given phenomenon. They both involve underlying assumptions related to: What is knowledge? How do we know? What is real? How do we understand meaning? How do we know something with certainty? How is research related to what we take as knowledge and reality? These are the key questions we will delve into in this chapter.

The questions above highlight a few basic research concepts, namely: epistemology, ontology, knowledge claims, action, and meaning. Fundamentally, these concepts all relate to how we make sense of the world, and the process of our sensemaking. This is relevant regardless of whether it is in the contexts of our informal experience in everyday life or formally through a research investigation. Thus, let's start with how we typically make sense of the world and our experiences in the everyday.

> **Pause and Reflect.** Jot down a few words or draw a picture that describes some of your basic understandings about the world. For example, what are some of the ways through which you know about things around you? What do you consider "real" in your experience (e.g., this book you are holding, invisible atoms that are the building blocks of all objects, ghosts, love)? How do you know something is true or not? What about knowing something is right and just? How do those things impact how you interact with others and the world, if at all?

NARRATIVE AND CONCEPTUAL INTERLUDES: DIFFERENT WAYS OF KNOWING

Let's consider a concrete phenomenon. Have you heard of chronic Lyme disease? Do you know someone who suffers from it? If you've never heard of it, where and how would you go about finding trustworthy information about it?

In fact, the use and meaning of "chronic Lyme disease" as a diagnostic category is considered controversial. Chronic Lyme disease is related to Lyme disease, a bacterial infection (called *Borrelia burgdorferi*) transmitted by ticks, with about 300,000 people diagnosed each year in the United States (Centers for Disease Control and Prevention, CDC). Theoretically, Lyme symptoms can be cured with conventional antibiotic treatment, but the actual clinical spectrum of this disease is far more complex. "Chronic Lyme disease" is often loosely used to describe a range of bodily responses where people suffer from prolonged debilitating symptoms, presumably associated with Lyme infection. For example, in some cases people who were diagnosed and received routine antibiotic treatment continue to deteriorate and develop more severe symptoms that may significantly impact basic functioning. In other cases, people struggle for years with symptoms that are not accurately diagnosed or treated, only to discover later the possibility or a confirmation of Lyme disease.

The controversy often reflects divided views between the medical community and patients/advocacy groups. Medical institutions, such as the Infectious Disease Society of America, the American Academy of Neurology, and the Centers for Disease Control and Prevention, hold a consensus that chronic Lyme disease is not a valid medical diagnosis. They only recognize *post–Lyme disease syndrome*, where people diagnosed with Lyme disease deteriorate after conventional antibiotic treatment. Their main argument, according to Henry Feder and colleagues, is that "there is no reproducible or convincing scientific evidence of any relationship to *B. burgdorferi* infection" (Feder et al., 2007, p. 1422). It is also argued that various debilitating symptoms that chronic Lyme disease patients experience do not resemble "objective manifestations" associated with Lyme disease. Those symptoms often overlap with clinical manifestations of other diseases. Thus, treatment guidelines warn against the prolonged use of antibiotics to treat post–Lyme disease symptoms, since a causal relationship between symptoms and a Lyme diagnosis cannot be established. Based on this, many medical insurance companies also refuse to recognize or cover chronic Lyme disease.

On the other hand, many chronic Lyme disease patients and patient advocacy groups (e.g., the International Lyme and Associated Diseases Society) take an affirmative stance that chronic Lyme disease is a valid diagnosis and they demand the right for patients to receive insurance-covered treatments (e.g., longer-term and more intense antibiotic treatment, and other alternatives). Their main arguments include (1) that a negative test result may simply relate to low sensitivity of current testing procedures, and (2) that there has been a lack of reliable and sensitive testing methods to accurately diagnose Lyme infection. The bacteria *B. burgdorferi* can remain inactive in patients' bodies, and thus can be shielded from detection for years. There are ample narratives and anecdotal accounts from people who identify as living with chronic Lyme disease. These stories reveal the devastating day-to-day struggles that people with chronic Lyme disease face trying to navigate care and coverage.

Epistemology and Ontology

We do not have the space here to thoroughly flesh out the controversies surrounding chronic Lyme disease, but we would like to use this context to explore those questions that we raised earlier: How do we know? Are there different ways of knowing? How do we know something really exists? In this example, both sides of the controversy make *claims* about a phenomenon known as "chronic Lyme disease." Those claims are *knowledge claims* that are not fundamentally different from claims made by a researcher during a research study. In fact, all of us are making knowledge claims all the time—at home, at work, or with friends. Even when we are thinking alone, as Erving Goffman (1978) has suggested, we tacitly make knowledge claims in relation to an (actual or imagined) audience.

In the context of social inquiry, we use the terms *epistemology* and *ontology* as formal expressions to capture our understanding about knowledge and the nature of reality, respectively. **Epistemology** is a theory about knowledge itself: How do we know what we know? For example, what is the process of knowing that you hear raindrops? How do you know you are hungry? How do you know someone is sad? **Ontology** refers to a theory about what exists and what is real. For instance, what is the nature of emotion? What is the nature of the self? Do UFOs exist? Is chronic Lyme disease a *real* thing? Throughout the human intellectual history, there have always been competing epistemological and ontological perspectives as people make sense of the world and the existence of things and themselves. Social inquiry, in a nutshell, is part of this ongoing quandary.

Each epistemological view always has a set of assumptions embedded within it, in terms of what is considered the ground for *valid* or *legitimate* knowledge. For instance, a scientific approach to knowing emphasizes the maxim "to see is to believe," whereby a claim is only valid or legitimate if one can demonstrate that what is claimed is observable or measurable. From this perspective, it is easier to prove that the claim "this is a rock" is valid in comparison to the claim "God is all-loving." Likewise, an ontological view includes assumptions about what there is to know and what is real. For example, one may assume something only exists if it is tangible and can be known through concrete senses. This person likely would not consider someone's claim that "I still speak to my grandmother, who passed away 2 years ago, now" to be real.

Epistemology, Methodology, and Method

You may wonder, what do these assumptions have to do with research? Well, they have everything to do with what we research, how to research something, what we consider research findings, and what to do about what we find in research. For example, if a researcher holds an ontological assumption that chronic Lyme disease does not exist, then this researcher will not be interested in developing a study about the nature of this "disease" or investigating the effectiveness of possible treatments. In contrast, if the researcher assumes that chronic Lyme disease is real and has an independent existence from other diseases, this researcher would likely pursue very different research questions and research plans. Similarly, if the researcher assumes the best way to generate valid knowledge about chronic Lyme disease is through direct observation and measurement of the symptoms and associated physiological indicators, this researcher would design a study that focuses on characterizing symptoms and indicators *externally*. This would be different from another researcher who values other ways of knowing the disease, such as patients' direct experiences, who likely would engage in some kinds of narrative-based methods to gather perspectives.

This illustrates that there is an internal logic between: (1) how we view and understand the nature of knowledge, what reality is, and the nature of doing research (epistemology and ontology); (2) what we deem appropriate approaches to carry out a research process in practice (methodology); and (3) down the stream, specific means and details of the design (methods). Let's use an analogy to explain this idea. Considering yourself an architect, you hold some philosophical ideas about architecture: what constitutes beauty, function, effectiveness, and style, or how to use space and materials. You might gravitate toward a modern style, and this orientation would influence how you actually design a specific building—the blueprint of the building. The modern style is the philosophical part, closely related to your epistemological and ontological views. The blueprint of the architecture aligns with *methodology,* and specific details of the design such as colors, materials, and shapes are all under *methods*. As we will discuss in Chapter 10, research methods such as interviews, focus groups, and questionnaires do not constitute a methodology themselves, since each can be applied by different types of research methodologies. For example, a questionnaire can be the main data generation method for a survey design, but it can also be embedded in a qualitative study to gather relevant demographic information. Interviews are commonly used in many types of qualitative methodologies such as narrative inquiry and ethnography but can be applied to understand how participants understand and respond to items on a questionnaire and thus enhance the validity of the questionnaire.

Theoretically, epistemological stance and research methodologies are not in a fixed relationship. For instance, a researcher who resonates with a feminist epistemological perspective may engage in a study with a quantitative experimental design, or another study that is guided by a narrative-based methodology. A researcher who identifies with a post-positivist epistemological stance (see below) or a researcher who takes on a critical epistemological stance may both apply statistical analysis in one study. In fact, Brett Stoudt's work (2014, for example) exemplifies a new, emerging field called "critical statistics." However, in reality many research methodologies have a specific, historical root and context from which they emerge, often influenced by the epistemological positions of the pioneers of a particular methodology. For example, the emergence of experimental design as a research methodology was associated with a positivist epistemological stance, prevalent in the natural sciences. As a result, certain associations are formed between epistemological/ontological perspectives and certain research methodologies, although such connections result more from historical reasons than methodological ones.

It is reasonable to assume that a researcher's epistemological, ontological, and ethical assumptions/stance all influence how and what research question they choose to inquire about, and their choice for certain methodological approaches and specific methods for a given study (more discussion in Chapter 8). Many scholars, such as Jonathan Grix (2002), advocate for a linear, directional relation among those components, in which a researcher's ontology determines their epistemology from which the research question, methodology, methods, and specific data sources naturally can follow. This is indeed a mainstream view among the research community, where you may hear the maxim, "Let your research question determine your methodology." In contrast, we hold a more fluid understanding of the relationships among those research concepts. Figure 5.1 illustrates a nonlinear and interpenetrating relationship among those components.

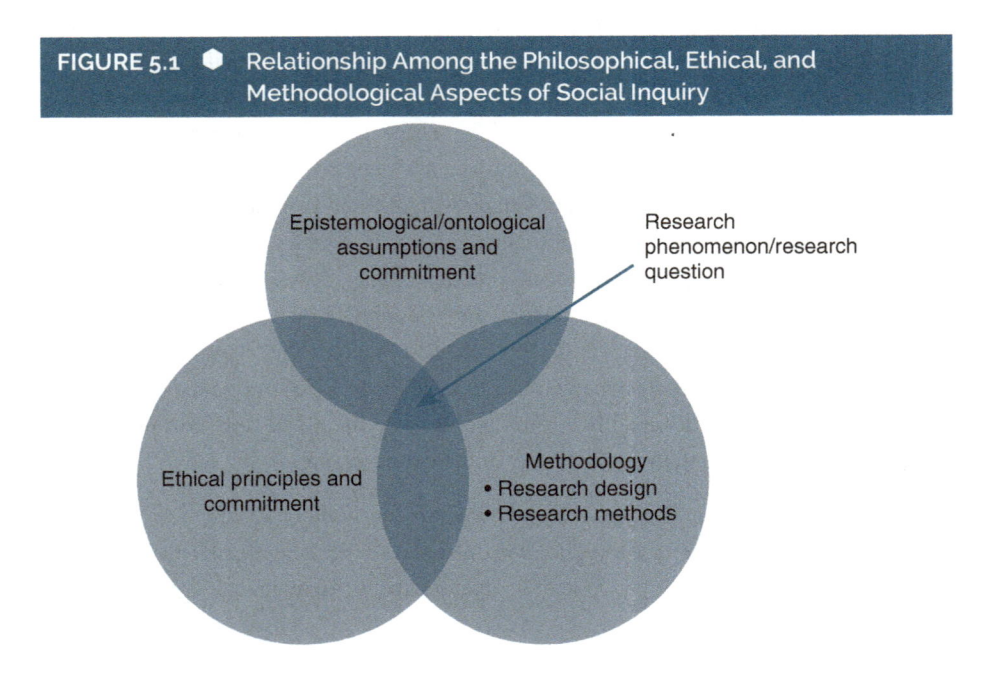

FIGURE 5.1 ● **Relationship Among the Philosophical, Ethical, and Methodological Aspects of Social Inquiry**

- Epistemological/ontological assumptions and commitment
- Research phenomenon/research question
- Ethical principles and commitment
- Methodology
  - Research design
  - Research methods

A researcher holistically grasps a research phenomenon and a research question informed by their epistemological, ontological, and ethical assumptions and commitments, and intertwined methodological considerations. They cannot be easily separated into a linear and sequential relationship. For example, a researcher may argue that their commitment to conduct research *with* participants, rather than *on* or *of* participants, means that they should use a methodology that better supports a collaborative and relational approach to research. Regardless of the specific research phenomenon and research question, this researcher gravitates toward this particular methodology rather than toward alternatives.

In this chapter we are introducing research concepts, such as epistemology and ontology, that are likely new to many readers. As you grapple with those new concepts, research language in this area can be confusing. For example, you may run into the term *research paradigm* in certain research literature, which at times is used to refer to different orientations to research (e.g., qualitative, quantitative, mixed-method, or action research). Other times, it refers to different epistemological positions (e.g., feminist paradigm, constructivist paradigm, etc.). In other contexts, the term may refer to different research methodology canons (e.g., experimental design, ethnography, phenomenology, etc.). To reduce confusion, in this text we refrain from using the term *paradigm* to describe either epistemology/ontology or methodology. Similarly, the terms **research design** and *methodology* are often used almost as synonyms. In our view, they are different concepts. A common use of "research design" links itself to established research methodologies such as experimental design, grounded theory, ethnography, and so on. In this way, "research design" becomes equated with canonized methodologies. Instead, we suggest that the use of "design" signifies the creative, fluid, and emerging nature that comes to design a study. For this reason, we conceptualize "design" not as a noun but as a verb—*designing*—to honor the fact that one can creatively design a study by integrating different methods guided by a cohesive and sound methodology (more discussion in Chapter 8).

> **Pause and Reflect.** There are quite a number of research vocabularies that we introduced above. To connect to your everyday experience, can you think of an example where you engaged in designing a comprehensive plan in a methodical way (e.g., planning a vacation or a large family gathering)? What were the overall methodology and methods involved in that plan?

The Contour of Typical Epistemology and Ontology Stances

Now that we have some baseline understanding of epistemology and ontology, we would like to offer a few examples to demonstrate how epistemological and ontological assumptions may influence how we conceptualize a research phenomenon and our decisions and choices related to a research process. Our discussion here is far from being adequate to account for the wide range of epistemologies and ontologies associated with social inquiry, or do justice to their unique roots and historical contexts. Our intention is to offer a sketch of the philosophical contours of social inquiry, as a starting point for your further explorations. For this purpose, we will discuss the stances of positivism, post-positivism, critical realism, and a countermovement carried by a set of diverging epistemologies.

Positivism

Let's go back to the Lyme example discussed earlier. The stance beneath the mainstream medical perspective assumes a reality of objects, forces, and events that exist independently from us (a realist ontological view) and that we can know this reality through observations and measurements (an empiricist epistemological view). This means that researchers need to "set aside" their personal opinions and interests and take on the role of an objective observer striving for unbiased observations. It is also assumed that since there is a single reality "out there," multiple researchers should be able to observe the same object or phenomenon and are expected to produce similar if not identical outcomes. This forms the foundation of an experimental approach to study a phenomenon, which centers around repeated observations/measurements and emphasizes the need for control to remove undue influences interfering with the accuracy and consistency of observations. In turn, observations provide the basis for generalizable patterns and "laws" about nature and social life, based on the logic of causal relations. Those patterns and laws are then used to predict occurrences of future phenomena. For instance, observations of patterns in weather become the basis for meteorological models, which are then used to predict future weather patterns. All of this is the foundation of an experimental design, which is the core of what is considered science, or the *scientific method*.

This combination of ontological and epistemological assumptions is often associated with *positivism*, which is most prevalent in the field of natural sciences (e.g., physics, biology, and chemistry). However, the social sciences have also adopted a *positivist* epistemological and ontological orientation and an experimental approach to research, especially in disciplines such as economics, psychology, education, and some subfields of sociology. This raises the question: Can social reality and social phenomena, such as communication, emotions, and identity formation, be deemed equivalent to physical reality and natural phenomena, such as gravity or genetics? Many scholars, such as Ted Benton and Ian Craib (2001) or Martin Hollis (1994), have argued that the social world and the natural world have fundamentally different ontological natures, and as such we come to know social and natural realities through different ways.

Post-Positivism and Critical Realism

Increasing dissatisfaction with a positivist approach to social inquiry had led to a *paradigmatic* shift to revise the underlying assumptions of positivism. American physicist and philosopher Thomas Kuhn, in his influential work *The Structure of*

Scientific Revolutions (1970), argues that a "paradigm shift" occurs when the scientific community goes through fundamental changes in its basic understanding and practice of science. In this context, "paradigm" refers to a prominent way of thinking about science in a given historical time. As an example, a new form of epistemology, *post-positivism,* was developed to challenge positivism in the 1970s and 1980s. Post-positivism challenges the notion that we are capable of fully knowing reality, and downplays the possibility that researchers can be completely impartial and objective in relation to what/whom they study. Although still acknowledging a reality that exists independently of us (a *realist* ontological view), a post-positivist view contends that we can only approximate our knowledge about reality. Our knowledge is always falsifiable, and we always fall short of knowing "the truth" with complete certainty.

This shift in epistemological assumptions also shows up at the methodological level: Instead of striving for universal laws, post-positivist researchers emphasize the probability of events. They acknowledge that there is no "pure" observation that is not already influenced, though usually implicitly, by the researcher's experience and given theoretical perspective. For instance, instead of focusing on whether chronic Lyme disease is real or not, post-positivist researchers would be more interested in understanding how likely it is that people struggling with Lyme disease may develop other symptoms, and the odds of curing those symptoms.

Similar to post-positivism, *critical realism* also grew out of rejecting some aspects of positivism. While upholding a realist ontological view about reality, it rejects the positivist take on "objectivity" and embraces a contextual view on knowledge: Our knowledge about reality is always situated in a given history, culture, and society. But critical realists also consider that not all accounts of reality are equally valid and there should be criteria to justify which accounts are better or worse. Later in this chapter, our guest contributor, Dr. Joe Maxwell, will further unpack this particular epistemology.

Diverging Epistemologies

Beyond the post-positivist movement, there have been multiple paradigmatic shifts in the more recent history of social sciences. Going back to the Lyme example, if we shift from medical explanations to patients' perspectives, the latter does not rely on observations and measurements but on direct experiences with the disease. Whether we call it chronic Lyme disease or post–Lyme disease syndrome, patients themselves have a unique access (others cannot have the same access) to knowing about the disease, based on subjective experiences. Do you consider patients' knowledge equally valid compared to scientific findings published in medical journals or lab testing results? Why or why not?

Constructivism. If you are a constructivist, you may say that we do not have a single "objective" reality, since individuals actively construct reality through their perceptions of their experiences. Knowledge is thus always created in this mediated way (a *constructivist* ontological position that there is no reality that exists independently from us). As a result, we do not have a single truth but *multiple truths* that are relative to a given individual and context (a *constructivist* epistemological position). Constructivism is a very popular ontological/epistemological stance, which many readers may resonate with, as it challenges positivist and post-positivist positions that there is an objective truth that exists independently from us. Meanwhile, constructivism implies a *relativist* view on reality and truth, which poses some challenging questions about what should be the ground for validating competing claims about a phenomenon. For instance, imagine different people claim their reality of living with chronic Lyme disease. Are those claims equally valid?

Postmodernism. The constructivist assumptions also find some echo in related epistemological/ontological stances like *postmodernism* (often used as a synonym for *poststructuralism*, even though they are distinct). For example, a postmodernist view, as implied by its name, assumes a skeptical attitude toward the master narratives representative of the modern era, which are marked by a taken-for-granted trust and reliance on scientific and technological knowledge and progress. In a nutshell, postmodernists, similar to constructivists, reject absolute truth and an independent existence of reality. They consider that knowledge production is always conditioned socially, culturally, and historically. As such, knowledge and the knower are never autonomous but intertwined in a given social, cultural, and political context. This suggests that knowledge production does not occur in a vacuum but is subject to various forces and the influence of power (more about this in Chapter 6). A postmodern approach thus focuses on destabilizing the notions of truth, reality, and the self, often perceived as coherent and continuous in nature. Postmodernists refuse to take those assumptions for granted, and often engage in efforts to destabilize the very foundation of those ideas. For the Lyme example, someone with a postmodernist orientation may likely question the privileged status of claims made by medical experts or from scientific findings. For example, they may examine how the medical model (re)produces the grand narrative about Lyme disease and positions doctors in power in relation to their patients.

Critical Theory. Meanwhile, if you identify with a critical orientation, you may accept that there is an objective reality "out there" consisting of objects, entities, and natural forces (a realist ontological stance), but there are also distinct ontological realms (more discussion below) other than the objective world, which we know through different access and means (a critical epistemological position). Similar to constructivism and postmodernism, a criticalist considers that knowledge always needs to be contextualized culturally, socially, historically, and politically. However, a criticalist likely does not assume a relativist view about multiple truths. While taking into account how power relations can distort knowledge, a criticalist does not equate power and knowledge, and believes that truth is possible. This demarcates a criticalist from either a constructivist or a postmodernist. A criticalist will also openly embrace a value orientation toward social betterment and justice. For example, someone with a critical stance may consider that multiple domains of existence are relevant to chronic Lyme disease, including the physiological mechanism and effects (the objective domain), patients' subjective experiences with the disease (the subjective domain), and the cultural/social formulation of the disease (the normative domain). All three domains are important for understanding and intervention (more discussion below).

Against Essentializing Epistemological Traditions. It is very important to note that none of the epistemological orientations described here—*positivist, post-positivist, critical realist, constructivist, postmodernist, and criticalist*—are clear-cut. Each of them is at best an umbrella term that includes diversity from within. Each orientation includes multiple suborientations that may come with overlapping and different sets of assumptions. For instance, there are multiple epistemologies associated with a critical stance: critical theory, critical race theory, critical disability theory, and so on. However, in this text we do not aim to provide a comprehensive introduction to this topic, or to offer a "complete" list of competing epistemologies. In fact, such a list probably does not and should not exist. Instead, we hope to equip you with some basic understanding and vocabulary so that you can further expand your knowledge basis in this area, if interested.

> **Pause and Reflect.** Which of the ontological/epistemological orientations discussed above resonate with you most? Do you think everything can be measured? Do you consider numbers more reliable than individual stories? Do you think researchers should assume a detached perspective in order to reduce bias?

All of those quandaries at their roots are epistemic and philosophical questions. That is why we find it necessary to introduce some key philosophical concepts in this earlier chapter so that you acquire a conceptual tool to engage in critical reflection and questioning. The latter is never abstract but always embedded in a concrete context and your life history.

Three Types of Knowledge Claims

After introducing some basic concepts and history regarding the philosophical foundations of social inquiry, we would like to offer a more concrete example of how epistemology and ontology become relevant in knowing and knowledge production. Our discussion below is largely influenced by the *critical communicative pragmatist* approach, drawing from the works of social theorist Jürgen Habermas (1984; 1987). Habermas articulates three types of knowledge claims, namely, objective, subjective, and normative claims. **Objective knowledge claims** make reference to the *objective ontological category* mostly consisting of objects, entities, and forces (e.g., I saw a computer in front of me); **subjective knowledge claims** make reference to a *subjective ontological category* of thoughts, feelings, intentions, motivations, experiences, etc. (e.g., I feel hungry and sad); and **normative knowledge claims** relate to the *normative ontological category* of agreement and mutual recognition among people in a given cultural and historical context (e.g., we should do no harm to others). Note that terms such as "objective" and "subjective" signify *ontological categories*, which is different from how they are often used in everyday contexts. We find this approach very compelling, although readers may develop your own opinions of how this approach resonates with you. Let's return to the Lyme example to put this discussion in context.

Objective Claims

As discussed earlier, the medical perspective focuses on whether "chronic Lyme disease" *exists*. This boils down to whether a causal chain between the *B. burgdorferi* bacteria and a series of alleged symptoms can be established. Or, in other words, whether the bacteria can be found in patients who experience those symptoms. This foregrounds the *objective* category of knowledge claims that mostly concerns the existence of an object or event. The disciplines of natural sciences such as physics, biology, and chemistry primarily work with this type of knowledge, using an approach to generating objective knowledge claims that is commonly understood as "to see is to believe." The experience of *seeing* is used as the primary ground to affirm the claim that something exists. In the Lyme case, since bacteria are too small to be seen directly by the naked eye, scientists have developed measurement methods to indirectly detect the presence of specific antibodies that are believed to be an indicator of a corresponding bacterial infection. Thus, observation and measurement become the pillar of knowing *about* the objective world. This is also the foundation of what we often call scientific knowledge.

Subjective Claims

In contrast, the patients' perspective foregrounds a different kind of knowledge claim and way of knowing—claims about experiences, sensations, feelings, emotions, and thoughts, which have a different kind of existence than an object that is presumably accessible by multiple people. Feeling pain, fatigue, fogginess, dizziness, and so on fall into the *subjective* category of knowledge claims to which only the patient themself has *privileged access*. However, the patient can communicate these experiences to others, and others may also infer about those subjective states based on observable behaviors that the patient exhibits. But the observer does not have the same access as the patient themself, and the observer can always be wrong. Imagine the scenario where an observer comments to the patient, "You look so tired," and the patient replies, "I actually don't feel tired." As you may see, at the end of the day, we have to rely on the patient to be honest and sincere about what they express. However, it is also possible that the patient could have a distorted perception of their experience—for example, experiencing psychological repression. Thus, we ultimately rely on subjective claims made by the patient to verify things in the subjective ontological domains, and count on the person being truthful and authentic in their claiming.

Normative Claims

The perspective of the Lyme disease advocacy groups highlights yet another distinctive domain of knowledge claims: It is *wrong* for doctors and insurance companies to dismiss chronic Lyme patients' experiences as illegitimate; the medical science community *should* allocate resources to better understand the mechanism of Lyme disease and develop ways to help alleviate suffering. Claims like these foreground the *normative* domain of knowledge about what is *right/wrong, appropriate/improper,* or *good/bad,* often expressed in the forms of "should," "ought to," and "must." Knowledge claims made in reference to this domain have an existence status that differs from both *objective* and *subjective* domains: They have to do with existing agreement on what constitutes the *rightness, goodness,* or *appropriateness* of our actions. Agreement like this is always shaped collectively by a group of people and is contingent on history and culture. And, of course, it is also prone to the influence of unequal power that occurs when we try to reach consensus (for example, who is present at the table when agreements are negotiated; who are subject to the benefits or disadvantages of such agreements; whose perspectives and voices are absent in a widely accepted norm). This connects right back to our discussion on the concept of *power* in Chapter 4, which will be further unpacked in Chapter 6.

Table 5.1 summarizes these three types of knowledge claims and their corresponding ontological categories, accompanied by some concrete examples of knowledge claims. Through this discussion, we hope to illustrate that we make different types of claims

TABLE 5.1 ● Types of Knowledge Claims

Types of Knowledge Claims	Ontological Categories	Examples of Research Claims
Objective knowledge claims	*The objective ontological category:* objects, entities, and forces in the physical world	• About 1 in 8 American women will develop breast cancer over the course of their lifetime. • The student walked out of the classroom after having an argument with the teacher.
Subjective knowledge claims	*The subjective ontological category:* experiences, sensations, feelings, emotions, and thoughts in the subjective world	• Yilin seems to be very anxious about meeting the therapist for the first time. • Omar is highly motivated to complete their education.
Normative knowledge claims	*The normative ontological category:* rightness, goodness, or appropriateness in social and civic participation	• We ought to address the rape culture on college campuses. • Patients should have rights to end their life when life is not worth living.

in relation to different ontological categories. Each type of knowledge claim is known through a form of distinct access. It is also important to note that any knowledge claim actually has all three aspects embedded, but those aspects are foregrounded and backgrounded in different ways. For example, if we examine the claim that "21% of children in the U.S. live in poverty," what is foregrounded is the *objective* aspect of the claim related to the prevalence and distribution of the poverty level. What is less foregrounded is how we define "poverty," which has a *normative* connotation in terms of how we reach consensus about what constitutes "poverty." What is much more backgrounded is the *subjective* experience of children living in poverty, which is also related to how we understand poverty. We will return to this discussion in Chapter 7, where we discuss the basis for verifying each type of knowledge claim to be true, valid, or trustworthy. That is, what are the *validity criteria* used to substantiate the claims we make.

Understanding Meaning

By now we have discussed the ideas of epistemology and ontology, and one way to conceptualize different types of knowledge claims; now we would like to introduce another fundamental concept in social inquiry—**meaning**—and how we **understand meaning**. Understanding meaning is relevant to all types of research endeavors, and to our everyday experiences. Going back to the funeral scenario introduced at the beginning of the chapter, how we make sense of the situation, and how we figure out how to act appropriately—both have to do with understanding meaning. For instance, if you grew up in a different culture and never attended a funeral in America, to understand what "funeral" means would require you to take the position of a *typical* person in the United States who has access to cultural knowledge about the situation. This includes being able to recognize the setting (e.g., this is a funeral), knowing how to *act* at a funeral in a culturally appropriate way (e.g., what to say, what to wear, what to bring, etc.), and understanding the possible intentions of other people who are also present at the funeral. In addition, you need not only grasp possible ways to respond to other people's actions, but also how your responses might be perceived by other people.

Let's translate this into a concrete scene. Imagine you have just walked into an American funeral home, and you quickly "read" the setting: People dress formally and mostly in dark colors; they are generally quiet and talk softly with one another. This forms a contrast to a birthday party, where you may hear laughter, music, and loud conversations as you open the door. Someone greets you and says, "Thank you so much for coming." You instantly recognize that this might be a close family member of the deceased. You understand that their intention is to show appreciation for your effort to attend the funeral. You also understand that to respond to their act, you may shake hands with this person and say something like, "I'm so sorry for your loss," with a matching facial expression. Or if you know the person well, you may offer a heartfelt hug. In contrast, you probably would not respond with a cheerful smile, "I'm so happy to see you!", or start to cry uncontrollably. If you actually do not feel sad at all, you probably would closely monitor how this might come across on your face when you interact with others.

Most of us who socialize in this culture instantly "get" this, that this is such and such a situation and I can act in this or that way. We grasp this all at once, holistically. But this occurs mostly tacitly, and is taken for granted in most of our everyday experiences, until we run into situations where we "misread" the situation or misunderstand the person with whom we interact. Being capable of understanding holistically what is going on is related to **cultural typification**, according to Phil Carspecken (1996). This refers to the competency to tacitly recognize a generality typical of a culture. This tacit recognition also involves being able to take multiple positions all at once: the person who attends the funeral (first-person), the people with whom you interact at the funeral (second-person), and the position of a typical person at an American funeral (third-person). In other words, understanding meaning involves acquiring the first-, second-, and third-person position all at once, moment by moment. In this way, we can anticipate what we are expected of by others and act in accordance with what is considered appropriate by people in general in a given culture.

This also highlights that words do not "contain" meaning in themselves (e.g., meaning of the word *funeral* does not reside in the word itself). Instead, meaning emerges from social interactions as we apprehend how to act next in a culturally competent way. In this sense, understanding meaning is *intersubjective* in nature, a concept that we first introduced in Chapter 2. We cannot help but use cultural typifications that we are most familiar with each time we try to make sense of a situation. Thus, the meaning we grasp might be off. For instance, imagine a person from the United States who tries to make sense of Chinese funerals based from their cultural typification of American funeral customs. This foregrounds another tacit process involved in understanding meaning—a "**hermeneutic circle**," a concept developed by social theorist Wilhelm Dilthey and illustrated in Figure 5.2. Basically, hermeneutic circles depict that when we interact with someone, we always start with an initial partial understanding based on a familiar cultural typification. We become aware of the cultural norms that bound this typification (but that we initially take for granted) only when we realize that our initial understanding of the situation differs from how the other person grasps the situation (Carspecken, 1996). This dissonance leads to a moment of integration where our prior and new understandings are synthesized into a new, holistic understanding. This process also involves *whole–part relations,* where a social action (a part) is always grasped in relation to a holistic situation and setting (whole). In the ongoing movements between the part and the whole, we modify our previous understanding and arrive at a

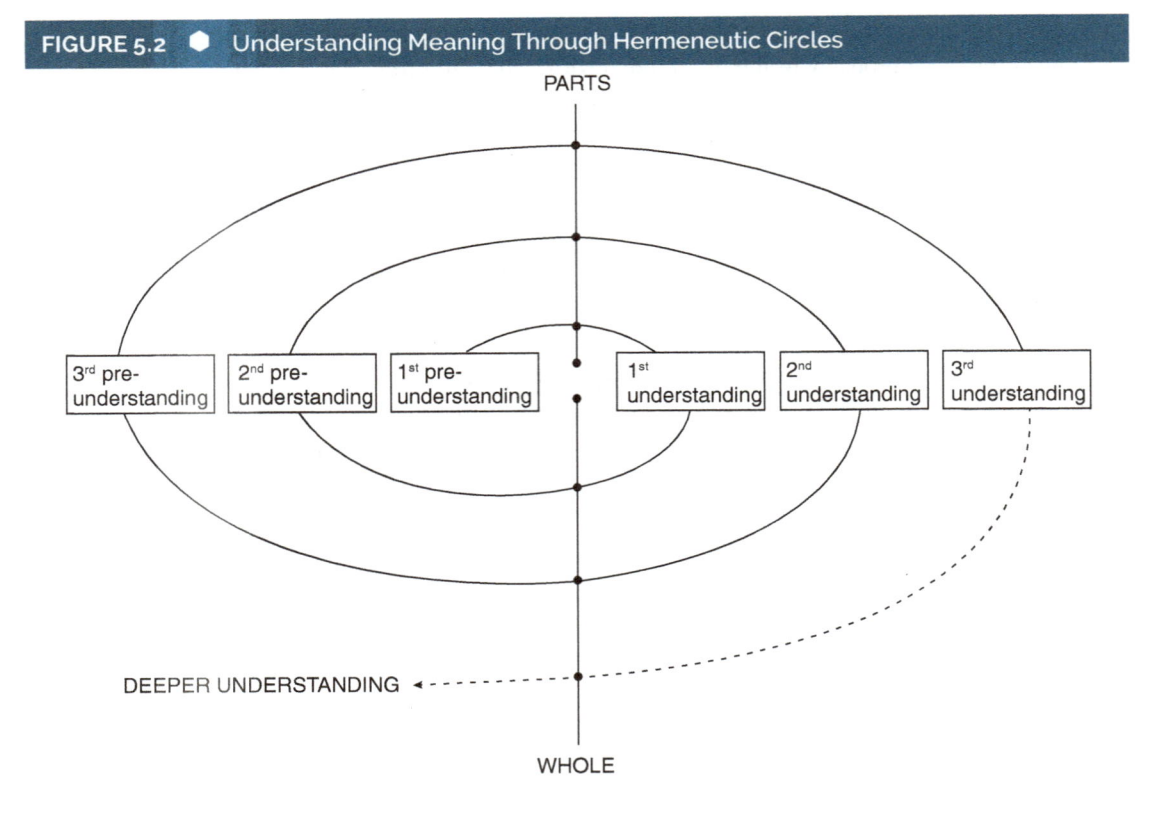

FIGURE 5.2 ● Understanding Meaning Through Hermeneutic Circles

PARTS

| 3rd pre-understanding | 2nd pre-understanding | 1st pre-understanding | 1st understanding | 2nd understanding | 3rd understanding |

DEEPER UNDERSTANDING ←-------

WHOLE

new understanding. This circle continues as our understanding deepens and meaning becomes clarified in contingency.

All social inquiry in fact involves how to understand meaning. Even when dealing with numbers and statistics, you are making inferences about the original social actions that those numbers represent. For example, someone may get a score on an anxiety inventory. But making sense of the score is making meaning about this person's *experience* of anxiety. Numbers themselves do not have fixed meaning internal to the numbers themselves. They are at best a truncated representation of more holistic and contextualized social experiences such as anxiety. Similar to the funeral example, to understand the meaning of numbers on an anxiety inventory, the researcher should be able to access as closely as possible the cultural typification of participants from whom those numbers are generated, through the *hermeneutic circle* and by taking multiple positions. At the end of the day, Robert Brandom explains that when we understand the meaning of an action or an expression, we know *how to act* in a way similar to the way the actor would act in a given situation (Brandom, 1994; Carspecken, 1999).

So why are we spending so much time talking about "meaning" here? This is because the concept of "meaning" and how we understand it is pertinent to all aspects of any research endeavor. For example, simply choosing a research phenomenon to study already involves intuitively grasping what we believe is salient and important to focus on. That is, we already try to understand meaning long before we initiate a formal research project. In particular, the process of making inferences of either numeric or linguistic representations (discussed in Chapters 12–15), the core of data analysis relevant to any research study, is essentially a process of understanding meaning in a fundamental way.

RESEARCH SCENARIO: MY "FAT GIRL COMPLEX"

To further illustrate how those philosophical issues are relevant to the research process, in this section we introduce a research scenario. We also invited a few scholars who approach their own research from different epistemological/ontological stances, a critical realist and a social constructive perspective, to respond to this scenario. We asked them how they would approach the study from their particular philosophical stance, and why. We hope to create a dialogue among those perspectives including your own, all of which are always open to being questioned as well. As you read through the research scenario and responses from the guest writers, keep track of your internal dialogue and reactions. Pay attention to how each perspective resonates with you, or not, and why that's the case.

Nowadays the term *body image* is woven into the fabric of our social and personal lives (at least in U.S. culture). It is pervasive whenever we turn on the TV, open a magazine, get on the internet and social media, or simply engage in our day-to-day interactions with people and with ourselves. Meanwhile, we have developed a fat-shaming culture in which the meaning of "fat" is loaded with judgment and being fat is automatically deemed negative, particularly if you are a woman. Mainstream research on body image and sexual health tends to implicitly assume that large-size women are unhealthy and desexualized. Consequently, size and weight become frequent targets of health promotion efforts.

Sonya Satinsky, the director of Health Promotion and Prevention Services at Princeton University, together with her collaborators, conducted some very interesting research targeting the intersection of women's body image and their experience with sexuality (see publications under Further Readings). Instead of following the traditional line of research focusing on body dissatisfaction and problems with sexual health, this group of researchers spotlighted the experiences of women of size and particularly size acceptance and "fat pride," where women experience body appreciation, love, and acceptance regardless of body size. They also challenged a taken-for-granted linkage between women's size and their sexual identity and satisfaction, for instance, that large body size correlates with sexual dissatisfaction and dysfunction—a common assumption that permeates both the research community and popular culture more broadly.

In one of their studies, titled *My "Fat Girl Complex": A Preliminary Investigation of Sexual Health and Body Image in Women of Size*, Satinsky and her colleagues Barbara Dennis, Michael Reece, Stephanie Sanders, and Shaowen Bardzell (2013) examined narratives from four participants who self-identify as women of size. Guided by feminist and critical theories, the study draws insights from Objectification Theory, which in a nutshell entails how women both are treated as objects and can view themselves in this way due to the constant evaluative gaze of others, which reduces women to "bodies." Using critical qualitative analyses, the researchers revealed that large body size is not necessarily linked to negative sexual health. Women of size in this study who hold a non-objectifying sense of self and an attitude of size acceptance did not make any association between body size and their sexual experiences. Meanwhile, women who internalized fat shame and the objectifying gaze of women's bodies reported a connection between having large body size, a lack of sexual self-assertiveness, and negative sexual experiences.

It is clear that the researchers are on the fringe of mainstream research on this very topic. The entire research project is conceptualized and approached from the perspective of a critical feminist epistemological position, which asserts that "knowledge" has historically been produced from the position of men, and has systemically excluded and obscured women's experiences. Critical feminists call for the abolishment of patriarchal norms, and the re-centering of women and other marginalized groups' perspectives and experiences in knowledge production.

This stance influenced their whole research process, starting from the development of research questions. The researchers did not just follow the established line of research and use it as a basis from which to further build. Instead, they first made explicit some of the embedded assumptions about "body," "fat," and "women" in current research discourse. Through this critical reflection they challenged the norm in existing literature that overly focuses on "body negativity," based on what are deemed "acceptable bodies" that are largely modeled after Western, heterosexual, young, white women.

This leads to the researchers' focus on the experience of women of size and their sexuality, an area riddled with unchecked assumptions but not actual empirical exploration. This is aligned with a critical feminist epistemology that does not take knowledge for granted, and aims to tease out how what we call "knowledge" could be distorted and contribute to (re)producing unequal and repressive structures in the society (e.g., women become objectified and reduced to their bodies; diversity among women is masked by assuming a single, dominant way of being a woman).

This epistemological stance also guides these researchers' decisions about every aspect of the research process: what kind of research design is most suitable; what constitutes meaningful data in relation to the research questions; how to generate data and from whom; and what are appropriate ways to analyze data and communicate findings. To be specific, a critical feminist orientation in this case is linked with a critical qualitative methodology that supports in-depth understanding of meaning and examination of assumptions embedded in knowledge claims. This is aligned with generating rich and reflective narrative data from women who self-identify as women of size—voices that were missing in the literature.

Similarly, a critical feminist orientation emphasizes advocating for positive social change rather than simply "describing" the reality without impacting it (assuming this is possible). Along this line, the authors call for an alternative approach to researching body image and sexual health: shifting away from size objectification and toward size acceptance, and from body-size change (e.g., weight loss) to attitude change (e.g., body appreciation and fat pride). They also stress the importance of resisting and transforming cultural stigma surrounding being "fat," and examining women's sexual health in "fully embodied," size-independent, and positive ways (Satinsky, Dennis, Reece, Sanders, & Bardzell, 2013).

Questions for the Guest Contributors (and to You)

To illustrate how researchers from different epistemological/ontological orientations may approach the same research context, we posed a set of questions to a few scholars and invited them to respond to the research scenario above. Those guiding questions include:

1. If you were to do a study about this topic (i.e., body image/"fatness" in American culture), how would you approach it? How would you approach this topic *similarly* or *differently* from the way Satinsky and her colleagues did?

2. What are the epistemological orientations that you bring to your own research? How do you see this orientation shaping how you respond to the study above?

3. What aspects of the Satinsky et al. approach would you challenge based on your own epistemological orientation? Or, on the other hand, what aspects resonate for you with this approach?

A Critical Realist Response to the Research Scenario: Joseph Maxwell

I'm responding to this scenario from what is often termed a "critical realist" stance, as described above. However, there are many different versions of this stance and its implications for research, and what I present below is based on my own understanding of this; see my book, A Realist Approach for Qualitative Research, *for a detailed explanation. In particular, I'm skeptical of the distinction that the authors of the present book make between "objective" and "subjective" ontological categories. For me, this distinction isn't ontological, but epistemological; the world is the way it is, but our understanding of the world can be based on quite different conceptual frameworks. My interpretation of this (which I draw from the philosopher Hilary Putnam) is that we tend to employ two very different conceptual frameworks in understanding the world (including the people and other animals in it). The physical framework, consisting of kinds of objects and forces, is what we normally use in making sense of the "external" world (the world of physical objects outside of our bodies), but also of the insides of our bodies (the muscles, bones, nerves, brain tissue, and so on that we can observe through dissection or imaging). The mental framework, consisting of ideas, beliefs, emotions, values, and so on, is what we use in understanding many things about people that are not directly observable, and are inferred from their speech and actions. (This framework is also regularly used to understand other animals that lack speech.) The meanings that people attach to things aren't an ontologically separate realm of reality; they are one framework for understanding the complex phenomena of people's lives, and these meanings have a causal effect on how people act and on how they think about other aspects of their lives.*

Here, Dr. Maxwell outlines some of the epistemological and ontological assumptions from a critical realist orientation. He raises an important point: that what is considered epistemological versus ontological is contested, something we also discussed earlier in the chapter. Dr. Maxwell voices his disagreement with how we demarcate subjective and objective ontological categories, and he explains an alternative approach that considers this distinction primarily epistemological rather than ontological. For example, he describes the distinction between a "physical" ("external") and "mental" ("internal") framework not as about different realities but rather as a distinction between the conceptual frameworks we use to make sense of the world.

Dr. Maxwell's perspective also highlights that a plurality of perspectives coexist. Not all perspectives are equally valid, but they can be challenged and critiqued. In fact, dialogues and debates are important to keep self-reflection alive so that different perspectives are not taken for granted as "everything goes." We are glad that he voiced his disagreement with our view. Imagine if he and we could engage in further conversation about this issue: Each side could clarify assumptions, potentially leading to new understandings even if as we continue to hold that disagreement.

This way of making sense of "physical" and "mental" phenomena has important implications for studying women's body images and their relationship to sexuality. First, it's essential to gain a valid understanding of the meanings that these women attach to body size, to others' reactions to this, and to their sexuality. As the authors note, it's dangerous to make assumptions about these based on prevalent social values; these women are undoubtedly influenced by such social judgments, but their own beliefs and perceptions don't necessarily reflect these. Narrative research is a powerful way to get at the women's actual concepts and values. However, like all methods, it doesn't give you a direct, "objective" account; there may be aspects of the women's beliefs that they are not consciously aware of, ones that can be gotten at by asking about (or observing) their behavior. Thus, it's important for researchers to test their conclusions by considering alternative plausible interpretations of the narratives, and seeking evidence that would challenge or support their interpretation. For example, asking teachers to describe how they respond to girls' and boys' questions in a science class may not reveal differences in their beliefs about girls' and boys' capabilities, ones that the teachers themselves may not be aware of; observations of their classroom behavior may uncover these differences, and provide a test of conclusions based entirely on interviews.

Dr. Maxwell illustrates how a critical realist orientation and related assumptions may guide his conceptualization of the original research scenario in terms of *what* to focus on, as well as *how* to carry out the study. For example, the emphasis on understanding how actors make meaning themselves lends itself to a narrative-based approach. But he also points out the importance of not only relying on narratives but also looking for alternative interpretations and using complementary methods (e.g., observations and interviews).

The other implication that I draw from a critical realist stance is that diversity and particularity are real and fundamental. Both quantitative and qualitative research have tendencies to treat generalizations as more important and "real" than the diverse meanings and experiences that they are based on. To use an example from earlier in this chapter, the Borrelia bacterium that typically causes Lyme disease is usually killed by doxycycline, curing the disease, but there are always exceptions that are real and need to be understood in order to provide the best treatment for each patient. Generalizations are often valuable and important, but each of these women's understanding of body size and sexuality is unique, and the researchers need to respect that uniqueness and not impose generalizations from their narratives that erase this.

Dr. Maxwell's point about the need to focus on the diversity and particularity of social phenomena, in contrast with generalization, taps into underlying assumptions about what is real and what is valuable to research. Again, you can see why epistemology and ontology are always important to engage with. This argument also foreshadows our further discussion on concepts such as "validity," "generalizability," and "research impact" in Chapters 7, 12, and 16, respectively.

A Constructivist Response to the Research Scenario: Sabine Siekmann and Joan Parker Webster

At the outset, we think it is important to mention that from our perspective there is not one definitive definition of constructivism. However, we do recognize there are basic principles underlying the continuum of constructivist onto-epistemological orientations—e.g., actors are knowers who co-create understanding of the world based in socially constructed knowledge claims and meaning is negotiated through interactions with others whose backgrounds and experiences are socially, historically, and culturally influenced (Creswell, 2013; Crotty, 1998; Denzin & Lincoln, 2000; Neuman, 2000). And, as the authors of this volume point out, similar principles are shared with other epistemological/ontological orientations like postmodernism and critical theory, each of which also comes with multiple, interrelated sets of assumptions.

Dr. Siekmann and Dr. Parker Webster use the term *onto-epistemological* to suggest deep interconnection of epistemological and ontological assumptions. The boundaries between different onto-epistemological orientations are never clear-cut—there can be overlapping assumptions, as the authors point out. Echoing our earlier discussion on the danger of taking a reductionist approach when trying to understand any epistemological and ontological traditions, the authors emphasize that a term like *constructivism* does not have a single, flat definition. Instead, it carries a school of internally diverse thoughts housed under one umbrella. Meanwhile, various constructivist orientations all share certain assumptions, such as: The knower plays an active role in creating knowledge; and knowledge is situated in specific social, cultural, and historical contexts.

We understand and articulate our onto-epistemological orientation as grounded in a social constructivist onto-epistemology; specifically, cultural historical activity theory (CHAT) put forward by Vygotsky (1978) and further developed by Wertsch (1985) and Engeström (1987). We also recognize CHAT, which assumes an active knower "doing" collaborative activity/work to co-create understandings of the world, is entangled with Western criticalist (Carspecken, 1996; Freire, 2000; Kinchloe & McLaren, 1994) and feminist new materialist (Dolphijn & van der Tuin, 2012; Hekman, 2010; Haraway, 2008) orientations.

Because these orientations intra-act with-in our work, which is socially and culturally situated with-in an Indigenous context, we find it critically important to diffractively read (Barad, 2007) these theories through Indigenous onto-epistemologies (John, 2010; Kawagley, 1995; Smith, 1999) in order to interrogate the familiar Western discourse of empiricist, interpretivist, and representationalist social science and the wider array of constructivist thought. We do this to gain new insights and make visible the differences that make a difference and better understand how matter comes to matter (Barad, 2003; 2017). And, because both new materialist philosophy and Indigenous onto-epistemology articulate "intra-secting" (Dennis & Parker Webster, 2018) theories and methodologies concerning the human and nonhuman, we also seek to trouble the assumptions about human–nonhuman agency and articulate an ethics that includes more than human-to-human relationships, expanding the concept of mediation beyond language and culture.

As the authors clarify their particular position on "social constructivist onto-epistemology," they flesh out *how* they draw insights from multiple social theories and schools of thought as the basis for their overall onto-epistemological orientation. This orientation problematizes Western views on human–nonhuman relations. The authors do so by placing *new materialist* and *Indigenous* onto-epistemologies in the forefront of their thinking. It is worthwhile to note that philosophical terms such as *western criticalist, feminist new materialist, interpretist,* and *representationalist* may be quite new to many readers. Again, each of those terms is part of a school of thought into which interested readers can delve deeper.

As part of our work with a research collaborative composed of Indigenous PhD students, we wanted to understand how individual and group researcher identities emerged and developed over the course of their graduate studies. We found that Engeström's model of third generation CHAT offered an analytic framework for investigating this highly complex activity system oriented around the activity of obtaining a graduate degree with the outcome of conducting research and writing a dissertation (see, for example, Siekmann & Parker Webster, 2019; Siekmann et al., 2019). Engeström (1987) built on Vygotsky's original mediational triangle consisting of "subject," "object," and "mediating artifacts/tools" by connecting the subjects to their dynamic relationships with "community," "rules," and "division of labor."

Yamagata-Lynch (2010) proposes activity systems analysis (ASA) as a process of identifying and describing each of the elements within an activity system, in order to uncover their systemic implications and thereby making visible systemic contradictions and tensions. Each node can be investigated by posing a series of questions as illustrated in Figure 5.3:

FIGURE 5.3 ● **Guiding Questions for Researchers Applying Activity Systems Analysis as an Analytic Framework**

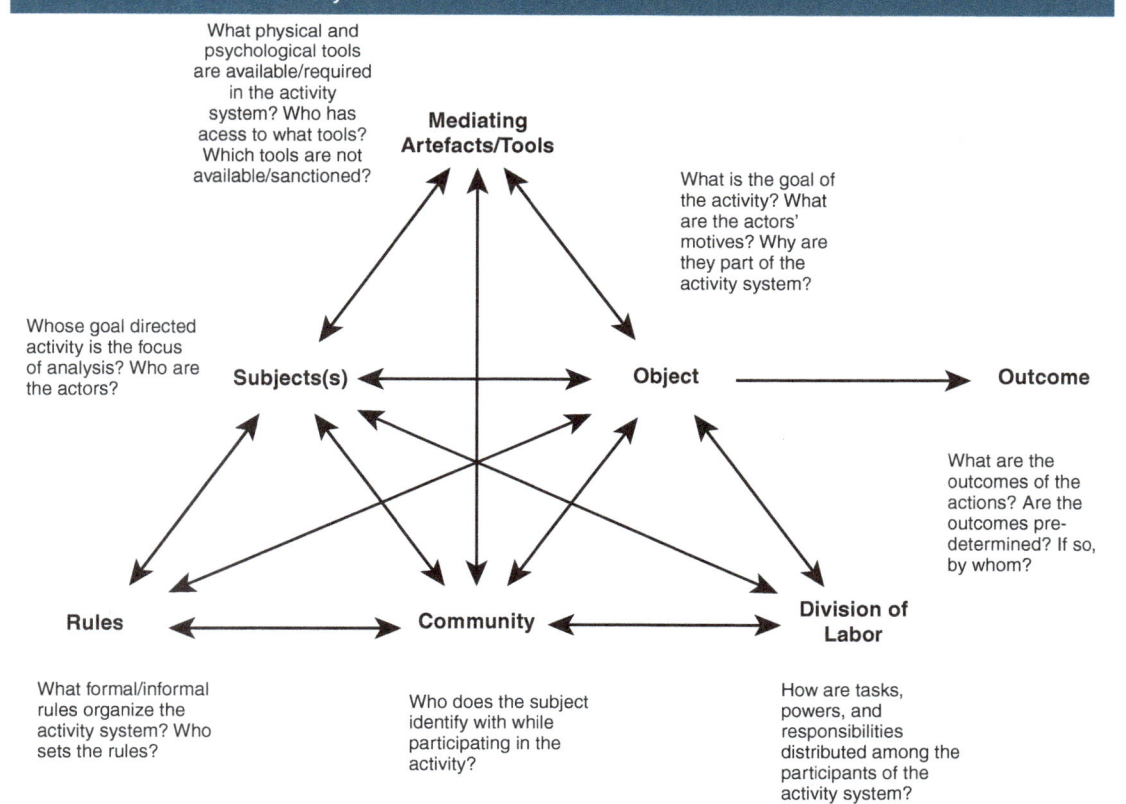

- **Mediating Artefacts/Tools**: What physical and psychological tools are available/required in the activity system? Who has access to what tools? Which tools are not available/sanctioned?
- **Subjects(s)**: Whose goal directed activity is the focus of analysis? Who are the actors?
- **Object**: What is the goal of the activity? What are the actors' motives? Why are they part of the activity system?
- **Outcome**: What are the outcomes of the actions? Are the outcomes predetermined? If so, by whom?
- **Rules**: What formal/informal rules organize the activity system? Who sets the rules?
- **Community**: Who does the subject identify with while participating in the activity?
- **Division of Labor**: How are tasks, powers, and responsibilities distributed among the participants of the activity system?

Activity systems are held together by the orientation of the activity (Engeström, 1993) and shaped by "historically accumulating structural tensions within and between activity systems" (Engeström, 2001, p. 136). Tensions may exist between each of the elements of the activity system. For example, participants within an activity system might have different and even conflicting reasons for participating in the activity system (object). The nature of the outcome, the rules, the division of labor, etc., might also be contested. As discussed in Siekmann and Parker Webster (2019), because subjects participate in multiple activity systems, each subject constitutes and is constituted by multiple positionalities. Actors have an array of positionalities to draw from, which allows them to position-take with other subjects and within the community of the activity system.

Here, the authors further unpack how their constructivist orientation influenced how they conceptualize the complexity of an activity system. In particular, this framework is positioned to "detect" contradictions and tensions, and carries an analytical capacity to explicate "systemic implications." Figure 5.3 embodies various onto-epistemological assumptions that the authors outlined earlier, which serve as the skeleton of this analytical framework that can be used for "activity system analysis" (ASA).

Applying ASA to the case of the "fat girls" first entails identifying actors in activity systems related to the problem space of body size, such as groups of women of size who share a common orientation. This shared orientation is established through questions relating to the subject, object, and outcomes nodes (see Figure 1). In collaboration and conversation with the participants, we would investigate each node in turn posing questions and identifying tensions and contradictions within the activity system. In addition, we would further examine and apply ASA to those related, nested activity systems (e.g., medical/health care, media/fashion) to make visible how these systems intra-act with one another in order to gain insight and open up possibilities for transformational systemic change.

Lastly, the authors explain how they would apply the ASA framework in the context of the research scenario. This conception will have further implications in terms of how they conceptualize and design a study in this context.

Overall, the study by Satinsky et al., alongside the critical realist and constructivist responses to it, illustrate that researchers may approach some social phenomena with different sets of philosophical assumptions and value orientations. In fact, all claim a "critical" stance to research, but those scholars may not have the same ideas about what it means to be "critical." Thus, further dialogue and clarification can be helpful so that we do not take those words for granted.

This dialogue also highlights that a researcher's philosophical orientation influences the researcher's methodological choices when investigating that phenomenon. However, it is not the same as a researcher *picking* a philosophical stance for a given study. It is not as though a researcher takes on a critical feminist stance when it comes to studying research phenomena related to women's experiences, and then becomes a critical realist when studying something else. A philosophical stance is not something one can "shop" for depending on the context, although it is often portrayed as such in research texts. While people do change their positions and values over time, a researcher's philosophical underpinnings tend to be consistent across studies.

The more important point is not for you to *choose* a philosophical stance but to reflect on the assumptions and values that you *already* carry as researchers and practitioners, and become aware of how they impact your research and professional practices. Without this, we may also risk falling into the trap of "value neutrality" that deprives researchers of opportunities for self-reflection. Doing so may, in fact, counterintuitively mask our blind spots and true biases that make research less objective and jeopardize the validity of a study (Harding, 1992; Peshkin, 1988).

YOU AND RESEARCH

Let's talk about how you might apply what we discussed in this chapter in your own context of engaging with research.

When Interpreting Research

If you do not see yourself doing formal research but mainly using research in informative ways, you may want to pay attention to whether author(s) of a research article explicitly reflect on their epistemological and ontological orientation/assumptions and how those things relate to their conceptualization and execution of a research study. If this information is missing, such absence at least may suggest a lack of awareness of the researcher's own epistemological positioning. Worse, it may perpetuate a culture of objectivity that works to conceal the hidden dominance of certain perspectives. On the other hand, if the author does acknowledge their positionality, you may gauge whether such philosophical positioning aligns with how the study is conceptualized and carried out. For example, if the researchers claim that they take a feminist position to study disordered eating in women, this position would entail that they not take "disordered eating" at face value—that is, only as an individual behavior issue. Instead, the research should take into consideration how gendered social and cultural norms may contribute to eating disorders. They may also be interested in learning about this

(Continued)

> (Continued)
>
> phenomenon from the perspectives of women who closely experience disordered eating to honor the voices of women, who have historically been repressed in a patriarchal society.
>
> What if the researcher claims a feminist position but carries out the study on the basis of a set of existing measurements that already have certain assumptions about what an eating disorder is and how to measure it? The measurements already frame responses from women who fill out the questionnaire, instead of creating space to hear from them directly and explore their conceptions. This would be an incongruence between epistemological stance and research methodology. Being able to spot the alignment or the lack thereof between epistemological positioning and research methodology helps to gauge the soundness and validity of a study—an important aspect of being a critical reader of research.
>
> ### When Doing Research
>
> For those of you who engage in informal research practices, you need to actively reflect on your own interests in and assumptions about knowing/knowledge in general, and in relation to a particular research phenomenon. To do so, you can examine how your past experiences may have influenced your interests and value orientation. As you become aware of those issues, you can monitor how your particular positionality may facilitate or hinder your effectiveness as a researcher for that given research context. As you explicate your epistemological assumptions, often in the form of personal theories, you will more easily be able to consciously design a study that best honors your values and commitments as a researcher and stay open to being challenged and to change.

SYNTHESIS: POINTS FOR REFLECTION

Conceptual Synthesis

In this chapter, we focused on foundational concepts embedded in social inquiry such as what constitutes knowledge, reality, and meaning. We explored related concepts including epistemology, ontology, knowledge claims, methodology, and method. As you've seen in various examples, the relevance of those concepts is not limited to the realm of research. They are also inherent in everyday life contexts and ordinary actions. It is just that in the context of social inquiry those concepts are picked up in a formal way. Any research activity has those concepts embedded as implicit assumptions, whether we consciously acknowledge them or not. Hopefully by now it's clear to readers that research doesn't exist in vacuum; it is never separated from the experiences, worldviews, and assumptions of the researchers and of research communities at large. In this sense, research is always contextualized and conditioned. We will have further discussion about the larger sociocultural-political contexts surrounding research in Chapter 6.

Methodological Synthesis

Related to research practice, carefully explicating and examining our epistemological and ontological orientations and assumptions help us better design and engage in a particular research study. Without this meta-level understanding and awareness, research is reduced to a set of mechanical exercises and procedures, divorced from the context, intended impact, or blind to negative consequences of the research endeavor (more discussion on this in Chapter 16). A good grasp on those meta-level concepts facilitates the process of developing a sound methodological design for a research study. As we discussed previously, epistemology, methodology, and methods form an inherent relationship. There is a close tie between how we conceptualize the nature of knowledge and research, our underlying epistemological orientations and values, and how we understand, approach, and design a given research phenomenon (methodology) and the particular methods that we choose.

Personal Synthesis

Throughout the chapter you have already had some moments to reflect on your own worldviews pertinent to epistemological and ontological issues. The next step might be to continue to expand this reflective practice into all of your scholarly activities and professional practices. An Indigenous scholar from New Zealand, Linda Tuhiwai Smith, provides a great set of questions for this ongoing reflection:

> Whose research is it? Who owns it? Whose interest does it serve? Who will benefit from it? Who has designed its questions and framed its scope? Who will carry it out? . . . Is the researchers' spirit clear? Does s/he have a good heart? What baggage are they carrying? Is the research useful to our community? Can it actually do anything right here right now that can help us grow? (Smith, 1999, p. 10)

You may substitute the word *research* with *practice* in this quote. This quote also nicely connects this chapter to core concepts introduced in Chapter 2 such as reflection, positionality, and criticality, and the discussions on identity in Chapter 3, and ethics in Chapter 4.

MOVING FORWARD

As we close this chapter, you might feel somewhat overwhelmed or still confused, given the dense nature of the concepts discussed here. For some of you, discussions in this chapter may deconstruct or even destabilize parts of your existing framework for understanding research. This is expected, and in fact welcomed. Without deconstruction, reconstruction cannot occur. The philosophical foundations discussed in this chapter are core to research and will be revisited throughout the book, so you will have ample opportunity to further digest these concepts. In the next chapter, we will further examine the nature of research and knowledge, in terms of how research is always embedded socially, culturally, historically, and politically, and the relationship between knowledge, social structures, and power. Keep holding onto the puzzle pieces that you try to put together. As we move along, the big picture will become clearer.

Further Readings

Allison, P., & Pomeroy, E. (2000). How shall we "know?" Epistemological concerns in research in experiential education. *Journal of Experiential Education, 23*(2), 91–98.

Grix, J. (2002). Introducing students to the generic terminology of social research. *Politics, 22*(3), 175–186.

Lehrer, J. (2010, December 13). The truth wears off: Is there something wrong with the scientific method? *The New Yorker*.

Paul, J. L. (2005). Historical and philosophical influences shaping perspectives of knowledge. In J. L. Paul (Ed.), *Introduction to the philosophies of research and criticism in education and the social sciences* (pp.1–20). Upper Saddle River, NJ: Prentice Hall.

Further Readings Related to the Research Scenario

Satinsky, S., Dennis, B., Reece, M., Sanders, S., & Bardzell, S. (2013). My "Fat Girl Complex": A preliminary investigation of sexual health and body image in women of size. *Culture, Health & Sexuality, 15*(6), 710–725.

Satinsky, S., & Ingraham, N. (2014). At the intersection of public health and fat studies: Critical perspectives on the measurement of body size. *Fat Studies, 3*(2), 143–154.

Winter, V. R., & Satinsky, S. (2014). Body appreciation, sexual relationship status, and protective sexual behaviors in women. *Body Image, 11*(1), 36–42.

Further Readings by Joseph Maxwell

Maxwell, J. A. (2012). The importance of qualitative research for causal explanation in education. *Qualitative Inquiry, 18*(8), 655–661.

Maxwell, J. A. (2017). Collecting qualitative data: A realist approach. In U. Flick (Ed.), *The SAGE handbook of qualitative data collection* (pp.19–32). London, UK: SAGE.

Maxwell, J. A. (2017). Using theory in qualitative research: A realist perspective. In M. Lipscomb (Ed.), *Social theory and nursing* (pp. 91–103). Abingdon, Oxon, UK: Routledge.

Further Readings by Sabine Siekmann and Joan Parker Webster

Siekmann, S., & Parker Webster, J. (2019). Critical intercultural conversations: Using activity systems analysis as a tool for educational ethnography. *Ethnography and Education: Special Issue on Multicultural Education, 14*(3), 377–393.

Siekmann, S., & Parker Webster, J., with Samson, S., Moses, C., John-Shields, A., & Wallace, S. (2019). *Pugtallgutkellriit*: Developing researcher identities in a participatory action research collaborative. *Journal of American Indian Education, 58*(1&2), 124–145.

6

SOCIOPOLITICAL CONDITIONS OF RESEARCH

In Chapter 6 we will continue to build on the concepts introduced in previous chapters, specifically intersubjectivity (Chapters 2 and 4), power (Chapter 4), normative claims (Chapter 5), and positionality (Chapters 3 and 4). We will examine how research practice is embedded in organizations, shaped by cultures, and influenced by large-scale trends such as globalization. Some researchers use "micro-level analysis" to describe the studies of interpersonal communication and "macro-level analysis" to denote the studies of large-scale social, cultural, and political issues. This chapter will locate our learning in-between the macro- and micro-levels to understand how research practice is both enabled and constrained by the macro-level social structure and how individual researchers position themselves in relation to structural factors in their everyday practice. Later, in Chapter 16, we will turn to this relationship again with a focus on the impact of social research—specifically, how we shall understand social research's potential to transform current structural injustice and hegemonic norms.

The framework introduced in this chapter is informed by and synthesized from several intellectual traditions, most noticeably British sociologist Anthony Giddens's theory of structuration (1979), German critical theorist Jürgen Habermas's communicative action theory (1987), and contemporary American sociological and methodological writings including Carspecken (1996, 2012) and William Sewell (1992). While the names and terms introduced in this chapter may sound intimidating, the "dry and abstract" theories are best understood when discussed using everyday examples. With this in mind, let's start this chapter with a scenario that many of us have encountered before: preparing attire for professional interviews. It then moves to a narrative, one that leads us to the heart of an environmentalist's decades-long endeavor to maintain a conscientious life.

MUSING UPON THE EVERYDAY

How Should I Dress for My First Job Interview?

At this point of your life, you have probably had several experiences attending interviews—for a job, an internship, or a graduate study program. These moments can be mixed with excitement and uncertainty, particularly around how to prepare in advance. In this section, we invite you to think about an important choice every candidate must make prior to any interview: what they will wear.

Over the past few years, many of Pengfei's friends left graduate school and joined the job market. She thus had multiple opportunities to help them prepare for job interviews and engage in conversations about interview dress codes. Several of her female friends found it hard to choose between pantsuits and dresses. Some felt more confident and comfortable in dresses but also understood that appearing more feminine could lead to their not being taken as seriously as their male counterparts. Her international friends were even less sure of how American employers would react to their interview attire.

In a different example, Pengfei's male friend, Alec, found it extremely uncomfortable and pretentious to wear suits. Alec grew up in a mountainous village in North China, where his family did not have money to purchase costly suits; nor did they need formal attire to attend social events. Alec himself had not purchased a suit until he was well into his graduate studies in the United States.

These examples raise interesting questions about the nature of rules. In our everyday life we encounter many rules from widely held expectations, such as wearing professional attire at a job interview, to institutionalized standards, such as a school's requirement for students to wear uniforms, and even nationwide laws. What are the similarities and differences among them? One may accurately point out that societal expectations, institutional regulations, and national laws vary in how fixed the rules are and what consequences an individual may suffer if found violating them. We can then further investigate what makes these differences possible. For instance, what compels us to follow certain rules habitually? Is it possible for individuals to negotiate and even change the rules? Furthermore, in what sense are our decisions, actions, emotions, and visceral feelings shaped by these rules? This chapter examines the cultural and sociopolitical structure that both conditions and enables our lived experience. We can then transfer our insights from looking at everyday life to understanding the impacts of rules on our research practice. Researchers do not research within a vacuum. Social research is shaped by the society in which it is embedded. This chapter introduces key concepts in understanding the relationship between social action and sociopolitical structure, and discusses their implications on research practice. Under this framework, we pose the question of how researchers can positively impact the world given that research itself is shaped and constrained by current social order.

NARRATIVE AND CONCEPTUAL INTERLUDES

Conceptualizing Social Action Through Looking at an Environmentalist's Dilemma

A few years ago, the authors' friend Cicada was searching for jobs after finishing his graduate studies and was invited by a university for an onsite visit. A self-identified environmentalist, he had been buying secondhand clothes since his college years. This time was no exception. He headed directly to Goodwill in the hopes of finding a secondhand suit for the interview. To his disappointment, Goodwill only carried a limited number of suits, and none were attractive or suitable. Leaving the store, Cicada found himself in a dilemma: On the one hand, he really needed that job and would like to look his best for the interview; on the other hand, he would consume more resources by purchasing a neat new suit. Buying new clothes simply countered the principle of reducing consumption, to which he was strongly dedicated.

Social Norms and Everyday Life

What can we learn about the relationship between an individual and society, from Cicada's story? First of all, we see a tension here: Cicada wanted to maintain a moral principle that he has been following for most of his adult life, but he could hardly do so. Why? Because he could not find appropriate clothes for a job interview in the local used clothing store, and a nice suit is a necessity for a successful interview. In order to understand Cicada's story better, Pengfei conducted a semistructured interview with him (a method of generating qualitative data; see Chapter 10). As he put bluntly in the interview,

> People always judge people by their clothes. And there is a certain expectation about what people should wear for interviews. If you don't meet some minimum standard of what people expect, then they will think less of you before you even get to talk with them. They see you and they think this person does not care that much about this interview. (Pengfei's interview with Cicada, January 10, 2017)

Cicada mentioned a "certain expectation" for his job interview attire. The expectation involves an implicit normative claim: Job candidates should wear formal, neat, and well-maintained clothes when they attend interviews. Employers may associate job candidates' clothes with their attitudes toward the new job; they may even, in some cases, use the investment candidates make on the suits to judge their commitments to the position.

In Chapter 5 we discussed the meaning of normative claims in relation to subjective and objective claims. Claims in the normative domain refer to what is good/bad, right/wrong, and appropriate/inappropriate. In this chapter, we will further situate the discussion of normative claims in the social world. In other words, we will examine when and how normative claims are enacted in everyday life and academic settings.

In our everyday life, normative claims underpin many of our activities: When we take a bus, we are expected to form a line and keep an appropriate distance from those in front of and behind us; when we get on the bus, we should not take the seats designated for passengers who are elderly, pregnant, or may have disabilities; if we have dinner with a friend in a restaurant, we are expected to talk in a low voice to avoid disturbing other guests; as we finish our meal and are ready to leave, we should tip our server for the service we received. These expectations, or normative claims, are widely held by societal members. We can find some norms cross different cultures, whereas others are unique to a single society; for instance, tipping servers 15–20% after dinner is practiced mostly in contemporary American society. Although people seldom make such expectations explicit, very often we implicitly refer to **social norms** to inform how we communicate with each other in a society.

Many social theorists agree that norms and expectations are "know-how" knowledge that we learn from doing (Carspecken, 1996; Habermas, 1987; Sewell, 1992), including anthropological theorist Sherry Ortner (1984). We do not follow a list of fixed rules in our social life, but implicitly know how to behave as a polite passenger or guest. We do not have to explicitly think about rules as we form a line, have our dinner, or ride a bus. We grasp the "know-how" knowledge habitually through our interactions with our parents when we are little, in our schools while playing with our classmates, and through observing the behavior of other members of society. As such, social norms are primarily instantiated through social actions and implicitly guide us when we interact with each other. When the two or more parties of social interaction consensually follow the norms, the social actors seldom question the implicit normative rules. However, a normative rule becomes a more foregrounded issue when one side of the interaction fails to follow it or starts to problematize its legitimacy. For instance, if Cicada chose a secondhand hippie-style jacket for his interview, the interviewer might wonder why he wore such casual clothes for a formal business event. They might even conclude Cicada was not very serious about the job.

> **Pause and Reflect.** In academia as well, people implicitly refer to normative claims to interpret what is a good researcher/research and what a researcher should do to produce legitimate knowledge. Consider the following scenarios and see if you can identify their backgrounded normative claims:
>
> - You submit a proposal to present an empirical study at a professional conference. The online submission system asks for the evidence of the IRB approval of the project.

- In graduate school, you have heard from multiple people that "doing this and that can build your CV," as if the single most important criterion you need to consider in planning your graduate studies is whether an activity can become a line on your CV.
- You notice that some academics in your program bring up the term *impact factor* often in discussing how one shall decide their publishing platforms. It seems that the higher the impact factors are, the more important and prestigious the journals are.

In some cases, social norms are patterned, which means we may find them instantiated recurrently in similar social settings. For instance, Cicada was interviewed for several professional positions offered by higher education institutions in the United States. In all of the interview settings, he had to dress up considerably. No one anticipated he would dress down or dress in any unique style. The phenomenon shows that this specific expectation about professional dress code is widely shared by a society, making it a patterned social norm. In this case, the dress code has become part of Western culture, which draws a clear line between work and family, job and leisure. People from non-Western countries, however, may not necessarily share the norms that prevail in U.S. society. We can also illustrate this point using a case closely related to social research. Some norms have been firmly established or even institutionalized in the United States, such as the statement mentioned above, in "Pause and Reflect," that one should obtain IRB approval if they plan to do research involving human subjects. But Mark Israel reminds us that the regulation of research ethics in other countries is often practiced differently from the committee-based, procedural-oriented model of Western-developed countries (Israel, 2020). Israel and his colleague Zheng-Rong Gan further argue that the prevalence of the American model ignores "the long-standing ways of conceiving ethics" connected with different cultural traditions (Gan & Israel, 2020). This example sheds light on the close relationship between social norms and **culture**.

Scholars conceptualize culture, one of the most intensely studied topics in social science, in many different ways. In this book, we propose to understand "culture" as patterned practice through which norms and values are formulated and enacted. Social norms, as an important part of culture, are represented symbolically and underpin the communications among the members of a cultural group. Recall the close connection between meaning-making and *cultural typification*—a term we introduced in Chapter 5. A cultural insider grasps meaning first through tacit position-taking and recognizing the communicative patterns in a culture. This process encompasses the implicit instantiation of social norms. Furthermore, whether or not certain norms are practiced often demarcates the often-blurred boundary of a cultural group.

If culture and social norms are so closely related, you may wonder: What is a cultural group? Is it determined by ethnicity, race, or nationality? Do the group members have to be identical in terms of their normative beliefs? Earlier studies on this topic tend to define a cultural group as homogeneous, such as a relatively isolated rural community. More recent studies, however, reveal the heterogeneity of a cultural group as understood in a traditional sense, and argue that different forms of social groups—such as an organization, a generation, or even a family—can all form their unique cultural practice in certain circumstances. A classic discussion on this topic is Paul Willis's *Learn to Labor: How Working Class Kids Get Working Class Jobs* (1976), which examines how, in the 1970s, British working-class youth formed their anti-mainstream and anti-school culture at the intersection of class (working class), gender (male), and generation (adolescents). In this subculture, which Willis coined as "the lads," the working-class youth enacted norms to distinguish themselves from and resist the mainstream culture. This analysis highlights the importance of the heterogeneity as opposed to the homogeneity of a cultural group, and also calls for us to attend to a social actor's enactment of norms in concrete and contextualized social interactions.

In the context of higher education, researchers can form different cultures and instantiate various norms regarding learning and knowledge. As we discussed before, social norms are derived from specific historical contexts and, in many cases, followed by social members habitually. This means that many social norms are practiced without being questioned. In the example of prioritizing CV-building activities in graduate schools, it is easier to follow what everybody else is doing and take this value orientation for granted. However, there are indeed moments in which one may see the need to explicate and/or challenge the norms. Two such moments are (1) clarifying a confusion or misunderstanding, and (2) voicing the oppression people have experienced by following the norms. If a friend suggests you prioritize activities that could add lines on your CV, you might follow up by asking them to clarify their meaning of CV-building activities. The follow-up question aims to explicate the tacit meaning in your conversation. Alternatively, you might question on what basis your friend makes this statement and even challenge it by laying out a different priority list. In the latter case, you might feel that the very idea of CV-building and self-branding has forced you to align your life with strategic calculation in order to secure a good position on the increasingly competitive academic job market. You could problematize this priority, as it deviates from your original goal for attending graduate school—namely, the pursuit of self-growth and self-realization. Your counterargument would problematize the legitimacy of the normative statement your friend presented.

The example of CV-building illustrates the dual aspects of social researchers' role in relation to critiquing and transforming norms and cultures. On the one hand, some prevalent norms are oppressive for or perpetuate a stereotype about a particular social group. These norms are heatedly contested, and many researchers use their research as a means to question the legitimacy of predominant social norms. Through disrupting the current norms, they advocate positive changes of a culture. On the other hand, researchers also need to reflect upon what norms are enacted through their research practice as well as what cultures are produced within their academic units, institutions, and disciplines. In addition to the advocacy for large-scale, societal-level changes, being reflective and mindful about what is immediate and close to us can also contribute to cultural transformation in small but meaningful ways.

Social Structure and Agency

Cicada and like-minded environmentalists strive to facilitate a positive change of consumerist culture. They challenge popular beliefs surrounding consumption in our society—specifically, the belief that buying new stuff is a way to stay abreast of the latest fashions and to display one's wealth and privilege. However, a question remains: How much change can Cicada's life choice realistically bring? As Cicada himself mentioned in the interview, a considerable part of our economy is driven by consumption. Can Cicada's environmentalism reshape our economy?

This question taps into the relationship between social actors and **social structure**, named for lack of a more appropriate term. Because of the multifacets of this term and its various meanings in different intellectual traditions, scholars note the term serves as "a kind of founding or epistemic metaphor," while to define it is "embarrassingly difficult" (Sewell, 1992, pp. 1–2). In this textbook, we take an approach of critical pragmatism to conceptualizing social structure as various heterogeneous, patterned rules and mechanisms that condition and enable social action, and are also consequentially impacted by social action. At first glance, it seems that social structure always runs at the macro-level: how economy works to distribute wealth and resources, the route capital follows across boundaries of nation-states, the systematic promotion of cultural beliefs by popular media, and the wide circulation of public opinions that demarcate the boundaries between "us" and "the other." However, the key of this definition lies in the connection between what we would consider as macro-structural dynamics and our everyday life, as social structure and social action are always so fused that it would be impossible to presume a static, fixed, and completely separate social structure that determines the course of social action. Furthermore, we would lose sight of the larger picture if we assume the complete autonomy of social actors without taking into consideration the enabling and constraining structural factors. Adapted from Carspecken's work (2012), Figure 6.1 illustrates the relationship between the two. In this figure, social structure is presented as both the conditions and consequences of social action. On the one hand, various forms of power (a term we will unpack later in this chapter) often mediate social structure's influence on actions; on the other hand, the more a social actor is able to articulate the connection between the two, the more the actor can reflect upon the structural condition in which the action is embedded.

120 Cluster 1 ■ Understanding Research

FIGURE 6.1 ● A Critical Approach to Conceptualizing Social Action

Action Consequences

Reproduction of	Cultural beliefs
Understanding of	Symbolic structure
	Institutionalized rules
Resistance against	Power relationship
	Social inequality
Repetition of	Identity
Transformation of	Everyday experience

Relation of Actor to Condition of Action

- Discursive awareness
- Tacit awareness
- Unacknowledged

Forms of power
Structural power–Interactive power

●ACT →

Become part of the conditions for next action

Conditions of Action [social structure]

Cultural structure	Institutionalized rules	Social system decoupled from culture	Material condition
Patterned social norms	Laws	Market	Environment
Typified cultural beliefs	Policies	Bureaucracy	Raw materials for production
Symbolic structure	Formal rules		Tools

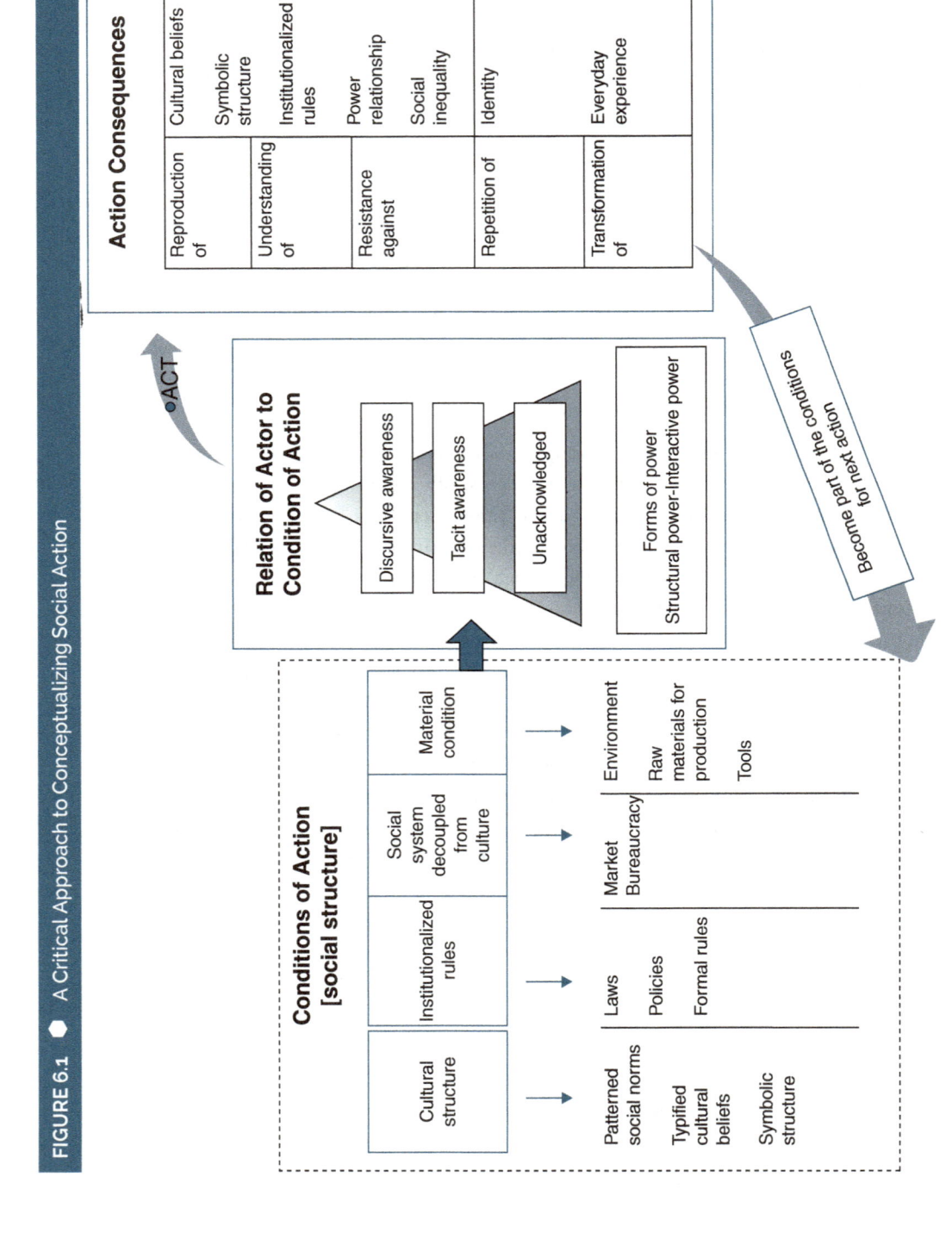

Let's think again about Cicada's story, this time focusing on the conditions of his action. Cicada notices two mutually reinforcing phenomena, that our society constantly encourages people to acquire more products, regardless of need, and that the capacity for consumption is associated with individuals' taste as well as their social and economic status. An expensive suit, for instance, indicates its owner's mainstream taste and their middle- to upper-middle-class social status. Meanwhile, our economy runs on the premise of pursuing profit. Manufacturers search for the cheapest human labor and material resources globally to maximize their profits. In order to sell their products to potential buyers, they also promote them in popular media. Below we identify two structural factors underlying these phenomena:

- The symbolic meaning system based on which social actors implicitly or explicitly enact social norms and formulate typified cultural meanings of their actions. Some anthropologists, for example, Robert Winthrop (1991), identify binaries as a significant component of a symbolic structure, such as those of female–male, culture–nature, or raw–cooked (see also Ortner, 1984). In Cicada's criticism of consumerism, we can reconstruct the juxtaposition of the binaries of new and used, economic success and failure, as well as environmental sustainability and overexploitation. Popular culture associates buying expensive clothes with economic success, whereas Cicada argues that endless consumption leads to the overexploitation of nature and that recycling secondhand goods can pave the way for a sustainable future.

- A social system that is decoupled from culture mainly runs on a different principle—in this case, the global market that runs on the principle of maximizing profit. The organization of workers, the division of labors, and the flow of capital are primarily driven by the chase of profit in contemporary societies.

Two other issues also contribute to configuring Cicada's dilemma:

- As Cicada was interviewing with an American public university, his employer needed to comply with relevant protocols, policies, and laws in the hiring process, such as the Equal Employment Opportunity Statement policies, which prohibit any form of discrimination in hiring. These rules differ from the social norms enacted in everyday communication in the sense that they are highly formalized, and violating them may incur institutionalized punitive consequences.

- Last but not least, the producers' capacity to manufacture clothes is shaped by material factors, such as the availability of raw materials and tools.

Going back to the idea that social structure is a founding or epistemic metaphor, we know that a metaphor never mimics what it refers to, for if that were the case, we would not call it a metaphor. Instead, a metaphor works in two ways—either bringing things far away closer to us or making things right in front of us unfamiliar. In either case, the idea of metaphor reminds us that we cannot take Figure 6.1 as a snapshot, a model, or a map to establish a one-on-one corresponding relationship between the figure and social reality. Instead, we can think to what extent this figure helps us see the connection between our social action and the macro-level trends, patterns, and dynamics—what at first glance seems to be so far removed from the action. It also sheds light on the action itself as we situate it firmly in its historical, cultural, and social context. As such, a metaphor provides us with the entry point and wondering space as we start to think critically while also leaving us enough freedom to problematize it. For instance, over the past years, many researchers have questioned the nature of a symbolic structure. They explored the debatable topic of the nature of a symbolic structure, and discussed whether it reflects human beings' universal cognitive features or a cultural group's unique historical development, as well as whether a structure can be reconstructed as a set of fixed rules or if it is more fluid and constantly changing. In this chapter, our analysis has been focusing on the connection among culture, social action, and social norms. We tend to look at culture as more porous and situational, as habitual yet also fluid, and as ever-changing structures enacted through social action.

> **Pause and Reflect.** Let's zoom in to explore the connections between formal rules and social norms in a research context using the example of IRBs. Institutional review boards (IRBs) are established to make sure researchers comply with relevant policies in protecting their research participants. In Chapter 4 we consider IRBs as a procedural approach to research ethics as opposed to a situational approach. What normative claims are institutionalized by IRBs? What normative claims are foregrounded when a researcher engages research participants in a concrete research scenario? How do the procedural and situational aspects of research ethics, intertwined as *the conditions of action*, shape research practice?

In the discussions above, we use Cicada's story to illustrate how actions are embedded in a social structure. Going back to Figure 6.1, we can raise a follow-up question about to what degree a social actor can be aware of the social structure that enables and conditions their action. Very often, people are encouraged to "be themselves," but can they be themselves regardless of the cultural and material contexts, or can they simply leave the traces of their class, gender, and ethnicity behind them? The degree to which a social actor can act independently and freely is usually termed "**agency**" in social sciences. The relationship between social structure and agency is at the center of social research. Going back to Cicada's case, when asked "How much change can Cicada realistically bring forward?" what were we really asking about? We were primarily concerned about how an individual could wrestle with structural constraints imposed on them through well-established social norms, predominant cultural beliefs, institutionalized production of material goods, and so on and so forth. In other words, we set off to explore the relationship between an individual and the social structure as it is manifested in Cicada's anti-consumerism lifestyle. To better tackle this question, it is important to introduce the concept of *power*.

Structural and Interactive Power

In Chapter 4 we investigated power dynamics in relation to ethical research practice, where we mainly focused on the researcher–research participant relationship—specifically, how power could be invoked on research participants by researchers to strategically achieve goals. In this section, we will continue to unpack the meaning of power and situate it in our analysis of the relationship between social actors and the social structure.

One way to look at power is to examine on what level power is invoked and who imposes power on whom. We can distinguish two types of power: macro-level structural power and micro-level interactive power. Macro-level power is usually imposed by organizations and institutions, such as the state and large companies, or on other social entities, such as individuals. Micro-level power primarily focuses on the interaction between different individuals. However, this does not mean that structural issues do not have an impact on interpersonal communication. As we have briefly discussed in Chapter 4 and will demonstrate later on, interpersonal communication is often mediated by widely held social norms, which can be considered a structural factor. On both levels, the initiator can use either a coercive or interactive form of power.

Let's use Cicada's story to explain this concept more concretely. A crucial question in this story is: Why did Cicada have to wear new clothes to his job interview? It is possible that he and his interviewers are in an unequal power relationship, which makes it difficult for him to maintain his environmentalist belief. To be clear, the unequal relationship is not based on coercion, although sometimes people do use coercion to force others to surrender. Cicada's interviewers did not beat him to the ground to force him to wear a new suit. On the contrary, there was a large chance that the interviewers would be polite and show him due respect during the interview. Cicada's predicament was largely due to the widely circulated social norm about what is considered appropriate attire for a job interview. Although the content of this specific job may have nothing to do with Cicada's personal taste, the interviewers might still judge him based on this social norm. Then, could he wear what he already owned and explain to the interviewers why he made this choice? It would be equally difficult for him to do so, as a job candidate is not supposed to mention such a topic in an interview. The power relationship between Cicada and his interviewers is mediated by the social norm about appropriate clothes in formal work settings.

Cicada's story serves as a good example illustrating the micro-level interactive power relationship. Power relationships at the micro-level can be very nuanced and vary from case to case. Therefore, researchers working on micro-level power analysis usually need to perform detailed and grounded analysis to uncover the micro-level power dynamics and their consequences. In Cicada's case, he intentionally chose to wear secondhand clothes in his everyday life, but if he would like to, he could afford new clothes. Imagine if the interviewee were a poor, single mom who needed the job to support her two young children. Where could she find the formal clothes for the job interview? She would probably be forced to choose between buying nutritious food for her children and a formal dress or pantsuit. Compared with Cicada, the single mom is in a more disadvantaged position. The comparison reveals how power relationships vary from case to case, and also how the structural issues such as gender and social status are folded into the formation of micro-level power relationships.

In Cicada's case, power dynamics are also manifested at the structural level. For instance, in the discussion of Figure 6.1, we identified the economic system as the second structural factor that contributes to configuring Cicada's predicament. In particular, we discussed the connection between the consumption and production of clothing in the contemporary world. It reveals how clothing producers intervened in the process of cultural production through shaping people's cultural imagination and reinforcing a normative understanding of appropriate clothing. This imagination and reinforcement, in turn, produce desire and needs for continued consumption of clothing, further driving the production of clothing and creating more profit for manufacturing companies. The impact of this power dynamic is not imposed on a singular individual, but rather on the society as a whole.

The analysis of structural and interactive power can be very complex, and therefore this brief discussion does not aim at fleshing out all the nuances in this theoretical framework, but opens the door for us to critically engage in the questions about power relationships. It also leads us to raise the question of how an individual, such as Cicada, can resist structural and interactive power and maintain his agency. Cicada did end up buying new clothes, but he managed to follow his life principles and buy as few as possible: He only bought a pair of suit pants, a shirt, and a tie, but not the coat. As to the larger issue regarding consumerism, in his interview, Cicada detailed how he was influenced by the hippie movement in his early years. When he was in college, he was involved in various countermainstream culture activities, such as antiwar activism and local co-operative businesses. He discussed his approach to environmentalism and anti-consumerism:

> To me, it has been quite individual. I have done some outreach to people through different groups I've been part of. But I cannot do a whole lot except for living my life and trying to make the best choices I can for myself. It's difficult because at one level, I feel I don't have the right to tell other people how

to live their life, but at another level, the way we make our lives can collectively destroy the planet. If you think about each individual person, one person does not make much differences. . . . But if all the people deal with it collectively, it will make a huge impact. It's a challenge to know how to address that other than speaking to people about it. I did write some of my musical . . . to address this issue. This is one way—through artistic expression. The other way is through activism, but I haven't done that a lot since I went back to school for a doctorate. (Pengfei's interview with Cicada, January 10, 2017)

Aesthetic activities and civic activism are the two approaches through which Cicada intervened, but he still struggled to find the best method for addressing the deep-seated cultural issues manifested in consumerism, because shifting a cultural belief would entail altering not only his lifestyle but also that of other social members. He is well aware of this tension, and meanwhile reflects deeply on his approach to balancing life between personal issues and public engagement. It would be difficult to discuss the effect of Cicada's efforts in a quantifiable manner, but identifying his strategies and self-understanding behind said strategies will help us understand where an individual's agency comes into play through interactions with those large-scale structural issues. In Figure 6.2 we first replace the term *act* in Figure 6.1 with Cicada's action of purchasing new suit pants and then explore the conditions and consequences of this action. The relationship between social structure and agency does not only reflect the relationship between the conditions of action and Cicada's act, but also can be located between his act and the consequences of the action. As we can see, even in the seemingly mundane example of purchasing clothes, the consequences of the action are multilayered: It reproduces the social norm around the formal dress code at job interviews and helps Cicada better understand his needs and moral commitments. Meanwhile, the action of buying pants but not a coat demonstrates Cicada's efforts to resist consumerism, as well as the environmental damage that the fashion industry incurs. This purchase effectively became a transformative moment when a long-term environmentalist took strategic action to negotiate with his reality. The consequences of action, which limit Cicada's participation in the consumerist market, then join the previous conditions of action and become the condition for the next social action.

> **Pause and Reflect.** Going back to Figure 6.1, what will happen if we replace the term *act* with *social research*? Can you try to redraw the figure, this time centering on social research? As we have demonstrated in the discussion of Cicada's clothes, one can develop a deeper understanding of a social action by comparing its conditions and potential consequences against the larger social and cultural context. Zooming in further, how will you redraw this figure if the focal point is your learning of social research?

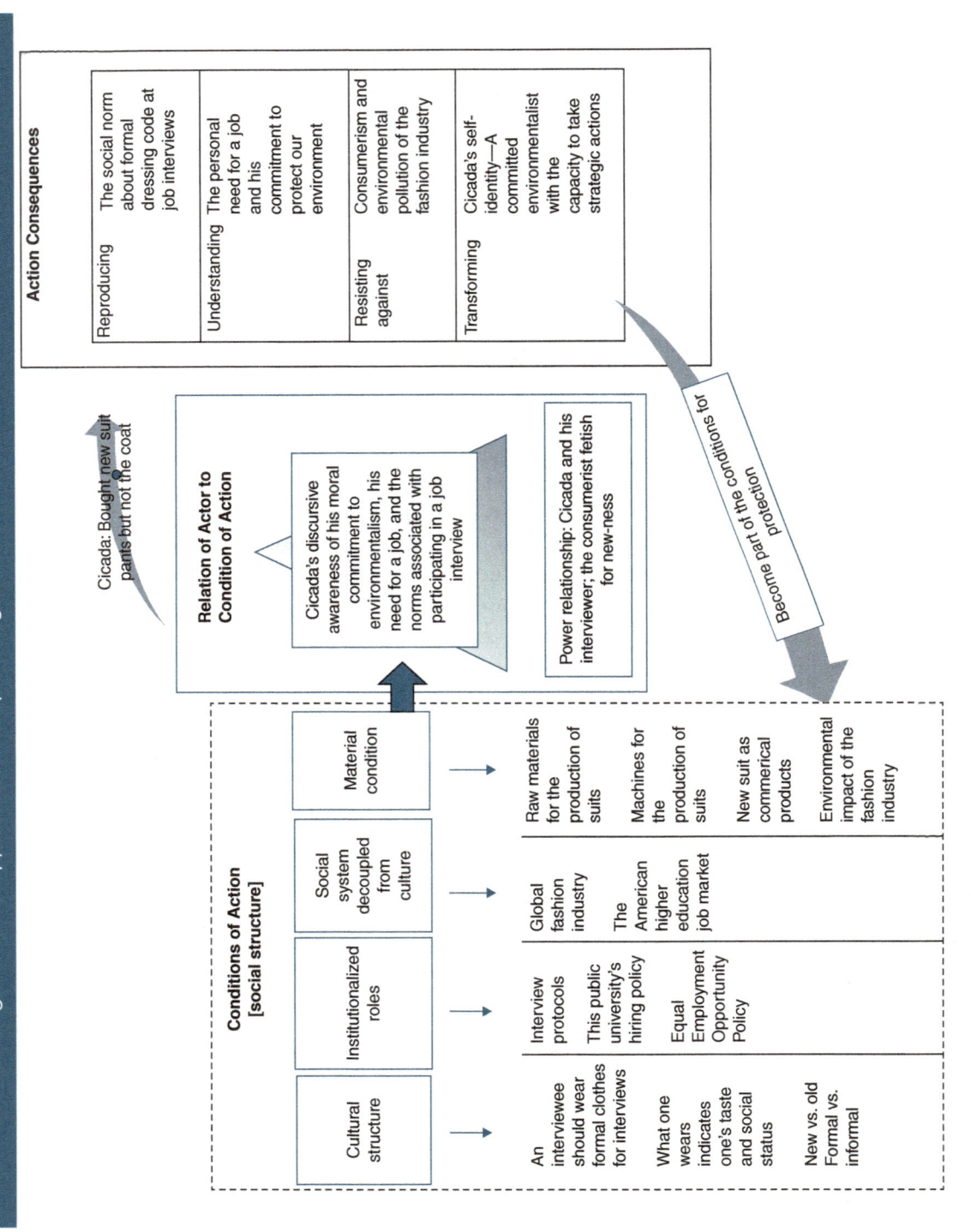

FIGURE 6.2 ● Using the Critical Approach to Conceptualizing Cicada's Action

Action Consequences

Reproducing	The social norm about formal dressing code at job interviews
Understanding	The personal need for a job and his commitment to protect our environment
Resisting against	Consumerism and environmental pollution of the fashion industry
Transforming	Cicada's self-identity—A committed environmentalist with the capacity to take strategic actions

Relation of Actor to Condition of Action

Cicada's discursive awareness of his moral commitment to environmentalism, his need for a job, and the norms associated with participating in a job interview

Power relationship: Cicada and his interviewer; the consumerist fetish for new-ness

Cicada: Bought new suit pants but not the coat

Become part of the conditions for protection

Conditions of Action [social structure]

Cultural structure	Institutionalized roles	Social system decoupled from culture	Material condition
An interviewee should wear formal clothes for interviews	Interview protocols	Global fashion industry	Raw materials for the production of suits
What one wears indicates one's taste and social status	This public university's hiring policy	The American higher education job market	Machines for the production of suits
New vs. old Formal vs. informal	Equal Employment Opportunity Policy		New suit as commerical products
			Environmental impact of the fashion industry

RESEARCH SCENARIO: MAKING A DIFFERENCE AS A RESEARCHER

As social researchers, how shall we study our society and bring about positive changes given that we are shaped and conditioned by various structural and interactive powers? Is this even possible? In this section, our guest authors engage with these questions from different perspectives. Sociologist Wei Luo, drawing on a study she completed with Julia Adams and Hannah Brückner, discusses how women researchers' voices are silenced in both the construction of discipline-based canons and crowd-sourced encyclopedias, such as Wikipedia. In this case, Luo and her colleagues' study critically examines how the production and dissemination of knowledge have resulted in the reproduction of the patriarchal social order.

Representation of Women Scholars in the Hybrid Space of Knowledge: Wei Luo

Many notable female scholars have vanished from canonical academic histories. For instance, the NASA mathematicians Katherine Johnson, Mary Jackson, and Dorothy Vaughan, whose stories inspired the critically acclaimed 2016 film Hidden Figures, *were nowhere to be found in the historiography of the Space Race for decades, despite their significant contribution. Matilda Gage, Marie Maynard Daly, and Chien-Shiung Wu, among numerous other female scientists, have been sidelined or dismissed as mere helpers of their male colleagues in the history of science for more than a century. (More underappreciated female scientists can be found here: https://www.smithsonianmag.com/science-nature/unheralded-women-scientists-finally-getting-their-due-180973082/.) In comparison to natural science disciplines, sociology has been relatively open to women since its founding, yet many notable female sociologists are still missing from public history of American sociology, both print and digital.*

As the most influential crowd-sourced encyclopedia, Wikipedia promises—but does not necessarily deliver—a democratic corrective to the generation of knowledge. Our research endeavors to trace the multiple pathways by which women either enter or disappear from the disciplinary records by analyzing the interaction between the canonical academic history and Wikipedia. Who are the vanished women? To approach this problem, we used two encyclopedic sourcebooks of early female sociologists as a comparative frame to scrutinize where leaks occur in the process of knowledge generation (Deegan, 1991; Lengermann & Niebrugge, 2007). The sourcebooks were attempts to reinstate and recover significant sociologists that are missing in the sociological canon. They represent the traditional way that encyclopedias assemble knowledge:

The entries are produced by experts in specific fields, largely based on reliable primary materials, and are usually peer-reviewed. Wikipedia, in contrast, signifies the trend of knowledge generation toward "amateurization," in which multiple anonymous editors collaborate on the same topic and assemble knowledge through existing online secondary sources. We then used Wikipedia's internal search engine to determine whether the names included in the sourcebooks appear on Wikipedia and/or other websites using Google search. We found that nearly 30% of the women in the sourcebook do not have a Wikipedia entry. We further dug into the archival materials of these missing women, which includes their scholarly writings and commentaries, correspondence, diaries, autobiographies, and other primary sources to investigate how they are presented in the sourcebooks and in Wikipedia entries.

By comparing disciplinary histories and Wikipedia, we found that women scholars are selectively underrepresented and misrepresented in the new digital repertoire. From a historical perspective, the presence or absence of a woman from written documents can be pinpointed in one or more layers in the pathways of knowledge formation. Each female scholar's work would have been assessed by contemporary commentators, who interacted with it via the cultural understandings and institutional arrangements and struggles of the time. These assessments, more or less contested, filtered into scholarly papers, reviews, editors' comments, personal correspondence, and non-academic records and representations of all sorts. These become forms of evidence that later scholars and investigators use as they select historical individuals in service of a particular narrative around the development of the discipline. Less-accredited academic or intellectual work may drop out at this stage, possibly to resurface later. The ongoing product of these narratives forms the academic history of the discipline.

Although it is highly likely that an editor of a crowd-sourced digital platform will rely on existing academic histories or other texts directly influenced by them to generate or edit entries about prominent disciplinary figures, those entries may instead arise from an earlier point in the chain of representation, for example, in primary archival sources. If so, however, the rules ensure that they are less likely to survive deletion challenges. And finally, meta-level analysts, like ourselves, who have access to both academic histories and Wikipedia or other digital platforms, seek to understand—and perhaps intervene in—the mechanisms that produce specific forms of representation of intellectuals in our contemporary world.

Two cross-cutting dimensions, or four logical possibilities, emerge as what has been the expert-led print and the crowd-sourced digital worlds intersect.

The baseline category—which we designate as "remembered"—includes female scholars who occupy important public positions in the discipline's history and who

FIGURE 6.3 ● Types of Canonical Textual Representation

	Academic History Yes	Academic History No
Wikipedia Yes	Remembered	Recovered
Wikipedia No	Neglected	Erased

Source: Luo et al. (2018).

also have a Wikipedia presence. The existence of this category enables us to clarify the other three, all of which are "missing."

The "neglected" category embraces those who are acknowledged in academia and have appeared in canonical histories but are missing from Wikipedia. This is a situation in which expert knowledge could help fill the gap on Wikipedia's more popular representation. This can only occur if page editors are persuaded to use more diverse and trustworthy academic sources, rather than other unvetted online information, as seems to be the case at present.

The category that we are calling "erased" includes those scholars who should have been recognized in the field or who were recognized by contemporaries, but who have been deleted from the discipline's history and, unsurprisingly, do not have a Wikipedia presence. These women made important academic contributions during the same period as their now more valued male counterparts.

The reconstruction of "erased" women in academic history and on Wikipedia is much more difficult than those in the "neglected" category. The foremost challenge is an acknowledgement—in some cases a re-acknowledgement—by the contemporary academic community of the important contribution of these early women intellectuals. Diligent research may then enable us to regain some of the lost information about the women themselves, as well as on the development of the discipline. However, Wikipedia's test of significance, which is based on existing online exposure, is likely to create further barriers to retrieving the missing women for the collective stock of knowledge.

Finally, with the category of "recovered" women, we suggest that there is at least a possibility, embedded in Wikipedia's crowdsourced approach to academic knowledge, of reintroducing the discipline's vanished women and reasserting their place in *intellectual history. Such cases are difficult to identify but illuminate the continuing utopian potential of mass knowledge generation in a digital age. This category is possible when Wikipedia editors consult previously marginalized sources in academic history, instead of relying on canonical history; in this way, they circumvent the gatekeepers in canonization.*

These four categories facilitate further excavation of the lives of female sociologists. They also have implications for better representation of not only the individuals in this specific discipline but also the various groups and organizations of which the women were, or should have been, in the counterfactual sense, members.

Wei and her colleagues critically examined two types of knowledge production and dissemination approaches, the canonical approach relying on conventional experts and the more recent crowd-sourced approach relying on multiple anonymous editors. They identified cases in which women sociologists were systematically excluded from the disciplinary history in both traditional canons and contemporary Wikipedia. Their study, although focusing on a specific social science discipline, serves as a good example to reveal the persistent structural discrimination against women in the knowledge production process. It calls for each and every researcher to deliberately reflect upon the entrenched power relationship in generating knowledge.

Moving from the macro- to the micro-level, in what follows Payal P. Shah discussed how she positioned herself in long-term ethnographic research in India, demonstrating that a researcher's reflection should be an ever-evolving process that connects one's identity, ethics, and philosophic commitments with critical examinations of the power relationships and cultural boundaries enacted by the research itself.

An Essay on My Positionality: Payal P. Shah

I strongly believe that a university's ability to develop critically reflective citizens who are able to thrive in an increasingly global world and promote innovative research that pushes the boundaries of current knowledge, requires building a cadre of faculty with diverse backgrounds, perspectives, and approaches to scholarship. As a South Asian American, I bring experiences in and perspectives on negotiating between an identity as an American and Indian to the academy. Coming to terms with my identity has been a process of navigating multiplicity in a society where we generally think in terms of binaries, e.g., Black/white, immigrant/native, etc. These dualities have often left me without a clear "space" to belong, and set me upon a journey seeking my ethnic identity, and interrogating what it means to be at once Indian and American, as well as a female navigating both cultures. I identify specifically with being Indian American, or an American of Indian heritage, as a way to specify my identity as neither only American nor Indian, but a unique fusion of the two, a fusion I have deliberately cultivated.

As a daughter of immigrant parents, I was often called upon to "translate" between these two cultures. I considered myself living two lives caught between two very different worlds—I had developed a close personal connection to India by spending summers there as a child, while being fully engaged in U.S. life through school, friends, and extracurricular activities. I constantly struggled with how these two worlds and identities could coherently come together in my everyday life. Throughout and following college, I intentionally engaged in academic and professional activities that forced me to explore and confront my multiple identities. This quest began in earnest during my tenure as a William J. Clinton Service Fellow in India where I worked with a grassroots education NGO for 1 year. This experience catalyzed my long-term engagement as a development professional and scholar in India that has spanned 15 years and allowed me to build a strong personal and professional relationship with Indian culture and society. I believe this in-depth understanding of both Indian and American culture and society, along with my efforts to reconcile a complex, multifaceted identity, enables me to bring unique perspectives to both my research and the academy.

My experience navigating two cultures has facilitated my ability to effectively conduct research in both the U.S. and India. As a female Indian American I am able to seamlessly move between insider and outsider perspectives—maintaining aspects of both in each context. In India, I share the same ethnicity as my research subjects and possess tacit and implicit cultural knowledge that enables me to integrate myself into the communities and lives of those I study. Likewise, my status as a female American positions me as an outsider and enables me to illuminate new understandings and insights and communicate these findings in a way that resonates with students, scholars, and development professionals in the West. However, this integration comes with significant challenges; challenges that stem from being neither Indian nor American in these contexts. Occupying this in-between space has demanded that I re-create my positionality so that it captures my unique positionality as it exists in a particular context; a positionality that is simultaneously and fluidly insider and outsider. Developing this positionality has demanded constant reflection, negotiation, and time with my participants to navigate between my understandings of my identity in relation to how my research participants perceive me.[1] This has not been an easy process to navigate as it is not straightforward and changes not only as my research sites and participants change, but also within a specific research site over time. Slightly more straightforwardly, in the U.S., I find that my insider status enables me to connect with mainstream American culture and society, while my outsider status allows me to engage meaningfully with our own diversity of ethnicities, races, classes, and perspectives. I believe that this has enhanced my ability to recognize and highlight how global issues, such as gender discrimination and poverty, manifest themselves in a variety of local cultural contexts. Consequently, I believe that my research and teaching add depth to issues related to social justice and inequality that provide insights that enhance both my scholarship and the perspectives that I bring to the academy here in the U.S. and in India.

As a critical feminist ethnographer, I adopt a scholarly position that cuts across traditional disciplinary boundaries, seeks to transform methodological approaches to research, and pays direct attention to the intersection of gender, class, race, and ethnicity. I conduct research that is multicultural, global, and postcolonial, and that also attempts to intentionally bring about social and individual change. My positionality, along with my professional and academic experiences, directly informs my commitment to higher education: a belief in the transformative potential of the teaching–learning dialectic and commitment to exposing individuals to issues of diversity—pushing individuals to, in Socratic terms, live the examined life and become citizens of the world.[1]

---

[1] See Shah, P. P. (2015), for a specific example of how I have engaged in this process of positionality re-creation.

YOU AND RESEARCH

When Interpreting Research

Your most direct encounter with theories will be the "theoretical framework" section of a research article, usually following either the introduction or the literature review section. Most "theoretical framework" sections succinctly summarize (1) the major points of the theories that the author engages and (2) in what sense the theory has informed the study. Often an author engages in a discussion of a series of interconnected epistemological and ontological statements in this section.

Compared with theories foregrounded in the section of theoretical framework, the integration of theories in a statement of positionality/motivation is more backgrounded. Many researchers do not have space in an article to dive into the conversation surrounding a theory. In these cases, pay attention to words such as *power*, *inequality*, or *culture*, as they will give you a clue to the influence of theories in the author(s)' reflection of their position to social structure.

In addition, in articles that present the author(s)' arguable opinions or disciplinary reflections, you may find valuable discussions on the social, cultural, and political conditions of research practice, as well as how this practice may impact the larger social world.

When Doing Research

This chapter focuses on social theories and their connection to research practice. Social theories differ from the epistemological theories we introduced in Chapter 5 in the sense that the former seeks to shed light on the interconnectedness between social actors and the social structure, whereas the latter is mainly concerned about the nature of truth and how we pursue truth. Regarding social theories, we think there are at least two approaches through which you can integrate them in your inquiry.

The first approach concerns how you will position yourself as a researcher in the social structure of our society, and how you understand your potentials and limits, positions and privileges. Just as Payal Shah Payal does, you can explicitly link this reflection with your statement of positionality/commitment (Chapter 3). The positionality statement serves only as a starting point of your inquiry journey and over the entire research process; engaging in this type of self-reflection allows you to better articulate the conditions of your research practice. When you juggle different ethical choices in the stream of acting, thinking with theories allows you to see your privileges in relation to your research participants. Thus, you will be more prepared to discern the potential power relationship revolving around research practice both at the structural and the interpersonal levels. As we have discussed previously, recognizing the potential inequality in a research process is vitally important to creating a democratic, egalitarian, and caring relationship between researchers and research participants, especially when researchers work with people from disadvantaged and minoritized social groups.

The second approach focuses on the substantive aspect of your study. If you are interested in developing a broadly defined critical orientation in your empirical work, the social theories introduced here offer a social ontology to conceptualize some of the foundational terms in critical research, such as power, culture, agency, and social structure. Integrating these into the inquiry process serves as a backdrop for you to understand the phenomenon in which you are interested.

SYNTHESIS: POINTS FOR REFLECTION

Conceptual Synthesis

In accordance with our conceptualization of research as practice/a constellation of social actions, Chapter 6 situates research practice in its social and political contexts, namely through the relationship between the agency of an individual social actor and the social structure. Regarding the latter, we discussed its two interconnected components: material conditions and a symbolic meaning system. The intrinsic connection between the symbolic meaning system, culture, and social norms connects this chapter to the discussion on different types of knowledge claims in Chapter 5. Of particular interest to this chapter are the dynamics of power relationships at both the interpersonal and the structural levels.

Methodological Synthesis

The key concepts we introduced in this chapter have important methodological implications. They can facilitate reflections on a researcher's own positionality, connect the micro-level analysis of social norms with predominant cultural beliefs, and deepen our understanding of power relationships. In the following chapters, we will continue to identify the moments when social theories are integrated into the processes of data generation and inference-making.

Researchers interested in critical research could also apply the theories introduced in this chapter to analyze their empirical data. There are rich potentials to develop in-depth analysis on, for instance, the enactment and reproduction of social norms in everyday communication, the multilevel power relationships, and how they shape people's social action. Due to the introductory nature of this textbook, we will refrain from further unpacking this topic, but we have included some readings to guide your further exploration at the end of this chapter.

Personal Synthesis

On the personal level, this chapter asks us to rethink the relationship between a researcher and the world as manifested in research practice. It raises a vitally important question: As social researchers, how shall we study our society and bring about positive changes given that we are shaped and conditioned by various structural and interactive powers? Foregrounding the "doing" aspect of research, this question is profoundly related to topics we discussed previously, such as identity and ethics. As contextualized as it is, there is no "one-size-fits-all" answer to this question, and we encourage you to actively devise your own approaches. Continuing our exploration of social inquiry, we will revisit the question by examining the impacts of research in Chapter 16.

MOVING FORWARD

The concept of validity is our focus in the next chapter. Previous literature tends to conceptualize this term in a technical fashion, highlighting the strategies that researchers can employ to validate their findings. In Chapter 7, "Engaging With Validity Through Research," we bring forth a discussion of validity rooted in our everyday communication with each other.

Further Readings

Brown, W. (2015). *Undoing the demos: Neoliberalism's stealth revolution* (Chapters 1 & 7). New York, NY: Zone Press.

Burawoy, M. (2017). The public university—battleground for real utopias. *Southeast Asian Social Science Review, 2*(1), 139–173.

Carspecken, P. F. (2012). Basic concepts in critical methodological theory: Action, structure and system within a communicative pragmatics framework. In S. Steinberg & G. Cannella (Eds.), *Critical qualitative research reader*. New York, NY: Peter Lang Publishing Group.

Collins, P. H. (1986). Learning from the outsider within: The sociological significance of Black feminist thought. *Social Problems, 33*(6), 14–32.

Ortner, S. B. (1984). Theory in anthropology since the sixties. *Comparative Studies in Society and History, 26*(1), 126–166.

Sewell, W. H., Jr. (1992). A theory of structure: Duality, agency, and transformation. *American Journal of Sociology, 98*(1), 1–29.

Further Readings by Wei Luo

Luo, W., Adams, J., & Brueckner, H. (2018). The ladies vanish? American sociology and the genealogy of its missing women on Wikipedia. *Comparative Sociology, 17*(5), 519–556.

Further Readings by Payal P. Shah

Shah, P. (2015). Spaces to speak: Photovoice and the reimagination of girls' education in India. *Comparative Education Review, 59*(1), 50–74.

Shah, P. P., & Khurshid, A. (2018). Writing against culture: Unveiling education and modernity for Hindu Indian and Muslim Pakistani women through an "ethnography of the particular." *International Journal of Qualitative Studies in Education, 31*(4), 257–271.

7

VALIDITY IN THE CONTEXT OF RESEARCH

As we approach the end of this cluster on foundational research concepts and issues related to identity, ethics, ontology, epistemology, meaning, norms, social structures, and power, we would like to zoom in on the concept of "validity" and how it connects to other concepts featured in this cluster. We have been using this term in previous chapters without formally defining it. This is because validity is also an ordinary concept that we engage with all the time without naming it as such. In this chapter, we define this concept and help you to draw further connections between your everyday experience and formal research contexts. We will explore: What makes us accept a knowledge claim as true, sound, reliable, or trustworthy? What is considered good research? How can we enhance the validity of a study? Again, we start our exploration with an everyday scenario that draws out the concept of validity in the context of everyday experience. From there we will move into a research narrative that further spotlights ideas pertinent to the understanding of validity. Our research scenario, a contribution from guest writer Dr. David Rutkowski, illustrates various ways that validity enters and influences concrete research practices. Finally, we reflect on the chapter and Cluster 1 as a whole to further forge interconnections among key concepts and issues.

MUSING UPON THE EVERYDAY: VALIDITY IN (MIS)UNDERSTANDING

Have you ever been misunderstood by someone? This probably happens often in your daily life—for example, being honked at by a driver behind you when you press the brake too suddenly to avoid a squirrel. Or you receive an email from your professor inquiring about your unexcused absence and questioning your level of engagement in class, without knowing that you had an emergency situation to respond to, which took your whole attention. Or you and an acquaintance carry on a conversation for quite a while before you realize that you were referring to different things!

> **Pause and Reflect.** Is there an experience of misunderstanding similar to those jumping out to you in the moment? What was your understanding about the situation then? How might the other person understand the situation? What could be some assumptions from either side? When and how did you recognize that there was actually a misunderstanding that just occurred? What did you do about the misunderstanding?

Let's stay with the scenario where the professor misunderstood the absence of a student. The professor might assume the absence to be a sign of disrespect and lack of engagement. This assumption could be linked to some general expectations implicitly agreed upon in educational settings, such as: Students should attend classes except in unforeseeable situations, a student should communicate with the professor in advance if they will miss class, and the professor has an evaluative role over the student. On the other hand, from the student's perspective, they might argue that they in fact did recognize and respect these norms, but were absorbed by the emergency situation and lost sight of other things. They might also argue that they have always been an earnest and engaged student who takes learning seriously. If the two parties discuss their respective understandings of the situation, fundamentally they are questioning and clarifying what is *truthful* and/or *valid* about what was really going on. This brings us to the idea of **validity**, a core concept that we engage in throughout this chapter.

As we progress through the chapter, hold on to the misunderstanding example you came up with. You can continue to examine the relationship of validity to your example as we deepen our discussion of the concept.

NARRATIVE AND CONCEPTUAL INTERLUDES: DO WE *REALLY* KNOW THE TRUTH?

We begin exploring the concept of validity in a concrete research context. According to the National Center for Education Statistics (NCES), there were about 9.4% English language learners (ELL) in American public schools during the 2014–2015 school year. ELL refers to students whose native tongue is not English. Imagine you were one of the fifth-grade teachers with a high percentage of students identified as ELLs. All students are required to take statewide standardized assessments in subject areas such as reading, math, and writing. Many of your ELL students are not fluent in English yet, and some arrived in the United States not long ago. You have repeatedly observed that your ELL students tend to score noticeably lower in those standardized assessments compared to other students. You wonder how you should interpret the score differences. The scores alone seem to suggest that your ELL students demonstrate lower academic abilities and learning in the areas tested. But you are not fully convinced: Is this the whole story? Can you take the numbers at face value? Are there other possible explanations that account for the differences? How can you evaluate which explanation holds more truth than others?

In fact, Jamal Abedi and Patricia Gándara (2006) reviewed an established line of research found to support the idea that test scores may not reflect a student's true abilities. Basically, researchers argue that the language used to construct tests can be too cumbersome to enable ELLs to accurately grasp the test questions. When a student answers a multiple-choice math question incorrectly, it could be related to not being able to understand the sentence structure or meaning of the test question rather than a deficit in mathematical reasoning. In this context, the student does not have the opportunity to demonstrate their math reasoning. Many researchers find that the linguistic complexity of assessments may significantly contribute to the gap between ELL and non-ELL learners. Unfortunately, the problem doesn't stop here. How policy-makers and teachers make inferences about these gaps has consequences, which can further fuel a vicious cycle. For example, ELL students are more likely to be classified as low-achieving students, and placed in slower-paced or lower-level instructional settings. This can delay their learning even further and amplify the achievement gap (Abedi & Gándara, 2006).

Meanwhile, research also points to other challenges associated with second language acquisition, such as parent education and poverty, which have been found also to contribute to lower test performance for ELL students. ELL students may also experience pressure to perform well on tests, since the stakes are very high for them and their families. In addition, many ELLs identify as racial/ethnic minorities in the United States. They may encounter and even internalize negative stereotypes that often associate certain racial/ethnic identity groups with lower intellectual abilities (Abedi & Gándara, 2006).

All those issues can intersect and exacerbate the vicious cycle that ends up reproducing a self-fulfilling prophecy confirming the perception that ELLs are "low achieving."

We can ask: Do achievement tests function in ways that we think they are supposed to function? Can we or should we trust the results derived from tests when we make inferences about learning and achievement? Even more concerning: Does use of standardized tests reproduce and deepen existing social and educational gaps for marginalized racial/ethnic groups, in the name of improving students learning? The answers to these questions have significant implications: Teachers, administrators, and policy-makers all use test results to guide their decision-making regarding instructional practices, program development, resource allocation, and educational policies. All of these impact students' educational experiences. This scenario provides a context for us to examine the methodological concept of *validity*.

Validity, Truth, and Objectivity

Defining Validity

So what is validity? How do we define it? How does validity get picked up throughout the research process? According to Sally Wehmeier, Colin McIntosh, and Joanna Turnbull, the *Oxford English Dictionary* defines "validity" as "the state of being logical and true" (Wehmeier, McIntosh, & Turnbull, 2010, p, 1692). It refers to the "soundness" and "truthfulness" of an argument or a statement. In the context of social inquiry, validity is closely tied to the concept of *truth* and knowledge claims, which we discussed in Chapter 5. Researchers probably would agree that truth and validity are what they all strive for in their research practice and in endeavors to make knowledge claims. A knowledge claim is an assertion that can be judged as true or false, right or wrong, good or bad, correct or incorrect (Carspecken, 1996). Therefore, the concept of validity has a close connection to how we conceptualize what *truth* is and how we derive criteria to evaluate knowledge claims, aiming at "telling the truth."

Going back to the ELL example above, how is validity relevant in that context? As we discussed above, if we take numbers at face value, we reach a certain set of interpretations and conclusions. But when we take into consideration various sociocultural, historical, and structural elements—the inevitable contexts where numbers are embedded—we likely will have second thoughts about whether we can attribute score discrepancies solely to differences in student ability. In other words, we may consider what is true and valid differently for the same phenomenon. Numbers don't automatically "have" validity, though this is a common perception (even within research communities) indicated by sayings like "numbers don't lie" or "numbers are hard facts" because "numbers are objective." This perception assumes that numbers have a thing-like existence that is independent from human opinions and values. In this way, numbers are routinely associated with "objectivity," without being questioned. Anything that involves human interpretation, on the other hand, is deemed "subjective." In this way, "objective" and "subjective" form a dichotomy, with the objective side given an implicit value of being true (and good), and the subjective side, biased (and bad). Right here the idea of what constitutes "truth" is tacitly taken up. We will return to the objective–subjective binary later in the chapter.

Truth, Validity, and Epistemological Assumptions

Validity in Relation to a Correspondence Theory of Truth. When we make a knowledge claim, we inevitably evoke an underlying notion of truth, often implicitly, based on which we justify the validity of that claim. The view that numbers better convey truth than people's opinions implies a **theory of truth** that is rooted in a subject–object orientation to knowing (truth), as we discussed in Chapter 5. This orientation often takes the form of an assertion about an existing *state of affairs* (e.g., student's achievement), claimed by taking an *external* and *disinterested* position to observe and measure that state of affairs (e.g., using standardized tests to measure achievement). With this assumption of truth, a knowledge claim can only be valid if it is testable and verifiable through observation, experimentation, and measurement. The claim can be judged by the accuracy and completeness of how well the assertion *represents* the state of affairs under study (e.g., how well test scores represent student achievement). Thus, there is a one-on-one correspondence between a truth claim (e.g., interpretation of test scores) and a state of affairs (e.g., student achievement). Validity theorists William Shadish, Thomas Cook, and Donald Campbell (2002) called this approach the **correspondence theory of truth**, which we discuss further in Chapter 8. The main idea is that a knowledge claim is some kind of "copy" of the original state of affairs that the researcher aims to "capture." One concept of validity can be derived from this conceptualization of truth. In this context, validity is regarded as an indicator that gauges the level of *correspondence* between a state of affairs and its representation as captured in the knowledge claim. This evokes the notion of "error." In this understanding, truth is deemed an *ideal* that is error-free. Knowledge claims in the forms of statements, descriptions, assertions, or inferences thus can be evaluated by their approximation to this ideal. The more valid a claim is, the less "confounding" error is involved and the closer it is to truth. This is why we often talk about controlling *confounding variables*. For example, in the ELL example, to enhance the validity of the study researchers would aim to include roughly equal numbers of boys and girls in both the ELL and non-ELL groups (assuming gender is conceptualized as a binary variable). In this way, researchers can be more confident in ruling out the possibility that gender differences, rather than ability, contribute to score differences. Similarly, researchers who conduct experiments often discuss eliminating *threats to validity*, or reducing statistical error—these ideas are based on an understanding of truth and error modeled on representation and correspondence, as described above. As a result, validity becomes a "yes" or "no" question: Does a study or a measurement "have" validity? This view is often associated with epistemological stances such as empiricism and (post)-positivism discussed in Chapter 5. This implies an underlying assumption about what truth is. This way of understanding validity historically has been the norm in the natural sciences and remains influential in many social science disciplines such as economics, psychology, and education.

> **Pause and Reflect.** Where do numbers come from? How are they generated? How is a measurement developed? Who makes decisions on what statistical procedures to use? How are numbers from research being used—used for whom and by whom?

These questions foreground a new, previously taken-for-granted horizon, a horizon of a set of *backgrounded* conditions that influence the process of number generation and statistical analysis. These conditions cannot be explained by numbers and statistics themselves. They include the use of language, researchers' theories that guide their conceptualization of research, decisions over which measurements to use and what statistical methods to apply, and the nature of their interactions with the participants (even indirectly through online surveys; more detailed discussion in Cluster 2 chapters). These areas are primarily communicative and relational in nature, and tap into the *intersubjective* foundation of research discussed in Chapters 2 and 3. This foregrounds a **subject–subject relation** rather than a **subject–object relation**.

Appearance Versus Reality. Reflecting on backgrounded conditions also raises questions about the premises on which representation and correspondence based on truth stand, which assume an implicit certainty about our visual perception ("seeing is believing"). This premise does not differentiate between two different levels of representation: the image of the object (e.g., the perception of an apple tree) and the object itself (e.g., the tree itself)—that is, a difference between *appearance* and *reality* (Benton & Craib, 2001). When we see an apple tree we take the image of an apple tree automatically as the tree itself. We rarely (and most of time there is no need to) question the difference between the image that forms on our retina and the actual tree itself, or ponder what makes it possible for us to perceive the tree. But as we move from the physical world to the social world, this problem becomes more profound because, as discussed in Chapter 5, social phenomena have a different ontological status than objects and entities in the physical world, for example, how we know a tree is different from how we know someone is learning. What we generate as numbers from a measurement that aims to measure achievement (a derived form of "appearance") is always different from the phenomenon of achievement itself ("reality"). Thus, numbers do not have truth embedded *within*: We still need to examine the contexts and processes of the number generation process when we gauge the validity of numeric results. This point is further illustrated in the research scenario presented later in the chapter.

The general logic of a correspondence theory of truth and the related conception of validity is illustrated in Figure 7.1. Those ideas will be further unpacked in Chapter 9 in the context of understanding "data" in research.

Validity and Other Conceptions of Truth. The discussion above illustrates that validity is tied to how we conceptualize truth, which comes with different sets of epistemological assumptions. Moving away from a correspondence theory of truth, therefore, we can arrive at different understandings of validity. For instance, if we hold a criticalist epistemological stance, the ultimate ground for truth rests on efforts toward consensus

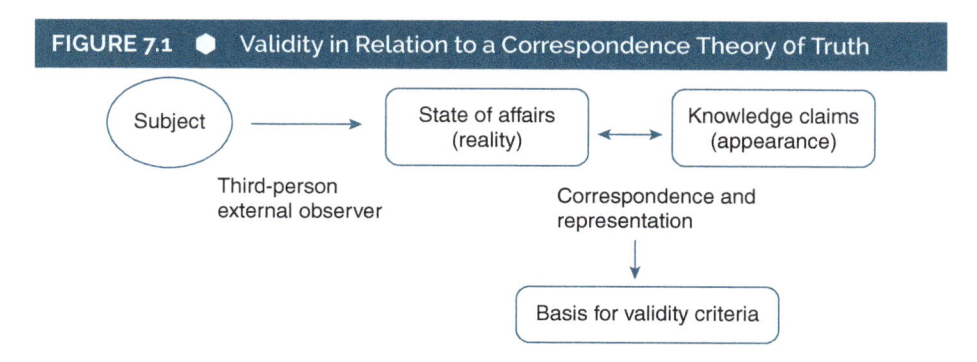

FIGURE 7.1 ● Validity in Relation to a Correspondence Theory of Truth

- Subject → State of affairs (reality) ↔ Knowledge claims (appearance)
- Third-person external observer
- Correspondence and representation → Basis for validity criteria

formation through dialogue. A metaphor associated with this way of understanding truth is a scene where multiple people come to the discussion table to share perspectives on some issue. People use sound reasoning and persuasion to gain understanding and consensus. This does not necessarily mean agreement, but an orientation toward mutual understanding. This shows some major differences between an empiricist and critical understanding of truth: truth as a precise copy of reality (an empiricist stance) versus truth as a dialogue that is always unfolding (a critical stance). This difference contrasts a subject–object relation versus a subject–subject relation as the basis for conceptualizing knowing.

Validity derived from the latter centers on how well a knowledge claim *wins* consensus from multiple perspectives, especially from people who are directly impacted by the research phenomenon. Following Habermas (1987), who thinks of this as communicative rationality, we can call this theory of truth a **dialogic theory of truth**. For example, when considering validity in relation to ELLs' achievement levels, a researcher with a critical orientation might ask ELL students how they understand test questions, about their thinking process, and what reasons they themselves give for not performing well on tests. The researchers may also want to gather input from teachers, parents, and the school district to contextualize their understanding about student achievement. This process is oriented to dialogue that is aimed toward consensus. Validity also means facilitating conditions for open and undistorted dialogic processes that support consensus formation. For instance, researchers might invest in developing relationships with participants, constantly reflect on their positionality and potential biases, provide space for deep listening to others' perspectives, and so on. Again, dialogue is the essence to validating knowledge claims from a critical epistemological stance. Figure 7.2 illustrates this conceptual shift in comparison to Figure 7.1.

In the next section we will discuss how the term *validity* is commonly discussed (differently) in various research communities and how it is often picked up in research practice. It is important to point out that the research community as a whole is far from reaching consensus about how we should conceptualize and apply the concept of validity. Many research terms have been used in reference to validity, as we discuss below.

FIGURE 7.2 ● Validity in Relation to a Dialogic Conception of Truth

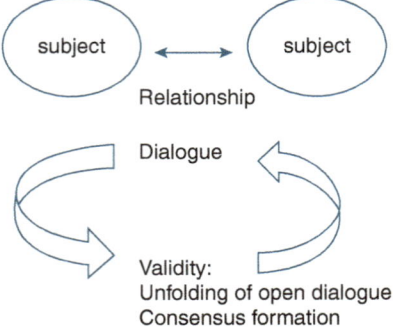

subject ↔ subject
Relationship

Dialogue

Validity:
Unfolding of open dialogue
Consensus formation

We know this can be confusing for readers who are relatively new to research. With this in mind, however, when we look at the current landscape of validity discussions, there are generally two major "camps" that roughly coincide with the boundary between quantitative research and qualitative research. We will briefly discuss the general trends in each camp before offering an alternative approach that may help transcend this divide.

Validity in the Context of Quantitative Research

Historically, the concept of validity has mostly been discussed in the context of experimentation and measurement in the context of quantitative research given its dominant status in social inquiry. In this context, a variety of validity concepts and procedures have been introduced to reduce or limit the scope of errors that occur in experimentation, measurement, and statistical inferences. These include the concepts of *internal validity, external validity, generalizability, construct validity, content validity, criteria-based validity, statistical conclusion validity,* and *ecological validity* as developed by scholars John Creswell and Timothy Guetterman (2019), Jack Frankael and Norman Wallen (2008), along with Shadish, Cook, and Campbell (2002). We won't discuss all of those terms in detail but want to draw out some conceptual themes to help readers understand how the terms are interrelated.

We can categorize these validity terms as fitting into three conceptual categories, as visually presented in Figure 7.3:

- In the context of *measurement* (relevant validity terms: construct validity, reliability, or inter-rater reliability), concepts examine whether items included in a measurement or instrument accurately and consistently measure a phenomenon being studied (e.g., whether a 50-item math test actually measures math ability, or whether those 50 items function consistently to measure math ability—that is, how consistent the test scores will be if we give the test today and then again tomorrow with the same participants);

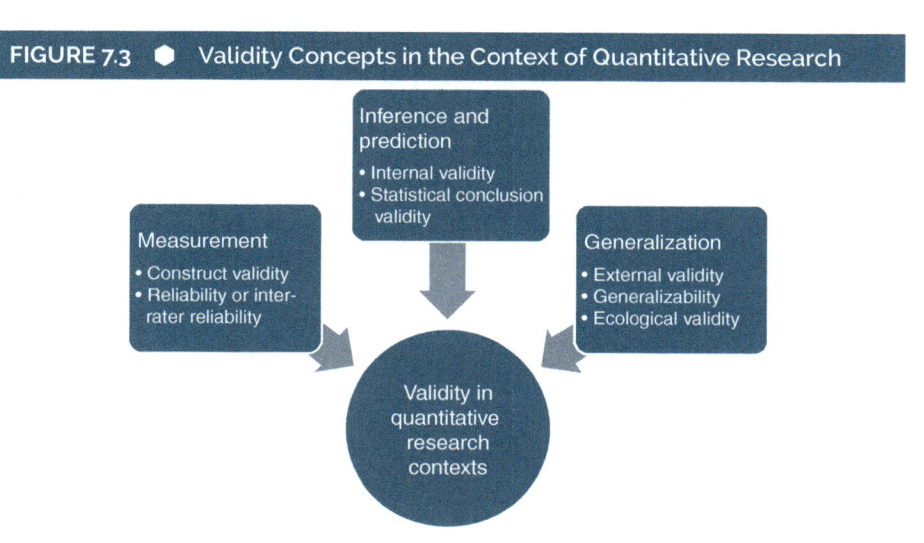

FIGURE 7.3 ● Validity Concepts in the Context of Quantitative Research

Inference and prediction
- Internal validity
- Statistical conclusion validity

Measurement
- Construct validity
- Reliability or inter-rater reliability

Generalization
- External validity
- Generalizability
- Ecological validity

→ Validity in quantitative research contexts

- In the context of *inference, prediction, and interpretation* (relevant validity terms: internal validity, statistical conclusion validity, etc.), validity concepts mainly gauge how well a statistical model or procedure can produce claims that we can confidently take as representing the phenomenon that we intend to study (e.g., we randomly assign participants to the treatment group and the control group so that if we find differences between the two groups we can more confidently conclude that the difference is due to the impact of the intervention instead of other confounding factors that we didn't take into consideration); and

- In the context of *generalization* (relevant validity terms: external validity, generalizability, and ecological validity), validity concepts determine how well findings from a limited group of participants can be extended to a larger population and across different settings (e.g., whether an ELL math program that is found effective in one school district and with one group of ELL students can be extended to other school districts and with other ELL students).

However, in actual research practice and publications, these three aspects of validity are not always addressed systematically. Validity-related parameters that you may encounter include *reliability* of a measurement, *internal validity*, and *generalizability* (more discussion on these in Chapters 11, 12, and 14). However, these concepts are often discussed disjointedly without a more cohesive, overarching theory focused on the meaning of validity in the context of measurement and experimentation.

Validity in the Context of Qualitative Research

The understanding of validity becomes even more complex and divergent in the context of qualitative research. In fact, according to Tony Onwuegbuzie and Nancy Leech (2005), there are more than 50 terms that have been used by qualitative researchers in reference to "validity." Many of those terms, to a large extent, are modified from the prototypes used in quantitative research. For instance, "dependability" is derived from the term "reliability," used in the context of measurement or instrument use; "credibility" and "trustworthiness" as articulated by Yvonna Lincoln and Egon Guba (1986) are formulated as analogs to "internal validity." Similarly, "transferability" may be considered as adapted from "external validity" or "generalizability." Table 7.1 highlights these kinds of correspondences.

This trend mirrors how qualitative research comes to the scene of social inquiry as an alternative or a challenger to the more established quantitative tradition. Qualitative research communities create those new validity terms to demarcate qualitative from quantitative research, but by modeling them after validity terms used in quantitative research context those new terms don't radically challenge the established understanding of validity from the bottom up. As a result, it is common in journal articles that authors first articulate, for instance, a feminist epistemological stance, but then apply a set of "conventional" validity procedures such as reliability and generalizability to describe the rigor and validity of the study. Using these terms provokes epistemological assumptions related to the correspondence of truth as discussed above. This is not consistent with a feminist epistemological position on objectivity and truth.

Meanwhile, various qualitative scholars have taken different points of departure to conceptualize validity, away from the framework established in quantitative research. Those new conceptualizations include the articulation of the "goodness" of research, Patti Lather's (1986) transformative potential of research in the name of "catalytic validity," Dennis's (2011) concern that validity be relevant to the democratic values of the society,

TABLE 7.1 ● Correspondence of Validity Concepts Between Quantitative and Qualitative Research

Validity in the Context of Quantitative Research	Validity in the Context of Qualitative Research
Reliability	Inter-rater reliability; dependability
Internal validity	Trustworthiness or creditability
External validity or generalizability	Transferability
Other Validity Terms	
Construct validity	Catalytic validity
Statistical conclusion validity	Communicative validity
Divergent or convergent validity	Psychopolitical validity

or Meagan Call-Cummings' (2017) notion of "communicative validity" to gauge how well the research process honors relationships with participants and communities. Similarly, Isaac Prilleltensky's *psychopolitical validity* has been used to foreground the potential of research to resist and transform oppression as an important criterion for evaluating validity (2003, 2008).

Overall, the issue of validity in qualitative research remains contested. Researchers would also benefit from a more unifying and meta-level understanding of validity across both quantitative and qualitative contexts (Dennis, 2013). With this intention, we attempt to ground the discussion of validity in the communicative context, in which research claims and arguments are made by people in interactions. That is, we shift from a subject–object to a subject–subject conception of validity, as discussed above. This involves a process of **understanding meaning** as it is relevant to all research, qualitative or quantitative. By attending to the connection between validity and meaning, the potential to dissolve the seemingly fixed boundary between quantitative and qualitative research becomes possible. We introduced the concept of "meaning" in Chapter 5, and develop it further below.

A Meta-Discussion: Validity in the Context of Understanding Meaning

Meaning and Validity: Intersubjectivity

To comprehend any type of knowledge claim, whether it is an objective claim (e.g., There is a pen on the table), a subjective claim (e.g., He is sad), or a normative claim (e.g., We should provide equitable educational opportunities to all students), we inevitably engage in a meaning-making process. Recall as we discussed in Chapter 5 that the process of understanding meaning implicitly involves *cultural typification* and *position-taking* (the latter is also discussed in Chapter 3): That is, you need to understand how a typical person in a given culture would act and what is considered an appropriate manner to do so. This requires us to grasp at least a *tacit communicative structure* that involves other people in that culture. We call it "tacit" because it is communicative in a way that does not necessarily involve the immediate presence of another person at the scene when you act.

This communicative nature of understanding meaning itself suggests that there is always a communicative context when we consider validity. To justify the validity of a knowledge claim involves other people, implicitly or explicitly. Most of the time we are not called to explain why we act in certain ways as long as communication goes smoothly. But when a misunderstanding occurs, we have to explicitly communicate our reasons and intentions to gain understanding or agreement from the other person. This process also invokes references to a more general group of people in the shared cultural context, who you expect would agree with your reasons for acting in some specific way. This was illustrated in the opening section of the chapter in terms of how the assumptions of both the professor and student are connected to related social norms; these norms always involve individuals beyond the two who are interacting. Therefore, validity has an *intersubjective* quality and an inherent *dialogical structure* aimed toward gaining agreement or consent from others. Validity is dynamic in the sense that it depends on a specific context, instead of being a fixed and a context-free property of a knowledge claim.

To understand the connection between validity, meaning, and intersubjectivity is significant because validity is related to whether we comprehend the meaning of a social action the way that *actors themselves* would. That is, validity is based on whether the knowledge claims we make about a social phenomenon are consistent with what actors involved in such a phenomenon would claim themselves. This requires that we as researchers be able to take the positions of the participants and their cultural reference groups (as we say, "being in their shoes"), via the intersubjective "infrastructure" of communication. Thus, enhancing validity, in terms of interpreting and making inferences about a social phenomenon, requires us to understand the meaning of social actions, which are always embedded in certain historical, social, cultural, and political conditions (as discussed in Chapter 6). This point also relates to the example of how we interpret an ELL student's performance on an achievement test.

Meaning and Validity: Meaning Field, Meaning Horizon

What is the process of understanding meaning exactly, you may ask? Going back to the opening puzzle about misunderstanding, you might have noticed that our actions usually come with intentions and reasons that we could use to justify a particular action if it is called into question. Understanding meaning is related to being able to *anticipate* those *possible* intentions and reasons. But most of the time we don't need to explicate them. In fact, intentions and reasons may not even be in the forefront of our awareness. We usually assume that the person/people with whom we are interacting share sufficient understanding of the possible intentions and reasons of our actions and would likely act similarly if in the same situation. In other words, whenever we act appropriately in a given context, we already grasp that there are a range of possible and reasonable ways to act. What constitutes the range of possible meanings of an action thus depends on the specific context.

There is not a fixed relationship between an action and a list of possible meanings of that action. And yet the range of possibilities is not unlimited and a possible meaning needs to be deemed reasonable for a given situation (Carspecken, 1996; Dennis, 2013). For example, back to the opening scenario about the misunderstanding between the student and the professor, there are a range of meanings that the student could pick up from the professor's email, such as: (1) "It is very disrespectful for students to miss class without notifying the professor," (2) "I'm disappointed about your action and I know you can do better," or (3) "I missed seeing you in class and I'm worried about you." The list can go on. But it would be a stretch to interpret the professor's email as, "You are doing very well in class," or "I don't care about you coming to class or not." This bounded range of possible meaning of a social action is called a "**meaning field**" (Carspecken, 1996).

Understanding what constitutes a meaning field for a given action is like tapping into a shared knowledge "stock" that we share with others in the same culture (Carspecken, 1996). This "stock" always forms the backdrop of our social interaction and makes it possible for us to understand meaning and act accordingly in daily life. The knowledge stock consists of culturally bounded language use, norms, practices, history, and narratives that we have learned since we were infants. Different aspects of the meaning field are more or less foregrounded and backgrounded for a given communicative context. For instance, going back to the example above, if the student and the professor don't know each other on a personal level, it's more likely that the student may perceive the professor's email as a reprimand. In contrast, if they have an established relationship, the student might perceive the email as constructive feedback, assuming the professor knows the behavior is not the norm for the student. Or if the student knows that the professor is deeply caring toward students, the student might interpret the email as an act of care. Again, meaning is always context dependent.

A set of possible meanings and the meaning field form a *part–whole relation*. It is through the contrasts between the part and the whole that we are able to grasp possible meaning (Carspecken, 1996). There can be multiple horizons of possible meaning for a given action, ranging from the most *immediate horizon* (e.g., in the above example, "you missed class without notification," foregrounding an objective aspect of the action), to the *intermediate foregrounded horizon* (e.g., "I'm concerned," a subjective aspect of the action), and more *backgrounded horizon* (e.g., it is inappropriate to miss class without notification, a normative aspect of the action). In this way the meaning field is grasped through a horizon-like structure when we understand the meaning of a social act, which Carspecken (1996) calls "**meaning horizon**." Figure 7.4 provides a visual representation that illustrates the connection between meaning field and meaning horizon.

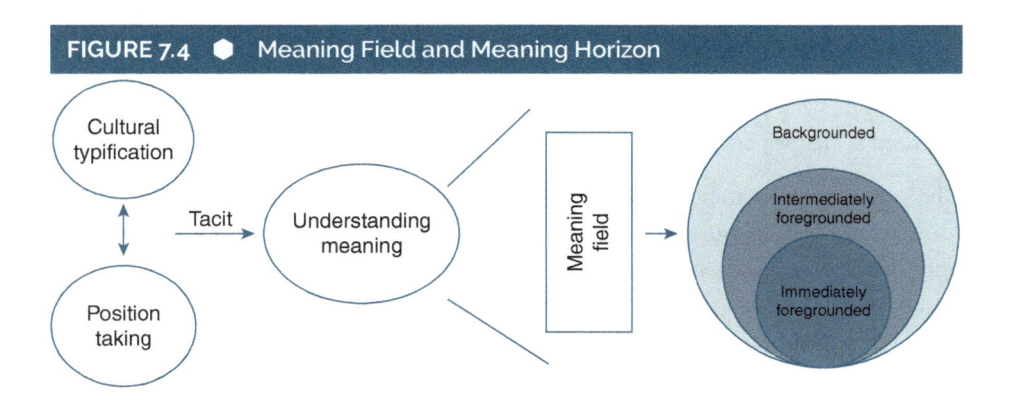

FIGURE 7.4 ● Meaning Field and Meaning Horizon

You may wonder: What do meaning field and meaning horizon have to do with validity? If we agree that social inquiry is about understanding social phenomena that consist of social actions and interactions, then to evaluate knowledge claims generated through social inquiry is to gauge whether the researchers appropriately grasp the meaning of those social actions and interactions. Given the subtle and complex nature and structure of meaning and what it involves to understand meaning, validity has some parallel features similar to the structure of understanding meaning. These include an "as if" quality and a fundamental uncertainty, which we will discuss in more detail below.

Meaning and Validity: An "as if" Quality

As discussed above, we learn how to tap into a knowledge stock so intuitively that we act most of the time not consciously aware we are drawing from this backdrop. We act toward one another "as if" each party has the same access to a shared knowledge stock. This "as if" quality allows us to communicate seamlessly without having to stop to explain every time why we act in a certain way. As discussed earlier, it is only when we realize a misunderstanding might have occurred or our actions are called into question that we realize we might not share the same knowledge stock after all.

The "as if" quality further manifests in the metaphorical quality of language in the sense that a word is always at best a metaphor in reference to what it signifies (Dennis, 2013). For instance, if you tell someone who has no idea what Facebook is, "You can Facebook me." The person might look puzzled and ask, "What do you mean by 'face book'?" You immediately realized that your assumption that "Facebook" is a shared language between you two didn't hold in this interaction. You reply, "Well, 'Facebook' is a popular social media platform that people use to communicate and share information." The other person continues, "Social media? What do you mean by that?" You keep going, "It's an online platform that anyone with a username can access so it becomes a virtual social network." It's possible this person may not even know what the internet is, and this conversation could go on until you reach a point where it becomes challenging to find another word to explain what is not being understood. By then you might have to pull out your computer and demonstrate what you can *do* with "Facebook" to help the other person "get" what you mean. But most of time this kind of clarifying conversation does not need to happen at all.

The important point to highlight through this example is that even when we try to clarify using words, we can't get out of the limitation of language. Language always functions only as a *representation* of something—at best as a metaphor. There is always a separation between the word that represents something and what is being represented. This is related to our earlier discussion about the difference between "appearance" and "reality," although this distinction here is not just limited to object-like things. To mitigate this inherent gap of representation, we may have to resort to acting out what we mean to make others understand. In fact, this is how we first learn language—thinking about how a baby first learns to point at things before they have a word to express what they intend to communicate. Even as linguistically competent individuals, when we are situated in a culture/linguistic community that we are not familiar with, it is not uncommon for us to have to use our hands and body to convey what we mean, right?

So what does this "as if" quality mean for validity? Similar to everyday communication, when you conduct research to understand a social phenomenon, the validity of our understanding and the knowledge claims we make rests on the degree to which we understand meaning. As such, a knowledge claim can be deemed *"as if" valid* as long as it is not being questioned. But there is always the potential that a claim can be called into question. Thus, validity is not a *yes/no* type of property but is pending, and can always be unpacked through further communication and unpacking. Therefore, any knowledge claims we make in research have to remain open to being questioned and challenged, and the validity of the claims can't be fixed even at the conclusion of a study.

Meaning and Validity: Uncertainty

This "as if" quality, taken together with the nature of meaning field (as a bounded range of possibilities), also suggests there is always uncertainty associated with understanding meaning. When we reach mutual understanding with someone (at least when we assume there is), it is not that we *converge* on a single meaning that is "out there." This is a common (mis)conception about validity in the use of the term *triangulation*—the idea that if we can triangulate multiple methods or have multiple people interpret the data, we surely can achieve validity since multiple perspectives should converge on the same truth. Again, underneath this is an epistemological assumption that truth is out there and is open to multiple access (a notion that collapses truth to the objective domain alone), instead of emerging from interactions and communication. The latter assumption suggests that we understand each other if no further query is necessary to reduce the ambiguity of possible meanings, and as a result we experience being "on the same page." We tend to have relatively higher certainty and can narrow down possible meanings in a culture or situation with which we are familiar. This sense of certainty allows us to act and communicate more smoothly and effortlessly in everyday life, in contrast with situations such as being in a foreign culture where we must make constant efforts to ensure we understand others.

Due to this nature of meaning, validity for knowledge claims that derive from our understanding about a social phenomenon has *uncertainty* built in as well. We can never make a knowledge claim with full certainty about it being valid; nor can we make totalizing claims that remain true in all time and space. Even what are considered natural laws discovered in natural sciences have been challenged and revised over time—for instance, Einstein's theories challenged the validity of Newton's laws, and quantum mechanisms in physics now continue to push the boundaries of Einstein's ideas. Instead, we need to acknowledge the *partialness* and *unfinishedness* of knowledge that we produce, and stay open to the potential for further dialogues with others to reach new understanding. We try to do this in everyday life all the time, and the world of research is no exception. Both the "as if" and uncertainty qualities suggest that *the validity of a knowledge claim may evolve as we open up to further investigation, debates, dialogues, and reflection to question the assumptions and premises of the claim.*

This *openness to fallibility* and to engagement with others also has an *ethical* dimension, as we discussed in Chapter 4. It implies that the meaning-making process can be corrupted by *unequal power relations* where the door to open communication and dialogues is blocked. For example, when only certain kinds of knowing and knowledge claims are deemed valid and legitimate, this creates a dominance or hierarchy in knowledge production and application that can do harm to certain groups of people and thus the society as an interconnected whole. Power distortion may close up researchers' awareness, or their capacity of self-reflection and engagement in a dynamic process of apprehending and approaching validity. When this happens, it erodes validity and ends up perpetuating *epistemological violence*, which we will discuss further in Chapter 16. As we connect validity to knowledge and *power*, an inherent connection between validity and ethics also becomes foregrounded. Again, we plant some seeds here for a more in-depth discussion in Chapter 16 on the epistemic and ethical dimensions of knowledge and research. Validity is at the center of this discussion. Figure 7.5 sums up our discussion above to illustrate the close relationship between understanding meaning and the nature of validity.

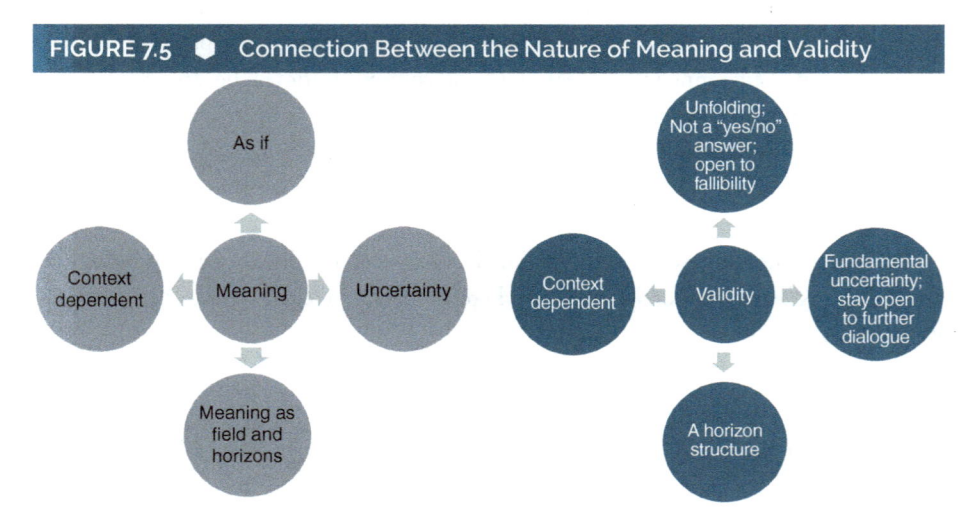

FIGURE 7.5 ● Connection Between the Nature of Meaning and Validity

A Unifying Approach to Validity: Validity Criteria for Different Types of Knowledge Claims

In the previous sections, we sketched out how the concept of validity is commonly conceptualized in the context of quantitative and qualitative research. We also discussed the current state of confusion and how the siloed approach to validity can be problematic. We advocate for a more unifying way of understanding validity that aims to transcend the entrenched divide between quantitative and qualitative research. This requires a meta-level methodological discussion that does not assume a fixed boundary between the two camps. For instance, understanding meaning can be the common ground to forge an alternative approach to understanding validity that is not bound to the quantitative and qualitative divide, as discussed above. Meanwhile, another approach to generating a unifying understanding of validity is to conceptualize **validity criteria** in relation to different types of knowledge claims in general (see below). This is in contrast with the common approach of tying validity to specific research orientations (quantitative or qualitative) or research designs (e.g., experiential design vs. narrative inquiry). Since all research, quantitative or qualitative research, makes three types of knowledge claims—objective, subjective, and normative claims—to varying degrees, focusing on validity in relation to types of knowledge claims helps to transcend seemingly fixed boundaries between research orientations and research designs.

Validity Criteria for Objective Knowledge Claim

Recall that in Chapter 5 we introduced a way of categorizing knowledge claims that originated from the perspective of a critical epistemology and ontology. This perspective differentiates three different types of knowledge claims, namely, the *objective*, *subjective*, and *normative* claims. Given their distinct epistemological and ontological nature, we also need different criteria to evaluate the validity of each type of claim. Going back to our Lyme disease example discussed in Chapter 5, objective claims (claims made in reference to the objective or physical domain of existence) such as "this patient is infected by Lyme disease" can be verified by a positive test result that shows that the Lyme-causing bacteria is present in a patient's body. Theoretically, multiple lab technicians should be able to perform the testing procedures and (supposedly) come to the same conclusion with some margin of error. In other words, the claim is open to *multiple access* by different observers. If a patient goes through a few tests and they all come back positive, doctors should have confidence that this patient has a Lyme infection. The validity criteria for objective claims like this rests on agreement reached by multiple observations. This principle of multiple access and reaching consensus is core to the scientific method that dominates natural sciences and is widely applied in social sciences as well. It is why we often talk about *repeated measures* and *replicated studies* to warrant the validity of a claim in this domain.

Similarly, when a patient is diagnosed with Lyme disease by a doctor, they will be prescribed remedies to eliminate Lyme-related symptoms and restore the patient's bodily functions. Here the claim that "this patient has Lyme disease" is associated with an existing theory about the cause and prognosis of this disease, based on which treatment guidelines are created (e.g., a course of antibiotic treatment). If the symptoms are relieved after routine treatment, the patient is believed to have recovered from Lyme disease. This outcome affirms a presumed causal chain between the bacterial infection and the symptoms, predicted by the diagnosis. This shows another hallmark of the validity of an objective claim: The *prediction* based on a knowledge claim (often in the form of a hypothesis) is upheld. Therefore, for objective claims, *multiple access* to observations, *agreement on multiple observations*, and *accuracy of prediction* are the main criteria by which we can judge the validity of such claims. The problem is that this set of principles is too often used for assessing other types of knowledge claims that are epistemologically and ontologically different from an objective claim, and thus should follow different validity principles.

Validity Criteria for Subjective Knowledge Claims

In contrast with objective claims, subjective claims made by patients such as "I feel extremely fatigued," "I am experiencing debilitating pain," or "I feel foggy" are not open to multiple access. Instead, the person making the claim has *privileged access* to knowing, in the domain of feelings, thoughts, emotions, experiences, intentions, sensations, etc. Other people can make observations and inferences about possible subjective states that this person *might* be experiencing, but ultimately they have to rely on the individual to tell the truth about what they are experiencing. This requires this person to be sincere, honest, and not in a self-deceptive state subconsciously or unconsciously (e.g., experiencing repressed pain or emotion). Since for subjective claims we rely on *privileged access*, we use the *sincerity* and *authenticity* of the actor as principles to evaluate the validity of this type of claim. Observation alone doesn't provide the basis for validity as it does for objective knowledge claims. For instance, to verify one's claim that "I am sad," other people may observe certain verbal or nonverbal behaviors that can be interpreted as sadness in a given culture. The person themself has the ultimate say about whether they are sad or not.

Objectivity–Subjectivity Dualism

The distinction made above between objective and subjective claims is important since "objectivity" and "subjectivity" are often pitted against each other as dichotomous. This is prevalent in both our everyday language and the context of research. Being "objective" as emphasized by the empiricist epistemological tradition (or a scientific worldview) is usually deemed the best way to know, regardless of categories of knowledge claims that are foregrounded in a given study. In this context, the meanings of "objective" and "objectivity" are often equated to "impartial," "rational," and "unbiased," with a value undertone of being "good" and "fair." In contrast, "subjective" or "subjectivity" are typically associated with the terms "partial," "biased," and "emotional," and thus perceived to be "unreliable" and "bad." This polarized conception alongside the attached value judgment is quite prevalent even among researchers themselves. This probably has something to do with the fact that the scientific worldview has been elevated to a dominant or privileged mode of knowing in modern times.

But this dynamic fails to give a full and accurate account of different types of knowledge claims that require different corresponding validity criteria, as discussed above. Here we would like to encourage readers to think carefully and critically about using the terms "objective" and "subjective." This can avoid reinforcing the misunderstanding that puts those two aspects of knowledge into a "good" and "bad" binary. Instead, we can treat objective and subjective knowledge claims as distinct knowledge domains that require different bases to verify their respective validity.

Validity Criteria for Normative Knowledge Claims

There is yet a third type of knowledge claim: normative claims—claims like, "It is wrong to deny medical treatment for people who are in need," or "The medical community should conduct more research to better understand the nature of Lyme disease." Those claims cannot be challenged or defended through multiple access of observations or the privileged access of experience. Instead, we understand normative claims through our ability to recognize the cultural norms and values implied within them. This requires us to understand things from the perspective of people in a given culture and context, which involves grasping assumptions about what is right, wrong, good, bad, largely accepted, and circulated in a given culture. This might include: how American society conceptualizes and approaches health care (e.g., is it a basic form of human right or a privilege?), what is deemed good and ethical medical practice, or whether and how we should use tax money to address issues related to public health.

Thus, the validity for normative knowledge claims is closely related to one's ability to position-take as closely as possible to a cultural insider, and to understand phenomena from this position (Carspecken, 1996). It also requires the ability to *recognize* cultural assumptions about rightness and goodness. Position-taking and recognition are both tacit and know-how types of knowledge, as discussed in Chapter 5, which makes it harder to translate them into explicit validity criteria. To generate valid claims about cultural norms requires the researcher to understand a culture as an insider–outsider and to know how to act properly following relevant norms. This has important implications for research. For instance, the researcher cannot rely solely on third-person observations or the researcher's own subjective experience about a research phenomenon to gain understanding about a culture or cultural norms. The researcher has to move toward becoming an insider, which takes time, effort, and relationship-building.

Validity in Research: A Recap

Given the different kinds of knowledge claims, the validity of each type of claim also requires different mechanisms to be upheld and evaluated. In social research we inevitably make claims in all three categories in any study. For instance, back to the study on academic achievement of ELL students, knowledge claims are made in relation to the cognitive ability of students based on their test scores. Cognitive ability itself is not primarily located in the objective domain but mostly in the subjective domain, to which students have privileged access. Meanwhile, we can come up with objective indicators (how students answer a series of test questions) to make inferences about cognitive ability. Regarding validity for this type of claim, we can include a test and retest procedure to see if test scores come back consistently (a frequently used validity strategy in the context of measurement), which is based on the principle of repeated measures through multiple access. This is associated with validity criteria for objective knowledge claims discussed above, and this procedure is typically termed **reliability**, or more precisely, *test-retest reliability*. But since the phenomenon of cognitive ability by nature follows the principle of privileged access, it is not fully open to multiple access by observers. Test score is only a possible objectified indicator to gauge cognitive ability.

We can become more certain about our interpretation of the scores by asking the students themselves whether and how they understood the test questions. This provides important information regarding whether the scores are consistent with what we assume they represent. This is a procedure called a *cognitive interview,* which can be included in any study that uses surveys or questionnaires. In addition, researchers for the ELL study made claims about various psychological, social, and cultural factors that might contribute to the achievement gap manifested in test scores. Some of those claims tap into the subjective domain (e.g., ELL students feel enormous pressure to perform) and the normative domain of knowledge (e.g., intellectual ability carries a negative stereotype for some racial minority groups). Accordingly, we need to use validity measures that are consistent with assessing subjective claims (e.g., by talking to the students to verify whether they do experience pressure, and if so, their experience with such pressure) or normative claims (e.g., through talking to members of a relevant racial minority in the community where the students live, and to check whether they consider intellectual ability a negative stereotype within their culture and community). This is a procedure usually called *member checking*. Basically, member checking is a validity procedure to check with actors themselves the possible meaning of their actions and experiences, which will then be put in dialogue with the researcher's own interpretations and understanding. In sum, we need multiple validity criteria and techniques to examine different types of knowledge claims we make in a study.

RESEARCH SCENARIO: VALIDITY AND ASSESSMENT: DAVID RUTKOWSKI

Thus far we have wrestled with various aspects of validity, a rather complex concept that may not be easy to grasp. In this section, we feature Dr. David Rutkowski, whose research focuses on the area of educational policy and technical topics within international large-scale assessment and program evaluation. Below, he shares how he encounters and approaches validity issues in his research across the globe.

When I teach and work with clients I often quip that for years I attempted to read at least one article a week about validity only to find that I am still confused. For a term that is used in academic, policy, evaluation, and everyday lexicons it is strange that we should find it such a heady and often misunderstood idea. In my field of international assessment and evaluation the term is readily used but I have come to discover that we rarely share exact definitions. When speaking with other academics, it is a bit easier to convey what I mean as I can cite specific scholarship that has informed my own understanding. However, such an approach is less helpful when working with policy-makers and other educational stakeholders such as parents and teachers. The truth is, my nerdy side could think of nothing more engaging than to have long conversations with a minister of education concerning the kinds of valid claims they can make from international assessment results. But I realize that is nothing more than a pipe dream. Yet, people are interested in validity and it has been my experience that nearly every stakeholder—from concerned parents to ministers of education—will want a "yes" or "no" answer when they ask me if the assessment results are valid. For obvious reasons they are often not impressed when I tell that I am not in the business of validating a test so I cannot give them a definitive answer (I will return to this point later).

I believe one reason that validity is crucial to most conversations around assessment is that results are often necessary criteria for judging the quality of modern educational systems. Schwandt (2001) writes that validity is an "epistemic criterion: To say that the findings of social scientific investigations are (or must be) valid is to argue that the findings are in fact (or must be) true and certain" (p. 319). Given that most modern societies invest a great deal into their educational systems it is logical that those societies want true and certain findings to judge the quality of that investment. Basically, if we have valid assessment results of student achievements we have a true measure and can thus hold people accountable.

At the national and international level there has been a growing use of assessment for accountability purposes. As one can imagine, accomplishing this task, most/many argue that we need valid assessments. But, why do people think an assessment, itself, can be universally valid? Moreover, how do educational stakeholders understand assessment validity? Finally, how do ideas around validity result in assessment use and misuse? These questions intrigue me, keep me up at night, and are where I focus a great deal of my research. As one example, over the past few years, along with two colleagues, Sam Sellar from the University of Manchester in the UK and Greg Thompson from Queensland University of Technology in Australia, I have had the privilege of working with teachers' unions in various countries. We started this work because some of the unions approached us requesting help with formulating a unified stance on "the validity of international assessments." The stance was needed because international assessments were billed by many in their respective governments as a true (e.g., valid) measure of national educational achievement and national success. Moreover, as assessment scores in some countries fell over time, policy-makers, the press, and many parents were placing a large burden of the blame for low performance on teachers. If the union could convince their members, politicians, and the public that the test was invalid, the argument would be moot. However, we felt that invalidating a major international assessment was well beyond our capacities and rather, we needed to have a nuanced and serious conversation about validity.

We agreed that we needed to explain to our union colleagues that we do not validate a test (i.e., validity is not a property of the test), but rather we validate the interpretations made of the test. We argued that each use of test scores required a new validity argument and in the absence of such an argument we could not deem the claim valid. In other words, assessments do not speak for themselves, nor do the data point to simple policy solutions. Individual scores, average scores, and comparative rankings do not constitute meaning but only provide a starting point for conversation. We further explained that the meaning attributed to test scores (at its most basic level, the notions of "good" or "bad" scores) requires a leap from the numbers to judgment about what these scores represent and, subsequently, what should be done. We further explained that the leap from numerical results to inferences was complex and is, at its core, the focus of validity.

Using Kane's (2016) work we defined validity in the context of assessment "as the extent to which the proposed interpretations and uses of test scores are justified," requiring "conceptual analysis of the coherence and completeness of the claims and empirical analyses of the inferences and assumptions inherent in the claims" (p. 198). We made the case to the unions that we could not and they should not attempt to provide a blanket statement on the validity of the assessments but rather should ask for evidence validating some of the more problematic claims and, when appropriate, attempt to falsify the claim. Falsifying claims was championed by Cronbach (1980, p. 103) when he explained: "The job of validation is not to support an interpretation, but to find out what might be wrong with it. A proposition deserves some degree of trust only when it has survived serious attempts to falsify it."

As an example, we used a popular inference among policy-makers and the press that one of the international assessments was measuring the quality of national educational systems. This claim was fairly straightforward to falsify because the assessment being used to make the claim did not assess the countries' curricula. Further, the assessment in question only assessed three subjects and focused on one age rather than a grade. Our union colleagues found the practice of falsifying the claim useful and empowering to them, affording them with useful information to counter some of the assessment's misuse.

I would be remiss if I did not concede that there is nothing stopping someone from making an invalid claim about assessment results. Assessment data are often reported as truth from which to make a claim. I believe this is where the misconception arises that the test is valid, rather the interpretations that we make from the results. As such, a basic appreciation of validity is central to appropriately using assessment data. Unfortunately, many of those that make invalid claims care little about validity and there is not much we can do. However, for the social science research community I can think of very few concepts that are more important.

In the context of large-scale assessment, Dr. Rutkowski demonstrates the importance of understanding and practicing validity when using test scores. As a researcher and evaluator, his work borders academia and non-academic problem solving. The research problems that he encounters, such as the teacher union's request to evaluate the validity of an international assessment, has a direct link to policy-making. This illustrates that how we understand validity has practical and political consequences (as discussed in Chapters 6 and 16). It is not surprising that policy-makers prefer a "yes/no" answer, out of a systemic desire for simplicity and certainty. But validity is not a yes/no concept. It has to be contextualized and understood in relation to inference-making (more discussion about this in the Cluster 3 chapters). In other words: Validity is not a property of an assessment. The idea that validity is best considered a "validity argument" is congruent with our discussion that advocates for a dialogic approach to understanding validity and the need to view validity as unfolding, always with uncertainty. Meanwhile, practices such as falsifying claims in specific contexts are effective and appropriate strategies to engaging validity, without falling into the trap of essentializing validity as a property of a test, or a research design. All in all, validity has to reside in a specific communicative context in order to be understood and evaluated.

YOU AND RESEARCH

Understanding the nature of validity is relevant when you are either interpreting or doing research. It is important to be savvy about evaluating the validity of research findings so that you can decide whether the study can be used to inform your professional practice. When doing research, validity is relevant to every aspect of the research process, from conceptualizing what idea is worth pursuing to what kind of impact one should aim to achieve through research.

When Interpreting Research

When you read research articles, do you find yourself pondering questions such as: Can I trust the findings of the study? Are the recommendations made by the authors warranted? Is the research design sound? Was the study carried out in a rigorous way as planned? What are the limitations that I need to be aware of? These questions all have connections to validity. How should you gauge the validity of a study reported in a journal article? A few things to highlight:

- Pay attention to the interlocking connection (or the lack thereof) between the epistemological stance that the researchers claim, as well as how the researchers go about choosing a research methodology. For example, if the author(s) claim a social constructivist position (e.g., reality doesn't exist independently but is constructed through our perception) to understand the phenomenon of disordered eating, it would make most sense that the participants' perspectives are included and valued during data collection and analysis.
- Typically, you can locate information relevant to validity as articulated by the author(s) in the methods section. For example, for quantitative research articles, you may find validity indicators such as reliability reported in the form of *Cronbach's alpha*, a statistical term that measures consistency among items used to measure a construct. Similarly, in the method section of a qualitative study, you may find a description of validity procedures and techniques used in the study (e.g., member checking, peer debriefing, etc.).
- When evaluating research claims made in the study, you should apply appropriate validity criteria to evaluate those findings and inferences. We provide a summary of the alignment between types of knowledge claims and corresponding validity principles that can be used to evaluate different knowledge claims in Table 7.2.
- You should expect to find a discussion toward the end of a research article that discusses the limitations of the study, which implies possible concerns that might impact the validity of the study.

When Doing Research

For those who are or will engage in formal research practice, take a moment to reflect on how you might apply your new understandings of validity to your research endeavors. Try to stay away from focusing on specific validity terms first (e.g., reliability, construct validity, trustworthiness). Instead, consider validity in a holistic way, as we discussed in this chapter. For instance, you should always be mindful of specific validity requirements in correspondence to the types of knowledge claims you make (Table 7.2 provides some concrete examples). Ask yourself: How do I know the inferences that I make in the study are sound? How as a researcher may I influence the research design, process, and outcome? What dynamics or factors might distort the findings? How would I like to interact with the participants? What kind of impact would I like to make through this study?

TABLE 7.2 ● Principles for Evaluating Knowledge Claims

Type of Knowledge Claim	Examples of Research Claims	Corresponding Validity Principles	Corresponding Validity Techniques
Objective claims	153 participants completed the survey	Multiple access and reaching consensus	**Repeated measure:** Count the number of participants multiple times
	Audio recordings of interviews are transcribed into written transcription		**Triangulation:** Ask another person to check the accuracy of the transcriptions by listening to the recordings
	1 in 6 children is living in poverty in the United States		**Representativeness:** Checking whether the sample where these statistics are derived from is actually representative of the U.S. population
Subjective claims	Participants experience depressive symptoms based on scores on a depression inventory	Privileged access; sincerity and authenticity	**Cognitive interview:** Check with participants if elevated depression scores correspond with their experience
	Participants shared their past experiences of failures during interviews		**Building trust and rapport** with participants prior to and throughout the interview process to encourage open sharing

(Continued)

(Continued)

TABLE 7.2 (Continued)

Type of Knowledge Claim	Examples of Research Claims	Corresponding Validity Principles	Corresponding Validity Techniques
	The student appears to be disinterested in the classroom activities		**Member checking:** Check with the student about this interpretation
Normative claims	Racist comments are deemed inappropriate in the classroom	Ability to position-take from the perspective of cultural insiders and gain recognition from them	**Member checking:** Ask people in the specific culture context where the claim is made whether they consent to the claim or disagree and why
	Unequal payment between men and women in the United States is not just		**Position-taking:** become familiar with a given culture and try to gain an insider perspective
	Marijuana should be legalized		

SYNTHESIS: POINTS FOR REFLECTION

As we conclude this chapter we anticipate readers might still be experiencing a sense of unfinishedness related to the many facets and layers of validity. This feeling is to be expected. After all, validity is perhaps one of the most foundational research concepts, and it always deserves more discussion and deeper understanding. Since validity is too often discussed in fragmented or overly simplified ways, our goal here is to create a more holistic and methodological understanding of the concept. We hope to demonstrate how validity is pertinent to all kinds of research inquiry, not trapped in an all-too-pervasive quantitative–qualitative schism.

Conceptual Synthesis

This unifying potential of validity starts with epistemology: the connection between knowing/knowledge and what we consider true and valid. As demonstrated earlier, this connection is always relevant to everyday experience, where knowledge claims are made all the time. For example, validity criteria are invoked when we gauge an email exchange between a professor and a student, an example used earlier. Similarly, in the formal research context, validity is about how well a knowledge claim meets the criteria for deeming the claim true or sound. Validity criteria have to do with how we understand truth, which depends on one's epistemological positions. But this does not mean everything goes. As Dr. Rutkowski reminds us: It is our *validity argument* that matters.

Methodological Synthesis

Meanwhile, we discussed how knowing involves understanding meaning, which is highly contextualized. We can never be fully certain about whether we grasp the meaning as intended. This shifts the focus of achieving validity from procedures that are external to a study (e.g., the default notion that we should use multiple methods to "triangulate" findings, or replicating a measurement or a study to enhance validity) to the communicative context of understanding meaning. Thus, validity always needs to be understood in layered contexts of a study and to the specific inference made. Understanding meaning, especially in a cross-cultural context, requires sufficient ability to take the position of research participants, and to examine the specific research phenomenon from the perspectives of the participants—for instance, how ELLs understand and experience standardized test questions.

Personal Synthesis

Developing a unifying understanding of validity doesn't mean this is or should be the only way to conceptualize validity. On the contrary, borrowing from the ancient Chinese wisdom of Yin and Yang as two opposing sides of a whole that depend on each other, unification relies on the existence of divergent views and differences. Without differences, sameness doesn't have a meaning. On the other hand, if we only discuss differences without unity, we miss the basis that makes comparison possible and we risk sliding into a relativist view that everything is equally right or good. As you work through this chapter, ask yourself: What ideas presented in this chapter did you find compelling or resonant with your own ideas and experiences about truth and validity? What did you find unconvincing, or where did you disagree? How would you go about challenging those ideas and underlying assumptions, which would include the perspectives of us, the authors?

MOVING FORWARD

As we reach the end of the first cluster, we now complete a full circle that moves from researcher's identity, intersubjectivity, and critical reflection (Chapters 2 and 3); ethics (Chapter 4); epistemology (Chapter 5); norms, social structure, and power (Chapter 6); to validity (Chapter 7). At bottom, all those concepts are meta-concepts that are inherently connected. The circle is not closed but will continue to expand as a spiral as we move to Cluster 2 chapters. In Cluster 2, we shift our focus from a conceptual discussion to more concrete research practices and methodological issues. We will further unpack how validity is also relevant to power relations that are embedded in knowledge production and dissemination. This reveals an ethical dimension in terms of how researchers either reproduce or resist unequal power relations through research practice, or what kind of impact we hope to accomplish, or how we evaluate what constitutes "good" and "significant" impact. Validity and ethics are deeply connected. We will discuss this in Chapter 16.

In Cluster 2, we will focus on the nature of "data" and data generation in a holistic discussion, again, without falling into the artificial divides between quantitative and qualitative research. We will also introduce various ways of generating data for the purpose of description, explanation, or understanding, and various issues that may arise during this process, such as sampling, outliers, and missing data. In the context of generating data, we will also embed discussions on what constitutes good research questions and the role of literature review in the research process. Meanwhile, meta-concepts introduced in Cluster 1 will continue to be *thematized* in new ways and new understandings. We look forward to continuing this exciting journey with you.

Further Readings

Call-Cummings, M. (2017). Establishing communicative validity: Discovering theory through practice. *Qualitative Inquiry*, *23*(3), 192–200.

Carspecken, P. (1996). *Critical ethnography in educational research: A theoretical and practical guide*. New York, NY, and London, UK: Routledge.

Dennis, B. (2013). "Validity crisis" in qualitative research. In B. Dennis, L. Carspecken, and P. F. Carspecken (Eds.), *Qualitative research: A reader in philosophy, core concepts, and practice* (pp. 3–37). New York, NY: Peter Lang.

Fine, M. (1994). Working the hyphens. In N. K. Denzin & Y. S. Lincoln (Eds.), *Handbook of qualitative research*. Thousand Oaks, CA: SAGE.

Lather, P. (1986). Issues of validity in openly ideological research: Between a rock and a soft place. *Interchange*, *17*(4), 63–84.

Lather, P. (1993). Fertile obsession: Validity after poststructuralism. *The Sociological Quarterly*, *34*(4), 673–693.

Further Readings by David Rutkowski

Rutkowski, D. (2018). Improving international assessment through evaluation. *Assessment in Education: Principles, Policy & Practice*, *25*(1), 127–136. (https://doi.org/10.1080/0969594X.2017.1300572)

Rutkowski, D., & Delandshere, G. (2016). Causal inferences with large scale assessment data: Using a validity framework. *Large-Scale Assessments in Education*, *4*(1). (https://doi.org/10.1186/s40536-016-0019-1)

Rutkowski, D., & Wild, J. (2015). Stakes matter: Student motivation and the validity of student assessments for teacher evaluation. *Educational Assessment*, *20*(3), 165–179. (https://doi.org/10.1080/10627197.2015.1059273)

WHAT IS THE MEANING OF "DATA"?

ROADMAP

In Cluster 1, we built up the landscape of concepts important to understanding, doing, and engaging with research. Those concepts will be deepened and put into practice in this cluster. We begin to look closely at the research process itself, specifically focusing on the concepts and practices of generating and acquiring data. We use the metaphor of a "roadmap" to bring these concepts and practices into view as we consider questions of what data are and how they are connected with the ways researchers ask questions and formulate plans for doing their research.

We are approaching the material differently than most introductory research texts. First, it is typical for information to be presented in a procedural way—that is, presenting research processes in the form of recipe-like procedures. Instead, we emphasize the *doing* nature of the research process as we provide touchstones, keys, and guides that function like roadmaps for engaging with and making decisions in the research process. While we acknowledge that presenting procedures in a step-by-step fashion serves a heuristic function, we expect that the guidance we provide in the chapters will broaden your capacity to apply knowledge across more complex engagements with research. Additionally, it is more realistic in the sense that understanding how decisions are made in the process of doing research is fundamental to being able to modify, apply, interpret, and evaluate research efforts.

Second, most research texts divide the doing of research into two or three categories, namely quantitative, qualitative, and possibly mixed methods. As you know by now, we are resisting using the quantitative/qualitative binary as our starting place. In the Cluster 2 chapters, important distinctions relevant to conducting studies with linguistic/textual or numeric data are addressed without using those distinctions as organizing features. Instead, in each of the chapters, the implications for quantitative and qualitative orientations toward data are presented as the distinction is relevant.

We are using the metaphor of a roadmap to steer these chapters. This metaphor works insofar as it suggests that there are purposes and goals related to the research process. Being effective and efficient in reaching those goals benefits from planning. There are often multiple routes to the desired point, as well as surprises and decision-making along the way. Having good equipment and knowledge facilitates good decision-making. Traveling with a roadmap is also an active process . . . no autopiloting! Travelers must be able to assess how the trip is going, judge the quality of decisions made so far, and anticipate and shift goals when needed.

To take the metaphor further, there is knowledge and there are skills that contribute to the success of the trip and that facilitate the traveling itself. There are aspects of *doing* research that have become commonplace within research communities. This is why it is possible to produce step-by step procedures as a helpful way of teaching people how to conduct research. As we build on our everyday ways of going about inquiry toward what is considered scholarly research, we will be making those accepted ways of *doing* research more explicit. In fact, each chapter begins with ordinary illustrations and then compares and contrasts them with relevant inquiry examples. As we do this, we invite you to be creative, inquisitive, and critical of this knowledge about *how to do research*. Entering research with an open and creative orientation resonates with what we know about how social science methodologies

FIGURE CL2.1 • Roadmap

Source: iStock.com/Swissmediavision

change and become better. Our knowledge and understanding of social life have developed over the centuries through both what we have learned through our successes as well as our mistakes. We can commit to the continuation of this kind of progress by remaining open and creative. As such, we will have new reasons and opportunities to advance what we are doing as social scientists and as practitioners who draw on social science knowledge.

There are four chapters in this cluster: a chapter on the process of doing research including how one identifies with the research process and with being a researcher (Chapter 8), conceptualizing data (Chapter 9), generating and acquiring data (Chapter 10), and assessing the quality and quantity of data (Chapter 11).

Chapter 8 is like a roadmap in the sense that it describes what a research process entails. We take seriously the aspect of traveling that has to do with being purposeful and goal oriented and guided. Knowing where you are headed and what you hope to accomplish helps you make decisions about which maps to use, the directions to take, and what will be needed to reach the destination. You also bring to bear your background knowledge of both maps and the specific terrains you are traversing, just as researchers review the literature to build up this background knowledge. We introduce the idea of creating a research proposal, which is like creating the specific path you will take in your travels. You will need to be clear about the goals.

In doing research this usually involves having clear questions to guide what you do and a clear idea about where you are positioned in the process (like putting a pin in your starting place on the map) and figuring out what you need in the process. The destination is not the only marker one pays attention to when traversing a research project. And, just as there are community-established protocols for driving or traveling on roads, there are such protocols for research.

Chapter 9 brings the concept of data into the foreground. As with any map, there are underlying conceptual understandings that are necessary for making sense of and creating maps. In traveling this might include concepts of distance and time. It might also include concepts of rest or feasibility. Chapter 9 develops such underlying concepts as purposive orientations and intersubjective aspects that are relevant to understanding data. Roadmaps help us understand the lay of the land, how we should interpret what we are witnessing as we travel. Modern roadmaps that like those generated through Google on our phones are specific to purposes and requests we enter. For example, I might ask the map on my phone to help me find a coffee shop nearby. Then the map will populate with nearby coffee shops. Consider these "coffee shops" to be data that were purposefully located on the map when requested by me. The roadmap then guides me, given my interests, to the data. In addition to being purposive, what the roadmap shows me is dependent on a common understanding of what I have asked for as well as concepts like "right" and "left," "north" and "south." As a researcher, I will have specific interests I use to generate data and establish the lay of the land relevant to those interests. In this way, Chapter 9 draws on the roadmap metaphor to establish how data that are relative to our purposes and current shared understandings can contribute to mapping out our research process.

Chapter 10 focuses on specific ways to generate and acquire data: It is the most procedural of our Cluster 2 chapters. In the chapter we argue for thinking of data through a process of doing rather than as a product. As such, you will be introduced to many things you might do to generate or acquire data. The chapter is not exhaustive but is illustrative of the possibilities. Most important, the chapter will help you understand what is involved in making decisions about data and how *processes* of generating or acquiring data connect to certain data *products* (which form the basis for later analysis). Chapter 10 furthers our roadmap metaphor in the sense that it provides guidance on how to choose specific pathways for travel. Just as you might consider the distance or length of different paths to your destination or the kind of terrain you must cross, in the data generation and acquisition process you must make similar choices, such as what protocols to use, how directly you wish to engage with research participants, and so on.

Chapter 11 brings us to questions like "What are enough data?" and "Are the data good enough?" We need to be able to think about the quality and quantity of the data we generate and acquire. In some instances there are standard rules of thumb, but always there are principles that underlie how we respond to such questions. As researchers we are accountable for our data, and as practitioners we want to hold researchers accountable for their data. No data are perfect, so we have to be aware of the limitations and challenges of the data along with their strengths. This chapter will help you learn the details of thinking through these issues. It is like a roadmap in that it helps us see the "yield" and "stop" signs in the data generating/acquiring processes, and it also helps us locate moments, turns, and transitions in those processes.

While we include traditional information relevant to the generation of data in the process of doing research, we treat conceptual insights as the centerpieces of the Cluster 2 chapters. Our goal is to provide rich roadmaps in which the detailed information—for example, how to write survey questions—might be located. As new methods are consistently being developed, the landscape and modes of decision-making entailed in the process might provide you with the most sustainable and transformative opportunities to engage with new methodologies. The roadmap metaphor that will orient you to Chapter 8 introduces you to the ideas of planning, proposing, and organizing research studies.

8

WHAT AM I LOOKING FOR?

REVISITING RESEARCH AND IDENTITY IN THE CONTEXT OF DATA

In Chapter 3 we began talking about intersecting connections between identity and research. In this chapter we want to move our thinking about identity along to look at the ways in which data are material created through interpretational engagements. The researcher's identity is unavoidably involved in the generation of data. Data do not just exist to be collected like eggs in a basket. That is, data are not things that exist outside of the researcher that the researcher gathers together. Neither do they exist inside the researcher's mind. This chapter will specifically focus on how research builds from background knowledge (including a literature review), what it means to have a researchable question (sometimes with a hypothesis for outcomes), and a design. These aspects of the research endeavor are linked to a particular conceptualization of data—data are the purposeful products of these research activities. In the "You and Research" section of the chapter, readers will be asked to imagine how the material of the chapter would be relevant to thinking about the construction of a research proposal or the creation of a rubric useful for examining research articles.

MUSING UPON THE EVERYDAY: SOLVING PROBLEMS THAT MATTER TO US

Think about a time you had a health symptom or watched a loved one with a recurring symptom or set of symptoms. Maybe it was a cough or a pain in your elbow. At some point in 2011, Barbara cannot remember precisely when it started, she was experiencing abdominal pain after eating. The pain was pretty severe, but it didn't last long.

At first, she just assumed it was some severe form of gas pain. The first several times, Barbara thought of the pain as being isolated events with gas as the probable explanation. One time after eating at a restaurant Barbara had cramping pain so severe, she was sure it must be food poisoning. It took a while of having these intermittent, short-lived pain episodes for her to decide there was a bigger problem. The persistence of recurrences prompted Barbara to wonder about what connected these episodes of abdominal pain. To gather information about possible explanations, Barbara decided to surf the internet. *Abdominal pain* alone is not a very precise search term, and, consequently, it was difficult to find very precise information about what might be causing the pain. Barbara used her initial hypothesis, that gas was causing the pain, to narrow her search. Alas, she could not find precise enough answers to solve the problem. Barbara's gas explanation was not holding up. Neither was the food poisoning hypothesis. Her description of symptoms was not specific enough to provide new information about the source of her pain.

Barbara needed more precise information about the pain and about its contexts of occurrence. She decided to keep a food journal. She meticulously and systematically recorded what she ate and drank along with notes about any pain episodes, including ratings about the severity of the episodes and how long they lasted. She set up the diary like what is shown in Table 8.1.

Eventually Barbara decided to systematically record what was going on with her body. To set up this record, Barbara drew on a hunch that the pain was likely related to eating and/or stress. She built into the diary the idea that the pain episodes varied one from another in terms of length of time and level of pain. She standardized how she recorded that

TABLE 8.1 ● Food Diary

Date/Day of the Week	Time	What I Ate/Drank	Stress Levels 1–10 (1 = low, 10 = high)	Pain Yes or No	Length of Episode in Minutes	Pain Rating 1–10 (1 = low, 10 = high)	Description of Pain Episode	Any Treatment
2/23 M	7:30am	Oatmeal, Tea	4	N				
	1 pm	Salad, Diet Coke	3	N				
	6:30pm	Fried tofu, tomatoes, cottage cheese	2	Y	45	4	Discomfort, cramping	Walking helped

information so that it was easy to synthesize information across episodes. For example, using minutes to note time meant that she could easily tell if some episodes were longer than others.

This more systematic approach resulted in increased informational precision about the pain episodes and strengthened validity of inferences she made as she mapped the pieces, patterns, and variations together. When Barbara reviewed her food diary, she could see that the pain was severe after eating foods that had higher oil/fat content. At one point during this process of record-keeping, Barbara experienced such severe pain that she ended up in the emergency room of a local hospital. Ultimately, an X-ray confirmed that her gall bladder (an organ that helps the body deal with fat and oil) was inflamed. Barbara's diary and the X-ray pointed to the same conclusions.

> **Pause and Reflect.** Let's pause for a moment and think about how data were generated for this everyday study.
>
> - Let's begin by numbering the steps in the process involved with Barbara's own exploration of symptoms. List out the various things she did or that you might do in a similar situation.
> - What specific differences/similarities do you notice between Barbara's surfing the internet and her diary-keeping?
> - What role did Barbara's assumptions and hypotheses play in generating the diary data?
> - What role did Barbara's commitments and motivations play in generating those data? How did her commitments and motivations intersect with the process of generating data? Where did they enhance the process, and where did those commitments and motivations inhibit the process?

The questions above indicate some important characteristics of research. All research has in its background a set of researcher commitments, which we introduced in Cluster 1. To conduct research, those commitments take concrete shape through organizational structures (which will be discussed below) and by engaging the characteristics of research-ability, systematicity, clarity, and openness. These four characteristics are infused through the research process and can serve as qualities of assessment for research studies.

Research-ability

Scholars like D. Kirk Hamilton (2012) and Sally Thorne (2016) write that the research-ability of a study speaks to the accessibility of the data, knowledge, participants, and so on. Research is a set of organized activities that involve subject-with-subject exchanges. Our ability to research depends on this communicative ground. Questions that cannot be answered are not researchable. For example, one cannot ask what God thinks, but one could ask what is reported in the Christian Bible. Similarly, we cannot conduct studies that require infants to talk. We cannot research intelligence without defining it and having ways to study it that fit that definition. Gabriel Stalianides and Andreas Stalianides (2020) reminded us that research-ability then involves how a researcher enacts the study in concrete ways that are communicable to others.

Openness

We contrast openness with neutrality. According to Andreas Schwab and William Starbuck (2016), neutrality is a nonrelational way of positioning data and researchers, whereas openness suggests that regardless of researcher commitments, the research should engage the process in an open manner. Openness requires researchers to structure the process in a way that is open to counter possibilities, including concluding that one's starting assumptions were flawed, as has been written about recently by Masoumeh Ghazinejad and colleagues (2018) and in the past by Ilja Maso and colleagues (1995). In general, when researchers describe their positions as neutral, they are describing a position that is open. This means that the researcher is not so invested in the particulars of the study (including outcomes) that they have made it impossible for counter perspectives to be generated.

Systematicity

Systematicity, according to Paul Hoyningen-Huene (2013), involves the careful meta-thinking of research *as a process* where one takes a third-person perspective on the trajectory of the process and its ramifications. This involves thinking about things like: "What are the questions or interests through which the research will be oriented?" "Who or what will be researched?" "What will the data be?" Basically, researchers must think about how they will systematically conduct their inquiries. That systematicity must be explicitly expressed. Context and background knowledge are implicitly linked to creating an external systematicity. Guy Paré and colleagues (2016) further point out that systematicity that is internal to the research project is established through some fairly standard touchpoints. For example, prior to collecting data, researchers identify a research design for their study consisting of ways of structuring the project that systematically guide the decision-making process.

Standardization

Standardization is a concept used to describe *how* we engage methods. It is part of the systematicity of a project. For some, but not all, designs, standardization is an important characteristic because it is part of how researchers ensure that their studies are fixed in the ways identified. This is how standardization works. Ronald Fischer and Taciano Milfont (2010) explain this nicely. When we standardize data collection we standardize the procedures, tools, and definitions necessary to ensure people collect the data in a similar manner. We also want to be sure that standard protocols are applied as intended.

Douglas Maynard and colleagues (2006) indicate that standardization is an important research characteristic for studies conducted using fixed designs. Standardizing provides each person with the same precise map and instructions, with the intention that people will take the same path to the end.

NARRATIVE AND CONCEPTUAL INTERLUDES: A RESEARCHER AND THEIR ORGANIZING

In this section of the chapter we explore structural organizing components of doing research, while also drawing attention to research-ability, systematicity, clarity, and openness. Researchers commonly structure and organize their work by (1) reviewing existing literature and establishing a conversation; (2) formulating interests, questions, and/or hypotheses; and (3) creating research designs. Researchers engage in these activities from a diversity of research approaches. Of course, our orientation in this book will be a relational one. To begin with, let's contrast that relational image of research with a more familiar way of thinking about research that looks something like Figure 8.1.

A scientist looks at something like a cell through a microscope and describes or measures what they see. Some scientists assume that the thing being looked at exists independent of

FIGURE 8.1 ● Image of a Scientist

Source: iStock.com/sanjeri

the scientist who is observing it and measuring how various treatments affect it. According to this way of conceptualizing research, the most valid study would be one conducted by researchers who are un-invested, separate beings from whatever phenomena they are examining. Though contemporary scientists do not tend to imagine their work through this image, many assumptions embedded in this way of thinking have been retained in general conceptions of doing research. One key assumption is the assumption of neutrality: Data are considered neutral, not to be distorted or biased by the (also neutral) researcher. Facts that are produced through research are considered valid to the extent that they can be assumed to match the actual state of affairs of that cell under the microscope.

In this chapter we offer a different way of thinking about data—one that asks for *openness,* not neutrality; *engagement,* not aloofness; and *criticality,* not proceduralism. If we think of data generation as an activity that involves interpretation and dialogue among researchers who do not enter the study as a blank slate, then we will begin to shift our thinking away from an idea that the microscope is the apparatus through which the researcher is connected with the data and instead think of dialogues among scientists as implicit to the generation of data about the cell.

In this section of the chapter, we will use narratives to explore the dialogue involved in conducting literature reviews; articulating research interests, questions, and/or hypotheses; and developing research designs. In order to do this, we are going to draw on a personal example. Barbara's niece Hannah was diagnosed with **Rett syndrome** near her second birthday. No one in the family had heard of this condition, and it put Barbara's family, particularly her sister, in a situation of having to gather a lot of new information not readily available. Within the first year of diagnosis, members of the family decided to attend a conference of the Rett Syndrome Association being held in Chicago. A lot of research was presented at this conference, but it was not always easy to figure out how to make sense of the information or how to use it. As users of research with a vested interest in understanding what it meant, they had to learn to compare, contrast, and judge not only research outcomes, but also the quality of the research processes. To understand the research, they had to understand background information, including researchers' goals and commitments, as well as ways of structuring the research.

Below we introduce three structuring activities that can help to organize and evaluate research projects:

- Reviewing existing knowledge;
- Formulating research interests, questions, and hypotheses; and
- Creating research designs.

We also note how the four characteristics (research-ability, openness, systematicity, and standardization) are differentially foregrounded throughout the research process. For example, research-ability and clarity foreground ways of assessing the articulation of research questions, interests, and hypotheses.

Reviewing Existing Knowledge and Establishing the Conversation

The helix is a common visual metaphor for research writ large.

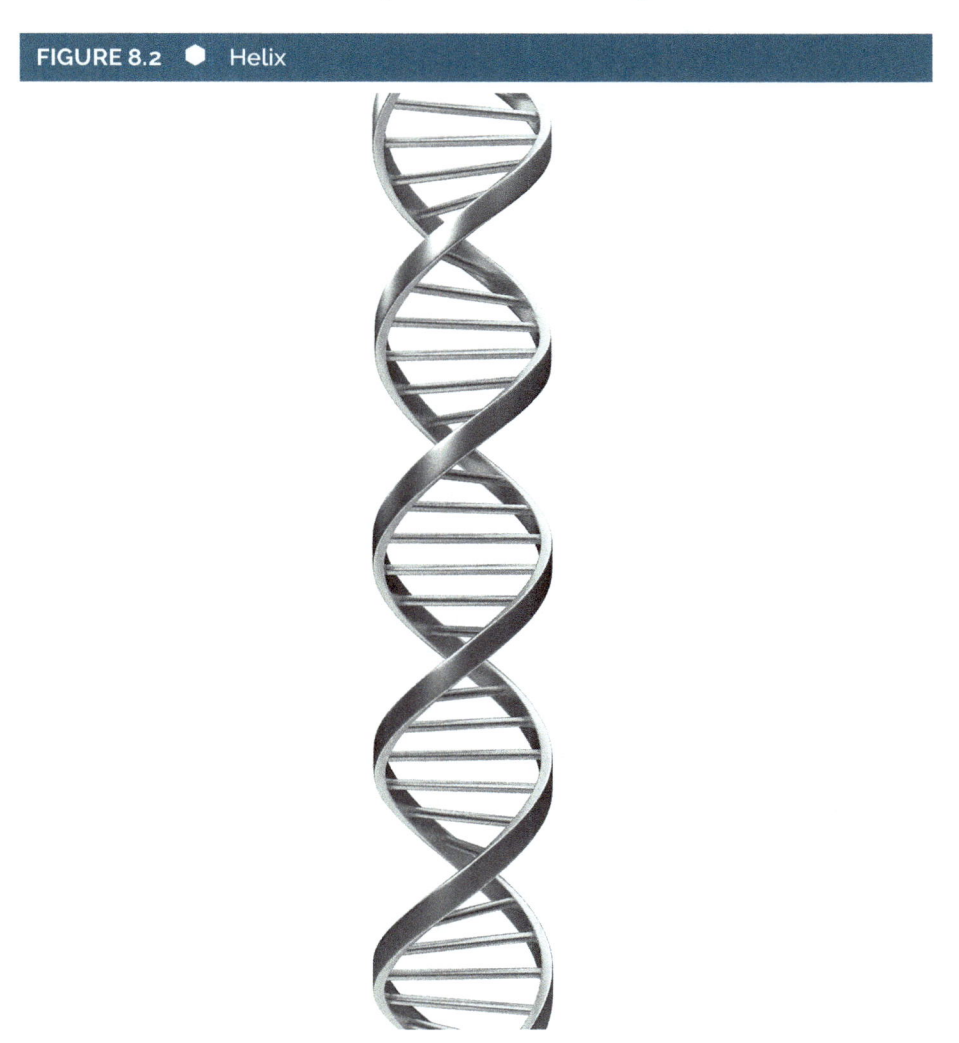

FIGURE 8.2 ● Helix

Source: iStock.com/luismmolina

This metaphor has worked well because it illuminates the ongoing, recursive, connected qualities of research efforts. Individual research studies are connected to both a past and a future. They are linked to an ongoing dialogue and they manifest a progressive momentum—that is, movement forward toward problem resolution, increased understanding, and in general a better world. No one study is the final last word or end of the story. Moreover, research is always conducted in a relational context that should be acknowledged as part of how the research itself is understood, including how we make sense of the results. Furthermore, this helix is regularly evident in the cycles of research when data are acquired as secondary sources from original studies. For example, there is a large-scale, population survey of Australian families with at least one child diagnosed with Rett syndrome being used to collect longitudinal data. These data have been important for many varying and related research projects—used by some researchers who are not actively involved in generating those survey data.

In order for research questions, hypotheses, and designs to be warranted, they must be set within an orienting context—one that can include statements of problems, needs, or interests that are not currently well addressed through existing knowledge. This is the responsibility of researchers at the outset. As research conversations move along, studies are sometimes connected in ways not initially envisioned by the researchers involved, but this does not detract from the originating context within which researchers locate their work from the outset.

Context: Establishing Interpretive Guideposts

Research context can be acknowledged in a number of ways—existing knowledge is part of the context, but site/location/participants/time frame of the study at hand are as well. Because all knowledge is contextual, understanding the context of the study is necessary to understanding, interpreting, and making sense of the research itself. This context helps to locate a study's purposes, interests, and design within its surroundings so that we understand how it connects to the broader conversation. If a rung on the helix is disconnected from all other aspects of the helix, free-floating, so to speak, its value to the ongoing dialogue is lost.

What constitutes the context of a study? Questions always involve some level of motivation on the part of the researcher. Sometimes motivations are personal: These are commonly reported in qualitative studies. For example, if Barbara was to conduct a study on the topic of educating girls who live with Rett syndrome, she most certainly would have a personal motivation, and as a qualitative researcher, she would be expected to share that with readers. Even quantitative researchers might be asked to identify their motivations. For example, Dr. Jenny Downs received a grant from the Rett Syndrome Association in the United States (Rettsyndrome.org) to conduct a study. An interviewer from the organization asked her "what prompted" her to do research related to Rett syndrome. Dr. Downs links her recent research on living a healthy life with Rett syndrome to her overarching career interests. She wrote:

> I have a strong interest in the benefits of movement and exercise for both children and adults and particularly for those with a neurodevelopmental disorder. My background is in both research and clinical practice and I have been able to work on projects in Rett syndrome about early development, functional abilities, physical activity and scoliosis. There is now increasing evidence that learning and development are favored in an enriched environment containing lots of physical activity, and some of this evidence relates specifically to Rett syndrome. I am very excited to be able to run this study which will investigate the effects of an enriched environment program for young girls in China who are newly diagnosed with Rett syndrome. (2017, https://www.Rettyndrome.org/for-researchers/investigator-spotlight; edits offered by Dr. Downs July 24, 2018)

Furthermore, she wrote about what she finds most rewarding: "For me, the single most rewarding aspect of conducting Rett syndrome research is linking research findings with the practical needs of these amazing girls, women and their families."

Dr. Downs indicated personal contexts for her funded study, including her passion and scholarly history. She also identified a social need and a specific country of study (China) as part of the context. Much of what she wrote in response to the questionnaire will not likely be included in a published article of the study because it is not traditional for researchers using quantitative approaches to share personal motivations. However, openly sharing the motivations speaks to the trajectory of research engagements that now form Dr. Downs's remarkable career.

Background Knowledge and More: Literature Review

The existing state of knowledge forms both a contextual background and a lively springboard for research activities. Background knowledge is generally built from what academics call the "literature," which predominantly includes publications but can also include formal presentations, personal communications, or unpublished documents. For example, at this point researchers know that Rett syndrome is comprised of multiple forms of mutations of the X chromosome so it can only really affect the lives of people with two X chromosomes, as those with only one X chromosome die at or before birth. This knowledge explains why studies focus on girls. Background knowledge can take the form of theories or concepts through which ideas might be framed. It can also take the form of previous research results. Many researchers situate their studies in the field of scholarship already conducted so that the new inquiry notes contributions their study will make to that field. With an emphasis on knowledge production, researchers both are positioned by and strategically position themselves within the knowledge context of their fields through the field's documented literature, particularly through peer-reviewed publications. When researchers review existing literature, they do so to both build up concepts and conceptual framework as well as examine the empirical work. When the researcher completes their study, outcomes of the research process are also situated within existing literature. And, sometimes, the literature becomes relevant to making informed decisions during the research process. Reviewing literature is thus an active rather than passive engagement with existing understandings—it is a purposeful effort to understand.

Literature reviews are not monolithic in form. There are different types of literature reviews—for example, Harris Cooper (1988) wrote about literature reviews that focus on a topic or those that bring forward a particular perspective. It is useful, then, to remember that literature reviews are complex strategic activities that can result in varying ways of presenting and discussing similar literature.

Richard Torraco (2005) provided guidelines for writing what is called an "integrative" literature review, where the review itself constitutes its own study by adding new insights and making substantive contributions to the field. This is exciting because we see the potential of literature reviews to push our conceptualizing and to provide a springboard for new knowledge and critique.

Literature reviews can serve different functions based on the type of research design being engaged and the purposes of the review. For example, for experimental designs, literature is used to establish the validity of the variables, justification of the design and/or subject selection, and the validity and reliability of the measures. The literature review also helps to establish definitional criteria for concepts used to conduct the study. For ethnographies, in contrast, the literature review might help to justify the questions or interests and/or selection of participants, but it will also be a much more fluid and ongoing part of the process, potentially changing in radical ways by the end of the ethnography. This seldom happens with an experimental design.

When we conduct literature reviews we have to keep several things about that literature in mind. We need to keep *the dates* of sources in mind. For example, if we are developing a conceptual or empirical history we want to be sure we include sources that span the life of the concept or empirical history, but if we are just interested in current literature then it is important to have reviewed the most current decade's publications and presentations. We also need to keep in mind *the credibility* of the sources. Credibility generally includes considerations of reputation/expertise of the scholars, and acceptability of the methodologies including tools and designs. However, one must think critically about credibility. For example, research that is topically marginalized in particular fields might also be interesting, relevant, and of high quality. Sonya Satinsky's work, about which you read in Chapter 5, is an example of this.

Another important aspect of the sources is *the purpose(s)* of the writers. The purpose will have implications for participant selection and generalizability of the studies as well as ways in which the concepts are presented. When writing or reading literature reviews, we want to make sense of the literature with the scholar's purpose in mind: We do not expect that knowledge reflected in that literature is neutral or unquestionable.

Writers of strong literature reviews also claim their own purposes so that their reviews might similarly be queried. This contributes to the dialogic potential of research. Sometimes writers intend to describe contemporary or historical developments through the literature, but other times writers intend to show gaps in the literature or critique faulty assumptions. Knowing these purposes helps readers position-take with the writer and assess the review based on the author's intentions. When the scholar's purposes are not made explicit in the literature review there is a risk that the knowledge presented will be read as neutral. However, remember from Chapter 5 that a relational epistemology locates the ways in which all knowledge is produced from particular positions, with particular access points and perspectives.

Researchers need to establish *inclusivity/exclusivity* criteria for literature in their reviews. Knowledge today is being mobilized globally at a pace never before imagined. Regardless of how researchers orient themselves toward the literature, they will make decisions that distinguish the results of a search for literature from the literature actually reviewed. This distinction already reflects the tension between inclusivity and exclusivity. Scholars should purposefully engage and explicate this tension. Writers should examine counterarguments, marginalized research efforts, complexities, and publication bias (the likelihood that papers reflecting nonmainstream orientations or not significant findings are *not published*).

Existing Knowledge and More: Meta-analysis

Gene Glass (1976) coined the term *meta-analysis* to refer to the process of statistically integrating primary research studies. In meta-analyses, published studies are examined with the goal of synthesizing findings, controversies, gaps, limitations, and so forth across the existing empirical literature. Meta-analytic studies use publications as their data. An example of a research question for a meta-analysis study might be: What do research findings suggest about the likelihood that girls with Rett syndrome can learn to read? Mark Crowther, Wendy Lim, and Mark A. Crowther (2010) articulate a methodology for meta-analytic studies that detail the methodological decision-making that must be both enumerated and justified, including all the criteria presented above for thinking about literature reviews. Meta-analytic studies generate new knowledge through close analysis and examination of the details of many studies in a field. Quantitative meta-analytic studies draw on a large sample of studies and purposefully look for trends using statistical analyses. More recently, there have been efforts to conduct qualitative meta-analyses of qualitative studies. George Noblit and R. Dwight Hare (1988) used small clusters (4–6) of closely related studies to engage meta-analytically with the literature while Rona Campbell and colleagues (2003) settled on 10 papers that fit clear criteria. The meta-analysis itself was also qualitative in its approach.

Informed Decision-Making: Justifying One's Decisions

Through a relational orientation toward research, we can imagine that all our research decisions are potential topics of conversation. When scholars describe their research, they open the implicit opportunity for others to question them about their decisions. Thus, every methodological and conceptual decision should be justifiable in dialogic ways. It would be impossible in terms of time, energy, and publication requirements to justify all decisions. Nevertheless, in principle, the potential to justify is always there. Remember that the sum of researcher decisions ultimately produces findings: knowledge that is positioned through those decisions. Each decision should therefore be made in an informed way so that it could be communicatively justified to others.

Formulating Research Interests, Questions, and Hypotheses

The justification process involves explaining the link between methodology and research interests, questions, and/or hypotheses. Have you heard the phrase, "The research methods should fit the question"? While there are multiple ways to consider a similar phenomenon, social scientists have tended toward both methodological and topical consistency. There is a link between question and methodology, but this does not mean the question always precedes the methodology. These tend to work together in tandem. In this section of the chapter, we look at how researchers engage with the research process by articulating interests, questions, and hypotheses. Later in the chapter, we see that these articulations are connected to how the research project is designed and how data are generated.

Also, some interests and questions are researchable and others are not. The researchability of a question is, in part, connected with the methodological orientation one takes. For example, the classic question, "What is the meaning of life?" is not an easily researchable question in the abstract, and we find we can only really study such questions in the context of specific lives, as in "What is the meaning of life for you?" With this research question, we could generate data that elicit understandings people might have on the meaning of their own lives. Similarly, it would be difficult to study a question like

"Is there a God?" This question suggests that the existence of God is something that can be verified objectively, and yet the very concept of God is a non-objectifiable form of existence. However, the question, "Do people, in general, believe there is a God?" is researchable because it asks about what people believe.

Research Interests

Research interests, generally, reflect an intersection of researcher-related motivations and expertise as well as field-related needs. For example, Dr. Downs has established a career studying symptomology and life attributes of children identified with Rett syndrome. If you search Dr. Jenny Downs's work, you will see that her interests and methodologies have a synergy to them. Even in studies where she utilizes some alternative methodologies, engaging in observations, for example, the consistency of her research interests shows through, including work with her colleagues Xinhua Bao (2013), Philippa Carter (2010), and others.

Research Questions

Most researchers identify questions that guide their studies. These questions fit within the generally identified research interests. Minimally, such questions imply the scope, specific focus, participants/subjects, and relevant design features of the study. The best research questions are precise (both clear and parsimonious).

Let's look at a few examples. Dr. Downs and her colleagues were interested in exploring the relationship between genotype and the presence/severity of epilepsy symptoms among girls enrolled in the large-scale project ARSD (Australian Rett Syndrome Database). This interest was sufficiently precise for the research to proceed without articulating a specific question. However, a question could be easily inferred: What is the relationship between genotype and the presence/severity of epilepsy symptoms? When we read this, we immediately know that a relationship is being examined, that we need a way to draw genotype and presence/severity of epilepsy from the database.

Some research questions are more open-ended, but still offer enough precision to guide how the study might be organized. For example, a researcher might ask: What stories do family members tell about early years in the life of their Rett daughter? You can see that this is researchable and it is clear. It indicates the kinds of stories that will be generated. The methodological implications of the question make clear the range of possible methods that could be used (for example, interviews, focus groups, or questionnaires). We can also assume from this question that we are not measuring stories and instead will use narrative approaches to describe or retell the stories.

> **Pause and Reflect.** Read the following questions and articulate what methodological decisions are implicit in the question itself:
>
> - How do the amount and severity of seizures of patients with Rett syndrome co-relate with caregivers' levels of anxiety?
> - How do the amount and severity of seizures of patients with Rett syndrome differ across patients using CBD oil and patients using Valium?
> - What happens in classrooms when students with Rett syndrome experience seizures?
>
> From the questions one can also note what concepts, participants, and contexts are relevant to the study.

Hypotheses

In our everyday language we think of hypotheses as informed hunches about how things are or what will happen. In research, hypotheses are used to articulate objective outcome expectations. This is a highly technical effort that is part of organizing quantitative studies. Technically, hypotheses are used in these studies to set the precise examination of the outcomes. This is called "**hypothesis testing**." Researchers articulate a hypothesis in terms of what they expect in response to the research questions (this is called a **research hypothesis**). Then the negation of that hypothesis (referred to as the **null hypothesis**) is articulated and tested. Let's say the research question is, "What is the relationship between genotype and the presence/severity of epilepsy symptoms?" A research hypothesis relevant to this question might be, "There is a [statistically significant] correlation between genotype and the presence/severity of epilepsy symptoms for girls included in the Australian database [ARSD]." This hypothesis clearly states the expected response to the research question. The null hypothesis would be: "There is no statistically significant correlation between genotype and the presence/severity of epilepsy symptoms for girls included in the ARSD."

This very technical process is meant to indicate the way in which the research question will be answered through statistical analyses. The null hypothesis is what is tested (the word researchers use to imply that the hypothesis is being examined statistically). To test a hypothesis, researchers try to find No Relationship/Difference, and they try to establish the extent to which this absence of a relationship is at all explainable by chance. For example, if researchers want to know that there is a relationship between genotype and the presence/severity of epilepsy symptoms, they will analyze the data assuming there is *no relationship* while also trying to make sure that chance does not explain the outcomes of the analysis. In this highly technical use of hypotheses, answers to questions are reduced to rejecting or accepting the null hypothesis. The main point to know here is that research hypotheses are direct articulations of answers to research questions. One then either accepts or rejects the hypothesis. The null hypothesis is the one tested because it is statistically possible to rule out a negative claim, but not to rule out a positive claim.

However, there are controversies regarding the use and articulation of hypotheses in social science. First, there is a long tradition of hypothesis testing that has been under scrutiny recently. The idea of statistical significance in hypothesis testing involves how confident researchers should feel about rejecting or accepting the null hypothesis—that is, how confident they are that chance alone does not suffice as the explanation of the outcomes. However, statistical determinations of significance are affected mathematically by things like the size of the sample. Moreover, researchers do not get a sense of the strength of the significance from this kind of statistical examination. For these reasons, some scholars are actively advocating for restraint in the use of hypothesis testing. Additionally, publishers of quantitative studies are reluctant to publish findings that do not show statistical significance as not important.

A second controversy involves the usefulness of articulating hypotheses for qualitative studies. Some qualitative researchers suggest that any anticipated outcome articulated by a researcher is a form of a hypothesis. In other words, if researchers expect that Rett families will tell stories related to their daughter's development and regression, this could be considered a hypothesis. However, it is not very precise and certainly would not be a testable statement in the statistical sense. Many qualitative researchers do not use hypotheses to organize our studies, but when they are used, they function to articulate what the researcher expects to happen.

Generating Data

Back to the Rett conference we described at the beginning of this section—let's zoom in. In each session at the conference, presenters shared interpretations and examples of data used in studies to explain, describe, argue, and discuss the various topics at hand. In one conference session researchers used biological descriptions to explain why some girls with Rett syndrome seemed better off than others (some could walk and others could not, for example). The data were biological accounts of cell activity. Scientists found that each cell only uses one X chromosome, so a girl will function more typically given the extent that more individual cells in her body use the healthy X chromosome instead of the mutated chromosome. These same findings also help illustrate a potential cure—training or tricking cells into using the healthy X chromosome rather than the mutated one. Each presenting researcher established what counted as data for their particular research purposes and questions, and shared that data to help convince others of what they found through the research.

Let's zoom out. Perhaps a member of the association's administrative team wants to know which conference sessions were most significant for participants. The administrator could take up session attendance records as data to see which sessions were most attended. Perhaps the administrator could use session evaluations as data for establishing the effectiveness of the session. In this context, attendance records and evaluation sheets become data as they are strategically taken up for research purposes. This transformation process varies depending on what kinds of records are being taken up. For example, with attendance counts, maybe someone stood at the door with a clicker, counting people who entered the session. Counters would have been taught standardized rules for counting (for example, whether or not to count the presenters). Once each session began, the counter entered the clicker number total into a conference administrator database for the corresponding session. Then this database would be transformed into data by examining for missing cases and errors *and* by migrating it into a software file and format that could be used for analysis. The transformation in this and every case would be purposeful and strategic, which means that producing data always involves a researcher's specific intentions.

Designing Research or Creating Research Designs

Designing research is a complex, but specifiable, set of activities. Research designs are similar to maps we might use to navigate the research process. Some of those maps have more flexibility to them and some of them are fixed from the outset. Mapping out an inquiry process is one way of recognizing one's responsibilities and commitments as researchers. A map is a systematic articulation of paths, terrains, and so forth using accepted conventions. The *systematicity* of a research endeavor is one of the characteristics that move us from the ordinary inquiry processes we engage in our everyday lives to something we would call "research." We might get hunches or anecdotal reports of experiences that we might articulate as we tell stories of our ordinary lived experiences or of our everyday inquiries. We don't think of these activities as research, in part, because as our language suggests, they lack systematicity. For example, Barbara had a hunch that something was wrong with her guts, but she had to get more systematic in order even to have a better idea of the symptoms' patterns. In order to move from an awareness that there must be some underlying explanation for her bodily experiences toward being able to describe the patterns of those experiences, Barbara had to introduce some mechanism that would facilitate a systematic view of those patterns. Designs can do this. Research designs are both produced through a researcher's designing process and used by researchers to engage in the research process.

Designs always provide researchers with guidance in the research process and as such are usually justified and developed somewhat early in the research process. Some fields center around a standardized and narrow set of designs typically used while others have a broader tradition of design usage; this is something we learn about our respective fields when we carefully examine the literature. Designs are also inherently bounded and limited. That's okay. This boundedness is part of what it means to do research, and by creating and describing our research designs we make it possible for the outcomes of our research to be better understood within the context of its boundedness and limitations. One can never do research that does not have boundaries and limitations. Oftentimes researchers will first orient themselves through one of three overarching approaches—quantitative, qualitative, or mixed methods. As you know by now, these three overarching approaches already carry forward epistemological assumptions. Thus, by the time one is creating a research design, the process will already imply a set of epistemological assumptions and broad approaches. In fields with strong homogeneity with respect to both epistemological assumptions and approaches there will typically be a narrower range of designs used. The creation and articulation of a research design makes these more concrete and systematically establishes the particularities of carrying out the research. We can liken the research design to creating a roadmap. There are already roads; there might even be very specific roads you would be asked to take. In some cases, there might be only one reasonable road to take; in other instances it might make sense to chart your own road—but be sure to bring along that all-terrain vehicle!

As the metaphor of the "roadmap" indicates, researchers will toggle between a view of the design that is a description of the map from a more or less static third-person perspective and a sense of the map as a mapping of the movement or process of research across both time and space. The vehicle in this metaphor is what we have come to think of as the concepts and epistemologies we draw on both to choose the appropriate map and describe how we move through that map. If researchers want to go off-road, then they must be able to provide a robust description of the epistemological framework that will carry them through the process, enabling them to move from beginning to end. This applies also to the mixed-methods approach, where the epistemologies must explain the mixing.

In this section of the chapter, we organize our discussion through layers. The first layer has to do with the fixed or flexible nature of the design, and the second layer engages with specific types of designs. We find Colin Robson and Kieran McCartan's (2016) descriptive categorization of designs between fixed and flexible designs to be particularly useful, so we use that heuristic to present various ways of creating research designs for studies.

Fixed Designs

Some studies are mapped out using a design that is fixed from the beginning, with very little expectation that shifts would be necessary in the process of reaching an anticipated conclusion to the study. In fixed design studies, many of the process decisions are front-loaded and researchers then carry out that process with fidelity to the original mapped out path. A prototypical fixed design is the **Randomized Control Trial (RCT)**. The RCT is a study through which researchers identify a precise expectation regarding the effects of a particular intervention or controlled variable on a specified population. This form of design represents the most fixed of all social science research designs because almost all decisions are made at the outset with maximum possible control over how the study is conducted. These studies are most frequently conducted by generating quantitative data. RCTs match what we have been taught to think of as experimental designs. These kinds of designs have traditionally been used to make causal inferences (more about causal inferences in Chapter 10). By establishing the effects of one variable on another we are suggesting the possibility that one variable *causes,* to some extent, change in another variable.

Variable is a technical term for a specific bit of information collected with some *standardized* precision (more on variables in Chapter 10). Variables are used as a way to pin down or "fix" the object of interest so it might be measurable through quantitative means. In other words, with fixed designs, even the information being examined gets pinned down as a variable by means of definition and, also, use. For example, "independent variables" are those that are controlled in the study in order to see their effects on what we call the "dependent variable." Thus, in a study seeking to see whether or not the particular mutation of the X chromosome gene linked with Rett syndrome affects particular walking outcomes, the gene is the independent variable and the walking behavior is the dependent variable. However, in a study that seeks to see if walking behaviors affect the amount of seizure activity, the walking behavior is the independent variable and the amount of seizure activity is the dependent variable. There are several types of variables, and it is important to pay attention to the use of the variable in the study and how that variable is being defined and measured. This kind of standardization is crucial for fixed design studies.

In addition to RCTs, social scientists conduct varying forms of correlational studies also using experimental designs. With correlational studies, researchers examine the relationship of variables to one another within a specified population. Contemporary statisticians have developed sophisticated ways of examining how one attribute might or might not be correlated with another attribute, even to the extent that they can talk about levels of influence across several attributes in relation to a specific characteristic of interest. With **correlational studies**, researchers identify the attributes or characteristics they expect to see co-related; sometimes they are able to identity the direction of that relationship at the outset. The studies help to establish whether or not there is a correlation and what the strength of that correlation is, as well as sometimes establishing the direction of the correlation. Correlations essentially demonstrate how various attributes, including things like symptoms, co-occur. Though correlations cannot tell us about causation, when very strong and persistent across time and settings, they can indirectly indicate potential causes, where it might be impossible to actually do studies to establish causation more directly. For example, we would never want to conduct an experimental study where we assign some children to a condition of poverty and other children not to such conditions in order to see if there is a causative relationship between poverty and learning. However, if we have persistent and strong enough correlations of economic conditions and learning outcomes, we have enough knowledge to know that programs improving economic conditions for children might also improve learning outcomes.

When fixed design studies are conducted in naturalistic settings, control of variables and specificity of population become more difficult. Approximations of experimental designs (referred to as quasi-experimental designs) are attempted. Quasi-experimental designs seek to control potential influences on desired outcomes so that lesser-understood influences might be articulated. For example, Dr. Downs and her colleagues conducted a study using video recording along with other forms of data. For their study, video protocols were designed so that families could record, in their everyday contexts, daily living activities of girls living with Rett syndrome—activities like eating, grooming, social interaction, and mobility. Researchers created a detailed list of behaviors to be coded through the videos, including definitions and examples of those behaviors. This study examined the feasibility and validity of use of video for research purposes, which meant developing a standardized protocol for both doing the video recording and coding the video recording along with creating parent checklists. To use naturalistic home settings as a site for data generation, laboratory controls are not possible. Standardizing becomes a way to narrow control in noncontrollable contexts. Control, like standardization, functions on a continuum in research. Dr. Downs and her colleagues established protocols, guidebooks to help parents follow the protocols, and checklists to use as a way of "checking" the use of the protocols. They also checked to see how consistently raters coded the videos—in other words, checking to see if their standardized protocol for coding the videos was doing its job. Such studies do not have enough control or standardization of variables to wear the label "experimental," but enough to warrant the label "quasi-experimental." Both experimentally and quasi-experimentally designed studies are relatively fixed in the ways they are conducted.

Flexible Designs

As the category name suggests, sometimes researchers map out their studies with flexibility. An ethnographer might enter a particular school interested in how teachers care for their students. How much data the ethnographer will collect in what specific ways is only loosely mapped out at the beginning. The specifics emerge over time. New questions might surface, refined foci might develop, new participants might be enlisted, and so on. One might wonder, "What gets designed in a flexible design study?" First, it is important to note that within the domain of flexible designs there are some specific design forms that have consistent characteristics. When one of those designs is used, the research community expects some engagement with the set of characteristics known to be associated with that design. However, in general, naming specific designs is less relevant to flexibly designed studies than it is to fixed design studies. Instead, researchers map out some possibilities (such as intending to make classroom observations and, also, to interview students over the period of an academic year) and some beginning commitments (or example, to be at the school 4 days a week in two different classrooms and interview the students in those two classes). A peer might respond to this proposal by saying, "Well, if you are trying to understand how teachers care for students, you should also interview teachers—and more than two of them." The design evolves within the structure of something we would call an ethnography: It becomes a range of possibilities and rules or norms for moving through the map—like don't go too fast or don't fail to stop at major sites along the way. With flexible designs, at the end of the day, researchers will want to carefully describe the path they took. This requires taking good notes along the way.

Let's look at a couple of common flexible designs. We have already mentioned ethnography. Though the precise definitions of ethnography continue to be debated, Martin Hammersley and Paul Atkinson (2007, p. 3) identify common characteristics: direct involvement and long-term engagement of a researcher in the ordinary, everyday contexts of participants "gathering whatever data are available to throw light on the issues that are the emerging focus of inquiry." Geoffrey Walford (2009), a highly respected educational ethnographer, argued that there needs to be "long-term engagement, multiple research methods, and the generation of rich data," "theory-led," and "systematic" (p. 273). "Theory-led" refers both to the theory through which one conceptualizes the field situation—the school and teacher–student relationship, for example—*and* the theory through which the methodology is animated—for example, the epistemological claims that underlie methodological decisions. Ethnographies can, and often do, include both quantitative and qualitative methods for generating data and for analyzing them; however, we would not call a study an ethnography if there were no qualitative data/analysis included. Ethnographers aim to articulate an understanding of the lived experiences and practices of participants, and quantitative approaches alone do not suffice for this.

Another common flexible design is known as **critical participatory action research** (CPAR). Michelle Fine, April Burns, Yasser Payne, and Maria Torre (2004, p. 173) introduce CPAR as "an epistemology that assumes knowledge is rooted in social relations and most powerful when produced collaboratively through action." Participants engaged with researchers help to establish the research questions and interests. Participants help conduct the study and are involved throughout the process with outcomes of the research including dissemination for the good of the communities engaged. It is through these epistemological principles and research processes that CPAR is recognized. We already introduced the idea of action research earlier.

> **Pause and Reflect.** In interview only studies, various forms of interviewing are used as instruments to survey populations to generate data. Knowing this alone does not give you enough information to understand the design of the study, what would you want to know in order to have a better idea about a flexible design study using interviewing?

RESEARCH SCENARIO: STUDYING A RARE CONDITION: JENNY DOWNS

In the following research scenario, authored by Dr. Jenny Downs, we can see how the career of a researcher unfolds somewhat systematically through their research, but we also see how the passion and motivations of the researcher are necessarily involved in the decisions one makes about the kind of research, the questions, and the methodologies one engages. In other words, the researcher designing the studies is integral and instrumental to any design that is produced.

I first qualified as a physical therapist and worked for many years in the field of pediatrics. But I always wanted to find out how to better manage some of the problems children and their families experienced and was drawn to working in research. I was awarded my PhD in 2003 and have been working at the Telethon Kids Institute since 2005, working toward improving our understanding about disability in childhood in order to improve health and functional outcomes.

In my work, I have engaged with several rare disorders and one of those is Rett syndrome. Families and clinicians often have little knowledge about the trajectory of a rare disorder and how clinical issues should best be managed. I work to build and maintain databases specific to Rett syndrome that can provide the data to understand their natural history: from the early years through growth and development and then through to adulthood.

With a background in physical therapy, it is not surprising that I have led projects that help girls with Rett syndrome to learn new motor skills and to use those skills by participating in more physical activity. For example, I recently received a grant from Rettsyndrome.org to work with 12 young girls in China to test the effects of an enriched environment for building gross motor skills. Working with young girls, I hoped to take advantage of neuroplasticity where you are more adaptable and able to learn when you are young. The intensive intervention was held in a kindergarten-like setting and with practice the girls did learn new skills. This study helps us to understand that education and practice will result in learning and greater capacity for young girls with Rett syndrome.

I recently developed a quality of life measure for children with developmental disabilities such as Rett syndrome. I want to know more about Rett syndrome and what the best treatments and managements are, to enable those living with Rett syndrome to live their best quality of life.

We can see from Dr. Downs's researcher scenario that she is studying questions for which there are no ready answers. She has not posed questions through which she is trying to prove particular answers, and she does not always know what will be the best approach for addressing her research questions. She cares about the ways in which her research might directly benefit those with Rett syndrome and their families, for example, and her questions and methodologies are aligned with those motivations.

YOU AND RESEARCH

As we wrap up this chapter we want to think about generating data as an active process in which researchers are seeking both understanding and outcomes. We want to use the map metaphor to think about the big picture aspects of engaging with data.

When Interpreting Research

As we read and apply research to our practices, we want to encourage you to think about the context of the research, which includes researcher positionality and background knowledge. It is important to begin to articulate our own expectations about the research, given the research questions and interests. It is important that we are able to gather information about the research design used to organize the research process. Most important, as we read research we should always remember that the data are produced through researcher activities—they are not neutral and they are always situated. Wise uses of studies involve interpreting the research with its own context, background commitments, and characteristics of research in view.

Good literature reviews are important for both doing and interpreting research. Minimally, we should pay attention to the credibility and dates of the sources, the authors' purposes, and how inclusive/exclusive the review is meant to be.

When Doing Research

It is important to remember that as researchers we play an active role in the generation of data. Our engagement with data is part of an ongoing relationship of research and ideas in a field, our own positionalities, and the theoretical landscape. We used the map metaphor to talk about the ways researchers organize their work around data. For producers this involves acknowledging our positionalities, reviewing the existing literature and raising clear and pertinent questions, and thinking about how to design the study.

> It is important that we, as researchers, acknowledge who we are in the research process. Some research designs involve less personal input into the process itself, but our identities are never a moot point.
>
> When you write research proposals and seek IRB approval, you will need to be sure that your research interests and questions are relevant for the field, fit your own positionality, and are in sync with the way you design the study. Methodological theories can tie these together. It is important to begin reflecting your own positionality and how this influences your methodological decisions. That decision-making process should be documented. These aspects of the research process put specifics onto the map that you will continue to lay out with increased precision.

SYNTHESIS: POINTS FOR REFLECTION

Conceptual Synthesis

This chapter introduces us to ways of conceptualizing data. The most important conceptual point is that data are generated. Data do not just exist. In order to produce data, researchers organize their work by drawing openly on background knowledge and positions, posing questions, and designing a path. The organizing process is an articulation of the openness, research-ability, and systematicity of the study. It is important to think about the ways in which researcher identity is, should, or can be integral to the design and data generation aspects of creating a map for a research process or for assessing research. We are proposing a relational conception of research that is at odds with the idea of the neutral lone observer studying phenomena that exist outside and separate from one's self. We proposed substituting the conception of being an open-minded researcher for being a neutral researcher. There are ripple effects that would be associated with giving up the assumption of neutrality. It would be interesting and important to imagine those ripple effects. Early in the chapter, we offered the following contrasts: *openness*, not neutrality; *engagement*, not aloofness; and *criticality*, not proceduralism. In what ways are these contrasts problematic? In what ways are they useful?

Methodological Synthesis

There are methodological consequences of thinking of data as being dialogically generated. It is important to think through how communities of researchers might engage in activities that promote open-mindedness and methodological openness across both quantitative and qualitative orientations to data generation.

This cluster of chapters brings more of the traditional procedures into the conversation. There are tensions associated with doing this. What balance should researchers strike between being creative and critical, investing personally and engaging procedurally? The scientific method has succeeded in important ways using the epistemological framework that if similar procedures, tools, and definitions are used multiple researchers should be able to reach the same conclusions and thereby establish a body of confirmable knowledge. How can we understand this success and still think more dialogically and relationally? What role does criticality play in the conduct of research? What are the limits? And similarly, what is the role of the researcher and what are limits of that role? Are there ways to think about research as creative activity? In this chapter we try to introduce the methodological means to think through these questions, but the tensions are not resolved.

We used the map as a metaphor in this chapter. What are the limits of that metaphor, and what conversations does it leave out? Where does the map facilitate our thinking?

Personal Synthesis

We hope this chapter has given you the opportunity to locate yourself as a researcher, or as someone who benefits from reading research. We would like to invite you to think about what differences it makes for you personally to be the one either to conduct or apply research. Why you, and what is it about you that matters? How are you relating to the data and to the study? If we move from the third-person map to a first-person wayfinding—what is your path? This gets us into the on-the-ground movements one takes—how one navigates the map.

MOVING FORWARD

This is the first chapter in the cluster on data. As such, it is big picture–oriented. The subsequent chapters in the cluster will pick up these big picture aspects and fill in the details much the way a large map might have finer details for varying cities or segments of the larger terrain.

Further Readings

Blaikie, N. (2009). *Designing social research* (2nd ed.). Cambridge, Oxford, Boston: Polity.

Calvino, I. (1983). *Mr. Palomar* (1st ed.). London, UK: Secker and Warburg.

Creswell, J., & Poth, C. (2017). *Qualitative inquiry and research design: Choosing among five traditions*. Thousand Oaks, CA: SAGE.

Greener, I. (2011). *Designing social research: A guide for the bewildered*. Thousand Oaks, CA: SAGE.

Salsburg, D. (2002). *The lady tasting tea: How statistics revolutionized the twentieth century.* New York, NY: Holt Paperbacks.

Thorne, S. (2016). *Interpretive description: Qualitative research for applied practice.* Abingdon-on-Thames, UK: Routledge.

Urban, J., & von Eeden-Moorefield, B. (2017). *Designing and proposing your research project (concise guides to conducting behavioral, health and social science research).* New York, NY: American Psychological Association.

Further Readings by Jenny Downs

Boban, S., Leonard, H., Wong, K., Wilson, A., & Downs, J. (2018). Sleep disturbances in Rett syndrome: Impact and management including use of sleep hygiene practices. *American Journal of Medical Genetics, Part A*, *176*(7), 1569–1577. doi:10.1002/ajmg.a.38829

Downs, J., Blackmore, A. M., Epstein, A., Skoss, R., Langdon, M., Jacoby, P., Whitehouse, A. J. O., Leonard, H., Rowe, P. W., & Glasson, E. J. On behalf of the Cerebral Palsy Mental Health Group. (2018). The prevalence of mental health disorders and symptoms in children and adolescents with cerebral palsy: A systematic review and meta-analysis. *Developmental Medicine and Child Neurology*, *60*(1), 30-38. doi:10.1111/dmcn.13555

Downs, J., Rodger, J., Chen, L., Xuesong, T., Hu, N., Wong, K., de Klerk, N., & Leonard, H. (2018). Environmental enrichment intervention for Rett syndrome: An individually randomised stepped wedge trial. *Orphanet Journal of Rare Diseases*, *13*(1), 3. doi.org/10.1186/s13023-017-0752-8

Ho, P., Downs, J., Bulsara, C., Patman, S., & Hill, A. M. (2018). Addressing challenges in gaining informed consent for a research study investigating falls in people with intellectual disability. *British Journal of Learning Disabilities*, *46*(2), 92–100.

MacKay, J., Leonard, H., Wong, K., Wilson, A., & Downs, J. (2018). Respiratory morbidity in Rett syndrome: An observational study. *Developmental Medicine & Child Neurology*, *60*(9), 951–957. doi:10.1111/dmcn.13726

Mori, Y., Downs, J., Wong, K., Heyworth, J., & Leonard, H. (2018). Comparing parental well-being and its determinants across three different genetic disorders causing intellectual disability. *Journal of Autism and Developmental Disorders*, *48*(5), 1651–1665.

Shields, N., Downs, J., de Haan, J. B., Taylor, N. F., Torr, J., Fernhall, B., . . . & Leonard, H. (2018). What effect does regular exercise have on oxidative stress in people with Down syndrome? A systematic review with meta-analyses. *Journal of Science and Medicine in Sport*, *21*(6), 596–603.

Stahlhut, M., Downs, J., Aadahl, M., Leonard, H., Bisgaard, A. M., & Nordmark, E. (2019). Patterns of sedentary time and ambulatory physical activity in a Danish population of girls and women with Rett syndrome. *Disability and Rehabilitation*, *41*(2), 133–141.

Wong, K., Downs, J., Ellaway, C., Baikie, G., Ravikumara, M., Jacoby, P., Christodoulou, J., Elliott, E., & Leonard, H. Impact of gastrostomy placement on nutritional status, physical health and parental well-being of females with Rett syndrome: A longitudinal study of an Australian population. *Journal of Pediatrics*. [in press].

9

DEFINING DATA

Chapter 9 explores the nature of data, namely, what it means to label something as data and what practices are involved in generating and acquiring data. In previous chapters, we explicated how a researcher's positionality and everyday experience shape their commitment to and interest in performing research. Specifically, in Chapter 8 we proposed openness as a key principle for engaging in research. In this chapter we continue to foreground research as a multifaceted practice embedded in modern societies, as opposed to procedures following a set of fixed guidelines or established canons. We conceptualize the process of generating and acquiring data as a type of social action that shares some common ground with everyday actions but also maintains unique characteristics. Furthermore, we analyze data generation and acquisition from two dimensions: goal-orientedness and communicativeness. While goal-orientedness emphasizes an "I" position and communicativeness centers a "you" position, the end of this chapter explores the possibilities to forge a "we" position through research practice.

MUSING UPON THE EVERYDAY: HOW MUCH SHOULD I PAY FOR MY FIRST HOME?

Imagine that you are a first-time home buyer. After shopping around on the housing market for a while, you finally find a dream townhome in a desirable neighborhood and decide to move ahead to make an offer. But how? With zero experience in purchasing a home, you have no idea about how much one should offer for a townhome listed for $170,000.

On the way home from work, you run into two neighbors, a young couple who bought a similar-size home 2 years ago, and naturally you start to chat about the local real estate market. One of them says, "A townhouse like what we bought is very popular right now. Often, they are listed for 1 or 2 days and gone. Ours is probably worth $180,000."

"Wow," you answer. "The market is already so active? There is probably little space for price negotiation."

You think to yourself, "Of course, I do not want to pay an inflated price for a new home, but I do not want to miss getting the home I want, either."

Feeling a little nervous after this chat, you research more information about the local real estate market from a popular online website and find that comparable homes in your area were sold for $111,000–$138,000, much lower than what the seller of your dream townhome is requesting. Meanwhile, you consider several other issues related to the purchase, including how much down payment you could offer, the process of getting a loan, the trend of the local real estate market, and the marketability of the townhome. It is not easy to make an offer that is both competitive and affordable. By the end of the day, you decide to meet with your real estate agent again before making the final decision.

The next day, you are waiting in a real estate company's meeting room with a mixture of excitement and uncertainty when your agent arrives with a folder in hand. She hands you the folder and explains, "All of the townhomes listed here were in the neighborhoods you like and sold recently—mostly last year—for 150–160K, with just one exception. See, this one was in a very bad condition when sold and its price dropped accordingly. Also, keep in mind there will be about 10% rise in price each year for a townhome like this."

All right, now you must make a decision. Over the past 24 hours, you have gathered three types of information: your neighbors' estimate of the value of a comparable townhome, the information listed online, and the records of home selling from a real estate company's database. Which information serves as the most reliable referential point? In addition to the selling records, other factors also play a part in your decision. Some of these factors are related to your personal situation, such as how long you plan to stay in this townhome and the security of your financial situation. Others are contextual factors that different home buyers may all want to consider, such as the trend of the local real estate market and the rate of the mortgage loan. Moreover, how much you trust the expert, your real estate agent, plays a role in processing the information and making an informed decision.

NARRATIVE AND CONCEPTUAL INTERLUDES

Generating and Acquiring Data as Social Action

How is the use of information in an everyday setting, such as purchasing a home, different from and similar to the gathering and processing of information in social research? To answer this question, let's first consider the following two research scenarios, both of which are reconstructed based on existing studies.

Research Scenario 1: In an autobiographical article, Black mathematics educator and researcher William Tate shared a story about his difficult negotiation with his high school counselor and administrator to stay in a college preparatory physics class (Tate, 1994). The counselor and the administrator attempted to remove several African American students—but no white students—from the class on the basis of their academic performance in that one particular course. In spite of this challenging situation, Tate and his classmates were able to collectively negotiate to remain in the class drawing on multiple pieces of evidence—from the expectations the instructor of this specific course held of them to their above-average scores in prerequisite STEM courses. Tate noted that this was just on of the struggles that African American students are forced to overcome in their lives. As a successful math teacher and educator, he knows a teacher's expectations matter and are often associated with the assumptions that instructors overtly or covertly make about students' objectifiable characteristics, such as skin tone. How, then, shall a researcher study teachers' expectations toward their students?

Research Scenario 2: Sociologist Lauren Rivera (2017) was interested in examining the persistent gender inequality in the American job market. Specifically, she noticed that existing literature on this topic rarely studies the hiring process in academia. She wondered whether the hiring of academics, such as faculty members, perpetuates gender inequality in the workplace of higher education. After reviewing the literature, she focused on entry-level faculty hires, as this position serves as the gatekeeper for entering an academic career and profoundly shapes the demographic composition of work units in higher education.

As you can see from these examples, in both everyday life and social research settings, we seek to improve our understandings, make decisions, and take action through purposively collecting, generating, and interpreting information. In a research context, these pieces of information are called **data**. Much of our discussion in this chapter will revolve around the characteristics of data and researchers' activities to **generate and acquire data**. In the scenarios discussed above, how shall the researchers move ahead with generating or acquiring data? If we compare these two research scenarios with the everyday example of purchasing a home, what are the differences and similarities between the two activities?

The first thing you may notice is that examining data from the everyday could range from being very informal and inaccurate to relatively formal and thorough, whereas social research is usually more systematic. In Chapter 8 we examined how systematicity is manifested in the entire research *process*, from designing the study, performing the research, to linking the research practice explicitly to our philosophical and ethical commitments. Generation and/or acquisition of data, in this sense, is a part of this systematic process. We advocate for approaching it in relation to other research efforts such as conducting a literature review, formulating **research questions**, and analyzing data.

Second, you may notice that in both the everyday and research scenarios, gathering and generating new information involves intensive communication and coordination. In the home purchase example, if we consider the real estate market to be part of the social structure that both enables and constrains our actions, by making an offer the buyers explicitly engage with the market. As rational as it appears, a complex social action like buying a new home is simultaneously emotional and embodied. Sometimes, even the direction of the sunlight coming through windows and the view in the backyard influence a buyer's decision-making process. Similarly, a researcher setting off to generate or acquire data most likely will need to interact with research participants and coordinate a series of social actions. One cannot conduct research in a vacuum void of social, political, and cultural influences. Only by actively recognizing and reflecting upon these influences can we democratize our research process and build a trustworthy relationship with our participants.

This chapter opens by musing upon the relationship between research and everyday life in terms of the generation and interpretation of information. Next, we will examine social research settings to unpack two characteristics of data generation and acquisition—goal-orientedness and communicativeness—and link them back to other components of research practice, such as inference-making, research ethics, and validity.

The Intention of Generating Data

You may have heard the term *empirical research* and its distinction from theoretical research. This book, in general, is designed to introduce the basics of conducting empirical studies, yet it says very little about theoretical contemplation. But why do we put so much emphasis on empirical research?

An obvious answer is that, in order to address an issue in the world, one needs to understand the current situation. Take the two research scenarios discussed above as examples: From surveying the current knowledge about the phenomena of interest, the researchers noticed that neither topic could be sufficiently addressed without new information, which justified their desire to conduct new studies. Sometimes the phenomenon may not be entirely new to researchers, but in the hope of proving a hypothesis, testing a theory, or establishing a new interpretive framework, researchers systematically gather more empirical information. In both cases, the action is to know.

To know is to perform an action that leads to new findings or interpretations of the world and ourselves. *Knowing* is the intention that researchers hold while they move from articulating their research questions to gathering empirical data.

This strong belief that you need to know the world first in order to improve it is rooted in the long empiricist tradition of the Western world. For researchers holding "knowing" as their main intention in conducting empirical work, the next step—applying the knowledge to impact the world—is usually not within their immediate horizon. Policy-makers, professionals, and practitioners are assumed to be the major force of change in a society and therefore are supposed to utilize the findings from empirical studies to improve policies and practice, whereas researchers' primary goal remains producing knowledge and reporting their findings. Along this line of thought, it is important to ask in what sense the term *data* is taken up by different parties and stakeholders, for there is a tendency to assume that the more data one has, the more accurate the findings. For instance, examining the link from data to evidence and then to practice, educational philosopher Gert Biesta (2010) cautions us about the use of evidence and data in the surging movement of evidence-based practice. In particular, he argues that evidence based on the study of empirical data should not dictate the practice of policy-makers and professionals, as the reign of data could harm the profoundly contextualized nature of educational practices, making it difficult to democratize the decision-making process. He also warns us of the tendency to prioritize effectiveness, as defined in a de-contextualized fashion by certain experts, over practitioners' insights on concrete situations or judgments on desired values and purposes.

While the separation of knowing and doing may be predominant in research influenced by the empiricist tradition, the two can never be fully de-coupled in some other cultural and/or philosophic traditions. For instance, in the Chinese tradition, self-cultivation is an important form of knowing, and a person who falls short of putting knowledge into practice cannot claim to be a true knower. As Confucian thinker Wang Yangming succinctly explains, "There never have been people who know but do not act. Those who 'know' but do not act simply do not yet know" (Wang, 2014, p. 267). In today's research context, we can also see this orientation, which considers that to know is already to practice. For instance, in Chapter 3 we introduced the concept of action research. Recall how action researchers intentionally blur the boundary between a researcher and a practitioner. In this type of research, to know simultaneously means to consciously act to change the status quo. Researchers remain closer to the social problems in which they are interested, thereby bringing altering reality directly into their research purview. The process enables researchers to participate in various social improvement projects, including but not limited to advocacy and activism, community-building, and professional development. Meanwhile, researchers and practitioners within the loop of the action emphasize reflexivity and embrace the self-growth and self-transformation that research practice cultivates.

> **Pause and Reflect.** Let's review Research Scenario 1. If a scholar wants to conduct an action research study to raise STEM teachers' awareness of racial justice in a local high school, where should they begin? In what sense does *knowing* simultaneously mean *doing* for researchers and teachers? How does the researcher's research intention differ across studies conducted through different means, such as examining to what degree being placed in a college preparatory course may improve a student's math performance?

Intentionally Foregrounding the Rationale of Data Generation and Acquisition

In performing research, it is not enough for a researcher merely to lay out their plan to generate and/or acquire data; they also need to justify their proposed plan by explaining why it is the best available.

For instance, in Research Scenario 2, about gender inequality in professional spaces, the researcher started by examining gender inequality in academia with a particular focus on junior faculty searches. Existing literature has shown that gender disparities in entry-level academic appointments are diminishing. Does that mean search committees generally do not discriminate against female job candidates based on their gender when making hiring decisions? The researcher realized that, if that were the case, it would counter the suggestions that academic career consultants typically give to junior female scholars about hiding their marital status during a job search. When the researcher started this project, very little was known about the decision-making process used in a junior faculty search. This puzzling situation indicates that more work could be done to address the issue. The researcher used this rationale to justify the necessity of conducting a new empirical study on this topic.

As this example has shown, the action of data generation and acquisition is embedded in a chain of social actions from reviewing literature to analyzing data. What we call "data" cannot be separated from these actions in which multiple parties are involved. This process also encompasses a series of inferences based on which researchers make methodological decisions.

When you deliberately work out your plan to generate or acquire data, here is a list of questions that you may want to ask yourself:

Questions About Research Rationale:

- Why do I need empirical data?
- What data do I need to answer my research questions?
- Why do I need to use this particular type of data as opposed to others?

Questions About Research Logistics:

- Where shall I go and whom shall I talk to in order to acquire/generate these data?
- How can I access the research site and/or connect to my potential research participants?
- How should I record and store my data?

- How should I prepare my data so that I can analyze them thoroughly?

Questions About the Quality of Data:

- How do I know I have enough data?
- How good are my data?

We compile this list of questions to demonstrate the deliberate and systematic nature of data generation, which we will examine in Chapters 10 and 11, in greater detail.

Different Levels of Goal-Orientedness

In our previous chapters, we have discussed two different approaches to social research: qualitative and quantitative. Specifically, we reject a tendency to essentialize the distinction between qualitative and quantitative studies. In Chapters 4, 5, and 7 we demonstrate the possibility of establishing guiding principles for both types of studies on research ethics, philosophic anchors, and validity issues. It is in the inferences revolving around data that we see the divergence of qualitative and quantitative studies most clearly. While qualitative researchers mainly use textual and visual data, quantitative researchers need to turn their data—letters, words, or visual representations—into numbers. Depending on the forms of data, researchers then employ different conceptual and methodological tools to analyze them. For qualitative researchers, this usually entails exploring the contextualized, pragmatic, and culturally situated meaning of the varying forms of data; for quantitative researchers, data analysis involves a series of statistical calculations and the establishment of relationships among variables. Following divergent routes to data, qualitative and quantitative researchers also differ in terms of to what degree they are purposively oriented toward answering their research questions.

The distinction of the intentions of researchers-in-action can be further tied to our discussion of relatively flexible or fixed research designs in Chapter 8. In other words, research employing these two different design approaches differ in their **goal-orientedness,** namely, to what degree a researcher strategically conducts actions in order to meet preset goals of research. Quantitative researchers are usually able to narrow down their research questions to focus on a few factors through reviewing the existing literature, and when designing their research the process is relatively more fixed. They define how they will turn a concept into measurable variables (a process called operationalization), formulate research hypotheses to establish relationships among variables, and use predetermined procedures to collect data. As quantitative researchers move from one step to the next, their purposive orientation is foregrounded.

They intend to test already formulated hypotheses and answer specific research questions.

Compared with quantitative studies, qualitative research preserves more flexibility and nonlinearity in the data generation and acquisition process. Because many qualitative studies are exploratory and open-ended in nature, it is very common for qualitative researchers to enter their field sites with only a very broad research topic in mind. They collect information as it appears relevant to their research topics, and adjust their research directions as needed. Doing so allows them to be sensitive to various encounters in their research sites and, in some cases, let their research participants introduce them to social and cultural worlds different from their own. As qualitative researchers very often formulate and reformulate their research questions, they keep their data generation and acquisition as open, emerging, and long-term processes. Accordingly, compared with quantitative researchers, they engage in setting, adjusting, and re-setting their research goals more frequently.

Operationalization

A unique aspect of quantitative studies is operationalization, through which researchers measure social phenomena and turn them into quantified data, namely, numbers. Recall how you measure things in your daily life. For example, if you want to measure the length of a desk to decide whether it fits in your study, you bring a ruler to measure the length of the desk top and the space where you want to put it. You also read the number on the ruler to get your results. If your friend disagrees with you, they can repeat what you did and see if they arrive at the same conclusion. This is what we do often in our daily life, but what if a researcher wants to measure more complex conceptual constructs, such as teachers' expectations for students of different races and ethnicities? Where can we find the ruler, or is it possible to measure it at all?

The answer is yes and no. In Chapters 5 and 7 we discussed the distinction between objective, subjective, and normative ontological claims. In which category do you think a teacher's expectations for a student fall? Such a statement is usually articulated as "I believe that xxx is a good student" and you probably can keenly point out that it foregrounds a subjective claim. However, such a subjective claim is often complemented by a few relatively more backgrounded normative or objective claims. For instance, if the statement is "I believe Pengfei is good at algebra," then a possible underlying connotation might be an evaluative/normative knowledge claim: "Asian students are good at mathematics" (a stereotype for Asian students). Unlike objective statements, we can hardly use a ruler to measure subjective and normative/evaluative statements. What we can do, then, is to create a conceptual map to transform this overarching construct of a teacher's expectations into a list of concrete and objectifiable questions. For instance, in a meta-analysis conducted by Harriet R. Tenenbaum and Martin D. Ruck, they divided the broadly defined concept of a teacher's expectations into three subcategories: teachers' expectations for students in terms of measuring their capacities; teachers' referrals; and teachers' positive, neutral, and/or negative speeches (Tenenbaum & Ruck, 2007). Some researchers—as analyzed by Tenenbaum and Martin—created or used existing questionnaires to measure how teachers rate their students' capacity, others examined who are more likely to be referred to special education programs by their teachers, and still others studied teachers' expectations as manifested in their interaction with students through observing and recording their communication with their pupils. Eventually, what the researchers compiled from the completed questionnaires, the referral records, and the observational notes are quantitative data with social meanings. A "5" on the questionnaire may connote a teacher's perception of how consistently a student is able to grasp new materials, whereas the same "5" in the observational notes may indicate that a teacher delivers five sets of positive comments to a student in a given amount of time. Further statistical analysis can be conducted after generating these quantitative data.

The process of **operationalization** turns claims derived from different ontological domains into objective claims, namely, statements involving numbers that multiple people can access. A series of inferences renders this transformation possible. In a procedural view of social research, people tend to associate inference-making with the stage of data analysis only. However, it is important to keep in mind that operationalization already involves a series of crucial inferential relationships. By performing operationalization, researchers can measure social phenomena across varying contexts and assemble a large amount of quantitative data. Operationalization then allows researchers to use data to describe large-scale trends and make generalizations: Both aspects will be unpacked further in Cluster 3.

As helpful as operationalization is in quantitative studies, its limitations are also worth noting. In using a relatively standardized and fixed procedure to measure a social phenomenon, researchers unavoidably flatten, reduce, and miss the rich contextual meaning of the situation. For instance, if we ask a teacher to evaluate how persistent one particular student in their class is in a face-to-face conversation, they may talk for 10 minutes about this student and give us many examples. By the end of the conversation, we may know that the teacher speaks highly of the student because the student can keep up with their academic work in challenging circumstances, such as when food or housing is insecure in their family, or when their school cannot provide strong support for their growth. However, a researcher could hardly obtain this information by asking the teacher to fill out a questionnaire about the student's persistence. Therefore, some methodologists have reminded us of the risk of overrelying on operationalization. They caution the meaning of social actions is always embedded in concrete contexts and cultural traditions and any attempt to uproot meaning from its social and cultural contexts risks generating misunderstandings and oversimplifications.

Generating Data as Communicative Action

The above discussion foregrounds research practice as goal-oriented. Research goals may differ in different research traditions (knowing as opposed to doing; knowing = self-cultivation; knowing = doing = making positive changes). The level to which researchers' intention of generating data is foregrounded also varies depending on differential research designs. The goal-orientation feature leads to a consideration of *the I aspect,* namely, the goals and plans of, as well as the products created by the researcher themself. Another aspect of the same process is the consideration of *you*—the other party involved in this action, research participants. In conceptualizing the data generation and acquisition practice, we also need to take into account *the you aspect*—your time, your experience, your feelings, and so on. In this section, we unpack the *you* aspect through understanding data generation as a communicative action.

Many daily inquiries involve communication. In the example of making an offer on a townhome, the communicative dimension is foregrounded when the new buyer chats with their neighbors and asks the real estate agent for advice. However, in analyzing data for the "Researching Research" project, we found that relatively fewer students noticed the communicative dimension of social research in the examples they gave. Many described an image of a solitary individual wrestling with a problem all by themselves, such as burying themselves in piles of books in a library, or experimenting with different ways to solve a problem. They depicted skillful and goal-driven inquirers, yet seldom mentioned the role of communication in inquiry.

We suspect this is due to the fact that many of our students unconsciously took a stereotypical image of natural science as the prototype of social research. Highlighting lab work, measurement tools, and mathematical calculations, our students' descriptions assumed a subject–object relation in social research. However, it is worth noticing that even in natural science, as Thomas Kuhn has demonstrated, intersubjectivity plays a significant role in developing agenda, formulating valid approaches, and evaluating findings (Kuhn, 2012 [1962]). If intersubjectivity is often in the background of natural science research, it is much more foregrounded in social scientists' work.

A basic form of communication in both everyday life and social inquires is to ask questions. By asking questions, we invite people to share with us their knowledge, insights, and experiences. In the everyday setting, people are more casual about whom we should ask and how the questions should be approached. For example, we may ask our friends or neighbors for opinions and suggestions in an informal chat, just like the young home buyer and the neighbors, but in many cases, we opt for experts. As expert culture becomes increasingly dominant in the modern era, many aspects of our daily life have become increasingly professionalized and specialized. We outsource parts of our lives to people who received professional training.

In social research, we view our research participants as experts about their lives. Asking questions can take various forms in social research. Recall the distinction we make between epistemology, methodology, and method in Chapter 5. We can locate the various forms of question-asking at the method level, namely, that different methods provide us with "forms" to construct and approach our communication with research participants. For instance, in most one-on-one and group interviews and some surveys, a researcher asks their research participants questions in a synchronous, face-to-face fashion, whereas in many other studies that generate quantitative data, questions are circulated and answered in an asynchronous and written form, and then transformed into quantifiable data. Compared with inquiries in everyday life, researchers are more selective in whom a researcher should include, what information is most relevant, and how the questions should be posed. Also, unlike in everyday life, social researchers do not typically search for experts with professional credentials. What they look for are experts of a different kind—ordinary people with first-hand, lived experience.

Content-wise, researchers across many social science disciplines are concerned with the ways in which our society is organized and how people connect with each other. Just as the English philosopher Thomas Hobbes (1588–1679) famously asked five centuries ago: Why do human beings live together without falling into a situation where everyone is against everyone? This fundamental question about sociality is manifested in concrete scenarios from teaching and learning, recreation, to medical services and market activities. Communication and intersubjectivity underlie the study of social phenomena in various disciplines. Sometimes researchers directly observe real-time communication taking place in a specific setting, such as an educator teaching mathematics in a classroom, a search committee holding a closed-door meeting to make a hiring decision, a nurse taking care of their patients, or a group of hikers trekking in a national park. In other situations, researchers analyze written texts addressing a specific audience, such as entries on social media, policy documents, and historical archives. In this sense, producing data in social research always involves the objectification of communicative actions.

The *communicative feature* of data generation and acquisition has several methodological and ethical implications. Most important, it requires researchers to interact with their research participants based on mutual trust, egalitarianism, and transparency. Instead of thinking of themselves as goal-driven social actors, researchers should consider the position of their research participants in approaching the relationship. This, then, calls for the consideration of *you,* your needs, your time, your benefits, the impact of my work on you, in addition to a single consideration of *I*, my goal, my work, my project, and my career.

If we take data generation as a process of charting a common ground for the communication between researchers and their research participants, it requires a researcher to ask themself the following questions:

Questions About Researcher–Participant Relationships:

- How can I offer a safe space to my research participants, one that makes them feel comfortable enough to share their experience and allows them to be vulnerable?

- What can I do to better respect my research participants' time, culture, and way of life?

- How can I turn this research process into a beneficial experience for my participants?

- What can I do to protect the privacy of my research participants and the confidentiality of the data in compliance with the IRB guidelines?

Questions About a Researcher's Positionality:

- How does a participant understand me as the researcher and how does this understanding evolve over time?

- What presumptions about the participants do I bring to the research process and how does that manifest in our interactions?

These are the crucial questions that a researcher needs to ask in the process of data generation. Compared with the questions listed in the last section about the *I* perspective, you will find that these questions are asked from a very different standpoint. While the questions in the last section are concerned with what a researcher can do to successfully achieve their goal of generating valid data, the questions listed above require a researcher to take the position of their research participants and ensure communication is transparent, open, and respectful.

> **Pause and Reflect.** Let's come back to the two empirical research scenarios we discussed in the previous sections. High school teachers are occupied with their teaching responsibilities, and if you want to invite all the teachers in STEM disciplines in an urban school district to participate in a survey about their expectations for their students, how are you going to approach them? In our other case, the fact that search committees usually hold closed-door meetings indicates the sensitivity of this issue. If you want to sit in and observe a search committee's meeting in a private research university, how are you going to make the search committee members comfortable with your presence?

Putting the Two Dimensions Together

The *I* perspective and the *you* perspective, or in other words, goal-orientedness and communicativeness, are not mutually exclusive. Going back to the idea that data generation and acquisition fundamentally involve social activities through which researchers and participants interact, goal-orientedness and communicativeness are two intrinsic facets of these activities. A thorough consideration of both perspectives will allow researchers to address issues such as validity and research ethics more comprehensively. To illustrate this point, let's use the example of conducting a survey on high school teachers' expectations for their students' STEM performance again. A researcher could use several procedures to strengthen the reliability of survey research: They could administer the same survey twice to the same group of research participants at an appropriate time interval to determine whether the two sets of results are positively correlated with each other (test-retest reliability); they could use two forms of questionnaires to measure the same variable and check if the results reflect the same trend (convergent validity); they could also examine whether the research participants' answers to different questions in a survey are internally consistent (internal consistency). All of these procedures, if articulated clearly, serve to enhance the overall validity of the study, but to achieve a deeper understanding of the meaning generation process, the researcher needs to go beyond the procedural and goal-driven orientation to understand the communicative aspect of the activities. For instance, the researcher in this survey study should also be concerned with whether the survey questions are framed in a precise and straightforward manner to minimize the possible misunderstandings and confusion of the research participants.

In Figure 9.1, we use a coordinate system to illustrate the two aspects of data generation and acquisition: the horizontal axis to represent the dimension of goal-orientation and the vertical axis to represent the communicative dimension. We can then locate research activities/data generation and acquisition methods at different parts of this figure to demonstrate their different levels of goal-orientedness and communicative-ness. For instance, large-scale assessment, located at the bottom right of this figure, is a highly goal-oriented activity with minimum communication between researchers and their research participants. This is due to the fact that many researchers who work on large-scale assessment will not collect their own data; instead, they retrieve data from an existing database and construct their own data set. Since the establishment of a large-scale database requires a lot of cross-regional coordination, financial support, and human resource input, the databases are usually created by resourceful institutions and made available for different researchers to use. Therefore, individual researchers are not usually directly involved in the interactions with the research participants who provide information to the database. The generation of the data in this case is mediated by the institutional efforts of establishing databases. In other examples, such as online and face-to-face surveys, researchers have a clearly defined agenda and are involved in limited communication with research participants. Ethnography and participatory action research, on the other hand, are located at the furthest point from large-scale assessment in our figure. One reason for identifying ethnography as very communicative yet less purposive is that many ethnographers, when they enter their field sites, have only a general topic of inquiry they would like to explore and often adjust their research focus and specific research questions while in the field, as they intermingle with the communities that interest them, spending time with them, doing participant observations, and immersing themselves into the culture. In the same vein, we can pinpoint other data collection methods on this figure, such as survey and various types of interviews, on this chart. Offering an overview of the characteristics of different data generation and acquisition methods, this illustration by no means exhausts all methods used by social researchers. In Chapter 10 we will continue the conceptual discussions laid out in this chapter and further unpack the varying practices involved in using each of these research methods.

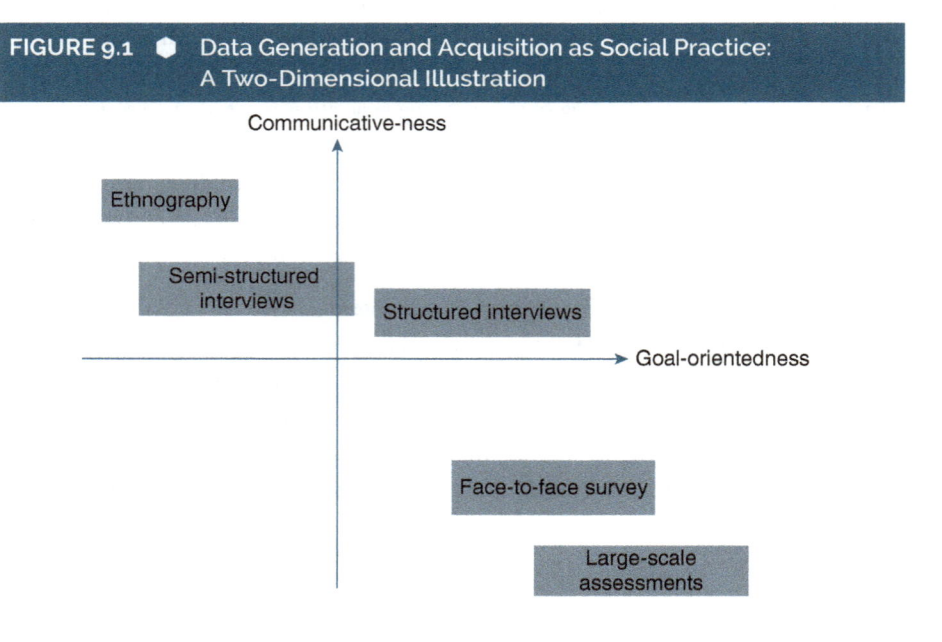

FIGURE 9.1 ● Data Generation and Acquisition as Social Practice: A Two-Dimensional Illustration

> **Pause and Reflect.** Putting the two dimensions together also allows us to explore the convergence of the *I* position and the *you* position. In some studies, it is possible for researchers and research participants to form a larger *we* position, which is born of a process through which data generation—as a nexus—lays a foundation for researchers and research participants to engage each other, explore a shared interest, and reflect upon the social phenomenon in question as well as their positionalities. By doing this, researchers and research participants may achieve consensuses and even forge a collective identity. Forging a *we* position requires both sides to be open to changes and to trust in the process as well as in each other.
>
> Going back to the two research scenarios we introduced at the beginning of this chapter, do you see any potential for the *we* position to emerge from those research processes?
>
> As researchers always need to deal with complex, concrete, and situated research scenarios, there are also situations when researchers and research participants find it hard to reach consensus. For instance, a participant may disagree with the researcher on the latter's interpretation of the data regarding the participant's experience. If you were this researcher, how would you address this disagreement?

RESEARCH SCENARIO: THE EFFECTS OF POWER ON ETHNOGRAPHIC RESEARCH: KE LI

As we explore the possibility of forming a *we* position in the process of data generation, it is important to notice the multiple layers of power relationships between researchers and research participants and the implication of this power relationship on the production of data. Researchers hold some privileges over research participants, as they are much more likely to be in a position to interpret and represent their research participants' experience. Being aware of this privilege and reflecting upon how it is manifested in different research contexts will help researchers democratize the research process. In reality, this power relationship can be very complex, especially when researchers work with a diverse group of research participants. In the following, our guest contributor, Ke Li, Assistant Professor at the John Jay College of Criminal Justice, discusses her fieldwork experience in rural areas of Southwest China, and candidly shares with us her challenges, struggles, and considerations of the fieldwork.

In an influential article, "The Extended Case Method," which was published in 1998, Michael Burawoy looked back at his experience as a white ethnographer studying the Zambian copper industry in the 1960s. To unpack how the whites had continued to dominate the industry, despite the formal dissolution of racism in the wake of Zambian independence, Burawoy enlisted the help of Zambian students to gather data. Doing so, as Burawoy noted, introduced layers of power relationships into his research: His own whiteness contrasted with the Blackness of Zambian students; and his status as the bwana *(boss) of the research team further thrust the latter group in a subordinate position in knowledge production. Indeed, we as ethnographers often find ourselves embedded in a matrix of power relationships. This matrix, I believe, is part of the very research process—intended to illuminate the domination, submission, and subjugation often at the heart of our research inquiries. Recognizing this reality means that we must carefully monitor the effects of power on the production of scholarly knowledge. In this regard, I have some firsthand experience.*

Between January 2010 and May 2011, I conducted field research in two rural townships in Southwest China. My goal was to examine how the rapid rise of divorce among an increasingly mobile population had impacted gender relationships, marriage, and family life in Chinese society. At the core of the research was my investigation of the grassroots court system's reactions to rural women's rights claims upon divorce. Shortly after my entry into the field, I spotted a hierarchy inside courtrooms, with judges sitting atop the official justice system, a market-based legal profession in the middle, and women litigants at the bottom—many with limited formal education, cash-strapped, and ill-informed of their lawful rights.

While navigating this hierarchized and gendered social space, I found myself wrestling with multiple power relationships. In the eyes of judges and court clerks, I was an intruder whose inquisitive gaze was unwelcomed. Not infrequently judges shut me out from court proceedings, even though litigants themselves had no opposition to my presence. When this exclusion happened, I had few options other than to endure it. The feeling of powerlessness and helplessness, in other words, permeated my interactions with institutional insiders. Meanwhile, a rather different set of power dynamics marked my interactions with women litigants. My status as a U.S.-educated researcher put me in a position of relative ascendency. From time to time, female litigants turned to me for legal advice and emotional support. Within this relational context, I became the one equipped with ample cultural capital and a clearer view of the official justice system. In short, I was holding plural positions in relation to my research participants.

This plurality of positioning vis-à-vis research participants was at once demanding and illuminating. It was mentally and emotionally demanding, because I had to frequently engage in power struggles with judges and court clerks on one side and disempowered women on the other. Regarding the former group, their permission was the key to my entry into crucial institutional settings (e.g., informal meetings between judges and litigants, mediation sessions, and divorce trials). To secure such access, I had to maintain a cooperative façade and to hold back negative emotions toward powerholders. These emotions ranged from mild irritation to outright moral indignation. In my interactions with the latter group, I was sympathetic and meanwhile had to constantly monitor my conduct, recognizing that I could subject divorcing women to a researcher's undue or unintended influences. For example, women litigants occasionally turned to me for legal advice for their divorce suits. This happened because some of them did not trust their paid legal counsel. As much as I sympathized with the women, I had to think long and hard, repeatedly assessing the potential consequences of my words and deeds. As a researcher, my job was to observe, document, and analyze women's interactions with the official justice system—not to alter such interactions. More important, my limited knowledge of judicial realities on the ground meant that my advice, even if consistent with the formal rules on paper, could wind up undermining, rather than helping, women's legal actions. To put it succinctly, from the plurality of my positioning as a researcher arose subordination to powerful institutional insiders in one scenario and potential, unintended harm to disempowered women in other scenarios.

Holding multiple positions in research processes, on the other hand, was immensely illuminating, for it enabled me to grasp research participants' lived experiences by situating myself in similar institutional environments. For example, as I struggled to access the court system, I came to discern the enormous power differentials between ordinary citizens and those on the bench. And I learned how judicial power was exercised oftentimes by controlling when, where, and in what conditions who could utter what. These firsthand experiences, in turn, helped me contextualize my inquiries into women's struggles with divorce litigation. Moreover, as I grappled with the salience of my status as a female researcher in interactions with male judges and legal professionals, I had to confront the entrenched gender order in Chinese society in a new light. To sum up, we ethnographers frequently hold complicated relationships with our research participants. These relationships, all too often, are a blessing and a curse at once, making it crucial for us to stay reflexive about the power dynamics that mediate our daily research experience.

✓ YOU AND RESEARCH

When Interpreting Research

When you read about empirical research, pay attention to the author's description of how the data were generated and/or acquired in their study. For a monograph, you can usually find such information in the introduction of the book, whereas for a journal article or a research report, most authors explain this process in the section about their methodologies and methods. First of all, pay attention to the description: What is considered data in the study? How does the author(s) generate and/or acquire them? Does the author(s) include a description of the research site? Who are the research participants? Do we know how large the data set is? How many types of data does the author(s) use in the study? Going beyond description, you can look

(Continued)

(Continued)

for the rationale that the author(s) provides to justify their methodological decisions regarding data. For instance, when looking at a case study, does the author(s) explain why this particular research site was chosen? If any questionnaires are used, then what makes the author think these questionnaires are most appropriate to measure certain variables? In terms of the researcher–research participant relationship, you may also want to look at how researchers interact with their research participants to build trust and democratize the research process. Researchers should also take explicit actions to ensure the quality of the data. Considering these aspects of an empirical study will help you examine and evaluate methodological decisions that the researchers made.

When Doing Research

Grounding yourself in a solid understanding of the research context and existing literature, you can now take one step further in your journey of social inquiry—generating and/or acquiring your data. We encourage researchers-in-action to notice the interconnections between what we have discussed in Cluster 1 and what is covered here, namely, that a researcher's practice of data generation is profoundly informed by the researcher's identity, positionality, and philosophic orientation. The awareness of this interconnectedness also taps into a key argument that we have been incrementally yet consistently building upon: that researchers make inferences at all stages of a project, not only that of data analysis. Sometimes, inference-making is manifested in a formal and explicit way, such as in the operationalization process in quantitative studies. In other situations, the research process is more exploratory, evolving, and iterative, and correspondingly, inference-making can occur in a more comprehensive and embodied manner. Either way, we stress that researchers should strive to be more reflexive and transparent about the assumptions and existing knowledge that they bring into their current practice and how the research process, while embedded and conditioned by the social structure and the material world, entails the production of a particular type of data.

In this essay, Ke found herself embedded in the very power relationships that she sought to unpack through her ethnographic work. She highlights self-reflexivity as the key approach to addressing the challenges she encountered in this process. Her insight sheds further light on the social context and structural issues behind research practice and leads us to probe the crucial question of the unbalanced power relationships in research practice.

SYNTHESIS: POINTS FOR REFLECTION

Conceptual Synthesis

In this chapter, we explored the methodological implications of understanding data generation and acquisition as social action. In particular, we discussed two dimensions of this action: the goal-oriented and the communicative dimensions. In our conceptualization, we demonstrate how the consideration from the "I" position and the "you" position entails a more comprehensive approach to the generation and acquisition of data. For instance, we noticed that, by conducting research, researchers set goals and employ various strategies to achieve them, but we also pointed out that the level of purposiveness varies across different research designs and scenarios. In the sense that data are always created by social actions, there are never raw data, but products of inter-subjective, objective-subjective, intra-group, and inter-group social practice.

Methodological Synthesis

In discussing each of the two characteristics mentioned above, we offered a list of questions to guide the move from conceptual understandings to methodological decision-making. We emphasized the need to justify our methodological approaches, which are both intrinsically linked to the validity of the study and reflective in nature. We also introduced the idea of operationalization and measurement. Both concepts are connected to our discussion of different types of knowledge claims in Cluster 1 and will be further unpacked in future chapters. Situating the researcher–research participant relationship in this context, we contend that building mutual trust with research participants and democratizing research processes simultaneously mean to address the power dynamics between researchers and their research participants.

Personal Synthesis

On the personal level, this chapter's topic is related to how we acquire and utilize information in general. We live in an era characterized by the explosion of information, which has become increasingly more accessible thanks to the development of digital technology and the prevalence of social media. However, the abundance of information, like a double-edged sword, creates both opportunities and challenges for our society. For instance, the popularization of social media has moved the burden of discerning the quality and validity of information from traditional gatekeepers to each societal member as demonstrated by the widely debated topic of "fake news" during and after the 2016 presidential election in the United States. In this sense, this chapter raised the question of how a responsible and concerned citizen can engage in informed public conversations. Meanwhile, it encouraged our readers to actively consider behind-the-scene issues when appraising and utilizing information presented by various media platforms.

MOVING FORWARD

In Chapter 10 we will introduce practical skills of data generation and acquisition. While it offers a survey of different methods widely used by social researchers, the chapter also uses concrete examples to demonstrate how researchers do their work in real-world research scenarios.

Further Readings

Fine, M. (1994). Working the hyphens. *Handbook of qualitative research.* Thousand Oaks, CA: SAGE.

Rivera, L. A. (2017). When two bodies are (not) a problem: Gender and relationship status discrimination in academic hiring. *American Sociological Review*, *82*(6), 1111–1138.

Tate, W. F. (1994). From inner city to ivory tower: Does my voice matter in the academy? *Urban Education*, *29*(3), 245–269.

Tenenbaum, H. R., & Ruck, M. D. (2007). Are teachers' expectations different for racial minority than for European American students? A meta-analysis. *Journal of Educational Psychology*, *99*(2), 253.

Further Readings by Ke Li

Li, K. (2015). "What he did was lawful": Divorce litigation and gender inequality in China. *Law & Policy*, *37*(3), 153–179.

Li, K. (2016). Relational embeddedness and socially motivated case screening in the practice of law in rural China. *Law & Society Review*, *50*(4), 920–952.

10

GENERATING AND ACQUIRING DATA

In the first two chapters of this cluster, we introduced data generation and acquisition from a conceptual standpoint. In Chapter 8 we discussed the nature of data generation and acquisition within the broader structure of the research process. Chapter 9 elaborated on the nature of data generation and acquisition in terms of the dimensions of goal orientation and communicative action. In this chapter we delve into exploring "what you do" in order to generate or acquire data as part of the research process. We begin by considering data generation and acquisition in the context of something many of us have done before: look for a recipe. We then turn to exploring different data generation and acquisition processes and products in the context of research. Our research scenario expands on this further using examples from our own "Researching Research" project, previously described in Chapters 1 and 2. Across the chapter, we raise questions related to ethical and relational dimensions of the data generation and acquisition process.

MUSING UPON THE EVERYDAY: HOW SHOULD I MAKE THAT LASAGNA?

In one of our introductory research methodology classes, an early assignment asked students to define research and inquiry. One student responded:

> *I will use my own recent experience as an example of research. A week ago I was interested in making the most perfect lasagna. My method of gaining information was to search recipes on trusted food sites. I analyzed data by finding both ratings and reviews of previously attempted recipes. My final conclusion was made by selecting the recipe with the highest average rating of success.*

The process this student described is likely familiar for many of us, either in the context of cooking, choosing which version of a certain product to buy, or otherwise in our daily lives. No matter the context, we all collect information to help us answer questions we need or want to answer. But how do we go about it? What filters do we use when there is so much information "out there"? What does it mean to acquire information that already exists, as opposed to generating new information? These are the questions we will focus on in this chapter. Before jumping into the discussion, take a moment to think about another kind of experience with information gathering.

> **Pause and Reflect.** Think about the last academic paper you wrote. What kinds of information did you use to formulate and substantiate your argument—what did you decide "counted" as evidence? How did you find that information and how did you decide which sources of information were best suited to addressing the points in your argument?

NARRATIVE AND CONCEPTUAL INTERLUDES: A DAY IN THE LIFE OF A RESEARCHER

In this section of the chapter, we use the narrative of an action research project undertaken by one of our students to deepen our discussion of data, and to introduce central concepts related to data generation and acquisition: data as *process* and data as *product*. We aim to tease apart the multiple dimensions of this term *data* that is used so often in research, to highlight assumptions often made about what kind of information can be generated, and to discuss how we can use that information as the basis for forming conclusions and/or making decisions.

In an assignment for one of our methodology courses, a student wrote about working for a local winery. She described her professionally oriented research in this way:

> *This past October, a local winery opened its first satellite location. We are essentially a wine bar, a tasting room, and a restaurant. We offer table service, tasting and bar service, and event space. Because this space is very different from the main winery location, there has been a lot of learn-as-we-go. When I read about action research for class, I thought this is what we do downtown! A group of us have worked there from day one and have gone through the bumps, the challenges, the ups, and the downs. Because of this, we have all become researchers. We have discovered things that do not work in this setting and we have discussed them as a team and come up with new ways of approaching the tasks. We have taken the time to observe if new ways are working and continued to make suggestions to fine-tune them into great practices. This really has been a team effort*

as well, which is something else that stuck out to me about action research while I was reading. We all use what we are learning on a day-to-day basis in order to help improve the way that work functions in this arena.

The process of opening a new eating/drinking facility is always challenging. Although this student's narrative is short, you can begin to get a sense from what she wrote that the winery opening involved an iterative process of gathering information. Let's talk about that in more detail.

Data as Process: Generating and Acquiring Data

In this narrative, our student writes about learning whether changes she and her colleagues made had worked. What the student refers to, though without using the term, is the process of **observation**, a form of data generation that emphasizes systematically paying attention to what is happening in one's research setting. It is sometimes referred to as "naturalistic observation," a term coined by Lincoln and Guba (1985) to highlight that the elements being observed are activities that occur naturally, rather than situations that are controlled or manipulated by researchers (as might occur in laboratory settings). In formal research contexts, observation as a data generation process often is utilized in settings where researchers are trying to understand cultures, groups, or relationships between groups. For instance, a researcher interested in the organizational culture of the new winery location might note where employees gather for informal conversations, what kinds of interactions occur between employees in different departments or at different levels of seniority, (lack of) hierarchy in staff culture, and so forth. These kinds of observations help the researcher learn more about the characteristics of the organization and what makes it unique (or not). Such observations may take different forms: Some situations call for **participant observation**, where the person doing the observing (the researcher) is also involved in what is happening. In other cases, the observer may be someone who comes from outside the context. For example, an outside consultant might observe workplace dynamics in order to provide feedback to employers about challenges faced by their employees. In this case the consultant will almost certainly not take part in any typical workplace activities but will likely act like a "fly on the wall" to try to understand what is going on from an outsider's perspective.

While our student mentioned observation, there are other ways she and her team could learn about what was working and what was not. Perhaps the winery could have asked customers to respond to a short set of written questions about what they enjoyed or was problematic about their experience. This would entail using **survey methods**: a form of data generation where researchers use questionnaires to ask a standard set of questions to a large number of research participants, often with a goal of understanding patterns. Surveying may take several forms, including telephone, paper and pencil, or electronic questionnaires disseminated via the internet. Most questionnaires primarily utilize closed-ended questions with limited response options to survey the population of interest. Multiple-choice questions or items where respondents indicate, with a set of 5–7 response options, how strongly they agree/disagree with some statement are most typical. Closed-ended questions facilitate analysis that allows for comparison across the responses provided by participants and enable researchers to make claims about patterns across respondents.

Another approach the winery staff could use to learn about what is (not) working is **experimental design**. This is a research design (rather than a specific data generation technique) that is used to make **causal** inferences, which we first discussed in Chapter 8, and which focus on whether a change in some **variable** being manipulated (the **independent variable**) leads to or *causes* change in another variable (the **dependent** variable). Remember that in Chapter 8 we defined variables as information collected with standardized precision. We can also think of variables as specific characteristics, which, as we discussed in Chapter 9, are operationalized or mapped onto the objective domain for measurement.

Experiments may use a number of techniques for generating data (such as surveys, structured observations, and so on). For instance, the Oliver Winery staff might conduct an experiment by manipulating just one aspect each evening about the room setup, such as where dining tables are placed: This would be the **independent variable**. Everything other than the room setup (e.g., how many people at a table, the way food/drink orders are taken, interaction between bar service and table service, and so on) would need to remain the same. These elements are **control variables**, which are kept the same under different experimental conditions in order to test whether it is actually the independent variable that leads to change in the dependent variable. By keeping everything but table locations the same, the team could test whether changes in the independent variable (room setup) lead to changes in a dependent variable of interest, such as the speed at which food arrives to diners once it is prepared. The relationship between these variables is summarized in Figure 10.1.

Let's talk a bit more about variables. When putting their experiment together, Oliver Winery staff will need to consider the **types of variables** they are examining. First, they will need to note whether these are **categorical** variables, which reflect distinct categories of some characteristic, or **continuous** variables, which have numerical values and can be measured on a continuum. An example of a categorical variable is an item on a survey asking someone about their religion, with five to six options listed. Although each option is different, there is no inherent value attributable to the different options a survey respondent might pick—"Jewish" as a category is no better or worse than "Agnostic" or "Protestant" or "Buddhist." When there is no rank order possible, categorical variables are called **nominal variables**. When a rank order *is* possible, categorical variables are

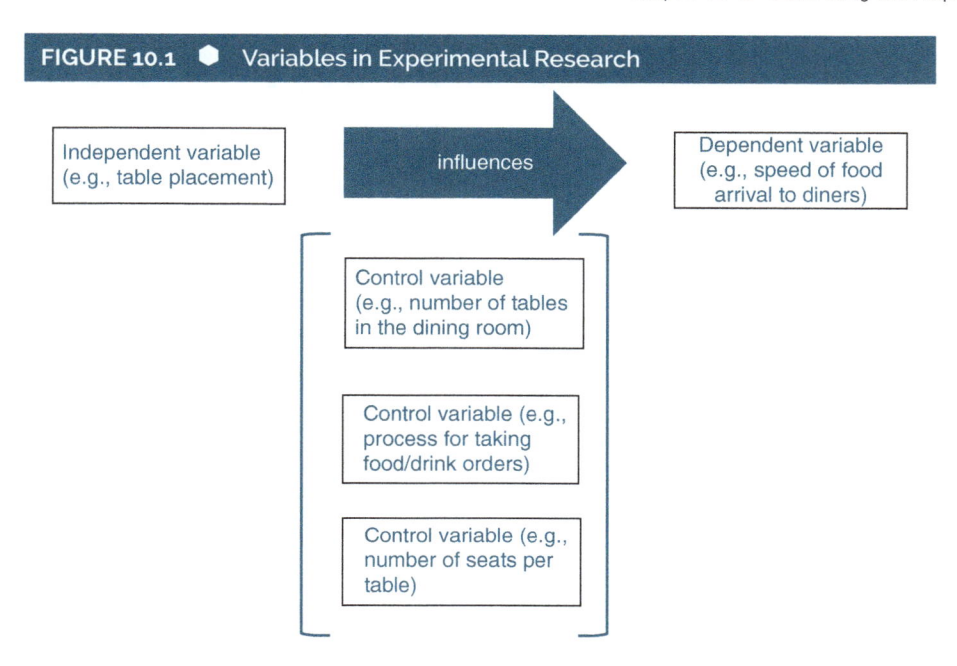

FIGURE 10.1 • Variables in Experimental Research

```
Independent variable          influences          Dependent variable
(e.g., table placement)      ──────────▶         (e.g., speed of food
                                                  arrival to diners)

                    Control variable
                    (e.g., number of tables
                    in the dining room)

                    Control variable (e.g.,
                    process for taking
                    food/drink orders)

                    Control variable (e.g.,
                    number of seats per
                    table)
```

called **ordinal variables**. Ordinal variables are ones that typically ask about things like how much you disagree/agree with some statement, or that ask you to give a response "on a scale of 1–5" (this is often referred to as a Likert item). While there is an assumed rank order between responses in ordinal variables (e.g., from least positive response [disagree] to most positive response [agree]), this rank order has no inherent numerical meaning.

Continuous variables (further classified into **interval** and **ratio** variables) differ from categorical variables in that they have inherent numerical properties. The difference between interval and ratio variables is in whether a measurement of zero on a numerical scale means that there is none of something. For instance, temperature measured in Fahrenheit uses an **interval** scale, because 0 degrees Fahrenheit does not mean absolute zero (this is only true when measuring temperature in degrees Kelvin). A measurement of distance, on the other hand, is a **ratio** variable, because 0 means that there is no distance between the units measured.

These variable types are summarized in Table 10.1.

Back to the winery learning processes the staff could use. Let's imagine that while cleaning out a back room in preparation for opening, staff members discovered notes taken by previous owners of the space, discussing the perfect setup for a restaurant. The team could examine these notes and make decisions based on what they state. In this case, the team would be using existing information rather than generating it themselves. This

TABLE 10.1 Variable Types

Categorical variables	**Nominal variables**: No rank order possible
	Ordinal variables: Assumed rank order, but order has no inherent numerical significance
Continuous variables	**Interval variables**: Numerically significant with equal distance assumed between numbers
	Ratio variables: Numerically significant with equal distance assumed between numbers; zero on a ratio scale means there is none of that unit of measurement

would therefore reflect what we refer to as **data acquisition**, the process of using existing data to create a new data set for analysis. An analogous example from the beginning of the chapter is trying to figure out the best recipe for lasagna by looking at different recipe sites. Data acquisition is common in social science research, such as when studies examine relationships between variables included in data from the U.S. Census. In this kind of research, researchers make choices not about what data to generate but about what components of existing data to use in analysis.

We can think of the treasure trove of notes from previous restaurant iterations as **archival data**. Archival data are not always originally generated for research purposes. For example, letters exchanged between individuals are often used sources for writing biographies. These letters were not initially written for research purposes but rather are historical artifacts, originally written for the purpose of personal correspondence. This makes the letters different than U.S. Census data or other data that were generated for research purposes but might be used by many different researchers to answer new or different research questions.

Finally, staff might speak directly to people who come to the winery to eat or drink. In one-on-one **interviews**, the staff might ask questions to learn more about the experience of these individuals at the new location. They might also conduct a **focus group**, bringing together a group of people to answer questions similar to those that might be asked in individual interviews. Both these techniques differ from survey research in that, even though questions are often set ahead of time (in the form of an **interview protocol**), the questions are open-ended. In the winery context, the team might use interviews or focus groups to try to learn from diners what was most enjoyable about their experience at the new winery location, what they felt was problematic, or about any ideas they might have for improvements. Individual interviews might be a better choice for situations where researchers (or the staff, in this case) are interested in understanding experiences of each participant in greater depth; focus groups, on the other hand, might be better suited for contexts where the research emphasis is on similarities and differences among multiple participants (for instance, in the winery case, where diners converge or diverge in terms of their perspectives on the dining experience overall).

In Table 10.2 we summarize some of the key aspects of the data generation and acquisition processes discussed earlier.

The processes we have discussed so far are only a few of the many different approaches used to generate or acquire data for research. Figure 10.2 includes these processes as well as other techniques for generating and acquiring data. The figure is nonetheless incomplete—these processes are developed, combined, and adapted constantly. The figure presents these processes in the context of *communicativeness* and *goal-orientedness* discussed in Chapter 9, illustrating the degree to which each method foregrounds communicative processes as well as the degree to which it is oriented toward an explicit, concrete goal (e.g., answering a very specific research question or set of questions). As you consider these approaches, think about which appeal to you most—and how you might connect these preferences with discussions earlier in the textbook about epistemological commitments and worldviews.

TABLE 10.2 ● Data Generation Processes

Data Generation Process	Used Primarily For	Example	Strengths and Limitations	Possible Ethical Issues
Observation (including participant observation, unstructured observation, structured/behavioral observation)	Understanding what occurs in a given research setting	Ongoing observation of a classroom in order to understand the ways that different groups of students interact	Can provide insight into behaviors and relationships as they occur in natural settings. Researchers may misunderstand what they observe without other forms of data as corroboration.	In contexts where researchers spend a lot of time in an observation setting, they may establish relationships with research participants that transcend the research relationship. This can blur the lines between observation and other forms of interaction and can result in misunderstandings or use of data in problematic ways.

(Continued)

(Continued)

Method	Purpose	Example	Strengths	Limitations
Survey methods (including face-to-face surveys and online/written surveys)	Exploring trends or patterns in a large population	Seeking feedback on instructors' approaches to integrating technology into language learning classrooms	Provide insight into patterns across a large group. Can provide easily standardizable data. Do not reflect nuance in respondents' perspectives. Survey items can be manipulated to produce certain results (such as the survey question about the Super califragilisticexpialidocious Antibullying Program in Chapter 4).	Wording of questions may render the identities of marginalized participants invisible. Decisions must be made about how to deal with missing data.
Experiments	Understanding cause and effect relationships between variables	Testing whether a new medication is effective (in comparison to another medication or to no medication)	When set up well, can provide evidence of causal relationships. Difficult to control for all variables.	Interventions may provide benefits only to treatment group members but not members of the control group.
Interviews (including unstructured interviews, semistructured interviews, structured interviews)	Understanding the perspectives or beliefs of individuals	Exploring the experiences of immigrants in terms of their adaptation to a new environment	Provide rich, nuanced insights into beliefs, opinions, and emotions. Difficult to get a representative sample. Time-consuming and thus often limited in terms of number of interviews conducted.	Decisions about location of interview, language used, etc., may potentially make participants uncomfortable. Power dynamics between researcher and participants may lead participants to feel they must respond to questions in certain ways.

| Focus groups (including sharing circles, interpersonal process recall discussions) | Understanding the perspectives or beliefs of a group | Survivors of domestic violence jointly discussing their experience of navigating the separation process from their partners | Can provide rich insights into a range of different perspectives. Groups are often not fully representative of the target population. | Choices about location and language may be more difficult because of differing needs among participants. Power dynamics between researcher and participants may lead participants to feel they must respond to questions in certain ways. |

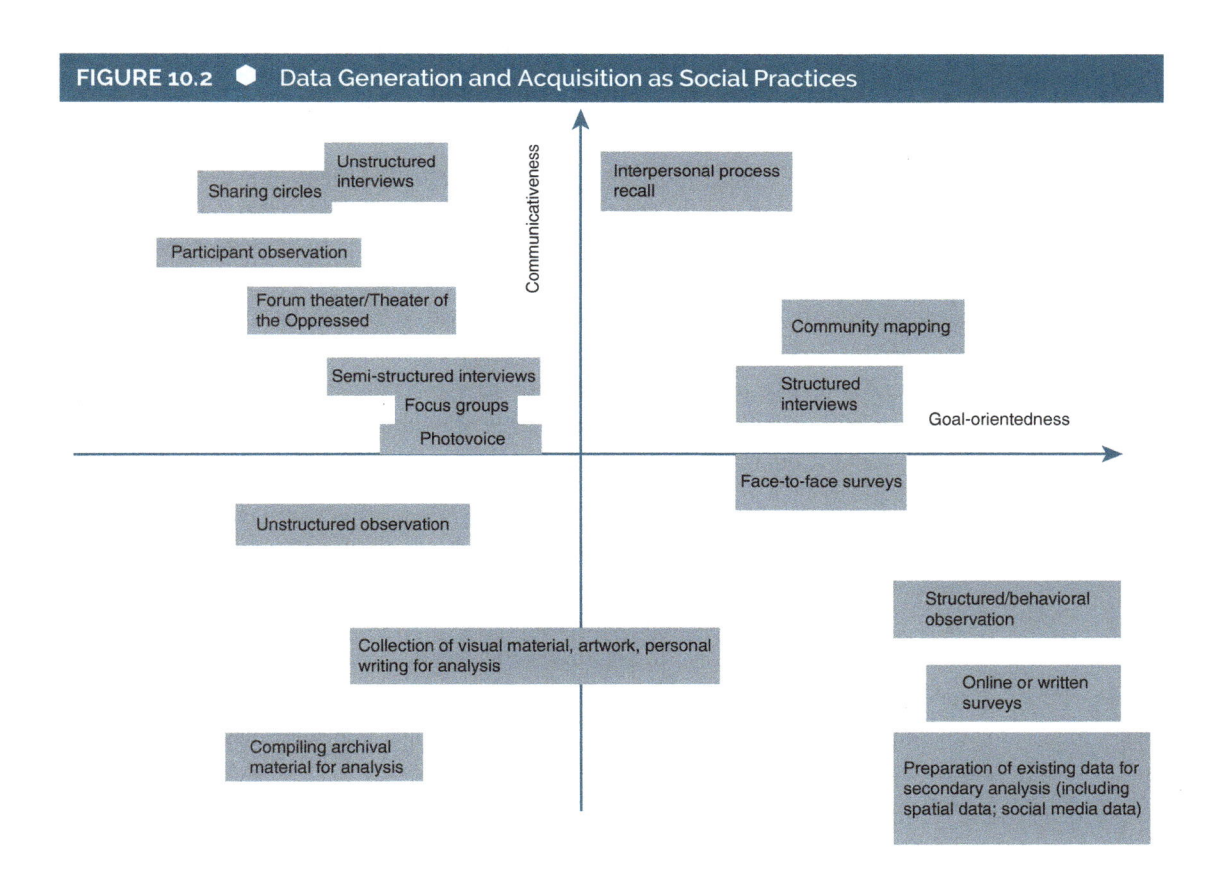

FIGURE 10.2 ● Data Generation and Acquisition as Social Practices

Axes: Communicativeness (vertical) and Goal-orientedness (horizontal)

Upper-left quadrant (high communicativeness, low goal-orientedness):
- Sharing circles
- Unstructured interviews
- Participant observation
- Forum theater/Theater of the Oppressed
- Semi-structured interviews
- Focus groups
- Photovoice

Upper-right quadrant (high communicativeness, high goal-orientedness):
- Interpersonal process recall
- Community mapping
- Structured interviews
- Face-to-face surveys

Lower-left quadrant (low communicativeness, low goal-orientedness):
- Unstructured observation
- Collection of visual material, artwork, personal writing for analysis
- Compiling archival material for analysis

Lower-right quadrant (low communicativeness, high goal-orientedness):
- Structured/behavioral observation
- Online or written surveys
- Preparation of existing data for secondary analysis (including spatial data; social media data)

The Process of Generating and Acquiring Data: What Researchers Do

Having thought about different data generation and acquisition processes, let's talk a bit about how researchers make choices about which approach to use and the implications of these choices.

Fundamentally, the basis for data generation and acquisition decisions is linked to beliefs about the nature of the world (ontology) and how we can know about that world (epistemology), as discussed in the Cluster 1 chapters. For instance, a researcher who believes that intelligence is "something that exists" independently of social interactions, and who believes that we can know about intelligence by measuring it in a standardized way, is more likely to conduct research about intelligence using standardized IQ tests than a researcher who believes that intelligence is a social construct that cannot be understood using only techniques that focus on objective knowledge claims. It is important to emphasize that data generation processes are not inherently tied to a specific kind of ontological or epistemological claim. Moreover, data generation techniques are not mutually exclusive—researchers can, and often do, use more than one.

The ontological and epistemological basis for decisions about data generation and acquisition processes is often very implicit, or backgrounded. Also fairly backgrounded are issues related to the individual identity of researchers. For example, researchers need to consider how comfortable they might be interacting directly with research participants or spending long periods of time "in the field." Some researchers might prefer a more distant form of data generation, such as survey research. The identity of researchers also needs to be considered in terms of their positionality with respect to both the research topic and specific elements of data generation. Researchers should be reflective about the way that their own background and experiences shape their understanding of certain topics, as well as how these can influence, for instance, the wording of questions they might use in interviews or questionnaires.

More explicitly, researchers make decisions based upon what they believe will generate data best addressing the research questions asked—a decision that is made within the broader context of methodological approaches and design considerations relevant to a particular study. As one example of this more foregrounded relationship between methods and research questions, interviews can be helpful for gaining an in-depth understanding of individual perspectives, but researchers are limited in how many interviews they can conduct compared with the number of people who might respond to similar, but less in-depth, questions using a survey. Thus, if researchers are interested in learning about patterns or trends among a large group, survey methods may make more sense.

When researchers make these decisions, multiple issues must be considered. For example, when conducting interviews or focus groups, researchers must choose who will be interviewed, or what their **sampling strategy** will be (something we will discuss more in Chapter 11). At the winery, the team might consider whether to interview regular diners or individuals coming in for the first time; whether to interview all patrons at a table or pick interviewees based on certain other characteristics, such as their food order or the day of the week when they are there. Each would lead them to learn about different aspects of the dining experience, so the team should consider whose perspectives are most important for addressing their research questions.

Once a sampling strategy is established, another important consideration is where and when to hold an interview, as this can shape interviewees' comfort levels. For instance, conducting an interview about someone's dining experience at a restaurant, where the waiter/waitress who served them and/or the chef who prepared their meal might be present, might lead an interviewee to feel uncomfortable about reflecting honestly. In focus groups, what is considered a "neutral" location also might differ from participant to participant. Moreover, researchers should consider relational and ethical dimensions of data generation, particularly as these are reflected in what they tell participants about themselves and the research project. As we discussed in Chapter 3, how researchers present themselves to interviewees shapes the kinds of relationships and levels of trust that are built with participants and thus how open they will be when sharing their thoughts, especially about topics they find emotionally challenging to discuss. In the micro-context of the researcher–participant interaction, it's also important to pay special attention to potential negative aspects of the interaction, and make decisions about how to proceed based on the concepts of intersubjectivity and care discussed in Chapter 4.

Conducting observations leads to similar considerations. Moreover, in long-term ethnographic studies as well as shorter research projects, researchers should consider what counts as data when they interact with individuals beyond the "formal" observation context. Here's an example: Someone brought into the winery to assess best approaches for setup might spend time there relaxing and having a drink, or informally conversing with kitchen and wait staff. At a certain point, this person will need to consider how to use any data that are generated in these moments—for instance, if a waiter/waitress complains about another member of the restaurant staff when carpooling home with the researcher, is this a piece of data? Decisions about issues like these entail considerations about situational as well as procedural ethics, care, and the process of community-building that are often a part of observational research.

Survey dissemination entails some of the same, but also different considerations than data generation processes that foreground personal interactions. For instance, researchers must decide how to word questions or what terms to use. An example in the winery context might be how to create a survey about ease of movement through the dining room. A survey question could state something like, "On a scale of 1–5, how comfortable did you feel getting from the front door to your table?" This would generate different responses than a question asking, "Was the space between tables sufficiently large so that you did not bump into anything on your walk from the front door to your seat? Please respond yes/no/other (if other, please explain)." Unlike the first question, which leaves the definition of "comfort" open, the second question asks about a specific issue that might affect comfort: space between tables. As we discussed in

Chapter 4, moreover, how questions are worded has implications for who benefits and who is harmed by certain definitions or terms. For example, many surveys include questions about demographics—age, race, and so on—where participants are provided with a list of options. Decisions about what categories to include in demographic questions about, say, sex or gender, or race and ethnicity, can potentially be harmful to participants from marginalized groups. As one example, choosing to limit options about gender to "male" and "female" normalizes a binary view of gender and renders invisible those individuals who identify as gender nonconforming, genderqueer, trans, or other.

Decisions to be made also arise in the context of experimental research. In the social sciences, "true" experiments—where participants are assigned randomly to be part of the "treatment" or "control" group, and where the environment itself is controlled in order to ensure that *only* the variables of interest are affected—are almost never possible. Instead, researchers generally conduct quasi-experiments, where participation in the "treatment" or "control" group is decided based on factors outside the researcher's control. For instance, in the winery experiment discussed earlier, the team would not be able to randomly assign diners (or even staff) to come to the restaurant on nights when there were different room configurations, but would have to rely upon the perspectives of the individuals who independently made the decision to show up (or were assigned to work) that night. Depending on what is most important to them to know about the room setup and how to ensure a smooth dining/working environment, the team would need to decide what specific characteristic of the winery should change in order to see whether it would affect another variable. They would also need to decide how long this change would last (one night? one week?) in order to determine whether it makes a difference, and on what basis they would establish that there is a causal relationship between the independent and dependent variables (e.g., a greater number of customers served each night).

In performing this experiment, the team might discover that a certain room configuration led to the dining and working experiences being significantly more pleasant than other room configurations. Should they invite back previous diners to re-experience the restaurant in that new configuration, perhaps at no or subsidized cost? In the context of a restaurant business, this is unlikely. However, in other research contexts, ethical considerations about how to address differences between members of "treatment" and "control" groups are paramount. For example, in school settings, research is often conducted in the form of comparing groups of students who are taught using different pedagogical approaches. Likewise, experimental approaches are often used to test new medications, and when individuals volunteer for medical studies, they are assigned either to treatment or control groups. Researchers must then decide how to ethically address the possibility that individuals in the control group will not benefit from the procedures or practices that are available to individuals in the treatment group.

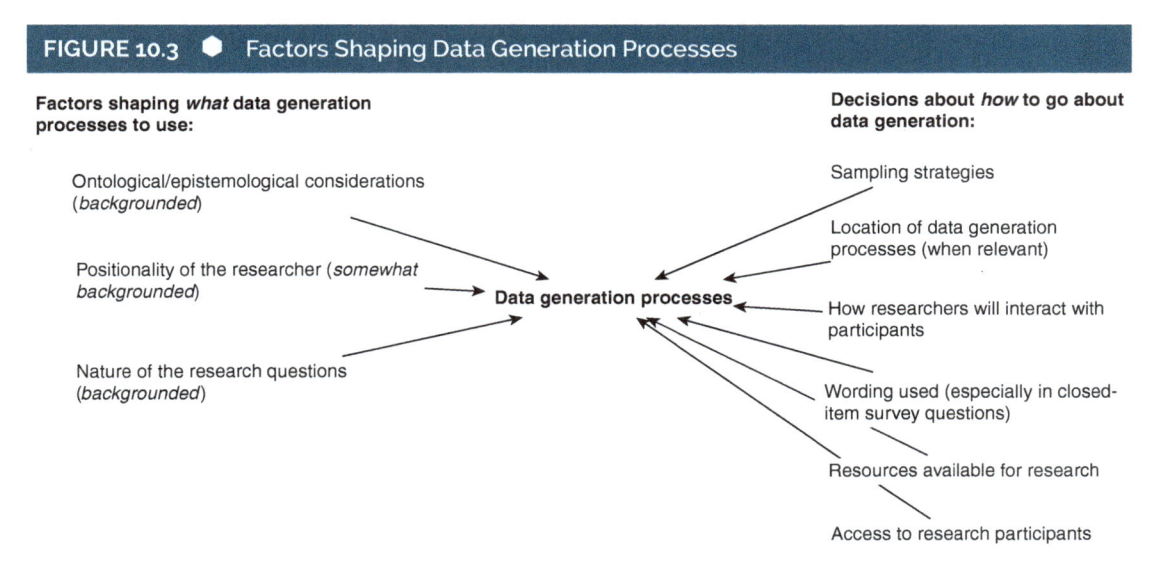

FIGURE 10.3 ● Factors Shaping Data Generation Processes

Factors shaping *what* data generation processes to use:

- Ontological/epistemological considerations (*backgrounded*)
- Positionality of the researcher (*somewhat backgrounded*)
- Nature of the research questions (*backgrounded*)

→ **Data generation processes** ←

Decisions about *how* to go about data generation:

- Sampling strategies
- Location of data generation processes (when relevant)
- How researchers will interact with participants
- Wording used (especially in closed-item survey questions)
- Resources available for research
- Access to research participants

The way that these various issues are connected to the process of data generation and acquisition can be seen in Figure 10.3. As you will note, there are both factors that shape *what kinds* of data generation processes are used, and decisions to be made about *how* that data generation occurs.

Before we move on, let's take a moment to reflect on some of this.

> **Pause and Reflect.** Think about your own personality and the kinds of situations with which you feel most and/or least comfortable. Are you an extrovert or an introvert? Do you like to hear stories? Do you find it nerve-wracking to approach people you haven't met? How do you feel about working with numbers? Your responses to these questions might give you some insight into the kinds of data generation approaches that make the most sense for you.

Data, Not Phenomenon

Our student wrote about the winery team discovering and discussing things that were not working. Perhaps members of the team made notes about things they perceived to be problematic about the new setup to use during discussions about what, if any, changes to make.

We can think about these notes as a form of data. Doing so raises the important notion that *data are different from the phenomenon of study*. In other words: In the research process we aim to understand some specific phenomenon. However, the data we generate are not *the same as* that phenomenon. To better explain this, let's go back to the possibility of surveying winery customers about what they felt was good/problematic about their dining experiences. By surveying customers, winery staff would seek to understand their perceptions about the most positive and negative aspects of their visit. The survey responses, however, are not *actually* customer perceptions, which are internal to each one of those individuals. Rather, the data would be customers' responses on the surveys, written at a particular moment in time.

We raise this point because it is closely linked to our view of knowledge creation as communicative. Recall that in Chapter 5 we wrote about meaning emerging from social interaction and shared social understandings. One of those implicit but shared understandings is that we can use data as a kind of "shorthand" that represents individuals' holistic experiences in a truncated form. This shared understanding about data representing a phenomenon is implied every time we engage in social inquiry.

This point is also linked to the ideas about different kinds of knowledge claims. Recall that knowledge claims map onto different ontological categories: "the" world, "my/her/your" world, and "our" world (Carspecken, 1996). As we will illustrate in the research scenario below, one way that phenomena can be represented is through the creation of **instruments**, tools such as tests or questionnaires used to measure certain concepts. These instruments map internal experiences—such as attitudes, emotions, or cognitive knowledge—onto the objective domain, so that they can be measured in a standardized manner. This means that the validity of these instruments needs to be assessed according to criteria for objective truth claims.

Understanding that the concept of data is not the same as the phenomenon being studied is important for several reasons. First, it has implications for how we judge the validity of knowledge claims. It also raises questions about whether "raw" data ever really exist; furthermore, it has ontological implications in that it suggests that data cannot be "out there" for us to collect. Finally, this idea highlights the intertwining of data generation, acquisition, and inference: When we choose "data" as reflective of some phenomenon, we have already made some basic inferences, based on shared understandings, about *how* or *in what form* we can use data to illustrate that phenomenon.

Let's take a second to reflect on this.

> **Pause and Reflect.** Think about a conversation you've had recently where you described a specific experience to your conversation partner. Do you feel the description was an authentic retelling of the experience? Were there moments that were challenging to describe? What was the difference between the experience itself and the description of that experience?

Data as Product

In the write-up of her experiences opening the new winery location, our student did not mention the result of data generation. But in any research context, the process of generating data leads to specific data *products*, which are used as the basis for conducting analyses and making inferences. These products are shaped by decisions researchers make about which of the data generated are sufficiently important to include in their analyses. This has important implications for what inferences a researcher ultimately makes.

Data products differ depending on the approach used to generate or acquire data. Some examples include:

- *Numerical data sets.* Data generated in the form of surveys, questionnaires, multiple-choice tests, or even some structured interviews are often used to conduct analyses showing patterns and trends across a large number of people. The product of this form of data generation is a data set that includes the responses collected from all research participants. For instance: Imagine the winery team collects 20 surveys asking respondents to rate different aspects of their experience at the new site, on a scale of 1–5. When they create the data set based on these responses, they compile results for each question. In doing so, however, they might need to make decisions about responses. For example, what if someone skips a question, or circles two responses, or doesn't circle anything but writes a response in the margins? When the team creates its database, it makes responses comparable and thus analyzable, but it also has already made inferences about what someone "meant" when they circled multiple options and has decided how to record that response in the database. Those decisions have important implications for inferences made based on later analysis. For instance, if the team were to decide that they would leave out responses when multiple options are circled, they would be drawing conclusions about their patrons' perspectives based on incomplete information.

- *Transcripts.* Interviews and focus group conversations are often recorded; these recordings are then written out as transcripts that form the basis for thematic, narrative, or other analyses. As with survey data sets, the creation of a transcript—the *product* of data generation—is itself a mix of data and inference. Researchers make choices about which nonverbal cues to include in their transcription, for instance. These choices are a form of interpretation that occurs prior to any "formal" analyses taking place.

- *Photographs and other visual products.* Photographs, videos, and other visual materials or artifacts can be used as the basis for data analysis. For example, in the winery context, staff could take photographs of the space to document different room configurations. Of significance: Visual materials are a data product, but also can serve as the basis for additional data generation. For instance, photographs can be used as stimuli for discussions in interview or focus group contexts.

- *Historical and archival data.* Historical/archival data provide insights into things that have happened in the past but may not be accessible through primary data generation processes (e.g., perspectives of individuals who have already passed away). Also in this category are data from social media posts (e.g., tweets, Facebook posts, or comments on electronic news articles). This form of digital data may have been created for nonresearch purposes but is increasingly a focus of empirical analysis. This raises both ethical issues (e.g., How might we think about gaining consent when analyzing public Twitter postings?) and practical concerns (e.g., How do we download digital data? How do we ensure representativeness?).

As you can see, "data" have several dimensions, all of which have important implications for understanding the social world. When we engage in research, we make choices about *what processes* to use as well as *how to represent* the information we collect in the form of data products we analyze. An important point to note is that products and processes can be intertwined, as mentioned with respect to visual data products above. In participatory action research, for example, co-researchers often generate data products that have a material basis but also are the foundation for ongoing *processes* of consciousness-raising and community engagement. In other words: The boundary between process and product is not always clear.

Another set of concepts that are often intertwined, as illustrated in the preceding pages, are data generation/acquisition and inference. In the winery scenario, the team engaged in an ongoing process of generating data, analyzing it, and using the inferences from their analyses to change the room layout. As we've discussed, it is a central characteristic of action research that analyses are used concretely to address a problem. The repetition of the data generation-inference cycle, as in the narrative presented, is also characteristic of action research. You will see other examples of this iterative approach in the "minifiction" examples below.

We emphasize this point because the processes of data generation and acquisition, and data analysis or inference, are usually presented linearly, with the former preceding the latter. We even do so in this textbook! The need to present information in a linear manner stands in tension with the elements of inference-making that characterize every aspect of the data generation process, including through choices that researchers make in creating data generation instruments or tools. We will return to these issues in Chapter 13.

RESEARCH SCENARIO: MAKING CHOICES ABOUT DATA GENERATION

In this section, we again draw on material from our "Researching Research" project, focusing on some of the challenges that can arise in the data generation process. The scenario draws from an assignment requiring students to choose an empirical article assigned for the course, and to pretend they were researchers spending a day working on the project discussed. Here is the assignment prompt:

For this assignment, we will use a method called "Mystory." This is a method utilized in qualitative research that blurs the lines between data and analysis, research and research participants, fact and faction, and stories told and experienced. The Mystory method was developed by the researcher Norman Denzin, who writes about it in his book Performance Ethnography *(Denzin, 2003). For the assignment, you will write a "mini-fiction" piece about this week's research articles. Utilizing either the Knoblauch and Hoy or Goddard and Foster articles as a basis—imagine you are the author and today you are going to collect data for your study. You (as an author of one of these articles) have already determined the research problem, purpose, and questions. Now imagine you are going to spend a day collecting data. What will happen today? Will you meet any difficulties? How will you solve them?*

The assignment was called a "mini-fiction" exercise because students were asked to pretend to be an author of one of the two articles for that week and to come up with *fictional* narratives based on their thoughts about what might have happened during the research process. However, the narratives reflect *real* possibilities, and therefore help illustrate different aspects of the data generation process.

A Day in the Life, I: Student Example

The first "mini-fiction" is based on a research study about self-efficacy among students and cooperating teachers in different contextual settings, as informed by a student's reading of Dee Knoblauch and Anita Hoy's 2008 article. The student writing this assignment created the following fictional account where they pretended to be one of the researchers analyzing data collected for the study described in the assigned article:

I've been researching "What happens to student teachers' efficacy beliefs when they are placed in urban settings?" and today I'm going to begin going through the multiple surveys we've collected over the course of the student teaching experience. We are now done with the 16-week student teaching experience, so I think it best that I begin looking at results.

> *First, I begin by sorting the various surveys: the Teacher Sense of Efficacy Scale (TSES), which was to be filled out by our participants before beginning student teaching, at the 8 week point, and after student teaching; the Collective Efficacy Scale which was administered at the 8 week point and at the 16 week point; and the Perceived Cooperating Teachers' Efficacy Scale.*

In this first part of the (fictional) researcher's process, she writes about three different **scales** used to collect data. A scale is a data generation instrument used to measure a specific **construct**. The "Teacher Sense of Efficacy Scale," for example, is a questionnaire that contains multiple **items** (questions or statements to which one must respond), each of which provides insight into that individual's sense of efficacy as a teacher.

In this study, the research team utilized existing scales rather than develop their own. This is fairly common, because the development of new scales is a long process. When developing scales, researchers must ensure that items accurately reflect the concepts of interest (this is often referred to as **construct validity**); they do this through processes such as conducting cognitive interviews.

Back to the narrative:

> *Since we administered the TSES the first time at the orientation meeting, we received all 196 of those forms (1 from each participant). I've been saving those for our data analysis. Now I'm looking at the number received at the 8 week mark . . . uh-oh . . . only 137 forms. Darn. Now I'll have to alphabetize the forms from the orientation meeting and the forms at the 8 week mark and see whose form was not returned. . . . Well, I suppose it's a good thing we have so many participants. Even without all the forms, we should still have a decent sample size.*

> *I've now entered all participant names into a spreadsheet. The first column contains pseudonyms, then the second column has the title, "8week TSES returned." I don't need a column for the initial TSES—the names of the participants is sufficient for that as that was where I collected the names from initially. Now, how can I show whether or not they have returned the 8 week TSES? Yes and No? That might be difficult to read over pages and pages. I think I'll place the number "1" in the cell from those that returned, and leave the cell blank if they didn't return. Blank cells are easier to read. Now I'll take the time to enter whether these were returned, and I'll immediately know which participants have to be removed from our data set.*

This part of the narrative highlights additional issues related to the data generation process. The researcher's discussion of number of forms received at orientation and at the 8-week mark refers to participant **response rates:** how many of the surveys distributed were completed by participants. Response rates for surveys and questionnaires have implications for how well the *sample* reflects the *population* of interest—a concept we will discuss further in Chapter 11. For now, we point this out because of implications regarding decisions the researcher needs to make about creating a database out of responses collected, and in particular about which survey responses to include (or not). Here the researcher decided to remove participants who did not return surveys at the 8- or 16-week mark. How might this decision shape inferences made later on? First, it means that inferences will be made based on information from an incomplete group. In addition, what does removing the partially completed questionnaires mean for those participants? One might ask whether it is ethical to discard data, given that a participant has taken the time to share responses based on an assumption that their responses will be included in the analysis.

Another set of choices emerging in this narrative has to do with how the researcher enters information into the database. Here we see once again the way that data generation and inference are closely connected: By choosing to structure her spreadsheet in a certain way, our researcher is already making choices about what is important.

Back from lunch. I think I'll look at another aspect of our data.

We also gave a "background information" sheet to each participant before student teaching began. We've already organized the information from the "background information" sheets, and have found that of the 196 participants in our study, 105 of them (53%) indicated that all 13 years of their own K–12 school experience were in a suburban setting, 35 (18%) of them reported that all 13 years were in a rural setting, 9 (5%) of them indicated that all 13 years occurred in an urban setting, and 47 (24%) of them said that they couldn't answer the question. Hmmm . . . we didn't ask them to identify why they couldn't answer the question. Speaking from my own experience, we moved around quite a bit during my childhood. I spent my first 2 years in a rural school setting, then 3 years in an inner-city school setting, then the rest of my K–12 years in the suburbs. Should we even display the information for the "can't answer the question" group? It really isn't detrimental to our research, and we'd likely have to take the time to list reasons why individuals couldn't answer. I'll have to think about that a little more. My first gut reaction is to not include it, but I'll mull it over for a little bit and talk to the other researchers about it. Oh, wait! I have to recalculate all those numbers based on those participants who didn't return all of the surveys. Man . . . so much for trying to get "ahead of the ballgame." I guess in the future I'll wait until all of the data are in before I start on any analysis.

The narrative from our researcher's afternoon suggests that she is wondering why participants couldn't answer the question asked. This points to one limitation of drawing on data collected using standardized scales or closed-ended questions: It doesn't let us acquire information in great depth. In this case, the researcher isn't entirely clear about what to do concerning the 47 respondents who said they could not answer this question, because she doesn't know *why* they responded this way. Unfortunately, with anonymous surveys, it is usually not possible to return to participants for follow-up. Sometimes, if researchers are designing a new instrument, they might test questions by conducting **cognitive interviews**, a special kind of structured interview used to assess how individuals understand the meaning of questions and the reasons they give for choosing specific option(s) in closed-ended items. Without some form of cognitive interviewing or other testing of the survey prior to broad distribution, researchers cannot be certain how well items capture the constructs they address.

Finally, our researcher mentions that in the future, she wants to "wait until all of the data are in before I start on my analysis." As her narrative shows, this clean break between data generation and analysis isn't really possible, given that she is making choices all along that will shape the inferences she makes.

This scenario highlights some key features of the data generation process when researchers are trying to understand broad patterns that occur across large numbers of individuals. In the next example, we focus on issues that arise when using data generation processes aimed at understanding specific phenomena in-depth.

A Day in the Life, II: Student Example

This second mini-fiction example draws from a study that examined the perceptions of students, parents, educators, and community members about the goals and purposes of schooling in a First Nation community in Northern Alberta, Canada, written about by J. Tim Goddard and Rosemary Foster (2002). In this assignment, the student's narrative was written in the voice of the district superintendent. Part of the "fiction" here (in contrast with the original study) was that the superintendent was the person doing the research—that is, generating data about their own school community. This is how the student-writing-as-superintendent described the data generation experience:

> *I am the superintendent in the northernmost community in Alberta. I am passionate about the future of our schools. Without a deeper understanding of who we are, how can anyone serve the needs of the students in the first place? Traditionally, there has been a strong disconnect between educational leadership and the cultural context of schools in Alberta. When I look around my district, I see parents who are Aboriginal and students who are a blend of many cultures. . . . I often ask myself, how can leadership really understand the people when they are disconnected from their cultural context? I believe we are not disconnected like*

the Southern schools in Alberta. I believe others can learn a lot from how we do things up here. Tomorrow, I will begin talking to my fellow educators, parents, and community members. I hope we can show others we have something really special. If not, we can learn where to go from here.

Even before the data generation process starts, this narrative points to some important identity issues. As the superintendent of the schools in the study, this individual's own professional identity is clearly linked to the focus of the research. As we discussed in Chapter 3, this has implications for the research process. Here, it might shape what the superintendent asks about in interviews, or how data are interpreted. Let's see what happens when data generation begins:

I arrived early at Church Point this morning to conduct my first round of focus groups. It was summer, so I assumed this would encourage all teachers to attend the focus group sessions. There are 11 teachers in the building but only 6 teachers showed. They were very difficult to manage and were not cooperative. They all talked over each other and I couldn't keep up with the discussion. They were really negative and they fed off of each other. I wanted the questions to emerge as the discussion progressed but it became apparent that I had little control. I was thinking it was good the conversation was taped, so the team could listen and transcribe it later. I was frustrated and tired by the end of the teacher focus group and decided to transition to one-on-one interviews with administrators. When we go to Moose River (another research site) I will arrange the groups so they are smaller and will have an interview procedure laid out.

The researcher's focus group clearly did not go as planned! As noted, the superintendent didn't explicitly plan out questions. Instead, the plan was to pose initial questions and then organically follow up. Kathryn Anderson and Dana Jack (1991) note that this kind of emergent approach can be beneficial in allowing for what *participants see as important* to come through, rather than only what the researchers deem salient for discussion. However, as in this case, it can also result in lack of control over the conversation. It's also important to note that only 6 of 11 teachers showed up for the focus group. This seems like a small number, but had all 11 teachers shown up, it may have been even more difficult for the researcher to maintain control. Because conversation *among* participants is a central benefit of focus groups, it is important to keep the group small. The researcher/superintendent wrote more about this below:

In the afternoon before my leadership interviews, I went to find the teachers that did not attend the focus group. The few teachers I was able to find indicated that they didn't want to be bullied by their peers and were afraid to attend the session.

> *I will plan to touch base with the teachers at Moose River to see their comfort level in being involved in the focus group. Otherwise, I will make other arrangements, so I can collect data from 100% of the teachers. I am disappointed but this may make up for the missing teachers at Church Point.*

The researcher's dilemma points to the importance of considering *how* someone might go about inviting participants to be part of a study. For individuals like those who feared speaking up in a focus group setting, individual interviews might be a better option. In some contexts, *who* conducts the interview might also shape people's willingness to participate. For instance, the unequal power relation between the superintendent/researcher and teachers in the school could negatively shape the desire of individuals to take part, which then influences what data are generated. (For an article that addresses this issue, see Razon and Ross, 2012.) The next section of the narrative focused on the superintendent/researcher's experiences conducting individual interviews at Church Point:

> *To prepare for one-on-one interviews, the research team wrote all the questions down ahead of time. I told the research team to allow the participants to ask if they didn't understand the meaning of the question. . . . I didn't want participants to feel influenced by my wording. Because of schedule conflicts, there were only two administrators I could meet at Church Point. This was really disappointing to me but I was relieved that both of the administrators were not shy and gave us lots of useful information. Now, I needed some students! The research team found two 10th grade students outside running the track. We pulled them into the school to get their perspectives. We bought them lunch for their time. We really had to encourage them to talk and prompted them with probing questions. . . . Later, our team started to listen to the recordings of the Moose River focus group to transcribe them. We had trouble discriminating between the voices since we didn't know the teachers well, and since time had passed since the conversation. We decided that next time we should have the teachers speak and say their first name so we at least have an idea of what they sound like.*

The narrative notes that the research team created questions ahead of time for individual interviews. Assuming these were fairly broad, open-ended questions, with some room for flexibility in the follow-up, this approach to interview design would fit into what is usually referred to as *semi-structured interviews*. These are about at the midpoint of the continuum between *unstructured* interviews, similar to the emergent design used in the morning focus group, and *structured* interviews, where the researcher fully dictates the substance of the conversation by using the same initial and follow-up questions with every participant. The narrative also mentions that in order to get students to participate in the interviews, the research team bought them lunch, but that even so they had difficulty getting students to say much. Lack of (potential) participant interest is another challenge that researchers conducting interviews may face, and one that is good to be prepared for. In fact, it is a challenge that is common across different forms of data generation—for example, in the first mini-fiction example, the student-as-researcher wrote about low response rates. To address this challenge, researchers sometimes offer incentives to encourage participation (e.g., money or gift cards, or being entered into a raffle for a more substantial prize). However, offering incentives can raise questions for researchers about *when* and *what kinds* of incentives are ethical.

Finally, in this narrative, the researcher mentioned challenges with the transcription process: difficulty in distinguishing among focus group member voices. Even in individual interviews, transcription can be challenging if participants do not speak clearly or if there are loud background noises. The length of the transcription process is also something to be aware of: It can sometimes take 3 or 4 minutes to listen and note down on paper every minute of an interview or focus group discussion.

The two scenarios discussed here highlight different data generation techniques as well as potential differences in sampling, decisions that must be made during the data generation process, and the kinds of challenges that might arise during the process. While these do not reflect the full range of decisions or challenges that can arise in the context of data generation, the scenarios provide some insight into some of the issues you might face when you begin generating data as part of an empirical research project. A brief summary of the differences in these two scenarios can be seen in Table 10.3.

TABLE 10.3 ● Mini-Fiction Research Scenario Summary		
	Research Scenario 1	**Research Scenario 2**
Data collection technique	Surveys (pre-validated; not created by researcher)	Focus groups and individual interviews
Sample size	196 respondents at point 1; 137 at point 2	6 participants in initial focus group (of 11 teachers) at site 1; 4 participants (2 administrators and 2 students) at site 2
Decisions to be made	How to enter data (especially how to deal with missing data)	How to recruit participants; how structured an interview/focus group context to establish
Challenges	Low response rates; missing data; timing of data entry	Lack of control over focus group; power dynamics affecting participant recruitment; difficulty distinguishing between focus group participant voices on recordings; superficial responses from participants

YOU AND RESEARCH

Before we wrap up, let's think through what data generation or acquisition processes might look like in your own work.

When Interpreting Research

When you read a research study, data generation and acquisition processes will be discussed in the Methodology or Methods section, often in terms of what processes were utilized, and if relevant, whether existing scales were used or new ones developed and validated for this study. Sample size (and/or response rate for survey and questionnaire-based studies), length of time over which data were generated (if relevant), and sometimes information about steps taken to protect the research participants (e.g., use of pseudonyms) will also be discussed. As you read this material, pay close attention to the relationship between research questions and data generation and acquisition processes. Does the evidence fit the questions being asked? Are the authors clear about who their research participants are (both in terms of numbers and in terms of the characteristics reflected among participants), so that you as a reader can assess how broadly or narrowly their findings might translate beyond the group of individuals who participated?

When Doing Research

Deciding how to generate data that addresses your research questions is key when preparing a research proposal. If your questions focus on the lived experience of certain individuals or groups, approaches like individual or focus group interviews, or ongoing observations, make more sense than disseminating a fixed-response or short-answer survey. On the other hand, if you want to obtain data from a large number of participants in order to assess broad patterns or trends, surveys will be a better option. In addition to the question/data fit, your choice of data generation or acquisition approach might be contingent upon the amount of time you have available for field research. It's also important to reflect upon your own personality, and how comfortable you feel with interpersonal relationships that might be formed through some forms of data generation. And of course, your ontological and epistemological commitments shape how you approach your research in terms of the questions that you ask and the data generation processes you plan to use.

As part of preparing an academic research proposal, you will need to justify the ethics of your study to an institutional research board. This includes justifying the data generation or acquisition processes you plan to use. Thus, you should think about issues such as: where and when interviews will be conducted (to ensure the comfort of interviewees); what you will do in order to make sure that all data generated are confidential and that your participants are not identifiable; and what potential risks may arise from participation in the research study and how these can be mitigated. You also should spend time reflecting on how participants will be recruited to ensure that opportunities for participation are fair and do not place disproportionate burdens on certain groups of people or exclude other groups. Moreover, it is important to reflect upon situational ethical issues that might arise during data generation—for instance, by thinking about the power dynamic that might exist between yourself and your research participants and what you can do to correct for power imbalances.

SYNTHESIS: POINTS FOR REFLECTION

Conceptual Synthesis

In this chapter, we've talked about different approaches to generating data and choices that are made about data generation and acquisition processes. We have also drawn upon discussions in the previous two chapters to show that data are products of data generation, but also are separate from the phenomenon we are investigating. Throughout the chapter, we have highlighted these issues in relation to broader concepts threaded throughout the textbook—identity, ethics, the relational nature of research, and validity.

Methodological Synthesis

At different points during the chapter we have raised questions about the choices that researchers make during data generation. As we noted, these choices are linked in large part to matching research questions with appropriate approaches for answering them. However, choices about data generation and acquisition involve much more than this: They include ethical choices as well as choices based on logistical concerns and personal preferences. All of these choices, in sum, shape how researchers approach the process of data generation and acquisition and, ultimately, the inferences they can make. We noted in Chapter 4 that research always has consequences that are embedded in our methodological choices—this is certainly true of data generation and acquisition, not only in terms of how they shape possibilities for analysis and inference-making, but also in how decisions about data generation have implications for relationships built with research participants.

Personal Synthesis

From a personal standpoint, one of the questions we raise throughout this chapter is what decisions *you* might make about data generation and acquisition, and why. Think about what processes most resonate with you among the approaches discussed, or about what kind of data you might seek to solve a problem. In terms of data generation and acquisition processes, it's also important to consider what evidence seems most compelling—for instance, if one of your friends or classmates says, "X approach to studying for an upcoming exam is more effective than Y approach," consider: What kind of evidence would convince you that this is actually the case? As we continue exploring data generation and acquisition and inference-making, we invite you to consider the approaches we discuss in light of these questions.

MOVING FORWARD

In this chapter, we discussed different elements of the data generation process and the products resulting from data generation and acquisition. In the next chapter we will look at what it means to have *enough* data and what it means to have *good* data. The discussion will build on our overview of the data generation and acquisition process as addressed in this chapter, emphasizing validity and ethics.

Further Readings

Ball, M. (2013, March). A more perfect poll. *The Atlantic.*

Briggs, C. L. (1986). *Learning how to ask: A sociolinguistic appraisal of the role of the interview in social science research.* Cambridge, UK: Cambridge University Press.

de Leeuw, E. D., Hox, J. J., & Dillman, D. A. (2008). The cornerstones of survey research. In E. D. de Leeuw, J. J. Hox, & D. A. Dillman (Eds.), *International handbook of survey methodology* (pp. 1–17). New York, NY: Lawrence Erlbaum Associates.

Evans, J., & Jones, P. (2011). The walking interview: Methodology, mobility and place. *Applied Geography, 31*(2), 849–858.

Fox, M. (2015). Embodied methodologies, participation, and the art of research. *Social and Personality Psychology Compass, 9*(7), 321–332.

Morgan, D. L. (1997). *Focus groups as qualitative research* (2nd ed.). Thousand Oaks, CA: SAGE.

Parker, B. (2006). Constructing community through maps? Power and praxis in community mapping. *The Professional Geographer, 58*(4), 470–484.

Salmons, J. (2015). *Doing qualitative research online.* Thousand Oaks, CA: SAGE.

Sloan, L., & Quan-Hasse, A. (Eds.). (2017). *The SAGE handbook of social media research methods.* Thousand Oaks, CA: SAGE.

Tachine, A. R., Bird, E. Y., & Cabrera, N. L. (2016). Sharing circles: An Indigenous methodological approach for researching with groups of Indigenous peoples. *International Review of Qualitative Research, 9*(3), 277–295.

Turner, D. W., III (2010). Qualitative interview design: A practical guide for novice investigators. *The Qualitative Report, 15*(3), 754–760.

Wang, C., & Burris, M. A. (1997). Photovoice: Concept, methodology, and use for participatory needs assessment. *Health Education & Behavior, 24*(3), 369–387.

11

HOW DO I KNOW I HAVE "ENOUGH" DATA? HOW DO I KNOW I HAVE "GOOD" DATA?

This chapter continues the exploration of data generation and acquisition that was introduced conceptually in Chapters 8 and 9 and discussed more concretely in Chapter 10. This chapter builds on the previous chapter's discussion of "how to" engage in data generation and acquisition processes by focusing on core concepts around knowing when we have acquired *enough* data to make inferences, and how we know our data are "good." The research scenario in this chapter draws out these concepts in the context of two research projects undertaken by scholars in different fields.

MUSING UPON THE EVERYDAY: HOW DID THE LASAGNA TURN OUT?

Let's start by re-examining our lasagna puzzle from the previous chapter. There, we quoted a student from one of our research methodology classes, who wrote,

A week ago I was interested in making the most perfect lasagna. My method of gaining information was to search recipes on trusted food sites. I analyzed data by finding both ratings and reviews of previously attempted recipes. My final conclusion was made by selecting the recipe with the highest average rating of success.

Imagine yourself in the shoes of this student, craving a slice of lasagna and seeking out the recipe with the right mix of cheese, sauce, noodles, and meat or vegetables or whatever your perfect lasagna includes. Now, think about the process you go through to find that perfect recipe. You read reviews, you look at ratings, maybe you look at ingredients . . . how long should you keep looking? How many recipe sites or cooking show reviews does it take before you decide you've found what you need?

Now, let's think about a different kind of scenario. Take a moment to recall the process you went through when you applied to graduate schools. Once you figured out what kind of program you were interested in, how did you decide where to apply? Maybe you sent emails to professors at different universities asking to speak to them about the program and its fit for you, or perhaps you spoke to a few current students at programs that interested you. Maybe you asked for advice from family and friends in your field of interest. When did you decide you had enough information to make a decision? And how did you decide what information was good, or credible?

In both of these situations, you need to filter through the data that are available to figure out what data are credible. Ultimately, you also need to decide when you have found enough data to make an informed choice about the problem or topic of interest, be it graduate school, lasagna, or anything else. How do you know this? And on what basis do you decide? In this chapter, we'll explore what it means to know you have enough data, and especially enough "good" data, in the context of the research process.

NARRATIVE AND CONCEPTUAL INTERLUDES: CREATING THE PERFECT RECIPE

In this section we use a narrative about developing a new recipe to introduce a number of conceptual elements, including sampling, data saturation, missing data, and generalizability/transferability. These concepts all address issues related to how one might think about collecting *enough* data and *good* data within the research process.

Let's start by taking a moment for reflection, keeping in mind the systematic nature of "data" as discussed in Chapter 8.

> **Pause and Reflect.** What are some of your initial thoughts about what constitute "good" data? Have you ever been in a situation where the information you collected was "bad" or insufficient in some way? What would have made the information better in the context for which you needed it?

Searching recipe websites is one way to find a "perfect" recipe. But if your search doesn't lead you to a recipe that's just right for you and you need to devise a new one, the process can be a little different. Here's an example: A few years ago, Karen was asked to bake several loaves of challah bread for a Rosh Hashanah (Jewish New Year) celebration. Rosh Hashanah is one of the holiest days of the Jewish calendar, and for the celebration, Karen wanted to make sure that the challah bread turned out just right. So she set about testing recipes. First, she looked up several existing challah recipes to get a sense of what she might want to do. Then she started experimenting: She made loaves with more and less whole-wheat flour, tried different amounts of yeast, and let them rise for different amounts of time before shaping them. Karen also tried different baking temperatures and a variety of techniques to make sure each loaf came out of the oven golden brown and fully baked, but not too dark. After each loaf baked, she asked friends and family to try some and give her feedback about which one was tastiest, keeping careful notes on ingredients and technique used for that particular loaf. After several rounds of testing, she finally felt her challah recipe was ready for the Rosh Hashanah celebration. (And the final products were delicious!)

Karen's process of recipe testing was similar to the process chefs might go through before putting a new dish on their restaurant menu, or while deciding what recipes to include in a cookbook. Karen is not a professional chef or baker, so her recipe-testing process was not as extensive as it would be for a restaurant or cookbook. Still, several aspects are relevant to discuss here in relation to research processes, in particular the concepts of sampling, data saturation, missing data, and generalizability/transferability.

Sampling

In the recipe-testing process, "sampling" comes up in a number of different ways. In colloquial terms, Karen's friends and family "sampled" (that is, ate) her test challah bread loaves in order to provide feedback. But Karen also had to make decisions about how many loaves of challah to bake as "test" loaves before landing on the best ingredient + technique combination for a delicious and beautifully browned loaf. These loaves were her sample loaves—that is, the loaves that she used to make broader inferences about what set of ingredients and what baking process should be used in order to ensure the best-tasting and best-looking challah possible for the Rosh Hashanah celebration. You can see this in Table 11.1: Karen's choices about baking temperatures and foil use for four *sample* loaves led her to a broader conclusion about what choices she should make in general when baking challah.

In the challah baking process as well as in formal research contexts, the concept of **sampling** focuses on numbers: It refers to how many participants take part in a study. This is a term usually used in studies where the purpose is to draw inferences about a certain group, called the population of interest or **target population**, which consists of the set of individuals meeting certain criteria that are important for the study. (It is important to distinguish this group from the **accessible population**, which is the part of the target

TABLE 11.1 ● Notes on Challah Baking

Sample Loaf #	Ingredient Changes	Baking Temperature	Other Relevant Factors	Conclusions
1	White flour, honey, 2 eggs	325 °F	Covered with foil after 20 min.	Needs more time to brown
2	White flour, honey, 2 eggs	350 °F	Covered with foil after 30 min.	Slightly overbaked
3	White flour, honey, 2 eggs	325 °F	No foil	Crust too thick
4	White flour, honey, 2 eggs	350 °F	Covered with foil after 20 min.	Perfect!

population that not only meets the researcher's criteria but is also accessible in terms of money, time, and other logistical constraints.)

Sampling occurs in social science research because in most instances, it is not possible to collect data from the entire population of interest or target population. For example, when companies want to understand consumer preferences, they cannot realistically reach out to *all* consumers or potential consumers of their products. Instead, a subset of that population, called a **sample**, is included in the study; the sample is the group of individuals who actually participate in the study (by completing a survey, participating in a laboratory-based experiment, or through otherwise engaging with the techniques used by researchers to generate and acquire data). In many quantitative studies, once researchers have collected and analyzed data about their participants (the sample), they use that analysis to draw inferences about the larger group (the population) from which the sample is drawn—this is called **generalizing** (we discuss this in more detail below). In the case of Karen's challah baking, for instance, she used a sample set of challah loaves (baked with different combinations of ingredients and using different baking techniques) to reach her conclusions about what makes the best-tasting and best-looking challah.

Sampling is a tool that allows researchers to draw broad inferences based on limited information (in particular, information from a limited number of individuals). In studies where inferences are being drawn about a broader population from a sample (the case in many quantitative studies), however, it is extremely important that characteristics of the sample match relevant characteristics in the population of interest (this is called a **representative sample**). If the sample characteristics do not match the population characteristics, it is likely that inferences drawn about the population based on the sample will be inaccurate, a problem known as **sampling error**. In order to ensure that the sample is representative, researchers utilize what are known as **probability sampling** approaches, where the chance of being selected as part of the sample is equal for any member of a population, or for segments of the population with certain relevant characteristics (see Table 11.2 for more on approaches to sampling).

When probability sampling is used, the larger the sample, the more likely it is that the sample and population characteristics will match, and the less likely it is that the results will be **biased**. In the context of sampling, bias refers to a situation where the characteristics of the sample do not match the characteristics of the population from which it was drawn because of over/underrepresentation of certain groups in the sample. It can occur because of differences in response rates among different groups, but sampling bias can also result from the decisions that researchers make about whom to target or how to recruit participants. For instance, a survey of community members conducted by telephone may be biased if individuals from certain groups within the community are less likely than individuals from other groups to own telephones. Sampling bias is similar to the concept of publication bias discussed in Chapter 8, where literature may not reflect the full spectrum of knowledge about some topic because certain kinds of studies are not published. As discussed further in Chapter 12, bias in both cases reflects a systematic difference between what statements about representativeness might be assumed to mean, and what they actually mean.

If a study is well designed, a smaller sample size can also often produce good results, where what researchers learn from the sample is reflective of the population more broadly. But even in a well-designed study, the actual sample may not perfectly match what was planned: Researchers' constraints, as well as individuals' decisions not to participate, or to participate only partially, can shape the representativeness of the study sample. Ultimately, the size of the sample depends on response rates (the percentage of individuals recruited to participate who actually do participate in a study); on researcher constraints (i.e., time or resources needed to recruit participants); and on statistical needs, such as the degree of precision needed in our estimates of population characteristics (we will return to this concept in Chapter 13).

Not all studies focus on drawing inferences about trends in a large population, however. In some studies—generally the kinds of studies we think of as qualitative studies—the emphasis is on understanding complex issues about human behavior among specific groups of people, such as the internal values or beliefs of the research participants. These may not necessarily be reflected in a broader population. For this reason, in these kinds of studies, researchers do not need to select a sample that is representative of a broader population. Instead, researchers aim to include participants with characteristics that are especially relevant to the research questions being asked. For instance, a study about the experiences of students who are English language learners would not recruit a random sample of students from the school where the study is being conducted. Instead, the researcher(s) would recruit participants who identify as English language learners. Of course, many other sampling criteria might be relevant as well, such as the age of the students, the length of their time in the United States, native language, and so on. Depending on the researchers' specific research questions, they might choose to compare students from different schools or different age groups and use a form of **quota sampling** to do so. The group of participants in this study will not be recruited through random selection; instead, decisions about participant recruitment will be made based on who researchers believe can provide the most insight into the perspectives and experiences of this specific group. For this reason, in this and other studies focused on understanding complex phenomena characterized by privileged access (see Chapters 5 and 7), you also may not find consistency in the way the term *sampling* is used. For example, some researchers use the term *population* rather than *subjects* or *sample* to describe those who participate in the study.

Figure 11.1 describes some of the main sampling strategies found in research studies.

FIGURE 11.1 ● Sampling Strategies

There are two main categories of sampling types, each of which includes several strategies.

A. PROBABILITY SAMPLING. Probability sampling refers to any kind of sampling strategy that involves a *random* selection of subjects (the sample) from a specific population. Types of probability sampling include the following:

1. SIMPLE RANDOM SAMPLING. From a target population including all important variables for the study, a sample is drawn by randomly selecting study participants from the larger population. The sample is considered random if every member of the target population has an equal chance of being selected.

2. STRATIFIED RANDOM SAMPLING. This type of sampling uses quotas for subgroups within the target population to ensure that all subgroups are fairly represented. With this strategy, participants are randomly selected from within the subgroups. The point is to be sure that the sample represents the population in terms of its proportions across subpopulations.

3. CLUSTER SAMPLING. Cluster sampling is similar to stratified sampling in that it is based in identifying subgroups. However, cluster sampling occurs in multiple stages. In the first stage, a random sample of the identified subgroups is selected, and then a random sample of individuals from each subgroup is selected from the sample of subgroups in the second stage.

4. SYSTEMATIC SAMPLING. In this type of sampling, every *nth* subject (the **sampling interval**) is selected from a list of all possible subjects (the population). For example, every 5th patient is selected from a list of individuals admitted to the hospital. The population listing must be random and the sample selection of the population must also start at a random point. For example, if you have an alphabetical listing of all subjects, you will not start with "A" but rather with a random point on the list, and then go by the nth interval.

B. NON-PROBABILITY SAMPLING. Non-probability sampling refers to sampling strategies that use a non-random method to select the sample. Because it is non-random, you cannot guarantee that every important characteristic in the population is fairly represented in the sample. Non-probability sampling is used when you are not really able to identify all the members of the population. It is often used in qualitative studies where the primary objective is to obtain specific information rather than make inferences about a larger group. Types of non-probability sampling include the following:

1. CONVENIENCE SAMPLING. This strategy is based on using the most readily available subjects. Convenience sampling is an easy method for recruiting study participants and is used when we cannot know who is in the population. However, it is important to consider what characteristics of the population are missed because individuals with those characteristics are not included in the sample.

2. QUOTA SAMPLING. In quota sampling, previous knowledge about the population (for example, from a literature review) and potentially important characteristics of the population are used to build some design into the sample. Each stratum of the population is represented proportionally.

3. PURPOSIVE SAMPLING. With purposive sampling strategies, researchers handpick subjects to participate in the study based on identified issues being examined. This type of sampling is used when the sample for a study is highly unique and there is a specific purpose that would render this sample particularly insightful or helpful (though it does not represent what is typical about the population). *Snowball sampling* is a special kind of purposive sampling where people already participating in the study recommend others who might agree to participate. This is especially useful when the sample is not easy to access.

How do purposive and quota sampling differ? Purposive sampling restricts the sample to a very specific population and then tends to use all of the subjects available. Quota sampling, on the other hand, uses individuals who represent a range of different characteristics considered important for the study.

3a. THEORETICAL SAMPLING. This is a form of sampling that is used with the explicit purpose of generating or developing theory. In theoretical sampling researchers make choices about participants based on the potential theoretical insights that can be gleaned through their inclusion in the study. It is most often used in an approach to research called **grounded theory**. When using this approach, researchers collect and analyze data in an iterative process, which allows for new subjects to be included throughout the course of the project so that the insights from their participation can help develop the theory.

3b. CRITICAL CASE SAMPLING (or extreme case sampling). Critical case sampling calls for picking a small number of cases for inclusion on the study based on their ability to provide the most information, given the research question. With critical case sampling, the goal is to select participants based on the assumption that they will be able to provide the most insight about the central phenomena explored. It is an approach that can be especially useful when there are limited funds and/or opportunities for including a larger group of participants.

3c. MAXIMUM VARIATION SAMPLING. This form of sampling is used when it is important to include participants who reflect a range of variation along some dimension of interest to the researcher. This approach is used to provide researchers with insights about the phenomenon of interest from the widest range of individuals along a specified criterion that is assumed to be important to the study.

How do you decide which sampling approach to use? In general, sampling decisions are made based how important it is for your sample to be representative of a broader population, what you already know (or don't know) about that population, and what kind of access you have to potential study participants. The decision tree in Figure 11.2 illustrates how this decision-making often occurs.

Before moving on, let's zoom out for a moment and explore some of the implications of sampling decisions that go beyond logistical concerns. In previous chapters, especially in Chapter 4, we have discussed how ethical considerations play out in different contexts related to the research process, including sampling decisions. In fact, the establishment of ethical review boards during the second half of the 20th century (such as institutional review boards in U.S. universities) resulted in part from the realization among researchers and policymakers that decisions about whether studies are ethical need to be based on who are included as study participants. The Belmont Report, a summary of ethical principles that serve as guidelines in the United States for conducting research with human subjects, addresses this issue under the principle of *justice*: the idea that study participation, especially when risks are entailed, should not disproportionately fall on vulnerable or marginalized groups.

Ethical considerations also arise in the context of sample size. For example, some studies focus on generating insights into individuals' internal experiences (for instance, their experiences with or perspectives on research, as in our "Researching Research" project). In these kinds of studies, additional data are not necessary for the inferential process once data saturation, which we discuss below, is reached. Thus, what happens if the sample is too *big*? Well, some might consider inclusion of a too-large sample to be a waste of research funds, if these could be used for other studies. If the research funds come from publicly funded grants (e.g., grants from government agencies, funded by tax dollars), what level of accountability might researchers have to the taxpayers, who are ultimately providing the funding for their research?

In addition, if the sample is too big, not all participants' responses may be used in the inference-making process. From an ethical standpoint, is it fair to our participants to ask them to invest time, and at times speak or write about topics that are emotionally taxing, if ultimately their thoughts may not be used for the purposes of knowledge generation? According to Jill Francis and colleagues (2010), similar questions arise in the context of sample sizes that are too small: In these cases, there may not be sufficient information to obtain informative results—leading, perhaps, to projects being discarded and participants' thoughts similarly not being utilized.

> **Pause and Reflect.** Take a moment to think back to our discussion of ethics in Chapter 4 and, in particular, the emphasis on an ethics of care. What do you think would be the ethical thing to do in a situation where you found yourself unable to incorporate the perspectives of research participants because you had either too much or too little information? Would your perspective on what would be the ethical thing to do change depending on whether you had too small or too big a sample?

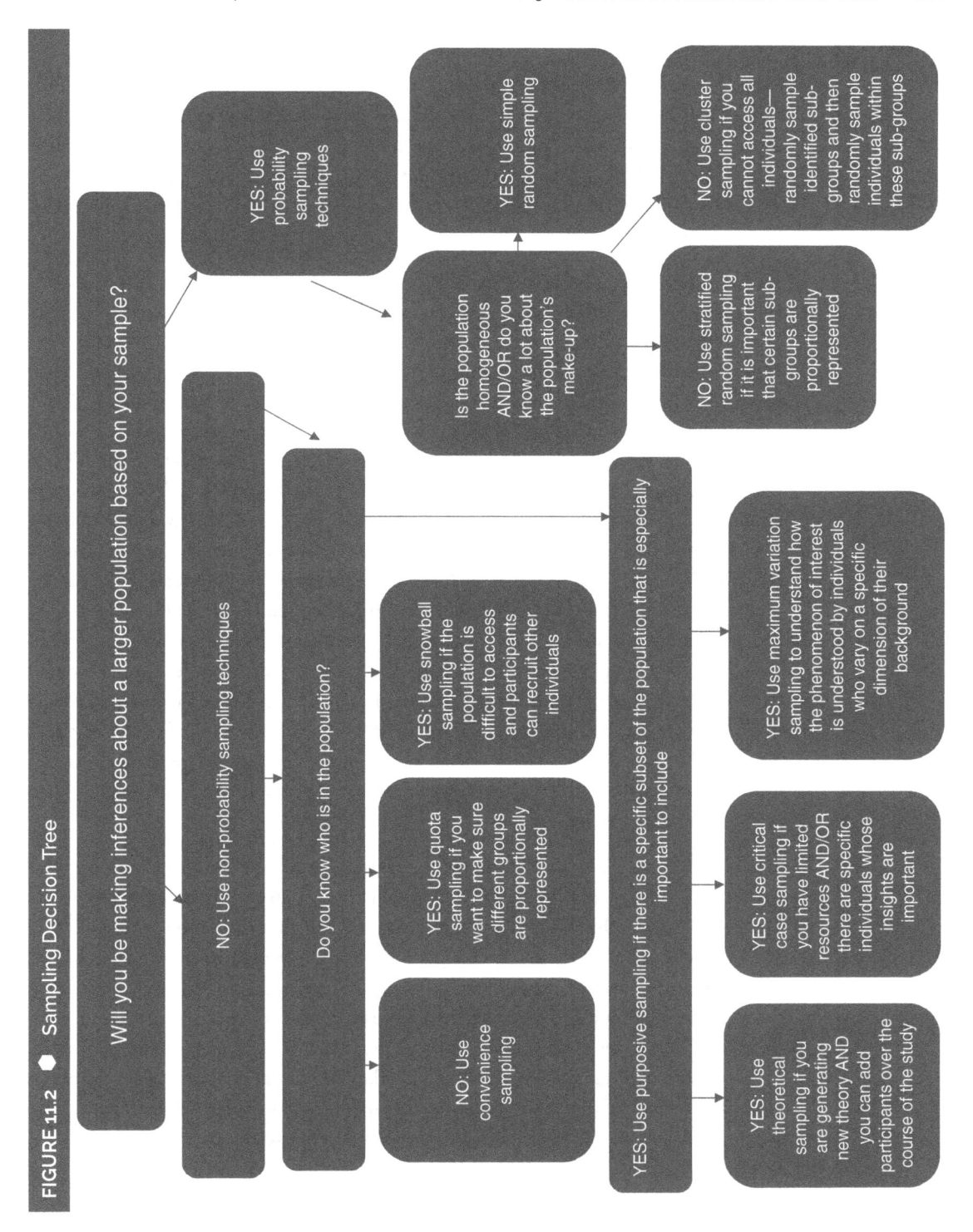

Chapter 11 ■ How Do I Know I Have "Enough" Data? How Do I Know I Have "Good" Data? 251

FIGURE 11.2 ⬢ Sampling Decision Tree

Will you be making inferences about a larger population based on your sample?

- **YES: Use probability sampling techniques**

  Is the population homogeneous AND/OR do you know a lot about the population's make-up?

  - **YES: Use simple random sampling**
    - NO: Use cluster sampling if you cannot access all individuals—randomly sample identified sub-groups and then randomly sample individuals within these sub-groups
  - NO: Use stratified random sampling if it is important that certain sub-groups are proportionally represented

- **NO: Use non-probability sampling techniques**

  Do you know who is in the population?

  - **YES:**
    - YES: Use snowball sampling if the population is difficult to access and participants can recruit other individuals
    - YES: Use quota sampling if you want to make sure different groups are proportionally represented
  - **NO: Use convenience sampling**

  YES: Use purposive sampling if there is a specific subset of the population that is especially important to include

  - YES: Use maximum variation sampling to understand how the phenomenon of interest is understood by individuals who vary on a specific dimension of their background
  - YES: Use critical case sampling if you have limited resources AND/OR there are specific individuals whose insights are important
  - YES: Use theoretical sampling if you are generating new theory AND you can add participants over the course of the study

Data Saturation

Recipe testing loaves of challah is not quite equivalent to conducting a research study where the aim is to make inferences about a large group from a smaller sample. Ultimately, Karen's goal in this endeavor was to make enough loaves of challah to ensure that she knew what combination of ingredients and baking techniques to utilize. At a certain point, Karen knew that further changes or tweaks to her recipe would not improve it. How did she know this?

Similarly, how does a researcher know they have enough data to ensure "good" results, when they are not relying on sampling approaches to ensure the representativeness of their participants? Well, an important point here is that "enough" data and "good" data are not equivalent terms: What makes a study "good" depends on a number of different criteria, which are a topic of debate within the methodological community (Tracy, 2010). For instance, because many qualitative studies focus on generating insights about the experiences of individual participants, it is not appropriate to talk about "enough" data with respect to number of participants, but rather the *depth* of data collected from each individual. One point that researchers such as Glenn Bowen (2008) or Michelle O'Reilly and Nicola Parker (2012) do agree upon in these smaller-scale studies is that there is a need for rich data that can highlight complexity and nuance—this is achieved, among other things, through what some scholars refer to as sample adequacy, or **data saturation**. This concept refers to a situation, mostly in qualitative studies, where acquiring additional data does not provide additional insights or nuance with respect to themes brought up through previous interviews, observations, or other data generation techniques: When this occurs, the sample is considered adequate for this particular study. Saturation is thus not related to quantity, but rather to the *quality* of the data already generated—that is, the depth of insights that can be reconstructed through thoughtful analysis of textual, visual, or other material.

Data saturation cannot be determined *a priori*; it is only after getting into the process of data analysis and inference-making that it is possible to know whether one has "enough" data—highlighting the intertwined nature of data generation and acquisition and inference. This intertwining characterized Karen's challah baking: Each loaf was baked (data generated) and then tasted by others (data analyzed) to provide feedback that then informed her next round of baking. Likewise, in many qualitative studies, researchers may not have a set number of participants in mind at the outset of the study. Instead, they may add additional study participants following initial data analysis, in order to more deeply understand the phenomenon in question. This differs from quantitative studies where researchers are looking to generalize from a sample to a target population: In many of these studies, the necessary sample size can be estimated prior to beginning data generation, based on statistical formulas.

It's also important to keep in mind that the need for saturation, as well as what saturation looks like, directly relates to the research questions and research design. In studies where inferences are drawn about a broader population, larger sample sizes allow researchers to be more confident that their participants are representative of the target population. In a study where a researcher is trying to understand, say, the range of experiences of students who identify as English language learners, it is similarly important to recruit participants who can provide different insights spanning that range, as well as to ask questions and use probes during interviews that allow for in-depth reflection. Likewise, when doing a study that involves observation of groups (such as ethnographic research), saturation may require spending enough time within the group or community to understand nuances in, for instance, the nature of interpersonal interactions, group dynamics, or cultural traditions within that community. In the context of this kind of fieldwork (as opposed to studies that are purely interview- or survey-based), reaching saturation may thus require spending longer periods of time "in the field" in order to see patterns and understand nuance.

On the other hand, in some kinds of research, sample size or saturation means very little. For instance, conversation analysis is a type of research that uses detailed transcripts of social interactions (including both verbal and nonverbal elements) to investigate *how* people interact. In research that utilizes this approach, studies can draw from a single transcript, and focus on elucidating sociopolitical and/or cultural norms as these are reflected in the transcribed conversation. In this kind of study, the concept of sample has little relevance.

Finally, it is important not to equate quantity with validity. As we discussed in Chapter 7, validity is intricately tied to understanding meaning; thus, the criteria for validity must emphasize whether we understand the knowledge claims that we make to be sound. Achieving data saturation can help us understand meaning in some ways, but *not* reaching saturation does not mean that research is not valid (see O'Reilly & Parker, 2012). Instead, it means that our understanding of meaning can be deeper and more nuanced. Keeping this in mind, we can see how having enough data to make robust inferences is different from having results that we can justify as valid.

Missing Data

In the context of Karen's challah testing, she worked from a set of existing recipes and tweaked them. However, let's imagine a situation where she was testing an old family recipe for challah, using a recipe card that listed necessary ingredients but didn't include quantities of those ingredients. In the context of recipe testing, Karen might have estimated the amounts to be used, based on other known recipes. Over the testing period she might try different combinations of flour, oil, and yeast amounts—but of course she wouldn't know for sure whether any of these amounts were "correct" based on the family recipe card. She might have also eliminated ingredients if it were not possible to include them in a way that would make for a delicious challah. Or she might have gone back to family members and asked for quantities—for instance, if the recipe were written down by Karen's grandmother (who is no longer alive), she might have asked her mother if she had any recollection of baking this challah and how much of each ingredient listed to use.

This situation is similar to dealing with **missing data**, a phenomenon that usually occurs in quantitative studies, specifically in the context of collecting large amounts of data for numerical analysis. The phenomenon of missing data refers to a situation where individuals do not respond to one or more items in a survey or questionnaire or where responses to an item are not inputted into a data set. This can influence the results of analyses and conclusions drawn from the findings, and is therefore important for considering whether we have "enough" or "good enough" data.

When there are missing responses in a questionnaire or a researcher forgets to input a data point, how should that be handled? As we have discussed before, these decisions are not simply procedural. For instance, it is important to consider the ethical ramifications of these different choices. In Chapter 4 we addressed marginalia as a focus of ethical concern. Here, let's think about the opposite situation, where researchers decide not to include some data provided by their participants when analyzing the data set as a whole. If someone takes the time and makes the effort to respond to a questionnaire, is it ethical to remove all of their responses when they skip one or a few questions? Similarly, what are the ethical implications of guessing what someone's response might be? These are not questions with a clear response, but they are important to consider in the context of making choices about how to handle missing data.

It is also important to consider how issues of validity play out with respect to missing data. Within the communicative framework that is the basis of our approach to research, validity is tied to the degree to which we can understand and explicate through our research how our participants make meaning of their own experiences (Carspecken, 1996). Knowing when we have "good" data, then, is inextricably linked to the interpretive process that we engage in as part of claiming validity (Dennis, 2013). This has implications for how we think about missing data. For example, can we claim that our interpretations are true and authentic to the experiences of our research participants when their perspectives are not included within our data set?

Procedurally, there are multiple ways to deal with missing data. If it is feasible, one might go back to the respondent/research participant and ask them to complete questions that were left blank. However, when questionnaires are completed anonymously, this is not

FIGURE 11.3 • The Intertwined Nature of Data Generation and Inferential Processes

- Return to respondents (*not always possible)
- Remove respondents who do not answer all questions from the database
- Make an educated guess (for example, input the mean for all missing responses)

possible. So, as with recipe testing, another possibility is to delete the case altogether: If a respondent skips two or three questions, one might choose not to include *any* of that respondent's survey responses as part of the analysis. Another possibility is essentially to take a guess, as when testing the challah recipe: For instance, if a respondent on a questionnaire leaves out their height, one might include the mean (average) height of all respondents in the sample as the data point from this individual. As Kristin Saisani (2005) suggests, the option that makes most sense will depend on what kinds of data are missing, how much are missing, and what kind of study is being conducted. Ultimately, making these decisions is itself part of the inference-making process, thus further highlighting the intertwined nature of data generation and inferential processes.

Generalizability and Transferability

When baking challah, there are certain ingredients and measures that change from recipe to recipe. But certain things stay the same, as well, and in the process of testing challah recipes, Karen always used unsalted butter, yeast, added egg to the dough, and so forth. Once she had baked several loaves she knew which ingredients or ratios were unique to each recipe she came across, and which ones were shared. In other words, she knew which ingredients and ingredient ratios transferred across loaves of challah or generalized from one loaf of challah to another.

In research contexts, generalizability and transferability are concepts that relate to the process of extending findings from one group to another. In research based on probability sampling, we use the term *generalizability* when making inferences about a target population based on a study sample. We always think of a sample in relation to the specific population it is drawn from and meant to generalize to—the target population—rather than the population in a generalized sense. For example, research findings from a sample of kindergarten students cannot be used to generalize to an entire population of elementary school students, but the findings can be generalized to the target population of kindergarten students.

As we saw with the concept of sampling and saturation, however, generalizing from sample to population makes little sense when research isn't conducted with the purpose of explaining trends or patterns in the population as a whole. In this case, we can think about generalizing in alternative ways, particularly in terms of **transferability**—that is, the degree to which results of a study might be transferable to other contexts or populations (Lincoln & Guba, 1986). In a cooking context, 30 different recipes might exist for tomato sauce, all with different proportions of sugar or salt or pepper. But it is quite possible that the "basic" elements of this sauce (say, garlic and onions and tomato paste) might be transferable in terms of their proportions from one recipe to another. In a research context, a study based on in-depth interviews with African American participants about their own views and experiences of racism can't be generalized to a broader population. However, we can think about how some findings or patterns in the data might transfer to other similar contexts, or how theoretical implications might align with inferences from research done with other individuals from marginalized demographic groups. The transferability of these findings always involves some element of recognizing what is particular about the study conclusions as well as what is universal, and considering how the universal elements might apply to a different context.

The concepts of generalizability and transferability have significance for considering the concept of "good" and "good enough" data because of the value research findings can have across different contexts (Tracy, 2010). Although we cannot expect that the experiences of individuals will be replicated or identically reflected in the experiences of others, *ideas* that emerge through generating in-depth data can be applicable or transferrable to other contexts. This points to an important distinction between generalizing in large-scale quantitative studies and in-depth studies about internal experiences. In large-scale quantitative studies, *researchers* determine the target population to which a sample can generalize. However, in qualitative studies that focus on explaining a phenomenon in-depth, it is the *readers* of the research who ultimately determine the relevance of the study to other contexts.

Table 11.2 compares the concepts of generalizability and transferability.

> **Pause and Reflect.** The concept of transferability is not one that is limited to experiences in the research world. Take a moment to think about a time when you applied information about one situation to a different situation. On what basis did you decide that the information was applicable to another context?

TABLE 11.2 ● Generalizability and Transferability

Generalizability	Transferability
• Generally applied to studies using numerical data for statistical analysis	• Generally applied to studies investigating a particular phenomenon in-depth using textual or visual data
• Focus is on making inferences about a population based on the study sample	• Focus is on explaining how findings from a study might apply to other empirical contexts *or* populations (transferability of *ideas*)
• Limited to the *target population* of a study	
• Conceptually important when explaining patterns or trends in some population	• Limited to the *universal elements* in study findings
• Onus is on *researchers* to explain to what extent study findings are generalizable	• Onus is on *readers* of the study to determine the transferability of findings to other contexts

RESEARCH SCENARIO: EVALUATING THE DATA GENERATION AND ACQUISITION PROCESS

In this section, we draw on two separate studies to highlight how issues related to collecting "enough" and in particular enough "good" data play out in the research process. The studies use very different approaches: One is based in the use of life history as a data generation tool to address broad theoretical questions, while the other is a survey study, using questionnaires to build a data set that highlights trends and patterns among a large number of organizations. The authors of each of the studies have written a "back story" to their project, which highlights their decision-making processes with respect to data generation.

How Do You Know You Have Enough Data? The Example of the Changing Fate Project: Pengfei Zhao

When I started to conceptualize my dissertation project, "Changing Fate: The Cultural Revolution's Rural Youth in Transition to Late-Socialist China," I began with a very broad theoretical question, namely, how people form and transform their identity in an era of radical social change. I came out with this question from my reading of social theories on identity. Most of the theories on identity highlight the intrinsic connection between social norms and self-understanding, by which they assume the social norms are relatively static in a society. Most of the existing theories have less to say about how people's identity transforms along with the changes in social norms and morality in an era of drastic social change. With this question in mind, I turned to the empirical world with which I was most familiar: China's rural society. The transition from socialism to late-socialism that rural China has gone through during the last three decades of the 20th century was fundamental and extensive. I thus felt that rural China would provide an empirical ground for me to explore the theoretical question I raised.

After discussing the issue of accessibility with my local informants, I decided to work with a former high school cohort (95 students in total): a group of people who received their school education in the Cultural Revolution (1966–1976), came of age during the transition from socialism to late-socialism, and were mostly in their late 50s when they participated in my project. Their school education exposed them to socialist collectivism and rural-oriented vocational knowledge, but as young adults, they had to establish themselves in an increasingly urbanized and privatized society. The theoretical question that I intended to explore—to put it in a simplified way— was translated into an empirical question of how this rural cohort transformed their identity from "socialist new peasants" to late-socialist subjects.

To develop an in-depth understanding of the experience of my research participants, I decided to employ the critical ethnographic approach in my study. In my field work, I widely employed qualitative methods such as life-history interviews, focus group discussions, participant observation, and archival research. Because of the nature of my work, I needed to work intensively with my research participants, and could only have a smaller sample size compared to most quantitative studies. My main goal in this project was to unpack the intricate connection between Chinese society's structural transformation and this group of former rural youth's individual experiences. As an empirical case, the project would shed light on the theoretical question in which I am interested. With this goal in mind, I was aware that strict generalizability based on a statistical relationship between the sample (my research participants) and the population (former Chinese rural youth who came of age in the same era as the research participants) did not apply to my study.

From 2011 to 2016, I spent multiple summers doing my field work in a county seat and surrounding rural areas in North China. I eventually interviewed 41 people from this former high school cohort through a combination of snowball and purposive sampling. I started with snowball sampling and with a few participants with whom I had long-term connections. Then these participants put me in touch with their former classmates, with whom I conducted more interviews. I also interviewed six former teachers of these participants, organized several focus group discussions, did archival research in two local archive departments, and joined my participants' social gatherings for participant observation.

After I was halfway through my fieldwork, I examined the demographic backgrounds and life paths of my participants to make sure that people of different genders, social statuses, life paths, and political backgrounds were included in my study. I found that the number of female participants was fewer than that of male participants. This was partly because males received more educational resources during the years when my research participants grew up, and consequentially the whole group of the 95 former students comprised only 29 women—much less than male students. I also realized that I interviewed more nonpeasant, middle-class participants than peasant participants, which might result in unintentionally silencing the voices of the peasant participants. Therefore, during the second half of my field work, I purposively recruited more female participants and more peasant participants to make sure that the less privileged subgroups in the cohort were well represented. As a result, I interviewed 15 female participants and 26 male participants in total. Fifty-two percent of the former female students and 39% of the former male students participated in my interviews. My interviewees also included 20 peasants (42% of the former students who are currently peasants) and 21 nonpeasants (45% of the former students who are currently nonpeasants).

Finally, my dissertation project data set includes 120 hours of audio/video-recorded interviews; 1,000+ pages of local archival documents; 4 focus group discussions; 100+ pages of field notes; and other visual or audio data either given by the research participants or retrieved from a variety of databases. I was able to identify recurrent themes across different narratives, triangulate relevant information, and discuss my interpretations with the participants.

I acknowledge that the findings of the project could not be generalized to all the rural youth in China. The value of the project lies in that, for the first time in both the Chinese and the English-speaking worlds, the Chinese rural youths' experiences of the transition to China's late-socialist era were documented and presented in a book-length study. What mattered most for me was to document their life stories in a rich, contextualized, and respectful way, as well as to bear witness to the country's difficult past. Meanwhile, the project also contributes to discussions about critical and social theories on the formation, reproduction, and transformation of identity.

Above, Pengfei discusses the steps she took to ensure that she was able to generate and acquire sufficient data in order to answer her empirical and theoretical research questions. As she points out, this study is not one that would be considered generalizable, because she focused on the in-depth experiences of a specific group: individuals in China who received their formal education during the period of the Cultural Revolution. Her emphasis on the formation and transformation of each of these individuals entailed a focus on inner meaning as constructed by her research participants. Yet, as Pengfei notes, her analysis highlighted broader links between individual identity formation and structural transformation at a societal level. These kinds of links might potentially transfer across contexts, even if the specifics of her participants' experiences cannot.

We can also see from Pengfei's discussion that her data generation and acquisition process enabled her to ensure different groups she thought could provide important theoretical insights (females and peasants) were well represented in her study. Her focus on making sure these groups were well represented helped ensure that Pengfei's data, and thus the inferences she drew, were an accurate representation of this cohort. Pengfei's use of multiple kinds of data in addition to her interviews—archival documents, focus group discussions, and other materials collected from interviewees and databases—was also important in ensuring she reached saturation and could see the same themes recurring across her data as a whole.

Global Survey of LGBT NGOs Working in Education: Oren Pizmony-Levy

My interest in LGBT nongovernmental organizations (NGOs) began in the early 2000s, when I joined the Israeli Gay Youth Organization. As a young activist I was always curious to learn from the experience of NGOs in other countries. The main reason was the simple fact that back then, there were no other LGBT organizations in Israel that focused on education or youth. More than a decade later, after I completed my doctoral degree, this curiosity led me to conduct a study of LGBT NGOs working in education. My reading of the literature led me to two research questions:

1. *How do LGBT NGOs challenge schools to be more open to different sexual orientations and gender identities?*

2. *To what extent does the work of LGBT NGOs vary across different social contexts (e.g., countries that are more or less accepting of homosexuality)?*

The main objective of the global survey was to document the services and programs that LGBT NGOs provide, and to discern patterns based on the social context in which they operate. Therefore, it was important to collect information about NGOs in diverse contexts.

The first task was to define the population. Our research team and I started with examining the "lay of the land." Overall, the LGBT movement worldwide is remarkably organized. There are many organizations (also known as social movement organizations

[SMOs]), and in many places there are well-established networks, such as the ILGA—*International Lesbian, Gay, Bisexual, Trans and Intersex Association*. *In some countries there are specialized organizations that focus solely on education and youth. However, this is not the case everywhere. In some countries, depending on resources and social acceptance of homosexuality, individuals work in alternative formats (e.g., groups, collectives, etc.). Thus, we decided to keep the term* NGO, *but also to include alternative terms for collective action around the issues of LGBT rights and education.*

We then conducted a census of all LGBT NGOs that work in formal and nonformal education. First, we searched websites of international and regional networks for NGOs that gave some indication of working with youth or schools. These included NGO directories and soft (electronic) copies of annual meeting programs/schedules. Second, we used Google to find additional links and references to relevant NGOs. For example, we found documents produced by NGOs and reports by foundations that gave money to LGBT organizations. In addition to English, our research team conducted searches in eight languages: French, Hebrew, Japanese, Portuguese, Russian, Spanish, and Traditional and Simplified Chinese. Although the term LGBT *is common worldwide, in some countries activists used other labels, such as sexual minorities and sexual diversity. Therefore, we used different search terms in order to minimize the effect of our search protocol on the census. Third, we conducted searches in two common social media platforms: Facebook and Twitter, using hashtags such as #LGBT and #LGBTyouth. We also created a Facebook page for the project to communicate with NGOs and activists worldwide (https://www.facebook.com/LGBTYouthNGOs2014).*

We entered the results of these searches into one, large Excel spreadsheet. For each organization, we entered basic contact information: name, location, website, social media, email, and phone number. Once the search was completed, we cleaned the data by combining duplicate records. These efforts yielded a database with 687 entries.

Our next task was to develop a sampling strategy for this population of organizations. Because our research team had limited resources, we decided to sample only NGOs that had a working email or active social media account. This way we could collect data through an online survey. This sampling approach is not free of limitations, and we had to recognize that our sample would be biased toward NGOs with greater capacity. In the future, we would like to extend the sampling to all NGOs by using alternative forms of data generation including mail surveys and face-to-face interviews in different locations.

To make sure we were not missing other NGOs, we also implemented a snowball sampling protocol. We asked respondents to share with us the names and email addresses of other LGBT NGOs working in education. Most of our respondents shared with us the contact information of one other NGO. In some cases, we already had the information for these additional NGOs in our census. However, overall the snowball sampling protocol yielded information for 152 additional NGOs that we had not previously included in our database.

Data generation (our survey dissemination) took place between July 2014 and July 2015. In the first phase (July–December 2014), we sent out invitations to participate in the survey. We sent two reminders: 2 weeks after the initial invitation and again 1 month after the initial invitation. In the second phase (April–July 2015) we contacted remaining NGOs (those from which we had not received a response to our survey) with an individualized message. By doing that we tried to better understand and address any concerns that activists had regarding the survey. We also contacted respondents who submitted partial responses (less than 75% of the questions answered) and invited them to complete the survey. This approach improved the quality of the data we obtained and prevented us from losing cases (due to missing data). In total our survey included full responses from 310 NGOs working in 110 countries.

During the data generation process, we monitored, on a weekly basis, the number of new responses to the survey. After 10 months and many efforts to encourage NGOs to participate in the survey, we observed that the survey reached a plateau. We compared the composition of the sample to the census (database) of organizations and found that overall our sample turned out to closely mirror the census in terms of geographic region, affluence (indicated by membership in OECD), and legal context for LGBT individuals. Therefore, we decided to close the survey and to move forward with analysis and writing.

Oren's discussion highlights a different approach to considering the main issues in collecting "enough" and "good" data. In this study, prior to determining a sample strategy, Oren and his research team needed to determine the population of organizations engaging in programming relevant to his topic of focus. Only after determining that population could a sampling strategy be decided upon. As Oren notes, the strategy of targeting only organizations with an established social media presence and/or email address limited the generalizability of findings, since these organizations also tended to be those with greater resources. Although this might be perceived as an indication that the data weren't sufficiently "good" to fully answer the research questions, in truth most studies are unable to include a fully representative sample. However, it is important to acknowledge (as Oren does here) the limitations of one's results, and in particular *in what ways* the inferences are limited. Also relevant here is the use of multiple terms—*collectives, groups, NGOs*—to define the population of the study. By using multiple terms, the researchers helped mitigate against potential bias in the study due to their Western-centric view of social organizations.

Another point to note about this study is how the research team addressed issues of missing data: by individually contacting organizations that had returned an incomplete survey in order to obtain responses to unanswered questions. This ensured a larger data set of survey responses to analyze, and prevented the research team from having to decide how to input or whether to exclude surveys with missing data.

Table 11.3 compares the two studies in terms of how methodological concepts were applied to these two study contexts. The table illustrates how in each study, the researchers dealt with some of the possible questions researchers might ask themselves with respect to ensuring "enough" data, "good" data, and results that might have significance beyond the study participants. From this comparison, you can see that the specifics of how these issued were addressed in each study varied quite a bit, highlighting both similarities in methodological concepts and their differences across different kinds of studies.

TABLE 11.3 ● Research Scenario Comparison

Questions Addressed	Changing Fate Project	Global Survey of LGBT NGOs
• Was I able to get responses across demographic groups? • Which perspectives or demographics may have been missed?	***Multiple Steps:*** • Snowball sampling to connect with the full cohort of students • Monitoring of demographic backgrounds of interviewees in order to ensure representation of different groups	***Multiple Steps:*** • Search for websites in multiple languages to create initial database • Snowball sampling to ensure NGOs were not missed
• What significance do results have beyond the study sample? • How did I ensure my results were representative of the population?	• Nongeneralizable study • Potential transferability of links between individual identity formation and structural transformation at a societal level	• Limited generalizability to LGBT NGOs as a whole because of focus on those with a web/social media presence • Use of multiple terms to mitigate against Western-centric understanding of "NGOs"
• How did I know I generated enough data? • How did I mitigate against missing data?	• Use of archival documents, focus group discussions, and other materials in addition to interview data, to ensure saturation	• Individual contact when surveys were incomplete to mitigate against missing data

YOU AND RESEARCH

As we wrap up this chapter, let's think about how the concepts we have discussed here might translate into your own empirical research processes.

When Interpreting Research

You will most explicitly come across discussions about "good" and "enough" data in the methodology section of a study, specifically in sections discussing how participants were recruited. These sections often also include information about response rates (where relevant), and demographic or other relevant information about participants, and sometimes address how missing data were handled (where relevant). As you read these sections, reflect upon the relationship between the research questions, target population (as relevant), and study participants. Does the sampling strategy make sense?

Another place to look for information pertaining to "good" and "enough" data will be in discussions about study limitations. Here researchers may address potential limitations that pertain to the representativeness of the sample, the number of participants, and so on. Not all studies will include this information, however. As you read empirical research, look to see whether and how researchers address these limitations.

Finally, think about the relationship between the research questions, the data presented, and the inferences made. Is there sufficient evidence to indicate data saturation? Are generalizations being made on the basis of a sufficient, or sufficiently representative, sample?

When Doing Research

As you prepare to undertake an empirical study and work on writing your research proposal, you will need to consider how much data you will generate or acquire and what forms that data might take. A central set of choices will address sampling and sample size. For example, if you are planning a large-scale survey study, your starting point will be the target population from which you will be recruiting study participants. You will need to ensure that your participants are representative of this population. (As noted above, there are statistical formulas that can help determine this.) You will also need to consider response rates, whether there are certain groups within the population that need greater representation in your sample, and so on.

A more in-depth project will require sampling decisions to be made based on estimations of how you can achieve saturation. As we saw with Pengfei's study, it may not be possible at the outset to know exactly what this number will be: Sarah Baker and Rosalind Edwards (2012) remind us that there is no exact formula for determining how much data are "enough." However, when submitting your proposal to your institutional review board, you will need to include an intended sample size and keep to this number or range. If the number of participants in your study changes by more than a few individuals, you will likely need to modify your study protocol. Table 11.1 earlier in the chapter may be a helpful resource for considering your sampling approach.

It is also important to reflect on how you might deal with having more data than you need, especially when you are doing time-bound research and will quite likely be focused on finding a way to complete your thesis/dissertation/study write-up. The need to complete your research project may stand in the way of an ideal situation where you are able to integrate all data. Thus, be realistic about what you think you will be able to do. Likewise, reflect upon how you might deal with missing data. What will be your approach?

SYNTHESIS: POINTS FOR REFLECTION

Conceptual Synthesis

In this chapter we continued the discussion begun in Chapter 10 about concrete elements of the data generation process, particularly as related to generating and acquiring appropriate data *quantities* as well as ensuring that the data are *quality* data. We focused on using validity and ethics as lenses for exploring whether the data generated or acquired are "good" and/or "enough." But it is worth considering the limitations of these lenses as well, and possibilities for other foundations upon which one might explore the "goodness" of data. For example, Pengfei's research scenario emphasizes the importance of bringing in voices that are generally not heard in research processes: The inclusiveness she discusses is another way of thinking about what might make data "good" that focuses on issues of social justice and emancipatory interests. Her decision about who to include suggests a certain perspective on what makes data "good" and the basis for quality inference-making.

Methodological Synthesis

There are a number of different choices about the specifics of data generation and acquisition that shape whether one has *enough* data to make generalizable or transferable inferences, and whether these are *good* or quality data. These choices primarily have to do with whether participants are representative of the target population (if this is important), how missing data from participants are treated, and so on. Depending on the kind of study conducted, we may or may not be able to make choices about who and how many individuals should be included in the research ahead of time; however, this is not always the case. Again, Pengfei's research scenario serves as a good example: It was only following her first few rounds of fieldwork that she realized the voices of women were not adequately included.

Personal Synthesis

As always, an important theme running through this chapter is providing space for you to reflect on your own perspective regarding what constitutes "good" or "enough" data. At this juncture, take a few minutes to think about the lens (or lenses) through which you might view "goodness." Also think about the logistical considerations that might shape your potential data generation processes. For instance, if you are conducting an empirical study, might you have the financial or other resources to make multiple trips for data generation? As we wrap up this cluster of chapters and move more explicitly into discussing inference-making, keep these questions in mind and remember that the choices made about data generation—both in terms of *what data* (discussed in Chapter 10) and *how much data* to generate and acquire—serve as the basis for the inferences that you might make.

MOVING FORWARD

This is the last chapter in the data cluster. The next section of the book moves into the process of making inferences. Chapter 12 will provide an overview of the inferential/analytical process. This discussion will build on our discussion of data generation and acquisition as addressed in this chapter and the previous chapters in the cluster.

Further Readings

Fusch, P. I., & Ness, L. R. (2015). Are we there yet? Data saturation in qualitative research. *The Qualitative Report, 20*(9), 1408–1416.

Groves, R. M., Cialdini, R. B., & Couper, M. P. (1992). Understanding the decision to participate in a survey. *Public Opinion Quarterly, 56*(4), 475–495.

Kaplowitz, M. D., Hadlock, T. D., & Levine, R. (2004). A comparison of web and mail survey response rates. *Public Opinion Quarterly, 68*(1), 94–101.

Weidmaier, B. (2017). Statistical power analysis. In M. Allen (Ed.), *The SAGE encyclopedia of communication research methods*. Retrieved from http://methods.sagepub.com/reference/the-sage-encyclopedia-of-communication-research-methods/i13981.xml?fromsearch=true

Further Readings by Oren Pizmony-Levy

Pizmony-Levy, O. (2011). Bridging the global and local in understanding curricula scripts: The case of environmental education. *Comparative Education Review, 55*(4), 600–633.

Pizmony-Levy, O., & Green Saraisky, N. (2016). *Who opts out and why? Results from a national survey on opting out of standardized tests* (Research report). New York, NY: Teachers College, Columbia University.

Pizmony-Levy, O., & Kosciw, J. G. (2016). School climate and the experience of LGBT students: A comparison of the United States and Israel. *Journal of LGBT Youth, 13*(1–2), 46–66.

HOW DO WE CONCEPTUALIZE "INFERENCE"?

CONNECTING THE DOTS

Often, approaching the end of a semester, we have students tell us, "I feel like, finally, I can connect the dots [about research methodology]." Their expression makes us think: What does it mean to connect the dots, and how do we do that?

Imagine you are working on a connect-the-dot puzzle. At the beginning, the dots seem to be discrete, dispersed, and do not make any sense to you. As you follow the order of the numbers and connect them one by one, gradually the contour of an object emerges. In the midst of the drawing, you may start to recognize what this picture could be, but you are not 100% sure. You are curious and sometimes skeptical about your own judgment, yet you keep going. You cannot wait to see the completion of the drawing, a moment when the picture reveals itself to you. As you connect the last two dots, a sense of relief and certainty rises. "Look! It's a snowflake," you tell yourself or your game partner (see Figure CL3.1).

Now, how shall we connect the dots in the journey of learning research methodology? For us, if the steps, procedures, and concepts are the dots in this space, it is inference that drives our move from one dot to another. Without inference, we may know what epistemology means or how a researcher goes about designing a survey, but we can lose sight of the interconnection between our onto-epistemological commitment and our practice of generating and acquiring data, or of the design of a survey and the interpretation of its results.

The chapters in Cluster 3 are designed to explore the inference-making process in social research. The chapters in this last cluster seek to establish dialogues about the concepts, types, and impacts of inference in the context of social research; tie together the previous chapters through identifying inferences in different stages and

268　Making Sense of Social Research Methodology

FIGURE CL3.1　Connect-the-Dot Puzzle

Draw a line from dot number 1 to dot number 2, then from dot number 2 to dot number 3, 3 to 4, and so on. Continue to join the dots until you have connected all the numbered dots. Then color the picture!

ANSWER:

iStock.com/ratselmeister

procedures of research; and eventually, address the impact of inferences on individual and societal levels. This opener briefly summarizes the features of our approach and gives you an overview of each chapter in this cluster.

In Chapter 12 we start our discussion of inference by exploring its relationship with meaning-making in our everyday life. At this level, the use of natural language, or symbolic mediated communication, is at the center of our investigation. Our discussion moves away from a correspondence theory of truth and problematizes the widely held belief that language is a form of representation. Meaning-making in everyday language is instead contingent upon context, culture, and norms, and is thus inherently uncertain. We introduce critical pragmatism as the theoretical orientation we use to grapple with the tentative and situated meaning in everyday language. Regardless of qualitative or quantitative approaches, the inference process in social science is first of all grounded in this everyday meaning-making. In this chapter, we re-conceptualize induction and deduction, two inferential approaches widely used by social researchers, from a critical pragmatist perspective.

Moving from Chapter 12 to Chapters 13 and 14, we zoom into the inferences we make during data analysis. Methodological texts tend to treat data analysis as a unique stage of research practice, separated from the generation and acquisition of data. From the perspective of inference-making, we contend that researchers are already making inferences about what we might consider data when we make choices about what data generation and/or acquisition approaches we can or should use. The interpretations that researchers make at the formalized stage of data analysis are connected to their previous work of conceptualizing and designing the study. Focusing on low-level and high-level inferences, respectively, Chapters 13 and 14 dive into the rationales and analytic techniques of data analysis. Our analysis will make the most sense if we start from low-level inference, which encompasses the description of numeric, textual, and visual data. Chapter 13 introduces several key terms and approaches used for low-level inference-making, such as descriptive statistics and thick description. High-level inferences, as unpacked in Chapter 14, lead us beyond description to identify larger trends and patterns. In this chapter, we look at a wide range of approaches to making high-level inferences, including correlation and causation, modeling, structural analysis, theorization, and consciousness raising.

Chapter 15 discusses the role of writing in facilitating the inference-making process. Writing is often perceived as a way to present findings, namely, the results of researchers' inferences. We argue that a product-oriented approach to writing tends to ignore the opportunities and spaces that writing itself offers for self-growth and mutual understanding. In this chapter, we suggest a process-oriented approach to writing, considering it a relationally responsible practice through which an author engages not only readers but also research participants and stakeholders.

Researchers do not make inferences in a vacuum. Instead, the inferences researchers make have profound social implications. Chapter 16 addresses the multifaceted impacts of inference-making at societal, cultural, organizational, and individual levels. In this chapter, we critically examine the current discourse of research impact that centers on the calculation of "impact factors" and expand how research impact could be conceptualized in relation to social structure, power, and empowerment, as well as cultural changes. Circling back to the relationship between social action/social research and social structure introduced in Chapter 6, Chapter 16 leads us to explore how the consequences of social research become the conditions of social actions.

Going back to the metaphor of the connect-the-dot puzzle, we call for continuously grappling with the relationship between the discrete dots and the line that links them together. In the context of social research, this means to critically engage two relationships: (1) the relationship between inferences and different stages and procedures in research, and (2) the relationship between inferences and discrete sets of analytic skills.

To address the first relationship, Cluster 3 ties the discussion of inference-making back to the foundational concepts of social inquiry introduced in Cluster 1. It revisits the key themes and concepts presented in the first cluster and looks at how they manifest in the process of inference-making. For instance, Cluster 3 explores the question of how a researcher can approach ethical issues in the process of analyzing data and making inferences. The philosophic principles we discuss in Cluster 1 continuously guide us in Cluster 3, not as abstract discourses but as the commitments that we strive to honor through doing the analysis. Meanwhile, we zoom out to look at how inference-making as a process starts far earlier than the analysis of data, and across different stages of research. Although Clusters 2 and 3 are organized in a way that follows the stages that a researcher goes through in research practice, it is important to remember that we are inferring, making connections among different concepts, and building rationales from the moment when we endeavor to articulate the background of our study and formulate our research questions.

To address the second relationship, we notice the tendency in today's methodological discourse to take qualitative and quantitative data analysis as two distinctive approaches hardly crossing paths. Sometimes, this distinction reduces inference-making to two sets of skills: coding and statistics. Going beyond the skill-oriented and dichotomous approach, we regroup these analytic skills not along the lines of quantitative and qualitative research but according to types of inferences that researchers can enact using these skills. Therefore, in the chapter on low-level inferences, we offer concepts and examples related to both quantitative and qualitative analysis. The same organizing approach applies to our discussion of high-level inferences. What we would like to emphasize in this cluster is the importance of justifying the chosen analytic approach(es) and reflectively appraising the applicability, limits, and boundaries of the chosen approach(es). Eventually, we hope to link the dots between our analysis of the data and the potential social impact of the research.

As you start to read the chapters in Cluster 3, pay attention to the questions, relationships, and organizational guidelines we discussed in this cluster opener. The end of Cluster 3 wraps up the entire journey of reading this book, yet your own journey with social research has just started. When the time comes for you to draw your own picture, what would you like to draw in your blueprint?

12

UNDERSTANDING INFERENCE AS A PROCESS

Imagine a student, having just finished the data collection aspects of their study, returns from their fieldwork experiencing both anxiety and excitement. The student is thinking to themselves, "Wow, I have all these data. Now what?" Yes. *Now what?* This question taps into the process of data analysis and indicates that the researcher must do something to get from data to findings. This movement from data to findings, broadly referred to as *analysis*, involves the researcher making inferences from the data. Inference-making is generally implicit in any interpretations we might think of as data analysis. Our goal is to raise awareness of the different types and levels of inference-making relevant for the analyses of data.

We begin by looking at the nature of inferencing through a couple of ordinary stories involving Pengfei and her daughter Iris; then we think about inferencing through an evaluation example. In the research scenario we learn about inferencing from Dr. Katharine Broton with respect to her research on food insecurity. We develop concepts related to inferencing (or inference-making) by moving from the ordinary context to research and we illustrate how inferences are linked with epistemology (from Chapters 2 and 3) and validity (from Chapters 5 and 7).

MUSING UPON THE EVERYDAY: THE WORLD OF IRIS

As a methodologist, Pengfei often receives requests from students and colleagues for suggestions on their data analysis. While helping people navigate their analysis processes, she wonders how everyday reasoning, in its very broad sense, is involved in how we come to understand, interpret, and make inferences within our ordinary interactions. To better understand these questions, she set off to observe her 3-year-old daughter, Iris. Pengfei was very interested in how Iris enacts the burgeoning forms of reasoning in her explorations of the world.

Iris, 3 years old, was raised bilingually (English and Chinese) and had spent most of her time with her parents in the United States. During the time Iris was between 2 and a half and 3 years old, both her English and Chinese vocabularies expanded rapidly. Each day, Iris explored the world with ceaseless curiosity, a little bit of caution—and, of course, some reasoning. She used her blossoming language to describe, suggest, argue, constantly negotiate, and occasionally agree with others. Communication is inherently linked with assumptions we make about reasoning. For example, when we understand someone, we understand their reasoning or the reasons they would give to explain or justify what they said or did. Here are two examples of Iris's thinking processes during that time:

Scene 1: Iris made a line of chairs, pretending she was on a train. Meanwhile, she opened her mom's umbrella, one of her favorite toys during this time.

Iris: *Mama, come here. To the umbrella.*

Pengfei: *Oh, why?*

Iris: *Inside* [Pengfei noticed that she meant inside the train] *is raining.*

Pengfei: *Really?*

Iris: *Yeah. Because I have the umbrella.*

Scene 2: Iris loved idly sucking her fingers. Pengfei tried to persuade her that she was too old to do that. One evening, Iris was relaxing on the sofa with two of her fingers in her mouth.

Pengfei: *Hey Iris, what are you doing?*

Iris: *I am a baby. Wawawa* [pretending to cry like a baby and meanwhile waving her legs and arms].

If one only pays attention to what was said in this conversation, the words would not make sense. For instance, in Scene 2 Iris did not directly answer Pengfei's question; instead, she claimed to be a baby. In Scene 1, Iris implied that holding the umbrella caused it to rain inside the train. Both scenes make the most sense when interpreted from within their contexts. In Scene 2, Iris was referencing the multiple prior conversations she had with her mom, in which Pengfei tried to convince her that she was a big girl already, and that a big girl does not suck her fingers. Iris was claiming the status of baby as a way for it to still be okay to suck her fingers without being disciplined by her mom. In order to meaningfully interpret Iris's playfulness in Scene 1, Pengfei noticed that Iris's imagination was inspired by what she was doing (holding the umbrella while sitting on the chair) and not the other way around (having the image of sitting on a train with rain falling on the inside and then deciding to enact that scene). Pengfei was interpreting Iris's words in light of what she was doing: arranging chairs like she was on a train, for example. When Pengfei drew inferences from what Iris said, she did so from within the context of the scene. This is how we make inferences all day long in our ordinary lives.

We are constantly making sense of one another by drawing on *implicit* inferences—that is, those inferences that are typically left unsaid. Through the narrative and conceptual interludes below, we will explore the ways in which our ordinary interpretation processes are both similar and different to how we make sense of data through analyses.

NARRATIVE AND CONCEPTUAL INTERLUDES I: MAKING SENSIBLE INTERPRETATIONS

While we ponder over the meaning-making process in our everyday life and in researchers' analysis of data, let's look at a different scenario. Imagine that you were an evaluator hired by a local high school to evaluate the effectiveness of a school-wide project. How would you decide what an effective evaluation might be?

One of our students from a research methodology class, Nathan Swinger, shared with us his high school experience of participating in a school-wide campaign. This specific campaign, the Tone of Decency Campaign, aimed at promoting polite social activities and reducing violence. In an online course discussion post, Nathan wrote:

> *During my sophomore year in high school, the administrators introduced a Tone of Decency campaign. They put up pictures of frogs with ToD written on them around the high school, had short introductions to basic conflict resolution, and set clear expectations for the ways that we should interact with each other and with the teachers. They also provided raffle tickets if you were caught by the teachers or staff being decent or kind. We thought this was stupid and we openly mocked "tone of decency." But we did so during times that people were being rude or unkind or conflict was beginning, short-circuiting these behaviors. I certainly did not think this was an effective method of decreasing violence and I can't imagine that any of my friends did either. But the funny thing is that violence did decrease. For the first time in over 30 years, there was not a single fight in the school. Detentions decreased, suspensions decreased. It was a fantastic success*

in sparking us to stop and reconsider whatever poor path we were starting down. Unfortunately, like many things, this program was derailed by a small, unlucky detail. During the Super Bowl that year, Budweiser unveiled their Bud-Weis-Er frog campaign. [Check this link to see the original version of this advertisement: https://www.youtube.com/watch? v=WkavReH4LE0. The Budweiser frog ad was successful at the beginning but also drew some growing concerns. Studies found that children showed affinity to the animated frogs in the advertisement, which made the public start to question the effect of this alcohol advertisement on minors (https://www.sfgate.com/business/article/Budweiser-s-Frogs-Beat-Out-Smokey-In-Study-of-Kids-2985200.php). The frog ad was discontinued in 1998.] *Some parents felt that the Tone of Decency frogs looked too similar to the Budweiser frogs and would encourage us to drink alcohol, so the program was stopped after the first year and unfortunately the school's incidence of violence returned to pre-intervention levels over the next 2 years. So was the program successful during its implementation? I'd argue from the behaviors that it was a fantastic success, but if you had given us Likert scales* [which were introduced in Chapter 10] *at the time, I think you would have had a very different impression.* (Swinger, 2018, online discussion post for "Strategies in Educational Research" course at Indiana University)

There are, as Nathan wrote in his post, many ways to think about effectiveness. Various ways of thinking about effectiveness are already implied through the evaluation process itself. We can think of the various ways to interpret a program as successful as potential inferences. Choices made regarding the design and data of the evaluation set parameters around what inferences were possible. For example, if program effectiveness is defined as a decrease in violence, then one's evaluation would necessarily involve counting violent incidents and comparing that with the number of incidents prior to implementing the program. Even if the evaluation is limited to examining whether or not the implementation of the Tone of Decency Campaign resulted in a decrease in the amount of violent activities recorded at the school, other factors could easily have contributed to a decrease in violence. In other words, to claim that the Campaign *caused* or even *contributed to* a decrease in violence, the evaluators would have to exclude other likely factors that could also have explained, influenced, or contributed to the decrease. For example, maybe the ways kids were making fun of the program might have resulted in less violence just because they were establishing camaraderie as a counter to the program itself. Moreover, even if you could pin down the Campaign as the major catalyst in decreasing students' violent behavior, as a responsible researcher, you would not want to neglect the potential side effects of this campaign, such as the potential that it encouraged students to drink alcohol. Just as we are suggesting with the ToD Campaign, when evaluators or researchers produce findings, they are essentially and inevitably producing outcomes of an inferential process—they are gathering up those inferences and deciding what to share.

In both the example of the Tone of Decency Campaign and the notes about Iris's interactions with Pengfei, we situate our highly abstract questions about inference-making in concrete situations. These examples help us complicate our understanding of some of the key ideas we will explore in this chapter. For instance, in our interactions with others, do we understand the interactions merely by the words used? What does it mean, in investigating a complex social phenomenon, to state that one phenomenon *causes* the other one? How is reasoning linked with inferencing? Do we have to exclude our emotions, embodied feelings, values, and other factors conventionally viewed as not strong enough reasoning to serve research purposes? These are all good questions for us to think with as we delve into more abstract theoretical discussions. Our hope is that, through the dynamic move between the concrete and the abstract, we will develop a more comprehensive and holistic understanding of what it means to make inferences in social science research. In the cluster chapters that follow, concrete forms of inferencing in social science will be presented and will build on the conceptual-theoretical foundations laid out in this chapter.

Correspondence Thinking and Its Problems

To get us started, let's take a moment to recall the correspondence theory of truth introduced in Chapter 7 because correspondence theory/thinking is deeply embedded in the social sciences. Correspondence theorists contend that a knowledge claim is best judged by "the accuracy and completeness of how well the assertion represents the state of affairs under study" (from Chapter 7). **Correspondence Theory of Meaning** (which we also refer to as correspondence thinking) suggests that there is a direct, one-to-one correspondence between a symbol and its meaning. This way of thinking is dependent upon a **Representational Theory of Meaning**, which argues that symbols (words and images, primarily) represent the meaning of the thing being symbolized, such as the word *umbrella* symbolizing the thing we call "umbrella." Important assumptions to correspondence thinking include:

1. The correspondence theory assumes that understanding is based on a word making a direct reference to the meaning it represents in a one-to-one correspondence. From these basic building blocks of words, a language user will build sentences and paragraphs.

2. Examining the correspondence between the word and what it represents assumes that a language user takes a position of an observer to judge the accuracy of the correspondence primarily through perception. For example, one would hear "rain" and observe to see or feel water drops from the sky. Perception

thus is prioritized in correspondence theories and can also be linked back the epistemological and ontological beliefs rooted in the empiricist-positivist/post-positivist intellectual tradition, as discussed in Chapter 5.

3. When an observer makes an inferential claim to know something, correspondence theorists would assume that it is best or most ideal for the observer to be value neutral as they report whatever they perceive, thereby ensuring that the one-to-one correspondence is not biased at all.

4. Correspondence theorists assume that inferences consist of representational connections between empirical phenomena and what they reference. Some correspondence theorists think of inference as a matter of identifying patterns of the observable associations between objects.

5. An important form of inference, along this line of thought, is induction, which infers the unobserved from what have been observed based on an assumed resemblance between them. For instance, let's assume that a researcher studied the implementation of the Tone of Decency Campaign in 20 high schools in Indiana and found all these campaigns effectively reduce the violent behaviors among students. They might feel confident to arrive at the conclusion that the Tone of Decency Campaign would be effective if implemented in other Indiana high schools. This conclusion would reflect an inductive form of inference because it would take as its starting point existing observations and use them to make inferences about other contexts that have not been observed.

Let's go back to the example of Iris's use of the word *rain*. A representational theory of meaning would suggest that *rain*, the word, represents the physical manifestation of falling moisture from the atmosphere. Correspondence thinking depends on this representational theory to indicate that the use of the word *rain* carries a one-to-one correspondence with the physical condition of rain. In this subsection we argue that induction is dependent upon a correspondence theory of meaning and that inferencing always involves both inductive and deductive ways of thinking. We suggest that correspondence thinking and representational theories are too direct and rigid to explain the amount of negotiation and uncertainty we encounter when we interact with one another and hope to understand one another. Similarly, we suggest that when our notions of research and interpretation are explained through representation or correspondence theories of meaning, that those explanations fail to account for the rich complexity of meaning and interpretation we find even among some of our youngest language users and knowledge seekers. For example, Iris's use of the word (symbol) *rain* cannot be well understood if there is only one way to interpret the meaning of rain. Instead, we can understand that Iris's use of the word *rain* (and its correspondence to the typical definition of the word) makes a game of the meaning that requires imagination. The imaginary is inferred—that is, it does not have to be said explicitly for us to understand what Iris means.

In Figure 12.1 we see a stack of rocks, but this stack of rocks has come to mean something more than its bare description. It has come to mean something of peace and balance. The correspondence between what we see (rocks of different sizes and colors stacked on top of each other) and the words we would use to describe what we see is insufficient for capturing the cultural interpretations of this stack of rocks.

FIGURE 12.1 ● The Richness of Meaning

Source: iStock/luismmolina.

Representation, or the idea that a symbol directly represents what it names, plays a crucial role in formulating correspondence-oriented truth claims. In other words, a researcher following the correspondence theory will both establish and assume a direct link between a sign and that to which the sign refers. For instance, we use the linguistic symbol "rain" to indicate a situation when "water falls from the sky in drops" (*Oxford Learner's Dictionary*). From this perspective, Iris's statement could not be considered meaningful or true since she was not directly referring to real rain. Instead, she used the word *raining* to describe an imagined situation. While that situation depends, in part, on understanding the reference to precipitation, it is not best understood through a one-to-one correspondence. As a participant in the interaction, Pengfei immediately understood Iris's imaginary play and its connection with the umbrella. If meaning-making starts with the word-by-word correspondence between the linguistic symbols and objects of phenomena being represented, how could Pengfei have known that Iris was engaging in imaginary play? This question reveals the first crack of the theoretical edifice of correspondence thinking. Certainly, we use correspondences to understand one another, but those relationships alone do not capture the way meaning and knowledge work on the whole. So while there might be a correspondence involved in thinking about the word *rain* and the phenomenon of precipitation, our understanding of the word *rain* when it is used must contextualize the correspondence in a way that includes how it is being used, for what purposes, and in what ways. In this situation, Iris was playing with her mom and she was using the word in an imaginary sense to help generate that play. While there was still a reference in Iris's use of the word *rain* to the precipitation we associate with the word, what she said would be considered nonsense without the pragmatic context of imaginary play.

> **Pause and Reflect.** Iris used the word *rain* to mean more than a one-to-one correspondence with precipitation. Her use of the word opened up an idea in our imagination that was facilitated by putting up the umbrella. The umbrella seemed to have caused the rain to appear in Iris's mind. The umbrella was real, but the rain was imagined. We would miss that the word *rain* was meant to conjure up an opportunity for playing with the umbrella if we did not have the context of her play as the situation through which we were making sense of use of the word. We want you to think about one of the following three examples of interpretation contexts in order to identify what might be the correspondence aspect of meaning, but then also consider how that correspondence is inadequate for producing a strong understanding of the situation: (1) a story in a local newspaper claims to accurately and faithfully report on criminal activity in the town the night before; (2) photographs of a wedding that claim to capture memorable moments of the event; and (3) an individual's IQ score is thought to reflect this person's intelligence. In each example you can identify the symbol (words for Example 1, images for Example 2, and test score for Example 3) with what it is meant to correspond. After doing that, think about how that correspondence would limit our understanding if what we knew was reduced to the correspondence. What else would you want to know in order to have a good knowledge or understanding in each case?

Problems With the Correspondence Theory and Its Representational Theory of Meaning

The correspondence theory has perpetuated a series of assumptions regarding truth, validity, objectivity, and bias. In previous chapters, we have questioned a taken-for-granted representational/correspondent relationship between the words and numbers we use on the one hand, and what they represent on the other hand. For instance, in Chapters 5 and 7, we pointed out that representational thinking reduces our understanding of human life experiences. We suggested that operationalization (a process for researchers to turn certain measurable characteristics of a social phenomenon into numbers; Chapter 9) can have similarly limiting effects. In Chapter 10 we introduced the idea that data are representations. In this section, we deepen our critique by examining:

1. the power structure underlying representational relationships; and
2. the challenge posed by probability thinking to sense certainty.

Let's use an everyday example to illustrate our first point. For instance, a person is visiting a doctor for a severe back pain, and then they are asked to use the "universal pain scale" to rate/measure their pain via a scale of 1–10 based on their own experiences of pain. The patient might wonder how this number they picked would accurately represent their embodied feeling of pain. They might want to add some clarifications about their pain—something like, "Actually, my pain is more subtle than Level 6, but I also feel very tired and dizzy." If the doctor showed no interest in listening to their explanation, and solely relied on the pain rating to establish the severity of their medical problem, how would they feel? Might they feel frustrated because the number itself would not fully express their feelings?

If the person with the power to evaluate medical needs and to plan possible treatments—a power established through expertise, cultural tradition, and legal frameworks—only took the numbers into account, the patient's reported number will have additional connotations related to the imbalance of power on how their pain becomes relevant to ensuing medical decisions. Is there a way for the patient to challenge the doctor? It seems to us that challenging the doctor's practice means simultaneously problematizing the power relationship between a doctor and their patients. Power issues sneak into knowledge production despite correspondence thinking being assumed to be value neutral.

Now let's consider our second point. While philosophers and social scientists probe the political connotations of representation, on the other end of the spectrum of knowledge production, natural scientists have, for a long time, endeavored to grapple with the nature of measurement. Their work leads us to recognize the problems with sense certainty (taking what we sense as certain or sure) upon which both correspondence thinking and representational theories are built. A common understanding about **measurement** holds that an observer can establish accurate ways to measure and calculate observations as outcomes of experiments, by relying on what is observable and measurable—that is, by relying on our senses to take in the information. Late-19th century British scientist Karl Pearson challenged social science assumptions of sense certainty by pointing out that all experiments are imperfect in nature. In other words, no matter how carefully the experimenter carries out their inquiries, they can never exclude all the unforeseeable or unobservable factors that might impact the experimentation results. A keen insight from Pearson lies in recognizing contingency as an inherent part of scientific exploration.

What Are Inductive and Deductive Reasoning? What's Their Relationship to Inference?

In this subsection we explore the meaning of induction and deduction, their connection with social science, and their relationship to making inferences. Our ordinary reasoning makes regular use of both induction and deduction. Likewise, all forms of research involve both induction and deduction.

FIGURE 12.2 ● Visualization of Induction

INDUCTION

Theory

Hypothesis

Confirmation

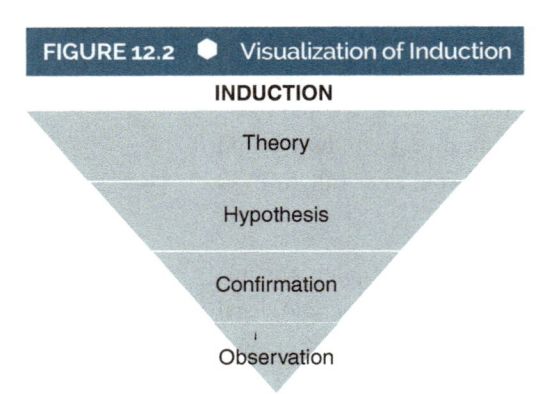

Observation

Induction

Induction involves making inferences based on external relationships of observations—that is, *drawing more general conclusions from particular observations*. These inferences imply an observable correspondence between or across the specific instances. For example, we might observe that day after day, during the Tone of Decency Campaign described earlier, there were no instances of violence. We might then make a general conclusion that the absence of violence means that the Campaign was successful. However, as you may have already noticed, there are some intrinsic risks of reducing our inference process to only induction. In the example of the Tone of Decency Campaign, the researcher cannot assume that the outcomes from the 20 schools studied would apply to the 21st school. For instance, at the 21st school, perhaps the decency expectations were not culturally sensitive and this resulted in increased rather than decreased altercations among students. More important, sometimes researchers fail to recognize that all observable facts depend on pre-existing categories as ways of observing, for example, not counting micro-aggressive activities as violence.

If an induction process is largely explained through correspondence theory, then the inferences reported will take these pre-existing categories for granted. In the case of the Tone of Decency Campaign, evaluators would have determined what counted as "effectiveness" prior to the empirical study: For instance, fewer incidents of violent acts on the part of students. What would have been observable would not only have a correspondence to a particular behavior (for example, hitting as a violent act), but would also imply something about effectiveness. In other words, the evaluators would decide whether the Campaign was "effective" based on whether they observed fewer incidents of hitting or other violent behaviors. However, other researchers could potentially challenge the conceptualization of "effectiveness" by putting forward a different way to think about it. For instance, we could approach "effectiveness" in terms of "student ratings of the program"—that is, if students like it could we consider the program effective? According to Nathan Swinger, students were not impressed with the Campaign and even made regular jokes about it. If effectiveness were defined in this way, it would impact how the researcher would collect empirical data to evaluate the Campaign—it would mean collecting data on student attitudes toward the Campaign rather than counting incidences of violence in the school.

When one relies on a correspondence theory to describe the inferential process of induction, the actual negotiation of meaning is ignored, such as how the school decides to define "effectiveness." Perhaps success is defined for the evaluation process without any reflection on what that definition leaves out or what its consequences are. This would be a problem. Later in the chapter we will come to think of induction through critical pragmatism, which frees the inferential process from the assumptions of correspondence theory.

Deduction

Induction starts from the assumption that knowledge is derived from the observation of the empirical world and becomes more general. That is, an inference is made from particular cases or instances to broader claims that primarily link observations. Now, what if we start from a different point—deduction? **Deduction** refers to a process through which we infer the truth of specific points by assuming the truth of more general premises. Both concepts, induction and deduction, have been generously debated in Western philosophy. Philosophers notice that, in deduction, as long as the general premise is true and the reasoning process is valid, the specific conclusion must be true. A typical example of a deduction is a syllogism. For instance, if I make the statements that "all babies suck their fingers" and "Iris is a baby," then I may arrive at the conclusion that "Iris must also suck her fingers." However, you may cast doubt on this inference, not because the inferential process is problematic, but by doubting either the first premise, "all babies suck their fingers," or the second premise, "Iris is a baby."

Contemporary social scientists often describe deduction as the movement from a general theory or set of assumptions/premises to specific conclusions that are logically inferred from those premises or theories. One could imagine an evaluation of a Tone of Decency Campaign that emphasizes deduction—it might be something like this: *If* we know that giving high school students alternative language for handling disagreements decreases the levels of violent activity among those same high school students *and* we know the Tone of Decency Campaign provides high school students with alternative language for handling disagreements, *then* we can expect that the Tone of Decency Campaign will result in a decrease in the levels of violent activity among high school students where the Campaign is implemented. Measuring levels of violent activity before and after would make sense and we would expect or hypothesize a decrease in the violent activity after the implementation of the Campaign.

FIGURE 12.3 ● Visualization of Deduction

DEDUCTION

Information

Pattern

Tentative Hypothesis

Theory

Induction and Deduction in Social Science

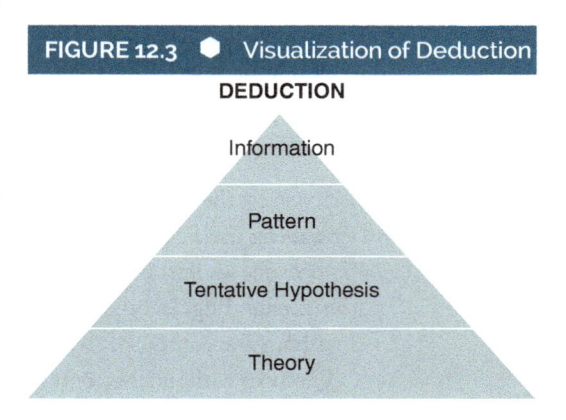

Perhaps you have heard people say that qualitative research is inductive and quantitative research is deductive. This fairly common contrast in the social sciences oversimplifies the inferencing process in several ways that will become clearer by the end of this conceptual interlude. Namely, (1) it oversimplifies both induction and deduction, and (2) it oversimplifies the interpretation process and how inferences are meaningfully conjectured. Even though both induction and deduction are used in all forms of research, it is possible for the overarching flow of a particular project to emphasize one or the other, as you will see in the research scenario presented later in the chapter. Nevertheless, it doesn't make sense to just equate one form of reasoning with a particular way of doing research. When we interpret both in research and in our ordinary lives, we do so by understanding communication by taking a broader view (more like induction) and by honing in (more like deduction). For example, we might imagine what are all the possible ways to interpret *rain* as if Iris's use of the word is poetic and, simultaneously, we can imagine examining the grammar of Iris's sentence in order to arrive at one logical, plausible meaning ruling out other possibilities. The specific situation (or context) of Iris's use of the word will guide us in how we might go about making sense of what she has said, just like a specific research context helps researchers grasp the interpretive expectations. For example, if a researcher is observing positive interactions among secondary students in public schools, it is helpful to know if students are joking around together as way of interpreting negative words to mean that they are having fun with one another.

One reason why people link induction with qualitative inquiry is that qualitative research is described as being capable of generating theories and being exploratory in the sense of its open design. Another reason why people link qualitative inquiry with an inductive process is that qualitative research is often designed in such a way as to focus intensely on single cases or small numbers from which more general propositions and understandings might be derived. For example, a qualitative researcher will generally enter the field open to learning how participants talk and act with respect to a particular interest—like an interest in how young children such as Iris avoid being reprimanded by their parents. In this situation, an ethnographer might spend lots of time with young children observing what they do in order to reach some general theories and ideas about how children act in order to avoid getting into trouble with adults. Researchers will take insights from each specific empirical example of an observable action to better understand the more general principles of acting.

However, the contextual aspect of the meaning must always be grasped as part of the meaning itself. That is, the inference of moving from particular empirical instances to a broader understanding of the phenomena should not erase the context as part of that understanding. In other words, we cannot adequately interpret Iris's use of the word *rain* without the context of imaginary play, and we cannot appropriately interpret a batch of IQ scores without the context that includes things like why the test was developed, for whom, and under what conditions.

In contrast, the reason why people tend to make the association between deduction and quantitative studies is because of how research hypotheses are formulated in these studies. In quantitative studies, researchers usually formulate research hypotheses based on existing empirical and theoretical literature. It is considered deduction because hypotheses are "deduced" from more generalizable statements. Therefore, literature reviews in quantitative studies are crucial in the sense that they provide the foundation from which specific research hypotheses are derived.

However, this view is, also, oversimplified. There is no one-way application of theories to research, because existing theories and findings in social science are always subject to re-examination and re-evaluation. Quantitative researchers are not satisfied with just testing whether or not their research hypotheses hold up. Instead, they further explore the implications of hypothesis testing results in relation to more general theoretical discourse or existing empirical findings. In other words, they loop back from the test results to the premises that they adopt and discuss their validity.

We must remember that meaning is generated in our social world primarily through natural language (as opposed to mathematical language or computational language) and is much more ambivalent, messy, and multifaceted. Accordingly, understanding and inferencing in our natural language cannot be reduced or fixed to a one-on-one relationship between a sign and what it represents. Studying the social world requires that researchers come up with ways to navigate this ambivalence and messiness of natural language.

> **Pause and Reflect.** Inductive and deductive reasoning might be easily thought of as opposites, but in social science, induction and deduction are inevitably interconnected. In the evaluation of the Tone of Decency Campaign, it is possible to imagine both inductive and deductive reasoning at work. To notice how induction might apply, think about how one would move from observations to general statements about how the program worked or didn't work. To notice how deduction might apply, think about how the theory of using positive talk to decrease violence might be evidenced over time.

Developing a Critical Pragmatist Perspective on Meaning Fields and Reconstruction

All theories of inferencing are at their heart theories of meaning. In this section of the chapter, we discuss important aspects of a pragmatic theory of meaning, which is different from the representational theory of meaning that we have linked with correspondence thinking or inferencing.

In what follows, we draw insights from **critical pragmatism**, which we introduced in Cluster 1, to elaborate on a different theory of meaning and inference-making. Critical pragmatism allows us to take context (contingency) and uncertainty into account in our research without assuming representational theories of meaning or giving up our capacity to critique.

The theory of critical pragmatism, as developed by theorists such as Habermas and Brandom, draws insights from a wide spectrum of intellectual traditions including classical American pragmatism and Frankfurt School critical theory (Brandom, 2003, p. 34). Like representational theories, the theory of critical pragmatism also pays attention to the way language mediates our inferences, yet it diverges from correspondence theory by taking uncertainty and contingency into account and by articulating a whole–part description of understanding. In this section of the chapter, we build on your understanding of these characteristics of meaning (as articulated in Chapter 7) to articulate the ideas of reconstruction and meaning fields as they relate to making inferences.

Reconstructing Meaning Fields

To better understand the approach of critical pragmatism, let's recall the concept of **meaning field** that we discussed in Chapter 7. There we introduced the tenets that guide our understanding of the connection between meaning and validity. To understand the meaning of a social action is to grasp the intentions and reasons actors would give to others when asked to explain their actions. In everyday life, these reasons are often not spoken unless there is a misunderstanding. That is, we often just imply or assume the reasons, and then when this creates problems we try to repair the misunderstanding by stating the reasons or explanations. Recall that a meaning field is a range of plausible inferences we make when we interpret or understand another's actions or words. For example, when Iris used the word *rain*, the meaning field would include inferences to her playing with her mom and her being able to imagine a reason to use the umbrella, while applying this imaginary scenario inside her home. Through critical pragmatism, meaning is not a matter of making a correspondence between a word and what it refers to. Instead, inferences are constituted of that which is implicit and meaning is thought of as a process of verbalizing what is often just assumed (Brandom, 2003). For critical pragmatists, this process is a reconstructive one rather than a correspondence or representational one (Carspecken, 1996; Dennis, 2018). In other words, as critical pragmatists we would articulate the range of interpretations, including the reasons and explanations relevant to the meaning of an action (including speech) as well as the context within which the action or words are being interpreted. Later in the chapter we provide examples of a reconstructive approach to analysis.

When Iris told Pengfei she was a baby, Pengfei simultaneously understood the range of possible meanings of this statement. She did not logically articulate all the various possible implications and inferences in order to respond to Iris. But this understanding was highly contextualized. For instance, Iris anticipated that her mom was going to tell her she was too old to suck fingers even before her mom said anything about her age, that is, because they had similar conversations before and she was stopped by Pengfei for similar reasons. Without this specific context, it would be difficult for outsiders to make sense of the conversation between Pengfei and Iris. In other words, we rely on the context about the mom and the preschooler to better understand their interactions. The meaning of the interaction is something that emerges between them communicatively—it's something they share, not something that only one of them is in possession of. Iris's statement already shows that she is aware of possible ways her mom might respond and so the inferences already include anticipated interpretations.

Since misunderstandings do happen, we must know how we can check out whether the two are making sense to each other. The best way to tell if meaning is shared is to observe how a dialogue continues from a participant position—that is, how the interactants act back toward each other. Each acting back implies a set of inferences that may or may not be shared. Reconstructive analysis, in this sense, allows us to see what inferences are missing and what ones are picked up by dialogue participants. Pengfei would recognize the misunderstanding through the continued interaction.

Iris's example shows that meaning-making is a holistic experience. We make sense of her words by understanding the context including culture and the history of interactions, inferences about Iris's possible intentions and how she could be thinking, as well as anticipations about Pengfei's intentions and possible responses. Reconstructive analysis allows us to start from the most salient meaning we grasp in a communicative scenario, and gradually make inferences about aspects of the meaning that are more implicitly nestled into our communications. From our critical pragmatist perspective, reconstruction is the description of how we make sense of each other in everyday life, but is always relevant to the analysis of data.

Reconstructing meaning fields is intuitively relevant for quantitative approaches to analysis as well, but you will not see statisticians talking about their analyses in these terms. This is because statistical interpretations have been largely standardized so the meaning fields are not as negotiable or open. For example, if practitioners wanted to determine how effective the Tone of Decency Campaign had been, they might start by trying to operationally define the term *effective* so that it could be observed or measured. A meaning field will always be involved in this process even if it isn't named. An evaluator might talk with others at the school and, maybe, also the developers of the Tone of Decency Campaign to determine what "effectiveness" might mean for them. Perhaps that meaning field would look something like this:

> *If the program is effective then there are fewer numbers of reported fights (both physical and verbal).* Or, *If the program is effective then, overall, discipline referrals at the school decrease.*

Then following the conversation where the range of possible meaning for "effectiveness" is narrowed, the evaluator could work from the more precise meaning. In other words, even when doing quantitative assessments, the definitions of terms will have to be worked out and such work always implies a meaning field. One could imagine an orientation to effectiveness that might involve the way the program was implemented or how satisfied the staff are with the program. You will also remember the various ways of thinking about effectiveness written about earlier in the chapter. We just mention this to illustrate that the meaning field could be different. Then the meaning field would be narrowed and standardized so that its clarity can guide observations and measurements. For example, the evaluator would want to employ the same definitions and reporting standards that were in place prior to implementing the program or comparing the rate of reported incidents before and after would not make sense.

Contrast Between Correspondence and Reconstructive Approaches to Interpretation

A reconstructive approach to understanding meaning is very different from correspondence thinking and representationalism. According to the correspondence theory, meaning-making starts with understanding the meaning of each word. We can understand the meaning of a sentence only if we know the meaning of all the words in this sentence. Furthermore, we determine the validity of a statement through examining whether there is a correspondence between a statement and the reality to which it refers. In the example of Iris and Pengfei's conversation, merely knowing the meaning of the four words "I"—"am"—"a"—"baby" may help us understand the literal meaning of the sentence "I am a baby," but it may not necessarily lead to a situational insight about for what reason and under what circumstances Iris uttered this sentence. Here we are not trying to deny the referential relationship between a symbol and what it represents in the real world (which is at the heart of representational theories of meaning), but what we have been trying to explain in this chapter is how this referential relationship, as a constitutive part of the meaning-making process, can only be enacted in a situational and action-oriented approach.

In studies that rely more on objectively standardizing or fixing meaning in order to gather measurements or make statements about causation, the parameters of interpretation (the meaning field) must be made quite explicit and held fairly constant through the research process. For example, how a professor grades an assignment should have some consistency in terms of meaning from one student to the next. That is, the grade should mean something roughly similar, so that if the teacher assessed Karen's assignment as a B and Pengfei's paper as an A, both students and the teacher ought to understand the meaning of those grades and their differences. The specificities would all be related to inferring what the grade represents as student learning. While we might be able to say that the grade represents student learning, the meaning field is a more precise way of specifying what that actually means in the context.

FIGURE 12.4 ● Image of Inferences in Checklists

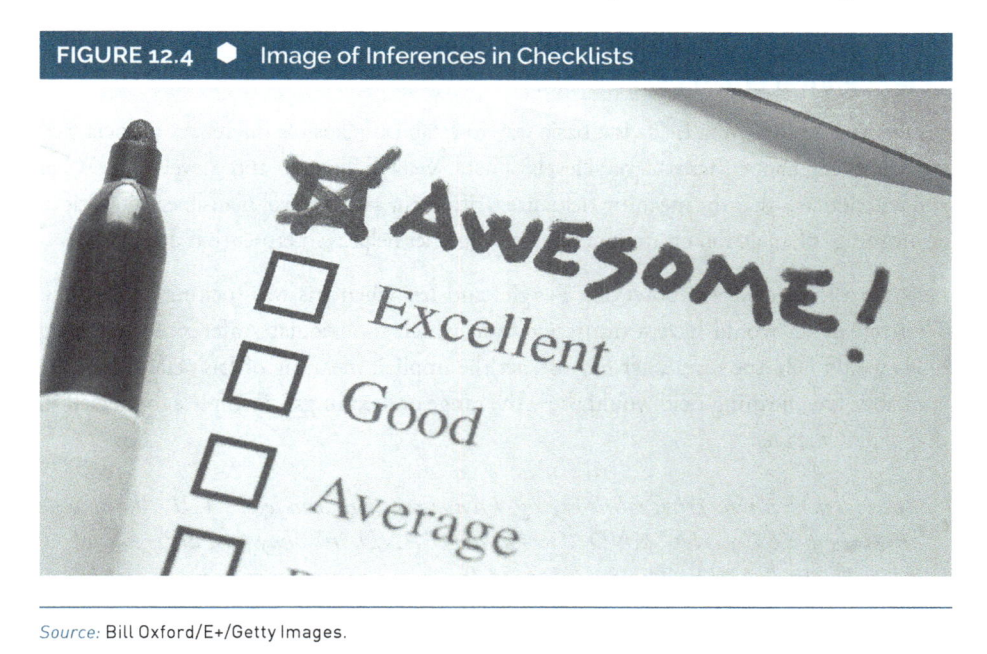

Source: Bill Oxford/E+/Getty Images.

In summary, a critical pragmatist perspective takes into account a broader context for making sense of any correspondences and representational connections between symbols and their meanings, whether those symbols are images, numbers, or words.

NARRATIVE AND CONCEPTUAL INTERLUDE II: APPLYING THE INSIGHTS OF CRITICAL PRAGMATISM TO SOCIAL RESEARCH

In this section, we apply the insights of critical pragmatism to social research. Critical pragmatism is capable of explaining correspondences, representations, positivist associations, and so on. Nevertheless, whatever theory of meaning a researcher finds themself drawing on, there will be relevant principles that will apply to the analysis process. Thus, we draw on critical pragmatism to propose a few principles that researchers may consider when making inferences in their research practices. These principles are by no means conclusive or exhaustive. On the contrary, we hope they can serve as guideposts orienting us toward a reconstructive understanding of analysis. As you will see below, these data analysis principles are not significantly different from the principles we implicitly enact to understand each other in our everyday life. What distinguishes the two processes lies more at levels of awareness, deliberation, and specification. In social research processes, researchers endeavor to be more transparent and reflective as they navigate through the meaning and inference-making process than they typically are in everyday life.

Reconstructing Meaning Fields as Social Science Inferencing

Reconstructing meaning fields is a basic way to establish plausible inferences in social science. This can happen across several levels of data. We will illustrate three levels here. What you will notice is that the meaning fields are written out as a range of plausible propositions or meanings of an action or utterance, which together help us interpret that data.

Let's say a researcher was observing Pengfei and Iris when Iris was sucking her fingers. That researcher would have a transcript from which to articulate inferences. Meaning fields would help the researcher reconstruct the implicit meaning of Iris's claim that she is a baby. The meaning field would show the range of meanings Iris implies for herself in that claim, such as:

> *"I am a person who cries; while crying, I wave my arms and legs." AND "I know this is how a baby cries." AND "I am a baby." AND "It's okay for babies to suck their fingers." AND "There is no need for moms to stop babies from sucking their fingers." AND "I expected you, mom, would want to stop me from sucking my fingers." AND "I know that you, my mom, do not think I am a baby anymore." AND "You, mom, think I should not suck my fingers." AND "I knew that you, mom, would say that I am not a baby anymore and so I shouldn't suck my fingers." AND "Still, I want to suck my fingers."*

Let us also articulate a meaning field for a simple claim that the Tone of Decency Campaign resulted in a decrease of violence at the school:

> *"There was more violence before we implemented the Tone of Decency Campaign." AND "We want the violence to decrease." AND "We attribute the decrease of violence to the Tone of Decency Campaign." AND "The numbers indicate individual events of violence." AND "Individual events of violence are each counted as equal to one another despite severity." AND "We are not paying attention to differences across gender or race in terms of events." AND "Though we know we do not catch all events of violence, we assume that if the events counted decreases that those not caught are also decreasing."*

This is what a meaning field might look like for a GRE score being considered by an admissions committee at a university:

> *"This score is within our range of acceptability." AND "This score is not high." AND "This student will probably do okay in our program." AND "This score indicates the amount of background knowledge the student has mastered." AND*

"GRE scores are relevant to performance in our graduate program." AND "GRE scores are similarly interpreted regardless of race or gender." AND "The higher the GRE score the better the student will perform in our program." AND "We want students with high GRE scores."

Some inferences in the above meaning fields are what we refer to as low, that is, closer to being explicit, and others are high, that is, more implied or assumed in the background of the meaning. It is helpful to think about reconstructing meaning through both low and high inferences.

Starting With Low-Level Inferences

When it comes to the inferencing that is specifically invoked as data analysis, a general rule is to start with low-level inferences. If we return to the example of Pengfei and Iris's interaction about finger sucking and look at the meaning field analysis we conducted, we can locate low-level inferences—that is, inferences that are quite close to how one might paraphrase or what one would say if asked, "What do you mean?" Low-level inferences from this particular meaning field would include the description of what Iris is doing (sucking her fingers), an association between what she is doing and what a baby might do, and a determination about whether or not Iris is a baby. (As an aside, one can see how these low-level inferences could be linked with the deductive reasoning: Babies suck their fingers. Iris is sucking her fingers. Therefore, Iris is a baby.) By starting with lower-level inferences, including descriptions (which we distinguish from inferences in Chapter 13), we first locate the part of the meaning that seems most salient to us, and then move to the meaning domains about which we are less certain. This process gives us more confidence about our analysis.

While there is no straight, linear relationship between doing lower-level inferencing and doing high-level inferencing, the articulation of higher-level inferences will almost always depend on an understanding of lower-level inferences. (More on higher-level inferences in Chapter 14.) This kind of precision is one of the things that can distinguish our meaning-making in the ordinary context from that of the research context. While our understanding will manifest as a toggling between the whole and the parts, the links between higher-level inferences and lower-level ones is crucial to any careful explication of that understanding.

> **Pause and Reflect.** Imagine, if you will, the last misunderstanding you had. Reflect on what aspects of the interaction were misunderstood. Write out a simple meaning field for the various actors that illustrates the differences in understanding. Then, generally locate the level of inference involved in the misunderstanding as low or high. What would have to be made explicit in order to avoid this misunderstanding in the future?

The Role of Substantive Theory

Throughout this textbook, we have been engaging with theories in multiple ways. Ontological and epistemological theories introduced in Chapter 5 lay a foundation for us to understand key methodological issues regarding meaning, knowing, knowledge, and truth. In Chapter 6, we introduced some basic concepts of social theories, which we use to understand social action, in particular the action of research practice. In the same chapter, we also distinguish philosophic and methodological theories from substantive and disciplinary-based theories. Now, what do the theories have to do with inference-making?

The inferences we make are not divorced from the theories that guide research practice in the first place, whether these are acknowledged or not. In fact, failure to acknowledge them could result in a bias. These include our ontological and epistemological beliefs about knowledge and knowledge production (as discussed in Chapter 5) as well as the different kinds of substantive theory that are used to conceptualize and/or explain human behavior. Even when they are not discussed explicitly, as in applied research that focuses on addressing immediate, concrete needs, these theories underlie the decisions that researchers make about what is important to emphasize in the analytical process (e.g., what data to code, describe, or otherwise analyze), as well as what conclusions are drawn.

Since we have extensively discussed metatheories in the first cluster of the book, here we will focus our discussion on the role of substantive theories. Remember that substantive theories are those that inform "the what" of your research—what you are studying. Researchers draw on substantive knowledge from the field to construct research hypotheses and questions, plan sampling strategies, and identify contexts or measures for conducting their studies. Substantive theories can, also, provide categories of analysis. For example, this is done in qualitative studies in content analysis and in quantitative studies through the operationalizing of variables. Substantive theories also supply rationale for analytic decisions (such as whether or not one should analyze causation), and establish definitional or meaning field parameters and foci (for example, narrowing one's analytic focus to parent–toddler interactions that involve reprimands).

Typically, the role of substantive theory is much more open and speculative for those using qualitative approaches to research than for those using quantitative analysis. Some researchers endeavor to construct theory from their empirical work. Others use theory to reveal complexities and paradoxes, to defamiliarize our everyday life, and to shed new light on social phenomena. Still others use theory as a way to think through possible interpretations.

Reconsidering Bias

Bias is an important concept in social science. It is often talked about with respect to the inferences a researcher makes. As you know, we advocate for a more inclusive, practice-centered and relational approach to research, which also has implications for how we think about the potential for bias in our analyses. Bias would be reflected in any statement produced through the analysis that cannot be expected to mean what it suggests it means—a mistake, mismatch, or misinterpretation between the statement and its probable interpretation. In other words, the likely interpretations of those statements would mislead a reasonable person or produce a systematic misunderstanding.

Bias can creep into analysis when researchers do not clarify the assumptions (including theoretical ones) and context of the research analyses. For example, perhaps someone studying the effects of the Tone of Decency Campaign experienced a lot of verbal bullying as a teenager. Perhaps this has some positive impacts on the analysis process in that the researcher might draw on their own experiences to be sure that verbal violence is measured and not just physical violence. However, perhaps an assumption about which is worse (verbal or physical violence) is implicitly made so that if physical violence decreases but verbal violence does not, the researcher might overvalue the failure of the program to decrease verbal violence in their assessment of the program's effectiveness when compared with how the implementers of the program might value those two forms of violence. This would be an example of bias. One cannot change their history of being bullied, but they can be mindful about how that history might influence inferences they are making. In terms of context, it also becomes important to know what is typical or not typical in order to spot when some behavior or outcome is atypical. Context also helps us understand the parameters necessary for the claims. If we study adult male hearts and then use our analysis to make conclusions about the human heart, we have not taken the context of our participants' gender into account in the analysis. This would produce a bias in those conclusions.

Another area of potential bias might be if our low-level interpretations are wrong—for example, if the operational definitions and the low-level inferences linking those definitions are a mismatch for how the variables are being measured, then our lower-level inferences could be inaccurate. Errors at lower levels of inference will bias the inferences we make at higher levels.

In the next section, Dr. Katharine Broton shares with us the way inductive and deductive reasoning are involved in her research on basic needs insecurity. This research scenario will help us further apply the concepts just presented to social science.

RESEARCH SCENARIO: UNDERSTANDING AND SERVING TODAY'S COLLEGE STUDENTS. THE PROBLEM OF BASIC NEEDS INSECURITY: KATHARINE BROTON

In the following research scenario, Katharine Broton, an Assistant Professor at the University of Iowa, writes about the different ways she has used induction and deduction to describe her research process. As you read her contribution, we encourage you to think about how her use of induction and deduction is complicated.

> *As a sociologist of education, I am interested in understanding how education matters for people's lives and in finding ways to improve people's lives through education. My research agenda is motivated by the increasingly consequential role of higher education in social stratification. Today, the economic, civic, and health benefits associated with a college credential are larger than ever (Hout, 2012; Oreopoulos & Petronijevic, 2013).*
>
> *During graduate school, I sought to understand the daily lived realities of undergraduates from historically marginalized backgrounds and how we could better support them. I joined Dr. Sara Goldrick-Rab's research team investigating need-based grant aid, a popular intervention designed to support students from low-income families (Goldrick-Rab, 2016). In interviews for that research project, some students reported that they were struggling to make ends meet. Due to limited financial resources, they were not able to get enough food to eat and find a safe, stable place to live. Although these challenges were not necessarily new, reports of basic needs insecurity were not part of the national discourse on higher education. Importantly, naming this problem challenged long-held assumptions and stereotypes about the experiences of college students. Too many people view college as a protected or even carefree time for self-exploration and emergent adulthood. In reality, most students are navigating college while managing significant work and family responsibilities, and they are doing so under considerable constraint (Goldrick-Rab & Stommel, 2018; U.S. Department of Education, 2015). In short, those interviews in which students identified food and housing insecurity as a barrier to their educational success illustrate the power of induction in inquiry. It enabled us to question what we thought we knew, add nuance to our understanding of student experiences, and generate new theories of student success.*
>
> *After some students shared that they experienced basic needs insecurity in interviews, we were interested in learning about the scope, depth, and*

distribution of this problem in which individuals lack the basic material goods necessary for decent human functioning. Surveys are the best tool for these types of research questions since their greatest strength lies in the ability to describe a particular target population on a large scale, such as college students. Dr. Goldrick-Rab's research team immediately added questions about food and housing insecurity to ongoing survey studies of college students in Wisconsin, and we started conducting surveys of basic needs insecurity at colleges and universities in diverse contexts across the nation. Additionally, we called on existing nationally representative studies of college students (e.g., National Postsecondary Student Aid Study) to add basic needs insecurity measures to their survey instruments since the cost of administering a high-quality, nationally representative survey is beyond the capacity of most research teams (e.g., Broton & Goldrick-Rab, 2013).

In our Educational Researcher *article, "Going Without: An Exploration of Food and Housing Insecurity Among Undergraduates," we share the results of four survey studies that provide some of the first multi-institutional estimates of basic needs insecurity among U.S. college students (Broton & Goldrick-Rab, 2018). The four survey studies have different strengths and weaknesses: Two have relatively high response rates of specific target populations while the other two have more diverse target populations, but lower response rates. Despite differences in survey research design and measurement, the results were largely consistent and the conclusion was clear: Food and housing insecurity is a problem for a substantial share of college students. Indeed, the conclusion was stronger because the results were not particularly sensitive to these methodological differences. Since we started doing this research a decade ago, there has been a proliferation of studies on this topic and recent systematic reviews confirm our findings and indicate that approximately half of undergraduates experience basic needs insecurity (Broton, 2019; Nazmi et al., 2018). More important, the problem of food and housing insecurity is now part of the national discourse on higher education and student success (e.g., Goldrick-Rab & Broton, 2015; Government Accountability Office, 2019).*

There is more to learn about the problem of basic needs insecurity in higher education, but researchers must not be complacent with describing a problem and its implications (Gamoran, 2014). In addition to studying the implications of basic needs insecurity for student success and well-being, I also investigate ways to alleviate it and promote college success. For example, Clare Cady, co-founder of the College and University Food Bank Alliance (CUFBA), and I are co-editing a book that explores the ways in which college and community leaders are fighting student hunger on our nation's college campuses (Broton & Cady, 2020). The actions range from short-term emergency responses like campus food pantries and small emergency grant programs to long-term systematic responses related to shifting university system policies and better aligning the public social safety net to serve college students. I am also working with Bunker Hill Community College to examine the causal impact of their meal voucher program on students' academic success and well-being using an experimental research design (Goldrick-Rab, Broton, & Hernandez, 2017). That is, we are using a deductive approach to test the hypothesis or premise that meal vouchers are an effective way to improve student success. This approach relies on counterfactual reasoning to study a cause-and-effect relationship in which the meal voucher program is the "cause" under study and the potential "effect" of interests is student success, including academic achievement and attainment.

The problem of basic needs security among college students is systematic and complex. In order to understand and address it, I use multiple methods to answer the research question at hand, engaging in the full research cycle from discovery and hypothesis generation to the testing of causal relationships. As an academic scholar, I conduct policy-relevant research and translate the findings for use by families, practitioners, and policy-makers. Together, the students, scholars, practitioners, and policy-makers working in this area make up the #RealCollege research agenda and movement to end basic needs insecurity in higher education.

Broton used multiple approaches to examine basic needs insecurity among college students. She wrote about different kinds of inferences involved in her studies—description; establishing causal relationships; the scope, depth, and distribution of food insecurity; and so on. Toward the end of her contribution she claimed that she "translate[s] the findings for use" by stakeholders. She admonishes people to take action to solve the problem, and she intends for her own research to contribute to such solutions. Some of the lower-level inferencing involved describing distributions of food insecurity. Higher-level inferencing would involve articulating causal relationships and establishing policy ramifications.

✓ YOU AND RESEARCH

Much of this chapter has explored inferences and data analysis by developing concepts and critiquing theoretical ideas. We develop critical pragmatism as a way of thinking through the meaning of inferencing and its potential impacts on analysis. Our critique of correspondence theories of meaning encourages us not to take regularly simplified terms like *induction* for granted in the research process.

When Interpreting Research

There is a lot of jargon associated with data analysis. As users, it can be difficult to make sense of the findings presented in research papers and conferences. Oftentimes results are presented without context and with little explanation of the inferencing process. Practitioners can feel stuck in terms of accepting the conclusions and having little idea about how to apply those conclusions. This chapter prepared us to challenge research that depends on a correspondence orientation. For example, we can note the extent to which context and complex ranges of meaning are taken into account by researchers. The chapter also prepared us to articulate meaning fields that are implicit in the presentation of the findings. This helps us raise pertinent questions about the gray area in studies: for example, asking if any data were left out of the final analysis/presentation or asking what assumptions are being taken for granted in the analysis of the data. The chapter also fostered an understanding of analysis that did not immediately separate qualitative and quantitative approaches. This makes it possible for us to orient conceptually toward research with questions about the inferencing process. It became clear that inferencing is not a set of procedures, but rather an articulation of awareness that is reconstructive and moves fluidly between whole and part relations just as we experience in our ordinary lives.

When Doing Research

As researchers design research and create data, they will already be making decisions that will impact potential analyses. Inferencing must be sensitive to both the contexts of the research process itself and of the phenomena of study. Researchers can trace their inferential decision-making, specifically when they arrive at particular definitions for variables, or when they decide what aspects of the context to include. While the chapter did not aim to provide researchers with specific analytic strategies, the introduction of key concepts of meaning field, reconstruction, uncertainty, and whole–part relationships provides researchers with the building blocks to conceptualize any interpretational and analytic process. Critical dialogue facilitates our awareness of how these aspects of meaning are at work in our research so researchers can develop ongoing critical peer relationships to provide feedback. For example, a critical friend might ask about the whole-to-part relationships implied by the research questions. The context of our research work can be reported by keeping a reflective journal as well as by employing multiple ways of recording the context (photos, drawings, audio files of discussions, or online blogs for establishing definitions and clarifying interpretations). With quantitative studies, one could get subject responses to the various questions by asking them to rephrase the question. This could help researchers understand the interpretive context for participants. The main point is to find ways to take seriously the complex and contextual nature of meaning and inference-making.

SYNTHESIS: POINTS FOR REFLECTION

Conceptual Synthesis

In this chapter we developed ideas of validity in relation to bias and inference from an understanding of critical pragmatism. We hope that you are able to resonate first with the way the concepts are part of your ordinary ways of relating with the people in your lives. As we better understand how inferences work in our everyday lives we are better able to hone in on this in our research work. You likely experienced the difference between correspondence thinking and critical pragmatism by thinking about misunderstandings you have experienced. In research work, it can be difficult to know when a misunderstanding has occurred, so we have to take extra care to be sure that our inferences are similar to those subjects or participants would offer. We offered a critique of what we think is an oversimplification of the concepts *induction* and *deduction* with respect to research. Most fundamentally, we argued that meaning is at the heart of analysis regardless of whether one is using qualitative or quantitative approaches.

Methodological Synthesis

We intended for our everyday understanding of inferences to become relevant for analysis. Though analysis is more specifically examined in the remaining chapters of this cluster, here we demonstrated how meaning fields were methodologically relevant across analytic approaches, and we provided examples for thinking about this. The division between qualitative and quantitative approaches was explored, but also called into question. We did this, in part, by suggesting that induction and deduction could be logical constituents of a meaning field but could not, on their own, account for methodological decisions or analytic processes. The specific analytic strategies presented in the chapters to come will build on the principles associated with inferencing. Furthermore, we provided a way of thinking about uncertainty as a kind of methodological openness linked to the way meaning works rather than as a kind of methodological limitation. Though this is not a common view in social science, we hope you will give it some thought. It is unusual to see the word *meaning* in methodology texts, so one main takeaway from this chapter is that all interpretations are inherently linked with meaning.

Personal Synthesis

For us, learning to explicate meaning fields, even if just in our own minds, helped to raise our awareness of meaning and heighten our ability to deal with misunderstandings. It helped us to understand how research findings can be misleading if depending on how they are presented and translated. We also came to see the uncertainty of meaning as linked with the uncertainty we experience through the self-recognition of others because our actions and identities are constantly being interpreted. Also, being able to unpack assumptions and meaning fosters personal reflection.

MOVING FORWARD

In this chapter we began to put terminology and concepts together in order to think about what it means for researchers to draw inferences from data. In the next chapter, these concepts will be useful as you learn about precise terminology and strategies associated with very specific ways to establish one's inferences as a researcher. For example, you will learn about some statistical strategies on concepts that help researchers make inferences about the *averages* or *means* of quantitative scores. The concept of meaning field allows us to conceptualize the meaning of statistical averages—that is, what inference is being made when scores are averaged together into a mean.

Further Readings

Grant, S., and Quiggin, J. (2013). Inductive reasoning about unawareness. *Economic Theory, 54*, 717–755.

Hayes, B. K., Heit, A., & Swendsen, H. (2010). Inductive reasoning. *Interdisciplinary Review of Cognitive Science, 1*(2), 278–292.

Lazarsfeld, P. (1958). On evidence and inference. *Daedalus, 87*(4), 99–130.

Palinkas, L. (2014). Causality and causal inference in social work: Quantitative and qualitative perspectives. *Research in Social Work Practice, 24*(5), 540–547.

Sobel, M. (2000). Causal inference in the social sciences. *Journal of the American Statistical Association, 95*(450), 647–651. Retrieved from https://www.thebalancecareers.com/inductive-reasoning-definition-with-examples-2059683

https://study.com/academy/lesson/inductive-and-deductive-reasoning.html

Further Readings by Katharine Broton

Broton, K. M. (2019). *A review of estimates of housing insecurity and homelessness among U.S. students in higher education.* (Working paper). Iowa City, IA: University of Iowa.

Broton, K., & Cady, C. (Eds.). (2020). *Food insecurity on campus: Action and intervention.* Baltimore, MD: Johns Hopkins University Press. https://jhupbooks.press.jhu.edu/title/food-insecurity-campus

Broton, K., & Goldrick-Rab, S. (2013). *Housing instability among college students.* (Research brief). Wisconsin Center for the Advancement of Postsecondary Education and the Center for Financial Security, University of Wisconsin–Madison.

Broton, K. M., & Goldrick-Rab, S. (2018). Going without: An exploration of food and housing insecurity among undergraduates. *Educational Researcher, 47*(2), 121–133.

Goldrick-Rab, S., & Broton, K. M. (2015, December 4). Hungry, homeless and in college. *The New York Times.*

Goldrick-Rab, S., Broton, K. M., & Hernandez, D. C. (2017). *Addressing basic needs security in higher education: An introduction to three evaluations of supports for food and housing at community colleges.* Madison, WI: Wisconsin HOPE Lab.

13

DESCRIPTION AND INFERENCE IN THE RESEARCH SPHERE

In the previous chapter, we discussed inference as a process, setting the stage for the remaining chapters in this cluster. Now we turn to an empirically grounded discussion of inference-making, emphasizing low-level inferences before moving to higher-level inference-making in Chapter 14. Here our focus is the challenges in distinguishing between description and inference. Our opening scenario focuses on the process of choosing the school district within which one lives. We then turn to discussing some of the core concepts around using description and making inferences during and following the process of data generation. The research scenario in this chapter draws out these concepts by presenting several "back stories" related to different kinds of analytical techniques.

MUSING UPON THE EVERYDAY: THE PROCESS OF MAKING CHOICES

In a previous chapter we focused on how we make choices about our lives, such as where to live. Here we continue that thread, with a specific focus on the process of choosing a school district—a process not too different from the process of deciding how much to pay for a home in Chapter 9.

If you have moved or bought a house in the United States, or know someone who has, you might be familiar with the fact that a selling point real estate agents often use to illustrate the attractiveness of a particular home is the school district for which a given neighborhood is zoned.

Choosing a school district as a parent, or as someone intending to raise children, can be challenging. How do you decide? Real estate agents often emphasize school rankings, which are based on things like average SAT score, percentage of students going on to 4-year colleges, student–teacher ratios, diversity of teaching staff and student body, and so on. What do you learn from these numbers and rankings? What meaning do you make of them, and how might you use them to make your decision?

Another approach to learning about a district might be to visit a school, or a few schools, to get a feel for what happens within the building walls. You might observe teachers with their students, speak with the principal about school values, or tour the campus to learn about opportunities and/or support systems that are available for students. This kind of approach to learning about a school district would provide a different kind of information than rankings. Would this kind of information provide the basis for making your decision?

If you think about these two possibilities, what becomes clear is that the basis for choosing a school (or school district), in either scenario, is linked with the kind of information you collect. In this context, the choice is about what school/school district is best. This entails making inferences about quality (based on specific kinds of information) and about what information to use in deciding which school/district is best.

The question here, and in the process of conducting research, has to do with how you make that inference—how *do* you decide what is best? Is it based on competitive rankings? Intuition? Concrete information about a specific teacher or school that you obtain by speaking with the educator, or perhaps through word of mouth from other parents in the school district? On the basis of these sources of information, you need to make choices both about what to focus on, and then about how to use that information. How do you do that? What processes do you use? Those questions form the focus of this chapter.

NARRATIVE AND CONCEPTUAL INTERLUDES: WHAT TO MAKE OF THE GRE?

These questions lead us to a number of concepts that we discuss in the following pages, specifically: the foundations of descriptive and inferential statistics, and descriptive and inferential processes in other analytical forms. We also clarify how these processes are linked to key concepts discussed earlier in the text. Fundamentally, these concepts address the basic distinctions, and simultaneous overlaps, in the process of *description* and the process of *inference-making*, or making meaning of information. Before we dive in, let's take a moment to reflect on the similarities and differences between these.

> **Pause and Reflect.** Jot down a description of the place where you live. Now, write about the place where you live in terms of why it is a significant place for you. What is the same about the way you wrote each of these? What makes each piece of writing distinct?

Our discussion of description and inference begins with an example that may be familiar to many of you: the General Record Examination (GRE) and its use as part of graduate school application packages. The GRE is a standardized examination required for admission to many graduate programs in the United States. While there are subject-specific GRE tests, the GRE General Test is just that—an exam focused on general knowledge. According to the Educational Testing Service (ETS), which administers the GRE, the test measures "skills that have been developed over a long period of time and are not related to a specific field of study but are important for all" (ETS, 2017).

When an individual takes the GRE, they receive a **raw score**: the number of questions answered correctly. This raw score is not what one sees when receiving a score report, however. Instead, the score report sent to graduate schools (and home to test-takers) is a **standardized score** between 130 and 170. This score is a conversion of the raw score that takes into account differences between versions of the test; it also takes into account differences in the difficulty level of questions answered correctly or incorrectly (see https://www.ets.org/gre/revised_general/scores/how for an explanation of how these scores are converted). The score report also includes a percentile value: This refers to the percentage of people taking the GRE whose scores fell below that of this particular test-taker.

GRE scores, when required, form just part of an application package used to determine student admission. As such, when we think about the GRE and the context in which it is taken and used, we can start to tease apart some of the different *descriptive* and *inferential* aspects of the examination's score and score reporting. While we don't have the space here to get into a deep discussion about the GRE specifically, it provides us with a useful example for addressing and clarifying broader concepts related to description and inference.

Description and Inference in Our Decisions About Data

To begin, it might be helpful to think back to Chapters 9 and 10, where we noted that "data" are already objectified: The very act of generating data requires acceptance of the idea that we can reconstruct individual experience through what are called "data." In other words, when we conduct interviews or gather information through other data generation techniques, there is an assumption that this information "counts" as data that are acceptable and appropriate for using to make sense of certain phenomena of interest. This means that what we think of as "raw data" are already bounded by certain interpretations of what we can use as data. That is, we already engage in interpretation even before we collect data, just by deciding what data we will collect.

GRE scores exemplify this kind of pre-interpretation. When graduate schools decide that the GRE is required as part of an application for admission—but not, for example, a writing sample—a decision has already been made that the GRE is an appropriate criterion for predicting success in graduate school, but that a writing sample is not. In other words, a decision has already been made about what is considered a legitimate form of "raw data" for assessing potential success. Yet there is evidence that GRE scores are not the same for all test-takers: Evidence shows that test-takers identified as belonging to one or more of several specific minority groups receive lower scores on the GRE than Caucasians (ETS, 2012). Thus, as others such as Corrie Wolf (2014) have noted, a decision to include the GRE as a requirement for graduate school admission, with a set minimum score criterion, means that certain groups of applicants may have less of a chance of admission, regardless of their other materials.

What does this mean with respect to description and inference? First of all, inferences about the applicant's potential (and, ultimately, decisions about admission) are based on what descriptions are included in the application materials. Yet the application requirements (e.g., how applicants are asked to describe themselves) reflect certain inferences by the graduate school department about what is important to include. As we have discussed in previous chapters, decisions about what kind of information should be included are a reflection of what is considered legitimate knowledge; this is shaped by cultural context and power dynamics. Thus, it's important to keep in mind that descriptive material from a certain source of data (like GRE score) may not fully capture an applicant's potential (as may be the case for certain groups of applicants). This raises questions about whether it is the most appropriate basis for making inferences. In some cases, these data may result in faulty inferences about individuals' applications.

More broadly, inference-making is not a single process but occurs from the inception of a research idea onward, so that inferences about meaning made toward the end of the process are based on both descriptions and previous inferences. The intertwining of inference-making with data generation can be seen in Figure 13.1.

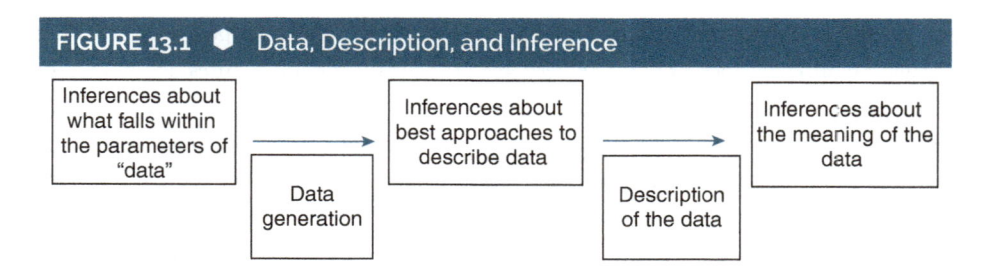

FIGURE 13.1 ● Data, Description, and Inference

Inferences about what falls within the parameters of "data" → Data generation → Inferences about best approaches to describe data → Description of the data → Inferences about the meaning of the data

Description and Inference With Numerical Data: An Introduction to Statistics

Let's go back for a minute to GRE scores and their interpretations. We can do that by using a hypothetical example of a prospective student applying to a master's program. Emma, our applicant, receives the following information in her score report: a score of 160 on the verbal reasoning section (percentile: 84), a score of 161 on the quantitative reasoning section (percentile: 80), and a score of 4.5/5 on the analytic writing section (percentile: 80). What do these numbers mean?

Emma's score is presented not only as an individual score that stands on its own. It also references broader trends or patterns among individuals who took the test when she did. These trends are expressed as **statistics** that are used as part of a process of making inferences and decisions. We want to note here that when we use the term *statistics* we are actually talking about two different things. First, there is the process of making inferences based on specific kinds of analyses of numerical data. Second, the term *statistics* is often used to refer to the output of those analyses. When someone talks about statistics in popular media, for example, the reference is often to the numbers that are the *output* of statistical analyses rather than the analyses themselves. That is also what we mean when we say that patterns related to the GRE are expressed as statistics.

Descriptive Statistics

Conceptually, statistics are a way of illustrating patterns or trends across numerical data sets. There are two general types of statistics: descriptive and inferential. **Descriptive statistics** are analyses that provide summaries of patterns seen in the sample. These summaries enable us to create useful "snapshots" of how data are distributed, and in doing so, help us understand trends in our data. While they are called "descriptive" statistics, as noted earlier, use of different kinds of descriptive data reflects choices already made about what patterns or trends are important and should be captured. Thus, they represent low-level inferences as well.

Generally, descriptive statistics consist of three main kinds of patterns, which we can see illustrated in our student's GRE scores. First, *measures of relative standing* tell us where a certain score falls relative to a group of scores. We can use **percentiles** or percentile rankings to show where a score lies in comparison with other scores. The "percentile" on a GRE score report is a measure of relative standing: It tells us how our student scored relative to other individuals who took the exam at the same time they did. From the scores listed above we know that Emma performed better than 84% of test-takers on the verbal reasoning section of the exam, and better than 80% of test-takers on the quantitative reasoning and analytical writing portions. This can be seen in Emma's sample GRE score report (Table 13.1).

TABLE 13.1	Sample GRE Score Report					
	Verbal Reasoning		Quantitative Reasoning		Analytical Writing	
Test date	Scaled score	Percentile	Scaled score	Percentile	Scaled score	Percentile
1/31/2020	160	84	161	80	4.5	80

Emma's score is presented as what is called a "scaled score" by the makers of the GRE. This is a standardized score, which is another measure of relative standing. The GRE, as noted, uses a standard score between 130 and 170 for the verbal and quantitative reasoning sections. Emma's verbal reasoning score is 160, but this is not the raw score: Remember that the score on each portion of the GRE is a conversion of the raw score that considers differences between versions of the test and differences in the difficulty level of questions answered correctly or incorrectly. The score of 160 in verbal reasoning, then, is a standardized way of showing how well Emma did on her GRE compared with other test-takers, when taking these issues into account. Outside of the specific context of the GRE, there are several generalized standard scores used in statistical analyses. **Z-scores** are standard scores that tell you how far away you are from the mean (or average, as we discuss below): A Z-score of 0 means that your score falls right at the mean; a Z-score of +1.57 means that your score falls 1.57 standard deviations above the mean. These Z-scores are used when you have data about a population that you know have, what statisticians call a **normal distribution. T-scores** tell us the same thing as Z-scores, but are used when the inference is expected to say something about the sample itself rather than the population that the sample is meant to generalize. T-scores are also generally used when the sample size is small (fewer than 30 units) or where you do not know whether the population data are normally distributed.

Let's say a bit more here about normally distributed data. When we talk about "distribution," what we are referring to is the way that data points fall on a curve—that is, the pattern that a curve creates. With data that are normally distributed, the curve is made up of data points that together look like a bell—hence, the normal distribution is sometimes referred to as the "bell curve." Many kinds of everyday data follow a normal distribution: for instance, the height of adults and intelligence quota (IQ) scores. When data are normally distributed, exactly 50% of data points fall below the center and 50% fall above the center. The center data point is the highest point in the curve; it is the **mean** (average) of all data points in the data set.

Getting back to descriptive statistics: With a standardized score of 130–170, scores in the middle range of the GRE for verbal and quantitative reasoning fall around 150. This middle set of scores is a *measure of central tendency*, the term that describes the "middle," or "typical" values within a data set. The average GRE score of students entering a specific graduate program is one example of this kind of descriptive statistic. In addition to the average, or mean value, another measure of central tendency is the **median**, which refers to the number in a data set that falls right in the middle and divides the scores in half. For example, if we are looking at the grades received on a quiz (see Table 13.2), and for a group of seven students whose scores are 41, 43, 43, 45, 48, 48, and 50, the median is 45. (If there is an even number of scores, the median will be the average of the two middle scores.) The median is sometimes a more useful way than the mean to describe a group of numbers, especially when there are *outliers*, or isolated numbers that differ considerably from the rest, that can lead to a distorted impression of the data when the mean is calculated (for instance, if a student received a 30 on the quiz above, when all the other scores were in the 40s, this score would be an outlier). Finally, the **mode** is used to describe the number in a data set that appears most frequently. It is particularly useful for describing categorical data, where numerical rankings have no meaning. It wouldn't make much sense to use the mean to describe the gender of students in the class, but the mode will tell us the gender with which the greatest number of students identify. In data that are normally distributed, the mean, median, and mode of the data set will be approximately equal.

Finally, *measures of variability* help us see how "spread out" scores can be—in other words, how much they vary. Measures of variability can help provide a more comprehensive picture than simply using measures of central tendency. For example, if you are looking to buy a house and comparing home prices in different neighborhoods, one neighborhood might have a mean price of $150,000 per home with very little variability (i.e., most of the houses fall relatively close to that mean price), while a nearby neighborhood might have the same mean home sale price, but a much wider range of prices overall. In combination, measures of variability and central tendency can give us a better

TABLE 13.2 ● Median, Mean, and Mode

Quiz Scores	Median Quiz Score		Mean Quiz Score	Mode	
41	41		(41 + 43 + 43 + 45 + 48 + 48 + 50)	41	
43	43		= 48 + 48 + 50)	43	43 and 48 appear twice each; this data set is **bimodal**
43	43	45 is the median; it falls in the middle of the scores		43	
45	(45) →		7	45	
48	48		= 45.42	48	
48	48			48	
50	50			50	

picture of what the situation is overall. The **range** is the simplest measure of variability to calculate: You get the range by taking the minimum score for a data set and subtracting it from the maximum score. For the GRE, the range of standard scores for verbal and quantitative reasoning is 40—that is, the difference between 130 and 170. The range is only a somewhat useful measure, however, because it doesn't tell you anything about the way that scores fall in between this lowest and highest value. However, the range can be useful if you are comparing data sets (for example, if you want to compare the range of test scores for two or more classes, or over multiple quizzes taken by the same class).

The **variance** and **standard deviation** indicate how close or far most scores fall from the mean. Going back to our house purchase example, if in one neighborhood prices are very closely clustered around the mean, the variance or standard deviation will be small compared with another neighborhood where the range of prices is much greater. From this last sentence you can also see how range is related to variance and standard deviation: A data set with a larger range will have a wider dispersion of scores around the mean. Visually, you can think about variance in terms of the width of the "bell" in a bell curve: A narrow bell indicates that most data cluster around the mean; a wider bell indicates data that are more dispersed, as in Figure 13.2.

In many statistical analyses, standard deviation (the square root of the variance), rather than variance itself, is utilized to indicate dispersion. Standard deviation is a measure that takes into account how far every data point in a data set is from the mean. The numerical value assigned to the standard deviation is the measure of how far a typical data point is from the data set average. As with the variance, the more spread out data points are around the mean, the larger the standard deviation will be.

In a normal distribution, we know that approximately 68% of scores fall between the mean and 1 standard deviation (expressed as +/− 1SD), 95% of scores will fall within +/− 2SD of the mean, and 99% of scores will fall within +/− 3 standard deviations from the mean. You can see this visually in Figure 13.3.

Here is an example: If the mean test score on an exam with normally distributed scores is 80, and the standard deviation is +/− 5, 68% of the test scores will fall between

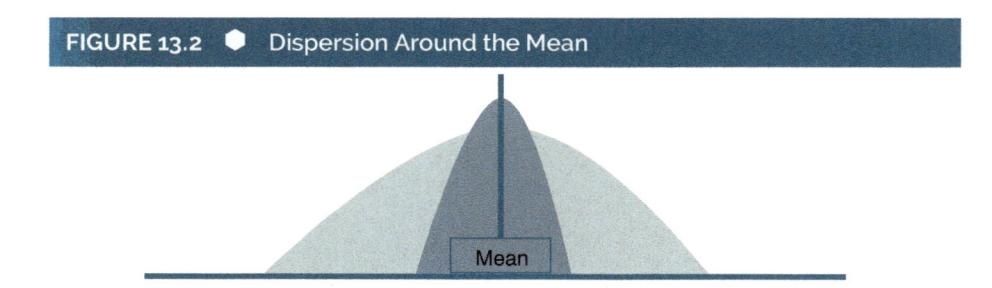

FIGURE 13.2 ● Dispersion Around the Mean

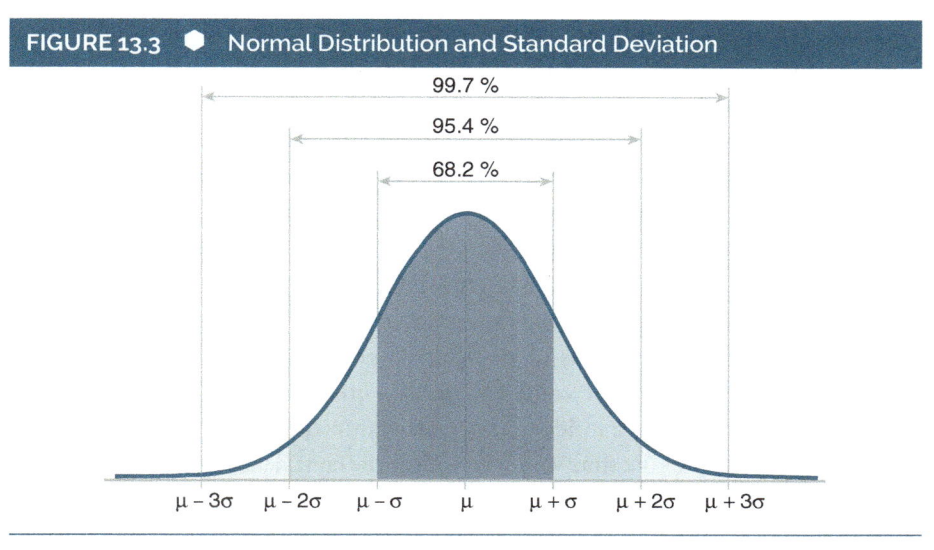

FIGURE 13.3 — Normal Distribution and Standard Deviation

Source: iStock.com/Peter Hermes Furian.

75 and 85, 95% of scores will fall between 70 and 90, and 99% of scores will fall between 65 and 95. If the standard deviation is larger than +/− 5, this means that the scores are more widely dispersed and the total range of scores will be larger.

Inferential Statistics

While descriptive statistics summarize data from a specific sample, **inferential statistics** allow us to extrapolate from this sample to the broader target population. Inferential statistics are based on data from our sample, but are used to provide information about characteristics we believe to be true about the population from which the sample is drawn. They are low-level inferences from sample data that we use to make higher-level inferences about the population.

Inferential statistical analyses are used for two purposes. First, they provide estimates about trends in the population as well as about the degree to which the sample reflects characteristics of the population (in other words, how generalizable our inferences might be). Second, inferential statistical analyses are utilized in order to make predictions about the population based on information gathered from the sample data. For example, you might be interested in knowing whether differences in GRE scores that are present in a sample of students from different racial/ethnic backgrounds are likely to be present in the target population, or whether those differences are due to chance; inferential statistical analyses can help you judge the probability of each of these possibilities.

In Chapter 11 we wrote about the importance of different approaches to sampling. Our sampling strategies have important implications for the degree to which data about our sample are applicable (or generalizable) to the broader population, thus highlighting how decisions about approaching the research process shape our descriptions of data and the inferences we make based on those descriptions. It is especially important for research drawing upon statistical analyses as the basis of the inference-making process to utilize representative samples in order to be generalizable to a broader population. The potential for sample data to reflect population parameters also depends on sample size: The larger the sample, the more likely it is that the results we see when we apply statistical analyses to our sample reflect results we are likely to see in our population. We can talk about how precise our estimates of the population parameters are by framing our statements in terms of a calculated **confidence interval**, which states the range within which we are confident that the true value of a parameter for the population exists. We state confidence intervals within the framework of **confidence level**: The percentage of the time we are confident the confidence interval contains the actual value of a population parameter.

There are many different inferential statistical analyses that are used to make estimates about population parameters or test hypotheses about a population. Learning how to conduct these analyses is beyond the scope of this textbook (although we do discuss inferential statistics more in Chapter 14), but we do want to highlight some of the primary factors influencing which test should be used. These include:

- The size of the sample;
- The kind of inference we are making, such as testing differences between groups, finding correlations (associations) between variables, finding the strength of the association between variables, or testing whether changes in one (or more) independent variable(s) predict a change in the dependent variable; and
- Whether we should use parametric or nonparametric statistical tests. These are the names given to two analogous sets of statistical procedures that can be used to do similar types of analyses (for example, there are both parametric and nonparametric tests that can be used to measure differences between two distinct or independent groups, such as differences in test scores resulting from students who have been taught with two different pedagogical approaches). The primary difference between parametric and nonparametric tests is that in order to use parametric tests, you must know (or be able to assume) the *parameters* of your target population—that is, information such as the mean and standard deviation (which we refer to as *estimates* when discussing the sample). When we have some knowledge about our population parameters and, in particular, whether the population data are normally distributed, we use parametric statistical tests to conduct analyses. Generally, these statistical tests also assume

that the dependent variable in the analysis can be measured continuously, meaning it is a variable for which mathematical operations make sense. (Recall that in Chapter 10 we discussed types of variables and the difference between categorical/nominal variables and variables that can be naturally measured in numerical form.)

As with choices about descriptive statistical analyses, each of the decisions that are made about which analysis to conduct itself reflects certain inferences about what is of central importance in the meaning-making process. Moreover, extending on our discussion of meaning fields in Chapter 12, the parameters that determine what statistical test we use also reflect certain boundaries around the possible meanings or inferences we can draw from the data we analyze.

Description and Inference With Textual and Visual Data

Just as with numerical data, when we analyze textual or visual data, description and inference are intertwined. To illustrate this, let's return to Emma's graduate school application. In addition to her GRE score, Emma's application might include her undergraduate GPA, a statement of purpose, perhaps a writing sample, and letters of recommendation from professors or employers. The admissions committee needs to interpret these materials holistically, considering each one on its own but also considering how together they illustrate Emma's interests and abilities in relation to the graduate program to which she has applied—in other words, considering each piece of the application in the context of the whole. The role of the admissions committee, ultimately, is to interpret each of these descriptive pieces and come to a conclusion about whether a given applicant will be a good fit for the program, will add unique characteristics to an incoming cohort, and/or is likely to succeed in graduate school.

The materials in Emma's application package can be thought of as an example of a **thick description** of her as a person, a concept that further highlights the inaccuracy inherent in the perception that "description" is separate from "inference." Thick description is a concept made salient in the field of anthropology by scholar Clifford Geertz (1973). It is an analytical technique that entails drawing on a lot of detail to provide insight into a phenomenon of study, such as a cultural group (or grad school applicant!). Although it uses the word *description,* it would be a misnomer to characterize "thick description" as solely descriptive. Thick description is different from simply presenting raw data: It uses very detailed rendering of a site or phenomenon of study to provide evidence for explanations made about that phenomenon—evidence that serves as the broader context within which one can draw meaning about specific instances of social action. In this sense, thick description is a technique utilized to establish the validity context for one's interpretations—that is, to justify one's findings. It allows readers, who were not present during the data collection process and do not have access to the data itself, to be, in a sense, brought into the experience of conducting this research. This means that readers can recognize some of the broader structural elements of a phenomenon or site of study (for example, gender rules or other norms) without the researcher having to write all of these out explicitly. Thick description is also inherently intersubjective: It lets readers position-take (understand by taking others' perspectives), which means it is always written with a dialogic orientation. Moreover, thick description allows readers to understand and make sense of contradictory information when these contradictions exist. Thus, it serves as a tool that allows readers to begin developing an insider's perspective into the phenomenon or site of study—similar to the kind of insider context, discussed in Chapter 12, that allowed Pengfei to make meaning of Iris's statements.

Let's zoom out for a minute and think about how thick description differs from the process of engaging in descriptive statistical analysis described earlier in the chapter. We can see some of the main similarities and differences in Table 13.3.

Now let's zoom back to discussing the intertwining of description and inference in textual data. We will use more of Emma's application package to illustrate this. One of Emma's former professors wrote the letter of recommendation seen in Figure 13.4.

This reference letter from Emma's former professor is descriptive: In it, the professor talks about Emma's actions in their class, interactions with Emma during office hours, and Emma's work over the course of the semester. However, the letter also helps contextualize

TABLE 13.3 — Thick Description and Descriptive Statistics

	Thick Description	Descriptive Statistics
Position of the researcher and reader	Based on an insider's understanding of a phenomenon of study Aims to allow readers to develop an insider's perspective into the phenomenon described	Based on an outsider's understanding of the topic studied Allows reader to develop an outsider's understanding of the topic
Objective of the analytical technique	To provide an understanding of the complexity of the phenomenon or study site described	To summarize patterns or trends in the data generated
Role of inference in the descriptive process	The researcher makes decisions about what aspects of the phenomenon or study site are important	The researcher must make decisions about which patterns in the data are important and should be summarized

FIGURE 13.4 Letter of Recommendation

To whom it may concern:

Emma was in my senior seminar on historical analysis. She always sat in the front row of class and took copious notes. She asked questions constantly and came to my office hours regularly, almost weekly during the last part of the semester when students in the class were working on original historical analyses for their final projects. Her time with me during office hours was characterized by further questions about course material as well as by seeking clarity on comments I made on drafts and final versions of her submitted work.

Emma was not a history major and did not have a clear grasp of the fundamentals of historical methods coming into the course; as a result, her grades during the early part of the class were low. Emma's grasp of the material improved tremendously over the course of the semester, and by the end of the class she proved herself capable of conducting a thorough historical analysis. Emma's grades during early assignments brought down her overall grade in the course. However, I do not believe this grade is reflective of her abilities as a student: her hard work and perseverance throughout the semester (while carrying a full course load in her own major field of study) are exceptional, and I believe that she is among the top 5% of all students I have had the privilege to teach in the last 15 years.

Sincerely

A.H. Prof
Associate Professor, XX University

Source: iStock.com/Valerie Loiseleux.

Emma's undergraduate transcript, which shows a fairly low grade for the course she took with this professor, and provides a more holistic picture of Emma as a student and what she was capable of achieving. In other words, it is a descriptive element that is used for interpretive purposes, and a tool that can help establish the basis for explaining the committee's admissions decision.

Figure 13.5 shows the notes one admissions committee member might have made on the recommendation letter in Emma's application file in order to capture what they thought was most important about this document.

These notes are an informal example of **coding**, the process of assigning categories or short-hand names (referred to as codes) to "chunks" of textual or visual data—a concept first introduced in Chapter 12. Johnny Saldána defines a code as "a word or short phrase

FIGURE 13.5 — Coded Letter of Recommendation

To whom it may concern:

Emma was in my senior seminar on historical analysis. She always sat in the front row of class and took copious notes. She asked questions constantly and came to my office hours regularly, almost weekly during the last part of the semester when students in the class were working on original historical analyses for their final projects. Her time with me during office hours was characterized by further questions about course material as well as by seeking clarity on comments I made on drafts and final versions of her submitted work.

Engaged student

Seeking improvement

Emma was not a history major and did not have a clear grasp of the fundamentals of historical methods coming into the course; as a result, her grades during the early part of the class were low. Emma's grasp of the material improved tremendously over the course of the semester, and by the end of the class she proved herself capable of conducting a thorough historical analysis. Emma's grades during early assignments brought down her overall grade in the course. However, I do not believe this grade is reflective of her abilities as a student: her hard work and perseverance throughout the semester (while carrying a full course load in her own major field of study) are exceptional, and I believe that she is among the top 5% of all students I have had the privilege to teach in the last 15 years.

Initial difficulties

Overall impressions:
- Improvement over time
- Desire to understand
- Willing to seek feedback to improve

Sincerely,

A.H. Prof
Associate Professor, XX University

---

that symbolically assigns a summative, salient, essence-capturing, and/or evocative attribute for a portion of language-based or visual data" (2009, p. 7). It is a process that can help organize large amounts of data, allowing for more focused analysis later on. When looking at applications, an admissions committee member may make notes on different parts of the application to help them remember key characteristics about the applicant—as in Figure 13.5. These notes might say things like "unclear connection to program focus" on the personal statement, "high scores!" about the GRE, or "mixed messages" in relation to letters of recommendation. With each of these short phrases, the admissions committee member captures the essence of what they feel is important to note about a particular candidate, knowing that they will not be able necessarily to reread every relevant part of the application when meeting to make decision, but that they will be able to glance at these notes as a way of remembering how they characterize the applicant overall. The codes are *descriptions* of the data that allow admissions committee members to make judgments or inferences about applicants. They also reflect decisions made by the admissions committee members about what is important to code.

In empirical research studies, coding serves a similar function. Researchers in early stages of analysis will go through material they have collected and assign data with codes that serve a particular meaning for the researcher. There are multiple ways to engage in the coding process with textual or visual data. Some researchers start with *a priori* codes—that is, codes created based on categories the researcher deems important (from existing scholarship, prior research, and so on) and then applied to the data. Other researchers use emergent coding procedures in which transcripts or other data to be analyzed are read through carefully, and codes created based on what are in the data. There are also different aspects of data that researchers might code. Most often, researchers use codes when focusing on the *substantive meaning* of the text. However, researchers also code chunks of data according to the *kind of language* used or the *structure* of the text. As we will discuss more in Chapter 14, this coding serves as a foundation for making broader or higher-order inferences about the meaning of our data as a whole.

In our "Researching Research" project, discussed in Chapters 1 and 2, we used several different coding approaches: In addition to assigning categories to what students said about their relationship to research (substance), we also coded the way they talked about research in terms of both language and structure: Was the structure of their writing formal or informal? Did they write about research in a way that showed a "distancing" of themselves from the research process, or did their responses suggest that they positioned themselves as researchers? In other words, through our coding process we addressed both the substance and structure of our students' essays. Moreover, our decision about *how* to code also shaped the kinds of descriptions we focused on in our analysis and, ultimately, the inferences we made.

Figure 13.6 shows one student's response to our initial prompt about how they define research as well as some of the codes we used to make sense of what was written. The figure includes *substantive* codes (about how research is defined, for example, and about the student's general perspective about research), but also codes about *language used* (informal) and about how the student positions themself in relation to the research process. In addition, you can see here both *a priori* or predetermined codes (such as "Definition of research") and examples of *emergent coding* (e.g., "Changing understanding of research," which is a code we created based on the data).

We want to emphasize that while it is a very important step in data analysis, coding is only *one step* in the process of making higher-level inferences. Regardless of what coding processes are used, following initial categorization of data into codes, researchers must then look at patterns or connections across the coded data (or themes, as in the process of **thematic analysis**) as well as disjunctures from those patterns in order to make sense of their material as a whole. For example, the codes in Figure 13.6 help us see how *one* student defined research. However, in order to develop our typology of the four ways students conceptualize research (as described in Chapter 2), we needed to look at data across *all* of

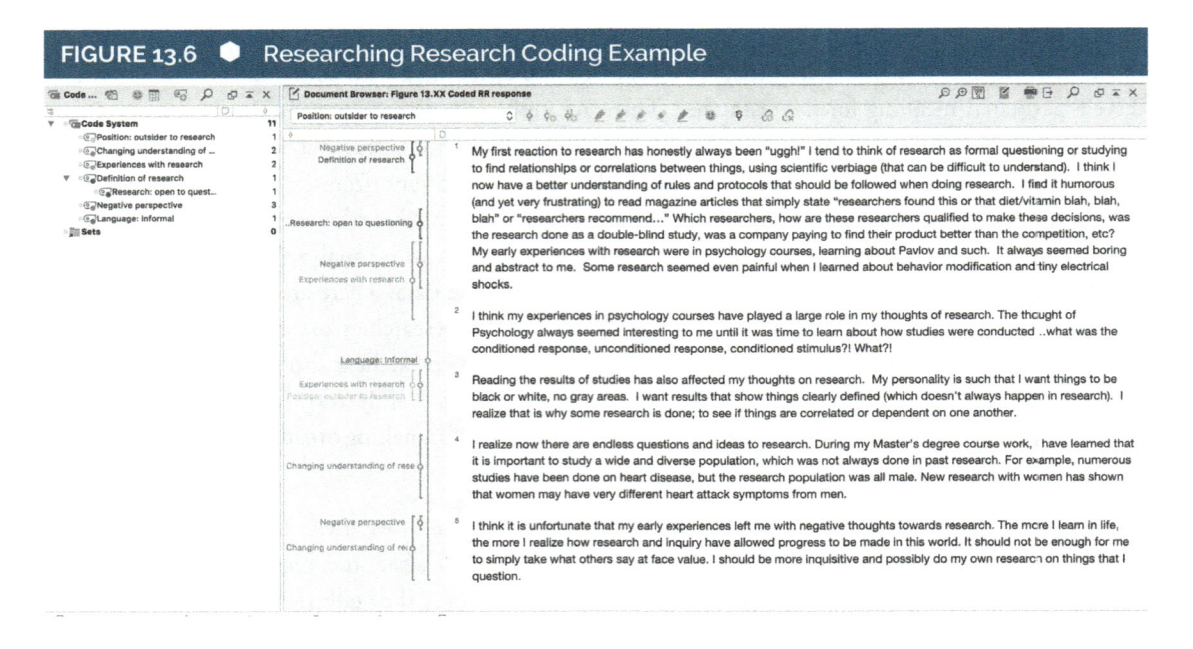

FIGURE 13.6 — Researching Research Coding Example

our student participants. We did this by first coding all student responses and then looking specifically at data related to defining research. Within this part of our data, we generated more detailed codes to categorize responses that defined research in different ways. Then we looked at data across these different codes to help us understand broader patterns and relationships across definitions. We will discuss this process further in Chapter 14.

> **Pause and Reflect.** To help make the concept of coding more concrete, take a few minutes to think about the way you take notes in class. As you hear your professor and fellow students speak, how do you decide what to write down? What kinds of things do you note that will help you remember important concepts, theories, terms, and so on? The notes that you take are similar in some ways to codes that a researcher might use when beginning systematic analysis: They are ways of capturing the essence of the discussions that take place in class.

Missing Data and Outliers in the Inferential Process

As we wrap up this part of the chapter, we want to briefly highlight how description and inference in data analysis tie back to some other concepts we have discussed. In Chapter 11 we addressed the concept of *missing data*, specifically as it relates to data collection or generation. As we mentioned there, deciding what to do about missing data is part of the inferential process, but it often occurs during data collection. This highlights the iterative rather than linear nature of the data generation–inference-making relationship. This is also true when making decisions about handling outliers. Our example of GRE scores, and how they are utilized as part of the admissions process, can help clarify how the concepts of missing data and outliers fit into the overall descriptive and inferential process. As we noted earlier, the GRE is just one part of an admissions package that includes a range of other materials. This means that the meaning of GRE scores needs to be interpreted in light of how they fit into the broader context of these other application materials—in some cases, they will be consistent with other elements of the application package, so that the way admissions committee members interpret these scores is fairly straightforward. However, imagine a situation where an applicant to a graduate program has very strong letters of recommendation, a personal statement that demonstrates a clear fit with the program goals, and high grades from their undergraduate study—but a GRE score that is under the minimum GRE score required according to the program guidelines. In this sense, the GRE score can be described as an **outlier** in comparison with the rest of the application materials. How do we make meaning of this outlier? Ultimately, the decision about whether to admit this applicant will need to be based on the admission committee's overall interpretation of materials—including, but not limited to, interpretation of this GRE score and whether it accurately describes the applicant in question. In other words, while the score might be an outlier in an absolute sense (it is not reflective of the applicant's other materials; it is lower than the minimum required score for admission), it is how that outlier is treated that ultimately determines the admissions outcome. Similarly, if a graduate program decides that the GRE is recommended for admission, but not mandatory, the admissions committee must decide how to proceed with applications that do not include the GRE—that is, in situations where there are missing data that could provide insight into the applicant's potential.

As we noted in Chapter 11, what researchers do—or don't do—with missing data has ethical implications as well as pragmatic ones. For instance, we might consider the ethics of applying inferences made about a sample or population to an individual whose data were excluded from a data set because of missing responses on a few survey questions. Likewise, in the case of outliers, we might ask about the ethical implications of making inferences based on either the inclusion or exclusion of outlier data. Again, these are situations that can be addressed in a variety of ways. However, as we move further into the research process, it is important to reflect on how ethical considerations come into play and build upon one another.

Coming Back to Validity

A second concept we briefly want to return to is validity, especially as it relates to both numerical and textual/visual data. There is a tendency among many to treat numbers and inferences based in numerical data as more accurate than inferences in studies based on generating textual, visual, or performative data. "Numbers don't lie!" is a phrase we often hear. Certainly, when we see numbers in front of us, it seems difficult to challenge them. Superficially, at least, there seems to be much less ambiguity in the number "63" than in a quotation from an interview.

However, when we consider the research process as a whole and the number of decisions involved in that process, things look a little bit different. In Chapter 10 we wrote about the process of acquiring or generating data, and the need for researchers to make decisions about what data collection tools or techniques to use. In the research scenarios from that chapter, further, we saw examples being made at different points along the process about how to make sense of those data. As we have discussed throughout the text, the data generation and inference processes are not linear but intertwined: Decisions and inferences must be made constantly. Thus, the "63" that you see is not an absolute truth, but rather an outcome of decisions: about what kind of item or scale to use in a questionnaire, about sampling strategies, about how to deal with missing data, and so on.

What we want to emphasize is that numerical data are not *a priori* more accurate than other forms of data. Instead, it is important to return to the concept of validity as we discussed it in Chapter 7, particularly in terms of ideas around providing justification for our claims, and consider the different kinds of knowledge claims that are being made when we engage in meaning-making (see also our discussion of correspondence theory in Chapter 12). When we generate numerical data, we are mapping onto the realm of *objective knowledge claims*; thus, our criteria for establishing a validity context for our claims should be based on the principle of agreement, drawing upon multiple observations/observers. When we make inferences based on other kinds of data, such as in-depth interviews about individuals' perspectives, our validity criteria should be compatible with the types of knowledge claims our inferences emphasize.

It is also important to keep in mind that the process of analyzing numerical data requires as many individual decisions to be made by researchers as in other kinds of studies. The primary difference is *when* these decisions occur. In large-scale studies based on numerical data, decision-making mostly takes place up-front: Researchers make decisions about which scales or rankings to use, about sampling strategies, and more. Before data are generated, researchers must decide how to operationalize the concepts they plan to study as variables—that is, strictly defined concepts that can be measured numerically. In other words, a large part of inference-making in this kind of research occurs early in the process; less decision-making is required after data are generated. In contrast, the process of generating and analyzing textual or visual data and reconstructing meaning requires researchers to engage with the data *after* they are collected to a much greater degree because concepts are not strictly operationalized in the same way (remembering, of course, that researchers collecting these kinds of data must also make many decisions before and during the data-gathering process).

RESEARCH SCENARIO: MAKING DECISIONS

In this section, we look at two studies to highlight the intertwining of description and inference in empirical inquiry. These studies illustrate different kinds of techniques that can be used in the inference-making process: **social network analysis** and **Photovoice**. Each of the examples shows *how* the process of making inferences occurs in the context of techniques that generate descriptive outputs. We highlight these techniques to show different kinds of approaches to data analysis. While we often think about textual or numerical data as the basis for meaning-making in empirical research, data used as the basis for analysis can take numerous other forms—including networks and images, as discussed below.

Network Analysis: Jeffrey Pugh

I am a question-driven researcher, a political scientist who is committed to interdisciplinary inquiry. That means that I do not have a strong allegiance to one particular method, adherence to strict disciplinary boundaries, or a need to label myself as an advocate of one of the big theoretical camps. Rather, I start with an empirical puzzle, often one emerging from practice or observations in the field, and select a research design and method that I think will provide the best test and most convincing evidence for inferences answering the question (Pugh, 2013). The other side of this is that I often rely on methods that I am still learning, applying them to a topical and regional context that I know well, rather than developing deep technical proficiency in a single method and then looking for topics to apply it to. During field work in Ecuador, in which I was studying the role of institutions in resolving conflict between refugees and their host communities, I began to notice some commonalities in the experiences people were sharing with me. Some programs were more effective than others at building trust and protecting refugee rights, but it did not seem to be only a function of budget amount, professionalism of staff, or program quality. I was relying mostly on interviews of Ecuadorian NGO and government officials, and surveys of Colombian refugees, asking questions about attitudes and experiences, economic livelihoods, and perceptions of security. The surveys showed a dramatic disjuncture in refugee trust toward state agencies versus non-state institutions like the church, NGOs, and the UN. At the same time, I kept hearing from interviewees about refugees coming to their offices, and although they could not help with the specific issue, they accompanied the refugees, who had developed trust in their staff, to the appropriate office and helped refer cases to trusted counterparts in other agencies (Balyk & Pugh, 2013). It seemed more and more that the relationships through which refugee-serving organizations coordinated and cooperated seemed to be especially important, as a large, well-funded organization with good programs in one area would not be very helpful to a refugee needing any other type of help if they did not have good networks among state agencies, NGOs, and the UN (Pugh, 2016). Likewise, the refugees themselves varied in how much interaction they had with each other, with the host community, and with different organizations, and those who were more isolated seemed to have a harder time (Pugh, 2018).

On the basis of this preliminary observation, I sought ways to systematically measure the structure of relationships among institutions and refugees, and to be able to compare them across different localities in order to determine how they might affect refugees' human security outcomes, as well as the way that migration policies and programs were negotiated. To do this, I built in a network question into to my survey. I asked refugees from what sources (NGOs, informal allies, state agencies, etc.) they had received help since coming to Ecuador, and what type of help they received. They could list whatever organizations or people they wanted, or indicate that they had not received any help. I coded the organizations that were mentioned, and noted a relationship between different organizations when they were mentioned by the same refugee, because this showed that they had a beneficiary in common and indicated they were likely to be in the same network. Using social network analysis software, I created a sociogram, a graph to visualize the structure of these relationships among the different organizations that allowed me to see which groups shared the most refugee beneficiaries, indicating a higher level of coordination, and which groups were peripheral to the network. Surprisingly, many of the state agencies that had the official responsibility for protection and migration governance were quite peripheral in the network, or were not mentioned at all by refugees. There was also a difference in the density of the network—how closely the organizations in the network cooperated—that corresponded with the reported discrimination and insecurity experienced by refugees, with localities having denser governance networks also reporting better security outcomes for refugees (Pugh, 2015).

In order to move from description to inference, I tested potential alternative explanations for variation in human security outcomes across six provinces in Ecuador, especially economic development and state institutional presence. Cities in the central region of Ecuador, and especially the capital city of Quito, had greater economic development and state institutional presence, but had worse outcomes for discrimination, experience with violent victimization, and intergroup attitudes than a border town in the jungle where economic development and institutionalization were lower but the governance network was denser and more diverse. Interviews with organizations and migrants provided additional evidence of the reasons for this correlation, as many participants in the localities with dense networks described being referred to help by different NGOs, while those in the cities with less dense networks reported not knowing where to go to solve problems, or they experienced more isolation and rejection that prevented them from getting what they needed. By triangulating network analysis, survey results, and qualitative interviews, I was able to examine more systematically the key question that my initial research had identified, and the evidence that the data produced was much more convincing than anecdotal claims made by key informants.

Dr. Pugh's narrative highlights how he used descriptive network diagrams as a way of making inferences about how organizations helped address conflicts refugees faced. In line with the intertwining of description and inference highlighted earlier in the chapter, his narrative also shows where inference is an inherent part of making decisions about which techniques to use to describe the data. Dr. Pugh used network analysis because of his belief that this approach could highlight relationships between organizations, and that these relationships might explain both policies pertaining to refugees/migrants and human security outcomes. Thus, Dr. Pugh's data generation drew on his own inferences about the utility of structural analyses to engage in the work of describing relationships and then making further explanatory inferences based on what the descriptions showed.

Our other example is based on another set of interpretive practices developed by Caroline Wang and Mary Ann Burris (1997) called Photovoice, which uses photography as the basis for meaning-making.

Photovoice in Our Community: Danielle Lansing

Our Photovoice inquiry was a result of a group of Native American families wanting to make a difference in the education of their children. The community came together in order to critically think about how to build culturally relevant curriculum for preschool classrooms. Families understood that this meant we would come together to think about the most essential skills and ideas that would support the development of young Native American children. We had a notion that much of these essential teachings would be connected with tribal language and culture. However, as a facilitator, I knew that within a diverse group, it was important that each parent's voice was heard. A shared history of boarding schools and generations of Native American parents not being consulted about the education their children served as a motivator. So we embarked on answering the following question as the basis of our inquiry: "What knowledge is needed to become a healthy Native American?"

As the facilitator, it was important that we take time to capture and highlight the unique experiences each of our families represented. Parents were eager to have their voices heard. They took time to develop their own photo collections that answered the research question. As each family completed their photo collection, we began small-group sharing for analysis.

Parents individually shared their photos through a reflection process that described both the literal and implicit meanings of their photos. This included describing the photo, telling the story of the photo, and then thinking about why it was important to them and the group. As parents shared their ideas with the others, some focused on the literal aspects of the photos while others addressed and discussed the meaning behind the images.

One family shared a photo of a baby boy being held in the arms of an elder. The woman held the infant close and had an expression of happiness and joy on her face. The family discussed how their grandmother had played an important role in maintaining the tribal language within the family through her interactions with family members. She often sang songs to the children in the language. As a participant observer, I carefully watched and listened as other parents nodded in agreement and also chimed in about how their grandparents also sang to their children. From these collective discussions, it was obvious that our group valued their elders as teachers of their children. There was an acknowledgement that elders were powerful teachers of language and culture.

As Dr. Lansing notes, parents in her group created their own collection of photos. At one level, each of these photographs was descriptive, in terms of providing initial data through illustrative responses to the research question. However, as the analytical process continued, underlying messages behind the images emerged as well. These underlying messages—inferences made about the photographs—were the basis for addressing the collective's broader questions about knowledge needed to become a healthy Native American. Again, we can see how the descriptive and inferential processes of inquiry intertwine in this example.

✓ YOU AND RESEARCH

Let's think about how you might find yourself grappling with issues of description and inference in the data analysis process as you read, or engage with, empirical research.

When Interpreting Research

Descriptions and explanations of data make up the bulk of what you see in "Results," "Findings," and/or "Discussion" sections of academic journal articles. As you read, pay attention to *what* information authors are utilizing to present their inferences and *how* those data are presented. Do authors provide demographic or other information about participants? What statistical tests, if doing statistical analyses, do the authors use? If working with nonnumerical data, what approach do authors utilize in order to make meaning of the data generated?

Not all research write-ups include discussions of ethical issue or validity. When these are discussed, as noted in earlier chapters, they are most often in the "Methodology" section of a study write-up. When you read, pay attention to the ways researchers address these concepts. Do they note treatment of missing data? Do their discussions of validity and validity techniques make sense in terms of the kinds of knowledge claims onto which their empirical data map?

Finally, think back to the research questions being asked, as well as any discussions about epistemological frameworks (or, if no such discussion exists, what you can glean about epistemological commitments from the choices made about various aspects of the research process). Reflect on whether decisions made about how to analyze, and then describe and explain the data, make sense in the context of the inquiry process as a whole.

When Doing Research

When planning your research, you will need to think about how to *describe* and *explain* the data you generate in ways that address your research questions and remain congruent with your epistemological commitments. If you are generating numerical data for statistical analysis, you will have already made decisions about creating a data set; this will shape your analytical process. You will likely engage in both descriptive and inferential statistical analyses, but *which* analyses you run will depend on a number of factors, including whether your data are continuous or noncontinuous, what your unit of analysis is (e.g., individual, classroom, or school-level data, or a combination of these), and/or whether your data are normally distributed. If your research questions lead you to generate data through interviews, focus groups, or visual techniques, you will also need to make decisions. Many analyses explore primary themes across respondents, but depending on your research questions, you might also consider analyzing narratives or using other analytical approaches.

When writing a research proposal for the institutional review board, the specifics of your analytical approach are likely to be of less concern than your data collection techniques, sampling strategy, and so on. However, your advisor(s)/committee members will want to see that you have fully thought through the logic of research questions, data generation, and analytical approach as you are designing your study. Thus, it is important to consider what you will do with your data in order to address your research questions. It is also important to reflect back to the underlying theoretical assumptions that shape the way you describe and analyze your data.

SYNTHESIS: POINTS FOR REFLECTION

Conceptual Synthesis

In this chapter we have explicitly addressed the intertwining of description and inference in the meaning-making process. Throughout the chapter, we have highlighted choices researchers make about describing their data, and how these choices shape the kinds of inferences that might be made. We also have noted that the relationship between description and inference is not unidirectional. Just as description shapes possibilities for meaning-making (both for researchers and for readers of their work), backgrounded inferences—such as the theoretical frameworks that undergird a study—lead to certain analytical approaches that influence the way data are described. This is true not only with respect to substantive theoretical frameworks but also when considering epistemological and methodological commitments. For instance, your approach to thinking about validity or ethics, as we have discussed in earlier chapters, will shape the way you decide to address issues such as missing data or contradictions within your data, when you engage in description and higher-level meaning-making.

Methodological Synthesis

As this chapter indicates, there is a wide range of analytical choices that researchers make in order to describe their data and engage in higher-level inferential processes. These include choices about *what* data to describe, but also *how* to describe data that have been generated. Dr. Pugh's research scenario is a good example of how such choices occur not only at the outset of a research project, but throughout the process as a whole: It was through his initial fieldwork that Dr. Pugh understood the need to be able to systematically explore relationships among and between organizations/institutions serving refugees, which led him to choose social network analysis as a way of both describing his data (including visualizing them through network diagrams), and as the basis for making inferences about differences in human security outcomes in the refugee community in Ecuador. It is important to note that the timing for making these kinds of choices will differ depending on the kinds of research questions asked and types of data generation techniques utilized. When generating numerical data for statistical analyses, for instance, many of the most significant decisions about approach must be made prior to data generation. It's also important to note that this chapter provides examples of only a few approaches to analysis. Many other approaches exist, and new approaches are continuously emerging.

Personal Synthesis

As we have already noted, a key theme of this chapter is the intertwining of data generation, description, and inference. In the reflective questions raised throughout this chapter we have offered opportunities for you to consider what choices you might make within this framework. We have also encouraged you to reflect further on how your ontological and epistemological beliefs might shape your choices when describing and interpreting data. It is also important to think about how you might react to descriptions or explanations that other researchers articulate: What might convince you that their inferences are justified, based on the data described? As you encounter research in academic and other settings, we invite you to continue to reflect on these questions and to articulate your own thoughts.

MOVING FORWARD

This chapter addressed distinctions between, and the intertwining of, description and inference in the research process. It sets the stage for the next chapter, where we will further explore inference-making as part of empirical research. We will continue to build on concepts discussed throughout Clusters 1 and 2.

Further Readings

Riessman, C. K. 1996. *Narrative analysis*. Thousand Oaks, CA: SAGE.

Starks, H., & Trinidad, S. B. (2007). Choose your method: A comparison of phenomenology, discourse analysis, and grounded theory. *Qualitative Health Research*, *17*(10), 1372–1380.

Wang, C. C. (1999). Photovoice: A participatory action research strategy applied to women's health. *Journal of Women's Health*, *8*(2), 185–192.

Wasserman, S., & Faust, K. (1994). *Social network analysis: Methods and applications*. Cambridge, UK: Cambridge University Press.

Further Readings by Jeffrey Pugh

Pugh, J. (2013). The short-term "bridge model" study abroad program: Peacebuilding in Latin America. *PS: Political Science & Politics*, *46*(4), 791–796.

Pugh, J. (2016). Peacebuilding among transnational youth in migrant-receiving border regions of Ecuador. *Journal of Peacebuilding and Development*, *11*(3), 83–97.

Pugh, J. (2018). Negotiating identity and belonging through the Invisibility Bargain: Colombian forced migrants in Ecuador. *International Migration Review*, *52*(4), 978–1010.

Further Readings by Danielle Lansing

Lansing, D. (2017). Learning from the community: Innovative partnerships that inform tribal college teacher education programming. In E. Petchauer & L. Mawhinney (Eds.), *Minority serving institutions: Programs, policies, and social justice* (pp. 35–50). New Brunswick, NJ: Rutgers University Press.

Lansing, D. (2017). Pathways to authentic community engagement: Phases of teacher development on a continuum of practice toward nation-building. *Tribal College and University Research Journal*, *1*(2), 59–79.

14

MAKING INFERENCES ABOUT TRENDS AND EXPERIENCES

Sometimes in life it becomes important to look for patterns within, across, and outside of the descriptive inferences talked about in Chapter 13. In Chapter 12 we established a theoretical conception of inferencing as an active process oriented toward understanding. In this chapter we want to develop knowledge of how to make broader inferences about the trends and experiences we initially articulate through the descriptive inferences we build up with data. In this chapter we learn how researchers make inferences about the ways variables might be related to one another and how experiences might be patterned—for example, one might wonder if there is a higher likelihood of being obese as an adult if one was obese as a child. Pondering this puts us in a position of comparing trends in childhood obesity with trends in adult obesity. In order to move forward with drawing inferences from these trends, we have to be willing to accept the trends that have been articulated as valid, while accepting the limitations of those inferences, including potential disputes in the definition and usefulness of "obesity" as a category (recall Chapter 5, where the concept of obesity was challenged). In other words, as researchers move forward in making inferences about trends and experiences, they bring with them a host of assumptions that become part of the inferencing process—assumptions about whether or not *obesity* itself is a health concept, as it is often pitched, or a sexist concept, as we saw in the work of Sonya Satinsky, sexual health expert at Yale University (Chapter 5).

MUSING UPON THE EVERYDAY: OBESITY IS CONTAGIOUS

Thus, it is necessary to articulate lurking assumptions. For example, one of those assumptions is that a woman's size is worthy of social comment. As discussed further along, this becomes of particular interest when both the health industry and the beauty industry converge on the value of being thin. As we muse upon the everyday context, we will experience the heaviness of sizeism and taken-for-granted assumptions common in U.S. culture. We will, once again, see how ordinary assumptions and social controversies are taken up wittingly or not through research efforts. Our position is that all research efforts should be open to critical perspectives on the level of such assumptions. In this section we explore typical ways in which we make inferences across trends and experiences with research efforts to do the same.

In the United States obesity is considered a national problem. This problem is not just talked about among health researchers. For example, ordinary magazine outlets often feature articles related to obesity, and people talk among themselves about obesity. One important point is that research projects, including what would be considered interesting questions to ask, are set within such sociocultural contexts. Not long ago, there was a rising cultural concern about something called "childhood obesity." People began to wonder whether or not there was a *rising* incidence of childhood obesity in the United States. This question asks us to make inferences about the rates of obesity in children over time. Notice that already we have to make assumptions about who counts as a child and how obesity is both defined and measured. Perhaps we link this trend (once we have it identified) with what is available in school lunches. When we do this, what is happening is that our minds are interpreting a meaningful connection between child weight and healthy eating options at school. Such mental links between healthy weights over time and what is served for school lunch involve making inferences—that is, interpreting what one means in relation to the other.

Once we have the building block structures for making inferences that would include broader claims, audiences, or applications, our minds easily want to do this. We start adding layers, and we have to assume the blocks underneath the new layers are there and will hold. This includes things like how we are conceptualizing obesity, for example, and on what underlying assumptions that conceptualization depends.

The cultural interest in obesity and health has been taken up through research. As you know, these would not be disconnected. Then research studies find their way back into our culture. We use one example of this here. People started to ask, "Are people more likely to be obese if they hang around others who are obese?" What trends would we need to observe in order to answer that question? What assumptions are we making about how to interpret even the word *obese*? Comparing trends is just one way to make inferences about trends and experiences. This chapter will explore the various ways researchers do this.

People in the popular press are asking, "Is obesity contagious?" To get to this question, one has to have already made descriptive inferences about the trends regarding obesity. Alan Mozes (2018) began an article for *Health Day Reporter* like this: "Living in a neighborhood with a high rate of obesity might raise the odds that you and your children will become plus-sized, too." In order to offer us this relationship between neighborhood obesity and personal trends toward obesity, one would have had to establish a trend toward obesity in individuals and trends toward obesity in neighborhoods. You would also have had to accept the definitions of "obesity" and "contagious." Reporting on the same study, Mike McRae (2018) wrote: "It's often described as an epidemic, but rising obesity figures might have more in common with infectious diseases than we ever realized." He went on to write: "New research has added evidence to the idea that being in a social network with a higher level of obesity puts us more at risk of increasing our body mass index (BMI), almost as if we were 'catching' behaviours that make us put on weight." Andrew Weil, well-known medical doctor and health commentator in the United States, posted an article reporting on the same study (2018) and contrasting it with an earlier study. His article was titled "Is Obesity Contagious? I Understand That Obesity Can Be Contagious. This Sounds Ridiculous to Me. Your Thoughts?" He started: "Some research does suggest that obesity is contagious, but not in the sense that you catch it as you would a cold or the flu. Instead, obesity appears to be 'socially contagious,' meaning people are more likely to become overweight or obese if those around them are." Each of these popular press articles drew from a study conducted by RAND Corporation researchers Ashlesha Datar and Nancy Nicosia (2018), with 1,519 army families across 38 U.S. military installations.

As a consumer of such popular reports of research, how might you decide whether or not to take the inferences of this reported study to heart? Of course, one can sometimes return to the original research to be sure that it is being accurately portrayed in the popular press. If it is, one still needs to figure out how to trust the inferences being drawn from the descriptive trends. Though the statements are produced as propositions—for example, "Obesity is contagious"—a host of inferences are being projected and, also, accepted. These inferences even involve leaps to our own lives and practices as people taking in the information. We are in the position of having to make inferences about how applicable, fitting, or relevant the information is for our situations, for us. In other words, how does this study matter for others?

Reading popular media in the United States puts us in the position of having to critically judge these inferential processes as a part of how we interpret research in our ordinary lives, but in this chapter we want to see how such inferences are built up in inquiry.

NARRATIVE AND CONCEPTUAL INTERLUDES: MAKING INFERENCES THAT MATTER

Ultimately, doing social research is tied up in wanting to advance knowledge that helps us create a better world, better lives, better opportunities, and so on. One of the ways researchers address those passions is by thinking about how much their studies might matter for the world—the question of "So what?" This question is not as easy to answer as it might sound. Answering the question requires a sophisticated set of analytic methods and conceptual tools. In this chapter we intend to introduce you to some of those methods and conceptual tools; however, the methods are constantly expanding. Moreover, the question of "So what?" always implies the question, "For whom?" For whom do these findings matter? There is more on the "So what?" question in Chapter 16.

Moving Beyond Description: Categories of Inferences

There are interesting differences across distinct inferential approaches in social science. **Statistical inferencing** has developed into a highly technical set of procedures, on the one hand, while **theoretical inferencing**, on the other hand, has expanded into a more amorphous collection of interpretational potentials. It is possible in statistics to create decision trees that help one determine the best statistical procedures to use given particular information about the study, but with theoretical inferencing, for example, one can explore a variety of interpretive possibilities in an effort to better understand the experiences and patterns/idiosyncrasies one is articulating. This difference will be evident in the ways broader inferences are both made and displayed across different studies. From the outside it looks as if statistical approaches have more precision and increased validity. It can appear as if the tight procedural and technical consistencies of statistical inferencing require expertise that is both intimidating and rigorous—less fuzzy, with more room for exactness and certainty. On the other hand, it can seem as if linguistic inferencing, as we saw with meaning fields, is more intuitive, but less certain. When novice researchers read statistical inferences, those inferences can seem incomprehensible, while the same novice researchers might read a narrative study and *feel* as though they intuitively get the more expansive meaning. The highly technical form of statistical inferencing also uses a very specific language that has, to a certain extent, become fixed. This contrasts with the more intuitive, fluid, and open-ended inference-making practiced by qualitative researchers, for example. In this section of the chapter, we focus on *conceptual* rather than procedural aspects of what it means to think beyond the descriptive inferences (both statistical and linguistic) because the procedural aspects always already depend on concepts being assumed. For this reason, we include some brief explanations of common inferential procedures in the appendices. These appendices will help you read such inferences when you are reviewing research.

Inferences that leap beyond the descriptions can be generally organized through the following categories: (1) causation, (2) correlation, (3) sociocultural structures, (4) insights and consciousness-raising, and (5) theory building. In building these inferences, researchers must draw on their initial descriptive interpretations.

Causation

Barbara's student Zayra is interested in studying the ways parents teach their young children (ages 3–4) healthy eating and drinking behaviors within the family because Zayra wants to support the development of healthy eating/drinking lifestyles with young children. Zayra could be advised to investigate this interest in many different ways. Let's think about two sharply contrasting ways to conceptualize this interest for the purposes of creating a methodological approach. First, Zayra can imagine that the parents' activities might cause (or at least correlate with) certain outcomes in the children's behaviors. Second, Zayra could wonder about the interactive processes involved in successful or failed efforts to help children eat and drink in healthy ways. In the first approach, Zayra would want to see how very clearly defined and measured variables relate or intersect with one another (for example, one variable could be what food/drink are available for the child, *and* a second variable could be what food/drink are consumed by the child). For the second interest, Zayra might want to look closely at interactive patterns in the family (for example, observations of parents and children interacting while sharing a meal together). By now you realize that even these ways of thinking about the interest carry forward assumptions from the interest itself—for example, identifying which food and drink are considered "healthy." There is no way to move to these higher forms of inference without carrying the baggage of necessary assumptions. The best we can do as researchers is to keep these assumptions as transparent as we can, and to clearly articulate them so that they are part of the conversation. There are also methodological assumptions. These two possible approaches to the study already begin to indicate whether or not causal inferences will become possible from the way the study is being conceived. The first approach seeks to examine if food availability (parental behavior) causes food choices (child behavior). The second approach does not try to establish cause; rather, it looks for interactive patterns involved with family eating. Some social scientists will never conceive of their interests in terms of causation and others will think that describing causation is the ultimate goal of any social science project.

In the obesity research cited above, would we conclude that a social network of more obese people will *cause* others who join it to become obese? Or would we say that there is some kind of correlation between any one individual's likelihood of being obese and the obesity of that individual's social network? The inference of causation indicates a particular way of thinking about the meaning of the descriptive inferences that is connected to differences in the way the subject of the research is conceived methodologically. In many (but not all) forms of qualitative inquiry, the subject has a more *agentic* conceptualization. This means that causality is rarely the inferential focus in qualitative inquiry. Instead, strong qualitative researchers will take a lot of care to describe the conditions within which participants are acting or telling their stories so that we come to understand the constraints and resources of their actions and agency. Doing this depends, at least tacitly, on the principle that the actor always could have acted otherwise. This is not to say that there are not strong influences and conditions that bear down on action. For example, perhaps a person's family eating patterns and genetic proclivities are strong influences over one's likelihood toward obesity, but a qualitative researcher would conceptualize these characteristics as influences and conditions for the person as they engage in eating decisions/activities rather than as causes for obesity. Given the diversity of the field of qualitative inquiry, this point is not universally articulated, but it does often show in the background methodological decisions researchers make—such as including detailed descriptions and artifacts indicative of the setting.

Social scientists use highly technical statistical procedures along with controlled research conditions to infer causation. Generally, when social scientists infer causation it is through a fixed design approach (discussed in Chapter 8) where variables are tightly controlled. In social science, it is difficult to have as much control as a scientist might have in a laboratory. Being able to locate the cause(s) of an outcome involves being able to rule out other plausible explanations as well as locate the effect of a variable (the independent variable) on at least one other variable (the dependent variable). Despite their difficulties, these Randomized Control Trials (RCTs) are quite popular—they are commonly referred to as the "Gold Standard" in the social sciences.

Establishing causation usually involves comparing the averages (or arithmetic means) on a dependent variable of at least two groups of people who match on important characteristics—one group without a **treatment**, or intervention, and the other group with a treatment administered. According to the RCT design, two samples would be randomly selected from the population and then randomly assigned either to the treatment group or to the nontreatment group. The randomness of the group assignment is supposed to help ensure that the two samples are similar enough to warrant comparing. In other words, it helps *control* for possible, even unforeseeable, variables that could influence the dependent variable (recall Chapter 8). However, to be safe, sometimes researchers do a *stratified* random sample in order to be sure that two groups match. (Recall the discussion on sampling in Chapter 11.) In this way if a difference is found across the two means, researchers don't have to worry whether that difference might best be explained by chance or by a skewed sample. When we make a causal inference in research, we are saying that one variable best explains effects on the dependent variable. Control must be sufficient so as to suggest that it is unlikely that other variables explain the outcome or effect. It is difficult to have so much control in social science research, especially research in naturalistic (i.e., the dinner table) as opposed to laboratory settings. Nevertheless, RCTs are used. It is impossible to imagine conducting an RCT for Zayra's research interests because it would be impossible to control all the possible influencing factors in the healthy eating behaviors of young children or the teaching activities of the parents. More important, for ethical reasons, researchers would not want to purposefully assign a group of young children to a research condition that we suspected was unhealthy because researchers would not want to put a participant at such a risk. Wanting the best for their participants is an important aspect of the researcher's ethical commitments.

How might an RCT work for Zayra's study? One could imagine establishing only two groups (Group A and Group B) to examine something like participation and outcomes of a particular exercise program in conjunction with a weight loss program. The independent (or treatment) variable could be participation in a specific exercise component in addition to a weight loss program. Members of both Group A and Group B are enrolled in the same weight loss program, but some were assigned an exercise component and others were not. All members of both groups have expressed a commitment to lose at least 10 pounds in 2 months. The members of the groups were randomly assigned to their groups and are equivalent in terms of gender, weight, social economic status, and workstyle (sedentary or active). Weight is the dependent variable—it is what one expects to change dependent on participation in the specific exercise program. It is measured in pounds. At the end of the 2 months, the average pounds lost across the two groups can be compared. Comparing the two groups (Group A weight loss program; Group B weight loss program with exercise component) will suggest whether or not a weight loss program coupled with an exercise program causes increased weight loss when compared with the group not involved in the specific exercise program. Do you see how some characteristics are "controlled" through the sample selection? Even with all this control, it might be difficult to rule out other plausible explanations—for example, perhaps there were differences in how the exercise component was implemented by people in Group B. If the components are implemented differently, then the outcomes might vary because of the implementation making it difficult to attribute any changes across the two groups more broadly to participation in the exercise components.

There are a variety of statistical tests used to check how the means of the two groups might compare. By comparing means, researchers are able to infer that difference across the means can be explained. In other words, researchers could tell whether or not the independent variable caused the difference across the two means. These statistical tests seek to rule out competing explanations so that the inference of causation (and the same will hold for correlational inferences, discussed in the next subsection) can be trusted. **Statistical significance** means that the inferences of causation (or correlation) are best explained by the variables identified and do not seem to be heavily influenced by chance or other unidentified or uncontrolled factors. Confidence intervals (which you might recall from Chapter 13) are another way that researchers try to establish the extent to which they can have confidence in their inferential claims. See Appendix A for explanations and illustrations of statistical tests commonly used to establish causation—specifically, T-tests, ANOVA, and Chi-square. The point of these tests is to determine whether particular variables might cause particular outcomes in contrast with the extent to which the outcome might have just happened by chance or through some other causative mechanism.

Making Relational Inferences

Another way researchers make inferential leaps is to establish *relationships* that draw on the descriptive interpretations. Establishing relationships helps social scientists better understand the ramifications of those descriptive interpretations. Establishing or articulating relationships can be accomplished through both statistical and textual approaches. Relationships can be visually displayed through charts and graphs. Relationships can also be indicated through metaphors, and they can be acknowledged narratively.

Correlation is a type of inference that is strongly associated with quantitative studies, not qualitative studies. There is an old adage—"Correlation is not causation"—and yet, as we will see in this subsection, social scientists have developed sophisticated ways of looking at stable correlations so as to imply causal inferences without using a cause/effect design. Correlational inferences are the most popular statistical inference across the social sciences. As the name suggests, correlational statistical analyses report on the likelihood that two or more variables co-occur, or co-relate. Here's how the logic works. In the study on obesity and social networks that was presented at the beginning of the chapter, the researcher wanted to determine whether the variables "obesity" and "social network" are correlated. In this case, researchers would gather information on both variables within a group or sample. Once they are able to describe the distribution of those variables, they want to look at whether or not those two variables co-relate. Perhaps as community-wide obesity goes up, individual obesity also goes up. Researchers call this a positive relationship.

Recall Satinsky's (2013) work from Chapter 5. Satinsky was interested in the relationship between size and self-image. She might have expected to find that as weight went up, self-image went down. Researchers call this an **inverse relationship**—when one variable goes down in direct relation with the other variable going up. Such a relationship could be depicted in a graph like Figure 14.1, where weight in pounds for U.S. women

FIGURE 14.1 • Weight and Self-Esteem

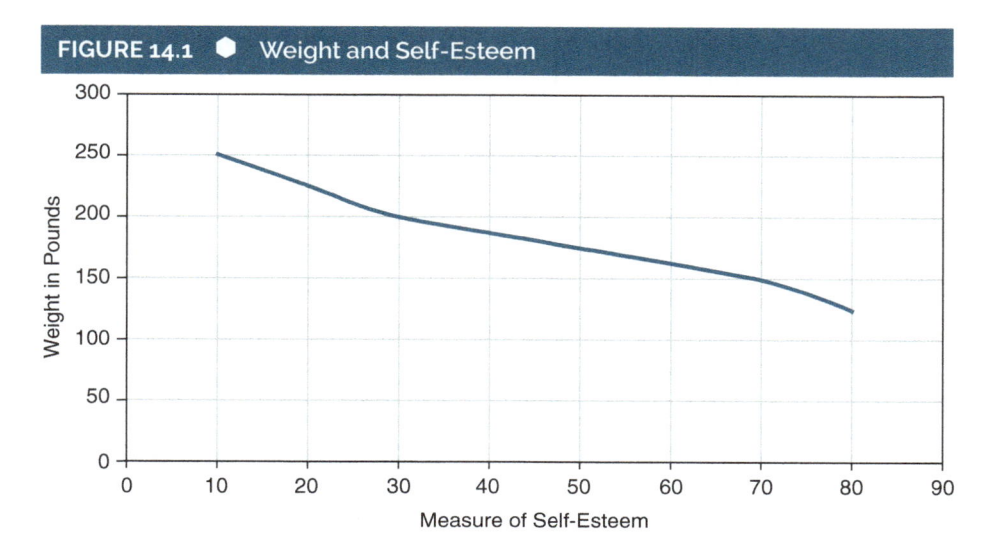

[Graph showing a downward-sloping line. Y-axis: Weight in Pounds (0–300). X-axis: Measure of Self-Esteem (0–90). The line starts near 250 pounds at self-esteem 10 and decreases to about 125 pounds at self-esteem 80.]

ages 21–50 is marked on the Y-axis and a measure of self-esteem where scores range from 0–100 with 100 being the highest is marked on the X-axis.

It's easy from this example to see that we cannot claim one variable causes the other, but if the relationship is strong enough and stable enough, we can conjecture a causal-like relationship. Nevertheless, we must be careful not to quickly translate a correlation into a causal inference. Correlations are usually reported as some fraction (using decimals) of 1 (or –1), like .80, for example. A perfect correlation is 1. The closer to 1, the stronger the correlation. Sometimes researchers are also able to report the direction of the relationship. A *positive direction* means that as one variable increases, the other also increases. A *negative direction* means that as one variable increases, the other variable decreases (an *inverse relationship* is described just above). The **Pearson Product Moment Correlation**, also known as r, is used to indicate the strength and direction of the relation between two distinct variables. For more information on common statistical tests used to establish correlation, see Appendix B.

Regression analysis is a sophisticated application of correlational statistics. These interesting statistical tests allow researchers opportunities to statistically control some variables in order to see how other variables might relate to one another. They allow us to compare the data with a **statistical model** of what the data *might* look like if the variables were controlled for ideal expected outcomes. For example, one might hypothesize that a woman's self-esteem would be lower if she weighed more. We could create a model of what that relationship might look like statistically and then we could compare our actual measurements with that model to see if the measurements fit the model.

The model is a hypothetical, a kind of ideal shape of the relationship given very particular ideas about those variables and how they act in relation to one another. For example, a **linear regression** suggests that if the relationship between two variables were plotted on a graph, it would resemble a straight line. We can imagine this straight line and what the data would look like mathematically, but rarely do data actually look like a straight line. The actual plotted relationship between the two variables can be compared to the imaginary straight line, also called the **line of regression**, which is assumed to match the actual data as plotted visually. If you look at the **scatterplot**, Figure 14.2, you can imagine the line that approximates the shape of the scatter of data points.

Regression analysis is used to predict future outcomes or explain the current situation. For example, we might be able to predict that if a person moves to a social location where there is a higher incidence of obesity, they are more likely to become obese themselves.

Reconstructing Logical Relationships

Qualitative researchers also articulate relationships in their analyses of verbal descriptions. In general, we would think of these as relationships that emerge within and across interpretive fields of meaning (which were discussed at length in Chapter 7). Researchers can, for example, read across their codes (discussed in Chapter 13) and note relationships in meaning and thereby create higher-level codes or what is sometimes referred to as themes or code families. This process includes organizing the codes into higher-order categories, but it also involves looking for other relationships across and within the codes. For example, in addition to categorical relationships (for example, soda is a kind of unhealthy drink), qualitative researchers might notice alternative relationships, such as drinking

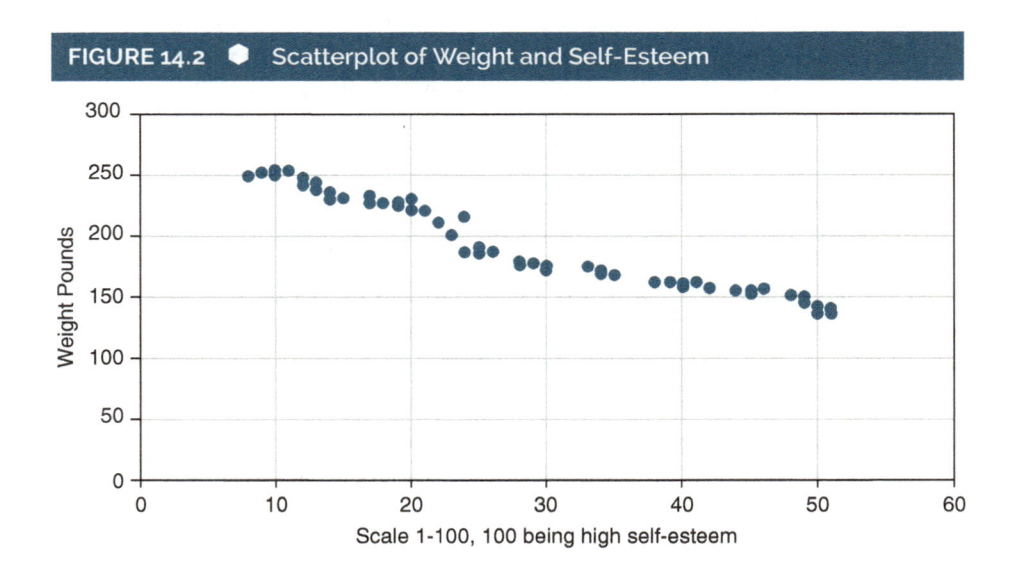

FIGURE 14.2 ● Scatterplot of Weight and Self-Esteem

soda is a way to celebrate and celebrating is psychologically healthy, but maybe not all ways of celebrating are healthy for the body. Articulating complex relationships is a matter of reconstructing the relationships of meaning that help participants understand one another and be understood. If there are several times in participants' stories when weight is talked about in relation to how one feels about one's self, then a qualitative researcher might reconstruct that relationship as "The weight of my self" or "The way I feel about myself," which could include codes such as "Fat is bad" or "Losing weight to feel better" or "My ideal weight" or "The me inside this body" and so forth. We can imagine such codes from women's narratives about their bodies and their self-perceptions. When we name these higher-level code themes, the name indicates the meaningful relationships across and within the codes that constitute those higher inferences.

Metaphors

Metaphors can be another way that researchers articulate relationships reconstructed from verbal data. Metaphors indicate relations by invoking implicit aspects of those inferred relationships. For example, during one of Barbara's studies on subjectivity, an interviewee kept referring to two types of beliefs—closed-fisted and open-fisted. Every time the interviewee would use this comparison, they would open their fist and close their fist. Sometimes this gesture was used in place of the words. This distinction was made explicit by one of the interviewees, but the contrast between beliefs one could not let go of (closed-fisted beliefs) and beliefs one could let go of and still be "the same person" (open-fisted beliefs) was important to every interviewee. *This metaphor helps us express and understand the relationship of the two types of beliefs to one another from participants' perspectives.* The metaphor also indicates the relationship of the person's sense of self to their beliefs. It helps us understand that beliefs were something that interviewees had agency over while also being internal to their senses of self. In Chapter 5 we read about Satinsky's (2013) "My Fat Girl Complex." Complex is a metaphor that indicates a relationship of *being* to *thinking* as complex and interdependent. The word *complex* is used in the United States to mean both a physical building that is complicated with levels, rooms, and so forth, as well as a mental state of being that seems to pre-reflectively structure one's thinking, though it is ultimately de-constructable—that is, we can see that it is uncertain and fallible.

Making Structural Inferences

Among qualitative researchers, some explicit attention has been paid to what "structures" humans' action—that is, what conditions provide structure to the meaning of our actions (as discussed in Chapter 6). *Structures do not determine outcomes, but indicate regularities and patterns of form.* We draw this idea primarily from the work of British sociologist Anthony Giddens (1979). For qualitative researchers, these conditions of action are cultural, political, economic, and material. Unlike biological or physical structures (like bridges), structures involved in meaningful social action must be inferred (Habermas, 1987). Though researchers using quantitative approaches do not tend to talk about their work using the same terminology, structures appear in the form of inferences about networks, models, or connections between variables. For example, in the United States there is a strong correlation between poverty and incarceration. One can identify structure through the variables that are examined in research on this correlation—variables such as education or reading level.

Modeling

Statisticians use math to create models that approximate the actual data in an idealized form—as if the data existed without any kind of error. Models are not deterministic—that is, they do not ordain what will happen. Instead, they are ways of thinking about the data that allow researchers to make predictions about future activity based on systematically understanding past activity. As such, *models are representations of the assumptions researchers are making about the system of variables under investigation and the conditions within which those variables take particular shape*. To be clear, all forms of inferential statistics *model* interrelationships (particularly causative relations and correlations), but **general linear modeling**, for example, is completed by using previously obtained inferential statistical information (such as T-tests) and *generalizing* to more than one dependent variable. In contrast, **multiple regression analysis** is conducted in order to map out the correlations of multiple independent variables with one dependent variable. This level of modeling (including general linear models) *generalizes* from inferential results of statistical tests like multiple T-tests. This approach to analysis provides opportunities to examine underlying regularities or patterns through which variables can be observed including conditions set by the researcher, such as particular geographic regions or socioeconomic statuses.

At the beginning of this chapter, we looked at some popular press reports of a study conducted by Datar and Nicosia (2018), who were interested in the links between the social community's generalized obesity and the obesity levels of individual members of the community. They wanted to establish conditions for the study that would rule out the possibility that people *chose* to live near those who were like them, so Datar and Nicosia decided to conduct the study with U.S. military families who did not get to *choose* where they lived. They studied the rates of obesity at the level of individual family member in relation to the obesity rate of the community, given the assignment of that family to that of their new community. To get their results, the researchers used linear and multiple regression modeling to correlate obesity measures with other variables—for example, over time. All families were military families who had been relocated, so this is the condition they had in common. The hypothesis was that if a family moved to a community with higher rates of obesity, this would increase that family's own obesity level. As such, the model would have a positive linear effect, and the researchers compared the line of the actual data with that model.

Social Network Analysis

Social scientists have long been interested in patterns of relationships that connect social actors (refer back to the Research Scenario in Chapter 13). Social network analysis is used to visually depict social structures using graphs or networks. This form of analysis identifies nodes and then maps out links between nodes. *Nodes* can represent individual actors, people, or things (phenomena of interest) within the network. Lines are used to depict connections. For example, one could study the spread of hashtag movements, like the #MeToo movement that surfaced in 2017 following the work of activist Tarana Burke (Burke, 2018). The nodes in this case would be the hashtag usage across time and place, and the lines would depict the spread of the hashtag. This form of analysis objectifies a meaningful phenomenon to observe its dispersion or connections. The visualization of the networks allows for broader inferences to be made about the networks. Network analysis articulates complex sets of relationships, from interpersonal to global. Network analysts organize their thinking through three categories: connections, distributions, and segmentations. For example, we would be able to see the spread of #MeToo, initiated by Alyssa Milano. We could see how many times it was used across the first 7 days and from where on the globe it was used. Then over time we could also see how it broke into other hashtags or was connected with other hashtag movements, like #TimesUp. These three categories (connections, distributions, and segmentations) describe different aspects of the structure of networks. It also becomes possible to note countermovements and strong affinities to infer types of purposes for using the hashtag. These inferences suggest how the use of the hashtag is structured over time and across space/users. Network analysis can be performed on numerical or narrative data.

> **Pause and Reflect.** Imagine that you can examine the historical and geographical spread of the use of the idea of "obesity." What would it mean to approach the spread of an idea numerically? Would it mean to track how many times it appeared in medical journals or as a headline in magazines? Would it mean establishing the time points at which obesity became medically diagnosable, coupled with the number of people diagnosed as obese? Would it involve looking at how much money was awarded in grant money? How about textually? Could one look across languages to study the word's history? Would it involve looking at the ways about which obesity is written cross-culturally? What common assumptions would the two network analyses (quantitative and narrative) share? What would be different about them?

Frame Analysis

Attributed to Erving Goffman (1974), frame analysis is a way to analyze *how* people writ large make sense of situations or activities such as social phenomena. Researchers will begin with the coded themes they articulated from qualitative data and use frame analysis to see how those themes are socially framed—the frame constitutes the structure of noticing the themes, as such. **Frames** are social phenomena that, sometimes unintentionally, coordinate activities across social actors in a large-scale way through organizing principles. For example, one could use a frame analysis to note large-scale differences/similarities in the way women's bodies were written about or visually depicted around the world or over time. One could examine what "frames" the concept of obesity across different cultures. For example, in Renaissance art, women were depicted as somewhat larger than the contemporary Western ideal. Perhaps what was framing the depiction of larger women during the Renaissance was wealth and health. Larger women were thought to have had enough wealth to be able to eat well, and thus were considered healthy and therefore desirable. In the contemporary Western world, thin is considered attractive, even though it is not considered particularly healthy. Large is considered both unattractive socially and unhealthy (even with contradictory studies). This is so much the case that the vast majority of the body positivity conversation has to do with helping larger women feel okay about their bodies in light of both social attractiveness propaganda and health/medical regimes. The medical aspect might be an important contemporary framing for obesity. With a privileging of medical expertise and information, talking about obesity from this perspective is a frame that casts size as a health issue. Such a frame contrasts sharply with size as an indicator of wealth. Researchers can use frames also to find the limits, contradictions, tensions, and so on entailed in the frame so as to not just take the frame for granted. For example, a researcher could gather diaries and observations of women who feel positive about their large bodies to note where this positivity breaks down and where the frames are fragile. Meanwhile, the researcher could also examine popular magazines of the time and culture to see the variety, prevalence, and strength of the frames from which inferences about body positivity might be made.

Bringing Inferences Into Dialogue With One Another

Once inquirers have reached a point where they can articulate things they learned or found through their analyses, it becomes possible to put that knowledge into conversation with others and with others' ideas. The point of doing this is to open up the opportunity for expanding the analyses further. This kind of expansion can take the form of *aha!* moments or what we might think of as having an insight, or it can take the form of developing theory. In both of these cases, a dialogue is forged that expands the analysis conceptually or substantively based on a broader set of interpretations.

This level of extension also brings researchers into identifying how their studies expand, challenge, and revise existing literatures.

Insights and Consciousness-Raising

One way that researchers think about the possibilities of trends from their coding has to do with how the codes, themes, or new knowledge inspire insights or consciousness-raising for both participants and for a field of readers. Barbara (using the last name Korth, 2002) published a paper in which she described consciousness-raising dialogues between herself and her participants based on what she was learning in the field. Others have also written about the way research can offer insights and help individuals/communities think anew about their experiences and situational contexts. With respect to obesity studies, consciousness-raising is closely related to de-stigmatization—consciousness-raising of the public encourages people not to label those who are large as "unhealthy" and to determine what actually increases the health, support, and accessibility of those who might be "diagnosed" as obese. When reading research, you will find the words *insight* and *consciousness-raising* used more often by those reporting on studies that use qualitative approaches, but studies reporting on quantitative findings could be thought about in this way as well. By bringing our analyses to the proverbial table for dialogue with either participants, scholars, or potential interpreters of the findings, the conversation itself can push researchers to see the analyses in novel ways or to reflect on the limits of the analyses to date. For example, in a study of an early-childhood classroom, Barbara noticed a difference in how teachers and students thought about the successes or challenges of students in the classroom based on gender. When Barbara shared these patterns with the teachers, they were surprised. In their minds, they thought of the differences as being related to the personalities of the children, not their genders. The new insight that emerged through the conversation between Barbara, the teachers, and the young children had to do with the point that choice in the classroom was already riddled with gendered assumptions because those assumptions are present in the culture. Together, Barbara, teachers, and students were able to identify how those cultural expectations were influencing participation in the class. They were able to change the practices of choice in the classroom to facilitate improved gender access to various activities (such as gaining noncompetitive access to the popular computer center for girls). What the analysis indicated was that girls had learned through the culture not to compete even as a way of getting what they wanted. Articulating this insight required bringing the analysis into dialogue and pushing toward greater understanding of that analysis. This same thing can happen when researchers use dialogue as a way of better understanding what they are finding statistically.

Consciousness-raising dialogues are not things that happen only among researchers or academicians. A good novel can raise one's awareness and shift one's thinking in fundamental ways. Consciousness-raising is an opportunity available to all of us when we are open to new ideas or ways of doing things and we are willing to acknowledge the fallibility of the ongoing ways of thinking/doing.

Theory Building

Another way of analyzing for broader trends and ideas is to put one's analyses into conversation with existing theories (recall our discussion in Chapter 11). Some researchers aim, from the beginning, to test theories. Statistical modeling can be used in this way. Researchers will explicitly draw on the constructs of theory, maybe even use these constructs as variables or to code the data and will thereby let the ongoing analyses "speak" to the theory. Moreover, new theory might emerge through the analyses and gain its articulation specifically through those analyses. In what is now considered a classic critical ethnography, Paul Willis (1977) studied a group of school-age boys. He drew on Marxist theory to analyze the data and in the process, he articulated a more agentic version of Marxism that accounted for the nuances of people actively reproducing cultural disadvantage for themselves. Willis developed critical theory and ideas of cultural reproduction through this study. Those ideas have been widely used since. In Chapter 9 you were introduced to Grounded Theory. The primary goal of Grounded Theory is reconstructing culturally salient, but largely implicit, theories underneath the everyday practices of a community of people. The implicit theories that are reconstructed through Grounded Theory can be placed into dialogue with existing theories in the literature about the ongoing practices. Since empirical studies will always also implicate theoretical assumptions, the conversation across practices and findings can benefit from theory building and articulation.

For Whom: Predictability, Generalizability, Transferability, and Commitments

Researchers also expand interpretations by thinking about their applicability. Over the years, the questions of applicability have been taken up in discussions of both analyses and validity. This basic question at hand is, "For whom are these analyses relevant?" The "for whom" question is methodological in the sense of thinking about the links between participants of a study and those others for whom the study's findings might directly apply. This question also requires practitioners to decide for themselves how a study might matter for them. The question also asks researchers to think about their own commitments to outcomes of their research projects. In this section, we present the four common forms of extending research analyses through the question of "For whom?" None of these forms of extension are absolute; rather, they are potentials.

Predictability

Predictability is an inference regarding the extent to which statistical results are able to predict outcomes related to particular variables with respect to the future. In statistical conversations, **predictive validity** refers to the extent to which current outcomes accurately predict future outcomes. Qualitative studies have the potential to articulate stable structures, which are likely to hold in future encounters, but these structures are not themselves predictive because they are not deterministic. Thus, we rarely see the concept of predictability used in qualitative investigations. In quantitative studies, predictability is desirable. Researchers hope to control their studies in such a way that it becomes possible for others to use their findings to predict outcomes in the future. Some studies, such as experimental designs and statistical modeling, are methodologically better suited to predictability than others.

Generalizability

Generalizability is an inference that links the sample to the population from which it was drawn (Chapter 11). This inference suggests the extent to which researchers can expect their findings to bear out with others in the population who were not included in the sample. This is one of the ways in which quantitative researchers have expressed the "So what" of their findings. In the field of statistics, generalizability is established through highly technical means. Conceptually speaking, if we can expect the findings from the sample (from Chapter 11) will repeat for the rest of the population, the researchers can say that their analyses are generalizable to others. In earlier decades, researchers who used quantitative data referred to generalizability as *external validity* because it indicated the extent to which the analyses might be valid for the population from which the sample of participants had been obtained. It is uncommon for people using narrative studies to generalize their analyses to other people. There are a couple of good reasons for this. First, *generalizing means extending the inferences from your sample to a population*, but most researchers doing qualitative studies do not draw samples from populations or use sampling strategies that would give us much confidence in such extensions. Nor are qualitative researchers typically interested in such generalizations. Second, there is a widespread belief that generalizing requires large samples, and most qualitative studies are conducted with smaller numbers of participants. Researchers distinguish this form of generalizability from theory building, consciousness-raising, and structural understanding—which generalize not to populations but to conceptualizations.

Transferability

Transferability is a way of thinking about how to use or apply research. Whereas generalizability is aimed at directly applying the outcomes from the sample to the population, transferability invites (at least implicitly) the reader to make connections to their own life experiences, conditions, and situations. Thick descriptions, clear articulation of examples, and rich understandings of participants and their experiences facilitate readers' abilities to transfer the interpretations into their own lives.

> **Pause and Reflect.** Think of a study about which you recently read or heard. How did your own experience inform the way you took in the information? How did you think about the relevance of the study's findings for your own life? How did the researcher either facilitate or limit your ability to determine that relevance?

Commitments to and for Whom

Researchers using qualitative approaches have been asked to locate their commitments in their projects. That is, they are expected to reflect on the question of who their research will impact. To whom and for whom are they committed? Having accepted that research itself is not a neutral act, inquirers must position their commitments within their knowledge production endeavors. Even when no controversies arise, and our commitments do not get problematized, acknowledging those commitments helps us all (practitioners and researchers) understand what is intended by conducting the study—what are the researcher's hopes for making the world a better place? In what ways might those hopes reproduce inequity despite our best intentions? These are the kinds of questions one can answer when taking seriously the call to reflect on one's commitments. We suggest that all research should have to answer these questions, but it is not typical among researchers who either use quantitative approaches or who believe that knowledge *is* neutral and that researchers' commitments are irrelevant to the application of research findings. This particular kind of extension of research interpretations is sociocultural and political (more to come on this in Chapter 16). It (re)locates the analyses in a sociopolitical context at the same time the researcher's commitments are also sociopolitically located. Feminist quantitative researchers Roberta Spalter-Roth and Heidi Hartmann (1991) provide an early example of explicating their commitments to women of color on which much of their later work has been built. They continue to build a network of researchers who use quantitative methods *and* also acknowledge their commitments. The Union of Concerned Scientists was formed in 1969 in the wake of nuclear weapons development. The nonprofit organization clearly articulates its sociopolitical commitments while simultaneously engaging in experimental studies that long assumed researcher neutrality on political issues. These examples are mentioned to illustrate that the question of "For whom?" is being taken up across a variety of researcher interests and methodologies.

> **Pause and Reflect.** Across the conceptual interludes, readers have had an opportunity to think about how analyses might be extended. If you were asked to describe the impact of a study, how might you use the various concepts above in your description? How is the idea of impact different across the various concepts—for example, insight versus generalizability? (Impact is discussed further in Chapter 16.)

RESEARCH SCENARIO: YOUTH ENCOUNTER PROGRAMS IN ISRAEL: KAREN ROSS

In the following research scenario, Karen Ross writes about how she analyzed her life history data to make inferences about trends and possibilities for change. In this excerpt, Karen discusses the potential application of the study in terms of impact.

As a doctoral student, I was interested in exploring how we might understand the "impact" of participation in encounter programs between Jewish and Palestinian[1] youth in Israel in a way that went beyond the short-term, cognitively, and affectively oriented change that was the focus of much of the scholarship on this topic. Many of these kinds of programs that bring together Jewish and Palestinian youth (or, for that matter, programs for youth in a wide range of contexts characterized by social identity conflicts) tout lofty aspirations to contribute to "peace writ large," or peace in society as a whole—but measure their contributions to that peacebuilding process in terms of short-term attitudinal or cognitive change among individual participants.

In my research, I wanted to try to understand how these kinds of programs can set the stage for change using a much broader conception of what that change might look like. To that end, I designed a study that tried to capture both depth and breadth of change.

My study took the form of a comparative case study with a focus on two aspects: the experiences of former participants in two Israeli encounter programs for Jewish and Palestinian youth, and the pedagogical choices as well as organizational structures that I believed could help explain some aspects of participants' experiences. Over 10 months, I collected data through observation of program activities, interviews with staff and board members of both organizations, and individual interviews with over 70 former program participants.

In order to capture the experiences of these program alumni both during and after participation in the encounter programs, I used a life history approach when conducting interviews, an unstructured interview approach in which I asked my research

---

[1] The term *Palestinian* is used here as a reference to citizens of Israel who describe their ethno-national heritage, and their national identity, as Palestinian. I use this term (rather than Israeli Arab or Arab Israeli) because this is how the majority of participants in my research refer to themselves.

participants to tell me about their lives and mostly followed their lead, rather than approaching the interviews with predetermined questions. In their telling of life stories, former participants in the encounter programs discussed their program experiences in the context of other salient experiences and relationships that shaped their personal and professional trajectories, thus allowing me, in my analysis, to reconstruct how their program participation enabled individual transformation (or not) in ways that were linked to broader societal discourses and sociopolitical events.

In my analysis of interviews with former encounter program participants, one of the things I focused on was the discourse that individuals used when speaking about different parts of their lives. As part of my interest in understanding the depth of change that encounter participation might facilitate, I was particularly focused on the narratives that individuals used to talk about themselves and "Others" (that is, the narratives Jews used when speaking about Palestinians, and Palestinians used when speaking about Jews), and how these narratives corresponded to or diverged from *what are referred to as the "master narratives" in conflict contexts: the stories into which members of a conflict group are socialized. By examining the correspondence of personal narratives and master narratives, I was able to make explicit some of the ways in which personal narratives changed, and how these changes were* attributed to *encounter program participation.*

My use of life history interviews also allowed me to explore how the experiences of individuals with whom I spoke fit into broader social contexts and structures as part of my focus on the breadth of change experienced by program participants. For instance, one of the patterns that emerged in my interview analysis had to do with the relationship *between experiences within each of the two programs I studied and action, in the form of continued participation over time in social change initiatives. When I analyzed my interviews as a whole, a number of trends emerged: Former participants from one of the two programs were far more socially engaged than alumni of the other organization's programs, a pattern I attributed to differences in the structure and pedagogical approaches utilized by each organization. I also found that other elements of individuals' social contexts—such as their identity as either Jewish or Palestinian, as well as personal experiences such as being direct recipients of anti-Palestinian discrimination or being at the site of a terrorist attack against Israeli Jews—played an important role in shaping their continued social change engagement.*

Karen's analysis involved higher-level inferences that were built up by examining the patterns related to her initial coding and descriptive inferences. Words emphasized in the above narrative indicate how Karen was conceptualizing the higher-level inferences. She reconstructed the experiences of her participants in order to articulate kinds of impacts that were significant or meaningful for them. She had to use the way they

YOU AND RESEARCH

Extending our inferences to think about trends and applicability ask something of both interpreters or research and researchers. For example, you will recall that transferability is an opportunity for readers to think about how the research is relevant to their own situations and experiences, but generalizability is an opportunity for researchers to take into account the ways in which their findings might accurately be applied to a population of people given the sample that was studied. Here we just point to a few things to think about when either interpreting or doing research.

When Interpreting Research

As interpreters of research, you will want to be able both to assess the ways in which the researchers are indicating the shape of their larger-scale inferences and be able to take responsibility for establishing the relevance of those studies to your own life. If a researcher concludes that Weight Loss Program A is more effective than Weight Loss Program B and you want to engage in successful weight loss, then you have to establish how much to trust the outcomes of the study and determine for yourself the extent to which the study is relevant (transferable and indicative of your own commitments) for you. This means that you cannot just read the findings section of a research report or take to heart a popular media article that tells you about a research study, without understanding or digging into the methodological details of the study, including the analytic details. While this chapter has not prepared you to read statistical outputs or qualitative analyses, you can use resources (particularly on the internet) to bolster your ability to critically read research articles, because the application of interpretation and the inferences that are made must be contextually understood. Many practitioners feel intimidated by statistical charts. In fact, the intuitiveness of qualitative approaches makes being a critical practitioner a little easier. Nevertheless, we can learn to assess quantitative studies with some fluency. Practice enables one's skills, but also turning to resources close at hand can jog your memory about terms and help you read materials with some confidence. Because fields tend to have preferences for particular research designs, one can begin by familiarizing oneself with those designs common to their particular fields.

When Doing Research

Researchers themselves will need to think about how they want to be able to extend their interpretations and analyses so as to design their studies with those possibilities in mind. No design predetermines that such extensions will be valid, but such thinking can create the opportunities. For example, if a researcher really wants to be able to generalize to particular populations, then an ethnographic design would not be a good choice.

When you think about the limitations or opportunities of your study, you will want to be precise about any difference between the potential of your study for offering such

(Continued)

> (Continued)
>
> extensions (like generalizability) and the extent to which your study actually made good on that potential. You should specifically describe any negative difference as a limitation.
>
> It is important to realize that not all studies can or should be broadened in all possible ways. The researcher is responsible for thinking about what appropriate possibilities are available for their particular project and to take these possibilities seriously. We would like to encourage all researchers to reflect on and engage their commitments and to imagine what effects these commitments have on how the research extends into the sociopolitical communities at hand. Furthermore, it is important for researchers to engage in larger-scale inferencing if the researcher intends to contribute directly to social change and policy conversations.

told their stories coupled with how various aspects of their experiences were connected to other aspects from their own ways of talking about those experiences. This required her to think across the codes and to look for patterns of connections. For example, Karen paid attention to the patterns of relationships that emerged through her participants' talk—specifically, patterns of experience and patterns of continued action. The impacts she found could be useful for examining or implementing similar programs.

SYNTHESIS: POINTS FOR REFLECTION

Conceptual Synthesis

In this chapter we make precise connections to earlier concepts—for example, we link sampling with generalizability, descriptive statistics with the ability to articulate inferences of causation and correlation, coding with thematic inferences, and identity of the researcher to the important question of "For whom?" The concepts in this chapter give us a way of talking about the relevancy of research claims beyond their own boundaries, for example, so that they might be relevant to a whole population or for a new way of thinking. We organized our thinking about the concepts through their potential impact, including producing broader sets of empirical interpretations, generating conceptual and theoretical interpretations, and identifying the study's application and relevance for different circumstances and situations.

Methodological Synthesis

Throughout the text, we have foregrounded dialogue in the research process and conceptualization. We are now able to look across the process to think intentionally about the kinds of dialogues that become possible across different methodologies. We begin to think about the opportunities for dialogue that are implied between researchers, between researchers and those who apply research, between researchers and participants. Some methodological decisions open up the possibility for generalizability, for example, while others create an opportunity for encouraging practitioners to reflect on how transferable the interpretations are to their own sets of experiences. These possibilities do not haphazardly emerge, but are part and parcel of the methodological process.

Personal Synthesis

Contemporary life is a bombardment of information. Sometimes we are seeking out the information and sometimes we are just hit in the face with soundbites, headlines, and attention grabbers. There is a cadre of public actors, known as influencers, who try to *influence* the behavior of the public—for example, Selena Gomez, who uses Instagram to influence perspectives on political issues. Many of the concepts presented in this chapter are also concepts we roughly use in our ordinary talk about influence and impact—generalizing knowledge, transferring knowledge, gaining insights, and so on. The divide between academia and "real life" coupled with the dysregulation of information in the public sphere produce a confusing moment in the intersection of research with the public life. Disinformation campaigns, political decrying of fake news, and media misrepresentations have heightened a desire for personal and public skepticism over knowledge, but without necessarily building the critical skills to manifest that scrutiny. We can use the more precise understandings of generalizability, for example, to nuance our personal abilities to be critical practitioners of knowledge, research outcomes, and research applications.

MOVING FORWARD

In this chapter we learned about making larger-scaled inferences across our data by drawing on lower-level inferences from our data. As you no doubt realize at this point, there is a broad array of possible inferences that can be drawn, and not all of these inferences will make it into our findings. Not all of these inferences will warrant being reported to the public. In Chapter 15 we confront what researchers must do to take the inferences they have established from the data into a coherent and legible set of valid findings that will make their contribution to practice and scholarship. Researchers are actively involved in the momentum that takes their inferences into what we think of as insights and findings.

Further Readings

Further Readings by Karen Ross

Ross, K. (2013). Promoting change within the constraints of conflict: Case study of Sadaka Reut in Israel. *Current Issues in Comparative Education, 15*(2), 35–52. (Special issue on *Education for Social Change and Transformation: Case Studies of Critical Praxis*).

Ross, K. (2014). Narratives of belonging (and not): Intergroup contact in Israel and the formation of ethno-national identity claims. *International Journal of Intercultural Relations, 42*, 38–52.

Ross, K. (2015). Quality as critique: Promoting critical reflection among youth in structured encounter programs. *Journal of Peace Education, 12*(2), 117–137.

Ross, K. (2016). Peace-building through inter-group encounters: Rethinking the contributions of "mainstream" and "politicized" approaches. *Peacebuilding, 4*(3), 317–330.

Ross, K. (2017). *Youth encounter programs in Israel: Pedagogy, identity, and social change.* Syracuse, NY: Syracuse University Press.

15

WRITING UP RESEARCH

Chapter 15 explores the conceptual and practical issues related to academic writing in its broad sense, which encompasses not only the writing completed in order to report and disseminate the findings of a study but also the writing composed before and during the process of data analysis. We propose to de-couple the close association between writing and its product and to foreground the opportunities that writing affords for self-growth and mutual understanding. Borrowing the term from Tineke Abma and Guy Widdershoven (2011), we consider writing to be a "relationally responsible practice," which provides a conceptual entry point for us to think through issues at the practical and procedural levels, such as genres, authorial voices, and choice of language.

MUSING UPON THE EVERYDAY

Professional Writing Revisited

If you are new to the world of social research, chances are you have not yet had many opportunities to develop your academic writing skills, but you may have ample experiences in writing other types of texts, such as course plans, professional reports, and letters. Recall the last time when you completed a relatively long piece of writing. This could be an essay you wrote for one of the classes you took last semester, a counseling memo, a report that you were appointed to draft on a professional committee, or even a long personal email to your friends. Take a few minutes to reflect on this very experience.

You can use the following questions to guide your reflection. As you engage with them, feel free to jot down your thoughts.

What process did it take for you to complete the writing?

How smooth was the process?

TABLE 15.1 ● Strengths and Challenges: Pengfei's Reflection on Her Dissertation Writing

Strengths	Challenges
Expressive	Made many grammatical mistakes
Had an aesthetic taste	Limited English vocabulary (her second language)
Patient and perseverant	Slow and procrastinated
Not afraid of sharing ugly drafts	Thought too much and wrote too little
Had a strong support system emotionally and scholarly	

How did you feel when you were working on this piece?

How do you feel about your writing product now?

What strengths and challenges did this experience manifest about your writing?

Now you may wonder: What does your personal or professional writing have to do with academic writing? Are there any connections or shared commonalities between the two? To answer these questions, we can start by brainstorming what our writing means to ourselves and others. This relational approach helps us understand why writing is a crucial component in social inquiry. For now, it is helpful to put forward one point bluntly; that is: We are all imperfect in our writing.

For instance, Table 15.1 is what Pengfei, one of the textbook authors, came up with as she worked on the last question of this activity. In this case, she was explicitly thinking about her experience of writing her dissertation.

In what follows, you will see, the goal of our writing is not perfection, but self-growth and mutual understanding. This message will pave our way to discuss writing on a more practical level.

NARRATIVE AND CONCEPTUAL INTERLUDES

A Morning With Metaphors

In the morning of late May, spring particularly hesitated to leave Urbana-Champaign, a Midwest college town. Wind danced through the high branches of the trees. In a quiet neighborhood, one or two cars occasionally drove by; we (the authors of the book) sat in the living room of a short-term rental house, where we were together for a writing retreat. Most of the time in the morning, we invested in a conversation on how we felt about our writing. At some point, Pengfei proposed that each of the dialogue participants use a metaphor to describe their writing experience.

When Peiwei's turn came, she leaned forward on the sofa, and started with a lower voice:

> What came to me is the four seasons, there's a kind of emotional quality to it. The images are like, I'm sitting on a porch with somebody and outside spring is coming. A lot of times, I feel like ideas are just emerging from this conversation. My conversation partner and I have our thinking, but then through the conversation, there's something stirring up. This helps me to become more aware of ideas that might be more implicit prior. And yeah, I feel like writing is a process. And then the summer, the temperature is warmer. There are a lot more activities, almost like trying to get into the material, writing, like get it out. And the fall feels like maturation and precipitation, like getting to a place I feel more grounded. And the winter is those things that I mentioned, sitting alone there and feeling a little bit cold. And in this mode, I don't know whom I'm talking to. I feel like I need to impress somebody, even this abstract sort of being accepted or rejected (makes me nervous). And sometimes we cycle through those emotional states.

An experienced Zen practitioner, Peiwei came up with metaphors that are fused with her love for nature. Do these metaphors resonate with you?

Writing as a Process

When we take time to write, we tend to locate our focus at its starting and ending poles. For instance, in the context of reporting academic findings, the two poles that draw most of our attentions are analyzing and thematizing findings on the one hand, and presenting the product of our research on the other. There are, indeed, many discourses revolving around the *product* of writing: style, productivity, impact, and so on, but relatively less attention is paid to the *process* of writing. That is why we jumpstart our discussion with Peiwei's metaphor about the four seasons—as it vividly captures writing as a process. By talking about the products, we may unintentionally create or reinforce a myth about writing, that it is a special talent owned by a small group of geniuses. One either has the talent to write or not. In this chapter, we have found it most important to debunk such a myth, for the existence of the myth makes it particularly hard to talk about the challenges, struggles, self-blaming, procrastination, and other mental, physical, and psychological issues that almost everyone experiences in writing.

Peiwei's metaphor richly reveals to us the ups and downs within the process of writing, starting from incubating ideas, to putting them into words, to coming up with a relatively complete piece. Moreover, Peiwei noticed that a writing process involves multiple cycles of writing, rewriting, self-evaluating, and further developing. In this sense, we think through writing, and writing itself is thinking. Writing and thinking are so infused with each other that a preconceived distinction between the two seems impossible. In the conversation among the authors during their writing retreat, Karen and Barbara commented on this point by emphasizing the significance of revision. Barbara's thinking evolves considerably during the writing and rewriting process, so she takes the opportunity of working on multiple rounds of drafts as a way to push herself to better articulate her thoughts. Similarly, Karen noted that focusing on the development of ideas, rather than worrying about the quality of her existing draft, makes her revision process relatively easier. If this is the case, a follow-up question is: How can we better integrate writing and thinking in the context of academic composition?

Acknowledging that writing is thinking, you do not expect yourself to create a well-thought-out piece in the first draft. In some cases, an author does not even have an argument at the beginning of the writing process. You can start with fragmented writing and see how these fragmented thoughts piece together a larger picture. As you put the words down, you may find that the writing process has helped you sort out different strands of thoughts entangled in your mind.

If we go back to the idea introduced in Chapter 12, that making inferences means to explicate implicit meanings, we can see that writing gives ambiguous and sophisticated thoughts a linguistic form. Many authors have the concerns that words cannot exhaust the nuances in their thinking. Once thoughts are turned into words, they worry, the insights in one's mind will escape from the fixated form of language. This concern is particularly evident in the context of reporting research findings. Researchers contend that as one analyzes and reports findings in a certain fixed way, they unavoidably flatten and reduce the richness and multifacetedness of the data. The concern is surely very valid. To fully address it, we will need to delve into a discussion of the nature of meaning and language, and how language is used in social research. While we have discussed some of these issues in the previous chapters, in this section, it suffices to mention that the approach to take writing as thinking facilitates our exploration of multiple potential ways to reconstruct the meaning of the data. In this sense, we can situate our writing in continuous efforts to seek understandings of a certain topic and to engage in conversations with our readers on this topic. In the context of reporting research findings, this means to make sense of multiple layers of the meaning of the data and/or to approach them from differential perspectives. In the context of writing research proposals, this means acknowledging the growth potential of the writing and adopting a developmental attitude toward what is put down in the proposal.

Closely related to the issue of fixating meanings, we notice that people often associate a sense of stability with writing. It may seem that once turned into words, the ideas are up for the others' judgment and evaluation. The sense of externalizing and materializing one's ideas could feel risky and particularly insecure. Taking writing as a thinking process will help us de-stabilize writing, as when words are put down, opportunities open up for revision. Closing and opening thus form a dialectical relationship, and the generation of ideas becomes more fluid. What we put on the paper may capture our thoughts at that specific moment, but does not necessarily represent us as a person who constantly seeks new growth.

> **TIPS FOR TO-BE GOOD WRITERS**
>
> Usually, people tend to think writing is a creative activity, but to practice it on a day-to-day basis requires some habituality. Here are some tips for you if you are interested in honing your writing skills:
>
> 1. Form your own writing habit. Many writing coaches and experienced writers recommend blocking a specific time to write every day. To do this, you may want to establish a writing ritual. A writing ritual is a relatively fixed set of activities that help you transition to a writing mode and build writing into your daily routine. It could be as simple as going to your favorite coffee house and opening your laptop, or as sophisticated as meditating for 20 minutes to search for your inner peace. Even if you are at the stage of brewing your ideas, you can start with writing those ideas down. As we have discussed above, the fragmented thoughts gradually will help you piece together your entire argument.
>
> 2. Learn your emotions associated with writing. Writing generates all kinds of emotions, but very often we tend to focus on the goal and the content of the writing instead of our feelings. Whether these feelings are negative emotions such as guilt (Oh, I missed a deadline again!), shame (What an ugly piece I just wrote!), and frustration (I could not come up with even one complete sentence . . .), or positive emotions such as pride (I cannot believe I've completed this assignment on time!), excitement (This is a great point to include in my literature review!), and relief (I am so happy I've addressed all my advisors' comments!), ignoring these emotions, especially the negative ones, often leads to a cumulative consequence of procrastination, unsustainable writing practice, and even mental health problems. Intentionally working on not only your writing skills but also the emotions associated with writing will bring you the much-needed writing–life balance.
>
> 3. Build a support system. Writing is a solitary journey. Sometimes you may feel like you are trapped into a fight with a windmill alone. To battle against the loneliness (or to better enjoy it) you will need
>
> *(Continued)*

> (Continued)
>
> a strong support system. Think about your support system at multiple levels. For instance, your academic advisors and mentors are familiar with the substantive content of your work, as well as the most appropriate way to speak to your audience. An interdisciplinary writing group lends you helpful eyes from the perspective of general educated readers. A professional proofreader helps you hone your skills at sentence and word levels. Your family and friends back you up in your life as you venture into the writing world.
>
> 4. Make feasible and concrete plans and dutifully follow them. Most of us plan our writing ahead of time, but very often we find it hard to follow through the plan, and eventually we end up writing less than we planned. Then, we start to doubt ourselves or feel anxious about the mounting work we still need to do. To address this issue, we can start with understanding our productivity better. For instance, some writing coaches recommend Francesco Cirillo's Pomodoro Time Management Technique (Cirillo, 2018), which divides work time into 25-minute intervals using a timer. Users can set up goals and track how many segments they use to complete a task. Several apps and software packages also facilitate the use of this technique. You may or may not use the Pomodoro Technique, depending on how comfortable you are with tracking your own writing.

Writing As a "Relationally Responsible Practice"

In this section, we borrow Abma and Widdershoven's expression to consider writing as a "relationally responsible practice" (2011). In previous chapters our discussion of relationality has mostly focused on the relationship between researcher and research participants in the process of understanding research commitment, constructing data, and making inferences. While the researcher–participant relationship is still within our horizon, we want to highlight another type of relationship in considering the process of writing: the **author–reader relationship**. Unlike the researcher–participant relationship, in which researchers may have the opportunity to communicate with their participants dual-directionally, the author–reader relationship usually is one-directional and mediated through the writing. Academic writing is distinguished from other types of writing as it assumes a specific kind of reader and thus a unique author–reader relationship.

Most academics write with the explicit or implicit presumptions that the readers have already grasped certain terms and knowledge prior to reading their work. By presenting their research to readers, academic authors invite conversations, constructive critiques, and future explorations. Therefore, in this author–reader relationship, readers are expected to

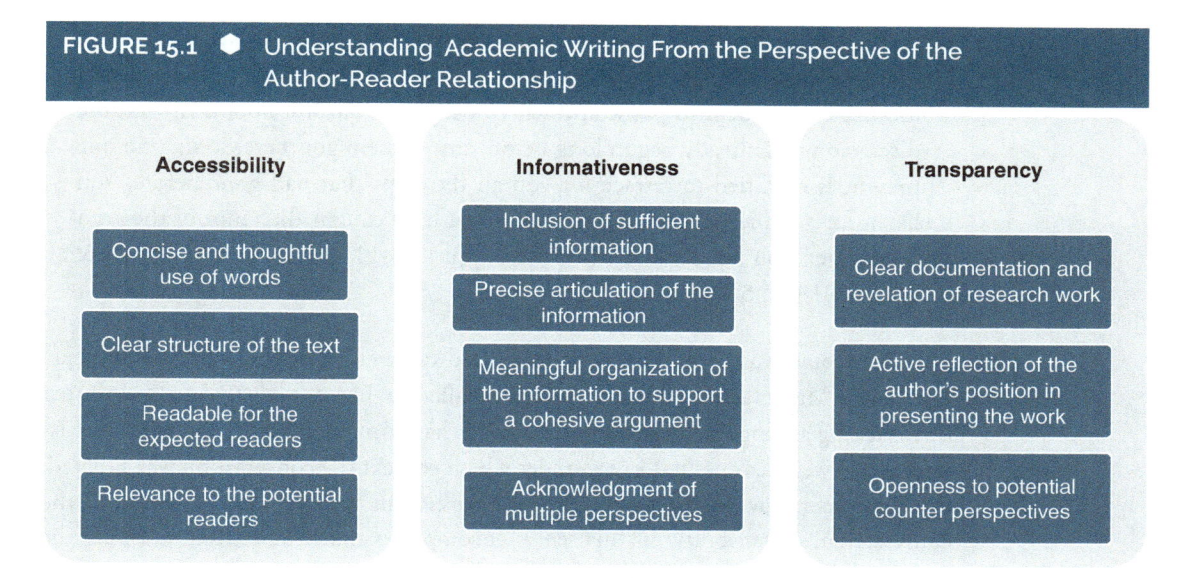

FIGURE 15.1 Understanding Academic Writing From the Perspective of the Author-Reader Relationship

Accessibility
- Concise and thoughtful use of words
- Clear structure of the text
- Readable for the expected readers
- Relevance to the potential readers

Informativeness
- Inclusion of sufficient information
- Precise articulation of the information
- Meaningful organization of the information to support a cohesive argument
- Acknowledgment of multiple perspectives

Transparency
- Clear documentation and revelation of research work
- Active reflection of the author's position in presenting the work
- Openness to potential counter perspectives

make judgments about the validity of the written claims and ask the "So what?" question (see also Chapter 14). Among different types of academic writings, there are nuanced variations in readership. For instance, a proposal for a master's thesis or doctoral dissertation is prepared to convince the author's committee—usually constituted of three to five experts in the field—of the significance and feasibility of the proposed study; a research report is written to present findings from an empirical study to the relevant stakeholders, such as policy-makers, practitioners, and researchers of a specific field. These are more conventional types of author–reader relationships, which sometimes overlap with other relationships such as those of advisor–advisee or evaluator–stakeholder, depending on different contexts. As shown in Figure 15.1, starting from the characteristic of relationality, we derive a list of principles to guide our understanding of academic writing.

Accessibility

We cannot talk about accessibility without referring to the relational nature of writing, for to produce an accessible text, we have to ask the question of "Accessible to whom?" The same piece may turn out to be a clear read for an experienced researcher, while it might be completely incomprehensible for people who are new to the field. Another snapshot from the authors' writing retreat may help illustrate this point. While continuing the conversation about metaphor and writing experience, Pengfei picked up a description of a cocktail party and asked her co-authors whether they could relate the description of the party scene to their writing. The scenario was first developed by Kenneth Burke (1941) and is referred to as "The Unending Conversation." It was included in an article written by Tim Huffman and Sarah Tracy (2018) and is presented below:

> Imagine that you enter a parlor. You come late. When you arrive, others have long preceded you, and they are engaged in a heated discussion, a discussion too heated for them to pause and tell you exactly what it is about. In fact, the discussion had already begun long before any of them got there, so that no one present is qualified to retrace for you all the steps that had gone before. You listen for a while, until you decide that you have caught the tenor of the argument; then you put in your oar. (Burke, pp. 110–111, cited from Huffman & Tracy, 2018, p. 559)

For a newcomer to the party, it would be hard to catch "the tenor of the argument" right away. Many factors contribute to this challenge: The participants are so invested in discussing an ongoing topic that they do not have time to recap the previous discussion; the newcomer does not know under which context the conversation was situated; the newcomer may not necessarily know how certain specific terms are used in the conversation. Accessibility, in this sense, encompasses much more than grasping the literal meaning of words, but also familiarizing oneself with the context, the previous discussion, and the implications of the current dialogue. As Figure 15.1 has shown, concise and thoughtful use of words, clear structure, readability, and relevance to the potential readers can be considered as a list of subcriteria under the overarching category of accessibility.

Informativeness

It may sound like a cliché, but it is worth repeating that academic writing should be informative. When explaining the term *informative,* we naturally think of including the necessary information for readers to understand the key aspects of the study. The term *informative,* thus understood, could be misleading because it perpetuates a view that researchers need to be held accountable for the "facts" they put down in the writing. While this is part of the picture in considering the author–reader relationship and its corresponding requirements for writing, in many cases being informative also means to decide what are the claims that researchers may want to foreground within a limited space. For instance, you probably have noticed that the philosophic underpinnings of a study are not included in most quantitative studies, whereas qualitative researchers put more emphasis on the congruence of philosophic approach, methodology, and methods. In this sense, we think that it is more helpful to conceptualize informativeness from the perspective of establishing a cohesive and well-supported argument and to ensure the inclusion of multiple perspectives. On the one hand, every study presumes a certain understanding of truth and validity; on the other hand, this presumption, regardless of being implicitly indicated or explicitly addressed, engenders different ways to understand what should be foregrounded in the writing and how a researcher shall present the work.

Transparency

Being transparent to readers is very often associated with research integrity. The term very often conjures up an idea of revealing what is behind the scene or what could otherwise be covered or hidden. This means that researchers should not only be explicit about the processes, findings, and potential limitations of the study but also actively reflect upon them, as noted by Rivka Tuval-Mashiach (2017). Several secondary concepts are introduced to assist researchers to produce transparent research. For instance, in qualitative studies, the term *audit trail* means that researchers keep track of the process of data collection and analysis, and report it when it is necessary. Going beyond dutifully keeping a record of the research process, being transparent also means reflecting upon your positionality in conducting the study so that your readers know that you present a view from a specific perspective.

> **Pause and Reflect.** In this section, we complicate writing-up research and presenting findings from the perspective of relationality. In a real research scenario, this may create tensions and ethical dilemmas as we position ourselves among different relations and endeavor to meet varying discipline-specific expectations. For instance, when the researcher's interpretation of the data differs from the research participant's interpretation, how shall the researcher present the findings?

Expanding the Author–Reader Relational Responsibility

The Relationship Is Multifold

There are things about which researchers are not transparent, most typically any identifiable information about research participants. This example demonstrates that we cannot fully address the author–reader relationship without also considering other overlapping relationships in a research process, most typically the researcher–participant relationship. As researchers and authors, we carry multifold relational responsibilities. Our reconstruction of research participants' experience will be more powerful and fundamentally more valid if it is recognized by the research participants themselves. This applies not only to qualitative studies aiming at understanding lived experience, but also to quantitative studies involving measuring human behaviors and attitudes. In this sense, we can anchor academic writing at the center of the author–reader framework and further expand it to include other types of relationships, such as those among researchers and participants, researchers and stakeholders, co-authors, as well as authors'/researchers' relationship to themselves. Due to the space limitations of the chapter, we cannot cover all aspects of the relational nature of writing. In what follows, we have chosen two aspects to further unpack: the researcher–participant relationship and the authors' relationship to themselves.

Typically, when an empirical study enters into the stage of reporting findings, researchers actively write about the patterns, trends, and lived experience of research participants;

unless being offered the opportunities, research participants have much less space to intervene in researchers' writing. This is particularly true if the participants belong to a marginalized social group and do not have a much-needed channel to voice for themselves. For instance, some researchers argue that, by studying marginalized social groups, researchers should give voice to the silenced, the unseen, and the marginalized. However, the good intentions of the researchers to speak *for* the participants could be problematic if researchers volunteer to represent the participants without checking in with them on the researchers' interpretation of their experience. The best way to handle this issue is always to democratize the writing process to include the participants themselves. By doing that, researchers are writing *with* the participants instead of merely *for* the participants. For instance, researchers from the participatory tradition have made meaningful efforts to democratize the writing process. In particular, they invite participants to co-write and to co-decide on how they would like the study to be presented.

In view of the overlapping of the author–reader and researcher–participant relationships, we can further expand Figure 15.1 to incorporate the latter into the figure.

As you could see from Figure 15.2, the incorporation of the researcher–participant relationship further complicates the figure we use to understand the quality of academic writing (Figure 15.1). While authors endeavor to make their texts more accessible for their readers, it is equally important for them to practice inclusivity in presenting the findings about their research participants. The writing products should provide sufficient information for the readers, but certain information regarding the participants' privacy should be kept confidential through the entire process (anonymization). Going beyond documentation and reflection, democratizing the writing process expands the space for

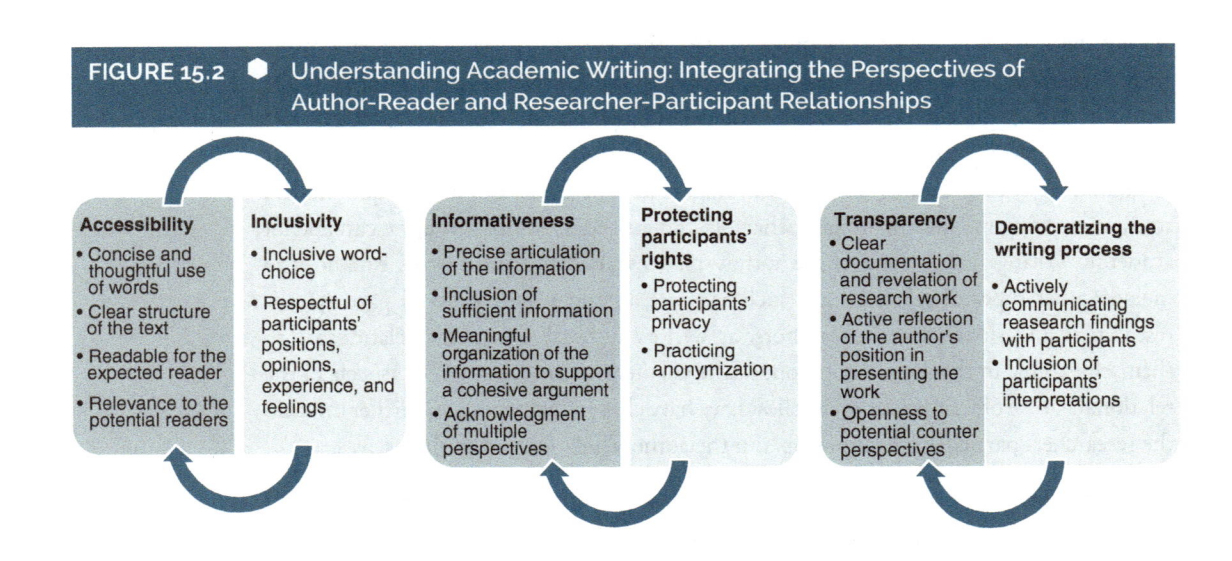

FIGURE 15.2 ● **Understanding Academic Writing: Integrating the Perspectives of Author-Reader and Researcher-Participant Relationships**

Accessibility
- Concise and thoughtful use of words
- Clear structure of the text
- Readable for the expected reader
- Relevance to the potential readers

Inclusivity
- Inclusive word-choice
- Respectful of participants' positions, opinions, experience, and feelings

Informativeness
- Precise articulation of the information
- Inclusion of sufficient information
- Meaningful organization of the information to support a cohesive argument
- Acknowledgment of multiple perspectives

Protecting participants' rights
- Protecting participants' privacy
- Practicing anonymization

Transparency
- Clear documentation and revelation of research work
- Active reflection of the author's position in presenting the work
- Openness to potential counter perspectives

Democratizing the writing process
- Actively communicating reasearch findings with participants
- Inclusion of participants' interpretations

transparency. Figure 15.2 thus demonstrates how integrating the two relational lenses allows us to understand writing more dynamically.

Figure 15.2 also cultivates our sensitivity toward the potential power relationship in the writing process. Without considering the researcher–participant relationship, an author could turn writing into a groundless monologue. The power dynamics could manifest themselves at different aspects of writing from inclusivity, to protecting participants' rights and democratizing the writing process. In this sense, even the choice of words has political ramifications. For instance, at the beginning of the textbook, we explained our use of pronouns: Instead of perpetuating a long-held heteronormativity, we decided to use the plural form of the pronouns to include people whose gender identity cannot easily fit into the binary structures.

> **Pause and Reflect.** A stakeholder for a research project is a person or an organization that can affect or be affected by the project, and that has an interest in the research. A stakeholder can be directly or indirectly involved in the research project, benefit or be negatively impacted by the study. Some researchers argue that when conducting applied social research, it is important to understand the stakeholders of the study, that is, who will benefit or be negatively influenced by the study, and who have an interest in the study. In writing, researchers need to explicitly or implicitly address their relationship with stakeholders. Considering the researcher–stakeholder relationship, how can we expand our understanding of accessibility, informativeness, and transparency in Figure 15.1?

Authors' Responsibility to Themselves

Through writing, we relate to our readers, but writing also encompasses a performative aspect, or to some degree, writers' relation to themselves. Going back to the conversation taking place during the authors' writing retreat: We (the authors) also discussed how anxiety sneaks into a writer's mind by creating a voice of an internal critic. When talking about the challenge she encountered in writing, Peiwei said:

> The first thing stood out to me is that writing feels very differently depending on whom I'm writing to. Sometimes when I'm expressing ideas through email to somebody, or contributing to a Google Doc . . . ideas just can flow much better. . . . Versus most of the time when I'm writing something when the audience could be a bit abstract. Then my writing constantly feels like a traffic jam, and sometimes I keep writing and rewriting one paragraph. I cannot really fully express what I want to say. And I think part of that is the audience that I am writing to. When I don't have a good sense of the discourse where my writing is supposed to belong, that's harder to trust. I think that doubt will come into a lot more throughout. Am I okay, good enough? How are people going to perceive this?

Most of us probably resonate with Peiwei's struggle. When we write, consciously or not, we create this internal critic in our mind, it being an internalization of a real authoritative voice in our life, or a voice representing an imagined critic. Engaging in an internal conversation with this voice may invoke various visceral feelings of self-doubt, anxiety, or even shame. There are different ways to work with this voice of self-critic. One of the best suggestions that we have heard is *forget yourself!* Taking a Zen Buddhist approach, this advice encourages writers to detach from their inner critics by forgetting the source of the anxiety —the self—and submerging oneself into the practice of writing.[1] As opposed to this forgetting-self approach, some writing coaches advocate for the disarming-the-inner-critic approach.[2] Sally Jensen suggests that writers can cultivate their awareness to be more aware of the mental, emotional, and physical signs of the inner critic's attack. By reflecting upon what the inner critic brings to the table, one can intentionally and creatively come up with unique strategies to counter the critic and to reaffirm the value of one's writing.

No matter which route you take, whether you cultivate your mindfulness of being present with your writing, or actively affirm yourself to conquer the negativity inside your mind, we think all writers can benefit from taking the attitude of writing as a constantly unfolding process. We do not necessarily have to fix an identical relationship between our self and our writing. Adopting this more fluid view will allow us to put more trust in ourselves, believing that our writing products, if they capture anything about ourselves, are the selves in the past tense. Through writing we will continue to grow and to explore—in varying ways—but none of these ways can be defined by our past works.

Genres and Voices, Conventions, and Innovations

In the following two sections, we locate writing at the nexus of the long-held academic writing conventions and the numerous possibilities of innovation opened up by the writing itself. Starting with the idea of genre and moving to the discussion of authorial voice, we demonstrate how a critical pragmatist approach affords us new insights to understand writing from its general contour, to the organization of paragraphs and the selection of words. We argue that the tension between conventions and innovations, as manifested at different levels of a writing product, can be productive if addressed appropriately.

Genre and Convention

When we compose academic writing, consciously or not, we are following certain conventions. These conventions are introduced to us in various ways and on

---

[1] This advice was shared by Dr. Lang Chen through personal communication. Dr. Chen learned it from her advisor, Koichi Shinohara, the now-retired expert of Buddhism at Yale University.

[2] Foote, S. M. (2019, June 21). Tame your inner critic. *Inside Higher Ed*. Retrieved from https://www.insidehighered.com/advice/2010/07/26/tame-your-inner-critic; Jensen, S. (2019, June 21). Dissertation survival skills: Disarming the inner critic. *Dissertation Doctor*. Retrieved from http://www.dissertationdoctor.com/articles/critic.html

different occasions: through our communication with our advisors and mentors, through following professional associations' guidelines, and by reading a journal's instructions to authors. They set up rules about how, for instance, a research proposal should be composed and what are some necessary elements that should be included. In this sense, we can consider academic writing as the use of different genres.

We do not talk about the term *genre* very often but do implicitly incorporate the requirements of certain genres in our writing. For instance, journal articles, research reports, and monographs are some of the widely used genres in disseminating research findings. For different genres, we employ different structures, tones, and progressions of inferences in our composition.

The insights from rhetoric and communication studies can shed light on the term *genre*. In alignment with the textbook's interest in social action, rhetoric scholar Carolyn R. Miller suggests that we understand **genre** as a typified action in response to and on the uptake of a recurrent situation (1984, 2015). Genres are culturally dependent forms for authors to adopt in performing their speech act. We understand genres through understanding their varying rules. Genres only make sense to us in relation to the concrete social situations in which they are adopted and used. In the case of academic writing, we learn how to write, for example, a research proposal, by understanding a set of rules about what should be included in a proposal and what should not, the style of the writing, and its typical structure. Furthermore, a research proposal is meaningful only if it is enacted in a concrete situation—namely, laying out the feasibility, significance, and plan of conducting a certain study.

Let's revisit the retreat conversation that the authors had to further illustrate how genres help the society to stabilize certain conventions. When asked to come up with a metaphor that best reflected their writing, Pengfei likened her writing experience to crafting a jar:

> If you're going to do a jar, the potter is actually, like, moving very fast. But you hold your hand still. I feel like my writing is like that. I'm just trying to make sense of the fast-changing experience. And I'm trying to, like, be very slow, patient, and careful.

The shape, detail, and size of a jar may vary, but different jars share some common properties and functions. Similarly, an academic genre distinguishes itself from other genres not only because of their different structures and forms but also due to the varying purposes that they serve in communication. Therefore, we can improve our academic writing by familiarizing ourselves with the general writing rules, goals, and formats of different academic genres.

RESEARCH PROPOSAL

Before novice researchers start to work on an empirical study, the first genre they need to grapple with is the research proposal—an example we will use to demonstrate how to integrate relationality and genre in our concrete writing practice. **A research proposal** is a written text mapping out the authors' research plan for a project and meanwhile requesting support, approval, or instruction from the targeted audience. It has its own generic format, which usually constitutes discussions of research purposes, questions, theoretical frameworks, methodological approaches and methods, and the proposed study's significance. If the researcher has conducted any pilot studies, they could also include a section on preliminary results and projected findings. However, merely piecing these parts together may not necessarily produce a satisfactory proposal, as we want to keep in mind that a research proposal is essentially a communicative endeavor to *convince* the readers of the significance and feasibility of the proposed study.

Think about what it takes to *convince* someone in your everyday life. For instance, if you want to persuade your undecided partner to see a couples therapist with you, what would you do?

In a proposal, we need to *convince* our committee members, reviewers, and colleagues that the proposed study is worthwhile to conduct. To achieve this goal, we present (1) what study we plan to do; (2) why it is important to do this study; (3) how we are going to do that; (4) what actions we will take to warrant the validity, ethical practice, and timely completion of the study. Sometimes, researchers tend to focus on Questions 1 and 3, but it is exactly the missing part—Questions 2 and 4—that justifies the need to conduct the study in the proposed way, according to methodologist Joseph Maxwell (see Maxwell, 2004, p. 118).

Remember that by the time you write a proposal, you probably know much more about this specific topic than does your audience. Even though they are your thesis or dissertation committee members, they may not claim their expertise on every aspect of your project, let alone research grant reviewers, who are selected not based on their knowledge on a specific topic. The non-expert nature of your audience has several implications in proposal writing: First of all, avoid jargon. If you can use accessible language to explain your work, go for it. Reviewers do not test you on your sophisticated use of terminology but evaluate your capacity to conceptualize and implement a research project. Second, give overviews but be cautious about being too detailed. In general, a proposal is not a place to unpack the literature review in full swing. By discussing what has been done previously, you develop a rationale for the proposed study. Third, the gap in literature is not the best way to justify a study. This argument helps, but we suggest moving one step further to explain why it is meaningful and much needed to fill in the gap. Fourth, researchers employing different research designs often find that they need to navigate the proposal stage of their work with varying degrees of flexibility. For instance, as we discussed before, some qualitative

> research designs are more emergent and flexible, whereas quantitative studies require relatively more fixed designs. Maxwell suggests that for researchers working with emergent designs, it is important to demonstrate their capacity to complete the research rather than pinning down the step-by-step procedures, which at this stage may not be realistic to project (Maxwell, 2004).
>
> Putting the tips above into practice, we include a rubric to facilitate your proposal writing in Appendix C.

The Change of Genre

Genre stabilizes writing forms, but that does not mean that the rules of different genres are fixed and unchangeable. Scholars Carol Berkenkotter and Thomas Huckin (1993) noticed that "genres are sites of contention between stability and change." Finding a balance between convention and innovation remains a productive tension in our writing.

New understandings of social research continuously broaden our horizons of academic writing. For instance, public scholarship requires us to engage with not only our academic audience but also the general public. Community-engaged work urges us to communicate our findings with the community members we serve. These new conceptualizations of research have given birth to new academic genres. The development of digital technology also incubates exciting creative ways to disseminate research through multimedia. Previously, academic work was mainly presented through writing, but now, artworks, websites, podcasts, and exhibitions have all become venues for discussing and disseminating social research.

> **Pause and Reflect.** Check out the following multimedia platforms for research dissemination. Who do you think is their targeted audience? In what sense do they break away from traditional academic writing? In your opinion, what are some of the criteria that we can use to evaluate the quality of the platforms here?
>
> *Digital Ethnography Lab*: https://digital-ethnography.com/labs/
>
> *New Books Network*: https://newbooksnetwork.com/
>
> *Project: Empowerment*: http://researchforempowerment.com

If you are new to the research world, you may wonder what are the best ways to navigate this productive tension between following conventions and pursuing innovation at the stage of writing, a question with which many scholars grapple. You may also notice that the tension not only manifests itself at the level of genre but also in the process of working on the structure of each text and at the more micro-level, such as the tone, the progression of inferences, and word choice. A particularly relevant concept related to this tension is "authorial voice," which we will unpack further in this chapter.

A Continuum of Academic Authorial Voice

In the context of conducting empirical social inquiry, we propose to conceptualize **authorial voice** as a combination of a series of factors within a specific genre that may impact the reporting of research and the communication between the author and the reader. This includes but is not limited to the structure of a text, the writer's positionality, the use of rhetoric techniques, and the choice of words.

A predominant understanding of authorial voice places qualitative and quantitative writings in a binary framework, within which quantitative writings employ a third-person position; passive voice; value-neutral and objective word choices; and a straightforward, argumentative writing style; whereas qualitative writings often use a first-person, reflective position; explicitly make value statements; and are more inclusive of varying writing styles (narrative, dramatic, poetic, etc.). However, this binary thinking needs to be problematized, as some researchers, such as Mark Applebaum and colleagues or Laura Ellingson, also notice the variation of voices within each of the traditions (Applebaum et al., 2018; Ellingson, 2011). Therefore, as Table 15.2 shows, we reconstruct a continuum of

TABLE 15.2 ● A Continuum of Academic Voices

	Literary Voice From the First-Person Position	Analytic Voice From the Third-Person Position
The writer's positionality	Use the first-person position Reflective Be explicit about the researchers' impact on the analysis of data, value, and ethical commitment	Use the third-person position (sometimes passive voice) Distant Implicitly presume the author's position does not influence the writing Value neutral
The structure of a text	Nonlinear and more flexible Inclusive of multiple voices, genres, and forms of presenting findings	Linear Standardized section demarcation Monolingual
The use of rhetoric techniques	Pursue varying aesthetic styles Use more literary techniques Expressive Experiential	Analytical Clear and concise Authoritative
The choice of words	Culturally sensitive Include rich contextual information	Use standardized language to explain analysis

academic voices in reference to the American Psychological Association's updated journal reporting standards that include the work of Applebaum and colleagues (2018), the work of Heidi Levitt and colleagues (2018), and Laura Ellingson's qualitative continuum (2011). To recognize the variation in writing practice within qualitative and quantitative traditions, we do not label quantitative writing at one pole of the continuum and qualitative writing at the other. Instead, we use "literary voice from the first-person position" and "analytic voice from the third-person position" to describe the two poles of writing.

In some disciplines, regardless of the qualitative or quantitative approaches that researchers take, they are highly encouraged to lean on the "analytic voice from the third-person position." As you will find out next, the formation of academic voices can never be separated from other components of research, such as disciplinary norms, philosophical approaches, and research designs.

When certain conventions of authorial voice become a disciplinary norm, following the convention can offer little space to engage in conversations about one's writing choice. For instance, sociologist Garry Gray in his article "Academic Voice in Scholarly Writing" shared a dilemma he encountered in his early career. As an instructor, he constantly encouraged students to adopt the first-person position by using "I," whereas in his own writing, the use of "I" was replaced by a journal managing editor with "This paper examines" or "This paper offers" (Gray, 2017). In this case, the normative expectation for the author to adopt a distant position from the writing was imposed on Gray externally by his editor. Gray suspects that the editor's choice of words reflects a predominant understanding within policy-oriented fields that associates "objectivity in voice with scientific legitimacy" (Gray, 2017).

Gray's example sheds light on the inherent connection between philosophical approaches and an author's voice. He notes this choice of the word "I" has profound implications on the writing of positionality, as the use of "I" creates more space for researchers to reflect upon their position in the knowledge production process. In various philosophical approaches that have moved away from the positivist/post-positivist paths, the author's/researcher's position matters, as the validity of knowledge is tightly related to how and by whom the knowledge is constructed. As such, one's philosophic approach often engenders a specific understanding of the author–reader and researcher–participant relationships and leads to distinctive writing practice.

The formation of writing conventions is also related to research designs. For instance, Xiaodi Zhou and Jori Hall (2018) ask how mixed-methods researchers shall construct their voice—given that qualitative writings often take the first-person position and quantitative writings prefer the third-person position. In their discussion, they advocate for more inclusion of first-person writing and propose an alternative approach to putting different writing styles in dialogue with each other in mixed-methods studies. Their work suggests that the continuous development of research designs also raises new challenges for academic writing.

Write to Your Own Voice

Have you ever discussed your writing with your advisors or editors and been told that "you need to find your own voice"? It is common advice people give, but you may end up at a loss and wonder, "How do I find my own voice?" or "Where is my own voice, after all?"

Instead of "finding" one's voice, we suggest that a better way to frame this issue is "cultivating" one's voice. As we have discussed, many factors may impact how a researcher presents their research to their audience. Rather than assuming this lost-and-found mode to approach authorial voices, "cultivating one's voice" offers space for us to reflect on the existing predominant writing practice, to explore the multifaceted connections between writing and other components of research, and to unlearn the judgments that we impose upon ourselves based on fixed yet ungrounded conventional academic norms. Only by first problematizing the taken-for-granted and loosening the seemingly unshakeable can we create this fluid space to better understand our research commitment and its connection to our writing.

You may still wonder how a novice researcher without much research experience can connect to the idea of cultivation. One way to connect is to return to the everyday example which we asked you to contemplate at the beginning of this chapter. Some of the everyday writing genres, such as letters and diaries, are very personal in nature. Although we may still follow well-established formats, it is much easier to recognize our own voices in these scenarios. When we write letters or diaries, it seems that we can bring ourselves into the asynchronous conversation we seek to establish and communicate more genuinely. Why? We suspect this is due to the fact that in these scenarios we can express ourselves relatively more freely. One does not need to worry about how the writing will be judged by the readers but may instead focus on communication and expression. To cultivate an authorial voice first of all means to cultivate this sincerity toward our readers and ourselves. There are surely countless techniques and rules that one could learn to improve writing, but without sincerity, the words created by techniques alone will fall flat.

RESEARCH SCENARIO: DOUBLE WRITING IN PARTICIPATORY ACTION RESEARCH: MEAGAN CALL-CUMMINGS

As you can see, we refrain from prescribing any "recipe" for cultivating one's own voice to be sensitive to the relational perspective we take in this book. All we can suggest is to develop your own approach to grappling with the productive tension between convention and innovation, while knowing that writing should first of all be a process of opening a dialogue between yourself and your audience. In this sense, procedure-oriented suggestions may create good writers, but every good writer will have to work out their unique, unrepeatable path to cultivating their own voice. This process may be particularly challenging but at the same time incredibly rewarding if a researcher adopts some innovative writing approaches. In the guest essay by Meagan Call-Cummings, Assistant Professor at George Mason University, she explains how she departed from conventional dissertation writing in her participatory action research project with Latinx youths. This departure was followed by a journey of innovative writing that led to a digital and multimedia dissertation.

I started my doctoral program in education policy in 2010. I was particularly interested in learning more about and conducting research around peace education and the ways in which everyday educational practices could be peaceful. After taking several courses in my program I felt like I was swimming, but not very well. I didn't know which way to turn or what to do next. It was only when I started taking methodology classes that I felt like I knew where I was headed. I felt deeply connected to the idea that methodological decisions and practices could also enact or build peace.

Participatory action research (PAR) is a methodological approach rooted in an onto-epistemological stance that argues every person has expertise, but particularly those who are closest to an issue, situation, or problem. Critical participatory action research (CPAR) suggests that people who have been pushed to the margins of society hold valuable expertise based in their experiences and that this expertise should be honored in research and play a central role in the creation of knowledge. The core of CPAR, then, is an ethic of peace, and that ethical stance should be met at every step of knowledge production (research) processes.

I began my dissertation research in 2013 with 52 Latinx high school students and one white teacher in a small, rural dairy town in Idaho. This town had in the preceding decade experienced a dramatic demographic shift from almost 100% white to about 50% white, 50% Latinx, mostly due to the growth in the dairy industry there. Almost all the students with whom I worked for my dissertation research identified as "undocumented" immigrants, meaning they lacked the papers required to be considered "legal" in the United States. This was a time of great turmoil. The Dream Act, which granted some people a temporary legal status, was just passed and these students and their siblings were in the process of applying. When we started our CPAR project together, their minds were tuned to this and other associated issues that were affecting their everyday lives. We honed in on a research question that was immediately important to them: Why are our teachers racist?

Over the course of 18 months together we engaged in several different types of participatory data collection and analysis, and shared our process and findings in several ways, including at a local school board meeting and through a video that shared the students' experiences with racism at their school and in their community. When it came time to write my dissertation, I was at a loss. I wondered, how could I maintain an ethic of peace and an onto-epistemological commitment to participation if I now turned my back on these students—my co-researchers—and wrote hundreds of pages they would never read or care about? How could I write something that their community would never see and would just collect metaphorical dust on a shelf?

I chose to create a digital dissertation (http://researchforempowerment.com/burned/) that would be co-created by these co-researchers and that could continue to be edited, added to, and most important, accessed beyond the life of the study itself. In order to be true to my ethico-onto-epistemological commitments and to CPAR's axiological tenets, we included comment boxes on every single webpage so that the co-researchers and community members from the research site could respond to our research findings and add their own insights and analysis. We chose not to transcribe all of our data but included them as close as possible to how they were originally collected. So, for example, we audio recorded students telling their stories of racism and put those audio files on the website. We scanned some of their research journal entries and made images of those writings available. We included some of the images they used for a Photovoice project we did. They introduced themselves in their own voices as co-researchers. We also included the reflections of Mrs. James, their white teacher, who was an integral member of the research team.

When I submitted this as my dissertation to my dissertation committee, there was a split reaction. While some of the committee members were immediately supportive, others were tentative. One committee member in particular told me something like, "This is all well and good, Meagan, but you need to get a job." The message behind that statement was kind and practical—it was that, although it's nice to stay true to one's ethico-onto-epistemological commitments, it might be hard to find a tenure-track position with a university that cares about participation in research more than numbers of publications and U.S. News rankings. It was then and there that I chose I would care more. And I continue to hold true to this commitment to caring more about people than I do about publications.

This commitment has led to tremendous satisfaction in the research I do. I'm now working with high school students and high school teachers on a project we call Courageous Conversations, which engages diverse high school students in arts-based inquiry as they engage each other in critical conversations that are often deemed taboo in typical classrooms. I meet with them every other Tuesday, and it is a highlight of those weeks. We are friends, confidants, allies, and colleagues. I am proud that we are co-authors on several publications and co-presenters at national and international scholarly conferences.

At the same time, this commitment has required that I often do double the work of some of my counterparts. For my dissertation, yes, I was able to do the website, which required a significant amount of writing, but I also had to write three scholarly publications. In my current position I often have to "double" write in order to fulfill practical requirements to move toward tenure as well as to fulfill my own personal commitment to sharing knowledge with those who create it and those who will use it. For example, for the Courageous Conversations project, in addition to co-authoring scholarly articles, our collective has begun to develop multimedia professional development materials in order to reach those we feel need our expertise the most. In the midst of the COVID-19 pandemic, I worked with the authors of this textbook and other colleagues to document acts of social solidarity through a virtual Photovoice project (https://knowledgedemocracy.org/projects-and-events/arna-social-solidarity-project/social-solidarity-project-gallery/). Because the reality of the situation was quickly evolving, and because we were committed not only to documenting social solidarity but also providing a space to build social solidarity, we needed to move faster than a journal outlet ever could. We chose to write short blog posts that were scholarly in nature but that were both accessible and useful to audiences beyond academia. We wrote blog posts, but for the work to "count" toward tenure, we also co-authored journal publications that took longer to reach audiences and most likely were not read by the people we were most committed to reaching.

In addition to "double writing," I also am repeatedly challenged by some scholarly journals' (and their reviewers') insistence on a particular way of writing, and a particular way of characterizing and reporting on the research (or knowledge creation) process. I often receive reviews of journal articles I have submitted that ask me to represent the collaborative analytic process in ways more recognizable to readers. Reviewers doubt the rigor of the work because either they have not seen an approach we have used before or they do not see its value. In these instances, of which there have been several, I have made different choices. Sometimes, I choose to fit what we actually did within our research collective into frames and ideas that would make more sense to audiences who are more familiar with traditional approaches. Other times, I choose not to do this and to find a different journal or outlet for a new submission. The decision that I make depends on many factors, including how much I and my co-authors care about what outlet we use and how much we feel like we need to change (or not) to satisfy reviewers and editors.

For one project, my evolving write-up was rejected three times by different outlets. In this instance, my co-author and I decided to hold onto the three different papers—to just wait for the right moment. About a year after those rejections, a call for book chapters came out related to the work that we had done. I submitted the chapter as a compilation of the three rejected papers. The submission was immediately accepted, with very few, minor changes. Considering it as one of the strongest chapters, the editor of the volume positioned it as the first chapter and praised it for making "for a perfect, rigorous way to lay the foundation for the rest of the approaches and examples covered in the book." Receiving that email was immensely satisfying. Staying true to my commitment to authentically represent participatory knowledge creation processes paid off!

In Meagan's research, including youth co-participants/co-researchers in the writing and reporting process complicates the singular form of the authorial voice; meanwhile, creating a digital dissertation defies the conventional practice of dissertating. There are indeed challenges, and at times well-intentioned advice cautioning against challenging the standard practice. However, she has been able to hold on tight to her commitment to her participants and to the enterprise about which she truly cares. Meagan's example demonstrates the complex nature of an authorial voice, which interweaves together one's ethical, onto-epistemological commitments in a concrete and contextualized research scenario.

✓ YOU AND RESEARCH

When Interpreting Research

If you mainly read and apply research in your own work rather than conducting formal research, the final products of research writing—reports, articles, and books—open the window for you to understand research processes and examine the findings. Correspondingly, it will be helpful if you develop your own strategies to read academic texts. Some of our previous students found it helpful to create a rubric to facilitate their reading, as it can serve two purposes: sorting out the key information in the text being studied and mapping out the evaluative criteria. In Appendix D we include an example of an article critique rubric for your reference. The example is relatively generic and you do not need to follow it exactly in your reading, but it is a starting point for you to create your own rubric that speaks to your discipline and your professional practice.

When Doing Research

If you are doing social research alone or with a team, chances are you will perform individual or collaborative writing in the research process. You may spend most of your time working on the question of "What to write?" This chapter offers the opportunity to explore writing itself. Writing can be a lonely journey, but if you can develop an understanding of the implicit relational components of writing—namely, how writers

> hold themselves responsible to their readers, participants, and themselves—this understanding will help you think through more concrete and practical questions, such as working on different academic genres and keeping writing a sustainable practice. Specifically, we use the research proposal as an example to demonstrate how relational thinking can help us better understand this genre. Another issue we identify in this chapter is how to navigate what we term "the productive tension between conventionality and creativity." Fundamentally, we encourage you to be an informed explorer in your writing.

SYNTHESIS: POINTS FOR REFLECTION

Conceptual Synthesis

In this chapter, we took up the idea of relationality and grappled with the question of what it means to conceptualize writing as a relationally responsible activity. We closely examined three types of relationship that writing involves: the writer–reader relationship, the researcher–participant relationship, and the writer's relationship with themself. Derived from this relational approach, we developed a series of guiding principles for academic writing. The writer–reader perspective leads us to the consideration of accessibility, informativeness, and transparency in academic writing. Introducing the researcher–participant perspective sheds light on the importance of inclusivity, protecting research participants' rights, and democratizing the writing process. Last, we suggest that a writer's relationship to themself also matters, as self-care is what eventually sustains writing. In the second half of the chapter, we focus on two key concepts in writing—genre and authorial voice—and reconstruct their meanings from a relational perspective. The conceptual discussion in this chapter feeds into our overall conversation about writing practice.

Methodological Synthesis

This chapter looks at writing that takes place at different moments of the research process and in different formats. As illustrated in the example of the research proposal, the concept of genre is helpful as it allows us to see how various communicative purposes are connected with different formats and conventions in writing. Writing also facilitates inferring as researchers iterate their understandings of existing literature and data. Moreover, the chapter discussed how different approaches to meaning and value give rise to differential authorial voices. To search for one's own voice is a journey of self-exploration, which encompasses not only how you would like to position yourself on a wide spectrum of philosophical traditions and discipline-specific research practice but also self-expression and self-cultivation.

Personal Synthesis

This chapter intentionally encourages a shift in the discourse on writing: Instead of focusing on the product of writing, we advocate for understanding writing as a process, which creates space for growth, reflection, and imperfection. Sometimes, writing can become a personal struggle—and no one can offer a one-size-fits-all prescription for these writing challenges. What we have found most helpful are two interconnected tips: (1) to start practicing without promising ourselves any answer prior to writing, and (2) to create a safe space to share our writing, get constructive feedback, and allow us to be vulnerable.

MOVING FORWARD

Reporting research findings through writing connects the process of inference-making with the dissemination of research. At first glance, it seems that researchers complete their mission as long as their findings are reported to the audience. In the next chapter, we will discuss the tracing of social research as it travels out of researchers' worksites and enters into the horizon of the public. We will focus on the term *impact* and locate social research's impact within the larger social, political, and cultural context.

Further Readings

Belcher, W. L. (2019). *Writing your journal article in twelve weeks: A guide to academic publishing success*. Chicago, IL: University of Chicago Press.

Bolker, J. (1998). *Writing your dissertation in fifteen minutes a day: A guide to starting, revising, and finishing your doctoral thesis*. New York, NY: Holt Paperbacks.

Joyner, R. L., Rouse, W. A., & Glatthorn, A. A. (2018). *Writing the winning thesis or dissertation: A step-by-step guide*. Thousand Oaks, CA: Corwin.

Maxwell, J. A. (2012). Research proposals: Presenting and justifying a qualitative study. In *Qualitative research design: An interactive approach*. Thousand Oaks, CA: SAGE.

Further Readings by Meagan Call-Cummings

Call-Cummings, M. (2017). Establishing communicative validity: Discovering theory through practice. *Qualitative Inquiry*, *23*(3), 192–200. Retrieved from: https://doi.org/10.1177/1077800416657101

Call-Cummings, M., & Dennis, B. (2019). Participation as entangled self-assertion. *Forum Qualitative Sozialforschung/Forum: Qualitative Social Research, 20*(2), Art. 24. Retrieved from: https://doi.org/10.17169/fqs-20.2.3203

Call-Cummings, M., Hauber-Özer, M., & Ross, K. (2019). Struggling with/against the unintentional reproduction of power structures in participatory research: Using reconstructive horizon analysis. *Action Research*. Advance online publication. Retrieved from: https://doi.org/10.1177/1476750319837324

Call-Cummings, M., & Martinez, S. (2016). Consciousness-raising or unintentionally oppressive? Potential negative consequences of photovoice. *The Qualitative Report*, *21*(5), 798–810. Retrieved from: https://nsuworks.nova.edu/tqr/vol21/iss5/1/

16

COMING BACK FULL CIRCLE

Implications of the Inferential Process

In both Chapters 6 and 14, we examined how inquiry doesn't exist in a vacuum but is always embedded in a given social, cultural, political, and historical context. As a form of social action, it is inevitable that research is conditioned by implicit social and institutional structures and norms, while having the potential either to reproduce or transform those structures and norms in small and big ways. In Cluster 3 chapters, we focused on the nature and process of making inferences in terms of descriptive accounts, or trends and patterns, through higher-level inferences. It seems like common sense to think that findings that we derive from an inferential process should land on certain practical applications, or in other words, make an impact on some level. The "So what?" raised in Chapters 14 and 15 continues to linger here. You may hear rhetoric such as "Research should inform practice," or "Policy decisions should be guided by research." We intuitively connect research with an effect in the real world. But how do these two aspects intersect, exactly? How do we know if research makes an impact? What do we consider a meaningful impact? And even more important, impactful for *what*, and for *whom*? *Who* gets to decide? Those questions already surfaced in Chapter 14, where we started to grapple with research applicability *for whom*? This chapter further unpacks how research circles back to the larger societal contexts within which it is based and that it intends to influence.

MUSING UPON THE EVERYDAY: WHAT IS IN MY FOOD?

Do you recall what you bought during your most recent visit to the grocery store? How did you decide which box of cereal to pick up from the shelf? What kinds of snacks did you put in your shopping cart? Today we face so many messages that compete for our attention—"low fat," "whole grain," "sugar free," "zero cholesterol," "non-GMO," "gluten free," "all natural," "organic," and so on. Are you someone who usually reads the "nutrition facts" on the food packaging and notes serving size, calories, and the fat, carbohydrate, and protein content disclosed in the nutrition panel? Does such information persuade you one way or the other when you try to decide between options? This ordinary scenario foregrounds the connection between policy, research, and our everyday practice.

It was not that long ago, in 1990, when nutrition labeling became mandatory in the United States. Supported by increased research findings that established a link between diet/nutrition and health/diseases (Institute of Medicine [IOM], 1990), consumers' demand for food labeling surged in the 1980s. As a result, the U.S. Food and Drug Administration drafted proposals and took comments from consumer groups, academia, the food industry, and IOM. This led to the passing of the Nutrition Labeling and Education Act (NLEA) and the ongoing development in food labeling today.

In this mundane example, research and consumers played an important role in shifting a policy that directly shapes everyday experiences. Can you think of an example in your professional lives as teachers, counselors, social workers, administrators, and so on where the practitioners' voices and actions and/or research in your field made an impact on a policy shift that in turn has a direct impact on your practice? Here are a couple of examples that come to mind. In February 2017, the West Virginia teacher strike resulted in increased teacher salary and other changes to improve student learning. Alia Wong (2019) reported that this collective action energized a nationwide teachers' movement to defend public education, marked by large-scale walkouts in Florida, Pennsylvania, Oklahoma, New York City, Denver, and Los Angeles. On the research side, Andrew Wakefield et al. (1998) published now-discredited research in the British medical journal *Lancet*, which linked the measles, mumps, and rubella (MMR) vaccine to autism. It was widely picked up in the media. This publication contributed to a drop in MMR vaccination rates and a rise in measles and mumps in countries such as the United Kingdom and the United States. Even worse, according to T. S. Sathyanarayana Rao and Chittaranjan Andrade (2011), it continues to perpetuate a climate of mistrust among parents regarding vaccination. In this case, a single research article manufactured a public health crisis and had a long-lasting impact.

What other examples did you come up with? How do you understand "impact" from those examples?

NARRATIVE AND CONCEPTUAL INTERLUDES: RESEARCH IMPACT—FOR WHAT, FOR WHOM, AND BY WHOM?

With those examples in mind, we explore what it means for research to be *impactful*. What constitutes research impact? How do we know impact is occurring? At first, these questions may appear abstract, so we would like to ground this discussion in the context of an actual research study—the Morris Justice Project (MJP).

In 2011 three mothers who lived in the same residential building in the South Bronx (New York City) began to compare notes. They shared their observations of the New York Police Department's (NYPD) presence on their street. They were outraged by frequent contacts by the police with their own sons and other young people of color in the neighborhood, occurring without basis. Intuitively, using their cell phones, these mothers documented day-to-day incidents of police activities around their building (Public Science Project, n.d.). Together, the mothers began to connect the dots. It became clear to them that policing in their community was problematic. Those three mothers became the impetus for a participatory action research project. A group of mothers, fathers, elders, and youth along with faculty members and graduate students, for example, Brett Stoudt and Maria Torre from the City University of New York (CUNY) and lawyers from Pace University Law School, came together to form a highly heterogeneous research collective. It aimed to document policing practice known as "stop-and-frisk," driven by "zero-tolerance" policies (Stoudt & Torre, 2014). The collective wanted to understand the perceptions of community members who were most impacted by this practice and these policies.

The group met weekly at a local public library. In time they mapped out a 42-block radius along Morris Street as their research site, just east of Yankee Stadium; thus they named the project "the Morris Justice Project." The research collective designed a survey and gathered more than 1,000 responses from residents about their perceptions of their neighborhood, and their attitudes toward police (Public Science Project, n.d.). After preliminary analyses of the survey data, the team took the findings back to the neighborhood. They asked residents for help to better make sense of the data. Incorporating feedback and perspectives from the locals, findings were highlighted and printed as "back-pocket reports," which were shared with residents, policy-makers, and elected officials. They also projected key research findings onto a tall neighborhood building. These findings were used to back up the argument that this community had been heavily targeted for "stop-and-frisk," although this policy and policing practices actually made residents feel more unsafe in their own homes. For example, 52% of survey respondents reported being stopped by police four times or more; 69% reported being stopped by police in the previous year. This coincides with NYPD's own statistics: NYPD conducted 4,882 stops in the 40-block neighborhood, but discovered only eight guns (Stoudt & Torre, 2014).

To disseminate the findings, the team organized block parties with the theme "Summer of Action," where community members made T-shirts and buttons featuring research findings. MJP also hosted a Bronx town hall meeting on community safety, where the team released a formal research report to the community. Meanwhile, the collective was involved in activism to advocate for policy changes regarding policing. MJP joined the effort of the Communities United for Police Report Coalition to support the successful passing of the Community Safety Act, a bill to increase accountability of the police force. They also closely followed a federal class action lawsuit, *Floyd et al. v. City of NY, et al.*, which challenged "stop-and-frisk" and racial profiling on the part of the NYPD. August 12, 2013, came with a historical ruling by a federal judge that found NYPD liable for a pattern of racial profiling and unconstitutional stops. In addition, in 2012 several members of MJP became the plaintiffs in another class-action lawsuit, *Ligon et al. v. City of New York,* challenging part of the "stop-and-frisk" program that allowed NYPD to patrol thousands of private apartment buildings in NYC. The federal judge on this case ruled NYPD's practice unconstitutional and appointed a monitor to oversee development and implementation of remedies in NYPD to address this problem (Public Science Project, n.d.).

> **Pause and Reflect.** What's your immediate reaction after reading about MJP? How is MJP similar to or different from some research projects with which you are familiar? Did this study make an impact? If so, how would you describe that impact from your own perspective?

MJP might have challenged some of your preconceptions about a research project, such as: The researcher adopts a neutral position in collecting and analyzing data, writing up findings, and publishing findings in an academic journal. It is hoped that academic publications can be used by policy-makers to influence policy decision-making. However, researchers themselves should refrain from direct political engagement. In contrast, MJP was steered by a group of people from a diverse background—foremost, community members directly impacted by the research phenomenon. Researchers offered their expertise but maintained a collaborative relationship with other members of the research collective. The collective shared an explicit value of advocating for justice and fairness in the criminal justice system. The project directly targeted policy change through participation and activism grounded in research findings. Traditional journal publications only came later in the project (see Stoudt & Torre, 2014; Stoudt et al., 2015). In addition, the collective diversified modes of research dissemination, including town hall meetings, neighborhood parties, sidewalk arts, pocket reports, illuminators, protest signs, and so on. Research findings were not primarily seen as a research product but as a conduit to facilitate further dialogues with community members to contextualize and verify or otherwise contest those findings. They also provided an opportunity for many community members to come together to share and hear their stories and perspectives, thus fostering a sense of community and solidarity.

Findings from MJP were also used to build evidence to persuade political stakeholders to take action, and to hold them accountable toward more just and fair policies and institutional practices. These efforts led to fruitful legislative and legal victories for the community and beyond. All of those processes also echo what we discussed in Chapter 14—that research inferences can become the catalyst for dialogue, which in turn has the potential to facilitate insights and consciousness-raising. And less obviously, the impact of MJP may be gauged in terms of employment of local community members (e.g., stipends for research associates) and career development opportunities (e.g., some community members went on to pursue higher education). Now, what do you consider "impact" from this study, similar to and different from what we articulate here?

What Does It Mean for Research to Have an Impact?

MJP highlights various ways that research may interact with the world that it aims to influence and change. More questions remain: How do we know if research makes an impact? Or should research make an impact at all? (For example: the argument of "pure basic science" that has value of its own, in comparison to "applied science.") Are there different types of impact? What principles can we use to evaluate research impact? To develop a more refined understanding about research impact, let's first take a look at some sample research studies:

A. A study that surveys the prevalence of sexual violence on college campuses.

B. A study that maps out the distribution of wealth around the world.

C. A study that tracks brain structures/activities involved in clinical depression by comparing the brain images of depression-free participants and those who experience a major depressive disorder.

D. A study that documents the effects of a community-engaged program for improving English language learners' academic achievement.

E. A historical analysis that examines conditions that facilitate or hinder the sustainability of a popular social movement.

F. A discourse analysis that examines how politicians discuss "terrorist attacks" in the media.

G. A narrative study that studies how people understand and experience "happiness."

H. An oral history project that documents the history of Native women and girls in North America.

I. An ethnographic study that aims to understand the impact of industry pollution on the health and life quality of local residents.

Explanation Versus Understanding

This set of studies focuses on a range of social phenomena on multiple levels. For instance, prevalence of sexual assault (Study A) and the distribution of wealth (Study B) both aim at documenting patterns and trends of a social or economic phenomenon, even though the scale of the individual study may vary. Study A works with a large sample from a number of colleges/universities in the United States, whereas study B addresses the even larger global geopolitical context. In contrast, the focus of Studies C and D shift toward categorizing relationships between phenomena: Study C examines the correlation between clinical depression and brain structures/activities, and Study D examines the effect of a particular intervention. As discussed in Chapter 14, both correlation and intervention effects rely on an underlying logic of *cause-effect*, or the model of *causality*, which relies on statistical procedures. Patterns of inferences such as *causation, correlation, regression,* and *modeling* may come into play in those studies. Meanwhile, in Study E, there is a shift from developing *explanations* based on causal and correlational relationships to historical and structural *understanding* of social phenomena. Instead of generating a correlational or causal pattern between factors, or evaluating the success or failure of a social movement, Study E focuses on understanding the processes and relationships that influence a social movement. And the phenomena being examined are also large-scale in nature.

Martin Hollis (1991) makes a formal distinction between *explanation* and *understanding* as two different modes of inquiry (see Figure 16.1). It is worth noting that the application of these two terms is different from their everyday use. Readers may consider them methodological terms that have specific meanings in the research context. **Explanation** primarily positions the researcher as a neutral third person external to the research phenomenon, who derives descriptive, correlational, or causal inferences based on systematic observations and measurements. **Understanding**, in contrast, requires the researcher to acquire an insider position as much as is possible, to understand the social phenomenon *from within*. As we discussed in Chapters 5, 7, and 12, understanding meaning requires gathering perspectives from people who are part of the research phenomenon, and more important, for the researcher themselves to position-take and gain perspective as an outside-insider.

This categorical difference between explanation and understanding becomes more salient as we move down to Study F and onward. These studies foreground an orientation toward understanding, with the research foci placed on people's narratives, lived experiences, or public discourses. The types of inferences we draw likely rely more on thematic, reconstructive logic relation, metaphor, social network analysis, frame analysis, and so on, also discussed in Chapter 14. In addition, researchers and participants in studies G, H, and I are brought into closer contact and proximity. This tendency becomes most pronounced in a participatory action research study, as embodied in MJP, where the boundary between researchers and participants becomes porous and fluid.

Most social and educational research may be recognized as oriented toward explanation, understanding, or a combination of both, as in mixed-method studies. Of course, this is only one way to conceptualize different types of social inquiry. Under the category of either explanation or understanding, studies may differ in terms of scale: those that focus on systemic or macro phenomena versus those that target individuals or small groups on the micro level. Table 16.1 helps to illustrate this differentiation. For a *macro-level* study that aims for explanation, it usually taps into the realm of the *system* (e.g., economic, legal, or political institutions). For a *micro-level*, explanation-oriented study, it primarily examines *individual* behaviors, motivations, attributions, or attitudes. In contrast, a macro-level study that orients toward understanding often focuses on apprehending a particular culture or a cultural (sub)group in the *lifeworld*. A micro study oriented toward understanding often delves into individual *actors*' narratives/story-telling, experiences, and understanding reasons that those actors would give to account for their actions. Note that we make a distinction between *system* and *lifeworld*, and between *individual* and *actor*.

Explaining the nuanced differences beyond these concepts is beyond the scope of this textbook. However, we make the following distinctions: The **lifeworld** is the sphere where we carry out everyday activities, socialize with others, and develop as individuals and as groups and cultures, whereas **system** manifests itself as industry, money market, legal and financial institutions, bureaucracy, political governance, physical and technological infrastructure, and so on. The two spheres are distinct in the sense that each is coordinated by different mechanisms. The *lifeworld* is maintained primarily through *communicative actions* and *communicative rationality*, through which two or more

TABLE 16.1 ● Research Orientations: Explanation and Understanding

Levels	Explanation	Understanding
Macro	System	Culture
Micro	Behavior; Individual	Action; Actor

Source: Adapted from Hollis (1994).

people interact with one another, grasp meaning intended by the other, and give reasons and back up their claims when being questioned. The explicit and implicit aim is to reach mutual understanding, or at times to repair and transcend miscommunications and misunderstandings. In contrast, the *system* is largely coordinated through *instrumental rationality*, which means various parts of the system operate almost exclusively based on a *means-to-the-end* focus, aiming for maximizing productivity, efficiency, profits, gains, and the accomplishment of goals. The system can run independently from the intentions and motivations of the individuals involved (Habermas, 1981, 1984). In other words, the systems operate in ways that everyday actors may not even be aware of; nor do they have direct control over them.

Another brief distinction we would like to make is between the notions of "behavior" and "action." Many readers may be more familiar with the term *behavior*, widely used in disciplines such as economics, psychology, education, social work, and popularized by behaviorism. **Behavior** is often understood as an occurrence and tendency of an individual that takes place in a given time and space, and thus is associated with the quality of being observable, measurable, and manipulatable. Behavior is tied to the notion of "individual." In contrast, an **action** may carry those qualities of a behavior, but it also emphasizes the intention or motivation of the person who carries out the action. Action may not always be visible (e.g., thinking, reflection, and other active forms of being). It is typically associated with an "actor" who always acts in a relational context to others, whereas behavior signifies a lone individual. You may wonder: Why this distinction? Those assumptions matter. For example, if we assume what we examine is behavior in social studies, we will generate findings that primarily shed light on factors, conditions, or mechanisms that would help to explain or modify behaviors. This often is the realm of *explanation*. But if we conceptualize findings in light of action and actor, the focus shifts to *understanding* intention, context, and meaning, as well as underlining structures and forces that shape actions, not as external and independent factors but as internal and mutually interdependent aspects that constitute the actor and their actions.

Nature of Research and Forms of Research Impact

Impact, Impactful, and Impacting. Keeping the typology in Table 16.1 in mind, let's further unpack how different types of research may shape the *potential* to make different forms of impact. This is a conversation we already initiated in Chapter 14. Depending on whether a study is oriented toward explanation or understanding, a macro versus micro focus, the potential and limitations of the study's impact may be anticipated. It is important to stress that we are *not* suggesting a deterministic relationship between the nature of the study and its possible impact. Research is always an unfolding and dynamic process. We can be surprised by what it can or fail to do. Our intention here is to provide a general conceptual tool for readers to better grasp the notion of research impact. On that note, we have yet to formally address what we mean by "research impact." The term *impact* was introduced in Chapter 14, where in the research scenario section Karen shared her research documenting the effects of a youth encounter program, tracing the action patterns and the self-understanding of participants across time. Impact is often taken as some sort of change and effect as a result of certain actions such as a research effort. To develop a more complex conception of research impact, we would like to contrast "impact," "impactful," and "impacting."

We often use the term **research impact** to describe *changes* resulting from a research endeavor, especially positive changes. The focus is often on characterizable and measurable effects and thus gives something of a *material* quality to the common conception of "impact." In other words, the term tends to privilege changes in time and space (e.g., increase or decrease in certain concrete measures). In contrast, if we use the term *impactful*, it shifts the focus from a material-like effect to a more general effect of change, including changes that are not so apparently defined in time and space. For example, think of consciousness-raising, or *aha!* moments of insights (discussed in Chapter 14) as forms of impact that don't involve change in space or concretely defined quantities. Similarly, the word *impacting* emphasizes the *process* rather than the product of making efforts toward change. It signifies that some changes may be ongoing, interlocking with other forms of change, and thus cannot be fully defined in a specific frame of time, such as at the end of a study. Accordingly, our use of "impact" in this chapter is not limited to the product-oriented understanding of change resulting from research. It also embodies the meanings of "impactful" and "impacting," which carry more *holistic*, *process-oriented*, and *nondeterminist* understandings of change. Figure 16.1 helps to recap the interconnection of those concepts.

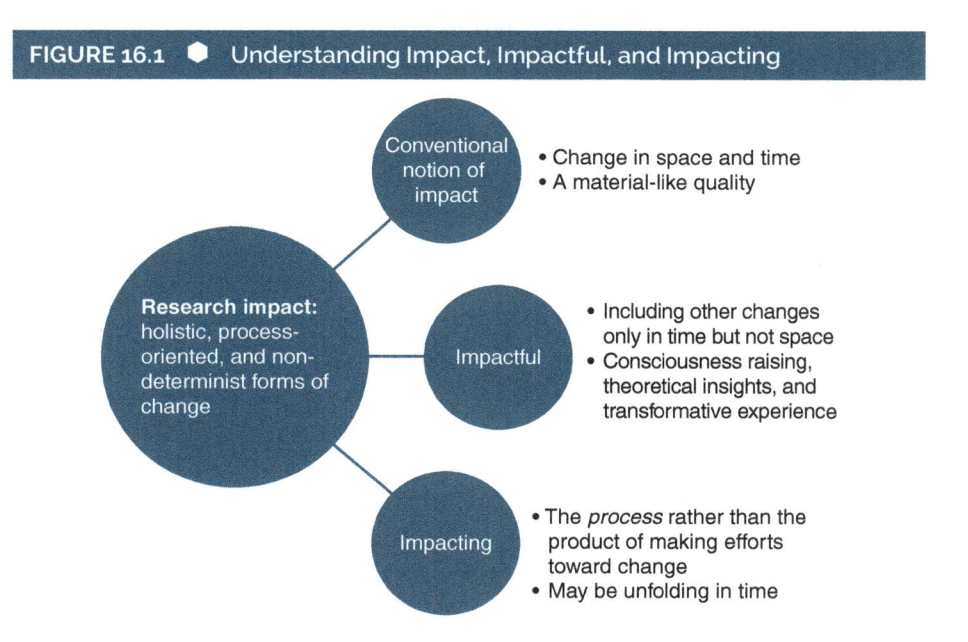

FIGURE 16.1 • Understanding Impact, Impactful, and Impacting

Research impact: holistic, process-oriented, and non-determinist forms of change

- Conventional notion of impact
  - Change in space and time
  - A material-like quality
- Impactful
  - Including other changes only in time but not space
  - Consciousness raising, theoretical insights, and transformative experience
- Impacting
  - The *process* rather than the product of making efforts toward change
  - May be unfolding in time

Conceptualizing Research Impact. With this clarification of what we mean by research impact, we will further examine the connection between types of research and possible impact. Some studies may aim to map out patterns of large-scale distribution of resources across a nation, or even transnationally (e.g., income, wealth, mortality, health or educational resources, consequences of climate change, etc.), or large patterns of social issues (e.g., sexual violence, bullying, drug addiction, hate crime, gun violence, civilian casualty in war zones, activities of police forces, and so on). Findings from those studies may provide pertinent evidence to raise public awareness, stir up debate in the public sphere, support social movements, or even shape policies and laws.

Policy and legal changes in turn may engender corrective courses of redistributing resources (e.g., tax laws; equal pay for women), intervention or prevention initiatives (e.g., social programs), or recognition of status and rights (e.g., the rights to sovereignty and land for First Nations) in light of equity and collective well-being. Of course, the assumption here is that our institutions function properly based on those principles, which is not always the case. It also implies a value-based judgment that we will touch on later. Meanwhile, on the micro level, research on developing and evaluating specific interventions that target desirable educational, health, psychological, and community outcomes (e.g., children's psychosocial development, addiction treatment, youth suicide prevention, gun violence intervention, etc.) can provide guidance and strategies to inform practitioners such as teachers, health providers, counselors, social workers, or community organizers to reflect on, improve, or diversify their practices.

Similarly, research that focuses on individuals' or a community's lived experiences, stories, and narratives can provide contextual understanding of the same social issues mentioned above. Rich and deep understanding, along with powerful stories, holds potential for consciousness-raising, precipitating public reflection and at times outrage, propelling social movements, and leading to policy and legislative changes. In particular, a focus on social actors' perspectives and experiences has the advantage of re-centering otherwise marginalized voices. Thus, this line of research has the unique potential to forge counternarratives that challenge and may even transform dominant discourses surrounding a social issue or about a group of people. For example, there is a common perception in American culture that living in poverty is a result of personal failure. Through ethnographic research, social researchers Kathryn Edin and Luke Shaefer (2015) provide different perspectives on this phenomenon based on lived stories and related historical and policy analyses. Their research findings are threaded together in the book *$2.00 a Day: Living on Almost Nothing in America*. The book serves as a powerful counternarrative that challenges false assumptions about the nature of poverty and about people who are affected by it. This kind of research has the effect of raising public consciousness and moral conscience, amplifying marginalized voices, and questioning accountability of the institutions. It may also contribute to social policy change in the larger scheme.

Note that we are not suggesting that only narrative and story-based research have the potential for consciousness-raising and creating counternarratives. In fact, large-scale studies aiming for explanation hold potential to achieve the same goal. We should not trap ourselves in a binary understanding that ties the scale of research and the mode of explanation or understanding to fixed research impact. Similarly, it is methodologically unsound to hold predetermined ideas of what a research study is capable of exerting influence on, only based on the dividing line between quantitative and qualitative research. Meanwhile, there is also a common (mis)conception that only large-scale quantitative studies can really make a difference. Chapter 14 already challenged this binary conception about research and what research can do. For example, as discussed in Chapter 14, theory building itself can be impactful for advancing the thinking of a scholarly community, which may have ripple effects outward. Overall, it is fair to say that depending on its specific nature and aim, a research study may bear certain potentials and limitations in relation to different types of impact. But none of these relationships are deterministic. There are various impacts that a particular research may ignite, some more predictable and some less so. Figure 16.2 sums up our discussion here.

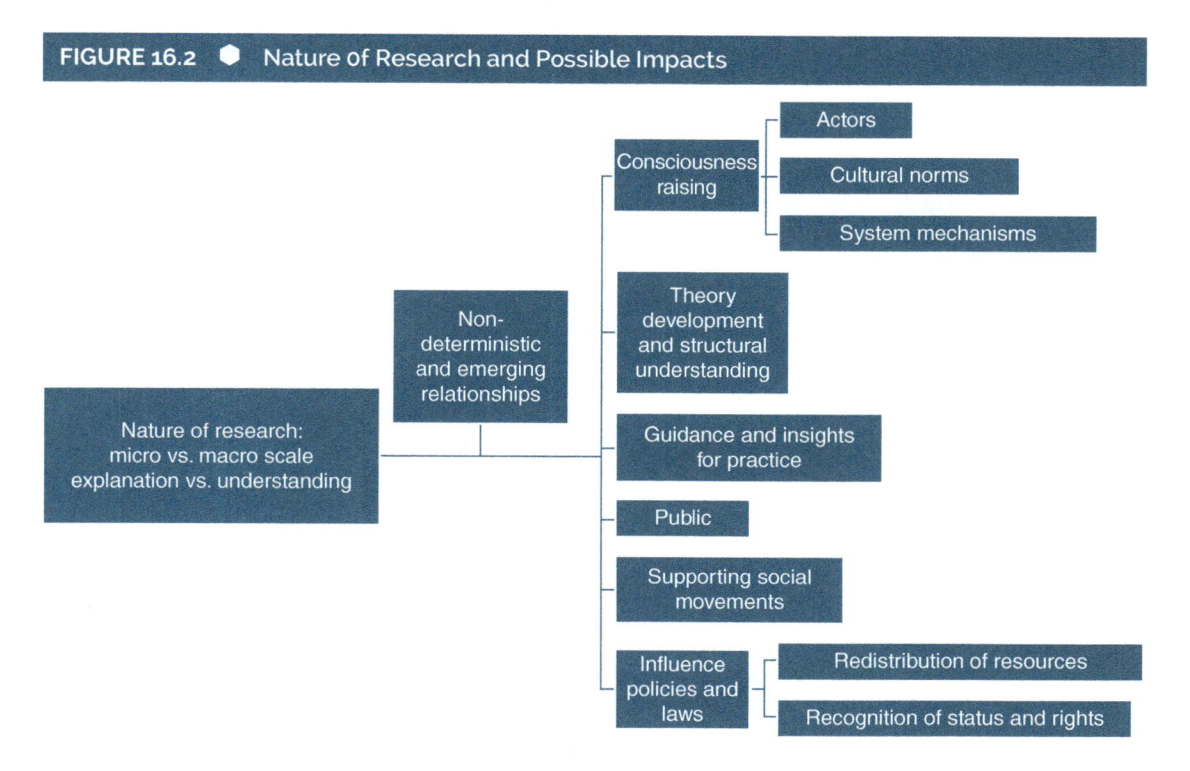

FIGURE 16.2 Nature of Research and Possible Impacts

- Nature of research: micro vs. macro scale, explanation vs. understanding
  - Non-deterministic and emerging relationships
    - Consciousness raising
      - Actors
      - Cultural norms
      - System mechanisms
    - Theory development and structural understanding
    - Guidance and insights for practice
    - Public
    - Supporting social movements
    - Influence policies and laws
      - Redistribution of resources
      - Recognition of status and rights

In addition, using the metaphor of a tree, Figure 16.3 suggests general domains through which research may make an impact.

- **Tree leaves** symbolize changes on the individual/actor level related to behaviors, actions, motivation, self-understanding, physical and psychological health, learning, development, and so on.
- **Tree branches** represent changes on the group, organizational, and community levels pertinent to collective well-being and livelihood, or productivity and efficiency, influenced by allocation of resources, safety and care, group dynamics, or communal culture, etc.
- The **tree trunk** embodies changes on a cultural level in terms of shifting cultural representations (e.g., mass media, literature and the arts, cultural discourses), or in terms of making visible repressive and oppressive cultural norms that are generally unacknowledged. Those norms operate to benefit certain groups of people while excluding others. They can either restrict or broaden the range of valid forms of being a community and societal member and thus are pertinent to identity and group development.
- **Tree roots** represent systemic-level changes in the realms of social, economic, and educational policies; political representation; laws; governmental bureaucracy; accountability; international relations; and more. Those system-level phenomena actively interact with the cultural-level phenomena, both of which are also inherently connected with individual and community phenomena.

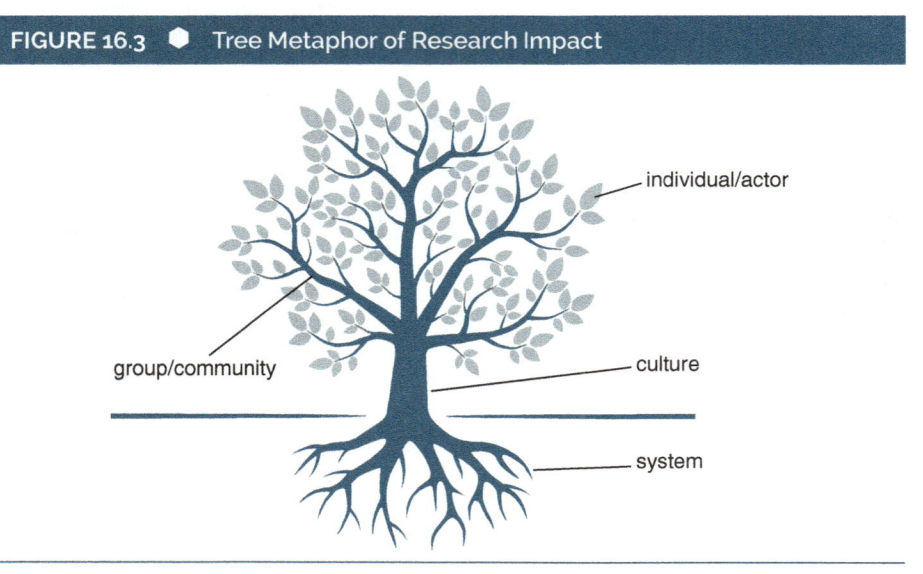

FIGURE 16.3 ● Tree Metaphor of Research Impact

Source: iStock.com/rolandtopor.

Since all of those aspects of potential changes are *interconnected*, it may be more accurate to say that one particular study usually foregrounds one or more aspect(s) of the whole, with the rest more or less backgrounded. On the other hand, one aspect of the whole may start a *cascade effect* in other domains simultaneously or in time. Thus, again, research impact is not a "neat" concept that can be easily pinpointed with full certainty. And yet it is possible to gauge and evaluate research impact without reaching a finite conclusion.

> **Pause and Reflect.** Looking at the tree and reflecting on your daily practices (including research endeavors), what kinds of influence or impact do you hope to be part of in your immediate and larger environment? What aspects make you feel frustrated or challenged in terms of facilitating change? Are there tensions and/or connections between these two sides of your experiences? If so, what to do about such tension?

How Do We Evaluate Research Impact?

Now that we have wrestled with the notion of *research impact* and suggested one possible approach to conceptualize it, we have more questions to ponder: Are there certain kinds of impact that are valued more than others? Why is this so? Who should get to decide? For example, within academia, a research study is primarily judged by its traditional output: academic publications. Meanwhile, the relative "worth" of a journal article is evaluated based on a mathematical indicator called "impact factor," assigned to a particular academic journal. Articles published in journals that have a high journal impact factor are generally deemed to have higher quality and prestige. However, this only addresses an evaluative framework of impact within the academic community. Thinking of the Morris Justice Project, what would happen if we opted only to use the citation rates or journal impact factors associated with the publications that came out of that project to judge the impact of this study? What would we gain or lose from using this approach?

Impact and Value

As you might have noticed, evaluating research impact inevitably evokes value judgments to discern what is good, useful, meaningful, or influential. Existing institutionalized matrices such as journal impact factor are so often picked up as taken-for-granted criteria for evaluating research impact, the matrix framework itself needs to be critically examined. This would involve demystifying surface-level perceptions of *objectivity* that are associated with quantification and standardization (discussed in Chapter 7), to unveil the *normative* basis of those criteria. These have to do with more fundamental values that propel the creation and application of those criteria in the first place. Recall in Chapter 5 that we discussed that knowledge production always has certain values embedded. Even saying "Research should be value-free" is a value statement. It is not surprising that when it comes to conceptualizing and evaluating research impact, multiple approaches and frameworks coexist, guided by different sets of values and epistemological assumptions about research and knowledge.

Chapter 14 discusses commonly applied concepts such as predictability, generalizability, and transferability as one set of criteria that are commonly used to evaluate the *applicability* of a research study. This set of criteria is based on the value that research should have an influence beyond its immediate context. It also carries the assumption that when a research study can exert an effect on future events or in broader/different contexts, the research becomes more useful or valuable. There are other approaches to evaluating research impact. For instance, we can gauge a study based on its contribution to making the world a better place. This evaluative framework is guided by an underlying assumption that connects research to justice and the common good. Similarly, there could be an evaluative framework built upon ethical and moral foundations, which examines how a research study may engender positive transformation, or on the other hand inflict harm. In the following section, we further unpack some of these approaches.

Is Generalizability Always Desirable?

In Chapter 14 we considered the desirable influence of research and the notion of *generalizability*. We tend to hold an implicit assumption that generalizability is always desirable. Generalizability implies the process of *replication*. That is, one observation or effect finds itself being replicated with another group of people, or in another context. This idea of generalizability is typically explained through a correspondence theory of truth, which we discussed in Chapters 5 and 9, instead of through a communicative theory of truth (Chapter 7). This notion of generalization is also tied to statistical analyses that largely rely on averages of aggregated data. In Chapters 11 and 13 we discussed how missing data and outliers are often thrown out to preserve the consistency of the majority of a trend or distribution. The reliance on *average* effects thus can overshadow the need to examine phenomena, groups, or individual actors that metaphorically constitute the outliers and missing data of the society. For instance, the practice of generalizability can be deeply biased when much of social science research has been done with white undergraduate students. Nonetheless, findings from those studies are routinely picked up as generalizable knowledge applicable to all people. This taken-for-granted affinity to "generalizability" has been challenged and questioned in social sciences. For instance, the emergence of new research vocabulary, such as "transferability" (see Chapter 14), offers a refreshing perspective that shifts the focus from outward generalization *by* the researcher, to readers' *own recognition* of similarities, usefulness, and applicability of a study. Since this concept is so pervasive, we encourage you to examine your own assumptions of generalizability: Where do your assumption(s) come from? When is generalizability desired and when is it not?

Research Impact and Social (In)justice

Meanwhile, when we discuss "impact," do you notice our tendency to tacitly associate impact with "positive," "useful," "transformative," "desirable," or "beneficial" change? It is common for us to say that we do research to engender positive social change. But what is considered positive and good necessarily taps into how we understand the ideals of society, which inevitably evokes the notion of social (in)justice. Social theorist Nancy Fraser, with her colleague Axel Honneth (Fraser, 1998, 2000; Fraser & Honneth, 2003), developed a theory of **social justice** that addresses justice in two distinct domains: *recognition* and *redistribution* (see Figure 16.4). **Recognition** refers to societal and cultural acceptance and respect for different social groups and associated identities, especially groups that have been historically marginalized (e.g., racial, sexual, and religious minorities; women, transgender individuals, people with disabilities, etc.). *Mis-recognition* is considered a form of social injustice, which contributes to status subordination and a wide range of subsequent damages to groups and individuals. Meanwhile, social injustice also manifests in *maldistribution*—that is, systemic and historical patterns of unequal distribution of resources, materials, and rights. Unfair distribution may manifest in increasing

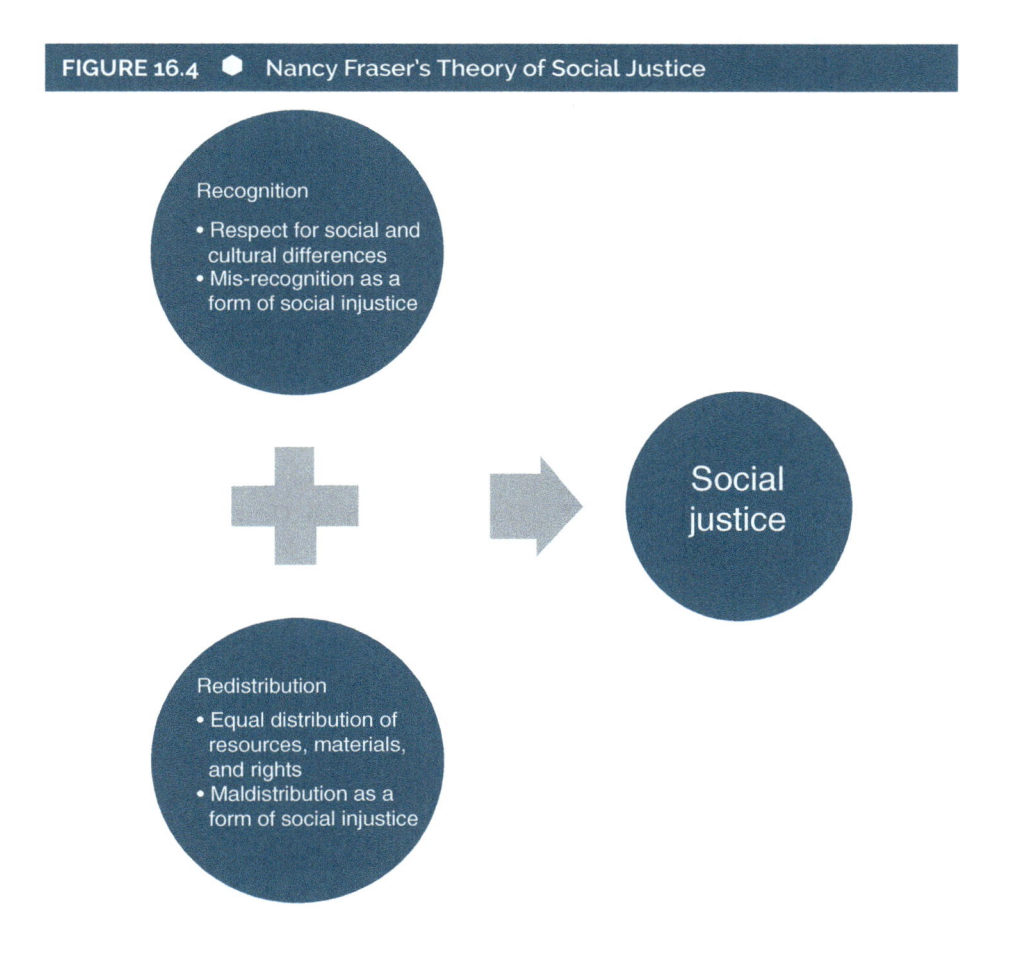

FIGURE 16.4 ● Nancy Fraser's Theory of Social Justice

Recognition
- Respect for social and cultural differences
- Mis-recognition as a form of social injustice

+

→

Social justice

Redistribution
- Equal distribution of resources, materials, and rights
- Maldistribution as a form of social injustice

polarization between the rich and the poor, disparity in educational opportunities, health care, social welfare, legal rights, and so on. Thus, **redistribution** is a form of justice.

Fraser argues that to address social justice we have to engage in both *recognitive* and *redistributive* efforts. The site of recognition prominently appears in the social and cultural milieu where institutionalized patterns of unequal status can be challenged and transformed, which can lead to increased inclusivity, equality, and participation. Redistribution requires changing the systems (e.g., economic, labor, political, and legal) through transformation in political agenda, social-economic policies, and laws that can lead to the redistribution of resources, opportunities, and rights. Fraser also asserts that the two domains intersect and are internally connected; both are needed to work toward social justice. Theories of justice like Fraser's foreground the link between research and social (in)justice pertinent to our conception of research impact. That is, we may gauge impact based on to what extent a study contributes or facilitates both recognitive and redistributive justice *in tandem*.

Back to the Morris Justice Project, we can examine its impact from this social justice perspective. MJP challenges various assumptions about crime rates and about communities that are associated with high crime rates. Just imagine that you are relocating for a new job. It is common sense to look up crime rates in various neighborhoods when choosing a safe or desirable place to live. Typically, high crime rates signify danger and chaos, which justifies policies like "stop-and-frisk" that elevate police presence and surveillance as the means to ensure safety. Inevitably, this logic stigmatizes communities and people who live in these neighborhoods as "unsafe," "dangerous," and very often this associates "poor" neighborhoods with large percentages of people of color. Those stereotypes seep deep into our everyday experience, often subconsciously, and perpetuate *mis-recognition* of people and communities. The voices from people who live in those communities are largely absent. As a result, dominant narratives reproduce themselves and have an array of consequences regarding distributive injustice. A myth of (un)safety makes fewer people want to live or buy properties in a "dangerous" neighborhood. Consequently, there are less desirable job opportunities, lack of tax revenue, and less investment in schools, health care, and public facilities. As you can see, recognitive injustice intertwines with redistributive injustice: They form a vicious cycle.

MJP set out to disrupt the cycle first by amplifying the experiences and perspectives of people and communities that were directly impacted by the "stop-and-frisk" policy. Through a consistent participatory research process, and ongoing inputs and verification from the community, MJP gathered data and findings demonstrating that "stop-and-frisk" policing is ineffective and in fact makes the community feel less safe. MJP also provided various platforms for community members to voice counternarratives about their own neighborhood. Those efforts directly challenged stereotypes and mis-recognition of *who they are*. Meanwhile, social and political activism interwoven in MJP led to redistributive outcomes regarding police presence. That is, the community did not need *more* police but rather community-based policing that builds relationships and trust. MJP helped to shift public dialogue on what makes a safe and prosperous neighborhood. This shift could have ripple effects in terms of future (re)distribution of resources to support the development of safe and prosperous communities.

Research as Power and Empowerment

Implicit in our discussion above is the concept of *power*. It was first introduced in Chapter 4, regarding power dynamics that can manifest in the relationships between researchers and participants. "Power" was further taken up in Chapter 6, where the sociopolitical context of research was discussed. Readers are likely more familiar with negative connotations of power in the forms of coercion, control, unequal status, exclusive practices, or repressive/oppressive cultural norms. But researchers also often talk about "bringing marginalized voices from the margin to the center" and amplifying marginalized voices so that they can no longer be silenced and ignored. In this sense, research also carries the potential to empower others and facilitate positive social changes. "Power" thus also refers to influences that can be positive, uplifting, transformative, and emancipatory.

Various scholars have argued that to make research valid and impactful it ought to embody a *transformative* dimension that facilitates changes in the world. For example, Sean Massey and Ricardo Barreras (2013) used the term *impact validity* to suggest a study needs to be gauged by the "extent to which research has the potential to play a role in social and political change or is useful as a tool for advocacy or activism" (p. 615). Similarly, Isaac Prilleltensky (2003) suggested the term *psychopolitical validity*, referring to how a study should be evaluated based on how oppression is addressed in the study, and how well the study facilitates "psychological and political liberation in the personal, relational, and collective domains" (p. 199). Jeasik Cho and Allen Trent (2006) prescribed "transformative validity" to denote the necessity to include "a progressive, emancipatory process leading toward social change that is to be achieved by the research endeavor itself" (p. 322). Patti Lather (1986) coined the term *catalytic validity*, the extent to which research empowers participants in the study, as an important validity indicator. All of those validity concepts share an underlying thread of connecting research to an *explicit* liberatory intent and aim. It connects power and research through *empowerment*, which was first discussed in Chapter 4. Taking MJP as an example, how well do you think it embodied impact, psychopolitical, transformative, or catalytic validity?

Meanwhile, we want to be cautious about use of the terms *empower* or *empowerment*, which were first introduced in Chapter 4. You may hear them used often with the best intention of bringing positive changes in the world. But let's take a moment to reflect on the meaning of "empowerment." To empower others already implies we have the power to do so (and others don't). Similarly, to "give others voice" sets a one-up power relation, positioning the researcher as the more powerful one, whereas the participants or community that we study are voiceless or powerless. Do you see how this can be problematic? It is critical that we also engage in self-reflection and critique our own positionality in relation to those with whom we do research. This is the essence of research *reflexivity*, discussed in Chapters 2 and 4.

Othering, Epistemological Violence, and Ethics

As we examine power relations and power dynamics in the context of research, we inevitably encounter the domain of ethics. We also need to think through research impact in light of research ethics. Feminist psychologist Michelle Fine once wrote an essay titled "Working the Hyphens: Reinventing Self and Other in Qualitative Research" (1994). "Hyphen" in this context refers to the line that simultaneously connects and separates self–other, which is always a dynamic process that depends on the context. Fine analyzed how social research, even with its best intention, may participate in various forms of *othering* the people that we study. She points out that too many studies in social sciences are positioned as research *on/of/about/for* other people. This conception already creates a separation between the researcher and the participants, which implies a power differential. For instance, in the name of giving voice and empowering others, researchers may end up reproducing similar dynamics of dominance that researchers intend to dismantle, contradictory to the intent of centering marginalized voices. Similarly, when studying elite social groups that are deemed privileged and powerful in society, researchers also need to be aware how power manifests in the hyphen between the researcher and the participant in nuanced ways.

Fine advocates that researchers wrestle with our own *privileged* positions. She emphasizes the imperative to avoid a tendency to flatten complex identities and reduce them to binaries. We need to avoid the tendency to essentialize race, class, and gender (and other identities) as neat and fixed categories that are free of their own internal tensions and contradictions. It is very important that we constantly challenge the academic discourse itself, which has been historically dominated by white-middle-class-male narratives—a form of mis-representation. Meanwhile, we may also commit to the pitfall of essentializing when we immediately discredit one's work because the researcher identifies as a white, middle-class man. This assumes that knowledge generated from people who occupy dominant positions is automatically invalid, without examining how power plays out in a specific context. Similarly, we essentialize when we assume that voices and perspectives from marginalized groups are homogenous and free of distortions because occupying marginalized positions guarantees access to truth. Equally important, this critique does not contradict the urgent need to center marginalized perspectives and defer to marginalized voices as our default practice. The key point here is that we need critical analysis of power at all times.

In a similar vein to Fine's critique, Gayatri Chakravorty Spivak (2010) used the term *epistemic violence* and Thomas Teo (2008, 2010, 2011) used the phrase *epistemological violence* to capture a unique form of violence. This concept cautions that researchers, in the name of "doing research," can do real harm to others, not necessarily in physical and outwardly recognizable forms of violence (though this can occur, too!), but in more covert, subtle, and potentially more long-lasting ways. Epistemic/epistemological violence occurs when knowledge becomes a tool to reproduce and intensify unequal power relations and systemically keep others marginalized. The term **epistemological violence** describes the situation in which the interpretation of research findings in the name of "knowledge" and "science" ends up creating or perpetuating the inferiority of certain cultural or racial groups. This happens when alternative explanations are available but excluded as illegitimate (Teo, 2011).

A clear (and outrageous) example of epistemological violence is related to the conceptualization and measurement of intelligence between Black and white children. According to historian Robert Guthrie (1976/2004), the earliest effort to use intelligence tests to compare Black and white children can be traced to 1897, when children were asked to repeat four stanzas of poetry. In this test, Black children outperformed white children, but the findings were discredited as invalid because they were not what the researchers expected. Again, in 1921, researchers from the University of South Carolina compared white children to three groups of Black children categorized by skin color (dark, medium, and light-colored), using an IQ test called the Binet Scale. The test scores showed that children with lighter skin scored higher on IQ scores. The researchers then concluded that "colored children" are intellectually "younger" than white children. This study, along with a series of similar studies, was cited as "scientific" knowledge and used to argue for separate educational programs for Black and white children. The use of IQ tests to differentiate individuals, which reflects racialized patterns, continued to be deemed legitimate practice in psychology until the 1980s and 1990s. Knowledge claims like those saying that Black–white IQ differences are due to genetic difference were widely accepted within academia (Teo, 2011), not even that long ago.

In this example, numerical differences on test scores were interpreted as "real" racial differences in intelligence, claims in the name of "scientific knowledge" that have led to profound consequences that continue today. These have far-reaching negative impacts for people of color, especially African Americans. This impact penetrates many areas including education, social mobility, identity development, self-esteem, vocational opportunities, the school-to-prison pipeline, and so on as evidenced by Michelle Fine's work with colleagues (Fine, Stoudt, Fox, & Santos, 2010). Research on intelligence contributed to school segregation policies prior to the Supreme Court decision in *Brown v. Board of Education,* as well as to today's desegregated but separate school districts, where white children and children of color continue to be segregated. As Suzette Speight notes, it has also seeped into an internalized sense of inferiority among African Americans (Speight, 2007).

Thus, epistemological violence is no less if not more harmful than physical violence, due to its long-lasting and institutionalized impact. It is particularly dangerous given its covert appearance and deceptive power in the name of "scientific knowledge," which shields epistemological violence from critical examination and refutation.

There is a double-edgedness of research in relation to liberation and repression, which foregrounds a fundamental ethical and moral question we inevitably become entangled with through research. That is, are we contributing to bringing positive changes to the world, or are we (un)consciously, even unwillingly, participating in the maintenance of systems of dominance and the status quo? In this context, ethics is not just a set of rules/regulations that are external to research. Instead, ethics constitutes the very foundation of what research is and how it should be conceptualized and approached. Circling back to our earlier discussion on a "value-free" or "value-neutral" stance on research (Chapter 7), such an assumption is dangerous because it may foreclose us from examining our motivations, interests, and the various power relationships manifested in our research practice. By doing so, we risk being blind to the effects of epistemological violence, which can undermine the good intention that draws us to research.

In sum, in this conceptual interlude we explored what it means for research to have an impact and various levels where research may make an impact, both positively and negatively. We unpacked the notion of "impact" and how it connects to underlying issues such as social justice and ethics. We also problematized how research may become entangled with empowerment, othering, and epistemological violence. This discussion builds upon key concepts introduced in Cluster 1: the nature of knowledge (epistemology), positionality, power, validity, and ethics, as well as the process and context of making inferences featured in Cluster 3 chapters.

> **Pause and Reflect.** What are some social issues that you care about deeply in your work and life? Are there any underlying values that guide your actions? How do you envision making a difference in your role as a student, professional, and/or researcher?

RESEARCH SCENARIO: EXTRAPOLATING SOCIAL CHANGE FROM RESEARCH: POSITIONALITY, ITERATIVITY, AND ENVISIONING: HAKIM MOHANDAS AMANI WILLIAMS

Now let's turn to a concrete, real-life research example—a long-term research endeavor by Dr. Hakim Mohandas Amani Williams. His research and writings center on school/structural violence, educational inequity, and youth/community empowerment. Below is a short essay prepared by Dr. Williams to share a decade-long research and advocacy effort with a school community in Trinidad. As you read through this research scenario, pay particular attention to how Dr. Williams and how you define *research impact* in this particular research context.

This essay uses a 9-year longitudinal study on school violence and educational inequity in Trinidad & Tobago (TT) to demonstrate how positionality, iterativity, and envisioning *play key roles in attempts to mobilize research as and toward social change. In other words, I have used findings from my research to inform certain interventions that may contribute, over the long term, to engineering social change; in so doing, I view my research agenda and the ways in which I operationalize it (including centering my positionality in an iterative process) as a form of social change as well.*

Some positivist conceptions of research insist on objectivity, while some critical conceptions of research are transparent about their decidedly conscious efforts to interrogate what they view as objectivism; my research falls into the latter camp. I start with the premise that all domains of human sociality, including research, are political. I believe that researcher positionality, whether acknowledged or not, influences research; I therefore view my positionality as constitutive of my research agenda.

I was born and raised in TT, a twin island republic (and former British colony) just off the coast of Venezuela. I grew up in Laventille, a community beset by a reputation for crime, violence, and poverty. Anecdotally, I was aware of some community members who—in attempting to dodge the consequences of the stigma of residing in Laventille—resorted to using different addresses on applications for jobs and for schools for their children; this was the start of my informal education around the larger implications of entrenched social class in postcolonial TT. It is this personal background that partially led to my interest in intra/interpersonal, and structural/systemic violence.

What has now become a near decade-long research project, commenced with a 7-month qualitative study at a secondary, co-ed school in Port-of-Spain (Trinidad) looking at school violence in 2009. It was scaffolded as a vertical case study; that is,

I considered various tiers of analysis—international, regional, national, community, school, classrooms, individuals—to deepen my understanding of violence in schools. The policies that have been created and enacted in TT around school violence (and in fact, in many parts of the world) often center on the individualized nature of school violence; in other words, schools and the educational system itself center their focus on student-to-student or student-to-teacher violence. My research (see Williams, 2013, for an elaboration) confirmed that there are varied (multidirectional) forms of and contributors to violence in schools, and I have used these very findings to inform a rather iterative research trajectory. Below I will describe in more detail how my positionality played a role in the research, and how I view research as process and platform for envisioning social change.

Researcher positionality refers to the values, beliefs, and background of the researcher; they can have an impact on the questions and methodologies we choose and even how we collect, analyze, and present/distribute the data. I intentionally chose a secondary school with students who came from working-class homes and socioeconomically disadvantaged communities very similar to Laventille because I saw my research as part of a critical lineage of postcolonial re-envisionings. My personal background from Laventille eased my entrée into the school site because many of the students, upon hearing my story, almost immediately opened up about their own lives in school and in their communities. In this case, the researcher served as a pivotal instrument in the data collection. The students shared stories of teacher-to-student violence and general violence at home and in their communities, all of which became the bedrock of my understanding that violence in schools could not be analyzed outside the wider context of the educational system; students' homes; communities; the colonially bequeathed structures, cultures, and processes of the nation-state; and regional and international influences.[1]

After the initial 7-month study, I returned for a few weeks each year to procure follow-up data and to ascertain if my findings would hold over time. It was during these follow-ups that I recognized how deeply entrenched systems are. Theoretically, I understood that to be the case but now the research, over a period of about 4 years, began to affirm that. I delved into the literature on dynamical systems theory, which provided the explanatory framework understanding how complex and nonlinear phenomena, like systems of violence, are fostered and maintained over long periods of time.[2]

Characterizing school violence as a complex system led to the recognition that any interventions had to be multipronged and self-sustaining. I wanted my research to reflect the kinds of decolonizing changes I wanted to see in TT society: increased inclusivity, less hierarchy, individual and community healing, capacity building, and empowerment. I created a Systemic Restorative Praxis model centered on three Rs: Remember, Repair (or Restore) and Re-envision. It is premised on (1) critical interrogation of the colonial impact on our bodies, minds, and structures, and the recollection of Indigenous/pre-colonial ways of being and knowing that were decimated/denigrated; (2) learning about and using restorative circles as an anticolonial form of conflict resolution, disinterring and unpacking our traumas, and by healing in community, restoring some of our historically ravaged dignities; and (3) building upon these two prior steps to re-envision our individual lives, communities, and postcolonial nation-states in more just, peaceful, and sustainable ways.

The 7-month initial study led to a critical youth participatory action research (CYPAR) project 2 years ago (with youth at the school collecting data and receiving training from me in conflict resolution and leadership development).[3] Additionally, in the past 2 years, the research has expanded into communities where I conduct workshops with parents in restorative circles, conflict resolution, and community activist training, and I return each year to offer follow-up training and to collect data on how they are utilizing the capacity-building skills. Over the past 9 years, the research itself has unfolded as a sort of iterative, dialogical, multivocal process as more findings have emerged. This research project will continue for quite some time, because I realize that if systems of violence do indeed become entrenched over long periods of time, then the decolonizing approaches will also require time and sustained effort. In sum, my vision is a multitiered intervention to match a multitiered problematique.[4]

---

[1] An example of international influences on the complex web of violence is analyzing the admixture of the increasing appetite for drugs in North America and the burgeoning drug supply in South America to feed this appetite, which adds to the global proliferation of small arms that accompany drugs on their way through the Caribbean. These two influences render disproportionate impacts on communities like Laventille because of the growth of gangs that partake in the drug trade.

[2] See Williams (2016), which elaborates on dynamical systems theory and how it is applied to my research and emergent interventions.

[3] I plan to follow up with these youth for the next 5 to 10 years to gauge their life trajectories.

[4] I even testified before a national parliamentary hearing in TT on school violence and got the opportunity to insist (in writing and in-person) on the necessity of approaching this topic in a systemic fashion.

This research story sounds inspiring, doesn't it? Did some of the key concepts that we discussed earlier stand out to you? For example, Dr. Williams emphasizes the importance of researcher's *positionality* (discussed in Chapter 3), *epistemological* orientation ("a critical lineage of postcolonial re-envisionings"), and how *impact* can be conceptualized during the research process. Dr. Williams demonstrated how his experience growing up in

Laventille has shaped how he conceptualizes school violence as an entrenched structural issue, and how he envisions impact as a long-term commitment to help build self-sustaining and transformative practices by and for the community. Shifting away from common discourse that attributes school violence to individual problems, Dr. Williams takes on a dynamic system theory and conceptualizes school violence as a complex manifestation of "intra/interpersonal, and structural/systemic violence." This informs his vision that "any interventions had to be multipronged and self-sustaining."

This research context embodies the notion of "impact" as *impact*, *impactful*, and *impacting* all at once. Oscillating between research, community practice, and theory building, the impact of this study is concrete but also constantly unfolding. Impact manifests in the process of CYPAR where youth and the community become empowered collaborators to directly address issues that impact them. Impact also manifests as a deepened theoretical understanding of school violence, which continues to be informed by ongoing practice. In addition, various forms of restorative practices enable concrete changes in individuals, schools, and the community, in the forms of consciousness-raising, building capability, and collaborative problem solving. This study also carries a deep yearning for social justice. Pertaining to *recognition*, voices and perspectives of the youth and community members are centered and amplified. They build up a counternarrative that shifts the conception of school violence to a form of structural/system violence. This iterative community-led process can in turn influence local and national educational policies and the allocation of resources, which may lead to *redistributional* justice as well.

What other forms/aspects of impact did you see?

✓ YOU AND RESEARCH

When Interpreting Research

When you read a research article, learning to take on a critical attitude toward the research is key. A set of self-reflective questions may help to grow your critical capacity: What do you consider useful and beneficial research? What is the basis for your evaluative framework? What kinds of research can make an impact on your professional practice? Who decides what is impactful? What research findings are considered transferable to your specific professional context and what not? Does this particular research perpetuate any form of othering and epistemological violence? In particular, nowadays the notion of "evidence-based practice/treatment" is a buzzword in many fields such as medicine, behavioral health, education, social work, counseling, and more. What's your understanding of credible "evidence"? How has the evidence-based rhetoric impacted your experience and your professional work? How do you critically apply relevant research evidence to your actual practice, while resisting the stifling effect of evidence-based discourse when it becomes too dominant?

> **When Doing Research**
>
> If you are currently involved in research or in the process of designing a study, it is important to reflect on your intention and values going into this project. How do these intentions and values manifest in choosing what (not) to study, what research questions (not) to ask, and how do you make methodological decisions along the way? Following Dr. Williams, you may also wrestle with: How might your positionality influence how you understand and pursue impact? How would you like your research to be picked up? By whom? What are possible small and big ways that your study can make a difference? On the other hand, how might your research participants react to your findings and conclusions? Can the claims and inferences that you make in the study harm someone, even in subtle ways? What's your responsibility as a researcher? To whom do you commit, and are you accountable?

SYNTHESIS: POINTS FOR REFLECTION

Conceptual Synthesis

In this chapter we illustrated that there are various ways to conceptualize "research impact," which may depend on the researcher's epistemological orientation. It does not mean all approaches are equal, and we can always question the underlying assumptions of each approach. At bottom, there is a normative plane based upon which we gauge what is valuable, good, useful, or beneficial. But we cannot examine these normative questions without also making explicit *for whom* and *by whom* these questions are relevant. Once again this reveals the *intersubjective* nature of research: No research exists independently of a relational context that devises meaning and intentionality. Meanwhile, issues of power become relevant when considering the impacts of a research process: Research can be the catalyst to *empower* others but can also perpetuate *othering* and *epistemological violence*. Research can never be neutral or value-free. In fact, claiming naive neutrality and objectivity can be a form of obscuring power. Counterintuitively, it makes research more legitimate if we are aware of our shifting positionality as a researcher in relation to the research context that we hope to influence. Thus, to understand research impact requires a deeper epistemological and practical reckoning that involves researcher's identity, self-reflection, and a critical analysis of power. In addition, the concept of research impact intertwines with our earlier discussions on validity and ethics. What makes a study valid has something to do with the extent to which a study may exert influence in the world in positive and transformative ways. The question about impact is simultaneously an ethical one because research can do harm in the names of "science," "evidence," and "neutrality." Therefore, research impact, validity, and ethics are intertwined and should always be examined together.

Methodological Synthesis

In this chapter we also discussed *nondeterminist* connections between the methodological design of a study and possible ways the study may make an impact. Studies can be roughly differentiated in terms of their internal logic toward *explanation* or *understanding*, on either *micro* or *macro* levels. We resist the fault line between quantitative and qualitative research, which reinforces an artificial divide. Instead, we encourage readers to examine methodological issues based on epistemological assumptions and researchers' commitments, instead of specific research designs. For instance, a macro-level correlational study and a micro-level narrative inquiry study have varying emphases with respect to explanation versus understanding. But both can work toward consciousness-raising, theory building, and persuasion of policy-makers. Meanwhile, in a taken-for-granted hierarchical knowledge system, the former (macro-level, causality-based) rationale tends to be valued more. This evaluative framework of legitimacy itself is worthy of critical examination.

Personal Synthesis

What does all this mean to us on the personal level? So far we have situated our discussion in the context of research, but as we have emphasized all along the way, research and everyday experience and practices are not separated. As we reflect on the ideas of making positive impact or on the contrary, the potential of epistemological violence, we can apply this discussion to our professional practice and everyday lives as well. This is the essence of *praxis* and *reflexivity* that we discussed in earlier chapters. Our knowing is deeply connected to our ways of being as a researcher, a professional, and as a person. How can we live our life in ways that uphold our epistemological, ethical, and moral commitments and responsibilities? What does it mean to make an impact in the world in which we live? How might we have also contributed to maintaining and supporting the status quo?

MOVING FORWARD

As we conclude Cluster 3, we are getting close to the end of our shared journey. Instead of seeing this as a linear process from a start to an end, we hope this is just the beginning of a lifelong journey that continues to unfold. Regardless of how formal research might play out in your specific context now or in the future, we hope many of those *how* and *why* quandaries will continue to find a home in your intellectual, professional, and everyday life. Moving ahead, we invite you to a dialogue and a metareflection among the co-authors, which "concludes" the text while keeping the text open for further dialogues.

Further Readings

Benton, T., & Craib, I. (2010). *Philosophy of social science: The philosophical foundations of social thought* (2nd ed.). London, UK: Red Globe Press.

Hollis, M. (1994). *The philosophy of social science: An introduction*. Cambridge, UK: Cambridge University Press.

Further Readings About the Morris Justice Project

The Public Science Project (PSP). (n.d.). *Morris Justice: A public science project.* http://publicscienceproject.org/

Stoudt, B. G., & Torre, M. E. (2014). *The Morris Justice Project: Participatory action research.* Thousand Oaks, CA: SAGE.

Stoudt, B. G., Torre, M. E., Bartley, P., Bracy, F., Caldwell, H., Downs, A., Greene, C., Haldipur, J., Hassan, P., Manoff, E., Sheppard, N., & Yates, J. (2015). "We come from a place of knowing": Experiences, challenges, advantages and possibilities of participating in Morris Justice Project. In C. Durose & L. Richardson (Eds.), *Re-thinking public policy making: Why co-production matters*. Bristol, UK: Policy Press.

Torre, M. E. (2009). Participatory action research and critical race theory: Fueling spaces for nos-otras to research. *Urban Review, 41*, 106–120.

Further Readings by Hakim Williams

Williams, H. M. A. (2013). Postcolonial structural violence: A study of school violence in Trinidad & Tobago. *International Journal of Peace Studies, 18*(2), 39–64.

Williams, H. M. A. (2016). Lingering colonialities as blockades to peace education: School violence in Trinidad. In M. Bajaj & M. Hantzopoulos (Eds.), *Peace education: International perspectives*, 141–156. New York, NY: Bloomsbury Publishing.

Williams, H. M. A. (2016). A neocolonial warp of outmoded hierarchies, curricula and disciplinary technologies in Trinidad's educational system. *Critical Studies in Education*. doi:10.1080/17508487.2016.1237982

Williams, H. M. A. (2017). Teachers' nascent praxes of care: Potentially decolonizing approaches to school violence in Trinidad. *Journal of Peace Education, 14*(1), 69–91. doi:10.1080/17400201.2016.1245656

17
POSTLUDE

We are quickly approaching the end of our dialogue with you. As we come to the close of this text, we want to reflect on a few core concepts that have characterized this textbook, both in terms of its *substance* and in terms of the *approach* we have taken.

One of our primary goals in this text has been to *open a dialogue* with you, our readers. And while the specifics of the dialogue between us and you are coming to an end, we hope that *you* will continue that dialogue with research and with the research process as you encounter it in professional, academic, and personal contexts.

Back in Chapter 1, we discussed the impetus for this book. You may remember that one of our inspirations for writing this text was coming to understand, through our teaching of classes such as the ones toward which this text is geared, that many students experienced what we called a *fissure* in how they related to research—that is, they experienced a tension between the way they defined research and the way they position themselves in relation to research (we discussed these fissures in detail in Chapter 3). Throughout the text, we have approached our discussion of concepts with the goal of *you being part of that conversation* and finding your own voice as a researcher. At this point, we hope that you feel confident to go out and continue being a part of research communities, be they in academic settings, your professional work, or in the context of your personal endeavors.

A central way through which we have modeled engaging in conversation *with* you through this textbook has been our use of multiple voices. Several times throughout the previous chapters we have discussed first-, second- and third-person positions (corresponding to use of I, you, and she/he/they) and the importance of drawing on multiple positions for understanding meaning. We have also modeled use of these multiple voices in order to draw attention to or make explicit taken-for-granted assumptions about relying on a third-person position in academic writing. Some of the ways through which we have done this include explicitly directing the "Musing Upon the Everyday" sections of each chapter toward you, our readers; drawing on an "I" or "we" position when discussing the narratives and conceptual interludes at the heart of each chapter; and bringing in a she/he/they perspective with research scenarios. In this way, each chapter has implicitly addressed our emphasis on multivocality and presented an alternative to the privileging of the third-person position in thinking about research.

In this last chapter, we want to be more explicit in our multivocal approach by modeling a dialogue among the four of us about research and about this text. We do this in the form of a dialogue around three key questions, presented in the form of two columns. All three of us have responded to these questions and to one another's responses in the first column. In the second column, we have drawn out some key ideas from the dialogue among ourselves as a way of reflecting explicitly on concepts that thread through this textbook. We also use this column to pose some questions for you, our readers—a symbolic space and a reminder that you are part of this conversation and that we want there to be a space for you as a contributor to, and not just a consumer of, these ideas about research.

We recognize that the format of the following pages may make them somewhat challenging to read. However, we wish to stay true to our intention of creating space for multiple voices and perspectives, particularly in this concluding chapter of the textbook. If you find this chapter visually challenging to take in, we encourage you to reflect on the reasons for this. For example, consider whether or how the discomfort may be related to what we take for granted in terms of how we understand what writing or text—especially academic writing or text—"should" look like: Does it have to be linear? If so, why might this be? In other words, what norms do we assume to be "true" when we accept that writing should occur in a certain way?

QUESTION 1

Share a Moment in Your Recent Life That Inspired/Motivated Your Research

Pengfei

An old, gray Nissan stopped by the curb. The driver rolled down the window and leaned toward me. "Are you Pe-ng-fii—?" I got into the second row of this car and briefly answered this stranger, whose name and face popped up when I requested a Lyft while visiting Florida.

We started to chat and he told me about the long journey that brought him to where he was: Years ago, he became interested in spiritual practice and traveled to India to pursue spirituality. Every day, he went to the temple to meditate. He traveled back and forth between the United States and India every year, but over time he started becoming very sick while he was in India. When he got older, the sickness became unbearable; he returned to the United States and settled down in Florida.

During our conversation, he told me, "After I started my spiritual practice, I felt my consciousness got better and better, but my body felt worse and worse." I asked him, "How do you feel about it?" He stopped and brooded over the question for several seconds. "I feel . . . I am still struggling with this . . . I perhaps should go back."

Several months have passed and the encounter with this driver still lingers in my mind. I have noticed, every time I think of this conversation, I revisit his silence. There is something special about it. At that moment, I was with him so profoundly. In fact, the more I thought about it, the more grateful I am to him, for he put so much trust in me that he was willing to share this vulnerable moment.

*Two of the key concepts that Pengfei highlights here are the salience of **relationships** in the research process, something we addressed all the way at the start of the textbook (in Chapter 2) and have continued to emphasize throughout, and the importance of **identity**—in this case the identity of Pengfei's driver. Pengfei's use of the phrase "mutual understanding" also draws out some key ideas about **intersubjectivity** and the importance of trust in communication—which is so central to the process of conducting research.*

There are many things about this moment that inspire me. Most important, it leads me to muse on what I have always been interested in, specifically, the dilemma of what is communicate-able and what is not, how we build up our trust and care toward each other, and how our mutual understanding starts with a commitment of being there with and for each other.

Peiwei

When I read Pengfei's story and reflection, I'm reminded of the simple profundity of communication: When two people open themselves up to each other with trust and care, we can tap into a deep interconnectedness. Perhaps this is the essence of intersubjectivity, a core concept threading through the textbook. It also illustrates my experience with a follow-up interview I recently conducted with a graduate student whom I got to know through a year-long ethnographic study. The intent of the interview was to gauge her experience and learning over time. I found myself deeply moved by how she came to understand other people and themselves on the plane of privilege and oppression with openness and honesty. At one moment, I asked her, "In all this learning, what does it mean for you?" She paused, her voice softened in her throat, tears slightly wet her eyes, and I could feel some emotions were coming up for her. Then she said, "Feels like fulfilment. And just . . . I don't know, I'm getting emotional about this. But just reaching my potential, I guess. Just doing what I'm supposed to be doing." In the moment, I felt very inspired by this young person who has committed to growth and deeper consciousness about herself and the world around her, and who is determined to interrogate what it means to be a white person and the nature of institutionalized whiteness.

*In this description of her interview, Peiwei notes a question she asked about the **meaning** of an experience as articulated by her participant. This is a concept we have explored throughout the textbook. In this example, we see how **meaning** is closely related to **identity**, in this case the identity claims of the participant as they relate to the experience of changes in her own understanding of her experiences. Peiwei's description of the changes in her participant's voice and her demeanor in response to being asked this question also is a reminder of how, in the context of discussing one's own sense of self, questions about **validity** (another key concept in the textbook) are addressed: specifically, through attempts to gauge the authenticity and honesty of the person with whom we speak. In this example, we can see how Peiwei's inspiration, drawn from her interaction with this student, is based in the authenticity of expression in that moment. This comes across in Peiwei's description of a sense of (possible) shared experience, which again illustrates the **intersubjective** nature of communication and, in a research context, of the data that are generated.*

I also felt a shared sense of freedom even though I can never be sure whether we were even close to experiencing the same thing. That experience has stayed with me ever since. Writing about it now reminds me that the essence of research at bottom has a relational foundation. Transformative potential is embedded in any research encounter.

Karen

So much is resonating for me in reading these two responses. I am particularly struck by Pengfei's comment about how special the *silences* of her driver were, and I find myself wondering, like her, what these silences meant and what they can communicate to us about who this man is. It reminds me of some interviews I did recently with men who are incarcerated, and how it felt to me that so much of what was important in the context of those interviews was not what was said, but the moments in which I felt there was a shared humanity between myself and the person with whom I was speaking. As Peiwei wrote, these were moments where sameness and differences were held simultaneously—so important in the context of the institutions where these men are incarcerated, where their humanity is stripped away every day. These moments are so grounding—a reminder, as for Pengfei and Peiwei, of the fundamental significance of relationships to research.

Barbara

One of the things that inspires my research is the act of silencing and the power of voice. A few years back I wrote a paper interpreting the failure of a secondary school principal to respond to my multiple attempts to meet with him in order to facilitate a conversation on making the school a safer, more robustly inclusive space for lesbian, gay, bisexual, trans, and queer youth. I took up his failure

*Karen's response to Peiwei and Pengfei further illustrates the salience of relationships to the research process. Another element of Karen's response, like Pengfei's, is a reaction to the notion of silence and the **meaning** of those silences. One thing we can take away from this is a reminder that meaning is more than what is easily observable, measurable, or translatable into text. From a research perspective, this means that what we can learn from any one approach to inquiry (for instance, focusing on what **is** part of the conversation, in terms of words stated) can only give us a partial understanding of what is experienced by our research participants in a holistic way.*

Pause and Reflect. At this point in time, what is your perspective about the relationship between meaning and what can (or cannot) be easily observed or expressed? When you think about how you "make meaning" of a given situation, what do you rely on to do so? What aspects of that meaning-making are based on what you can see or hear, and what aspects are not?

to respond as both a silence on his part—that is, a silence that I could interpret to mean things like "We don't need you here. Our school is fine." AND "I am not interested in what you have to say." AND/OR "We can't talk about this here." AND/OR "No making waves." However, his silence was also a silencing of me and the youth with whom I work. It had consequences because of his power to open or keep closed doors. He essentially cut off the opportunity for dialogue with others in the school.

This story turned into something quite positive—the youth I work with trained all the teachers in their school district at a professional development day—including that principal who had failed to respond. Together, we have been studying the learning engagements of youth educators who aim to equip schools with more positive learning cultures for their gender and sexual nonconforming students. These youth are empowered and empowering. The inquiry that is tightly nestled within their work has me working with them in ways that I could never have conjured up on my own. I am inspired to do research by these students, and by others who want to make the world a better place, who forge opportunities to share their voices and learn from being engaged in a dialogue, and who are willing do the hard work of self-reflection and advocacy.

Barbara's conjectures about the secondary school principal referenced here reiterate the significance of silence as a form of nonverbal communication that can be analyzed.

*Her comments are also an important reminder that there is always a fundamental uncertainty about our interpretations—something we have tried to emphasize throughout the textbook. To expand upon what we wrote about Karen's response to this question—in a research encounter (and in nonresearch contexts as well), even when we **do** take into account the meaning of what is not said, we can never claim to be certain that we fully understand another's perspective. As Barbara notes, the possible meanings she attributes to the principal's silence are just that—possible meanings, rather than definitive ones.*

QUESTION 2

How Does This Textbook Reflect the Value That You Place on Research?

Karen

Some of the key concepts that come to mind as I think about both this textbook and, more broadly, the values I place on social research include: collaborative, dialogic, iterative, nonlinear, and process/product. I think these concepts are encapsulated visually in Image 17.1, which we drew during one of the first retreats we held as part of the process of writing this textbook (June 2016).

IMAGE 17.1 ● Early Conceptualization of the Textbook

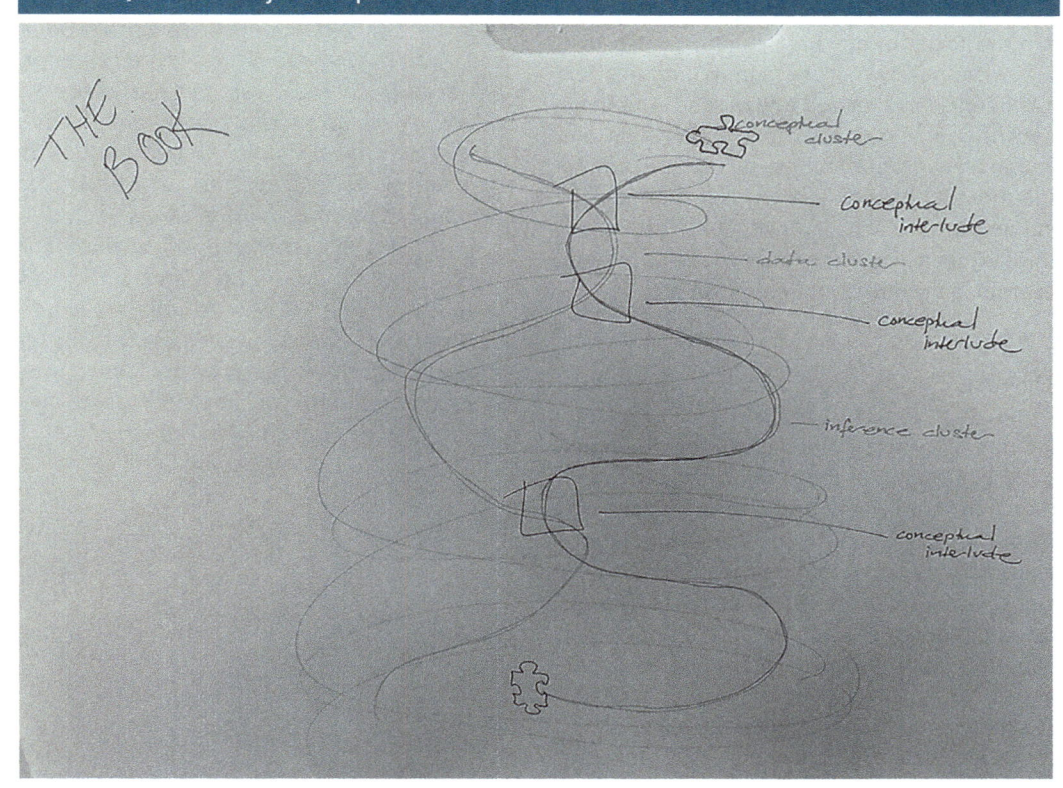

When we drew this image, the four of us were engaged in coming up with a way of conceptualizing the textbook. As we worked on teasing this out, this image became a centerpoint for us: a way of visually illustrating some of the themes that come through in this text. Now, as I look at this image, I see it as a way to illustrate multiple layers: the *form* of our textbook, the *substance* of our textbook, and how both of these reflect our own values or commitments to the research process.

For instance, I think about how in their intersections with one another, these three sets of lines represent parts of the research process that progress in dialogue. Data and inference occur simultaneously, each moving on their own, but they connect and shape one another in tandem with broader concepts (ethics, relationships, identity, epistemology, etc.) that are the focus of our first cluster in this text. Likewise, our own process in writing this text has been characterized by dialogue. And I connect this dialogue also to collaboration and collaborative approaches, which are among the most foundational of my commitments to inquiry, and which are reflected throughout this textbook in terms of our process and in the examples we have highlighted substantively.

Barbara

The dialogue is deepened and broadened when the implicit aspects are explicitly included. For example, we can locate underlying assumptions that might have lain dormant in our work and conversation, but through questioning we articulate these assumptions and examine them. This is crucial to a reflective research practice as well. Another aspect of dialogue that has been part of our textbook writing process and is important to research is the space and permission to disagree without penalty. Disagreements require an orientation toward understanding; otherwise it is easy to resolve disagreements in unequitable ways—even without intending to do this. For example, it might be easy for

*One of the ideas that comes up in our conversation here is the importance of explicitly creating **a space for dialogue** to occur. In different ways throughout the previous chapters, we have emphasized this idea of dialogue as central to the way that we four, as researchers, understand the purposes of research as well as the ways we try to approach relationship-building with our research participants. But Barbara's point here, about the space for disagreement, also speaks to the need for the research community itself to be a space that is open to differing views. This is something that is important to reflect upon in relation to, for example, **academic writing** as discussed in Chapter 15, and **dissemination of findings/broader issues of impact and policy** as discussed in Chapter 16. An idea we would like to re-emphasize is the importance of research findings and write-ups as themselves part of a conversation that is always open to new and different perspectives.*

us to let the voice of "most experience" sway the outcomes of disagreements. This would not foster a deeper understanding or open a space for new ideas. Our disagreements were always conversations that pushed our thinking and allowed new ideas to emerge collaboratively. The same can happen in research, when dialogues do not easily foreclose on agreements.

Pengfei

Like Barbara, writing the textbook for me is a process of making explicit what is implicit. What was not entirely clear to me initially but has become increasingly explicit is the close connection between research and everyday life. Writing the textbook has allowed us to unpack the multilayered connection between the two, for example, by using examples from our everyday life to demonstrate how insights from the daily life can be transferred to the research domain. More important, research is both constrained and shaped by our practice in other social domains (policy, administration, social activism, etc.) and needs to find its way to circle back to our civic, professional, and everyday life. In general, I found that I see a lot of values from research that feel the pulse of time, develop an intimate relationship between theoretical innovation and the needs of the world, and eventually help us envision and create a better future.

Peiwei

I resonate with the idea that research is a process that is not separate from the world we live in or from the researcher. We engage in this process in the company of others, and through dialogues and reflection our implicit and intuitive understanding becomes enriched, sometimes crystallized and sometimes transformed.

The values of grounding research in praxis, reflection, dialogue, and relationship go back to the very beginnings of writing this book, as

An additional idea that is articulated explicitly in Peiwei and Pengfei's responses is the notion of **research as action**, *and that is shaped by and shapes our personal, professional, social, and civic lives. This idea has indeed been at the core of every chapter of this textbook in our emphasis on the relationship between everyday experiences and the "formal" research context. It is also an important idea to hold on to, we believe, in the context of thinking of research as a collective, collaborative endeavor that each one of us comes to with different kinds of expertise.*

Pause and Reflect. The responses in this section raise the question of what collaboration can, or should, look like. Can you picture yourself engaging in collaborative research, or is this something with which you have had experience? What kind of dynamics did you experience or would you like to see in collaborative research? How (if at all) does this differ for you from collaborations in other contexts?

IMAGE 17.2 ● Guiding Values of This Textbook

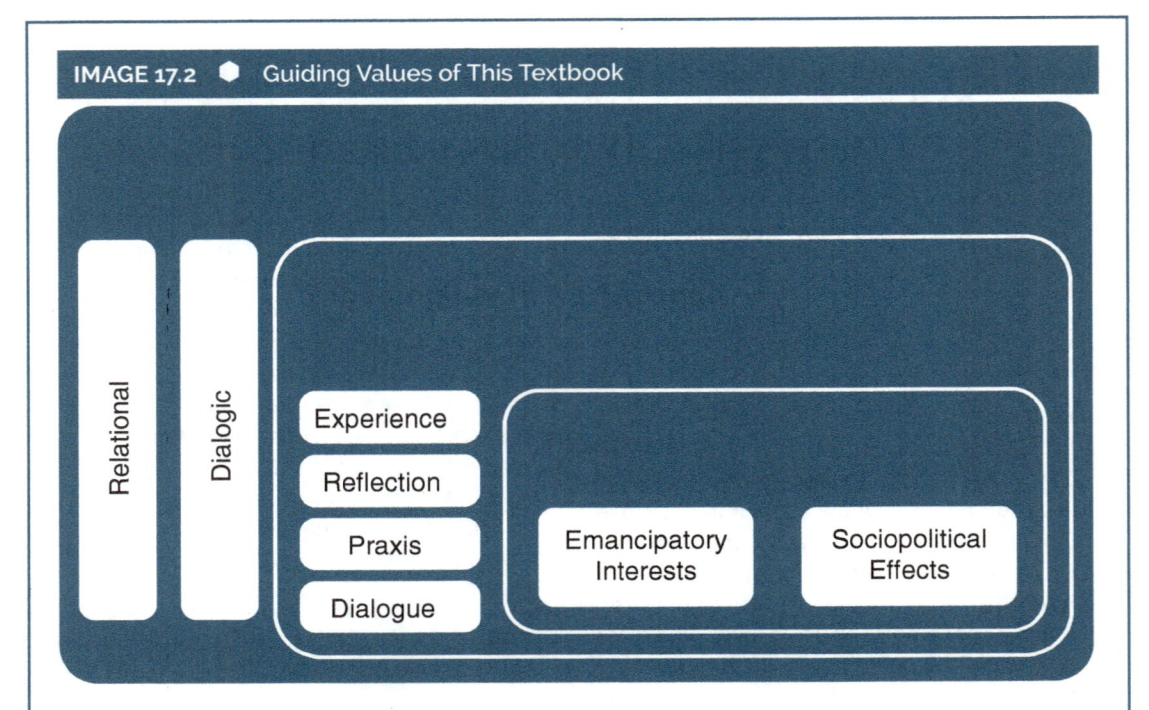

- Relational
- Dialogic
  - Experience
  - Reflection
  - Praxis
  - Dialogue
  - Emancipatory Interests
  - Sociopolitical Effects

in Image 17.2, which was featured in our book proposal. The values informed how we developed the structure and content of this book, and they also guide our teaching practices and our engagement with one another in our writing process. We do not always succeed in putting them into practice, but they help us recognize when we fall short and to find ways of re-engaging in ways that better honor our intentions.

Sadly, those values often find themselves at odds with an academic culture that rewards individual achievement, efficiency, and productivity, which are largely defined *externally* in numbers and matrix. However, the practice of praxis, relationship, dialogue, and reflection serves the best antidote to this culture and what philosopher Jürgen Habermas calls the colonization of the lifeworld by the system. The creation of this textbook is a way to hold space for us—and our readers—to imagine other ways to understand and engage in research that fosters wholeness and creativity.

Peiwei's comment about concepts being defined **externally** *brings up issues we have visited several times throughout the chapters of this textbook: measurement and standardization. In her comment here, Peiwei connects the concept of standardized/universal measurement indicators to the broader values that shape this methodological approach. In this way, Peiwei's comment is also a reminder that there is no approach to research that is "value free" or "value neutral." Whatever approaches to research or practice you resonate with most strongly, we encourage you to think about the underlying* **epistemological commitments and values** *within which these approaches make sense.*

QUESTION 3

Based on Our Conceptual Framing and Values, How Do You Approach (or Understand) the Process of Doing Research?

Peiwei

I briefly shared in Chapter 1 that I was a chemistry major as an undergraduate student and continued to pursue doctoral training in biochemistry for a few years. Leaving science behind and embarking on a new path to become a psychotherapist and a qualitative researcher has forged new horizons in my understanding. As I started to reflect on once taken-for-granted knowledge and its framing, I realized that implicit assumptions and stances have been packed into what appeared to be a "neutral" and indifferent scientific attitude. Over time I also grasped how knowledge is always produced in relational and communicative contexts, and often shaped by power structures that condition what is considered legitimate knowledge. To be a conscious researcher I need to ask critical questions about research itself (e.g., research for what, by whom, and who will benefit?) and about my role. This requires never-ending self-reflection to expand on my awareness of complexity, relational dynamics with others and with myself, as well as the connection between specific research context and larger structural issues. And no less important: my openness and humility to possible fallacy due to my blind spots and limited horizons of understanding at a given time, which will always be the case.

Today, research to me is a process of engaging with others relationally and collaboratively to address social issues that impact people who are more vulnerable. Research has a deeper meaning fused with the pursuit of freedom and inclusivity for all. These

*Peiwei raises a critical point here that highlights something we have tried to address throughout this text: the need to ask critical questions not only about what our data "mean," but more broadly about **how** we go about research, **what** the implications of our approach are (for our participants, for us, for policy, for practice), and **who** benefits or is disadvantaged in the process. Raising these critical questions leads us to a place of foregrounding relationships, ethics, and epistemological commitments as part of research: something that we do explicitly in this book by addressing these issues as **foundational** to the process of inquiry. Also important to note here is the fact that asking critical questions is a way of stepping back from taken-for-granted assumptions about our culture(s) and cultural norms. As we noted when discussing legitimate knowledge in Chapter 3, norms about how to do research are contextual. And as Peiwei notes, fallacy or misunderstanding due to cultural limitations requires us to remain open to other contexts and ways of understanding the world.*

Pause and Reflect. Throughout the textbook, we have been explicit about our own epistemological orientation. However, we recognize that this orientation is not universally shared, and we encourage readers to spend some time reflecting on their own priorities and commitments as they relate to research—whether in the academic, professional, or personal realm. Over the course of this textbook, what understandings have you come to about your own priorities? What commitments do you feel you hold as primary in the research process?

assumptions and commitments propel me to approach research in more ethnographic and participatory-oriented ways, and to facilitate a more democratic and equitable context for all who are involved in a research process with me. To this end, I experience a strong impetus to learn and incorporate participatory action research and elements of creative expression in the research process. This has become my current yearning as my being continuously becomes anew as a researcher.

Pengfei

I resonate with what Peiwei wrote above about research as an ethical, relational, and democratic engagement with others. Peiwei has also articulated beautifully how the research process, viewed from a longer span of time in an individual's personal history, can be understood as a journey of self-cultivation and self-realization. When I read her paragraphs, I found myself connecting personal histories with the larger history of our time. I cannot help but ask: What kind of research do we need in this day and time? Admittedly, this is a question impossible to answer within a few paragraphs, but this question brings me back to the thought that we need to move away from a canonical approach to research. If research is our response to an ever-changing world, then eventually, what matters most is our vision of what we would like to bring forward to the world through our research. By this, I am not suggesting abandoning the canons of social science research, but trying to put into words how research is a way to embed me and maybe us in this world. Canons, methods, and procedures matter in the sense that they provide us inspirations, food for thought, and suggested routes, but ultimately, we all need to navigate our own journeys.

*In her response to Peiwei, Pengfei's emphasis on the **journey** of doing and approaching research connects with the importance of questioning why we engage in social science inquiry. It also is a salient reminder of the personal journey we all take in developing our own understandings of both the technical aspects of research and reflecting on our answer to the question of why (and how) we engage. As we approach the last few pages of this text, we encourage you to reflect on what you have taken from your journey with us so far—and we encourage you to continue your journey through and with social science research.*

Barbara

This approach has raised for me something new about the ways in which methods and canons can foreclose on deep listening and understanding. I have discovered, in quite personal ways, how it is that standardizing a canon and set of methods limits our openness as persons to one another and to the research process itself, including its vulnerabilities and errors. Through this collaborative effort, I have learned to open up to new methodological challenges, even critiquing my own previously published ideas. Previously I have done most of my writing work alone, albeit much of my research has been inclusive and collaborative. Writing together has surfaced new ways of being in research that are critical. For example, reading the words of my colleagues has brought tears to my eyes as their words both challenge and heighten my own experiences.

Karen

Thinking about this question and the responses my colleagues have written brings me back to the start of the textbook writing process, and what I wrote in Chapter 1 about shifts along the way in my conceptions of research. As this writing process draws to a close, what is clearest for me now is a view of research as a process oriented toward understanding—like Barbara, the collaborative effort has been a big part of that. Something has shifted for me over the past 2 years as we have found different ways to connect and write this text, and have challenged each other to think through taken-for-granted elements of research. The integration of the process and the product (this book) has been so tight, and that integration has really become foregrounded for me as central to research.

Karen's and Barbara's contributions to this dialogue illustrate another concept that has permeated this text: the importance of learning **with** *and* **from** *others. This is connected to concepts we raised in Chapters 2, 3, 5, and 7 about relationships and identity, as well as thinking about research from the perspective of intersubjectivity, rather than understanding research based on a subject–object orientation.*

The references to dialogue and collaboration also are emblematic of the approach to understanding **validity** *we emphasize in this text, which foregrounds a process of openness, dialogue, and questioning rather than fixed notions of "truth."*

Our own understandings of research have been shaped, not only by years of engaging in the inquiry process, but also—and perhaps especially—by working together to produce this textbook. But these understandings are never complete and are constantly shifting as we are exposed to new ideas, practices, and relationships. We would love to learn from you how you view the process of research and what ideas you have about pushing the field of social science research methodology—as it applies in professional and academic contexts—forward in different ways.

Here, we conclude our textbook and with it, our dialogue with you, our readers. As we wrap up, we want to thank you for being part of the conversation throughout this textbook, and we hope that some of the ideas we have raised in this and in the previous chapters will inspire you to continue engaging in thoughtful, relationally focused research. As you move forward as researchers in your professional, personal, and academic lives, we encourage you to surround yourselves with a community: people with whom you can dialogue about decisions you make, challenges you encounter, and of course the high points you inevitably will experience as part of the process! We wish you all the best.

# APPENDIX A

STATISTICAL TESTS USED TO ESTABLISH CAUSAL INFERENCES

With statistical tests there will be a difference between when it is appropriate to use parametric or nonparametric tests.

TABLE A.1 ◆ Comparing Parametric and Nonparametric Tests

Parametric Tests	Nonparametric Tests
Assume a normal distribution of the variable(s) in the population	Do not assume a normal distribution of the variable(s) in the population
Should be used with ratio or interval data	Can be used with categorical and ordinal data, as well as ratio and interval data
Are more precise	Are less precise

t-test

This is a parametric test that is used when you want to compare *mean scores* of two groups in a randomized experimental design, specifically the post-test mean results. The *t*-test measures whether there is a *statistically significant* difference between the results of a treatment and control group.

Variables: One independent, one dependent, both continuous.

Assumptions: Normal population, values are sampled independently, populations being sampled have the same variance.

Test statistic = t (t value).

When reading the results of a *t*-test, you will want to look for the degrees of freedom (that sum of N − 1, for each group), the mean, and the standard deviation.

Example: A school conducted nonviolence training with its seniors. This table indicates a before and after comparison of 15 people who take a before and after test of school violence indicators. The score on indicators goes down after nonviolence training.

TABLE A.2 ● Making Sense of *t*-Tests

Variable	Number of Cases	Mean	Standard Deviation	SE of Mean	Degrees of Freedom *df*	*t*
Before	15	207.9333	28.56188			
After	15	197	24.39262			
Difference	15	10.93333	6.329824	1.634353	14	6.6897*

Confidence Interval at 95%

Lower: 7.427994

Upper: 14.43867

Alpha = .05

*Significant at .05 level

To read the table you want to pay attention to the *t* value and whether or not it is significant and at what level. This particular difference is significant at the 0.05 level. The 0.05 level means that with 95% confidence the outcome was not determined by chance. We can see that the mean value of the difference (10.93333) falls within the confidence interval of 7.427994 and 14.43867.

ANOVA (Analysis of Variance)

This is a parametric statistic used when you want to compare two or more means. The analysis focuses on whether there is statistically significant *variance* between the means being compared (hence, analysis of *variance*). An ANOVA is called a one-way ANOVA when there is a single independent variable; it is a two-way ANOVA when the effect of two independent variables on a dependent variable is being measured. An ANOVA test can be used to measure variance in means *between groups* (called a between-subjects variable), or variance in means *within* a group (e.g., testing different conditions within a group, such as differences in dosage levels for the same set of patients—this is called a within-subjects variable or a repeated-measures variable).

Assumptions: Normal population, values are sampled independently (for a between-subjects design), populations being sampled have the same variance.

Variable Types: One or more independent, one dependent, independent can be categorical, dependent must be continuous.

Test statistic = F

Example: Let's say that a researcher is interested in how well people learn nonviolent attitudes across three different scenarios: (1) nonviolence training, (2) empathy training, and (3) no training. We want to compare the learning of attitudes (scores on a test) across the three groups to see if there is a difference and if that difference is attributable to the direct nonviolent training. When we read Table A.3, we can see that the mean (or average) differences across the three groups is much larger than the mean (or average) differences within each of the groups. The differences across the three groups is statistically significant.

TABLE A.3 ● Making Sense of ANOVA

Source	Df (degrees of freedom)	SS (sum of the squares)	MS (mean squares or average of the squares)	F statistic	P value
Treatment (sometimes labeled "between" because it is examining differences between the groups)	2 (because there are 3 groups and DF would equal N − 1 or 3 − 1)	2510.5	1255.3	93.44	0.000
Error (sometimes labeled "within" because it looks for differences within each group under the assumption that the groups should be relatively homogeneous)	12 (because there are 13 subjects in each of the 3 groups, so N − 1 or 13 − 1 = 12)	161.2	13.4		
Total	14	2671.7			

The p value is $P(F(2,12) \geq 93.44) < 0.001$

Wilcoxon Signed-Rank Test

The Wilcoxon signed-rank test is a nonparametric test that examines *paired differences*, similar to the T-test, used to compare whether means in a population differ for a *dependent* variable of interest—for instance, it might evaluate data from a quasi-experimental study that looks at differences in reading ability of students before and after receiving a specific kind of instruction. Unlike the T-test, it is used when distributions of differences for the samples cannot be assumed to follow a normal distribution.

Assumptions: Data are paired (either as matched samples or repeated measures on a single sample—e.g., students *before* and *after* receiving instruction in a specific reading approach), data are measured on a ranked or ordinal (categorical) scale, the distribution across the two groups needs to be symmetrical (or related).

Variables: Two categorical independent variables from related or matched groups, one dependent variable measured at the ordinal or continuous level.

Test statistic = W

Mann-Whitney U Test

The Mann-Whitney U Test is another nonparametric *paired difference* test, similar to the T-test, used to compare whether means in a population differ for an *independent* variable of interest. Unlike the T-test, it is used when distributions of differences for the samples cannot be assumed to follow a normal distribution.

Assumptions: Non-normal distribution, independence of groups being compared.

Variables: One independent, one dependent, independent can be categorical, dependent must be continuous.

Test statistic = U

Pearson Chi-Square

This popular nonparametric test is particularly useful with categorical data to establish causal inferences. It is often used to establish that two variables are independent of one another or how likely it is that a difference we find in the data is the result of chance.

Assumptions: Non-normal distribution, variables assumed to function independent of one another.

Variables: One independent and one dependent variable, both categorical.

Test statistic = X^2

Example: Let's say we are looking at categories of students and comparing those categories with the prevalence of saying positive things to peers (yes or no) during the Tone of Decency Campaign (see Chapter 14). We will use the Pearson Chi-Square statistic to see if there are any differences between the categories.

TABLE A.4 Understanding Pearson's Chi-Square						
Says positive things to peers		Athletes	Musicians	Nerds	Other	Total
Yes	Count	8	6	6	6	26
	Expected Count	6.2	7.3	6.8	5.7	26.0
	Residual	1.8	−1.3	−.8	0.3	
No	Count	4	8	7	5	24
	Expected Count	5.8	6.7	6.2	5.3	24.0
	Residual	−1.8	1.3	0.8	−.3	
Total	Count	12	14	13	11	50
	Expected Count	12.0	14.0	13.0	11.0	50

Note: Pearson Chi-Square Value = 1.710, *df* = 3, Asymptotic Sig (2-sided) = .635 (*p* value).

APPENDIX B

STATISTICAL TESTS USED TO ESTABLISH CORRELATIONAL INFERENCES

There are parametric and nonparametric tests to test for correlations. In this appendix we present one of each.

Pearson Product Moment Correlation (for linear relationships), Spearman's Rank Correlation Coefficient

The Pearson Product Moment Correlation is the most common parametric test for looking at relations between two variables. This statistic can tell us both the strength and the direction of the relationship. The Pearson Product Moment Correlation generates a coefficient between 0 and 1 or −1 and 0. The closer the value is to 1[−1], the stronger the correlation. In social sciences, generally researchers expect the coefficient to be over +/−.7 to be considered strong enough to report.

Assumptions: That the two variables are independent of one another, that their distribution in the population follows a normal curve.

Variables: Two continuous or ordinal variables.

Statistic: r

TABLE B.1 Positive Correlation

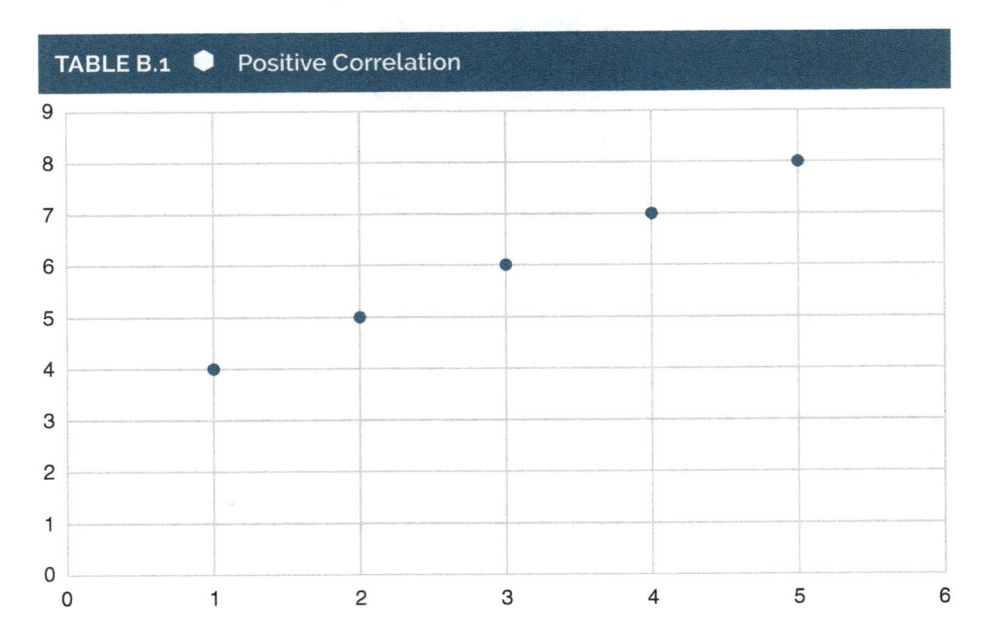

x	y
1	4
2	5
3	6
4	7
5	8

In Table B.1, we can imagine two variables, let's say "wellness" and "exercise": as one increases the other, also, increases.

TABLE B.2 Pearson Product Moment Correlation

	Self-Esteem	Positive Self-Talk	Care for Others	Happiness
Self-Esteem	-			
Positive Self-Talk	.742***	-		
Care for Others	.949***	.530***	-	
Happiness	.336***	.189**	.332***	-

Table B.2 reports on Pearson Product Moment Correlations. One can see that all of the correlations are reported in the positive direction. The dashes mark spaces on the Table where we would not test a correlation since it is with the same variable. Three asterisks mark that the correlation is statistically significant at the .001 level.

Spearman Rank Order Correlation

This is a nonparametric test that examines correlations using the concept of rank. Researchers will rank the data across the two or more variables and then look to see if they are related. Let's say subjects took tests of their levels of happiness and then second took tests of their helping behavior. Their scores would be ranked from highest to lowest. Then the ranks in each variable would be correlated. The coefficient produced will range between 0 and 1, either positive or negative.

Assumptions: The variables must be independent. No assumption that they are distributed normally in the population.

Variables: Two or more continuous or ordinal variables

Statistic: r

TABLE B.3 ● Spearman Rank-Order Correlation

	Happiness	Helping Behavior
Happiness	1	.669**
Helping Behavior	.669**	1

** Indicates at the .05 level.

Chi-Square

Chi-square examines relationships across two variables using a nonparametric approach.

Assumptions: Does not assume the variables are normally distributed in the population. Assumes the variables are independent of one another.

Variables: Two categorical variables.

Statistic: X^2

Example: Look at the results of examining college degree (as either obtained or not obtained) and dog ownership (as yes or no) among 25–30-year-olds using a chi-square. There were 300 people, and given the U.S. population is 37% we would expect that the value of college completion would be 37 yes and 63 no. Thirty-eight percent of U.S. households own dogs. We don't have rates specific to the age group of study, so we will use this to set our expected rates at 38 for yes and 62 for no.

TABLE B.4 — Chi-Square

	Dog Owners	Not Dog Owners	Total
College Degree	44	68	112 *(111)*
Expected Value	42.18	68.82	
No College Degree	163	25	188 *(189)*
Expected Value	71.82	117.18	
Total	207 *(114)*	93 *(186)*	300

The X^2 college degree dog owners is 46.01, which is not too far off the expected value, but the X^2 for noncollege degree non–dog owners is 72.51, which is fairly different from the expected value.

APPENDIX C

GETTING CLARITY ABOUT THE VISION OF YOUR PROJECT

Step 1: What is the phenomenon or topic that you are interested in studying and understanding more?

I. Delineating a broad research topic:

The topic of my proposed research project is:

_____
_____
_____
_____

I am interested in:

_____
_____
_____
_____

Step 2: A moment of self-reflexivity:

My interest stems from:

_____
_____
_____

I anticipate these of my previous experiences may impact my involvement in this project in several possible ways:

_____
_____
_____

The following onto-epistemological commitments of mine will possibly inform my research in this study:

_____
_____
_____

The following ethical commitments of mine will possibly inform my research in this study:

_____
_____
_____

Step 3: Specify your research purpose statement:

I. Zooming into one or a few research problem(s):

Within this broad research topic that I am interested in, one of several problems are particularly worth exploration. They are:

_____
_____
_____
_____

The reasons that these problems are worthy of more exploration are:

_____
_____
_____
_____

II. Articulating your research purposes:

I hope this study can:

_____
_____
_____
_____

III: Narrowing down the research questions:

What could be a few research questions related to your topic/interest that you would be interested in asking and exploring? Jot down a few below:

1. _____
   _____
2. _____
   _____
3. _____
   _____
4. _____
   _____

Step 4: Brainstorm a working draft of your proposal abstract and synthesize some key information of your proposed study *into one short paragraph*—imagine you are writing to a friend of yours about your preliminary ideas about this project.

_____
_____
_____
_____

APPENDIX D

A GENERIC RUBRIC FOR EVALUATING EMPIRICAL RESEARCH ARTICLES

Title of the article:

Citation:

This rubric is divided into two sections: The first section helps readers identify an empirical article's methodological approach and key information pertinent to understanding the quality of a study; the second section leads readers to explore the interconnections among different parts of an article/a study, the rationale and inferences made by the authors, the limitations and impact of the study, and the relevance of the study to the reader's research and/or professional practice.

Moving from Section One to Section Two demonstrates a growing understanding of an article, that is, that the reader is not only making sense of what is presented in an article in a literal manner but also grappling with the strengths and limitations of the study. Eventually, an important goal of reading an empirical research article is to be able to see in what sense a reader's research and/or professional practice may or may not be informed by the study.

Section One: Identifying Key Information

TABLE D.1 — Identifying Key Information in an Empirical Research Article

Components of an empirical article	Guiding questions	Your notes
Research topics and questions	What general topics and issues is the researcher concerned about? What are the more focused research questions that the researcher addresses? Has the researcher provided any information to discuss why this given topic and questions were chosen? For quantitative studies, what are the research hypotheses tested by the researcher?	
Theoretical frameworks or perspectives	What theoretical framework or perspective is employed in the study and what are the key tenets of this framework or perspective? Does the researcher provide any rationale to justify their choice?	
Literature review	What key concepts, themes, and/or constructs does the researcher use to organize the literature review? What criteria does the researcher use to include/exclude existing literature? In what ways is the review of existing literature integrated into the study being reported?	
Methodology and data generation and acquisition	Is there an onto-epistemological orientation explicitly employed to inform the study? If so, what is it? What are the methodological approach and research design of the study? Are there any sampling strategies involved, and if so, what are they? Who are the research participants, and what is the site? Are there any instruments used and if so, what are they? What activities are involved in generating and/or acquiring data? How many types of data are generated and/or acquired and how large is the dataset?	

Ethics	Does the study comply with the institutional standard of ethical research?	
	Has the study taken prudent measures to protect the privacy of the participants and the confidentiality of the data?	
Data interpretation and analysis	What analytic approaches are employed in interpreting and analyzing the data?	
	Do we know the process through which the analysis is conducted? If so, what is the process?	
	What methods and techniques are reported to enhance the validity of the study?	
Implications of the findings	Does the researcher reflect upon the limitations and future directions of the study? If so, what are they?	
	Does the researcher address the implications of the study on the societies (professional practice, policy-making, etc.)? If so, what are they?	

Section Two: Exploring Assumptions and Evaluating Quality

Purposes, Assumptions, and Perspectives of the Study

- What key claims about the researcher's identity and positionality are foregrounded or can be reconstructed from the article?

- What implicit assumptions or motivations does the researcher bring into the research as they position themselves in the way discussed above?

- To what degree does the study achieve its purposes and goals?

Ethics

- What are the potential risks and benefits for participants who have taken part in the study?

- In interacting with the participants, presenting their lived experience, and attending to their unique cultural backgrounds, what efforts has the researcher made to build the researcher–participant relationship to ensure it is egalitarian, respectful, and trustworthy?

- How may the transferring or generalization of the research findings negatively or positively influence the social groups or communities that share similar characteristics with the participants?

Onto-Epistemological Orientation

- To what degree does the researcher actively reflect on their onto-epistemological commitments?
- How coherently is the researcher's onto-epistemological orientation connected with their conceptualization of validity, the choice of the methodology, the interpretation and analysis of the data, and the discussion of the findings and limitations?

Inferences

- How strong is the rationale that the researcher offers to justify the need and significance of the study and their methodological decisions?
- In what sense does the researcher critically examine the implications of the study's sampling strategy in relation to the generalizability and transferability of the findings?
- How soundly and sufficiently does the researcher make their low-level inferences?
- How convincing is the connection made between low-level and high-level inferences?
- Does the writing of the study convey the inference and the process of the study well?

Impact and Relevance

- What impact might the study produce at the individual, group, and/or societal levels?
- Have you learned anything from the study? If so, what have you learned and what findings are transferrable to your research and professional contexts?

GLOSSARY OF TERMS

Accessible population: The accessible population is the segment of the target population that is accessible to researchers. Members of a target population may not all be accessible to recruit for participation (due to time, money, or other logistical constraints).

Action: An action is similar to *behavior* in the sense that *action* involves doing something, but it also emphasizes the intention or motivation of the person who carries out the action. Action may not always be visible (e.g., thinking, reflection, and other active forms of being).

Action research: Action research is a form of inquiry that is oriented toward explicitly and immediately addressing concrete problems. In contrast with some forms of research that are primarily focused on adding to the body of knowledge about some topic, action research projects aim to *use* that knowledge in an immediate and practical way.

Agency: Agency refers to the degree to which a social actor can act independently and freely within a given social condition.

Alternative hypothesis, or Research hypothesis: The research or alternative hypothesis is a statement of the outcomes of difference or relationship across variables that the researcher expects. If the null hypothesis is rejected, then this means we can often accept the research or alternative hypothesis. However, sometimes researchers will reject both.

Archival data: Archival data consist of materials that may not have been originally generated for research purposes, but that are compiled and used to answer empirical research questions.

Author–reader relationship: In a research setting, the author–reader relationship refers to the communication between the reader of a research-related text and its author(s) primarily mediated through the text. Sometimes, the author–reader relationship in academia is institutionalized, such as when student's dissertation committee is expected to read their dissertation. Conducting social research often involves navigating several relationships including the author–reader relationship.

Authorial voice: In an academic setting, authorial voice refers to a combination of different factors that influence the delivery of the study discussed in a text. Typically, it includes the structure of a text, the writer's positionality, the use of rhetoric techniques, and the choice of words.

Behavior: Often understood as an occurrence and tendency of an individual capable of doing something that takes place in a given time and space, and thus is associated with the quality of being observable, measurable, and manipulatable. Behavior is tied to the notion of "individual."

Bias/Biased: There are controversies about the meaning of bias in social science research. We conceptualize bias as a mistake in interpretation or a misunderstanding of data. Bias can be the result of a mismatch between the sample and population or between the interpretation of a score and the meaning of the phenomena tested.

Categorical variables: Categorical variables are variables that measure a characteristic with no inherent numerical properties, such as gender. These include both nominal variables that have no rank order, and ordinal variables, which can be ranked.

Causal: Causal inference refers to the process of drawing the conclusion that there is a causal connection between two variables—that is, that manipulation or change in one or more independent variables is the cause of change in a dependent variable of interest.

Coding: Coding is a part of the analytical process that entails assignment categories or short-hand referents (codes) to portions of textual or visual data.

Cognitive interview: A cognitive interview is a special kind of structured interview that is used to assess how individuals understand the meaning of survey questions when they are worded in certain ways, and to understand the reasons for the option(s) individuals choose when responding to closed-ended survey items. Cognitive interviews are used so that researchers can ensure that their items capture the constructs their survey or other data collection instrument addresses.

Communicativeness: Communicativeness refers to the interpersonal and intersubjective aspects of data generation and acquisition with dialogue as the ideal image.

Confidence interval: The confidence interval refers to the range within which we are confident that the true value for a population parameter exists.

Confidence level: Confidence levels are a way of describing the percentage of the time that we are relatively sure that the identified confidence interval contains the actual value of a population parameter.

Construct: A construct is a specific attribute that is being measured through a data collection instrument. Because constructs in the social sciences generally are internal and thus not able to be measured directly, data collection instruments often include multiple items that are used to indirectly get at the construct in question.

Construct validity: This form of validity is concerned that items in a scale accurately measure the concept of interest.

Content analysis: Content analysis is a technique for systematically analyzing textual data through the patterns and/or quantities of words, concepts, or themes related to a research question of interest.

Continuous variables are variables measuring a characteristic with inherent numerical properties that can be placed on a continuum. Generally speaking continuous variables are contrasted with categorical variables. There are two types of continuous variables: ratio and interval.

Control variable: A control variable is a variable that is "controlled for," or kept constant. Control variables are variables that researchers think might affect the dependent variable but are not the primary variables of interest in the study. In social science research, control variables are often demographic variables (age, ethnicity, race, gender, etc.).

Correlation/Correlational studies: Research that attempts to establish if and to what extent (strength or direction) two or more variables might relate with one another. Generally, correlational studies do not indicate causation.

Correspondence theory of meaning: This theory of meaning suggests that there is a direct, one-to-one correspondence between a symbol and its meaning.

Correspondence theory of truth: A particular theory of truth that considers knowing as making an assertion about an existing state of affairs by taking an external and disinterested position to observe and measure that state of affairs. The truthfulness of knowledge claims can be judged by the accuracy and completeness of how well the assertion represents the state of affairs under study. Thus, there is a one-on-one correspondence between a truth claim and a state of affairs.

Criticalism: While the epistemological stance referred to as critical or criticalism is defined in various ways, it has some common aspects. First and foremost is the idea of not taking knowledge and truth for granted—that is, being willing to call into question any underlying assumptions on which one's knowledge might rest.

Critical participatory action research: Through this research design the line between researchers and subjects/participants is blurred. Designs emphasize democratic values, participation, and relevancy for the communities involved. It is a flexible design approach to research.

Critical pragmatism: This theoretical perspective, associated with the work of Jürgen Habermas and Robert Brandom, assumes that knowledge is a matter of social action through which meaning is mediated by language use and context. It is "critical" in the sense that it always seeks to examine the normative aspects of actions and communication, and to interrogate power relationships in our social life. Critical pragmatists examine the use of language in communicative actions and in the context of actors' intention and commitment. The approach considers knowing is essentially tied with doing.

Cultural typification: Cultural typification is the competency to tacitly recognize a generality typical of a culture. This tacit recognition also involves being able to take multiple positions all at once.

Culture: Culture refers to patterned practice through which norms and values are formulated and enacted.

Data: In everyday language, the term *data*—the plural form of *datum*—refers to the information that researchers collect in order to examine their research questions. Critically engaging with this term, we argue that there are no ready-made data for researchers to collect, but what is more critical is to look at how data are constructed in research processes.

Data acquisition: The phrase *data acquisition* is used to indicate 'the process of transforming/using pre-existing data for a new study.

Data saturation: Data saturation refers to a situation where few or no additional insights about important themes relevant to a research study will be gained by generating additional data. The concept of data saturation is related to the quality (not quantity) of data generated.

Deduction: Deduction refers to a process through which we infer the truth of specific conclusions from assuming the truth of more general premises.

Dependent variable: A dependent variable is a variable that is being tested to see whether it changes due to change or manipulation in another (independent) variable, or more than one independent variable.

Descriptive statistics: Descriptive statistics are analyses that provide summaries of patterns in data collected from a given sample.

Dialogic theory of truth: A theory of truth. It considers that the ultimate ground for truth rests on the effort of consensus formation among people through dialogue. People use sound reasons and persuasion to win mutual understanding and consensus from one another.

Epistemic violence: Epistemic violence describes a situation when the interpretation of research findings in the name of "knowledge" and "science" ends up creating or perpetuating inferiority of certain social groups. This happens when alternative explanations are available but excluded as illegitimate. In this way, research leads to a unique form of harm and violence. *See also* **Epistemological violence**.

Epistemological violence: Epistemological violence describes a situation when the interpretation of research findings in the name of "knowledge" and "science" ends up creating or perpetuating inferiority of certain social groups. This happens when alternative explanations are available but excluded as illegitimate. In this way, research leads to a unique form of harm and violence.

Epistemology: *Epistemology* is the root word philosophers and social scientists use to talk about assumptions regarding knowledge and knowing. These assumptions will always be embedded in how a person thinks of research because research engages knowledge. Epistemology can be considered a theory about knowing and knowledge: How do we know what we know? What is the nature of knowledge? What are limitations of knowing and knowledge?

Ethnography: A field-based study of a group of people that engages researchers in participating in, observing, and otherwise gathering information about the norms, culture, practices, routines, rituals, language, and so on of a group of people. Ethnography is a flexible design approach to research.

Experiment: An experiment is a form of data generation that tests whether a change in a single (dependent) variable is caused by change in a dependent variable (or multiple dependent variables).

Experimental design: This is a form of research design that seeks to control enough of the context of the study so as to be able to gather data that can identify whether change can be attributed to a particular cause. Many of us were introduced to this design as the scientific method. Experimental designs are fixed design approaches to research.

Explanation: Explanation, as a mode of inquiry, primarily positions the researcher as a neutral third person external to the research phenomenon, who derives descriptive, correlational, or causal inferences based on systematic observations and measurements.

Fallibility: Fallibility in research involves acknowledging the potential risk that we are wrong in what we are claiming. This fallibility is linked to openness in the research process because when we orient ourselves toward understanding, we are open to hearing that perhaps our ideas, plans, claims, and so forth are not right or correct. We are open to seeing that we are wrong somehow.

Focus group: A focus group is a type of group interview where multiple individuals come together to answer questions together rather than individually.

Frames: We follow Erving Goffman (1974), who thought of frames as social phenomena that, sometimes unintentionally, coordinate activities across social actors in a large-scale way through organizing principles.

General linear modeling: General linear modeling is a statistical way to model inter-relationships using previously obtained inferential statistical information (such as T-tests) and generalizing to more than one dependent variable.

Generalizing: Generalizing refers to the process of using findings from a sample to make inferences about the broader population from which that sample is drawn. The capacity for generalizing in research is called generalizability.

Genre: We adopt Carolyn R. Miller's pragmatic approach to genre, which suggests that genre is a typified action in response to and on the uptake of a recurrent situation (Miller, 1984, 2015). An academic genre is enacted in a concrete communicative situation, where an author implicitly applies certain rules to write and to communicate with the readers.

Goal-orientedness: Goal-orientedness refers to what degree the researcher strategically conducts actions in order to meet the goals of research.

Grounded theory: Grounded theory is a way of designing research that focuses on constructing new theories through generation of data, rather than using an existing theoretical framework as the basis for data generation and analysis. Grounded theory uses a specific set of procedures for analysis in order to create conceptual categories whose relationships are explained as theoretical insights.

Hermeneutic circle: A hermeneutic circle describes the unfolding process of reaching understanding. People who engage in social interaction always start with their initial understanding, and from there acquire new perspectives through recognizing different perspective of the other.

Hypothesis testing: This phrase is used in research to indicate a specific kind of experimental study where a hypothesis is articulated and researchers test or check to see if that hypothesis must be rejected or if it can be accepted. Hypotheses are not proved through research; they are tested through research in order to accept or reject them.

Identity: A person's identity consists of the full set of traits or characteristics that, in total, distinguish them from other people.

Identity claim: We use the term identity claim to emphasize the fact that whenever we engage in some form of social action, we are making a claim about who we are through that interaction with others. The identity claim we make is always shaped by others with whom we are interacting. In other words, identity claims are constituted relationally. They are also partial, in the sense that the instantiation of an identity claim can never encompass in total who we are.

Independent variable: An independent variable is a variable that is changed or manipulated by researchers in order to test whether it causes or leads to change in the dependent variable.

Induction: Induction is a form of reasoning that starts from the assumption that knowledge is derived from the observation of the empirical world and becomes more general.

Inferential statistics: Inferential statistics are analyses that extrapolate from sample data to a broader target population.

Instruments: The term *instrument* is used in formal research contexts to refer to tools that researchers use to measure certain concepts or constructs. (*Instrument* is a generic term that is used to refer to surveys, questionnaires, tests, and so on.) These instruments map internal experiences—such as attitudes, emotions, or cognitive knowledge—onto the objective domain, so that they can be measured in a standardized way.

Intersubjectivity: This philosophical idea suggests that understanding involves two or more perspectives relative to one another. The point is something like this: In order for two people to understand one another, they must (at least in principle) expect that they can each articulate the other person's point of view. We use the word *expect* because, of course, sometimes this breaks down, but when we talk, we do so with the expectation that the other person will be able to take our perspective. Without this expectation, our motivation to talk and reach understanding would be lacking.

Interval: Interval variables can be placed on a continuum; however, a "0" on an interval scale does not mean that there is none of that characteristic (e.g., degrees Fahrenheit).

Interview: An interview is a data generation technique that usually consists of one-on-one interactions between a researcher (interviewer) and participant (interviewee), where the interviewer asks interviewee questions. Interviews can be structured (the same questions are asked of all interviewees); semi-structured (interviewees are asked the same general questions, but follow up questions may differ from one individual to the next); or unstructured (which may focus on certain topics but generally does not include set questions and has a much more conversational format).

Interview protocol: An interview protocol refers to the set of questions or topics that researchers use as reference when conducting interviews. Interview protocols can take many forms: Some will include a list of questions; others may focus on topics of discussion with sample questions and/or follow-up questions.

Inverse relationship: An inverse statistical relationship is when one variable goes down in direct relation with the other variable going up.

Items: In a data collection instrument, an item is a specific question or statement to which a participant must respond.

Know-how: Know-how foregrounds knowledge related to knowing how to act next.

Know-what: Know-what foregrounds knowledge claims about what is type of knowledge.

Lifeworld: Lifeworld is the sphere in which we carry out everyday activities, socialize with others, and develop as a person and as groups and cultures. The lifeworld is maintained primarily through *communicative actions* and *communicative rationality*, during which two or more people interact with one another, grasp meaning intended by the other, and give reasons and back up their claims when being questioned.

Linear regression: Linear regression describes the relationship of two variables that, when plotted, resembles a straight line.

Line of regression: The actual line plotted through a linear regression statistical analysis.

Mean: The mean is a measure of central tendency that is used to describe the average number or score.

Meaning: Meaning does not have a direct correspondence to a word or expression but can only be grasped through position-taking and an intersubjective process of understanding a situation.

Meaning field: A symbolic expression does not "contain" a predetermined meaning within, but is related to a range of possible meanings. This bounded range of possible meanings of a social action is called "meaning field." There is no fixed relationship between an action and a list of possible meanings of that action. And yet the range of possibilities is not unlimited, and a possible meaning needs to be deemed reasonable for a given situation.

Meaning horizon: Meaning field is grasped through a horizon-like structure when we understand the meaning of a social action, which is called "meaning horizon." This horizon structure can range from immediate foregrounded horizon, to mid-range horizon, to backgrounded horizon.

Measurement: In research, measurement refers to using a tool (like a ruler or scale) to observe phenomena and get a sense of its attributes, like size or degree.

Median: In descriptive statistics, the median is used to refer to the number in a data set that falls in the middle of the sample and divides the sample in half.

Methodology: While often used interchangeably with methods, we use the term *methodology* to refer to an orientation toward knowledge production in the planning and conduct of research. For example, one might use a grounded theory methodology.

Methods: We use the term *methods* to refer to the specific strategies that are used in relation to one's methodology. For example, one might use interview methods with a grounded theory methodology.

Missing data: Missing data occur when individuals do not respond to one or more items in a questionnaire or survey. They also occur when researchers fail to input participant responses into the data set created for analysis.

Mode: The mode describes the number in a data set that appears most frequently. A data set is bimodal when two numbers appear with the same frequency.

Multiple regression analysis: This is a statistical analysis conducted in order to map out the correlations of multiple independent variables with one dependent variable.

Nominal variable: Nominal variables, a type of categorical variable, are variables that name categories with no intrinsic association with order or number, such as gender.

Normal distribution/Normally distributed: Data are considered "normally distributed" when they appear as a bell curve. A data set is considered to be normally distributed when 50% of values fall below the mean and 50% of values fall above the mean; and where the mean, median, and mode are the same.

Normative knowledge claims: Normative knowledge claims make reference to the normative ontological category of agreement and mutual recognition among people in a given cultural and historical context.

Null hypothesis: This kind of hypothesis makes a statement that claims there will be no relationship or differences across variables measured in the study. This is the hypothesis that is typically examined through experimental designed studies. Researchers will either reject or accept the null hypothesis.

Objective knowledge claims: Objective knowledge claims that make reference to the objective ontological category mostly consisting of objects, entities, and forces.

Observation: This is a form of data generation that emphasizes systematically paying attention to what occurs in one's research setting.

Ontology: Ontology refers to a theory about what exists and what is real. We understand ontology to be about the nature of being, or existence.

Operationalization: Operationalization is a process through which researchers clearly define how a social phenomenon or a concept, typically not directly measurable, will be measured indirectly so that researchers can construct quantifiable data based on the measurement. In social sciences, the inferences in the process of operationalization involve turning claims that fall into different ontological domains into objective claims.

Ordinal variables: This type of categorical variable can be interpreted according to a ranking—for example, lightest color to darkest color.

Outlier: An outlier is a data point that is distant from other data points.

Participant observation: This is a specific type of observation where the person doing the observing is somewhat involved with their research setting and thus cannot be considered an external, disconnected observer.

Partisanship: This is the claim that all knowledge is partial and that it simultaneously is knowledge from a particular perspective or set of perspectives. This means it always carries with it the perspective from which it is produced. The opposite of partisanship is a belief that knowledge can and should be neutral.

Pearson Product Moment Correlation: A statistic known as *r* that is used to indicate the strength and direction of the relation between two distinct variables.

Percentiles: Percentiles are a form of descriptive statistics (specifically, a measure of relative standing) that show where a score falls in comparison with other scores.

Photovoice: Photovoice is an interdisciplinary approach to inquiry that knits together documentary, feminist, and participatory orientations to inquiry.

Position-taking: Position-taking refers to the idea that any time we engage in a communicative act, we are doing so either implicitly or explicitly for someone else—in other words, that we are always communicating for an audience and therefore our expressions always reflect an attempt to ensure that these expressions will be recognized by others. We implicitly try to use how we understand as others' perspectives in order to communicate our ideas in a way that will be understandable to them. Position-taking is the mental and communicative act of understanding another perspective, including how they might interpret and respond to you.

Positionality: Positionality is a term we define as a way of referencing the way a researcher discusses their own background and experiences, and/or their identity, in relation to the empirical research process in which they are engaged. This is also referred to as reflexivity.

Power relationship: Power relationship refers to the interaction through which a social actor's capacity to act freely is shaped, impacted, or controlled by other social actors or certain social structural factors. In this book, we take power not as a thing or a property that people own but as a relational feature enacted through social actions. In terms of its effects, a power relationship often results in social actors' abandoning of mutual understanding as the primary focus of interaction and quest for knowledge.

Predictive validity: As the name suggests, predictive validity reports the extent to which current outcomes accurately predict future outcomes.

Probability sampling: Probability sampling is an approach to sampling where any member of a target population, or member of a segment of that population, has an equal chance of being selected to participate in a research study as part of the study sample.

Procedural approach to ethics: This way of thinking about ethics is largely identified as broadly applicable rules of behavior guiding right action with others.

Prove: Proving was a prominent idea of 20th century social research. The idea was that if one could accumulate enough evidence, one could claim to have proven something to be true once and for all. Social scientists have been moving away from this idea. It is counter to the idea of openness (which asks us to keep the potential fallibility of our assumptions in mind) and also to the idea of situatedness of knowledge (which would suggest that if situations change, the knowledge also will change). Instead of prove, we use the idea of claim. We make claims, but these claims are always subject to scrutiny through which we may validate them, but not prove them.

Quota sampling: Quota sampling affords researchers an opportunity to compare subgroups of the population by setting quotas for particular contingents of the population.

Randomized Control Trial (RCT): The RCT is an experimental design where the sample is both randomly drawn from the population and where the members of the sample are randomly assigned to specific experimental conditions—that is, to specific treatment groups or no-treatment groups (a control group) in an effort to pinpoint what might cause differences in outcomes. RCTs are fixed design approaches to research.

Range: Range refers to a descriptive statistic that is calculated by taking the difference between the highest and lowest score in a sample data set.

Ratio: Ratio variables are set so that a "0" on the continuum means that there is *none of* that characteristic (e.g., measurement of distance).

Raw score: A raw score refers to a score that has not been adjusted or standardized in any way. For instance, the number of problems answered correctly on an exam is the raw score.

Recognition: Recognition refers to societal and cultural acceptance and respect for different social groups and associated identities, especially groups that have been historically marginalized (e.g., racial, sexual, religious minorities, women, transgender individuals, people with disabilities, etc.). Mis-recognition is considered a form of social injustice, which contributes to status subordination and a wide range of subsequent damage to groups and individuals.

Redistribution: Redistribution concerns how income, resources, and rights are distributed among societal members. Social injustice can manifest in systemic and historical patterns of unequal distribution of resources, materials, and rights. Unfair distribution may manifest in increasing polarization between the rich and the poor, disparity in educational opportunities, health care, social welfare, legal rights, and so on.

Reflection: Reflection is an inherent quality of knowledge, when we conceptualize knowledge as a product of subject-to-subject endeavors. This means that there is always a way to indicate how the knowledge manifests the subject-to-subject relations from which it emerges or through which it is engaged.

Regression analysis: Researchers can examine correlations in a sophisticated way by statistically controlling some variables in order to see how other variables might relate to one another.

Reliability: A term related to the conception of validity. It is often used in the context of measurement and repeated observations. Basically, it indicates how well a test stably and consistently measures a construct, or how well two raters reach consensus regarding their respective ratings.

Representation: Representation refers to the idea that a symbol directly means what it names in a one-to-one correspondence.

Representational Theory of Meaning: A representational theory of meaning argues that symbols (words and images, primarily) represent the meaning of the thing being symbolized, such as the word *umbrella* symbolizing the thing we call "umbrella."

Representative sample: A representative sample refers to a group of individuals participating in a study whose characteristics are proportionally representative of relevant characteristics in the target population as a whole.

Research as action: Thinking of research as action provides us with an opportunity to consider what the research is doing in the social world.

Research design: Research design refers to the process to engender an overarching plan for a research study, which can be a creative and dynamic process.

Research hypothesis, or Alternative hypothesis: The research or alternative hypothesis is a statement of the outcomes of difference or relationship across variables that the researcher expects. If the null hypothesis is rejected this means we can often accept the research or alternative hypothesis. However, sometimes researchers will reject both.

Research impact: Research impact describes *changes* resulting from a research endeavor, especially positive changes. But it should not be limited to characterizable and measurable effects that can be easily defined in time and space. Impact also includes "impactful**,**" where the focus shifts from a thing-like effect to a more general effect of change, including changes that are not so apparently defined in time and space. Similarly, impact may also signify the process of "impacting" and the possibility that some changes may be ongoing, interlocking with other forms of change, and thus cannot be fully defined in the frame of time, such as at the end of a study. Overall, our use of "impact" in this text is not limited to the product-oriented understanding of change resulted from research. It also embodies the meanings of "impactful" and "impacting," which carry a more holistic, process-oriented, and nondeterministic understanding of change.

Research method: Research method includes a wide range of specific means and procedures applied in a research study.

Research methodology: Research methodology can be understood as a philosophical/theoretical "blueprint" that guides conceptualizing, designing, and implementing a research study.

Research proposal: A research proposal is a written text mapping out the authors' commitments and research plan for a project and meanwhile requesting support, approval, or instruction from the targeted audience. Usually, it includes the purposes, questions, rationale, design, and action plan for the proposed study. It is also important to demonstrate the significance and feasibility of the study in a proposal.

Research question: A research question is a narrowed question that indicates exactly what the researcher hopes to answer by conducting the study. Researchers must ask questions that are answerable.

Response rates: Response rates reflect a ratio of those responding to an invitation to participate in research and the number of people invited or a ratio of the number of responses to items in relation to the number of items.

Rett syndrome: Rett syndrome is a rare neurodevelopmental disorder that occurs in 1 in 9,000 live female births. It was first described a little more than 50 years ago by Dr. Andreas Rett in Austria, and in 1999 its genetic cause—a mutation on the *MECP2* gene on the X chromosome—was identified. As for most rare disorders, children are affected, and it has severe impacts.

Girls with Rett syndrome experience largely normal early development but at around 6 to 18 months, they then experience developmental regression. For example, the young child loses hand and/or communication skills, she develops hand stereotypies (repetitive and meaningless hand movements), and walking becomes impaired. There are additional health problems such as episodes of hyperventilation and breath holding, the development of scoliosis and epilepsy, sleep disturbances, and poor growth.

At the same time, girls with Rett syndrome are capable of learning new skills, building strong relationships with their family and caregivers, and enjoying social interactions in a variety of activities, especially when in nature and the outdoors.

The best treatments for Rett syndrome are not yet clear, but living an active life with opportunities for communication contributes to optimal quality of life.

Sample: A sample refers to those individuals who take part in a research study. The data that are generated by participation of this group of individuals are used to make inferences about predicted responses of the target population as a whole.

Sampling: Sampling refers to the process of choosing participants to take part in a study. Methods for sampling depend on the kind of study being conducted.

Sampling error: Sampling error occurs when incorrect inferences are made about a target population due to characteristics of the sample of research participants not matching the characteristics of the population.

Sampling strategy: Sampling strategy refers to the approach a researcher or group of researchers plan to use to recruit participants for a study.

Scales: Scales are a type of data collection instrument used to measure specific constructs. They are generally used to measure affective characteristics (emotions or attitudes). They differ from tests, which are used to measure knowledge or competence.

Scatterplot: A scatterplot is a visual depiction of data on a graph so that relationships between two variables can be displayed—one variable is reflected on the x-axis and the other is located on the y-axis.

Situational ethics: This category of ethics is thought of as right action given specific contexts and local implications—what we do in the stream of acting, making decisions, and interacting through our research.

Social justice: Social justice is a normative concept that gauges what is good, right, equitable, and just in terms of the experiences and treatments of all members of the society. There are various theories to conceptualize social justice. We introduced in Chapter 16 one particular social political theory of social justice advocated by political philosopher Nancy Fraser, who conceives of social justice as existing in two interwoven domains: *recognition* and *redistribution*. Mis-recognition and mal-distribution are both deemed a form of social injustice.

Social network analysis: Social network analysis uses the concept of network to display social structure as connections across nodes (individuals, actors, things, and so on).

Social norms: Social norms are patterned normative claims about what are considered appropriate actions. They are rooted in societal members' shared cultural beliefs and often enacted implicitly through social actions.

Social structure: Social structure is the various heterogeneous, patterned rules and mechanisms that on the one hand, condition and enable social action, and on the other hand, are consequentially impacted by social action.

Standard deviation: Standard deviation is a term used to indicate the dispersion of values from a sample data set around the mean—that is, how close or far most scores fall from the mean value. The standard deviation is calculated by taking the square root of the variance.

Standardized score: A standardized score is a measure of relative standing (a form of descriptive statistics). Specifically, it refers to a raw score that has been converted to take into account differences in measurements and report scores in a consistent form.

Statistical inferencing: Statistical inferencing is a process by which researchers interpret the meanings of statistical outputs with respect to the analysis of data.

Statistical model: Statistical models are statistical possibilities for hypothetical patterns in the data. These are used as comparisons for the actual patterns obtained from the data.

Statistical significance: Statistical significance indicates that the inferences of causation (or correlation) are best explained by the variables identified and do not seem to be heavily influenced by chance or other unidentified or uncontrolled factors.

Statistics: Statistics refers to the process of generating and analyzing numerical data, typically in large quantities, to categorize, classify, and/or illustrate patterns in those data. The term *statistics* is also often used to refer to the output of the analyses.

Subject–object relation: Subject to object relations refer to an epistemological orientation that conceptualizes knowledge production primarily as a knowing subject making knowledge claims about an object or object-like existence. Typically, a subject–object relation describes a lone researcher who simply makes observations about the object of their study as a third person.

Subject–subject relation: Subject to subject relations refer to an epistemological orientation that conceptualizes knowledge production primarily as a relational process between two or more knowing subjects. A subject–subject relation describes an intersubjective process that foregrounds the relationships between people as a basis for social inquiry.

Subjective knowledge claims: Subjective knowledge claims make reference to a subjective ontological category of thought awareness, feelings, intentions, motivations, and experiences.

Survey methods: Survey methods are a form of data generation where researchers ask sets of systematic/standardized questions (surveys) of a large number of participants in order to understand patterns or trends across a large group.

System: System manifests itself as industry, money market, legal and financial institutions, bureaucracy, political governance, physical and technological infrastructure, and so on. The system is largely coordinated through *instrumental rationality*, which means various parts of the system operate almost exclusively based on a *means-to-the-end* rationality, aiming for maximizing productivity, efficiency, profits, gains, and the accomplishment of goals.

Systematicity: Systematicity is a characteristic of research that describes the way the research itself functions as a whole system.

T-scores: T-scores are a form of standardized score that is used with sample data, or with population data that may not be normally distributed. They are used to show the distance of a score from the mean.

Target population: The target population in a research study is the set of individuals within a population who meet specific criteria important for the study.

Tests: Tests are a form of data collection instrument used to measure constructs that focus on cognitive knowledge or competence.

Thematic analysis: Thematic analysis is an approach to analyzing narrative or textual data that focuses on understanding common themes—topics, ideas, or patterns of meaning—that come up repeatedly in a data set.

Theoretical inferencing: Theoretical inferencing involves drawing on concepts in order to explore meaningful connections across cases in qualitative research.

Theory of truth: Refers to competing theories about what is considered truth. It can be explicit or implicit.

Thick description: This description refers to the use of detail to provide insight into a phenomenon of study. Specifically, it entails detailed rendering of a phenomenon or site of study that helps justify explanations made about that phenomenon.

Transcendental I: The concept of the "transcendental I," as described by Immanuel Kant, which suggests that there is always a part of our self that is beyond our capacity to reflect upon.

Transferability: Transferability is a term used primarily with qualitative studies because of the inapplicability of sample to population generalizability to this kind of research. It refers to the degree to which results of a study where researchers use nonprobability sampling techniques can provide relevant insights in other contexts or with different populations.

Treatment: A treatment in research is a planned intervention whose effects are studied.

Types of variables: Variables are discreet qualities and categories of interest in a study. There are multiple types of variables, and the type has consequences for the kind of statistical analyses one uses.

Understanding: Understanding, in contrast to explanation, requires the researcher to acquire as much as possible an insider position to understand the social phenomenon from within. This involves a capacity of position-taking and understanding meaning.

Understand meaning: To understand meaning requires a cultural competency to tacitly recognize a cultural and social scene holistically and the ability to know how to act next through position-taking. Understanding meaning involves the ability to take the position of a typical person in a given cultural and historical context, who recognizes and has access to the cultural knowledge about the situation.

This also involves hermeneutic understanding where pre-understanding becomes unpacked and expanded in interaction with the other. Meanwhile, meaning is grasped through discerning a field of possible meanings, which forms a horizon-like structure in a given interactive context.

Validity: Validity refers to the *soundness* and *truthfulness* of an argument or a statement. In the context of social inquiry, validity is closely tied to the concept of truth and knowledge claims.

Validity criteria: Validity criteria are a set of principles based on which we gauge the validity of certain types of knowledge claims. Different types of knowledge claims (objective, subjective, and normative claims) require different sets of validity principles and related criteria.

Variable: Variable is a technical term for a specific bit of information collected with some *standardized* precision across people that we expect varies in some way across those people. A variable is a measurable characteristic that can change between or among research participants. The characteristic is defined and operationalized by researchers in order to be measurable in a standard manner across all research participants. For example, if we said socio-economic status was a variable we would say that it varies by amount of economic income and access one might have.

Variance: Variance is a descriptive statistic used to indicate the dispersion of values around the mean.

Z-score: A Z-score is a form of standardized score that shows how far a score is from the mean, or average. Z-scores at the mean are represented by a 0; a positive or negative Z-score tells you how many standard deviations a score is from the mean. Z-scores are used for population data that are normally distributed.

ABOUT THE CONTRIBUTORS

Katharine Broton is an Assistant Professor of Educational Sociology in the Departments of Educational Policy and Leadership Studies and Sociology (courtesy) at the University of Iowa. She is a faculty affiliate with the Hope Center for College, Community and Justice at Temple University and the Center for Research on Undergraduate Education at the University of Iowa. Broton studies educational inequalities with a focus on higher education, and her work has appeared in *Educational Researcher, Educational Evaluation and Policy Analysis, The New York Times*, and *Wisconsin Public Television*, among others. Her formative scholarship on basic needs insecurity among college students has received awards from the American Educational Research Association Division of Postsecondary Education and Iowa Academy of Education, and it was cited in a recent Government Accountability Office report calling for federal investment to end hunger in higher education. The National Science Foundation, Kresge Foundation, Lumina Foundation, and others have supported her research. She teaches graduate courses on research methods, finance in higher education, and higher education policy. She has a PhD in Sociology from the University of Wisconsin–Madison.

Meagan Call-Cummings (PhD, Indiana University, Bloomington) is an Assistant Professor of Research Methods in the School of Education, College of Education and Human Development, at George Mason University in Fairfax, Virginia. She teaches qualitative methodology courses as well as a course in participatory action research. Her writing most often engages questions of ethics and validity in the context of participatory action research. Her research most often takes the form of youth participatory action research, where she works with high school students and their teachers to evaluate the effects of school-level, local, and federal educational policies on students.

Jenny Downs is Program Head of Child Disability at Telethon Kids Institute in Perth, Australia. She works toward improving the health, mental health, and quality of life of children with disability and their families. This includes research on the natural history of rare disorders including Rett syndrome, the CDKL5 deficiency disorder, Prader-Willi syndrome, and Duchenne muscular dystrophy, as well as disorders such as Down syndrome, cerebral palsy, and autism, which occur more commonly. She also works on the development and validation of outcome measures for use in clinical monitoring and clinical trials. She has evaluated treatments including the impacts of powered standing wheelchair devices on the physical and mental health of teenagers with Duchenne muscular dystrophy, gastrostomy for children with feeding difficulties, and early developmental intervention for Rett syndrome.

The Feminist Research Collective began at Indiana University, Bloomington, in 2017. It started as a small group of women devoted to complicating what it means to be a woman in patriarchal heterosexist spaces, while promoting positive and empowering opportunities for collective engagement.

Danielle Lansing is a faculty member at Southwestern Indian Polytechnic Institute (SIPI) within the Early Childhood Education (ECE) Program. Prior to entering higher education, she served as an educator for 15 years. She has taught in Bureau of Indian Education and tribal contract schools in New Mexico and Arizona with various tribes in Arizona and New Mexico. Lansing's research interests include Native teacher education, community-based participatory research, and Indigenous research methodologies. Danielle's research experience includes qualitative research methodologies including phenomenological studies and grounded theory. Lansing is an enrolled member of the Navajo Nation. She credits her family's educational experience as the motivation for her continued interest and commitment to Indigenous education.

Ke Li is an Assistant Professor of Law and Society at John Jay College of Criminal Justice, the City University of New York. She received a joint PhD in sociology and criminal justice at Indiana University, Bloomington, and her research focuses on law and society in contemporary China with particular attention to interplay of dispute management, social inequality, and power relationships in everyday life. So far, her works have been published in the *Law & Society Review* and *Law & Policy*. With the support of the American Council of Learned Societies, she is currently developing a book manuscript titled *Marriage Unbound: Divorce Litigation, Power, and Inequality in Contemporary China* (under contract with Stanford University Press).

Wei Luo is a postdoctoral fellow at the Center on Philanthropy and Civil Society at Stanford University. Trained as a historical sociologist, she is broadly interested in understanding the coevolution of economic and associational life in different historical contexts. Her two co-authors of the presented project are Julia Adams, Professor of Sociology and International & Area Studies at Yale University, and Hannah Brückner, Professor of Social Research and Public Policy at New York University–Abu Dhabi.

Joseph Maxwell is a Professor (Emeritus) in the Research Methods program in the College of Education and Human Development at George Mason University. His doctoral degree is in anthropology, but for the past 40 years his research and teaching have mainly been in education, with an increasing focus on methodology. He is the author of *Qualitative Research Design: An Interactive Approach* (3rd edition, 2013) and *A Realist Approach* *for Qualitative Research* (2012), as well as articles on qualitative and mixed-methods research, Native American societies, and medical education. His current research deals with using qualitative and mixed methods for causal explanation, validity in qualitative and quantitative research, the history and breadth of mixed-methods research, the value of philosophic realism for social research, and the importance of diversity and dialogue across research paradigms and methods.

Sara McClelland is Associate Professor Psychology and Gender in the Departments of Women's and Gender Studies and Psychology at the University of Michigan. Her research focuses on the development of critical research methods to study how discrimination has become normalized and, therefore, difficult to study. Her recent work on the politics of measurement has ranged from studies of attitudes toward abortion, sex education policies, lesbian and bisexual women's experiences of discrimination from friends and family, and sexual health near the end of life.

Joan Parker Webster is a retired Associate Professor of Education at the University of Alaska Fairbanks (UAF), where she developed the Reading Endorsement for Alaska state licensure and the Master's of Reading and Literacy program at UAF. Specializing in literacies and cross-cultural communications, she also taught courses in qualitative research methodologies. Currently, she is affiliated faculty in the Center for Cross-Cultural Studies at UAF. She also works as an educational research consultant, primarily as evaluator for federally funded grant programs. Parker Webster continues to conduct ethnographic research and publish in the areas of qualitative and online research methodologies, multiliteracies, cross/intercultural communication, and Indigenous education.

Oren Pizmony-Levy is an Associate Professor of International and Comparative Education at Teachers College, Columbia University. Prior to graduate school in the United States, Pizmony-Levy worked in the Education Department of the Society for the Protection of Nature in Israel (NGO) and served as the research coordinator at the Israeli Gay Youth Organization. Trained as a sociologist, his research focuses on global educational movements—including international large-scale assessments, environmental and sustainability education, and LGBT education—and their impact on policy/practice. Oren is the founding director of the Teachers College Center for Sustainable Futures; he leads a research–practice partnership with the New York City Department of Education to promote and advance sustainability education in public schools.

Jeffrey D. Pugh is Assistant Professor of Conflict Resolution at the University of Massachusetts Boston. He received his PhD in political science from the Johns Hopkins University, and is the executive director of the Center for Mediation, Peace, and Resolution of Conflict (CEMPROC), based in Quito, Ecuador. Pugh's research focuses on the role of non-state actors and international institutions influencing governance and peacebuilding in the Global South, especially in migrant-receiving areas of Ecuador. His multimethod, interdisciplinary research has been published in more than a dozen peer-reviewed journal articles and in a forthcoming book. He has received many research awards from national and international associations, including the American Political Science Association, International Studies Association, Peace & Justice Studies Association, and others. Pugh has taught courses on Negotiation, International Relations, Immigration, International Conflict Resolution, and Latin American Politics, as well as experiential courses abroad.

David Rutkowski is an Associate Professor with a joint appointment in Educational Policy and Educational Inquiry at Indiana University (IU). Prior to IU David was a Professor of Educational Measurement at the University of Oslo, Norway, where he still holds a Professor II appointment. David also worked as a researcher for the International Association for the Evaluation of Educational Achievement in Hamburg, Germany. David's research focuses on educational measurement and policy. He has collaborated with or consulted for national and international organizations including the U.S. State Department, USAID, UNESCO, World Bank, IEA, and the OECD. David has worked on and led evaluations and assessment projects in over 20 countries. He currently is the editor of the IEA policy brief series, co-editor of the journal *Discourse*, serves on the IEA publication editorial committee, and is a board member of several academic journals. He also co-leads a project on improving assessment literacy among teachers in Indiana. David has published numerous peer-reviewed articles, is co-editor of *The Handbook of International Large-Scale Assessment*, and recently co-authored the book *The Global Education Race: Taking the Measure of PISA and International Testing*.

Payal Shah (Associate Professor, University of South Carolina) conducts ethnographic research at the intersection of education, gender, culture, and society. She explores these themes by examining the sociocultural context of female marginalization and the role of formal and nonformal educational initiatives in promoting gender equity in South Asia. She has been engaged with research and practice on educational issues in India for over 15 years. Payal teaches courses in comparative education, social foundations of education, and qualitative research. She holds a PhD in Education Policy Studies, an MA in International and Comparative Education, and an MA in Sociology, all from Indiana University.

Sabine Siekmann is Professor of Linguistics and Foreign Languages at the University of Alaska Fairbanks. She holds a PhD in Second Language Acquisition and Instructional Technology from the University of South Florida. Her research interests include bilingualism at home and at school, Indigenous language maintenance and revitalization, sociocultural theory and second language teaching, technology integration in language learning, and teacher professional development. She has been involved in a series of large-scale federally funded grant projects supporting Alaska Native (Language) Education through graduate education and materials development, as well as in establishing the Second Language Acquisition, Bilingual Education, and Literacy endorsement.

Nathan Swinger is a pediatric critical care doctor at Indiana University and Riley Hospital for Children. He is passionate about finding new and better ways to provide graduate medical education and empower learners.

Hakim Mohandas Amani Williams, a native of Laventille, Trinidad & Tobago, is Associate Professor and Interim Chair of Africana Studies, Director of Peace and Justice Studies, and affiliate in Education, Globalization Studies, and Public Policy at Gettysburg College. He also adjuncts at the Morton Deutsch International Center for Cooperation and Conflict Resolution at Teachers College (NYC), and completed his doctorate at Columbia University in International Educational Development and Peace Education. He researches school/structural violence, educational inequities, and youth/community empowerment, and has conducted workshops/trainings on mediation, conflict resolution, intercultural communication, restorative circles, leadership development, and activism in diverse settings.

REFERENCES

Abedi, J., & Gándara, P. (2006). Performance of English language learners as a subgroup in large-scale assessment: Interaction of research and policy. *Educational Measurement: Issues and Practice*, 25(4), 36–46.

Abma, T. A., & Widdershoven, G. A. (2011). Evaluation as a relationally responsible practice. In Y. Lincoln & N. Denzin (Eds.), *Handbook for qualitative inquiry* (pp. 669–680). Thousand Oaks, CA: SAGE.

Anderson, K., & Jack, D. C. (1991). Learning to listen: Interview techniques and analyses. In S. B. Gluck & D. Patai (Eds.), *Women's words: The feminist practice of oral history* (pp. 11–26). New York, NY: Routledge.

Appelbaum, M., Cooper, H., Kline, R. B., Mayo-Wilson, E., Nezu, A. M., & Rao, S. M. (2018). Journal article reporting standards for quantitative research in psychology: The APA Publications and Communications Board task force report. *American Psychologist*, 73(1), 3.

Baker, S. E., & Edwards, R. (Eds.). (2012). *How many qualitative interviews is enough?* National Centre for Research Methods.

Balyk, L., & Pugh, J. (2013). Governance networks in Ecuador's border region. *Forced Migration Review*, 43, 47–49.

Bao, X., Downs, J., Wong, K., Williams, S., & Leonard, H. (2013). Using a large international sample to investigate epilepsy in Rett syndrome. *Developmental Medicine & Child Neurology*, 55(6), 553–558.

Barad, K. (2003). Posthumanist performativity: How matter comes to matter. *Signs: Journal of Women in Culture and Society*, 28(3), 801–831.

Barad, K. (2007). *Meeting the universe halfway: Quantum physics and the entanglement of matter and meaning*. Durham, NC: Duke University Press.

Baranek, G. (1999). Autism during infancy: A retrospective video analysis of sensory-motor and social behaviors at 9–12 months of age. *Journal of Autism and Developmental Disorders*, 29(3), 213–224.

Benton, T., & Braib, I. (2001). *Philosophy of Social Science*. New York, NY: Palgrave.

Berkenkotter, C., & Huckin, T. N. (1993). Rethinking genre from a sociocognitive perspective. *Written Communication*, 10(4), 475–509.

Biesta, G. J. (2010). Why "what works" still won't work: From evidence-based education to value-based education. *Studies in Philosophy and Education*, 29(5), 491–503.

Bowen, G. A. (2008). Naturalistic inquiry and the saturation concept: A research note. *Qualitative Research*, 8(1), 137–152.

Brandom, R. (1994). *Making it explicit: Reasoning, representing, and discursive commitment*. Cambridge, MA: Harvard University Press.

Broton, K. M. (2019). *A review of estimates of housing insecurity and homelessness among U.S. students in higher education*. Iowa City, IA: University of Iowa Press.

Broton, K. M., & Cady, C. (Eds.). (2020). *Food insecurity on campus: Action and intervention*. Baltimore, MD: Johns Hopkins University Press. https://jhupbooks.press.jhu.edu/title/food-insecurity-campus

Broton, K. M., & Goldrick-Rab, S. (2013). *Housing instability among college students*. Research Brief, Wisconsin Center for the Advancement of Postsecondary Education and the Center for Financial Security, University of Wisconsin–Madison. Madison, WI: University of Wisconsin Press.

Broton, K. M., & Goldrick-Rab, S. (2018). Going without: An exploration of food and housing insecurity among undergraduates. *Educational Researcher*, 47(2), 121–133.

Burawoy, M. (1998). The extended case method. *Sociological Theory, 16*(1), 4–33.

Burke, T. (2018, November). *Me Too is a movement not a moment*. [TEDWomen]. https://www.ted.com/talks/tarana_burke_me_too_is_a_movement_not_a_moment?language=en

Call-Cummings, M. (2017). Establishing communicative validity: Discovering theory through practice. *Qualitative Inquiry, 23*(3), 192–200.

Campbell, R., Pound, P., Pope, C., Britten, N., Pill, R., Morgan, M., & Donovan, J. (2003). Evaluating meta-ethnography: A synthesis of qualitative research on lay experiences of diabetes and diabetes care. *Social Science and Medicine, 56*(4), 671–684.

Carspecken, P. F. (1996). *Critical ethnography in educational research*. New York, NY, and London, UK: Routledge.

Carspecken, P. F. (1999). *Four scenes for posing the question of meaning and other essays in critical philosophy and critical methodology*. New York, NY: Peter Lang Inc.

Carspecken, P. F. (2003). Ocularcentrism, phonocentrism and the counter enlightenment problematic: Clarifying contested terrain in our schools of education. *Teachers College Record, 105*(6), 978–1047.

Carspecken, P. F. (2012). Basic concepts in critical methodological theory: Action, Structure and System within a communicative pragmatics framework. In S. Steinberg & G. Cannella (Eds.), *Critical qualitative research reader* (pp. 43–66). New York, NY: Peter Lang Inc.

Carter, P., Downs, J., Bebbington, A., Williams, S., Jacoby, P., Kaufmann, W., & Leonard, H. (2010). Stereotypical hand movements from 144 subjects with Rett syndrome from the population-based Australian database. *Movement Disorders, 25*(3), 282–288.

Centers for Disease Control and Prevention (CDC). Lyme disease. https://www.cdc.gov/lyme/stats/humancases.html

Cho, J., & Trent, A. (2006). Validity in qualitative research revisited. *Qualitative Research, 6*(3), 319–340.

Cirillo, F. (2018). *The Pomodoro technique: The life-changing time-management system*. New York, NY: Random House.

Cooper, H. (1988). Organizing knowledge syntheses: A taxonomy of literature reviews. *Knowledge in Society, 1*, 104–124.

Creswell, J. (2013). *Qualitative inquiry and research design: Choosing among five approaches*. Thousand Oaks, CA: SAGE.

Creswell, J. W., & Guetterman, T. (2019). *Educational research: Planning, conducting, and evaluating quantitative and qualitative research*. Upper Saddle River, NJ: Pearson.

Cronbach, L. J. (1980). Validity on parole: How can we go straight? *New Directions for Testing and Measurement, 5*(1), 99–108.

Crotty, M. (1998). *The Foundations of Social Research: Meaning and Perspective in the Research Process*. Thousand Oaks, CA: SAGE.

Crowther, M., Lim, W., & Crowther, M. S. (2010). Systematic review and meta-analysis methodology. *Blood, 116*(7), 3140–3146.

Datar, A., & Nicosia, N. (2018). Association of exposure to communities with higher ratios of obesity with increased body mass index and risk of overweight and obesity among parents and children. *Journal of American Medical Association, 172*(3), 239–246.

Deegan, M. J. (1991). *Women in sociology: A bio-bibliographical sourcebook*. Westport, CT: Greenwood Press.

Dennis, B. (2013). "Validity crisis" in qualitative research: Still? Movement toward a unified approach. In B. Dennis, L. Carsepcken, & P. Carspecken (Eds.), *Qualitative research: A reader on philosophy, core concepts, and practice* (pp. 1–49). New York, NY, & Frankfurt, Germany: Peter Lang Inc., 1–49.

Dennis, B. (2018). Working without/against a compass: Ethical dilemmas in educational ethnography. In D. Beach, C. Bagley, & S. Marques da Silva (Eds.), *Handbook on ethnography of education* (pp. 51–70). Hoboken, NJ: Wiley.

Dennis, B., & Parker Webster, J. (2018). *Entangling ethnography: Agency, diffractivity, and difference that makes a difference* [conference presentation]. Oxford Ethnography and Education Conference, New College, Oxford University, 2018.

Denzin, N. (2003). *Performance ethnography: Critical pedagogy and the politics of culture*. Thousand Oaks, CA: SAGE.

Denzin, N. K., & Lincoln, Y.S. (2000). Introduction: The discipline and practice of qualitative research. In N. K. Denzin & Y. S. Lincoln (Eds.), *Handbook of qualitative research* (2nd ed., pp. 1–29). Thousand Oaks, CA: SAGE.

Dolphijn, R., & van der Tuin, I. (2012). *New materialism: Interviews & cartographies*. Ann Arbor, MI: Open Humanities Press.

Downs, J. (2017). Investigator spotlight—Dr. Jenny Downs Telethon Kids Institute in Australia. https://www.Rettyndrome.org/for-researchers/investigator-spotlight

Downs, J., Géranton, S., Bebbington, A., Jacoby, P., Bahi-Buisson, N., Ravine, D., & Leonard, H. (2010). Linking MEPC2 and pain sensitivity: The example of Rett syndrome. *American Journal of Medical Genetics, 152a*(5), 1197–1205.

Downs, J., Leonard, H., & Hill, K. (2012). Initial assessment of the Stepwatch Activity Monitor™ to measure activity in Rett syndrome. *Journal of Disability and Rehabilitation, 34*(12), 1010–1015.

Downs, J., Leonard, H., Jacoby, P., Brisco, L., Baikie, G., & Hill, K. (2015). Rett syndrome: Establishing a novel outcome measure in an era of clinical trials for rare disorders. *Disability and Rehabilitation, 37*(21), 1992–1996.

Du Bois, W. E. B. (1920). The souls of white folks. In W. E. B. Du Bois, *Darkwater: Voices from within the veil* (pp. 15–25). New York, NY: Harcourt, Brace & Co.

Ducharme, J. (2018, July 12). About half of Americans say they're trying to lose weight. *Time*. http://time.com/5334532/weight-loss-americans/

Edin, K. J., & Shaefer, H. L. (2015). *$2.00 a day: Living on almost nothing in America*. Boston, MA: Houghton Mifflin Harcourt.

Educational Testing Service. (2012). *GRE general test score information by ethnicity/racial groups, 2009–2010*. https://www.ets.org/s/gre/pdf/gre_general_test_score_information_by_ethnicity_2009_2010.pdf

Educational Testing Service. (2017). *Test content and structure*. https://www.ets.org/gre/revised_general/about/content

Ellingson, L. (2011). Analysis and representation across the continuum. In *Handbook for qualitative inquiry* (pp. 595–611). Thousand Oaks, CA: SAGE.

Engeström, Y. (1987). *Learning by expanding: An activity-theoretical approach to developmental research*. Helsinki, Finland: Orienta-Konsultit Oy.

Engeström, Y. (1993). Developmental studies of work as a testbench of activity theory: The case of primary care medical practice. In S. Chaniklin & J. Lave (Eds.), *Understanding practice: Perspectives on activity and context* (pp. 64–103). New York, NY, & Cambridge, UK: Cambridge University Press.

Engeström, Y. (2001). Expansive learning at work: Toward an activity theoretical reconceptualization. *Journal of Education and Work, 14*(1), 133–156.

Feder, H. M., Jr., Johnson, B. J., O'Connell, S., Shapiro, E. D., Steere, A. C., Wormser, G. P., & Ad Hoc International Lyme Disease Group. (2007). A critical appraisal of "chronic Lyme disease." *New England Journal of Medicine, 357*(14), 1422–1430.

Federal Policy for the Protection of Human Subjects (2017, January 19). *Federal Register, 82*(12), 7149–7274.

Fine, M. (1994). Working the hyphens. *Handbook of qualitative research*. In N. Denzin & Y. S. Lincoln (Eds.), *Handbook of qualitative research* (pp. 70–82). Thousand Oaks, CA: SAGE.

Fine, M., Stoudt, B., Fox, M., & Santos, M. (2010). The uneven distribution of social suffering: Documenting the social health consequences of neo-liberal social policy on marginalized youth. *The European Health Psychologist, 12*(3), 30–35.

Fischer, R., & Milfont, T. L. (2010). Standardization in psychological research. *International Journal of Psychological Research, 3*(1), 88–96.

Foote, S. M. (2010, July 7). Tame your inner critic. *Inside Higher Ed.* https://www.insidehighered.com/advice/2010/07/26/tame-your-inner-critic

Fox, D., Prilleltensky, I., & Austin, S. (Eds.) (2009). *Critical psychology: An introduction.* Thousand Oaks, CA: SAGE.

Fraenkel, J. R., & Wallen, N. E. (2008). *How to design and evaluate research in education* (7th ed.). New York, NY: McGraw-Hill.

Francis, J. J., Johnston, M., Robertson, C., Glidewell, L., Entwistle, V., Eccles, M. P., & Grimshaw, J. (2010). What is an adequate sample size? Operationalising data saturation for theory-based interview studies. *Psychological Health, 25*(10), 1229–1245.

Fraser, N. (1998). *Social justice in the age of identity politics: Redistribution, recognition, participation* (No. FS I 98-108). WZB Berlin Social Science Center.

Fraser, N. (2000). Rethinking recognition. *New Left Review, 3,* 107.

Fraser, N., & Honneth, A. (2003). *Redistribution or recognition? A political-philosophical exchange.* New York, NY: Verso.

Freire, P. (1972). *Pedagogy of the oppressed* (M. B. Ramos, Trans.). New York, NY: Herder.

Fyfe, F., Downs, J., McIlroy, O., Burford, B., Lister, J., Reilly, S., Laurvick, L., Phillippe, C., Msall, M., Kaufmann, W., Ellaway, C., & Leonard, H. (2007). Evaluation of a video-based evaluation tool in Rett syndrome. *Journal of Autism and Developmental Disorders, 37*(9), 1636–1646.

Gamoran, A. (2014). *Inequality is the problem: Prioritizing research on reducing inequality.* New York, NY: William T. Grant Foundation.

Gan, Z., & Israel, M. (2020). Transnational policy migration, interdisciplinary policy transfer and decolonization: Tracing the patterns of research ethics regulation in Taiwan. *Developing World Bioethics, 20*(1), 5–15.

Geertz, C. (1973). *The interpretation of cultures.* New York, NY: Basic Books.

Ghazinejad, M., Hussein, B. A., & Zidane, Y. J. T. (2018). Impact of trust, commitment, and openness on research project performance: Case study in a research institute. *Social Sciences, 7*(2), 22–33.

Giddens, A. (1979). *Central problems in social theory: Action, structure, and contradiction in social analysis* (Vol. 241). Berkeley, CA: University of California Press.

Goddard, J. T., & Foster, R. R. Y. (2002). Adapting to diversity: Where cultures collide: Educational issues in Northern Alberta. *Canadian Journal of Education/Revue Canadienne De L'éducation, 27*(1), 1–20.

Goffman, E. (1956). *The presentation of self in everyday life.* New York, NY: Anchor Books.

Goldrick-Rab, S. (2016). *Paying the price: College costs, financial aid, and the betrayal of the American dream.* Chicago, IL: University of Chicago Press.

Goldrick-Rab, S., & Broton, K. M. (2015, December 4). Hungry, homeless and in college. *The New York Times.*

Goldrick-Rab, S., Broton, K. M., & Hernandez, D. C. (2017). *Addressing basic needs security in higher education: An introduction to three evaluations of supports for food and housing at community colleges.* Madison, WI: Wisconsin HOPE Lab.

Goldrick-Rab, S., & Stommel, J. (2018, December 10). Teaching the students we have, not the students we wish we had. *The Chronicle of Higher Education.*

Government Accountability Office. (2019). *Food insecurity: Better information could help eligible college students access federal food assistance benefits.* Washington, DC: Author.

Gray, G. (2017). Academic voice in scholarly writing. *The Qualitative Report, 22*(1), 179–196. https://nsuworks.nova.edu/tqr/vol22/iss1/10

Grix, J. (2002). Introducing students to the generic terminology of social research. *Politics, 22*(3), 175–186.

Guthrie, R. V. (1976/2004). *Even the rat was white: A historical view of psychology.* Upper Saddle River, NJ: Pearson.

Habermas, J. (1984a). *The theory of communicative action—Volume 1: Reason and the rationalization of society* (T. McCarthy, Trans.). Boston, MA: Beacon Press. (Original work published 1981)

Habermas, J. (1984b). *The theory of communicative action—Volume 2: Lifeworld and system: A critique of functionalist reason* (T. McCarthy, Trans.). Boston, MA: Beacon Press. (Original work published 1981)

Habermas, J. (2015). *Knowledge and human interests* (J. J. Shapiro, Trans.). Hoboken, NJ: Wiley. (Original work published 1968).

Hamilton, D. K. (2012). Design and the researchable question. *HERD, 5*(4), 139–141.

Hammersley, M., & Atkinson, P. (2007). *Ethnography: Principles and practice* (3rd ed.). London, UK: Routledge.

Haraway, D.J. (2008). *When species meet*. Minneapolis, MN: University of Minnesota Press.

Harding, S. (1992). Rethinking standpoint epistemology: What is "strong objectivity"? *The Centennial Review, 36*(3), 437–470.

Hartsock, N. (1983). The feminist standpoint: Developing the ground for a specifically feminist historical materialism. In S. Harding & M. B. Hintikka (Eds.), *Discovering reality. Synthese Library Vol. 161* (pp. 283–310). Dordrecht, Germany: D. Reidel Publishing Company.

Hegel, G. W. F. (1979). *Phenomenology of spirit* (A. V. Miller, Trans.). New York, NY: Oxford University Press.

Hekman, S. (2010). *The material of knowledge: Feminist disclosures*. Bloomington/Indianapolis, IN: Indiana University Press.

Hollis, M. (1994). *The philosophy of social science: An introduction*. Cambridge, UK: Cambridge University Press.

hooks, b. (1984). *From margin to center*. Boston, MA: South End Press.

Hout, M. (2012). Social and economic returns to college education in the United States. *Annual Review of Sociology, 38*(1), 379–400.

Hoyningen-Huene, P. (2013). *Systematicity: The nature of science*. Oxford, UK: Oxford University Press.

Huffman, T., & Tracy, S. J. (2018). Making claims that matter: Heuristics for theoretical and social impact in qualitative research. *Qualitative Inquiry, 24*(8), 558–570.

Institute of Medicine (IOM). (1990). Nutrition labeling, issues and directions for the 1990s. Washington, DC: National Academy Press.

Israel, M. (2020). Organizing and contesting research ethics. In R. Iphofen (Ed.), *Handbook of research ethics and scientific integrity*. Basel, Switzerland: Springer.

Jensen, S. (n.d.). *Dissertation survival skills: Disarming the inner critic*. Dissertation doctor. http://www.dissertationdoctor.com/articles/critic.html

John, T. (2010). *Yuraryararput kangiit-llu: Our ways of dance and their meanings*. PhD diss., University of Alaska Fairbanks.

Kane, M. T. (2016). Explicating validity. *Assessment in Education: Principles, Policy & Practice, 23*(2), 198–211. https://doi.org/10.1080/0969594X.2015.1060192

Kant, I. (1996). *Critique of pure reason* (W. S. Pluhar, Trans.). Indianapolis, IN: Hackett Publishing.

Kawagley, O. (1995). *A Yupiaq worldview: A pathway to ecology and spirit*. Fairbanks, AK: Alaska Native Knowledge Network.

Kincheloe, J. L., & McLaren, P. L. (1994). Rethinking critical theory and qualitative research. In N. K. Denzin & Y. S. Lincoln (Eds.), *Handbook of qualitative research* (pp. 138–157). Thousand Oaks, CA: SAGE.

Knoblauch, D., & Hoy, A.W. (2008). "Maybe I can teach those kids": The influence of contextual factors on student teachers efficacy beliefs. *Teaching and Teacher Education, 24*(1), 166–179.

Kofoed, J., & Staunæs, D. (2015). Hesitancy as ethics. *Reconceptualizing Educational Research Methodology, 6*(1), 24–39.

Korth, B. (2002). Critical qualitative research as consciousness-raising: The dialogic texts of researcher/researchee interactions. *Qualitative Inquiry, 8*(3), 381–403.

Kuhn, T. S. (1970). The structure of scientific revolutions. *International encyclopedia of unified science* (Vol. 2, no. 2).

Kuhn, T. S. (2012). *The structure of scientific revolutions* (4th ed.). Chicago, IL: University of Chicago Press.

Kuntz, A. (2015). *The responsible methodologist: Inquiry, truth-telling, and social justice.* Walnut Creek, CA: Left Coast Press, Inc.

Lather, P. (1986). Issues of validity in openly ideological research: Between a rock and a soft place. *Interchange, 17*(4), 63–84.

Lengermann, P. M., & Niebrugge, G. (2006). *The women founders: Sociology and social theory 1830–1930: A text/reader.* Waveland Press. IL: Long Grove.

Levitt, H. M., Bamberg, M., Creswell, J. W., Frost, D., Josselson, R., & Suárez-Orozco, C. (2018). Journal article reporting standards for qualitative research in psychology: The APA publications and communications board task force report. *American Psychologist, 73*, 26–46.

Lincoln, E. G., & Lincoln, Y. S. (1985). *Naturalistic inquiry.* Newbury Park, CA: SAGE.

Lincoln, Y. S., & Guba, E. G. (1986). But is it rigorous? Trustworthiness and authenticity in naturalistic evaluation. *New Directions for Evaluation, 1986*(30), 73–84.

Maso, I., Atkinson, P., Delamont, S., & Vehoeven, J. (1995). *Openness in research: The tension between self and other.* Assen, Netherlands: van Gorcum and Company.

Massey, S. G., & Barreras, R. E. (2013). Introducing "impact validity." *Journal of Social Issues, 69*(4), 615–632.

Maynard, D. W., Schaeffer, N. C., Drew, I. P., Raymond, G., & Weinberg, D. (2006). Standardization-in-interaction: The survey interview. In P. Drew, G. Raymond, & D. Weinberg (Eds.), *Talk and interaction in social research methods* (pp. 9–27). Thousand Oaks, CA: SAGE.

McCambridge, J., Witton, J., & Elbourne, D. (2014). Systematic review of the Hawthorne effect: New concepts are needed to study research participation effects. *Journal of Clinical Epidemiology, 67*(3), 267–277.

McClelland, S. I. (2016). Speaking back from the margins: Participant marginalia in survey and interview research. *Qualitative Psychology, 3*(2), 159–165.

McClelland, S. I., & Holland, K. J. (2016). Toward better measurement: The role of survey marginalia in critical sexuality research. *Qualitative Psychology, 3*(2), 166–185.

McRae, M. (2018, January 24). We should consider obesity as a kind of contagious disease, study shows. *Health: ScienceAlert.* https://www.sciencealert.com/study-finds-obesity-socially-contagious-behaviour

Miller, C. R. (1984). Genre as social action. *Quarterly Journal of Speech, 70*(2), 151–167.

Miller, C. R. (2015). Genre as social action (1984), revisited 30 years later (2014). *Letras & Letras, 31*(3), 56–72.

Modecki, K., Minchin, J., Harbaugh, A., Guerra, N., & Runions, K. (2014). Bullying prevalence across contexts: A meta-analysis measuring cyber and traditional bullying. *Journal of Adolescent Health, 55*(5), 602–611.

Mozes, A. (2018, January 28). Is obesity "contagious"? HeatlhyDay News, *HealthyDay Reporter.* https://www.webmd.com/diet/obesity/news/20180123/is-obesity-contagious#1

National Center for Education Statistics (NCES). (2017, July 24). https://nces.ed.gov/programs/coe/indicator_cgf.asp

Nazmi, A., Martinez, S., Byrd, A., Robinson, D., Bianco, S., Maguire, J., Crutchfield, R. M., Condron, K., & Ritchie, L. (2018). A systematic review of food insecurity among U.S. students in higher education. *Journal of Hunger & Environmental Nutrition,* 1–16.

Newman, W. L. (2000). *Social research methods: Qualitative and quantitative approaches.* Boston, MA: Allyn and Bacon.

Noblit, G., & Hare, R. (1988). *Meta-ethnography: Synthesizing qualitative studies.* Thousand Oaks, CA: SAGE.

Onwuegbuzie, A., & Leech, N. (2005, March 10). A typology of errors and myths perpetuated in educational research textbooks. *Current Issues in Education* [online], *8*(7). http://cie.ed.asu.edu/volume8/number7/

O'Reilly, M., & Parker, N. (2012). "Unsatisfactory saturation": A critical exploration of the notion of saturated sample sizes in qualitative research. *Qualitative Research, 13*(2), 190–197.

Oreopoulos, P., & Petronijevic, U. (2013). Making college worth it: A review of the returns to higher education. *The Future of Children, 23*(1), 41–65.

Ortner, S. B. (1984). Theory in anthropology since the sixties. *Comparative Studies in Society and History*, *26*(1), 126–166.

Paré, G., Tate, M., Johnstone, D., & Spyros, K. (2016). Conceptualizing the twin concepts of systematicity and transparency in information systems literature reviews. *European Journal of Information Systems*, *25*(6), 493–508.

Peshkin, A. (1988). In search of subjectivity—one's own. *Educational Researcher*, *17*(7), 17–21.

Prilleltensky, I. (2003). Understanding, resisting, and overcoming oppression: Toward psychopolitical validity. *American Journal of Community Psychology*, *31*(1–2), 195–201.

Prilleltensky, I. (2008). The role of power in wellness, oppression, and liberation: The promise of psychopolitical validity. *Journal of Community Psychology*, *36*(2), 116–136.

The Public Science Project (PSP). (n.d.). *Morris Justice: A public science project*. http://publicscienceproject.org/

Pugh, J. (2013). The short-term "bridge model" study abroad program: Peacebuilding in Latin America. *PS: Political Science & Politics*, *46*(4), 791–796.

Pugh, J. (2015). Redes de migrantes y refugiados en Ecuador: Un estudio de Quito, Lago Agrio, Esmeraldas, e Ibarra. *CEMPROC Working Paper Series in Peace, Conflict, and Development*.

Pugh, J. (2016). Peacebuilding among transnational youth in migrant-receiving border regions of Ecuador. *Journal of Peacebuilding and Development*, *11*(3), 83–97.

Pugh, J. (2018). Negotiating identity and belonging through the invisibility bargain: Colombian forced migrants in Ecuador. *International Migration Review*, *52*(4), 978–1010.

Rao, T. S., & Andrade, C. (2011). The MMR vaccine and autism: Sensation, refutation, retraction, and fraud. *Indian Journal of Psychiatry*, *53*(2), 95–96.

Razon, N., & Ross, K. (2012). Negotiating fluid identities: Alliance-building in qualitative interviews. *Qualitative Inquiry*, *18*(6), 494–503.

Rivera, L. A. (2017). When two bodies are (not) a problem: Gender and relationship status discrimination in academic hiring. *American Sociological Review*, *82*(6), 1111–1138.

Robson, C., & McCartan, K. (2016). *Real world research* (4th ed.). Hoboken, NJ: Wiley.

Ross, K., Dennis, B., Zhao, P., & Lei, P. (2017). Exploring graduate students' conceptions of research: Links between identity and research conceptions. *International Journal of Teaching and Learning in Higher Education*, *29*(1), 73–86.

Sainani, K. L. (2015). Dealing with missing data. *PM R*, *7*(9), 990–994.

Saldaña, J. (2009). *The coding manual for qualitative researchers*. Thousand Oaks, CA: SAGE.

Satinsky, S., Dennis, B., Reece, M., Sanders, S., & Bardzell, S. (2013). My "fat girl complex": A preliminary analysis of sexual health and body image in women of size. *Culture, Health and Sexuality: An International Journal for Research, Intervention and Care*, *15*(6), 710–725.

Satinsky, S., & Ingraham, N. (2014). At the intersection of public health and fat studies: Critical perspectives on the measurement of body size. *Fat Studies*, *3*(2), 143–154.

Schwab, A., & Starbuck, W. (2016). A call for openness in research reporting: How to turn covert practices into helpful tools. *Academy of Management Learning and Education*, *16*(1), 125–141.

Schwandt, T. A. (2014). *The SAGE Dictionary of Qualitative Inquiry*. Thousand Oaks, CA: SAGE.

Sewell, W. H., Jr. (1992). A theory of structure: Duality, agency, and transformation. *American Journal of Sociology*, *98*(1), 1–29.

Shadish, W. R., Cook, T. D., & Campbell, D. T. (2002). *Experimental and quasi-experimental designs for generalized causal inference*. Boston, MA: Houghton Mifflin Company.

Shah, P. (2015). Spaces to speak: Photovoice and the reimagination of girls' education in India. *Comparative Education Review*, *59*(1), 50–74.

Siekmann, S., & Webster, J. (2019). Critical intercultural conversations: Using activity systems analysis as a tool for educational ethnography. *Ethnography and Education: Special Issue on Multicultural Education, 14*(3), 377–393.

Siekmann, S., & Webster, J., with Samson, S., Moses, C., John-Shields, A., & Wallace, S. (2019). *Pugtallgutkellriit*: Developing researcher identities in a participatory action research collaborative. *Journal of American Indian Education, 58*(1&2), 124–145.

Smith, D. (2003). Five principles for research ethics: Covering your bases with these ethical strategies. *Monitor on Psychology, 34*(1), 56.

Smith, L. T. (1999). *Decolonizing methodologies: Research and Indigenous peoples*. London, UK: Zedbooks.

Smith, L. T. (2006). Choosing the margins: The role of research in Indigenous struggles for social justice. In N. K. Denzin & M. D. Giardina (Eds.), *Qualitative inquiry and the conservative challenge* (pp. 151–173). Walnut Creek, CA: Left Coast Press.

Smith, M. V. (2008). Pain experience and the imagined researcher. *Sociology of Health & Illness, 30*(7), 992–1006.

Speight, S. L. (2007). Internalized racism: One more piece of the puzzle. *The Counseling Psychologist, 35*(1), 126–134.

Spivak, G. C. (1990). Poststructuralism, marginality, postcoloniality and value. *Literary Theory Today*, 219–244.

Spivak, G. C. (2010). Can the subaltern speak? In R. Morris (Ed.), *Can the subaltern speak? Reflections on the history of an idea*. New York, NY: Columbia University Press.

Stalianides, G., & Stalianides, A. (2020). Posing new researchable questions as a dynamic process in educational research. *International Journal of Science and Mathematics Education*.

Stoudt, B. G. (2014). Critical statistics. In T. Teo (Ed.), *Encyclopedia of critical psychology*. New York, NY: Springer.

Stoudt, B. G., Fox, M., & Fine, M. (2012). Contesting privilege with critical participatory action research. *Journal of Social Issues, 68*(1), 178–193.

Stoudt, B. G., & Torre, M. E. (2014). *The Morris Justice Project: Participatory action research*. Thousand Oaks, CA: SAGE.

Stoudt, B. G., Torre, M. E., Bartley, P., Bracy, F., Caldwell, H., Downs, A., Greene, C., Haldipur, J., Hassan, P., Manoff, E., Sheppard, N., & Yates, J. (2015). "We come from a place of knowing": Experiences, challenges, advantages and possibilities of participating in Morris Justice Project. In C. Durose & L. Richardson (Eds.), *Re-thinking public policy making: Why co-production matters* (pp. 125–137). Bristol, UK: Policy Press.

Tate, W. F. (1994). From inner city to ivory tower: Does my voice matter in the academy? *Urban Education, 29*(3), 245–269.

Tenenbaum, H. R., & Ruck, M. D. (2007). Are teachers' expectations different for racial minority than for European American students? A meta-analysis. *Journal of Educational Psychology, 99*(2), 253.

Teo, T. (2008). From speculation to epistemological violence in psychology: A critical-hermeneutic reconstruction. *Theory & Psychology, 18*(1), 47–67.

Teo, T. (2010). What is epistemological violence in the empirical social sciences? *Social and Personality Psychology Compass, 4*(5), 295–303.

Teo, T. (2011). Empirical race psychology and the hermeneutics of epistemological violence. *Human Studies, 34*(3), 237–255.

Thorne, S. (2016). *Interpretive description: Qualitative research for applied practice*. London, UK: Routledge.

Torraco, R. (2005). Writing integrative literature reviews: Guidelines and examples. *Human Resource Development Review, 4*(3), 356–367.

Tracy, S. (2010). Qualitative quality: Eight "big-tent" criteria for excellent qualitative research. *Qualitative Inquiry, 16*(10), 837–851.

Tuval-Mashiach, R. (2017). Raising the curtain: The importance of transparency in qualitative research. *Qualitative Psychology, 4*(2), 126.

Unger, R. K. (1998). Positive marginality: Antecedents and consequences. *Journal of Adult Development, 5*, 163–170.

U.S. Department of Education. (2015). *Demographic and enrollment characteristics of nontraditional undergraduates: 2011–12.* Washington, DC: Author.

Vygotsky, L. S. (1978). *Mind in society: The development of higher psychological processes.* Cambridge, MA: Harvard University Press.

Wakefield, A. J., Murch, S. H., Anthony, A., Linnell, J., Casson, D. M., Malik, M., et al. (1998). Ileal-lymphoid-nodular hyperplasia, non-specific colitis, and pervasive developmental disorder in children. *Lancet, 351,* 637–641.

Walford, G. (2009). For ethnography. *Ethnography and Education, 4*(3), 271–282.

Wang, C., & Burris, M. A. (1997). Photovoice: Concept, methodology, and use for participatory needs assessment. *Health Education & Behavior, 24*(3), 369–387.

Wang, J., Iannotti, R., & Nansel, T. (2009). School bullying amongst US adolescents: Physical, verbal, relational, and cyber. *Journal of Adolescent Health, 45*(4), 368–375.

Wang, Y. (2014). *A record for practice* (P. Ivanhoe, Trans.). In J. Tiwald & B. W. V. Norden (Eds.), *Readings in later Chinese philosophy: Han to the twentieth century.* Indianapolis, IN: Hackett Publishing.

Wehmeier, S., McIntosh, C., & Turnbull, J. (Eds.). (2010). *Oxford advanced learner's dictionary of current English* (7th ed.). New York, NY: Oxford University Press.

Weil, A. (2018, May 7). *Is obesity contagious?* Drweil.com. https://www.drweil.com/diet-nutrition/diets-weight-loss/is-obesity-contagious/

Wertsch, J. V. (1985). *Vygotsky and the social formation of mind.* Cambridge, MA: Harvard University Press.

Willis, P. (1977). *Learning to labour: How working class kids get working class jobs.* London, UK: Saxon House.

Winter, V. R., & Satinsky, S. (2014). Body appreciation, sexual relationship status, and protective sexual behaviors in women. *Body Image, 11*(1), 36–42.

Winthrop, R. H. (1991). *Dictionary of concepts in cultural anthropology.* New York, NY: Greenwood Press.

Wolf, C. (2014). The effect of Graduate Record Examination on minority applications: Experience at New York Institute of Technology. *Journal of Allied Health, 43*(4), 65E–67E.

Wong, A. (2019, January 22). America's teachers are furious: From West Virginia to Los Angeles, educators are ushering in a new era of labor activism. *The Atlantic.* https://www.theatlantic.com/education/archive/2019/01/teachers-are-launching-a-rebellion/580975/

Yamagata-Lynch, Lisa. (2010). *Activity systems analysis methods: Understanding complex learning environments.* New York, NY: Springer.

Zhou, X., & Hall, J. N. (2018). Mixed methods papers in first-person and third-person: Writing voices in dialogue. *Journal of Mixed Methods Research, 12*(3), 344–357.

INDEX

Abdominal pain, 172
Abedi, J., 139
Abma, T. A., 351, 356
Academic history and Wikipedia, 127–130
Academic Voice in Scholarly Writing (Gray), 367
Accessibility, 357–358
Accessible population, 245
Activity systems analysis (ASA), 105–106
Agency, 122–123
American Psychological Association, 64–65
Anderson, K., 237
Andrade, C., 378
ANOVA (analysis of variance), 420–421
Anti-consumerism, 124–125
Appearance, 142
Applebaum, M., 366, 367
Applicability, 390
Archival data, 222
ASA. *See* Activity systems analysis (ASA)
Atkinson, P., 190
Audit trail, 359
Australian Rett Syndrome Database (ARSD), 183
Authenticity, 154
Authorial voice, 366–368
Author-reader relationship, 356–357
    authors' responsibility, 361–362
    multifold relational responsibility, 359–361

Backgrounded horizon, 149
Bao, X., 183
Barreras, R., 393
Behavior, 384
Bell curve, 306
Benton, T., 90
Berkenkotter, C., 365
Bias, 247, 293
Biesta, G., 201
Binet Scale, 395
Body image, 99
Body mass index (BMI), 329

Borrelia burgdorferi, 85–86, 94
Bowen, G., 252
Brandom, R., 98
Broton, K., 294–296
Bullying, 65–66, 68–70, 72
Burke, K., 357
Burns, A., 190
Burris, M. A., 321

Call-Cummings, M., 147, 368–372
Campbell, D. T., 141, 144
Campbell, R., 182
Care and openness, 70–72
Carspecken, P. F., 49, 97, 113, 119, 149
Carter, P., 183
Cascade effect, 389
Catalytic validity, 146
Categorical variables, 220
Causal inferences, 220
    statistical tests to, 419–423
Causation, 331–334
CHAT. *See* Cultural historical activity theory (CHAT)
Chi-square, 427–428
Cho, J., 393
Chronic Lyme disease, 85–87, 91–95
Cirillo, F., 356
Cluster, 14–15
Cluster sampling, 248
Coding, 313–316
Cognitive ability, 156
Cognitive interviews, 156, 161, 236
Collaborative action research project, 50–55
Combahee River Collective (CRC), 32
Commitments, 344
Communication
    data generation and acquisition, 206–210
    in inquiry, 206
    interpersonal, 113, 123
    and intersubjectivity, 207

Communicative validity, 147
Confidence interval, 310, 334
Confidence level, 310
Consciousness-raising, 341–342
Construct, 234
Constructivism, 91–92
Construct validity, 234
Contagious, 329
Continuous variables, 220, 221
Control variables, 220
Convenience sampling, 249
Convention, 362–363
Cook, T. D., 141, 144
Cooper, H., 180
Correlation inferences, 334–336
    statistical tests to, 425–428
Correlations, 188–189
Correspondence theory
    of meaning, 277–281
    and reconstructive approach, 288–289
    of truth, 141
Craib, I., 90
Credibility, 146, 180
Creswell, J., 144
Critical case sampling, 249
Criticalism, 28–29
Critical participatory action research
    (CPAR), 190–191, 369, 370
Critical pragmatism, 285–286, 289
Critical realism, 90–91
Critical statistics, 88
Critical theory, 92–93
Critical youth participatory action research
    (CYPAR) project, 399–400
Cronbach, L. J., 159
Crowther, M., 181
Crowther, M. S., 181
Cultural historical activity theory (CHAT), 104, 105
Cultural typification, 97
Culture and social norms, 117–119
CV-building activities, 118–119
Cyber and traditional bullying/aggression, 66
Cyberbullying, 68

Data, 199, 218, 303–304
    acquisition, 222
    generalizability and transferability, 255–257
    missing, 251, 253–255
    sampling, 245–251
    saturation, 252–253
    transformation, 185–186
Data generation and acquisition
    communication, 206–210
    goal-orientedness, 203–204, 209–210
    knowing and doing, 200–201
    operationalization, 204–205
    phenomenon, 229–230
    planning, 202–203
    power relationship, 211–213
    process of, 219–229, 257–263
    products, 231–232
    social action, 198–200
    and students, 233–239
Datar, A., 329, 338
Decision-making, 139, 168, 170, 174, 181, 182, 200–202,
    215, 250, 257, 297, 318–322, 380
Deduction, 283–285
Dennis, B., 1–3, 5–7, 10, 25–27, 30–32, 34, 44, 48, 51,
    66–68, 70, 100, 146, 171–173, 176, 178, 186, 331,
    337, 341, 354, 409–410, 412, 413, 417
Dependability, 146
Dependent variable, 220
Description and inference, 301–303
    data, 303–304
    descriptive statistics, 305–309
    inferential statistics, 309–311
    missing data and outliers, 316–317
    network analysis, 319–321
    photovoice, 321–322
    textual and visual data, 311–316
    validity, 317–318
Descriptive statistics, 305–309, 312
Designing research, 186–191
Dialogical structure, 148
Dialogic approach, 1, 13
Dialogic theory of truth, 143
Dilthey, W., 97
Double writing, 368–372
Downs, J., 178–179, 183, 189, 191–192
Du Bois, W. E. B., 13

Edin, K. J., 386
Educational Testing Service (ETS), 303
Effectiveness, 282–283
Elbourne, D., 73
Ellingson, L., 366, 367

Embarrassingly difficult, 119
Emergent coding, 315
Empirical research, 200
    article, 433–436
Empowerment, 73, 393–394
Engeström, Y., 105
English language learners (ELL), 138–141, 143, 145, 148, 156, 163
Environmentalism, 124–125
Epistemology, 26–28, 86–93, 96, 99–104
    constructivism, 91–92
    critical theory, 92–93
    postmodernism, 92
    traditions, 93
    violence, 152, 395, 396
Equal Employment Opportunity Statement, 121
Ethics, 59–61, 396
    bullying, 65–66, 68–70, 72
    care and openness, 70–72
    guidelines, 64–65
    intersubjectivity, 69–70
    morals and, 60
    positionality, 67–69
    power, 72–74
    principles, 60
    procedural and situational, 63–65
    in research, 62
Experimental design, 220
Explanation, 382–384
External validity, 146, 343

Fallibility, 71, 152
Fat, 99–101
Fate project, 257–260
Feder, H., 85
Feminist Research Collective (FRC), 32–36
Fine, M., 190, 394–396
Fischer, R., 174
Fixed designs, 187–189
Flexible designs, 189–191
Focus group, 222
Food diary, 172–173
Foster, R., 236
Frame analysis, 340
Frames, 340
Francis, J. J., 250
Frankael, J., 144
Fraser, N., 391–392

Gan, Z. -R., 117
Gándara, P., 139
Geertz, C., 311
Gender inequality, 202
Generalizability, 145, 146, 246, 255–257, 343, 390
General linear modeling, 338
General Record Examination (GRE), 303–307, 316–317
Generate and acquire data, 199. *See also* Data generation and acquisition
Genre, 362–363, 365–366
Ghazinejad, M., 174
Giddens, A., 113, 337
Glass, G., 181
Goal-orientedness, 203–204, 206, 209–210
Goddard, J. T., 236
Goffman, E., 86, 340
Gray, G., 367
GRE. *See* General Record Examination (GRE)
Grix, J., 88
Grounded theory, 249, 342
Guba, E. G., 146, 219
Guerra, N., 65
Guetterman, T., 144
Guthrie, R., 395

Habermas, J., 12, 28, 31, 93, 113, 143, 286, 414
Hall, J. N., 367
Hamilton, D. K., 173
Hammersley, M., 190
Harbaugh, A., 65
Hare, R. D., 182
Hartmann, H., 344
Hartsock, N., 67
Hawthorne effect, 73
Hegel, G. W. F., 13
Heinz Dilemma, 60
Helix, 177–178
Hermeneutic circle, 97, 98
High-level inferences, 291
Historical/archival data, 232
Hobbes, T., 207
Hollis, M., 90, 382
Honneth, A., 391
Hoy, A.W., 233
Hoyningen-Huene, P., 174
Huckin, T. N., 365
Huffman, T., 357–358
Hypotheses, 184–185

Iannotti, R., 65
Identity, 41–42, 407
   and identity claim, 37, 42–49, 51–54, 56, 67, 68, 408
   in research, 43
Immediate horizon, 149
Impactful, 385
Impact validity, 393
Inclusivity/exclusivity, 181
Independent variable, 220
Induction, 282–285
Inference-making, 273–275
   bias, 293
   Broton and, 294–296
   correspondence and reconstructive approach, 288–289
   correspondence theory, 277–281
   induction and deduction, 281–285
   meaning field, 286–288, 290–291
   representational theory, 277–281
   substantive theory, 292
   See also Description and inference
Inferences, 15, 145, 330–331
   causation, 331–334
   correlation, 334–336
   frame analysis, 340
   insights and consciousness-raising, 341–342
   metaphors, 337
   modeling, 338–339
   social network analysis, 339
   structural, 337–340
   theory building, 342
Inferential statistics, 309–311
Informativeness, 358
Insights, 341–342
Institutional review boards (IRBs), 59, 63
Instrumental rationality, 384
Integrative literature review, 180
Intelligence quota (IQ) test, 226, 306, 395
Intermediate foregrounded horizon, 149
Internal validity, 145
Interpretation, 145
Intersubjectivity, 31, 69–70, 147–148, 407
Interval scale, 221
Interval variable, 221
Interview protocol, 222
Interviews, 222
Inverse relationship, 334–335

Israel, M., 117
Items, 234

Jack, D., 237
Jensen, S., 362
Job interviews, 114, 115
Justification process, 182

Kane, M. T., 158
Kant, I., 45
Ke Li, 211–213
Knoblauch, D., 233
Knowing and doing, 200–201
Knowledge
   legitimate, 8, 43, 47–50, 86, 304
   stock, 149
Knowledge claims, 93–94, 153–156
   normative, 95–96, 155–156
   objective, 94, 153–154
   principles, 161–162
   subjective, 94, 154
Kofoed, J., 66
Kuhn, T., 90–91, 206
Kuntz, A., 60

Language, 150–151
Lansing, D., 321–322
Lather, P., 146, 393
Learn to Labor: How Working Class Kids Get Working Class Jobs, 118
Legitimate knowledge, 8, 43, 47–50, 86, 304
Levitt, H. M., 367
LGBT nongovernmental organizations (NGOs), 260–263
Li, P., 3, 6, 7, 353, 361, 362, 408–409, 413–416
Lifeworld, 383–384
Lim, W., 181
Lincoln, Y. S., 146, 219
Linear regression, 336
Line of regression, 336
Literature review, 179–181
Low-level inferences, 291
Luo, W., 127–130

McCambridge, J., 73
McCartan, K., 187
McClelland, S., 74–76
McIntosh, C., 140

McRae, M., 329
Macro-level power, 123–124
Macro-level study, 383
Maldistribution, 391
Mann-Whitney U Test, 422
Mapping, 186
Marxist theory, 342
Maso, I., 174
Massey, S., 393
Maximum variation sampling, 249
Maxwell, J., 101–103, 364
Maynard, D., 175
Meaning, 96, 98–99
Meaning fields, 148–150, 286–288
  reconstructing, 290–291
Meaning horizon, 148–150
Means-to-the-end focus, 384
Measurement, 144, 281
Median, 307
Member checking, 156, 162
Meta-analysis, 181–182
Metaphors, 337
Methodology, 87–89, 91
#MeToo movement, 339
Micro-level power, 123–124
Micro-level study, 383
Milano, A., 339
Milfont, T., 174
Miller, C. R., 363
Minchin, J., 65
Mini-fiction exercise, 232–239
Mis-recognition, 391
Missing data, 251, 253–255, 316–317
Mode, 307
Modecki, K., 65, 68, 69
Modeling, 338–339
Morris Justice Project (MJP), 379–383, 389, 392–393
Motivations
  and engagements, 24
  personal, 2, 178, 179
  researcher-related, 183
Mozes, A., 329
Multifold relational responsibility, 359–361
Multiple regression, 338
My "Fat Girl Complex": A Preliminary Investigation of Sexual Health and Body Image in Women of Size (Satinsky), 100, 337

Nansel, T., 65
National Center for Education Statistics (NCES), 138
Naturalistic observation, 219
Negative direction, 335
Nicosia, N., 329, 338
Noblit, G., 182
Nodes, 339
Nominal variables, 220
Nonparametric test, 310, 419, 422, 425, 427
Non-probability sampling, 249
Normal distribution, 306
Normative knowledge claims, 94–96, 155–156
Numerical data sets, 231

Obesity, 327–332, 334, 336, 338–341
Objective knowledge claims, 93–95, 153–154, 318
Objectivity-subjectivity dualism, 154–155
Observation process, 219
Ontology, 86–93
Openness, 174
Operationalization, 204–205
Ordinal variables, 220–221
O'Reilly, M., 252
Othering, 394
Outliers, 316–317

Paradigm shift, 91
Parametric test, 310, 419, 420, 425
Paré, G., 174
Parker, N., 252
Parker Webster, J., 103–107
Participant observation, 219
Participatory action research (PAR), 369
Partisanship, 29–30, 67
Payne, Y., 190
Pearson, K., 281
Pearson Chi-Square, 422–423
Pearson Product Moment Correlation, 335, 425–426
Percentiles, 305
Peshkin, A., 67
Photographs, 231–232
Photovoice, 321–322
Pizmony-Levy, O., 260–263
Pomodoro Time Management Technique (Cirillo), 356
Positionality, 47, 67–69, 79
Position-taking, 46, 69, 162
Positive direction, 335
Positivism, 90

Postmodernism, 92
Post-positivism, 90–91
Power, 72–74, 393–394
Power, interactive, 123–126
Pragmatic fissures, 51, 52, 56
Predictability, 343
Prediction, 145
Predictive validity, 343
Prilleltensky, I., 147, 393
Priori codes, 315
Privileged access, 154
Probability sampling, 247, 248
Procedural approach to ethics, 63–65
Psychopolitical validity, 147, 393
Pugh, J., 319–321
Purposive sampling, 249

Qualitative research, 145–147, 203, 204
Quality, 150–151
Quantitative research, 144–145, 203, 204
Quasi-experimental designs, 189
Quota sampling, 248, 249

Randomized Control Trial (RCT), 188, 332, 333
Rao, T. S., 378
Ratio variable, 221
Reality, 142
Recognition, 391
Recognitive effort, 392
Reconstructing meaning fields, 287
Reconstructive analysis, 287
Reconstructive approach, 288–289
Redistribution, 391, 392
Reflection, 31–32
Reflexivity, 47
Regression analysis, 335–336
Relationally responsible practice, 356–359
Relationships, 334–339
Reliability, 145, 146, 156
Repeated measures, 153, 156, 161
Replication, 390
Representation, 279–280
Representational theory of meaning, 277–281
Representativeness, 161
Representative sample, 246
Research
    as action, 413
    designs, 89, 186–191
    interests, 183

paradigm, 89
proposal, 364–365
questions, 183, 199
See also Research impact
Research-ability, 173–174
Researcher-participant relationship, 359–361
Researchers Applying Activity Systems Analysis, 105
Research impact, 379–382, 385
    explanation and understanding, 382–384
    generalizability, 390
    impact, impactful, and impacting, 384–385
    nature, 386–387
    othering, epistemological violence, and ethics, 394–396
    power and empowerment, 393–394
    and social justice, 390–393
    tree metaphor of, 388–389
    and value, 389–390
    Williams and, 397–400
Researching Research project, 38, 50–52, 206, 217, 233, 250, 315, 316
Response rates, 234
Responsible Methodologist, The (Kuntz), 60
Rett syndrome, 176, 178, 179, 181, 183, 185, 188, 189, 191–192
Rivera, L. A., 199
Robson, C., 187
Ross, K., 4, 6, 7, 25–27, 30–32, 43, 44, 46–48, 244–246, 252–255, 288, 345–348, 354, 385, 409–412, 417
Ruck, M. D., 204–205
Runions, K., 65
Rutkowski, D., 137, 157–159

Saisani, K., 255
Sample, 246
Sampling, 245–251
    error, 246
    strategy, 226
    See also Individual sampling
Satinsky, S., 99, 100, 106, 181, 334, 337
Scaled score, 306
Scales, 234
Scatterplot, 336
Schwab, A., 174
Schwandt, T. A., 157
Scientist, 175–176
Self-expression, 42, 44, 373
Self-reflection, 3, 12, 45–47, 107, 152
Semi-structured interviews, 238

Sewell, W., 113
Shadish, W. R., 141, 144
Shaefer, H. L., 386
Shah, P. P., 130–132
Siekmann, S., 103–107
Simple random sampling, 248
Sincerity, 154
Situational ethics, 63–65
Smith, D., 64
Smith, L. T., 109
Snowball sampling, 249
Social
   inquiry, 1, 8, 9, 86, 88–90, 93, 96, 98, 108, 134, 140, 144, 146, 150, 366
   justice, 390–393
   network analysis, 319–321, 339
   norms, 115–119
   system, 121
Social structure, 119–123
   agency, 122–123
   and interactive power, 123–126
Spalter-Roth, R., 344
Spearman Rank-Order Correlation, 427
Speight, S., 396
Spival, G. C., 395
Stalianides, A., 174
Stalianides, G., 174
Standard deviation, 308
Standardization, 174–175
Standardized score, 303
Starbuck, W., 174
Statistics, 305
   descriptive, 305–309
   inferencing, 330
   inferential, 309–311
   model, 335
   significance, 334
Staunæs, D., 66
Stoudt, B., 88
Stratified random sampling, 248
Structured interviews, 238
Structure of Scientific Revolutions, The (Kuhn), 90–91
Student
   ELL, 138, 139, 143, 145, 148, 156
   identity claim, 37, 42–49, 51–54, 56, 67, 68, 408
   insecurity, 294–296
   and schooling, 236–239
   self-efficacy, 233–236
Student-centered approach, 11

Subjective knowledge claims, 93–95, 154
Subject-object relation, 142, 143
Subject-subject relation, 142, 143
Subject-to-subject relationship, 32
Substantive codes, 315
Substantive theory, 292
Supercalifragilisticexpialidocious Antibullying Program, 72–73
Survey methods, 219–220
Symbolic meaning system, 121
System, 383
Systematicity, 174, 186
Systematic sampling, 248

Tacit communicative structure, 147
Target population, 245
Tate, W., 199
Teacher Sense of Efficacy Scale, 234
Tenenbaum, H. R., 204–205
Teo, T., 395
Test-retest reliability, 156
Thematic analysis, 315
Thematization, 14–15
Theoretical inferencing, 330
Theoretical sampling, 249
Theory building, 342
Theory-led, 190
Theory of truth, 140–144
Thick description, 311–312
Thorne, S., 173
Tone of Decency Campaign, 275–278, 282, 283, 287, 290, 293, 423
Torraco, R., 180
Torre, M., 190
Tracy, S. J., 357–358
Transcendental I, 45
Transcripts, 231
Transferability, 146, 255–257, 343–344, 390
Transformative validity, 393
Transparency, 359
Treatment, 332
Tree branches, 388
Tree leaves, 388
Tree roots, 388
Tree trunk, 388
Trent, A., 393
Triangulation, 151, 161
Trust and rapport, 161
Trustworthiness, 146

T-scores, 306
T-test, 419–420
Turnbull, J., 140
Tuval-Mashiach, R., 359
$2.00 a Day: Living on Almost Nothing in America (Edin and Shaefer), 386–387

Uncertainty, 151–152
Understanding, 382–384
Understanding meaning, 96–99, 147–152
Union of Concerned Scientists, 344
Unstructured interviews, 238

Validity, 137–140, 143, 317–318
    appearance and reality, 142
    criteria, 153
    defining, 140
    intersubjectivity, 147–148
    and knowledge claims, 153–156
    meaning field and meaning horizon, 148–150
    qualitative research, 145–147
    quality, 150–151
    quantitative research, 144–145
    reliability, 156
    Rutkowski and, 157–159
    theory of truth, 140–144
    uncertainty, 151–152
Variability, 307–308
Variable, 188
    types, 220–222
Variance, 308
Visual products, 231–232

Wakefield, A. J., 378
Walford, G., 190
Wallen, N., 144
Wang, C., 321

Wang, J., 65
Wang Yangming, 201
Wehmeier, S., 140
Weil, A., 329
Whole-part relations, 97
Widdershoven, G. A., 351, 356
Wikipedia, academic history and, 127–130
Wilcoxon signed-rank test, 422
Williams, H. M. A., 397–400
Willis, P., 118, 342
Wilton, J., 73
Winthrop, R., 121
Wolf, C., 304
WomenWeLove research project, 32, 33
Wong, A., 378
Working the Hyphens: Reinventing Self and Other in Qualitative Research (Fine), 394
Writing
    accessibility, 357–358
    authorial voice, 366–368
    authors' responsibility, 361–362
    Call-Cummings and, 368–372
    convention, 362–363
    genre, 362–363, 365–366
    informativeness, 358
    multifold relational responsibility, 359–361
    process of, 353–356
    transparency, 359
    and voice, 368

Yamagata-Lynch, L., 105

Zhao, P., 4–7, 25, 26, 30–35, 51, 114, 115, 125, 204, 257–260, 264, 265, 273–275, 277, 279, 286–288, 290, 291, 312, 352, 353, 357, 363, 407–409, 413, 416
Zhou, X., 367
Z-scores, 306